Dictionary of Literary Biography

Documentary Series

Yearbooks

Concise Series

Dictionary of Literary Biography
Yearbook: 1997

Dictionary of Literary Biography
Yearbook: 1997

Edited by
Matthew J. Bruccoli

and

George Garrett

With the assistance of L. Kay Webster

A Bruccoli Clark Layman Book
Gale Research
Detroit, Washington, D.C., London

The paper used in this publication meets the minimum requirements
of American National Standard for Information Sciences–Permanence
Paper for Printed Library Materials, ANSI Z39.48-1984 ∞ ™

ISBN 0-7876-2519-1
ISSN 0731-7867

10 9 8 7 6 5 4 3 2 1

To George Terry

Contents

Plan of the Series

The advisory board, the editors, and the publisher of the *Dictionary of Literary Biography* are joined in endorsing Mark Twain's declaration. The literature of a nation provides an inexhaustible resource of permanent worth. We intend to make literature and its creators better understood and more accessible to students and the reading public, while satisfying the standards of teachers and scholars.

To meet these requirements, *literary biography* has been construed in terms of the author's achievement. The most important thing about a writer is his writing. Accordingly, the entries in *DLB* are career biographies, tracing the development of the author's canon and the evolution of his reputation.

The purpose of *DLB* is not only to provide reliable information in a convenient format but also to place the figures in the larger perspective of literary history and to offer appraisals of their accomplishments by qualified scholars.

The publication plan for *DLB* resulted from two years of preparation. The project was proposed to Bruccoli Clark by Frederick C. Ruffner, president of the Gale Research Company, in November 1975. After specimen entries were prepared and typeset, an advisory board was formed to refine the entry format and develop the series rationale. In meetings held during 1976, the publisher, series editors, and advisory board approved the scheme for a comprehensive biographical dictionary of persons who contributed to North American literature. Editorial work on the first volume began in January 1977, and it was published in 1978. In order to make *DLB* more than a reference tool and to compile volumes that individually have claim to status as literary history, it was decided to organize volumes by

topic, period, or genre. Each of these freestanding volumes provides a biographical-bibliographical guide and overview for a particular area of literature. We are convinced that this organization—as opposed to a single alphabet method—constitutes a valuable innovation in the presentation of reference material. The volume plan necessarily requires many decisions for the placement and treatment of authors who might properly be included in two or three volumes. In some instances a major figure will be included in separate volumes, but with different entries emphasizing the aspect of his career appropriate to each volume. Ernest Hemingway, for example, is represented in *American Writers in Paris, 1920–1939* by an entry focusing on his expatriate apprenticeship; he is also in *American Novelists, 1910–1945* with an entry surveying his entire career, as well as in *American Short-Story Writers, 1910–1945, Second Series* with an entry concentrating on his short stories. Each volume includes a cumulative index of the subject authors and articles. Comprehensive indexes to the entire series are planned.

The series has been further augmented by the *DLB Yearbooks* (since 1981) which update published entries and add new entries to keep the *DLB* current with contemporary activity. There have also been *DLB Documentary Series* volumes which provide biographical and critical source materials for figures whose work is judged to have particular interest for students. One of these companion volumes is entirely devoted to Tennessee Williams.

We define literature as the *intellectual commerce of a nation:* not merely as belles lettres but as that ample and complex process by which ideas are generated, shaped, and transmitted. *DLB* entries are not limited to "creative writers" but extend to other figures who in their time and in their way influenced the mind of a people. Thus the series encompasses historians, journalists, publishers, book collectors, and screenwriters. By this means readers of *DLB* may be aided to perceive literature not as cult scripture in the keeping of intellectual high priests but firmly positioned at the center of a nation's life.

DLB includes the major writers appropriate to each volume and those standing in the ranks behind them. Scholarly and critical counsel has been sought in deciding which minor figures to include and how full their entries should be. Wherever possible, useful references are made to figures who do not warrant separate entries.

Each *DLB* volume has an expert volume editor responsible for planning the volume, selecting the figures for inclusion, and assigning the entries. Volume editors are also responsible for preparing, where appropriate, appendices surveying the major periodicals and literary and intellectual movements for their volumes, as well as lists of further readings. Work on the series as a whole is coordinated at the Bruccoli Clark Layman editorial center in Columbia, South Carolina, where the editorial staff is responsible for accuracy and utility of the published volumes.

One feature that distinguishes *DLB* is the illustration policy—its concern with the iconography of literature. Just as an author is influenced by his sur-roundings, so is the reader's understanding of the author enhanced by a knowledge of his environment. Therefore *DLB* volumes include not only drawings, paintings, and photographs of authors, often depicting them at various stages in their careers, but also illustrations of their families and places where they lived. Title pages are regularly reproduced in facsimile along with dust jackets for modern authors. The dust jackets are a special feature of *DLB* because they often document better than anything else the way in which an author's work was perceived in its own time. Specimens of the writers' manuscripts and letters are included when feasible.

Samuel Johnson rightly decreed that "The chief glory of every people arises from its authors." The purpose of the *Dictionary of Literary Biography* is to compile literary history in the surest way available to us—by accurate and comprehensive treatment of the lives and work of those who contributed to it.

The *DLB* Advisory Board

Foreword

The *Dictionary of Literary Biography Yearbook* is guided by the same principles that have provided the basic rationale for the entire *DLB* series: 1) the literature of a nation represents an inexhaustible resource of permanent worth; 2) the surest way to trace the outlines of literary history is by a comprehensive treatment of our lives and works of those who contributed to it; and 3) the greatest service the series can provide is to make literary achievements better understood and more accessible to students and the literate public, while serving the needs of scholars. In keeping with those principles, the *Yearbook* has been planned to augment *DLB* by reflecting the vitality of contemporary literature and summarizing current literary activity. The librarian, scholar, or student attempting to stay informed of literary developments is faced with an endless task. The purpose of the *DLB Yearbook* is to serve those readers while at the same time enlarging the scope of the *DLB*.

The *Yearbook* includes articles about the past year's literary events or topics, as well as obituaries and tributes. Each *Yearbook* also includes a list of literary prizes and awards, a necrology, and a checklist of literary histories and biographies published during the year. This *Yearbook* continues the *Dictionary of Literary Biography Yearbook* Awards for the novel, first novel, poetry, children's book, and literary biography.

From the outset, the *DLB* series has undertaken to compile literary history as it is revealed in the lives and works of authors. The *Yearbook* supports that commitment, providing a useful and necessary current record.

Acknowledgments

This book was produced by Bruccoli Clark Layman, Inc. Karen L. Rood is senior editor for the *Dictionary of Literary Biography* series. L. Kay Webster and Denis Thomas were the in-house editors.

Administrative support was provided by Ann M. Cheschi and Brenda A. Gillie.

Bookkeeper is Joyce Fowler.

Copyediting supervisor is Samuel W. Bruce. The copyediting staff includes Phyllis A. Avant, Patricia Coate, Christine Copeland, Thom Harman, and William L. Thomas Jr. Freelance copyeditor is Rebecca Mayo.

Editorial associate is Jeff Miller.

Layout and graphics staff includes Janet E. Hill and Mark J. McEwan.

Office manager is Kathy Lawler Merlette.

Photography editors are Margaret Meriwether and Paul Talbot. Photographic copy work was performed by Joseph M. Bruccoli.

Production manager is Philip B. Dematteis.

Systems manager is Marie L. Parker.

Typesetting supervisor is Kathleen M. Flanagan. The typesetting staff includes Pamela D. Norton and Patricia Flanagan Salisbury. Freelance typesetters include Deidre Murphy and Delores Plastow.

Walter W. Ross, Steven Gross, and Ronald Aikman did library research. They were assisted by the following librarians at the Thomas Cooper Library of the University of South Carolina: Linda Holderfield and the interlibrary-loan staff; reference-department head Virginia Weathers; reference librarians Marilee Birchfield, Stefanie Buck, Stefanie DuBose, Rebecca Feind, Karen Joseph, Donna Lehman, Charlene Loope, Anthony McKissick, Jean Rhyne, and Kwamine Simpson; circulation-department head Caroline Taylor; and acquisitions-searching supervisor David Haggard.

Dictionary of Literary Biography
Yearbook: 1997

The 1997 Nobel Prize in Literature

Dario Fo
(1926 -   )

Donato Santeramo
Queen's University

SELECTED WORKS BY DARIO FO AND FRANCA RAME: *Mistero buffo; Giullarata popolare,* edited by Franca Rame (Cremona: Tip. Lombarda, 1969);

Pum, pum! Chi è? La polizia! Con cronologia storico-politica 1969–1972 della strage di Stato (Verona: Bertani, 1972);

Guerra di popolo in Cile (Verona: Bertani, 1973);

Le commedie, Vol. 1: Gli arcangeli non giocano a flipper; Aveva due pistole con gli occhi bianchi e neri; Chi ruba un piede è fortunato in amore (Turin: Einaudi, 1974);

Le commedie, Vol. 2: Isabella, tre caravelle e un cacciaballe; Settimo: ruba un po' meno; La colpa è sempre del diavolo (Turin: Einaudi, 1974);

Il Fanfani rapito (Verona: Bertani, 1975);

La marjuana della mamma è la più bella (Verona: Bertani, 1976);

Le commedie, Vol. 3: Grande pantomima con bandiere e pupazzi piccoli e medi; L'Operaio conosce 100 parole e il padrone 1000 per questo lui è padrone (Turin: Einaudi, 1977);

Le commedie, Vol. 4: Vorrei morire anche stasera . . . ; Tutti uniti! Tutti insieme! Ma scusa, quello non è il padrone? Fedayn, edited by Rame (Turin: Einuadi, 1977);

Le commedie, Vol. 5: Mistero buffo; Ci ragiono e canto, edited by Rame (Turin: Einaudi, 1977);

Tutta casa, letto e chiesa, by Fo and Rame (Verona: Bertani, 1978);

Le commedie, Vol. 6: La Marcolfa; Gli imbianchini non hanno ricordi; I Tre bravi; Non tutti i ladri vengono per nuocere; Un morto da vendere . . . (Turin: Einaudi, 1984);

Manuale minimo dell'attore (Turin: Einaudi, 1987)—includes an essay by Rame;

Parti femminili: Una giornata qualunque; Una coppia aperta (Milan: F. R. La Comune, 1987);

Le commedie, Vol. 7: Morte accidentale di un anarchico; La signora è da buttare (Turin: Einaudi, 1988);

Le commedie, Vol. 8: Venticinque monologhi per una donna, edited by Rame (Turin: Einaudi, 1989);

Dialogo provocatorio sul comico, il tragico, la follia e la ragione (Rome: Laterza, 1990);

Totò Manuale dell'attor comico (Turin, 1991);

Johan Padan a la descoverta de le Americhe (Florence: Giunti, 1992);

Il papa e la strega e altre commedie, edited by Rame (Turin: Einaudi, 1994).

Editions in English: *We Can't Pay? We Won't Pay!,* translated by Lino Pertile, adapted by Bill Colvill and Robert Walker (London: Pluto, 1978); republished as *Can't Pay? Won't Pay!* (London: Pluto, 1982);

Accidental Death of an Anarchist, translated, with an introduction by Duzanne Cowan, in *Theater,* 10, no. 2 (Spring 1979); revised edition (London: Methuen, 1987);

Female Parts, translated by Margaret Kunzle and Stuart Hood, adapted by Olwen Wymark (London: Pluto, 1981);

Trumpets and Raspberries, translated and adapted by Robert McAvoy and Anna-Mariea Giugini (London: Pluto, 1984);

An Open Couple–Very Open, translated by Stuart Hood, in *Theater,* 17, no. 1 (Winter 1985);

Archangels Don't Play Pinball, translated by McAvoy and Giugini, with an introduction by Hood (London: Methuen, 1987);

Elizabeth, Almost by Chance a Woman, translated by Gillian Hanna, with an introduction by Stuart Hood (London: Methuen, 1987);

Mistero Buffo: Comic Mysteries, translated by Ed Emery, with an introduction by Hood (London: Methuen, 1988);

Dario Fo Plays: One (Mistero Buffo, Accidental Death of an Anarchist, Trumpets and Raspberries, The Virtuous Burglar, One Was Nude and One Wore Tails), with an introduction by Hood (London: Methuen, 1994);

Dario Fo Plays: Two (Can't Pay? Won't Pay!, Elisabeth, The Open Couple, An Ordinary Day), with an introduction by Hood (London: Methuen, 1994).

In his impressive study of Rabelais's work, Mikhail Bakhtin pointed to the revolutionary nature of medieval carnival in which kings were decapitated and crowds were crowned. According to Bakhtin, then, carnival is a discursive mode that subverts the monologism of authoritarian discourse. In "L'essence du rire" (1855) Charles Baudelaire states that laughter is solely human and essentially contradictory as it is a sign of infinite grandeur and infinite misery. According to the French poet, it is from the perpetual shock between the two that laughter arises. He then makes a fundamental distinction between comedy and the grotesque by stating that the former is imitation whereas the latter, which he also calls "absolute comedy," is creation. More than fifty years later, Luigi Pirandello, in his essay *On Humor* (1908), makes a similar distinction between comedy and humor by stating that the comic is the perception of the opposite, while humor is the feeling of the opposite produced by the "special activity" of reflection.

This is the cultural tradition or, rather, countertradition within which Dario Fo's work can be best understood as it is profoundly carnivalesque, thoroughly grotesque, and, thus, humorous. Virtually all his theatrical pieces are truly subversive, as they do not allow catharsis. For Fo the essential element of dramaturgy is ideology, as theater is considered to be a thorough investigation of society; its primary function is to scrutinize the powerful and, thus, subvert official culture. He pursues this objective through his performative texts with his own idiosyncratic use of voice and body language and by the unique and courageous production politics he has adopted over the years.

One of the characteristic features of Fo's distinguishing performative strategies is his thorough reliance on epic acting; yet it must be understood that there is a profound difference with Bertolt Brecht's theory. In the latter case the actors' detachment from the character is fundamental in order to achieve the didactic effect that is the ultimate goal of the theatrical experience. In Fo's vision the actor is humorously in and out of the character: on the one hand, actors have to "live" their part, but on the

other they must be able to detach themselves from the characters and view them critically. His style derives from the long-standing tradition of realism in Italian theater and, as he has pointed out, not that of naturalism. Furthermore, his stagings are thus characterized by the actor being detached and critical of what is being acted out, and not the actor being alienated from the character. This way the actor can provide the audience not with mere information but rather with the necessary data for reconstructing meaning.

Style is thus central in the understanding of a play, and it is also essential for reaching didactic purposes. Fo states that the only key to the grotesque dimension is tragedy, and yet he maintains that the only way to act out tragedy is to take it to the limit of the grotesque. Another influential tradition in the process of definition of his personal style is the commedia dell'arte, and yet he warns that there are indeed two different traditions: one that worked in the courts and serviced the aristocracy, performing only certain types of commedie, that is, plays that were downright conservative in content; and others that never were performed for courts and nobility but only were acted in taverns and town streets. Obviously he embraced the latter and more subversive tradition of the commedia dell'arte.

Fo is the only Italian playwright to enjoy international acclaim since Luigi Pirandello. Yet it is virtually impossible to provide a unifying and unambiguous definition of his work, as his theater is continuously "on the move." This constant transformation is the result of its mirroring and questioning the ever-changing political and social realities of the world. His many productions, almost one a year for the past forty years, constitute an exception for the Italian theatrical scene, which has been extremely poor, and his endeavors as playwright, actor, director, and producer embody the concept of total theater.

In Italy, Fo has been often criticized for not being an author or a playwright but only a stage improviser. His shows have provoked political debates that ultimately have become the generating power behind his mises en scènes and represent the stagings of his ideological stances as his theater performances have become a form of agitprop. At the same time, more than anyone else, Fo has taken his shows "to" his audience, and the targeted audience also underwent transformation over the years as Fo's ideological stand changed. His performances are often political speeches outside traditional political settings. Between 1962, when he and his companion, Franca Rame, were forced out as hosts of the popular television show *Canzonissima,* and 1977, when he was allowed to perform on state television again, his personal and public history is characterized by expulsions, "excommunications," and provocations.

Fo's troubled and intriguing tale began in San Giano in Lombardy in 1926. Son of a railway worker and of a peasant, he attended the Accademia di Brera, an art school, and subsequently enrolled at the University of Milan in the Department of Architecture. However, he abandoned his degree shortly before completing his studies. He then started writing and acting, but his main activity at the time was painting. In 1952 he began to collaborate with the Italian state radio, RAI, for which he wrote comic monologues later broadcast as an eighteen-week series titled *Poer Nano* (Poor Dwarf). From 1953 to 1956 he worked for the movie industry as a writer, and he also acted in *Lo svitato* (Screwloose), directed by Carlo Lizzani.

In this period, however, Fo was still searching for a personal voice. Such a process was contemporary with a major general transformation of the Italian theatrical scene, which was then experiencing the decline of the author and the rise of the director. Fo's first works were in satirical-cabaret style, and the main stratagem in his performances was to overturn and ridicule common beliefs. At this time he was laying the foundations for a new theatrical machine, similar to that of the pre-commedia dell'arte, one which was not yet absorbed by the establishment and accepted as a practice. His Fool-like attitude–that is, the typical behavior of someone who basically lives at the margins of society–enabled him to seek truth without ever having to compromise. His debut was titled *Dito nell'occhio* (A Finger in the Eye, 1953) and scripted with Franco Parenti and Giustino Durano. It was indeed an extremely ambitious project as it comprised twenty-one sketches on the history of humanity. The idea behind the play was to reexamine historical myths such as the building of Cheops's pyramids by concentrating on the thousands of slaves who lost their lives in the effort; the giving of credit for the idea of the Trojan horse to Ulysses when instead an unknown soldier had come up with it; and the presentation of Napoleon and Nelson as two little boys squabbling. Satires of American movies and allusions to contemporary Italian politics filled the second part of the show, which ended with the actors taking pictures of the audience. *Sani da legare* (Fit to Be Tied Up, 1954), also written with Parenti and Durano, was forced to close before the end of the season because of its political content. With his next play, *Gli arcangeli non giocano a flipper* (1959; translated as *Archangels Don't Play Pinball,* 1987), Fo introduced two new elements

Fo as Harlequin (Dario Fo, The Tricks of the Trade, *1991)*

to Italian satire. The first novelty was a progressive growth of the absurd characters, and the second the social class of the characters, who all belonged to the "lumpenproletariat." In the plot of the play the protagonist, a petty criminal, is tricked by his friends into believing he is marrying a beautiful young girl, who is really a prostitute. A series of complications arise with bureaucratic overtones till the end, when the young man is "saved" by the archangels whose intervention recalls the deus ex machina of classical theater.

That same year Fo and Rame formed their own theater company named "La compagnia Dario Fo–Franca Rame." They enjoyed increasing success as they moved from a socially satirical setting to a politically satirical one. After *Gli arcangeli non giocano a flipper* the company staged several other plays, including *Aveva due pistole con gli occhi bianchi e neri* (He Had Two Pistols and White and Black Eyes, 1960), *Chi ruba un piede è fortunato in amore* (He Who Steals a Foot is Lucky in Love, 1961), *Isabella, tre caravelle e un cacciaballe* (Isabella, Three Sailing Ships and a Con Man, 1963), *Settimo, ruba un pò meno* (Seventh, Steal a Bit Less, 1964), and *La signora è da buttare* (Throw the Lady Out, 1967).

Aveva due pistole con occhi bianchi e neri includes fifteen songs and a chorus. The play takes jabs at authority, and Fo almost ended up in prison because he refused to submit the text for approval by the authorities under censorship laws. *Chi ruba un piede è fortunato in amore* is a modern version of the classical myth of Daphne. This play can be considered Fo's most "written" piece. It tackles issues relating to corruption in the construction industry, a "disease" which was afflicting Italy during the postwar economic boom. In fact, many builders were ruining Italy's natural landscape by developing new residential areas with no city planning, but with the aid of corrupted politicians.

Settimo, ruba un pò meno, staged in 1964, can be considered a synthesis of Fo's various attempts to achieve a stage text. It was then rewritten in the 1990s to fit the "Tangentopoli" bribe scandal that rocked Italy and brought the Christian Democrats down after more than forty years in power. In the original version of the play, Fo presented dramatic happenings that ridiculed the political Left in Italy in a grotesque manner as onstage the police killed several protesters. *La colpa è sempre del diavolo* (Always Blame the Devil, 1965) can be considered the first step toward Fo's theatrical maturity. The play presented imaginary events of the Middle Ages, and Fo later declared that what he had staged was the "unofficial" history, the one that cannot be found in textbooks. That is, the play was a farce of devils and witches which denounced the support given by the Catholic Church to temporal powers, and in which Fo portrayed the heretics as the counterforces. At the same time the play alluded to American imperialism and later became the basis for *Mistero Buffo* (1969).

La signora è da buttare was an allegory of American history, filled with an interplay of metaphors staged in a circuslike environment. It was a straightforward attack against the American presence in Vietnam organized in a thoroughly fragmented plot. The play indeed closed a period, as Franca Rame officially joined the Italian Communist Party; the Fo-Rame Company dissolved, and the couple formed a new theater company named Nuova Scena.

At this point Fo and Rame had become celebrities; they appeared in several television commercials, and his plays were being performed throughout Europe. However, they became aware of the great contradiction they were living. Their performances were "comfortable" denunciations of bourgeois society, and the people they criticized were not only paying them but applauding them at their shows. Indeed the bourgeoisie could accept such satire only because it was being produced within its system. Fo and Rame believed they had become like those fools who were actually paid by the royals to make fun of them, and became increasingly tired of

being the "jesters of the bourgeois." They decided to leave the official theater circuit. Their gesture was not an isolated one in Europe: Jean-Louis Barrault was fired as director of the Odéon Theater in Paris for publicly supporting the protest of the university students, and Giorgio Strehler resigned from the Piccolo Teatro in Milan for political reasons.

Fo and Rame's first mise-en-scène after leaving the official circuit was *Grande pantomima con bandiere e pupazzi piccoli e medi* (Grand Pantomime with Small and Middle-Sized Puppets, 1968). With this move they acquired a new audience of peasants, pensioners, and subproletarians. They decided to debut in a small town on the outskirts of Cesena, Sant'Egidio. The venue was new, and the play presented several novelties from their previous productions. Above all there were no characters, strictly speaking, but the audience was placed in the presence of the representation of pure social functions: the Capital, the Business Association, the Bishop, the Puppet-King and the Dragon. Their new theater company had decided that all members would receive the same pay and would alternatively play the major roles. Later on Dario Fo admitted this to be unworkable. The play covers thirty years of Italian history from the Resistance to 1968. The language is simple and immediate. This play, along with all the others of this period, found their circuit in the alternative structure of ARCI, the Italian Communist Party's recreational organization.

Mistero Buffo, produced in 1968, marked a new beginning for the Italian theater. It was a one-act and one-man play. The show was composed of a tapestry of medieval texts and apocryphal Gospels. The language used was a mixture of northern dialects, and the entire text was profoundly subversive of established theatrical, historical, and social practices. At the time Fo had left the main theatrical circuit and had gone to underground theater with a play titled *Fedayin*. On the stage real Palestinian guerrillas sang their songs and told their story; however, Fo was seeking a sort of compromise between the Palestinians and the Israelis.

Because of the political content of this and other plays of his he was watched closely by the censorship committee, and often brought to police stations and threatened. Yet in 1962, probably thanks to a center-left coalition in government, Fo was invited to host Italy's most popular television show, *Canzonissima.* During this atypical experience, Fo and Rame developed an original approach as they criticized and satirized popular song-competition shows just like *Canzonissima.* However, their political satire would doom them, as their critique of Italian contemporary society and political entourage eventually led to their dismissal. A skit that is still one of their best was about a worker who is so grateful to his employer for his job that, when his aunt visits him and ends up in a meat-grinding machine, he does not interrupt production and eventually returns home not with his aunt but with 150 cans of her meat. The show was fiercely attacked by center and right-wing newspapers, and Fo and Rame were rebuked by the directors of RAI, who decided to censor their scripts. As a consequence, they left the show in protest against censorship. In 1966 he was asked to direct *Ci ragiono e ci canto* (I Reason and I Sing), a show produced by the Nuovo Canzoniere Italiano. He was thus exposed to the history of Italian popular music and to the history of the working class. This encounter with popular culture was crucial to the development of Fo's future research and production as he left the official theatrical circuit. With *L'operaio conosce soltanto trecento parole, il padrone mille, per questo lui è padrone* (The Worker Knows Three Hundred Words, the Boss Knows a Thousand—That's Why He Is the Boss, 1969) Fo's satire reached the Italian Communist Party for its policies and thus ended his collaboration with ARCI.

Once again Fo and Rame moved on and founded a new theatrical company, "Collettivo Teatrale La Comune." Then they toured off-off theaters, natural grounds of the ultraleft groups of the extraparliamentary area. The new intellectual/political direction taken by their theater was that of "theater-news," that is, a purely informational theater that would promote awareness. The first staging of this period was *Vorrei morire anche stasera se dovessi pensare che non è servito a niente* (I'd Rather Die Tonight If I Didn't Think It Had Been Worth It, 1970), a piece in support of the Palestinian movement, which is compared to the Italian Resistance. It was followed by *Morte accidentale di un anarchico* (Accidental Death of an Anarchist, 1970), a text engendered by anger over the explosion of a bomb in Piazza Fontana in Milan and the death of an anarchist, Pinelli, while in police custody. The play also proposes a counter theory on terrorist actions in Italy and lays bare the threads of state terrorism. *Pum! Pum! chi è? La polizia!* (Knock, Knock! Who's There? Police!, 1972) was an example of Fo's personal interpretation of didactic theater and was seen by more than a million people. Fo stated that didactic theater should not be cold and detached but has to be a machine that makes the audience laugh about dramatic situations. Furthermore, catharsis is to be avoided so that anger remains inside one and action follows.

The lives of Fo and Rame were thereafter characterized by conflicts with authorities and opposi-

Dario Fo and Franca Rame; photograph by Luigi Ciminaghi on the front cover of Fo's 1989 play, translated in 1992

tion. For instance, in 1973 Rame was attacked by a squad of Fascists, and Fo was arrested for allegedly having disregarded theater rental agreements. He was soon released when thousands protested in his defense. Upon returning from a staging in Paris, Fo and Rame decided to occupy a building in Milan, the Palazzina Liberty, to build a theater. Hundreds joined in the occupation.

In 1974 Fo staged *Non si paga* (translated as *We Can't Pay? We Won't Pay!*, 1978) and in 1975 *Il Fanfani rapito* (Fanfani Kidnapped). These two productions revived the 1958–1959 farces. In 1977 he and Franca returned to state television and worked for Channel Two, which was then controlled by both Socialists and Communists. The programming of *Mistero Buffo* angered the establishment and provoked condemnation from right-wing newspapers and the Vatican. By this time Fo had become the most-performed and translated Italian author abroad. His plays were staged throughout Europe. Nevertheless, the couple was not granted visas to enter the United States in 1980 because of their involvement in *Soccorso Rosso* (Red Aide), a group of lawyers who defended left-wing extremists in trials. In 1983 their play *Coppia Aperta, quasi spalancata* (translated as *An Open Couple–Very Open,* 1985) tackled the crisis of a relationship and condemned the chauvinistic attempts of the husband to set down the rules of the marriage. Fo and Rame were finally granted visas for the United States in 1985 and toured only the eastern part of the States. *Il diavolo con le zinne* (The Devil with Tits, 1997), Fo's latest play, dwells on the contemporary political situation in Italy, and particularly on the role of some magistrates, especially Antonio Di Pietro, in the *Mani Pulite* (Clean Hands) affair.

Mani Pulite was an earthquake that hit not only the Italian political scene but also the whole country. It was initiated by a group of magistrates based in Milan who uncovered a widespread system of bribery and corruption in government agencies and parties. The investigation brought down the government coalition–the Christian Democratic Party, the Socialist Party, the Socialist Democratic Party, the Liberal Party, and the Republican Party. The scandal brought these parties to their knees, and they all eventually dissolved. The Christian Democrats, who had been in power since 1948, split into several political formations and lost millions of votes. The Socialist Party, which had been in the government coalitions since the 1960s, virtually disappeared, and Bettino Craxi, its leader and former prime minister of Italy, fled the country and is presently hiding from Italian magistrates in Tunisia. The only two major parties that were not caught in the scandal were the Italian Communist Party and the Italian Social Movement–the former Fascist Party. They, however, also were transformed, and each eventually split into two formations.

One of the substantial effects of Mani Pulite is that in 1996, for the first time after the constitution of the Republic, the renewed Italian Communist party–now called Democratic Party of the Left (PDS)–gained power in a center-left coalition, in which it holds the majority. Ironically, the corruption that had plagued Italian political life for decades and was finally uncovered by the investigation of the Milanese magistrates had been relentlessly denounced by Fo and Rame for thirty years. What had been experienced as a voice in the desert by a blinded country became a blunt reality, or rather, the "truth." Fo and Rame's commitment to addressing international issues such as the Israeli-Palestinian conflict, the abuse of women, AIDS, and the capitalist exploitation of labor has been equally central to their work. This commit-

ment was one of the prompting factors in the awarding of the Nobel Prize to Dario Fo.

He has been a candidate for the Nobel Prize in literature since 1977, and in 1997 he was finally awarded the prize in recognition of his relentless contribution, not only to the development of contemporary theater but also for his critique of authoritarian and imperialistic practices in the Western world. The Nobel Prize in literature has been, for the first time, awarded to a true person of theater–that is, Dario Fo: playwright, actor, producer, and theater theorist.

References:

Erminia Artese, *Dario Fo parla di Dario Fo* (Cosenza: Lerici, 1977).

Dario Fo and Franca Rame: Theatre Workshops at Riverside Studios, London (London: Red Notes, 1983);

Claudio Meldolesi, *Su un comico in rivolta: Dario Fo il bufalo il bambino* (Rome: Bulzoni, 1978);

Tony Mitchell, *Dario Fo, People's Court Jester* (London: Methuen, 1984);

Mitchell, ed., *File on Dario Fo* (London: Methuen, 1989);

Marisa Pizza, *Il gesto, la parola, l'azione: Poetica, drammaturgia e storia dei monologhi di Dario Fo* (Rome: Bulzoni, 1996);

Paolo Puppa, *Il teatro di Dario Fo: Dalla scena alla piazza* (Venice: Marsilio, 1978);

Michele Straniero, *Giullari e Fo* (Rome: Lato Side, 1978);

Chiara Valentini, *La storia di Fo* (Milan: Feltrinelli, 1977).

Nobel Lecture 1997

Dario Fo

Contra Jogulatores Obloquentes

["Against jesters who defame and insult"]

Law issued by Emperor Frederick II (Messina 1221), declaring that anyone may commit violence against jesters without incurring punishment or sanction.

The drawings I'm showing you are mine. Copies of these, slightly reduced in size, have been distributed among you.

For some time it's been my habit to use images when preparing a speech: rather than write it down, I illustrate it. This allows me to improvise, to exercise my imagination—and to oblige you to use yours.

As I proceed, I will from time to time, indicate to you where we are in the manuscript. That way you won't lose the thread. This will be of help especially to those of you who don't understand either Italian or Swedish. English-speakers will have a tremendous advantage over the rest because they will imagine things I've neither said nor thought. There is of course the problem of the two laughters: those who understand Italian will laugh immediately, those who don't will have to wait for Anna [Barsotti]'s Swedish translation. And then there are those of you who won't know whether to laugh the first time or the second. Anyway, let's get started.

Ladies and gentlemen, the title I've selected for this little chat is "contra jogulatores obloquentes," which you all recognize as Latin, mediaeval Latin to be precise. It's the title of a law issued in Sicily in 1221 by Emperor Frederick II of Swabia, an emperor "anointed by God," who we were taught in school to regard a sovereign of extraordinary enlightenment, a liberal. "Jogulatores obloquentes" means "jesters who defame and insult." The law in question allowed any and all citizens to insult jesters, to beat them and even—if they were in that mood—to kill them, without running any risk of being brought to trial and condemned. I hasten to assure you that this law no longer is in vigour, so I can safely continue.

Ladies and gentlemen,

Friends of mine, noted men of letters, have in various radio and television interviews declared: "The highest prize should no doubt be awarded to the members of the Swedish Academy, for having had the courage this year to award the Nobel Prize to a jester." I agree. Yours is an act of courage that borders on provocation.

It's enough to take stock of the uproar it has caused: sublime poets and writers who normally occupy the loftiest of spheres, and who rarely take interest in those who live and toil on humbler planes, are suddenly bowled over by some kind of whirlwind.

Like I said, I applaud and concur with my friends.

These poets had already ascended to the Parnassian heights when you, through your insolence, sent them toppling to earth, where they fell face and belly down in the mire of normality.

Insults and abuse are hurled at the Swedish Academy, at its members and their relatives back to the seventh generation. The wildest of them clamour: "Down with the King . . . of Norway!" It appears they got the dynasty wrong in the confusion.

(At this point you may turn the page. As you see there is an image of a naked poet bowled over by a whirlwind.)

Some landed pretty hard on their nether parts. There were reports of poets and writers whose nerves and livers suffered terribly. For a few days thereafter there was not a pharmacy in Italy that could muster up a single tranquillizer.

But, dear members of the Academy, let's admit it, this time you've overdone it. I mean come on, first you give the prize to a black man, then to a Jewish writer. Now you give it to a clown. What gives? As they say in Naples: pazziàmme? Have we lost our senses?

Also the higher clergy have suffered their moments of madness. Sundry potentates—great electors of the Pope, bishops, cardinals and prelates of Opus Dei—have all gone through the ceiling, to the point that they've even petitioned for the reinstatement of the law that allowed jesters to be burned at the stake. Over a slow fire.

On the other hand I can tell you there is an extraordinary number of people who rejoice with me over your choice. And so I bring you the most festive thanks, in the name of a multitude of mummers, jesters, clowns, tumblers and storytellers.

(This is where we are now [indicates a page].)

And speaking of storytellers, I mustn't forget those of the small town on Lago Maggiore where I was born and raised, a town with a rich oral tradition.

They were the old storytellers, the master glass blowers who taught me and other children the craftsmanship, the art, of spinning fantastic yarns. We would listen to them, bursting with laughter—laughter that would stick in our throats as the tragic allusion that surmounted each sarcasm would dawn on us. To this day I keep fresh in my mind the story of the Rock of Caldé.

"Many years ago," began the old glass blower, "way up on the crest of that steep cliff that rises from the lake there was a town called Caldé. As it happened, this town was sitting on a loose splinter of rock that slowly, day by day, was sliding down towards the precipice. It was a splendid little town, with a campanile, a fortified tower at the very peak and a cluster of houses, one after the other. It's a town that once was and that now is gone. It disappeared in the 15th Century.

Five of the twenty-five cartoons distributed by Dario Fo at the Nobel Prize ceremony (translated by Faust F. Pauluzzi). #1. The Italian words translate as: Against Throat-cutting Hecklers; Friends, Men of Letters, Famous Artists; Members of the Academy; Interview; Jester; Provocation; Uproar.

#8. Personally I Owe Much to Master Blowers; Crazily; Explosive.

#9. Thunderous and Solemn the Greeting Arises; Shakespeare, Molière; Both Disparaged by Know-It-Alls and Wise-Guys

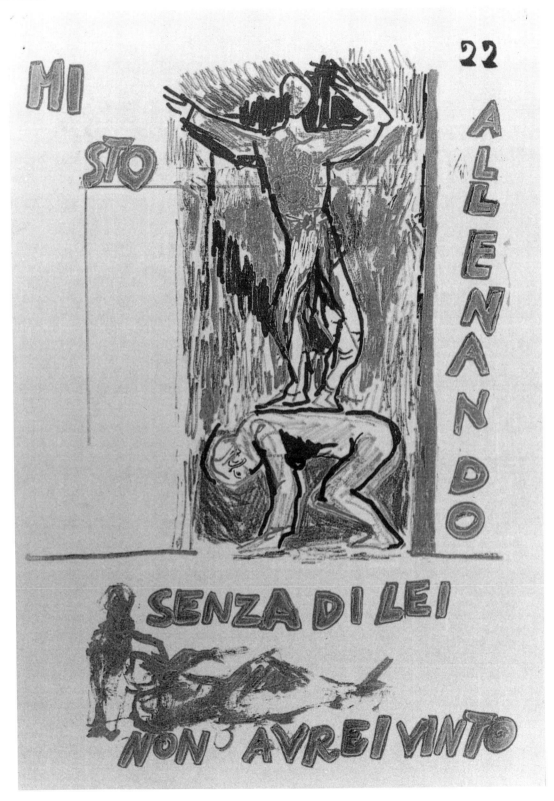

#22. I Am in Training; without Her I Would Not Have Won

#24. Franca! Where Is Franca?

"'Hey,' shouted the peasants and fishermen down in the valley below. 'You're sliding, you'll fall down from there.'

"But the cliff dwellers wouldn't listen to them, they even laughed and made fun of them: 'You think you're pretty smart, trying to scare us into running away from our houses and our land so you can grab them instead. But we're not that stupid.'

"So they continued to prune their vines, sow their fields, marry and make love. They went to mass. They felt the rock slide under their houses but they didn't think much about it. 'Just the rock settling. Quite normal,' they said, reassuring each other.

"The great splinter of rock was about to sink into the lake. 'Watch out, you've got water up to your ankles,' shouted the people along the shore. 'Nonsense, that's just drainage water from the fountains, it's just a bit humid,' said the people of the town, and so, slowly but surely, the whole town was swallowed by the lake.

"Gurgle . . . gurgle . . . splash . . . they sink . . . houses, men, women, two horses, three donkeys . . . heehaw . . . gurgle. Undaunted, the priest continued to receive the confession of a nun: 'Te absolvi . . . animus . . . santi . . . gurgle . . . Aame . . . gurgle . . .' The tower disappeared, the campanile sank with bells and all: Dong . . . ding . . . dop . . . plock . . .

"Even today," continued the old glass blower, "if you look down into the water from that outcrop that still juts out from the lake, and if in that same moment a thunderstorm breaks out, and the lightning illuminates the bottom of the lake, you can still see—incredible as it may seem!—the submerged town, with its streets still intact and even the inhabitants themselves, walking around and glibly repeating to themselves: 'Nothing has happened.' The fish swim back and forth before their eyes, even into their ears. But they just brush them off: 'Nothing to worry about. It's just some kind of fish that's learned to swim in the air.'

"'Atchoo!' 'God bless you!' 'Thank you . . . it's a bit humid today . . . more than yesterday . . . but everything's fine.' They've reached rock bottom, but as far as they're concerned, nothing has happened at all."

Disturbing though it may be, there's no denying that a tale like this still has something to tell us.

I repeat, I owe much to these master glass blowers of mine, and they—I assure you—are immensely grateful to you, members of this Academy, for rewarding one of their disciples.

And they express their gratitude with explosive exuberance. In my home town, people swear that on the night the news arrived that one of their own storytellers was to be awarded the Nobel Prize, a kiln that had been standing cold for some fifty years suddenly erupted in a broadside of flames, spraying high into the air—like a fireworks *finale*—a myriad splinters of coloured glass, which then showered down on the surface of the lake, releasing an impressive cloud of steam.

(While you applaud, I'll have a drink of water. [Turning to the interpreter:] Would you like some?

It's important that you talk among yourselves while we drink, because if you try to hear the gurgle gurgle gurgle the water makes as we swallow we'll choke on it and start coughing. So instead you can exchange niceties like "Oh, what a lovely evening it is, isn't it?"

End of intermission: we turn to a new page, but don't worry, it'll go faster from here.)

Above all others, this evening you're due the loud and solemn thanks of an extraordinary master of the stage, little-known not only to you and to people in France, Norway, Finland . . . but also to the people of Italy. Yet he was, until Shakespeare, doubtless the greatest playwright of renaissance Europe. I'm referring to Ruzzante Beolco, my greatest master along with Molière: both actors-playwrights, both mocked by the leading men of letters of their times. Above all, they were despised for bringing onto the stage the everyday life, joys and desperation of the common people; the hypocrisy and the arrogance of the high and mighty; and the incessant injustice. And their major, unforgivable fault was this: in telling these things, they made people laugh. Laughter does not please the mighty.

Ruzzante, the true father of the *Commedia dell'Arte,* also constructed a language of his own, a language of and for the theatre, based on a variety of tongues: the dialects of the Po Valley, expressions in Latin, Spanish, even German, all mixed with onomatopoeic sounds of his own invention. It is from him, from Beolco Ruzzante, that I've learned to free myself from conventional literary writing and to express myself with words that you can chew, with unusual sounds, with various techniques of rhythm and breathing, even with the rambling nonsense-speech of the *grammelot.*

Allow me to dedicate a part of this prestigious prize to Ruzzante.

A few days ago, a young actor of great talent said to me: "Maestro, you should try to project your energy, your enthusiasm, to young people. You have to give them this charge of yours. You have to share your professional knowledge and experience with them." Franca—that's my wife—and I looked at each other and said: "He's right." But when we teach others our art, and share this charge of fantasy, what end will it serve? Where will it lead?

In the past couple of months, Franca and I have visited a number of university campuses to hold workshops and seminars before young audiences. It has been surprising—not to say disturbing—to discover their ignorance about the times we live in. We told them about the proceedings now in course in Turkey against the accused culprits of the massacre in Sivas. Thirty-seven of the country's foremost democratic intellectuals, meeting in the Anatolian town to celebrate the memory of a famous mediaeval jester of the Ottoman period, were burned alive in the dark of the night, trapped inside their hotel. The fire was the handiwork of a group of fanatical fundamentalists that enjoyed protection from elements within the Government itself. In one night, thirty-seven of the country's most celebrated artists, writers, directors, actors and Kurdish dancers were erased from this Earth.

In one blow these fanatics destroyed some of the most important exponents of Turkish culture.

Thousands of students listened to us. The looks in their faces spoke of their astonishment and incredulity. They had never heard of the massacre. But what impressed me the most is that not even the teachers and professors present had heard of it. There Turkey is, on the Mediterranean, practically in front of us, insisting on joining the European Community, yet no one had heard of the massacre. Salvini, a noted Italian democrat, was right on the mark when he observed: "The widespread ignorance of events is the main buttress of injustice." But this absent-mindedness on the part of the young has been conferred upon them by those who are charged to educate and inform them: among the absent-minded and uninformed, school teachers and other educators deserve first mention.

Young people easily succumb to the bombardment of gratuitous banalities and obscenities that each day is served to them by the mass media: heartless TV action films where in the space of ten minutes they are treated to three rapes, two assassinations, one beating and a serial crash involving ten cars on a bridge that then collapses, whereupon everything—cars, drivers and passengers—precipitates into the sea . . . only one person survives the fall, but he doesn't know how to swim and so drowns, to the cheers of the crowd of curious onlookers that suddenly has appeared on the scene.

At another university we spoofed the project—alas well under way—to manipulate genetic material, or more specifically, the proposal by the European Parliament to allow patent rights on living organisms. We could feel how the subject sent a chill through the audience. Franca and I explained how our Eurocrats, kindled by powerful and ubiquitous multinationals, are preparing a scheme worthy of the plot of a sci-fi/horror movie entitled "Frankenstein's pig brother." They're trying to get the approval of a directive which (and get this!) would authorize industries to take patents on living beings, or on parts of them, created with techniques of genetic manipulation that seem taken straight out of "The Sorcerer's Apprentice."

This is how it would work: by manipulating the genetic make-up of a pig, a scientist succeeds in making the pig more human-like. By this arrangement it becomes much easier to remove from the pig the organ of your choice—a liver, a kidney—and to transplant it in a human. But to assure that the transplanted pig-organs aren't rejected, it's also necessary to transfer certain pieces of genetic information from the pig to the human. The result: a human pig (even though you will say that there are already plenty of those).

And every part of this new creature, this humanized pig, will be subject to patent laws; and whosoever wishes a part of it will have to pay copyright fees to the company that "invented" it. Secondary illnesses, monstrous deformations, infectious diseases—all are optionals, included in the price . . .

The Pope has forcefully condemned this monstrous genetic witchcraft. He has called it an offence against humanity, against the dignity of man, and has gone to pains to underscore the project's total and irrefutable lack of moral value.

The astonishing thing is that while this is happening, an American scientist, a remarkable magician—you've probably read about him in the papers—has succeeded in transplanting the head of a baboon. He cut the heads off two baboons and switched them. The baboons didn't feel all that great after the operation. In fact, it left them paralysed, and they both died shortly thereafter, but the experiment worked, and that's the great thing.

But here's the rub: this modern-day Frankenstein, a certain Professor White, is all the while a distinguished member of the Vatican Academy of Sciences. Somebody should warn the Pope.

So, we enacted these criminal farces to the kids at the universities, and they laughed their heads off. They would say of Franca and me: "They're a riot, they come up with the most fantastic stories." Not for a moment, not even with an inkling in their spines, did they grasp that the stories we told were true.

These encounters have strengthened us in our conviction that our job is—in keeping with the exhortation of the great Italian poet Savinio—"to tell our own story." Our task as intellectuals, as persons who mount the pulpit or the stage, and who, most importantly, address to young people, our task is not just to teach them method, like how to use the arms, how to control breathing, how to use the stomach, the voice, the falsetto, the *contraccampo*. It's not enough to teach a technique or a style: we have to show them what is happening around us. They have to be able to tell their own story. A theatre, a literature, an artistic expression that does not speak for its own time has no relevance.

Recently I took part in a large conference with lots of people where I tried to explain, especially to the younger participants, the ins and outs of a particular Italian court case. The original case resulted in seven separate proceedings, at the end of which three Italian left-wing politicians were sentenced to 21 years of imprisonment each, accused of having murdered a police commissioner. I've studied the documents of the case—as I did when I prepared *Accidental Death of an Anarchist*—and at the conference I recounted the facts pertaining to it, which are really quite absurd, even farcical. But at a certain point I realized I was speaking to deaf ears, for the simple reason that my audience was ignorant not only of the case itself, but of what had happened five years earlier, ten years earlier: the violence, the terrorism. They knew nothing about the massacres that occurred in Italy, the trains that blew up, the bombs in the *piazze* or the farcical court cases that have dragged on since then.

The terribly difficult thing is that in order to talk about what is happening today, I have to start with what happened thirty years ago and then work my way forward. It's not enough to speak about the present. And pay attention, this isn't just about Italy: the same thing happens everywhere, all over Europe. I've tried in Spain and encountered the same difficulty; I've tried in France, in Germany, I've yet to try in Sweden, but I will.

To conclude, let me share this medal with Franca.

Franca Rame, my companion in life and in art who you, members of the Academy, acknowledge in your motivation of the prize as actress and author; who has had a hand in many of the texts of our theatre.

(At this very moment, Franca is on stage in a theatre in Italy but will join me the day after tomorrow. Her flight arrives midday, if you like we can all head out together to pick her up at the airport.)

Franca has a very sharp wit, I assure you. A journalist put the following question to her: "So how does it feel to be the wife of a Nobel Prize winner? To have a monument in your home?" To which she answered: "I'm not worried. Nor do I feel at all at a disadvantage; I've been in training for a long time. I do my exercises each morning: I go down on my hands and knees, and that way I've accustomed myself to becoming a pedestal to a monument. I'm pretty good at it."

Like I said, she has a sharp wit. At times she even turns her irony against herself.

Without her at my side, where she has been for a lifetime, I would never have accomplished the work you have seen fit to honour. Together we've staged and recited thousands of performances, in theatres, occupied factories, at university sit-ins, even in deconsecrated churches, in prisons and city parks, in sunshine and pouring rain, always together. We've had to endure abuse, assaults by the police, insults from the right-thinking and violence. And it is Franca who has had to suffer the most atrocious aggression. She has had to pay more dearly than any one of us, with her neck and limb in the balance, for the solidarity with the humble and the beaten that has been our premise.

The day it was announced that I was to be awarded the Nobel Prize I found myself in front of the theatre on Via di Porta Romana in Milan where Franca, together with Giorgio Albertazzi, was performing *The Devil with Tits*. Suddenly I was surrounded by a throng of reporters, photographers and camera-wielding TV-crews. A passing tram stopped, unexpectedly, the driver stepped out to greet me, then all the passengers stepped out too, they applauded me, and everyone wanted to shake my hand and congratulate me . . . when at a certain point they all stopped in their tracks and, as with a single voice, shouted "Where's Franca?" They began to holler "Francaaa" until, after a little while, she appeared. Discombobulated and moved to tears, she came down to embrace me.

At that moment, as if out of nowhere, a band appeared, playing nothing but wind instruments and drums. It was made up of kids from all parts of the city and, as it happened, they were playing together for the first time. They struck up "Porta Romana bella, Porta Romana" in samba beat. I've never heard anything played so out of tune, but it was the most beautiful music Franca and I had ever heard.

Believe me, this prize belongs to both of us.

Thank you.

translation: Paul Claesson

The Year in Fiction

George Garrett
University of Virginia

Everybody's up in arms, more than usual these days, about how commercial fiction is driving out the literary kind and soon we'll all be buying either Michael Crichton or Danielle Steel at one of the many Barnes & Nobles; or, failing that, we'll all be watching very bad movies or worse TV, and that will be that.

—Carolyn See, *The Washington Post*
(28 November)

"We have an uneducated class of people. They're too stupid to read. So now we're catering to them."

—publisher Roger Straus, quoted in the
New York Observer (18 August)

Sometime in late September or early October, someone at the *Washington Post Book World* called and asked me to write a few hundred words on my favorite literary novels of 1997 for their special holiday issue. And I did so, hurrying to get it in by deadline, because I was off to Venice for a brief vacation and a Smithsonian tour. My little piece had a short lead-in paragraph in which I noted with dutiful pleasure that there had been some good books by well-known masters—Saul Bellow, Bernard Malamud, Peter Matthiessen, Norman Mailer, Philip Roth, John Updike, Joyce Carol Oates, and others (not a bad batting order); these had likely enough earned plenty of critical attention elsewhere. My four or five books, as good as anything mentioned above, would maybe be less known to the casual reader.

This defensive little paragraph was edited out by the people at the *Post*. Otherwise they left my account of "Literary Fiction" under the general rubric of "Informed Opinions" (*Washington Post Book World*, 7 December) as is. And here it is:

Literary Fiction

On the Road with the Archangel, by Frederick Buechner (Harper San Francisco). Buechner has been a hero of mine since 1950, when his first novel, *A Long Day's Dying,* appeared. Since then there have been 15 books of nonfiction and 14 more novels, each a new adventure. This latest, told in the first person by the Archangel Raphael, is a version of the fabulous and apocryphal Book of Tobit. It sings and dances, wealthy with laughter and deeply moving. Buechner is as good as we have.

Byrne, by Anthony Burgess (Carroll & Graf). The farewell address of the late Anthony Burgess, brief as it is, has enough story about several generations of wild Irishmen to fill a fat epic. With economy and bravado Burgess chose to write his novel in verse, four parts in ottava rima, invented by Ariosto, beloved by Byron in "Don Juan," and one part in the nine line stanza of Edmund Spenser. Sound formidable? It isn't. It's great fun and games and easily accessible. How appropriate for *Byrne* to be Burgess's final novel, that he shouldn't have to rest in peace.

A God Strolling in the Cool of the Evening, by Mario de Carvalho (LSU Press). Set in the twilight of the Roman Empire, this Portuguese novel tells the story of a good man in bad times, a man who might be called noble except that his irony and honesty won't allow it.

Frenzy, by Percival Everett (Graywolf). One of the best and most original of our younger American novelists is Percival Everett, and his 11th book, *Frenzy,* an altogether indescribable accounting of the story of Dionysos and his "mortal bookmark" and buddy Vlepo, is like no other I know of. Let it happen and it will work for you, creating a strange world we may have lived in once upon a time.

Nashville 1864: The Dying of the Light, by Madison Jones (J. S. Sanders). This book, by veteran novelist Madison Jones, is specific in time and place, a splendidly realized account of the fall of the Confederacy in the west as experienced by 12-year-old Steven Moore, as quirky and credible as Huck Finn. In a year of Civil War novels, including a couple of enormously successful ones, this one is, for my money, the best of the lot.

The only other year's end list of outstanding fiction limited to five titles ("The Best Books of 1997") appeared in *Time* 5 January 1998 in the following order: *Mason & Dixon* (Holt), by Thomas Pynchon; *Underworld* (Scribners), by Don DeLillo; *Cold Mountain* (Atlantic Monthly), by Charles Frazier; *American Pastoral* (Houghton Mifflin), by Philip Roth; and *The God of Small Things* (Random House), by Arundhati Roy. I am pleased and relieved to report that all five of these also appear on the *DLB* list of notable books of 1997 below.

I stand firm in my choices and support of those wonderful books and, as well and just as much, in support of the longer list of favorite books of 1997 that follows. I note that many of these novels and collections of stories are also to be found in *The New York Times Book Review* under "Notable Books of the Year 1997" (7 December), 136 titles, including poetry with fiction, and some are not. Another way of putting it: not everything on the *Times* list, by any means, made my own personal list of notable books for the *DLB Yearbook 1997*.

In any case, after much moaning and groaning (at the bar) about the fate of literary fiction in the hands of bottom-line-worshiping publishers and megalomaniacal chain stores, supermarkets of books, and not counting what things, good and bad and indifferent, that may have fallen by the wayside, it was a year with, after all, a full share of excellent literary fiction, far more than can be suggested by any list, short or long. It seems, then, fitting and proper to begin this annual look at the state of fiction with my list of favorite works that came to my attention, one way and another, during the year:

Lee K. Abbott, *Wet Places at Noon* (Iowa). Eight stories by one of our most gifted, lively, and highly praised story writers. "Abbott's community is pure Americana," his publisher writes, "a wild world inhabited by gloriously street-smart smartasses: overeducated, under-employed men mourning for the confident women who have left them. . . . His urgent, maximalist style allows their exhilarating voices to be heard and remembered." Here is one of those voices from "The Talk Talked between Worms":

> For company, I had turned the TV on—*General Hospital,* I recall, in which attractive inhabitants from a made-up metropolis were falling in love or scheming diligently against one another. They were named Scorpio and Monica and Laura and Bobbi, and for a moment, it as long as one in war, I desired to be at the center of them: Reilly Jay Hamsey in a fancy Italian suit, his teeth as white as Chiclets, him with lines to orate and a well-groomed crowd happy to hear them.

Rilla Askew, *The Mercy Seat* (Viking). A large-scale, closely observed, fully imagined novel of the settlement of the West in the late 1880s. Told by multiple voices and from various points of view, it is at heart the story of two brothers, John and Lafayette Lodi, whose differences have biblical parallels in Cain and Abel, Jacob and Esau. Madison Smartt Bell writes (for the jacket) that "the story of *The Mercy Seat* feels as elemental and strong as something from Greek mythology, or the Old Testament." The language is at once apt and poetic. The

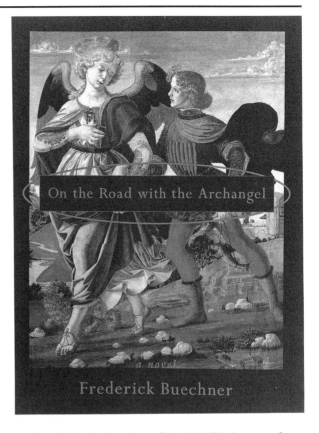

Dust jacket for the winner of the 1997 Dictionary of Literary Biography *novel award*

sense of place, Oklahoma and the Ouachita Mountains, is abiding. A powerful new novel by the author of *Strange Business*:

> I followed them on the white horse miles and miles going slow on the wagon road to Latham because her eyes told me, because her mouth said, Come go with us, but her eyes said You are going to die if you do not. And I did die to something, because I fell unconscious for seven days, they said a death mark came on me, Jessie said I was dead, she wanted to bury me, but Thula told them I was not dead but in the other world receiving my instructions, and I remembered what it was then, for a little time I remembered.

Louis Auchincloss, *The Atonement and Other Stories* (Houghton Mifflin). This strikingly prolific writer (thirty-nine books of fiction, fifteen of nonfiction in fifty years) here offers twelve stories, versions of his eastern WASP world, its honorable virtues, its often disguised and concealed vices. Auchincloss has long since mastered and refined the narrative style, marked by control, clarity, and a full range of irony. These stories show no falling off of energy nor any sense that he has finished his exploration and exploitation of a vanishing social class:

It was like her to waste no time in what they both recognized, without a word exchanged, as a compact. He could always beat her at backgammon; for the hundreds of dollars lost she expected some market tips. Though supported by the carefully doled-out allowance of a rich but exasperated mother, Ilona was usually as broke as she had left each husband and always in search of a windfall.

Paul Auster, *Hand to Mouth: A Chronicle of Early Failure* (Holt). Auster's first in a multiple-book contract with Holt, *Hand to Mouth* is an oddly interesting marriage of fact and fiction. Basically a memoir of hard times with no money, the book includes three plays, a tabletop baseball game complete with cards and rules, and Auster's first full-length novel, "Squeeze Play," a detective story written under the name Paul Benjamin:

It's all a matter of details, coincidence, the chance gesture, the unconsciously spoken word. You have to be alert at every moment. On the lookout for the slightest note of discord, the subtle hint that things are not what they seem to be. . . . If you're not careful, you can get lost in the labyrinth of other people's lives and never find a way out. But those are the risks. Once you get involved with human beings, there are no straight roads anymore.

Howard Bahr, *The Black Flower: A Novel of the Civil War* (Nautical and Aviation Publishing). Bahr, a former curator of William Faulkner's house, Rowan Oak, has set his novel in and around the November 1864 battle at Franklin, Tennessee. The principal character, in a large cast, is twenty-six-year-old Bushrod Carter, a rifleman from Mississippi. Shelby Foote has called *The Black Flower* the best account written of the battle of Franklin:

And in the field of trampled grass, amid the false twilight and the rush of living water, Bushrod Carter looked at his hands. He was not afraid now—the worst of that was over, back at the foot of the hills when they could see the long plain stretching out before them and the works where the Strangers waited. He was not afraid, he just wasn't ready, and he knew that if he had a hundred years he would be unready still. Too many things to say, too many thoughts he hadn't shaped yet, too much life.

John Banville, *The Untouchable* (Knopf). Starting from the facts of the life and times of Anthony Blount and the Cambridge circle of spies, Banville, in this, his eleventh novel, has fully imagined and created an alternative or parallel life, that of Victor Maskell, like his model a spy, probably a double agent, and a distinguished critic and art historian. Basically a sustained monologue by Maskell, addressed to an ambiguous (perhaps false) biographer, Miss Vanderleur; layered in irony, intelligence, and, appropriately, a keen sensitivity which gives the sensuous affective surfaces a glittering reality; the story, told from old age and illness, follows Maskell and his fellows from the 1920s through the 1930s and the Spanish civil war, World War II, and the Cold War. The fully realized character of Maskell, a complex man of vices and follies and surprising virtues, is a tribute to the power of fiction to summon up truth:

Everybody nowadays disparages the 1950s, saying what a dreary decade it was—and they are right, if you think of McCarthyism, and Korea, the Hungarian rebellion, all that serious historical stuff; I suspect, however, that it is not public but private affairs that people are complaining of. Quite simply they did not get enough of sex. . . . Whereas—O my friends!—to be queer was very bliss. The fifties was the last great age of queerdom.

Frederick Barthelme, *Bob the Gambler* (Houghton Mifflin). Ray (Adam) and Jewel (Eve) play at the fall of man in a casino called Paradise on the tacky Mississippi Gulf Coast. As the *Washington Post* (12 October) put it: "*Bob the Gambler* is ultimately about how utter ruin can give fresh meaning to life, and it's a strangely bouncy tale."

Rick Bass, *The Sky, the Stars, the Wilderness* (Houghton Mifflin). Equally adept in fiction and nonfiction, story and essay, Rick Bass here presents three short novels, various in setting, form, and content, yet linked by a lyrical evocation of the wilderness. In the title novella a woman, the last of her family, which has owned and occupied a ten-thousand-acre ranch since 1846, tells of her life growing up there and returning and of her unconditional love for the wildness of uncorrupted nature:

I live here on the Prade Ranch alone—already years beyond the age of my mother when she returned to the ranch—to the particular elements of the earth: soil, water, carbon, sky. You can rot or you can burn but either way, if you're lucky, a place will shape and cut and bend you, will strengthen you and weaken you. You trade your life for the privilege of this experience—the joy of a place, the joy of blood family; the job of knowledge gotten by listening and observing.

Charles Baxter, *Believers* (Pantheon). This collection, Baxter's fourth, consists of seven short stories and the title novella. Baxter's fiction, widely admired, is accurately described on the jacket as an "unparalleled gift for revealing the unexpected in the ordinary, for capturing the fleeting moments that indelibly define a life, for articulating the moral and emotional quandaries that can besiege us as we balance love and responsibility." Forms, settings, subjects, points of view are different from story to story, and he is an adventurous innovator; but at the center is a voice and a vision all his own:

> All this happened a long time ago. Most of the witnesses are gone or, if they are still alive are deeply irritable, as my mother is, with the crankiness of aging people who do not want to give up their treasures to someone who is not likely to appreciate them. Today I have brought flowers to brighten up her room and a new biography of Susan B. Anthony.

Ann Beattie, *My Life, Starring Dara Falcon* (Knopf). Ann Beattie's eleventh book—she is author of five other novels and five collections of short stories—tells the story of the brilliant, manipulative, and seductive Dara Falcon and her profound and unsettling influence on Jean Warner, the narrator of the story. Subtle and complex, this story of an unlikely friendship opened to mixed notices from reviewers. Particularly injurious was the negative review in *The New York Times* (24 April) by Michiko Kakutani, jumping the gun—the book's publication date was 12 May. A response by John O'Brien in the *Review of Contemporary Fiction* (Summer) took issue and umbrage with Kakutani's point of view:

> So what *is* Kakutani's problem? Putting aside her general mediocrity as a reviewer, why does she have such objections to this book? The answer would seem to reside in the fact that the narrator is an upper-middle-class housewife who, in trying to escape the drudgery of her life, turns to a figure such as Dara as a model. In brief, this is the 1950s, Madame Bovary is dead, Beattie isn't being politically correct and thus provides no models for real American women to emulate, which is after all the sole purpose of literary art. Yes?

Beyond the usual boundaries of praise and blame, Beattie's new book is one of her best and most mature works so far.

Saul Bellow, *The Actual* (Viking). A short, evocative, wonderful book, as rich and sardonic and funny as any of Bellow, early or late. Harry Trellman tells all, including his love for Amy Wustrin, and a love story (with a well-earned happy ending) is what it proves to be. Meanwhile Bellow gives us a good look at Chicago and some memorable characters there:

> With my chink or Jap looks, I am seldom taken for a Jew. I suppose there is some advantage in this. When you are identified as a Jew, you are fair game. The rules of behavior change, and you become in a sense expendable. Now, Adletsky, as one of the richest men in the world, didn't need to care whether you esteemed him or not. He was openly Jewish, because it was altogether too clear. Besides, your opinion didn't matter a damn to him.

Doris Betts, *The Sharp Teeth of Love* (Knopf). This book is Doris Betts's ninth book of fiction, a novel set mainly in the West, the High Sierras, and featuring (in a cast of well-realized, interesting characters) Luna Stone, a good and a troubled young woman, trying to find herself and a life worth living. In a wonderful surprise a ghost (coming to us through the sensitive imagination of Luna), the ghost of Tamsen Donner of the Donner Party, becomes an important and believable character:

> Like Luna, Tamsen Donner had come to this place the long way around, had lived in North Carolina, too. Had taught school there at Elizabeth City on the Pasquotank River. From that land of fish and duck hunting and Dismal Swamp she had ended up here in the blizzards, and one man had eaten her time and her strength and her nursing care while another one—though he always denied it—had possibly eaten her flesh.

Heinrich Böll, *The Mad Dog: Stories* (St. Martin's Press). This book consists of ten stories, most of them about Germany and Germans during and after World War II, originally written by Böll in the 1940s and 1950s:

> If only he would wake up. His face was so insanely happy it made her sick. She saw nothing of herself in his face. It was horrible to be so alone, to sit by his couch and not know what he had written, or whether it would be published, or if they would get any money for it. Not to know why he was smiling so happily, not to know where he found the money or credit to get drunk.

Ron Carlson, *The Hotel Eden: Stories* (Norton). Carlson's third collection of stories (he is also author of two novels), twelve stories, varied in form and subject, first published in literary magazines as well as *Esquire, Harper's,* and *Gentleman's Quarterly,* is marked by clarity, balance, fully dimensional characterization, and a wealth of voices who are easy to listen to. Beyond these things, however, Carlson demonstrates a fine-tuned and subtle sense of the inward feelings of his characters and, as well, an irrepressible and generous sense of humor.

> I took my stupid question and the great load of other stupid questions forming in my ordinary skull out of the girls' room and through the dark hallways of Granger High and out into the great sad night. The parking lot was empty and I stood by the red scooter as if it were a shrine to the woman I loved, I ached for, in other words Betsy, who now walked toward me across the pavement, and who now, I realized, wasn't exactly my

brother's lover anymore, a notion that gave me an odd shiver. I was as confused as bakers get to be.

Mario de Carvalho, *A God Strolling in the Cool of the Evening* (Louisiana State University Press). Winner of the Pegasus Prize for Literature, this Portuguese novel, translated by Gregory Rabassa, is outwardly a kind of historical thriller, set in the vividly evoked world of the Roman Empire. But it is more than that, as well. It is also the story of a good man in bad times, Lucius Valerius Quincius, a man who could be called noble except for his own honesty and irony which won't allow that. Though set in ancient times, this story is as pertinent as this morning's headlines:

> I set about reviewing my own case coldly, as if sitting in judgment on myself. A procedural question: had I indeed been bewitched by Iunia? I went over all my encounters with her, acknowledging the strange and subtle pleasure I got from them, even though most of the time my words and attitudes had seemed ungentle and distasteful to me, even though I had been constantly testing the limits of my self-control as I tried to shake back my fury. It was true that Iunia attracted me, even against my will, like these magical crags that loom loftily over the sea and call ships to them, smashing their hulls against the rocks.

Stephanie Cowell, *The Players: A Novel of the Young Shakespeare* (Norton). This third novel in the author's Elizabethan/Jacobean series, basically a biographical novel of Shakespeare's life up to 1595, takes great risks and triumphs over them. Not everyone, by any means, will agree with all details of Cowell's characterization and motivation of Shakespeare. But the time and place are vividly, sensuously realized, shoring up her authority with an expressive, poetic authenticity. And her characterizations of others—Marlowe, Jonson, Greene, Heminges, Henslowe, the Earl of Southhampton among others—are solidly based in reality. Finally there is a personal engagement, the effort of a gifted writer of the present to understand and to summon up a greater writer of the past. As she writes in her excellent "Historical Notes":

> As a writer I have taken great interest in following the path of the slowly emerging artist, always an individual matter and one of much personal struggle. I believe Shakespeare was in his youth a charming man who moved with grace, danced, was much drawn to music and laughter, and was deeply sensual. It is no wonder his colleagues loved him so much. Even after four hundred years, his words speak to us of his astonishing empathy for his fellow man.

Elizabeth Cox, *Night Talk* (Graywolf). Elizabeth Cox's third novel, set during the civil rights struggles of the 1950s and 1960s, and today, deals mainly with the complex, long friendship of Evie, who is white, and Janey Louise, who is black, and their mothers, Agnes and Volusia. Of the daughters of Janey and herself Evie writes (in the "Epilogue, 1991"):

> These girls whom we imagined would be close friends, are not. But they know how to tolerate each other with politeness learned from schools and politicians. They speak guardedly about their feelings, because they have been told that words can start a riot. They do not yet believe that love can stop one.

Harry Crews, *Celebration* (Simon and Schuster). This is the twenty-first book by Crews in a busy and productive career as a highly original Southern novelist whose "narrative magic" is aptly described by Joseph Heller as "weird, funny, and starkly powerful." Here a gothic but altogether credible geriatric set lives in a Florida trailer park called Forever and Forever. "A beautiful young bombshell" named Too Much arrives to wake up the neighborhood:

> She was standing now, her naked young-girl's breasts cantilevered ninety degrees from her rib cage. Without leaning more than a foot, he could have taken a nipple in his mouth. At that moment, he would have given his other hand to know that she would have welcomed him to do it.

Lydia Davis, *Almost No Memory* (Farrar, Straus). A decade after her collection of stories *Break It Down,* Davis has gathered fifty-one stories in less than two hundred pages (some are very short, less than a page) various in form and content but bound together by her own highly developed, sophisticated, funny-sad voice. Her work, freighted with high praise from high places, is described by Jonathan Franzen as "delicious, hilarious, dismaying." Here is the complete text of the story "The Outing":

> An outburst of anger near the road, a refusal to speak on the path, a silence in the pine woods, a silence across the old railroad bridge, an attempt to be friendly in the water, a refusal to end the argument on the flat stones, a cry of anger on the steep bank of dirt, a weeping among the bushes.

Nicholas Delbanco, *Old Scores* (Warner). Delbanco's twelfth novel—he is also author of two collections of stories and three works of nonfiction—*Old Scores* is an old-fashioned, well-plotted, allusive, and moving love story, beginning with a student-teacher affair at Catamount College (read Bennington) between gifted philosopher Paul Ballard and a beautiful idealist, Elizabeth Sieverdsen, in the late 1960s and ending here and now, after years of difficulty for the world and these people in it:

> There are few men and women who have what can fairly be called a great passion, and she was one of the few. She shared her youth and middle age with someone she adored and who adored her equally. She had been, she told herself, blessed. The love had transfigured them each and both; the record of their devotion was hers to remember and keep.

Don DeLillo, *Underworld* (Scribner). Hugely hyped, massively and expensively promoted, widely reviewed, DeLillo's latest, and his eleventh, novel was (briefly) a best-seller and at more than eight hundred pages, hard to heft and even harder to describe briefly by anyone, including the busy publisher. What can be said is that it is the story of (among other things) the lives and times (our times) of Nick Shay and Klara Sax. Shay is, appropriately for our age, a waste-disposal specialist; Klara is an artist. There are a host of other cameo characters, "real" and fictional. And the whole thing gets under way with a brilliant fifty-page account of the home run Bobby Thomson hit off of Ralph Branca, giving the Giants the 1951 pennant. Which also happens to be the same day the news arrived that the Cold War was deadly serious—the Soviets tested an atomic bomb. This wildly ambitious novel, full of stories, is linked by the selfsame baseball that Thomson hit. In the jacket copy of the publisher it is "fought over and scuffed, generates the narrative that follows. It takes the reader deeply into the lives of Nick and Klara and into modern memory and the soul of American culture—from Bronx tenements to grand ballrooms to a B-52 bombing raid over Vietnam." Like this year's *Mason & Dixon,* this one will take some time and some sorting out at leisure to be truly known. Meanwhile there is DeLillo's style, which is, unquestionably, at its finest hour (so far):

> You know about families and their video cameras. You know how kids get involved, how the camera shows them that every subject is potentially changed, a million things that they never see with the unaided eye. They investigate the meaning of inert objects and dumb pets and they poke at family privacy. They learn to see things twice.

Thomas Dyja, *Play for a Kingdom* (Harcourt Brace). In a year marked by several outstanding Civil War novels, this one benefits from a new and

Dust jacket for an aggressively promoted and well-received novel

imaginative twist. A company from the 14th Brooklyn encounters a company of Alabama infantry, both on peripheral picket duty following the Battle of the Wilderness. Over a period of time, leading up to Spotsylvania, they play a series of four baseball games against each other:

> There were now two outs, though Lyman could hear the Rebs grumbling about some new trick pitch. He held the ball, listening for whatever was there, but all he heard now was Burridge urging him to get on with it. Arlette was up and he'd doubled twice already. Another here would clear the bases and stretch the lead, possibly beyond reach. . . . He ignored Wesley's motion for a speed ball and threw a snap.

John Dufresne, *Love Warps the Mind a Little* (Norton). Dufresne's third book (he is author of a well-received novel, *Louisiana Power & Light,* and a collection of stories, *The Way That Water Enters Stone*), is a delicate mixture of humor and high seriousness. In the setting of Worcester, Massachusetts, would-be (and mostly blocked) writer Lafayette

Proulx falls in love with Judi Dubey, then loses her to cancer. It is a love story with truth at the center of it:

> My story "Figure of Fun" touched an exposed nerve with Mr. Thom Blake, the editor of the *Brooklyn Review*. He took me to task in a noxious and ferocious letter, just bubbling with vitriol. "Please," he wrote, "no more of these insufferable rustic septic tank rural stories. No more grotesque bumpkins or genetically damaged rednecks. Enough of these afflicted, desperate, ugly, indigent freaks, these marginal and insignificant wallowers in misery. These dysfunctional misfits do not represent the way we live now in America. We have indoor plumbing in America and medicines to cure rickets and fathers who are not alcoholic child abusers." Right there on the classy *Brooklyn Review* stationery was a thick, blotchy period.

Dominick Dunne, *Another City, Not My Own* (Crown). Pop writing, pure and simple. But what makes this one interesting and worthy is its complex (sometimes confusing) fusion of fact and fiction. Setting out, on assignment, to cover the O. J. Simpson trials and story, Dunne elected to use the tools of metafiction by replacing himself with a mirror-image protagonist named Gus Bailey, calling the form "a novel in the form of a memoir." The very confusion of fact and fiction serves his subtextual theme—the question, in a world of images and symbols, of what is true and what is false (and what is grotesquely funny):

> That night at Harry Evans and Tina Brown's dinner for Gore Vidal at L'Orangerie, to celebrate the publication of his memoir *Palimpsest,* Gus arrived late after appearing on *Larry King Live.* He said to his old friend, Tina Brown, whom he hadn't seen for ten months, "If I act peculiar, tell me, Tina. I feel like I'm flipping out. I've become a zealot over this trial. I can't think of anything else. I even *dream* about O. J."

Deborah Eisenberg, *All around Atlantis* (Farrar, Straus). This book, the sixth by one of the most highly regarded and widely praised contemporary story writers, contains seven stories of varying length and diverse subject matter, solidly linked together by Eisenberg's subtle vision and inimitable style:

> The man who stood at the door of the apartment (K. McIntyre, # 4B) was nice-looking. Nice-looking, and weirdly unfamiliar, as if the whole thing, maybe, were a complete mistake. Francie thought over and over in the striated extrusion of eternity (this was then and this is then; that was now and this is now) it had taken the door to open.

Leslie Epstein, *Pandaemonium* (St. Martin's Press). Clearly one of the best novels of the year. A brilliant and adventurous fiction, telling much of the history of Hollywood as well as the rise of the Third Reich, roughly set between February 1938 and 1942, all told to us through the stylish, knowing, and credible first-person narrator—Peter Lorre. Real and fictional characters (including the author's father and uncle, twins who were prominent screenwriters of the era and co-authors of *Casablanca*) mix in easy consort, as do real and fictional events and documents—there are some wonderfully realized columns by Louella Parsons. It is a book at once savage and savagely funny, a mixture of slapstick and mythopoeic tragedy. It is the seventh and finest book to date by this greatly gifted writer:

> By then the sun had dropped well down the sky and the shadows of the trees fell over the road. The people in the truck began to shiver. Drahomira asked her companion where they were going. "We're in a woods," he answered. "There are trees on every side." Then the road ended and the truck came to a stop. The Jews—for that, of course, is who they were—got out. Carrying their bundles, they followed the men in uniforms to a little clearing. Then they had to take off their clothes.

Richard Ford, *Women with Men* (Knopf). Ford's seventh book is a collection of three long stories, linked thematically according to the title, dealing with the love and war of the sexes. Two are set in an elegantly evoked Paris; the other takes place in Montana. The writing is strong and thoughtful; the voice is Ford at his best:

> He reached what he thought on the map should be rue d'Assas, with the Luxembourg directly across the street. But instead he found a different street, rue Notre-Dame-des-Champs, and ahead of him was not the great garden with the seventeenth-century palace built by the Medicis, but once again the Boulevard Raspail, a part of it he hadn't been on. Though the Luxembourg Gardens still had to be on his right. He should simply take the first street that way, even though that meant going back out onto Raspail, clogged now with spewing, honking traffic, stalled in both directions. It was smart, he felt, to be on foot.

Charles Frazier, *Cold Mountain* (Atlantic Monthly). This is the book that surprised the literary world by rising, then camping out, for more than half of the year, as number one on most best-seller lists, and by winning, against the formidable opposition of DeLillo's *Underworld,* the National Book Award. Much of the credit for its commercial success goes to Atlantic's Morgan Entrekin.

But Frazier helped things enormously, with this his first novel, by a wealth of beautiful writing and by a powerful and gripping story. It tells the picaresque tale of a Confederate deserter, Inman, trying to escape the Civil War and to find his way home to Cold Mountain and to his prewar sweetheart, Ada. This story is intercut with the story of Ada and her friend Ruby trying to bring an Appalachian farm back to life. Deeply felt, keenly observed in general and in a multitude of details, *Cold Mountain* rediscovers for our time a period lost in larger historical events, in a place seldom (except, perhaps, in the fiction of Fred Chappell) so gracefully summoned. And with Inman, his solitary dedication, Frazier comes close to Archetype:

> Inman rubbed at its cylinder and barrel and thought about the fright in the town and the river crossing and the preacher and how he might have done things differently in each case. He wished not to be smirched with the mess of other people. A part of him wanted to hide in the woods far from any road. Be like an owl, move only at dark. Or a ghost. Another part yearned to wear the big pistol openly on his hip and to travel by day under a black flag, respecting all who let him be, fighting all who would seek to fight him, letting rage be his guide against anything that ran counter to his will.

Castle Freeman Jr., *Judgment Hill* (University Press of New England). This is a first novel by a writer whose short stories and essays have earned high praise, set in southern Vermont, and featuring Garrett Benteen and his long, complex, expressive, and finally losing battle against commercialism and development. In an afterword Freeman states that his intention has been "to produce a kind of written landscape-with-figures, a picture." In this he has succeeded admirably: "That day an end-of-summer noon, the air blown out clean and the sky as high and keen as a steeple with those big white clouds like freight cars going by, but up in the real mountains a few leaves are turning, the old men always the first to spot them and bring the news."

Carlos Fuentes, *The Crystal Frontier: A Novel in Nine Stories* (Farrar, Straus). As the subtitle indicates, Fuentes's latest is a sequence of short stories linked together to fit the flexible definition of a novel. What holds the stories together is that all of them have something to do, one way or another, with the Mexican oligarch Leonardo Barroso and his family. Each also involves some kind of clash between Americans and Mexicans. A wealthy Mexican who has lived much of his life elsewhere, including years in the United States, Fuentes is the ideal creator of these tales:

Ad for the 1997 National Book Award for Fiction, the author's first novel

Don Leonardo Barroso was in the first-class section of Delta's nonstop flight from Mexico City to New York. With him was an incredibly beautiful woman with a mane of black shiny hair. The hair was like a frame for the striking cleft in her chin, her face's star. Don Leonardo, in his fifties, felt proud of his female companion. Seated by the window, she was imagining herself in the irregularity, the variety, the beauty, and the distance of the landscape and the sky. Her lovers had always told her she had cloudlike eyelids and a slight storm in the shadows under her eyes. Mexican boy friends speak in serenades.

Mary Gaitskill, *Because They Wanted To* (Simon and Schuster). With her first collection, *Bad Behavior,* Mary Gaitskill established herself as a vital and gifted writer and took control of her particular territory—the complex wars of the sexes and the unending struggle between flesh and spirit, all of these things captured and exposed in a deadpan style. The dozen stories of *Because They Wanted To* continue her explorations with a mature authority:

> The ugliness of the hospital pleased him; it seemed appropriate. The lounge was furnished with smudged plastic chairs, a vinyl couch with a strip of duct tape on it, and a candy machine. People sat in various attitudes of unhappiness. Daniel looked at them. One man looked back. His hair was standing up, and his hands

appeared numb. He looked as though he might say something hostile. Daniel looked away.

Robert Girardi, *Valporetto 13* (Delacorte). Girardi's third novel, the story of a young foreign-exchange trader who finds love and mystery and finally a new and better life, may not be strikingly original in its subject matter and general message. Yet his fine, evocative sense of place, the power and the glory of it, especially in ancient Venice where most of this takes place, lifts this novel to its feet and earns applause:

> The vast cemetery of San Michele glowed softly in the flicker of candle flame and echoed with the sound of human voices. Everywhere I looked I saw groups of people gathered in the wavering shadows among the tombs, with the bottles of wine and picnic suppers they had brought over from the city. San Michele was full of light and motion tonight as a summer field back home is full of fireflies at dusk.

Arthur Golden, *Memoirs of a Geisha* (Knopf). This is a first novel which attracted much notice and favorable attention because of its remarkable imaginative authenticity. Here Golden has written a lyrical first-person accounting, in the voice of a Japanese woman, of her life as a geisha in Japan from girlhood to old age (in New York City):

> Perhaps it seems odd to you that we all bathed together, men and women, and that we planned to sleep in the same room later that night. But actually, geisha do this sort of thing all the time with their best customers—or at least they did in my day. A single geisha who values her reputation will certainly never be caught alone with a man who isn't her *Danna*. But to bathe innocently in a group like this, with the murky water cloaking us . . . that's quite another matter.

Brian Griffin, *Sparkman in the Sky & Other Stories* (Sarabande). This first collection, winner of the Mary McCarthy Prize in Short Fiction (judged by Barry Hannah), consists of seven stories set in and around eastern Tennessee and mainly during the 1960s. As Barry Hannah has written in his foreword:

> The Griffin stories are remarkable. Without the hectoring and false tones you might find in yet another chronicle of cozy or lunatic Dixiana, Griffin offers a natural persuasion about these citizens in Tennessee. Mostly the voice comes to him as easily as a walk in the park, it seems, and I find this an imperative in writers of the first order. I hold that in all the best writing there is a natural pace, an unwilled but inevitable current. We do not want the manufactured feeling, the forced plastic, the bogus rhetoric.

Jim Grimsley, *My Drowning* (Algonquin). In playwright Grimsley's third novel, he writes beautifully about southern rural life and poverty from the point of view of complex, fully dimensional characters who, even as young children, possess an identity and inwardness:

> Alma Laura grew, and I watched her progress when she was with me, and I never wondered how she could be here if she were really dead. . . . She grew as I grew, a little behind me. Sometimes when she was not with me, I would see her walking in the distance, usually at the edge of the woods, or in some empty building near whatever house we lived in.

Allan Gurganus, *Plays Well with Others* (Knopf). Author of the highly successful and prizewinning first novel *Oldest Living Confederate Widow Tells All* (1989) and of the story collection *White People* (1991), Gurganus here tells the story of three greatly gifted young people in New York in the 1980s and the coming of the plague of AIDS, which changes and tests their community and civility to the quick:

> The truth is, our community would meet a waiting test beyond imagining. Picture that last tea-dance in the first-class ballroom of the Titanic, just before the ice. Imagine how all these pretty people presently being charming and sociable and complimenting each other's fox trotting will soon line up for too few life boats.

Amy Hempel, *Tumble Home* (Scribner). Hempel's fiction is original enough to ask for an acquired taste. But for those who delight in it (and there are plenty), this third collection, presenting seven stories and the novella "Tumble Home," is her finest work so far. The title novella, a long, rambling letter written by a patient in a mental institution to a painter she once briefly met, is an extraordinary, virtuoso piece, at once funny and deeply moving. The other stories, building to the finale of "Tumble Home," are quite short, as in "Housewife," here complete:

> She would always sleep with her husband and with another man in the course of the same day, and then the rest of the day, for whatever was left to her of that day, she would exploit by incanting, "French film, French film."

George V. Higgins, *A Change of Gravity* (Holt). With twenty-eight books in a career that began with a bang and *The Friends of Eddie Coyle* (1972), Higgins has long since crossed over from genre fiction to the novel as his own genre—the Higgins novel. This is the full-steam-ahead story of the lives and times, the

ways and means of two old-time Massachusetts politicians—Ambrose Merrion, clerk of the court in Canterbury, and Danny Hilliard, chairman of Ways and
Means in the state House of Representatives. Higgins has no rival for showing how things work in the
worlds of law and politics, crime and punishment,
and showing and telling it with an impeccable ear
for inimitable dialogue. Here, Geoffrey Cohen, representing Danny at a deposition, has a few professional words (among many others) to say to the
prosecutorial Feds:

> The idea's preposterous on its face, but grant it,
> *arguendo:* Dan Hilliard last sought elective office well
> over ten years ago. The state Statute of Limitations is
> six years. The federal one is five. Except for murder or
> treason, of course—neither of which I've heard my
> learned friend here mention, at least as yet. So: why in
> the world is the federal watchdog prowling out here
> with his Operation Rolling Blunder, snarling and
> snapping at Danny Hilliard, and the people who backed
> him for the office he filled so well?

Ha Jin, *Under the Red Flag* (Georgia). Jin's previous collection, *Ocean of Words,* won the 1997
PEN/Hemingway award, and this latest, twelve stories set in the rural town of Dismount Fort during
the time of the Cultural Revolution, is the winner of
the Flannery O'Connor Award for Short Fiction.
Sex and violence and the narrative interest and
power of the exotic give these stories a special quality:

> Naturally some men in the League of Mao Zedong
> Thought began to think how to punish Li Wan. That
> was not easy because Li was from a poor peasant
> family, was a Party member, and seemed to be red
> inside and out. Nonetheless they kept an eye on him
> and assigned a young man, Tong Fei, to prepare a file
> and collect material against him. While the whole town
> was busy making revolution, how could they tolerate a
> man who would ride a motorcycle to the mountains
> with a shiny fowling piece across his back and hunt
> pheasants every weekend?

Denis Johnson, *Already Dead: A California Gothic*
(HarperCollins). Johnson, who has already earned a
kind of cult status, and a variety of prizes and
awards, with his poems and his fiction, here presents a large-scale thriller—1990 dope deals, sex and
violence, dopers who read Herman Melville and argue among themselves about Ludwig Wittgen-
stein—set on the high coast of northern California.
Not quite parody, not altogether a send-up, the
story is fast paced, gripping, at times moving, and,
above all, always cool and knowing:

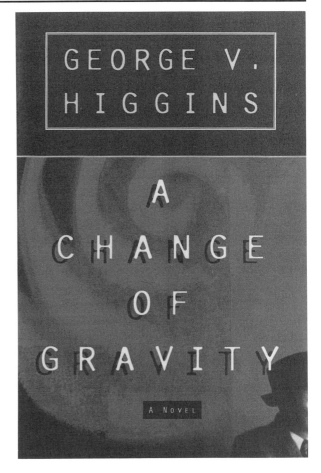

*Dust jacket for Higgins's novel about politics and friendship
in Massachusetts*

> Others joined them, other hands at short glasses like
> shivering newborn puppies—the randomly incised and
> greasy hands of bikers—carpenters' hands with their
> discompleted fingers—sawyers' hands epoxied with
> pitch and dirt—and they all got right with shots and
> watched the images on the tube.... Not bad people, not
> evil people, but actually storms of innocence. Dead-
> heads telling their tears. The town where Jesus got his
> swastika removed. . . . Fairchild wondered about the
> possibility of living here forever.

Madison Jones, *Nashville 1864: The Dying of the
Light* (J. S. Sanders). This slender, evocative, and
haunting novel, a "memoir" of Steven Moore circa
1900, describes events thirty-six years earlier when
he, aged twelve, and his slave companion, Dink, left
the family's hardscrabble farm hoping to find Steven's father, a soldier of the Confederacy. They
stumble innocently into the middle of the battles
around Franklin and Nashville:

> There were certain things I later remembered with
> special trenchancy, though at the time these registered

only as stock events of the battle. One was a shot evidently delivered from close range, from a cannon or howitzer that must have been loaded with pieces of chain. Its path was straight through a huddle of writhing figures, carrying with it, as seemed to me, limbs and heads and torsos like fragments expelled from a quarry blast. That and one more special thing recalled in the hours after. It was all the fallen shapes in the wake of the battle line, lying at random and motionless in death, or struggling, twisting in final efforts to escape death's tightening hand. But these were horrors to me only in the remembering.

Matthew F. Jones, *Blind Pursuit* (Farrar, Straus). This well-written thriller is Jones's fourth novel, a fast-paced account of the desperate search ("blind pursuit") of her parents and the police for a kidnapped little girl named Jennifer. The characters—men and women, police and suspects—are solidly drawn and above any usual stereotyping. The situation is as real as the headlines. The style is transparent and accessible:

The man did as she'd told him. In the darkness created by or indigenous to him he felt ashamed that he should have to suffer such indignities, though he understood himself to be the world and all other earthly inhabitants as existing solely for or to aid in his evolvement. Recent events saddened him most in that they reminded him that he, and thus the universe, would someday die.

Ward Just, *Echo House* (Houghton Mifflin). *Echo House,* Just's thirteenth novel and seventeenth book, was, justly, a short-listed finalist for the National Book Award. This wise and entertaining story is set mainly in Washington, D.C., and follows the fortunes of an American political family, the Behls, from roughly the first term of Woodrow Wilson to the early years of the twenty-first century. Here, on election night of 1952 we see Governor Adlai Stevenson losing the election:

Then the governor was in the room, smiling, shaking hands, accepting praise for the campaign he had waged. The news from Hartford was bad, but Bridgeport was still to come. Be of good spirit. The governor made his slow transit of the room, exuding a host's warmth. His bald head reflected the glare of the electric lights and he looked much older than in his pictures.

Ismail Kadare, *The Three-Arched Bridge* (Arcade). Here the Albanian master gathers together myths, fables, and stories (told by a monk named Jjon), chiefly concerned with a bridge (at once real and metaphorical) built in 1378 between East and West, the Christian and the Muslim worlds in the Balkans:

Late last Sunday night, when I had gone out to walk on the sandbanks, I saw the idiot Gjelosh Ukmarkaj walking on the bridge. He was laughing to himself, guffawing and making crazy signs with his hands. The shadows of his limbs pranced over the spine of the bridge, stretching down past the arches to the water. I struggled to imagine how all these recent events might have imprinted themselves on his disordered mind, and I told myself how foolish people are to laugh whenever they see him crossing the bridge, bellowing and waving his arms, thinking he is riding a horse. In fact, what people know about this bridge is no less confused than the inventions of the mind of a madman.

Nanci Kincaid, *Pretending the Bed Is a Raft* (Algonquin). This is a collection of eight stories by the author of *Crossing Blood,* a novel which received high praise and considerable attention. Kinkaid is a native of Tallahassee, Florida, who now lives in Tucson. Though she has set her stories in the South (Georgia, Alabama, Florida), and her manners and habits are part of the Southern literary tradition, she is more than a "regional writer." This collection arrives with book-jacket blessings from Richard Bausch, Mary Hood, and the celebrated Henry Louis Gates Jr.:

Myself, I don't have a thing against Jeff. As far as I'm concerned he's just a man who over-married. That's all. You know, like a good-natured puppet, whose wife has got all his strings wrapped around her little finger and tied into a tangle of convoluted knots. If you ask me, he's secretly afraid of her. Brother laughed when I said that. Brother has a sense of humor that just won't quit. He can get a good laugh out of just about anything.

Hanif Kureishi, *Love in a Blue Time* (Scribner). This book consists of ten stories that are chiefly concerned with the trials and tribulations of Pakistanis in England. Kureishi is a brilliant young writer whose *Buddha of Suburbia* won a Whitbread Prize and whose screenplays for *My Beautiful Launderette, Sammy and Rosie Get Laid,* and *London Kills Me* have won him acclaim and awards:

Daily there were many hapless people in that bar: Somnolent junkies from the local rehab, the unemployed and unemployable, pinball pillocks. Eshan nodded at many of them, but if one sat at his table without asking, he could become truculent. Often, however, he would chat to people as he passed to and fro, being more grateful than he knew for distracting conversation. He had become, without meaning to, one of the bar's characters.

Starling Lawrence, *Montenegro* (Farrar, Straus). In this elegantly written and deeply imagined first novel, British agent Auberon Harwell goes into the dangerous Balkans in the first years of the century, a place described (in a jacket blurb) by the master Patrick O'Brien as "a world quite unlike Western Europe, formed by a spartan life in the mountains in a time of pitiless war with the Turks, by ethnic hatreds and long-lasting blood feuds." Not since Rebecca West's *Black Lamb, Gray Falcon* and Joyce Cary's *Memoir of the Bobotes* have we had so complete a picture of the Balkans at that crucial time:

> At Kolasin they turned east, and entered a forest of evergreens that rose to meet the snow. Janko showed him a road that would take them to his parents' house. Over the pass they went, where the cold wind encouraged Harwell to think that there were weeks of spring left, with mats of bloom following the retreating snow higher and higher into the bare rock above the tree line. The road began its descent towards the border, and Beranc, and the Sandzak beyond. From time to time the forest opened out to show them the land below, where stark limestone needles rose like islands out of that dark green sea.

Bernard Malamud, *Bernard Malamud: The Complete Stories* (Farrar, Straus). This book contains fifty-five stories, written from the 1940s to the 1980s, a posthumous collection by a great American master of the art, together with an introduction by his editor, Robert Giroux, with an appendix including a checklist of all Malamud's stories—eight previous collections together with several stories uncollected until now. Though most of the stories have already been published in books over the years, the new collection is a valuable contribution to our literary history: "One morning, to escape the noises of war, she dragged herself to the river Ouse, there removed shoes, stockings, underpants, and waded slowly into the muddy water. The large rock she had forced into her coat pocket pulled her down till she could see the earth in her green eyes."

Pamela Marcantel, *An Army of Angels* (St. Martin's Press). This is a large-scale novel of the life and times of Joan of Arc, beginning with her childhood as the peasant girl, Jhanette, and ending with the martyrdom of (as she came to be called) Jehanne the Maid. This novel is at once vividly authentic and deeply imaginative, large in scope, yet altogether intimate:

> She sought solace in the past. Her thoughts drifted back to Domremy, to the days of her childhood before the advent of the visions which had set her upon her path. How simple life was then. She had nothing to worry about but marauding skinners. Her more immediate concerns had revolved around the day-to-day habits of village life, dictated by the seasons.

Dust jacket for the winner of the 1997 Dictionary of Literary Biography *first novel award*

Larry McMurtry, *Comanche Moon* (Simon and Schuster.) Billed by the publisher as "The Final Volume of the *Lonesome Dove* Saga," this capacious and wonderfully inventive novel deals with the central characters of all the novels of that series of linked novels—Augustus McCrae and Woodrow F. Call, in the years leading up to the Civil War and after, focusing especially on the Comanche wars and the great raid led by Chief Buffalo Hump in 1856. It is a story rich with old and new characters of every kind, including some deeply imagined and utterly human Indians: "I'm bored to death with the 19th century west," McMurtry said in a *New York Times Magazine* profile ("Larry McMurtry's Dream Job," by Mark Horowitz, 30 November). "I wrote more about it than I ever intended to." His admirers can be grateful that he overcame his good intentions and gave us four first-rate novels among which *Comanche Moon* is as good and necessary as any:

> The rain clouds hovering to the south had been dancing away from them for a week; the Brazos River, still a full two days to the south, might have to be their salvation, as it had been for many travellers. Once again he had to

carry with him, on a long trip home, a sense of incompletion. They had travelled a long way, hung ten bandits, but missed their leader, Blue Duck, murderer of his own father, and many others besides.

Peter Matthiessen, *Lost Man's River* (Random House). This is Matthiessen's seventh novel and his second in a projected trilogy about the mysterious Watson family and the Florida Everglades. (The first, *Killing Mister Watson,* appeared in 1990.) Deeply rooted in an extraordinary place and peopled with real and imaginary pioneer families, densely written and rich with authentic detail, *Lost Man's River* is, like much of Matthiessen's fiction, uniquely his own blend of voices. Southwest Florida is not his region, but he has almost made it so: "A man came out of the fire mist, crossing the shadow land of the killed woods. He drifted, disappeared, and came again through smoke and blackened thorn, moving from willow clump to bush like a panther traveling across open savanna."

Rick Moody, *Purple America* (Little, Brown). Rick Moody has earned an enviable reputation among younger novelists, his two earlier novels, *Garden State* (1992) and *The Ice Storm* (1994), and his collection of stories *The Ring of Brightest Angels Around Heaven* (1995) having received extravagant critical attention and praise. *Purple America,* set in one night and told by multiple voices and visions, follows Hex Raitliffe, who has come home to care for his dying mother. The prose is densely layered, the style as textural and rhythmic as poetry:

> She had been a talker. She had been able to put the awkward at ease; she had been able to comfort children; she had been able to sweet-talk truculent shopkeepers. But her voice was gone, was consigned now to the netherworld of widowed socks and earrings. She began to cry, in the living room, and her tears were of the specifically disabled sort. They came without pounding of fists or oaths, they simply fell, like summer drizzle, no sound accompanying them, just their erratic progress along her cheeks.

Haruki Murakami, *The Wind-Up Bird Chronicle* (Knopf). Set in the present in Japan, Murakami's latest novel is built on flashbacks to the Japanese wars with Manchuria, Mongolia, and China. Reviews were mixed, but Philip Weiss of the *New York Observer* did his best to do some justice to the Japanese author and cult figure ("Forget DeLillo, Pynchon—Murakami is My Man!," 22 December). "For three days last month," Weiss wrote of this novel, "a book was the most important thing in my life again. At page 200, I was looking at the last page,

611, and ruing that it was that short." Here a Mongolian shepherd deals with a captured Japanese spy:

> The man started by slitting open Yamamoto's shoulder and proceeded to peel off the skin of his right arm from the top down—slowly, carefully, almost lovingly. As the Russian officer had said, it was something like a work of art. One would never have imagined there was pain involved if it weren't for the screams.

Lewis Nordan, *Lightning Song* (Algonquin). In his seventh book Lewis Nordan, master of the Southern version of magic realism, tells the story of Leroy Dearman, twelve, who lives with his family on a farm and learns a lot about love and lust—and magical electricity. Here Leroy considers the incredible drum majorette, Ruby Rae: "He wanted with all his heart to reach out—indeed he was terrified he would do so—and touch her body with his hand and explain that he had had many erections but never one so painful as this, even in uncle Harris's room with the magazines, never one that endured for so long, through time and heat and stressful activity." Later, carrying a baton given to him by Ruby Rae, he is struck by lightning: "Elsie watched her son light up like a bulb. . . . Flames rose from his hair, flashed out like torches from his heels. All of his dark history was suddenly bathed in light. Ruby Rae was revealed."

Charles T. Powers, *In the Memory of the Forest* (Scribner). Powers, a highly regarded journalist who died before this novel, his only book, appeared, writes here of rural Poland as the Eastern Bloc began to collapse. Leszek, a young farmer, sets out to investigate the murder of a friend near the village of Jadowia, a quest which turns into a discovery process revealing the hidden and suppressed past of modern Poland:

> Already there were trainloads going by, nearly every day. Loaded with Jews. Nobody knew where then, but it was Treblinka they were going to. In the village the Jews were frantic. They were frantic in every village. They knew. So they were going to try. . . . In the dark they would get their guard to turn his back. That would get them to the edge of town. Then the fields. We were supposed to watch for them.

Thomas Pynchon, *Mason & Dixon* (Holt). This large story (773 pages of small print) based on the lives and times of British surveyors Charles Mason and Jeremiah Dixon, is, in the publisher's words, "reimagined by Thomas Pynchon, in an updated 18th century novel featuring Native Americans and frontier folk, ripped bodies, naval warfare, conspiracies erotic and political and major caffeine abuse."

Long awaited, it appeared to mixed if not widespread reviews and soon made a brief appearance on the best-seller list in *The New York Times*. It created a second literary stir, and no little publicity, when it was, justly or unjustly, not selected as a finalist for the National Book Award. The book can speak for itself (and will for years to come). Among the many reviews of all kinds, two seemed to me especially well done and valuable—that (untitled) by Robert L. McLaughlin in the *Review of Contemporary Fiction* (Fall 1997) and eighteenth-century scholar Martin Battestin's "A Novel for Listeners" in the *Sewanee Review* (Summer 1997): "Thomas Pynchon in this long-awaited novel about the British astronomers who from 1763 to 1767 hacked out of the wilderness the ominous 'Line' that divided Maryland from Pennsylvania, South from North, seems very much Laurence Sterne's heir in a narrative as deep as it is eccentric and whimsical."

Philip Roth, *American Pastoral* (Houghton Mifflin). Nathan Zuckerman (again) is the narrator of this story, set on the occasion of a forty-fifth high-school reunion, of a high-school hero—Seymour "Swede" Levov, whose life and times are our life and times and memories. *American Pastoral* received mixed notices, from high praise to shrugging indifference, but in any case it is Roth's most "public" novel in a good while, playing at its fable in a powerfully evoked historical context:

> At dinner the conversation was about Watergate and about *Deep Throat*. Except for the Swede's parents and the Orcutts, everybody at the table had been to see the X-rated movie starring a young porno actress named Linda Lovelace. The picture was no longer playing only in the adult houses but had become a sensation in neighborhood theaters all over Jersey. What surprised him, Shelly Salzman was saying, was that the electorate who overwhelmingly chose as president and vice president Republican politicians hypocritically pretending to deep moral piety should make a hit out of a movie that so graphically caricatured acts of oral sex.
>
> "Maybe it's not the same people," said Dawn, "who are going to the movie."

Arundhati Roy, *The God of Small Things* (Random House). This first novel by a native of Delhi is a family saga concerning the anglophile Muslim family, the Ipes, who live in Ayemenem. Its inventive narrative and rich rhetoric made it a best-seller for a time:

> Wet leaves in the trees shimmered like beaten metal. Dense clumps of yellow bamboo drooped into the river as though grieving in advance for what they knew was going to happen. The river itself was dark and quiet. An

absence rather than a presence, betraying no sign of how high and strong it really was.

Richard Russo, *Straight Man* (Random House). The academic novel runs the risk of accumulated clichés and tedium, but in this, his fourth novel, Richard Russo triumphs over these risks with a neatly plotted story and, above all, with the lively, sardonic, and inimitable voice of his protagonist and first-person narrator, William Henry Devereaux Jr., who is entirely credible as a gifted (if blocked) writer and a second-generation academic fighting for survival in the grungy town of Railton and the equally grungy faculty of West Central Pennsylvania University. The result is the best novel with a setting in the groves of academe since Mark Harris's *Wake Up, Stupid!* (1959):

> We hadn't, any of us, intended to allow the pettiness of committee work, departmental politics, daily lesson plans, and the increasingly militant ignorance of our students let so many years slip by. And now in advancing middle age we've chosen, wisely perhaps, to be angry with each other rather than ourselves. We've preferred not to face the distinct possibility that if we'd been made for better things, we'd have done those things.

Bernhard Schlink, *The Reader* (Pantheon). German Law professor and author of several crime novels, Schlink here tells a complex literary narrative, one which has been widely praised and a best-seller in Europe, of a first-person narrator who much later remembers an intense, passionate affair he had with an older woman when he was a fifteen-year-old student. The woman disappears and years later serves as a concentration-camp guard during the war and is subsequently tried and given life imprisonment for her crimes. This is a thoughtful, painful, richly layered short novel told in an engaging and evocative style:

> At first I was embarrassed to meander home through the Alsatian villages looking for a restaurant where I could have lunch. But my awkwardness was not the result of real feeling, but of thinking about the way one is supposed to feel after visiting a concentration camp. I noticed this myself, shrugged, and found a restaurant called Au Petit Garcon in a village on a slope of the Vosges. My table looked out over the plain. Hanna had called me kid.

Joseph Skibell, *A Blessing on the Moon* (Algonquin). This is an extraordinary first novel, partly factual and partly a magic-realist fairy tale, dealing with the death in the Holocaust of Chaim Skibelski and his family. Critic Sanford Pinsker described it in the *Washington Post* (4 December) as "a novel in which the usual lines separating this world from the world to come, the fantastical from the real, and the horrible from gallows humor become increasingly blurred." Firmly rooted in the long traditions of Jewish fables and folktales, it is a cornucopia of stories of the death of the European Jews:

> The woman he had traded his house to for a hiding place reported him at once. And who can blame her? With Lipski curled into a circle below her staircase, she was in danger and her family as well. But the soldiers danced him out in that jolly way of theirs, flushing him so merrily from his hutch and into the bright streets that even Lipski had to laugh, as they beat his head into the curb.

Lee Smith, *News of the Spirit* (Putnam). The six stories in this, Smith's third collection, all have diverse subjects but are thoroughly southern in place and voice. Smith is also the author of nine well-received novels. Clarity, humor, compassion, and high energy are essential qualities of her work. This collection received mixed notices and deserved better:

> Then Lily announced that she was in love, *really in love* this time, with a young poet she'd met that summer on Cape Cod where she'd been waitressing. We waited while she lit a cigarette. "We lived together for two months," Lily said, "in his room at the inn, where we could look out and see the water." We stared at her. None of us had ever lived with anybody, or known anyone who had. "It was wonderful," she said. "It was heaven. But it was not what you might think," she added enigmatically, "living with a man."

Muriel Spark, *Reality and Dreams* (Houghton Mifflin). Tom Richards, the protagonist of this small novel, is a sixty-three-year-old film director in England, working on a movie titled "The Hamburger Girl." Injured, he considers his somewhat troubled family and tries to make some sense out of his life and art. As reviewer Carolyn See ("The Ordinary Face of Evil," *Washington Post,* 27 June) puts it: "He waits for images to smack him on the side of the head." Here Tom watches one of his daughters on TV:

> Tom watched Marigold launching her book on a late night talk show. . . . He admired her magnetism, so that it didn't matter that as a woman she looked hideous—quite deliberately so. She described with bitter passion her adventures looking for a job, insults leveled at her and the people she "represented," insolent interrogations. Whether these were real or invented, they made good televised material.

Les Standiford, *Deal on Ice* (HarperCollins). This is the latest John Deal book, fourth in the series featuring the Miami private eye, by a gifted writer who has earned high praise from Elmore Leonard, James Ellroy, Robert Parker, and others. This one pits a murderous plot by big, multimedia chain stores against the independent bookstore wherever it can still be found:

> That's their strategy, you see. Look around, find a thriving bookstore, drive a stake into its heart, then take over once the corpse has been buried. You can stop giving your big discounts then, trim your hours back to whatever's reasonable, cut your staff to the bone, cut your list of titles to the bone, forget about your bands and all that, and run your big hairy store like a supermarket. Somebody comes in to ask for a copy of the *Paris Review,* the kid at the counter says maybe it's in the travel section. Go have a look.

Darcey Steinke, *Jesus Saves* (Atlantic Monthly). This, Steinke's third novel, follows the fate of two girls—Sandy Patrick, who has been abducted, and Ginger, daughter of a preacher, who is obsessed with finding the missing Sandy. The result, an authentic picture of the downside of the world we find ourselves living in (and dying in), is a hard-edged, lyrical book described in the *Library Journal* as "a tour through an American hell as vivid and upsetting as any imagined by Hieronymus Bosch." Here Ginger witnesses the funeral of Sandy:

> If Ginger hadn't turned down the familiar road between the two strip malls, she wouldn't have recognized the dump. The new parking lot was filled with Saturns and minivans and the white gravel path that led past a cement birdbath and a wooden bench to the pond's center. These stones arranged like a child's game of hopscotch and covered now with tokens of bereavement: stuffed bunnies and baby dolls, carnations wrapped in cellophane, candles burning in tall glass holders, Hallmark sympathy cards and homemade construction paper ones sitting upright on slabs of stone.

Robert Stone, *Bear and His Daughter: Stories* (Houghton Mifflin). This is novelist Stone's first collection of stories, consisting of six short stories and a novella ("Bear and His Daughter") written between 1969 and the present. A variety of characters and settings—New England, New Jersey, Mexico, the Caribbean, Oregon—does not disguise a common concern (in all but one of the stories) with dope addiction and alcoholism and an urgent sense of the disintegration of the society and culture as perceived by its walking wounded. Nobody writing to-

Dust jacket for the volume Vonnegut has announced will be his last novel

day equals his uncanny mastery of the intense, crumbling consciousness of his drunks and dopers, as here in "Helping":

> It was possible to imagine larval dreams traveling in suspended animation undetectable in a host brain. They could be divided and regenerate like flatworms, hide in seams and bedding, in war stories, laughter, snapshots. They could rot your socks and turn your memory into a black and green blister. Green for the hills, black for the sky above. At daybreak they hung themselves in rows like bats. At dusk they went out to look for dreamers.

Randeane Tetu, *Flying Horses, Secret Souls* (Papier-Mache Press). This slender volume, Tetu's second, offers seventeen stories and the title novella, all linked by her concern for a variety of characters and a voice like no other. Of this work poet Brendan Galvin has written: "Randeane Tetu writes to us from where we live, but with this difference: she sees so deeply into quotidian life that she gives it back to us with the commonplace elevated toward the miraculous."

Harry Turtledove, *How Few Remain* (Ballantine). The author is a master of the genre of alternate history, with twenty books to his credit. This one, elegantly worked out, presupposes that the South won the Civil War and deals with the *second* civil war in 1881. Real and imaginary characters, leftovers and new faces jostle each other. Here a somewhat older and less impetuous Jeb Stuart considers the orders of his still-adventurous commander—Stonewall Jackson:

> The longer he studied the map, the less happy he got. To carry out General Jackson's orders, he would have to pull troops from as far away as Arkansas, and that would result in weakening a different frontier with the USA. He would also have to call down the Fifth Cavalry and to denude the rest of the garrisons protecting west Texas from the Comanche raiders who took refuge in New Mexico Territory. If the Yankees turned the Comanches loose, there was liable to be hell to pay among the ranchers and farmers in that part of the country.
> But there would be hell to pay if he did not obey Jackson's order in every particular.

John Updike, *Toward the End of Time* (Knopf). Updike's eighteenth novel (his forty-ninth book) is set in 2020, a future much like the downside of the present only more so, and centers on a retired Boston banker, Ben Turnbull, who tries his best to have a private life in a time of great public disorder. Part satire, part meditation, this book opened to mixed reviews, but is outstanding work by an adventurous professional and an impeccable stylist:

> The mornings have a nip to them now when I walk down for the *Globe*. Certain tall yellow-headed weeds–hawkweed, I think–have taken root in the cracks of the broken concrete dying yard and I bend down to pull a few on my way, and throw them onto the burning pile as I pass. Since childhood I have loved this month–the flat dry taste of it, the brown-lawn look of it, bouncing the heat back up against your bare legs, and the lack of any importunate holiday marring the blank days on this side of Labor Day and the return to school.

Katherine Vaz, *Fado & Other Stories* (Pittsburgh). This book consists of twelve stories by a California novelist of Portuguese-Azorean descent, mostly dealing with this special ethnic subculture in a variety of free-wheeling, lyrical forms. This book won the coveted Drew Heinz Literature Prize for 1997. "The author has wit and humor as well as a strong sense of urgency that keeps the reader turning pages," wrote the contest judge, George Garrett. "There is a magic 'touch' that transcends magic realism."

> The old stories said that our Azorean homeland was Atlantis rising broken from the sea. We all have marks and patches surfacing on our skin. I have a fierce dark animal erupting from my side.

Kurt Vonnegut, *Timequake* (Putnam). The premise of this classic Vonnegut gathering of jokes and memories, fact and fiction, real and imaginary, is that on 13 February 2001 a little glitch in time forces us all to relive the decade of the Nineties exactly as it was. The central characters, full of beans and good and bad ideas, are Vonnegut himself and his imaginary colleague Kilgore Trout. The form allows plenty of room for a rosary of Vonnegut's speculations and reactions:

> Into the news store I go. Relatively poor people, with lives not strikingly worth living, are lined up to buy lottery tickets and other crap. All keep their cool. They pretend they don't know I'm a celebrity.

Fay Weldon, *Wicked Women* (Atlantic Monthly). Her fourth collection of stories (Fay Weldon is also the author of twenty-six other books, twenty-one of them novels) offers twenty stories created between 1972 and the present. Various in form and subject, they are united by a uniform clarity, by an often merciless satirical point of view, by high energy and high spirits, and by a stylish technical authority:

> Edward once explained to Hetty that "Ira" meant "rage" in Latin; why was she calling his grandchild "rage"? But Hetty just laughed and said Ira was the Hebraic for "watcher" anyway, and she thought it sounded nice; who cared what it meant; and Rory said it was a Po-Mo name.
> "Po-Mo?" I asked.
> "Post-modern," Rory replied. "A post-modernist is someone who knows the meaning of everything and the value of nothing."

Paul West, *Terrestrials* (Scribner). An extravagantly wonderful novel, this is the author's sixteenth and his best and brightest so far. It follows the story and fates of two spy-plane pilots, Booth and Clegg, as viewed and written about by an alien:

> The narrator, whose name is One Eighth Humbly has particular trouble with the concept of seasons and with that of espionage. His notion of the novel, based more on movies and TV transmissions than on literature proper, tends to be sketchy, but he has gleaned from sundry sources what the novel is like, and the form haunts him. He does his best.

Tom Wolfe, *Ambush at Fort Bragg* (Bantam Doubleday Dell Audio). Advertised as "not available in print" though a version of the short novel was, in fact, just published in *Rolling Stone* (December 1996) and though it was published in book form in France, Brazil, Spain, and other countries, *Ambush* deals with a television producer, Irv Dutcher, and his sensational attempt to trick three redneck soldiers into an inadvertent public confession of a murder. It is, in the tradition of *The Bonfire of the Vanities,* savagely satiric, parodic, and a passionate critique of contemporary journalism. Not all the critics were pleased. David Streitfeld's review ("A Wolfe in Sheepish Clothing," *Washington Post,* 29 August) was a full-fledged tomahawk chop: "It's possible that Tom Wolfe is too famous to do reporting anymore, and so he has to sit back in New York and write about what he thinks is going on out there. If so, it would be an odd fate; back in the heyday of the New Journalism, Wolfe used to accuse famous novelists of hiding out from the real world, a place so much more interesting than their fiction."

It was a season during which much was written and said about the shabby fate of the "literary" novel. The blockbusters continued their overall domination of the market though there were extraordinary exceptions—*Cold Mountain* sat atop the best-seller list of *The New York Times* for more than half a year, and *The God of Small Things,* energized by the British Booker Prize, was firmly on the list for an equal length of time. Other literary books—*American Pastoral, Underworld, Mason & Dixon, Comanche Moon*—made brief appearances. And the number of literary titles remained enormous.

There were other good books of fiction by American literary heavyweights and contenders. Joyce Carol Oates's *Man Crazy* (Dutton), dealing with a dysfunctional family on her familiar turf in upstate New York, centered on the hard times of a young girl, Ingrid. It is a story riddled with sex, violence, and in the words of Michiko Kakutani of the *Times* (29 August), "Emotional chaos in life." Kakutani strongly criticized this novel: "Although more than a dozen people in this novel die horrible and in some cases, truly gruesome deaths, Ms. Oates tacks on one of her contrived happy endings. It is an absurd conclusion to an inept and gratuitously lurid story." Cynthia Ozick fared better (she was nominated for the National Book Award among other things) with the *Puttermesser Papers* (Knopf), the story of the life and times of Ruth Puttermesser, who was born in the Bronx and murdered on the Upper East Side sixty years later. Alice Hoffman's novel, *Here On Earth* (Putnam), concerned an odd love affair between a good woman and a ruthless manipulator. In *Larry's Party* (Viking) Pulitzer Prize–winner Carol Shields tells the story of Larry Weller, a Canadian landscape designer. Howard Fast, eighty-two years old and with eighty-five books to his credit, brought out the sixth and final book of his Immigrants series—*An Independent Woman* (Harcourt Brace). Edmund White finished off his autobiographical trilogy with *The Farewell Symphony* (Knopf). As much memoir as novel, it deals with gay life in the 1970s and 1980s. Bharati Mukherjee brought out her ninth novel, *Leave It to Me* (Knopf). It was described by critic Nicholas A. Basbanes as "a free-wheeling version of 'Electra,' that ancient Greek tale of parental dysfunction carried to the extreme." Craig Nova's eighth novel, *The Universal Donor* (Houghton Mifflin), is a medical thriller set in Los Angeles. It follows physician Terry McKechnie as he tries to treat a serious and complex case of snakebite. The irrepressible Robert Coover plays a sequence of highbrow, virtuoso variations on "The Sleeping Beauty" story in *Briar Rose* (Grove). Michael Dorris's posthumous novel, *Cloud Chamber,* concerns five generations of a fictional American family. The prolific Stephen Dobyns writes of what

happens in the small town of Aurelius, New York, when three young girls disappear in *The Church of the Dead Girls* (Metropolitan). In Donald E. Westlake's *The Ax* (Warner) Burke Devore, a downsized executive, sets out, with considerable success, to murder all the known rivals in his particular specialty and to get his job again. Westlake also brought out *Comeback* (Mysterious). Writing under the pen name Richard Stark, he reintroduces Parker, the protagonist of sixteen of his early novels, who this time goes after a sleazy televangelist.

Various veterans brought out new novels this year. Ellen Gilchrist's fifteenth book, *Sarah Conley* (Little, Brown), concerns the conflict between a woman's career and her first love. J. P. Donleavy in *The Lady Who Liked Clean Restrooms* (St. Martin's Press) tells the story of one Jocelyn Jones, a South Carolinian who ended up in Scarsdale. In *Le Divorce* (Dutton), a nominee for the National Book Award, Diane Johnson offers an old story (innocent Americans abroad) refurbished with any number of new and ironic twists. John Hawkes's *An Irish Eye* (Viking) is the odd story of Dervla O'Shannon, a foundling. Old pro Hortense Calisher presents the life of Carol Smith, who, having spent twenty years in prison for her part in a 1970s bomb plot, is now trying to adjust to life in Spanish Harlem and the 1990s in *In the Slammer with Carol Smith* (Marion Boyars).

Younger, upwardly mobile professionals made their mark, too. In Jay Parini's *Benjamin's Crossing* (Holt) the center of attention is the philosopher Walter Benjamin and his attempt to escape the Nazis in World War II, an episode which ended with his suicide. Walter Mosley's latest is not another adventure of Easy Rawlins. In *Always Outnumbered, Always Outgunned* (Norton) Mosley introduces a brand new protagonist, Socrates Fortlow, an ex-con who devotes his life and his great strength to doing "good works" in honor of a "murky pledge." In Robert Olen Butler's *The Deep Green Sea* (Holt) Ben, a Vietnam veteran, returns to Saigon many years later and falls in love with his guide, Tien, who may also, it turns out, be his own illegitimate daughter. For his eighth thriller in the Thorn series, *Red Sky at Night* (Delacorte), James W. Hall has his hero crippled and disabled. Thomas Mallon's *Dewey Defeats Truman* (Pantheon) is a story of love and politics set in the summer of the 1948 election. Douglas Bauer's *The Book of Famous Iowans* (Holt) follows fifty years in the life of Will Vaughn, a small-town Iowan. Tim McLaurin's fifth book, *The Last Great Snake Show,* was described in *Brightleaf* as "a comic road novel." Commenting on the cast and crew of male characters in Lawrence Naumoff's *A Plan for Women* (Harcourt Brace), Carolyn See (*Washington Post*, 22 August) summed up: "These are the men who drive women bats." The latest off-the-wall creation by *Esquire* columnist Mark Leyner, *The Tetherballs of Bouganville* (Harmony), is about (among all kinds of things) a young tetherball obsessive named—what else?—Mark Leyner. Paul Theroux's *Kowloon Tong* (Houghton Mifflin) is mainly the story of expatriate Brits Betty Mulland and her son, Bunt, who are owners of a company in Hong Kong called Imperial Stitching. Concerns here are the end of empire and the coming of the Chinese. Like Paul Auster's *Hand to Mouth,* Barry Gifford's *The Phantom Father* (Harcourt Brace) is a mixture of the factual and the fictional. Gifford defines it himself as being what the Japanese call *shosetsu*—primarily factual, but also imaginary. *Saint Leibowitz and the Wild Horse Woman* (Bantam) is a posthumous novel and Walter M. Miller's first book since the celebrated *A Canticle for Leibowitz* (1959). It is set in the future of a postholocaust America when the Great Plains are swept by warring nomadic hordes. Gary Jenning's *Aztec Autumn* (Forge) is set in mid-sixteenth-century Mexico and follows the audacious attempts of a young Aztec, Tenamaxtli, to overthrow the Spanish conquerors. Cristina Garcia's *The Aguero Sisters* (Knopf) is a meditation on Cuba and the Cubans in the early 1990s. Alison Leslie Gold's *The Devil's Mistress* (Faber & Faber) takes the form of an imaginary diary of Hitler's mistress and wife, Eva Braun. Jean McGarry's *Gallagher's Travels* (Johns Hopkins University Press) is a (needless to say) satirical novel about the life of Cathy Gallagher and her search for "an interesting life."

There were, as ever, many hopeful first novels published during the year. Here are several from among those who earned some significant attention or were exceptionally interesting and worthwhile: Chris Offutt's *The Good Brother* (Simon and Schuster), widely reviewed and praised, deals with Virgil Caudill from the hill country of Kentucky. Having avenged the murder of his brother, he takes on a new identity and goes to live in Montana. Rafi Zabor's *The Bear Comes Home* (Norton) is about a talking bear who is also a jazz saxophone player. Christopher Dickey's thriller, *Innocent Blood* (Simon and Schuster), tells the story of Kurt Kurtovic, an Army Ranger who fights in Panama, Kuwait, and Bosnia and, for a time and purpose, must become a terrorist. *Los Alamos* (Broadway) by Joseph Kanon is framed in the form of a murder mystery. To solve it, Michael Conolly is sent into the midst of that famous, top-secret assembly of atomic scientists during the spring of 1945. Martha McPhee's *Bright Angel Time* (Random House)—a somewhat autobio-

graphical novel set in the 1970s and told mostly by eight-year-old Kate—was highly praised. *The Light of Falling Stars* (Riverhead), by J. Robert Lennon, concerning the results of an airline crash near Marshall, Montana, was likewise the recipient of many favorable notices. Mark Jacobs's *Stone Cowboy* (Soho) is about an American drifter named Roger who is released from prison in Bolivia and promptly falls into a series of misadventures. Writing in the *Washington Post* (30 September), David Nicholson called it "a remarkable debut from a writer of great promise." Lorenzo Carcaterra's *Apaches* (Ballantine) is a first novel if you elect not to count *Sleepers* (1995), which purported to be fact, nonfiction, but seems now to have been mostly fiction. In *Apaches* a renegade group of crippled cops goes up against a peculiarly sleazy form of the drug trade. In Dionne Brand's *In Another Place, Not Here* (Grove) two women, Lizete and Verlia, meet on a Caribbean island and have an affair. Suzanne Matson's *The Hunger Moon* (Norton) is a series of interrelated stories about three lonely women. John Mulligan's *Shopping Cart Soldiers* (Curbstone) is an autobiographical novel, replete with the visions and hallucinations of Vietnam veteran Finn MacDonald. Two novels which, though worthwhile on their own, gained attention for extraliterary reasons were filmmaker Oliver Stone's autobiographical *A Child's Night Dream* (Knopf) and Astro Teller's *Exegesis* (Vintage).

Of course, there were a gracious plenty of other good books by good novelists published in 1997, both by Americans and by foreign writers. The latter category seems to be growing as a larger and larger part of the literary scene, in part because several of the major publishing companies are now owned by European conglomerates who need an outlet for the European "product," and partly because what American publishers have come to classify as a kind of subgenre, "literary fiction," is much more commonly encouraged and produced over there. For blockbusting commercial novels, worldwide publishers tend to look to American commercial fiction in translation. In any event, there was a lot of literary fiction, both foreign and domestic in origin, published in the United States during 1997.

Most of the books mentioned below were widely reviewed from beginning (*Kirkus, PW*) to the tag end (literary magazines) of their short shelf season. And many, the majority, were well received also. In the meantime others appeared and vanished without attracting my attention or anybody else's. It's the way of the literary world. . . . Among the more prominent imports from Britain were Peter Ackroyd's *Milton in America* (Doubleday). This, his ninth novel, is a "what if " book—what if John Milton had fled the Restoration and come to live in New England? Stevie Davies's *Four Dreamers and Emily* (St. Martin's Press) is a satire of the world of academic Brontë scholarship. Penelope Fitzgerald's *The Blue Flower* (Houghton Mifflin) is a novelized biography of the eighteenth-century German writer Novalis. Caryl Phillips moves toward complex metafiction with *The Nature of Blood* (Knopf), his sixth novel. This one, focused on European tribalism, has a variety of plots and settings in different historical periods. The latest Inspector Wexford mystery by Ruth Rendell, *Road Rage* (Crown), involves the kidnapping of Wexford's wife, Dora, by Sacred Globe, a malevolent environmental group. *Great Apes* (Grove) by Will Self is a kind of cerebral "Planet of the Apes," described by *The List* as "a bastard offspring of Oliver Sacks and the Marquis de Sade." Canadian fiction continues to develop on its own, not dominated by Britain or the United States. Ann Michaels's *Fugitive Pieces* (Knopf), basically a holocaust story told in the journals of Jakob Beer, received attention and critical praise. So did Mordecai Richler's tenth novel, *Barney's Version* (Knopf), an autobiographical novel set in the Montreal Jewish community of St. Urban Street and featuring Barney Panofsky. A well-received first novel and winner of Canada's Trillium Award was Wayson Choy's *The Jade Peony*, a coming-of-age novel set in Vancouver's Chinatown in the late 1930s and early 1940s.

The Irish story continues to appeal to American readers and publishers. *Reading in the Dark* (Knopf), the autobiographical story of a boy named Seamus coming of age in troubled Northern Ireland, earned kudos for Seamus Deane. Novelist and playwright Ellis Ni Dhuibhne created a sequence of related stories, intercut with episodes from an ongoing folktale ("The Search for the Lost Husband") in *The Inland Ice* (Blackstaff). The lives and loves and intractable problems of people in the rural Irish town of Creevagh are the subjects of Walter Keady's *Celibates and Other Lovers* (MacMurray & Beck). Bernard MacLaverty's *Grace Notes* (Norton), set variously in Ireland, Glasgow, and Kiev, is the story of a young composer–Catherine McKenna. Edna O'Brien's latest, *Down by the River* (Farrar, Straus), shows a rural teenage Irish girl who is raped and impregnated by her father and becomes a tragic public figure. Colm Toibin's *The Story of the Night* (Holt), his third novel, is set in Argentina during the Falklands (Malvinas) War, centering on the gay and half-English Richard Garay.

France's ninety-six-year-old author, Nathalie Surraute, produced a highly experimental, postmodern novel–*Here* (Brazilier). George Hyvernaud's *The Cattle Car* (Northwestern) was first published in 1953 in France and is based on the author's experiences in Pomeranian Prison Camps in World War II. From Belgium came *Oedipus on the Road* (Arcade) by Henry Bauchau. The author, an eighty-four-year-old psychoanalyst, writes of the life of Oedipus between the events in *Oedipus Rex* and *Oedipus at Colonus*.

There were many translations from the German published this year. Among those which were widely noted: Marcel Beyer's *The Kaknau Tapes* (Harcourt Brace). Set during the time of the Third Reich, it is the story of an expert at recording voices. Goebbels's daughter, Helga, is an alternate narrator. Christoph Ransmayr's *The Dog King* (Knopf) is a "what if" book of alternative history based on the premise that the Morgenthau Plan for the complete deindustrialization of Germany and Austria had been carried out. *Jacob the Liar* (Arcade), by Jurek Becker: in a dying ghetto a Jew with a hidden radio misreports the news so as to give some hope to his fellow sufferers. Concerning a German writer, Andreas, who had worked as a Nazi journalist in World War II, Grete Well's *Last Trolley from Beethovenstraat* (Godine) shifts back and forth from the 1940s to the present. *Heroes Like Us* (Farrar, Straus) by Thomas Brussig offers a satirical view of the times leading up to the fall of the Berlin Wall. In Sten Nadolny's *The God of Impertinence* (Viking) Hermes and Hephaestus continue their age-old quarrel in a thoroughly contemporary setting. *Magdalena the Sinner* (HarperCollins) is the first novel by Lilian Faschinger. Magdalena kidnaps a priest and makes him listen to her confess to the murders of seven men (among other things). From Austria we have *Lover, Traitor: A Jerusalem Story* (Metropolitan) by Anna Mitgutsch, the account of a doomed love affair between Deborah, an Austrian Jew, and Sivan, a Palestinian terrorist.

Hungarian Peter Esterhazy has ninety-seven short chapters, each of them a separate love story, in *She Loves Me* (Northwestern). Highly praised and sometimes compared to Faulkner's *Absalom, Absalom!* (1936) was Peter Nadas's *A Book of Memories* (Farrar, Straus). It is told by three voices–an actor in modern East Berlin; Thomas Thoenisuen, who is an imaginary nineteenth-century figure; and Krisztian, a contemporary technocrat. Two books by Polish nineteenth-century realist Boleslaw Pruss were at last published in English–*The Doll* (Central European University) and *The Sins of Childhood* (Northwestern). From troubled Croatia came *The Taste of a Man* (Penguin), a story of cannibalism in New York City, by Slavenka Drakulic.

Moving eastward, from Israel we had *Panther in the Basement* (Harcourt Brace), by Amos Oz, which is set in Jerusalem in 1947 and is the story of a twelve-year-old boy named Proffy and his Freedom or Death organization. A young student becomes completely obsessed and involved with a book called "The New Life" in Turkish novelist Orhan Pamuk's *The New Life* (Farrar, Straus). This novel was described in *The World & I* (September) as "a postmodernist fantasy, a complex novel of identity changes and twists of fate that wrestles with the East-West schism in the Turkish soul." From Syria came Ulfat Idilbi's *Damascus Bitter Sweet* (Interlink), the sad life and the sudden death of a woman named Sabriya, a book described in *The New York Times Book Review* (7 September) as "operatic in its self-pity."

The University of Arkansas published a translation from the Arabic, *Improvisations on a Missing String,* by Nazek Saba Yared. India continues to produce energetic and interesting and influential writers. One of these is Vikram Chandra, whose *Love and Longing in Bombay* (Little, Brown) is a sequence of stories told by Rajit Sharma, a computer programmer who hangs out in a Bombay bar called Fisherman's Rest. The brilliant young writer Amitav Ghosh brought out *The Calcutta Chromosome* (Avon). Set in the future and written in a metafictional high style, it tells the story of some disparate people (a movie star, a reporter, a computer expert) who send for a missing Nobel Prize–winning scientist. *Lajja=Shame* (Penguin), the story of a Hindu family living near Dacca, produced a *fatwa* and exile for its Bangladeshi author, Taslima Nasrin, without the public-relations benefits that earlier accrued to Salman Rushdie. Among the well-reviewed novels from Asia were *Comfort Woman* (Penguin) by Nora Okja Keller (who is, in fact, an American), the story of the Korean "Comfort Women" who "serviced" the Japanese military in World War II. And, finally, from Japan, a gathering of short stories, originally published in the 1920s, half of them delicate miniatures and the others autobiographical–*The Dancing Girl of Izu* (Counterpoint), by Yasunari Kawabata.

Latin America offered fiction in translation from several languages and nationalities. Patrick Chamoiseau from Martinique published his fifth novel set there, *Texaco* (Pantheon), which won the Prix Goncourt in Paris in 1992. In *The Ministry of Hope* (Marion Boyars) Roy Heath produced a comic novel about a professional healer in postcolonial Guyana. Francisco Goldman's *The Ordinary Seaman* (Atlantic Monthly) was widely reviewed and praised for its surrealistic story of fifteen Central Americans trapped on a dead ship in Brooklyn. In *In the Palm of Darkness* (HarperCollins) Mayra Montero tells the story, set in Haiti, of the search for an elusive frog. This work was described in *The New Yorker* as a "dazzling, original fugue on love and extinction." Angeles Mastretta writes of a Latin American woman living a double life with two utterly

different men in *Lovesick* (Riverhead). From the Portuguese we have the life and times of a hit man in São Paulo in Patricia Melo's *The Killer* (Ecco).

With backlists becoming more and more a thing of the past (for many reasons), reprints and new editions of out-of-print novels and stories are becoming more important as the business of small presses and university presses. Two of the best and most influential publishers of reprints in a crowded and increasingly competitive field are Louisiana State University Press, with its Voices of the South series, and Dalkey Archive, which has become a major player in literary reprints. An incomplete sampling of the most recent additions to their extraordinary list–and one should remember that Dalkey Archive also publishes originals and translations and, as well, the *Review of Contemporary Fiction,* which is arguably the most important literary magazine for contemporary book reviews–gives some idea of the industry and service being performed by Dalkey Archive. Here are a few of the books from 1997–1998: Aldous Huxley, *Those Barren Leaves;* Nicholas Mosley, *Children of Darkness and Light;* Louis-Ferdinand Celine, *Castle to Castle* and *Rigadoon;* Felipe Alfau, *Locos; The Conversions* and *The Journalist,* by Harry Matthews; Leslie Fiedler, *Love and Death in the American Novel;* and *The Complete Fiction of W. M. Spackman,* edited by Steven Moore.

Added to the LSU Voices of the South series in 1997 were Ellen Douglas's *A Family Affair; Lives of the Saints,* by Nancy LeMann; William Humphrey, *The Ordways;* Max Steele, *Debby;* Doris Betts, *The Gentle Insurrection;* Donald Hays, *The Dixie Association;* Joan Williams, *The Wintering;* and *A Place Without Twilight,* by Peter Feibleman–bringing to twenty-six the number of books reprinted in the series. Johns Hopkins University Press brought out two titles by Michel Tournier–*Friday* and *The Ogre.* Counterpoint published a new edition of James Salter's first novel–*The Hunters.* The University of Illinois Press continued its series The Radical Novel Reconsidered with two novels of the 1940s: Ira Wolfert's *Tucker's People* and Alexander Saxton's *The Great Midland.* Syracuse University Press brought out six titles in its Library of Modern Jewish Literature: *My Own Ground,* by Hugh Nissenson; Ludwig Lewisohn's *Island Within;* Merrill Joan Gerber's *Anna in Chains; The Suicide Academy* and *The Rose Rabbi,* by Daniel Stern; and *While the Messiah Tarries,* by Melvin Jules Bukiet. The University Press of Virginia reprinted *The Shad Treatment,* by Garrett Epps, for its new Classics of Virginia series. Sun and Moon Press published *Six Early Stories,* by Thomas Mann. Coffee House published volume three of *Collected Works* by Paul Metcalfe. Owl Books brought out new editions in paperback of *Shame* and *The Satanic*

Verses, by Salman Rushdie. And all the above are just examples of the activity in the reprint market.

In the meantime the commercial presses have not been altogether idle or indifferent. Viking Penguin is reprinting (twelve so far) the books of Wallace Stegner. Viking also brought out a fortieth-anniversary edition of Jack Kerouac's *On the Road* along with *Some of the Dharma,* composed of previously unpublished work by Kerouac. As the first in a planned series of paperback reprints of her work, Grove Press published a new edition of Jacqueline Susann's *Valley of the Dolls.* The Library of America brought out volumes of Wallace Stevens and Nathaniel West and a two-volume set of *Crime Novels.* Carrol and Graf published a revised edition, with a new translation by Brian Murphy, of Mikhail Sholokhov's *Quiet Flows the Don,* the celebrated Soviet novel dealing with the days of czarist and Revolutionary Russia.

Small presses and university presses are more and more involved in the publication of short fiction, though most of the commercial houses are involved as well. What has gradually happened is that small-press and university-press fiction are no longer considered to be inferior venues for the publication of short fiction and are just as likely to be reviewed in the major reviewing publications. Still, on the evidence, it seems that the commercial houses are publishing short fiction by well-known and beginning writers. New Directions, not her usual publisher (Houghton Mifflin), brought out Muriel Spark's *Open to the Public: New & Collected Stories.* Meanwhile, however, Houghton Mifflin did publish Maeve Brennan's *The Springs of Affection,* twenty-one stories set in the same Dublin neighborhood, and Harlan Ellison's *Slippage,* stories written over forty years by a leading science-fiction writer. Houghton Mifflin also published collections by talented newcomers such as Carolyn Ferrell's stories of the inner lives of inner-city children—*Don't Erase Me.* And one which captured the attention of book reviewers all across the country, Peter Ho Davies's *The Ugliest House in the World,* a rich and multicultural variety of which Jay Fernandez (*Washington Post,* 4 January 1998) wrote: "He writes with equal authenticity about the Communist Revolution in China, present-day tensions in Wales and ostrich herding in Patagonia, evoking time and place with what appears to be an impressive acuity." Viking published *The Collected Stories* by Paul Theroux. Here are sixty-odd stories and 660 pages, various in subject and substance and mostly set in Singapore, Central Africa, and London. Harold Brodkey's *The World Is the Home of Love and Death* (Holt) is a posthumous collection, most of the stories closely autobiographical and mostly about the Silenowicz family and about Wiley, who acts as Brodkey's stand-in. Also from Holt came Francine

Prose's *Guided Tours of Hell,* two novellas about Americans abroad; and *The Embroidered Shoes,* by Can Xue, a collection described as featuring "strange, disordered worlds where people speak in riddles and time and setting are as fickle as the wind." Alice Mattison's third collection of stories, *Men Giving Money, Women Yelling* (Morrow), is all set in New Haven and furnished with a cast of linked and recurring characters. Molly Giles's *Creek Walk* and William Boyd's *The Destiny of Nathalie X* were brought out by Knopf; Julie Hecht's *Do the Windows Open?* came from Random House. Ethan Mordden's *Some Men Are Lookers* (St. Martin's Press) is a series of interrelated stories about gay life in Manhattan. Ida Fink's *Traces* (Metropolitan) has stories set in Poland during the Nazi era and after. There are a dozen stories, various in form and subject matter, in *Not Her Real Name* (Anchor), by young New Zealander Emily Perkins. In *Busted Scotch* (Norton) James Kelman brings together stories of two decades, set in urban Scotland and England. Another Scotsman, Jeff Torrington, has a group of grim stories of Scots workers on the assembly line ("the Devil's Carousel") of a dying auto company in *The Devil's Carousel* (Harcourt Brace).

Other stories of interest and value published by smaller presses follow. Janet Kaufman's third collection, *Characters On the Loose* (Gray Wolf) is a series of minimalist stories, as much concerned with language as with anything else. Sharon Solwitz's *Blood and Milk* comes from Sarabande. Morehouse published Sara Maitland's *Angel and Me.* The nine stories set in and around Detroit which form *Within the Lighted City* (Iowa) won the John Simmons Short Fiction Award, judged by Ann Beattie. Charlotte Bacon's *A Private State* (Massachusetts), consisting of eleven stories ranging across a variety of geographical and thematic boundaries, was winner of the Associated Writing Programs' Award for Short Fiction. Also from the University of Massachusetts Press is Jay Neugeboren's *Don't Worry about the Kids,* a selection of stories by this novelist from the work of the past twenty-five years. Forty years' work is to be found in veteran Gordon Weaver's new and selected gathering—*Four Decades* (Missouri). Another longtime story writer, Mario Benedetti, gathers stories of various kinds dating from the 1940s through the 1970s in *Blood Pact & Other Stories* (Curbstone). Peter Bacho's *Dark Blue Suit* (Washington) has twelve stories about Filipino immigrants in Seattle from the 1950s to the present. Harvey Grossinger's five stories and a novella in *The Quarry* (Georgia) concern Jewish characters while the seven stories of Lynn Luria-Sukenick, posthumously published in *Danger Wall May Fall* (Zoland), are all about troubled women. Jere Hoar's debut collection, *Body Parts* (Mississippi), arrived on the scene with high praise, including this judgment by Barry Hannah–"Profound and superb!"

Most readers come to know the writers of short fiction, for better or worse, through the means of anthologies. Probably the two most important are the annual gatherings–*The Best American Short Stories* (Houghton Mifflin) and *Prize Stories: The O. Henry Awards*–for a spot in either or both of which most writers of short fiction would gladly kill or be killed.

Larry Dark, who came on board as the new editor for *Prize Stories 1997: The O. Henry Awards* (Doubleday), has made some changes for that annual volume. In his introduction Dark mentions that, in addition to a new look and format, he has expanded the list of magazines covered and consulted, allowed Canadian magazines and writers to be eligible for the first time, added a list of fifty Honorable Mention stories, and shifted the publication from spring to fall. Moreover, he has, for the first time since the 1940s, used a jury–in this case well-known writers Louise Erdrich, Thom Jones, and David Foster Wallace–to assist him. He does not mention that, as the acknowledgments and permissions clearly indicate, only one of the twenty stories in this volume was actually published in 1997–Mary Gaitskill's "Comfort," originally published in *Fourteen Hills*. Of the others, fifteen were published in magazines and books during calendar year 1996, and four are from 1995. Of the stories, a surprising number, seventeen, came from little magazines; the other three came from *The New Yorker*. Four of the stories, 20 percent, appeared in Cornell's *Epoch,* which is singled out as (also a new twist) "this year's O. Henry Award–winning magazine." This year's gathering offers some familiar names (Lee K. Abbott, John Barth, Andre Dubus, Deborah Eisenberg, Mary Gordon, Alice Monro, Susan Fromberg Schaeffer), but it also presents some brilliant newer voices, among them Arthur Bradford, Carolyn Cooke, Matthew Klam, and Christine Schutt. *The Best American Short Stories 1997* is edited by E. Annie Proulx. It has twenty-one stories from a variety of journals with a variety of authors. Stars like Robert Stone, Richard Bausch, Cynthia Ozick, Lydia Davis, Tobias Wolff, T. Coraghessan Boyle, and Clyde Edgerton appear together with newer voices, among them Karen E. Bender, Junot Diaz, June Spence, Alyson Hagy, Michael Byers, and Tim Gatreaux. This anthology also picks three stories from *The New Yorker* as well as one each from the slick magazines *Esquire* and *Oxford American*. The remaining sixteen stories come from literary magazines, with both the *Paris Review* and *Southern Review* having two stories.

Other anthologies of interest and quality in 1997 included: *Hard-Boiled: An Anthology of Crime Stories,* ed-ited by Bill Pronzini and Jack Adrian (Oxford), which contains thirty-six stories from the times of Raymond Chandler to the present (James Ellroy and Ed Gorman); *Nothing But You: Love Stories from The New Yorker* (Random House), edited by Roger Angell, with a variety of *New Yorker* authors from elders such as (the late) I. B. Singer, V. S. Pritchett, and Jean Rhys to newer people such as Mary Gaitskill, Michael Chabon, and Judy Troy; *25 And Under/Fiction* (Norton), edited by Susan Ketchin and Neil Giordano, had fifteen short stories by fourteen young writers, nine of whom are somewhat older than twenty-five, but no matter–a lively and various collection; and *Scribner's Best of the Fiction Workshops 1998* (Scribner), edited by John Kulka and Natalie Danford, with Carol Shields as guest editor, is derived from participating workshops (113 in the United States and 9 in Canada). The various editors selected twenty-two stories from twenty-one writing programs (New York's Columbia was allotted two stories). The work is, as might be expected, uneven, and perhaps more reflective of the editors' tastes and abilities than any noteworthy trends; but the level of creative competence is uniformly high. Probably some of these writers will be heard from in the future. *Sixty Years of Great Fiction from the Partisan Review* (Partisan Review Press): in addition to the usual suspects (Styron, Sontag, et al.), this one has an impressive gathering of real heavyweights–Beckett, Bellow, Calvino, Camus, Dos Passos, Ellison, Farrell, Faulkner, Kafka, Malraux, Moravia, Silone, Singer, Gertrude Stein, and Robert Penn Warren. The recently formed Texas Review Press, edited by Paul Ruffin, has published *Three Novellas:* "And Earth on Its Frozen Journey," by Tom Whalen; "Days of Captivity," by John S. Walker; and "Deaths by Drowning," by Richard Plant. These are the three winners of the 1996 Southern and Southwestern Novella Competition, a contest which summoned up more than 150 manuscripts. The first-place winner, by Tom Whalen, is described by the editor as "the bittersweet initiation chronicle of a group of tightly knit neighborhood kids who live an almost enchanted life. . . . This lyrical piece, reminiscent of so much of Whalen's work, is pure magic in its interweaving of outer reality and inner. It is as much poetry as it is prose." Two anthologies with foreign roots have more than literary interest. *Daylight in Nightclub Inferno* (Catbird), edited by Elena Lappin, is a gathering of work by sixteen Czech writers. *Acid Plaid: New Scottish Writing* (Arcade), edited by Harry Ritchie, has on board some old hands (William Boyd, Iain Crichton Smith, Shena Mackay), as well as many newer voices from the trainspotting generation.

Dictionary of Literary Biography Yearbook Awards for Distinguished Novels Published in 1997

Frederick Buechner

Starling Lawrence

NOVEL

For fifty years and more Frederick Buechner has been writing fiction of all kinds—from straightforward stories to myths and fables, all of it of the highest quality. Intelligence, wit, and unsentimental compassion (and faith) shine through his pages. Except for the common characteristic of excellence and an ease and fluency he has possessed and maintained from the beginning of his career until today, his books are highly original, kin to but not clones of each other. This year's novel, *On the Road with the Archangel* (Harper, San Francisco), is a slender, evocative, imaginative retelling of the Apocryphal Book of Tobit, narrated in this case by the witty, civilized, charitable, and delightful Archangel Raphael. Dedicated to the late poet James Merrill ("to the memory of James Merrill, who spoke with archangels, and a friendship of fifty-five years"), it is appropriately a kind of prose poem and, at one and the same time, a fable, a yarn, a kind of prayer.

–George Garrett

FIRST NOVEL

The story of the adventures of Auberon Harwell, an unlikely spy in Montenegro before the beginning of World War I whose cover is a collection of botanical specimens, is here told with style, energy, and page-turning excitement by Starling Lawrence, editor in chief at Norton and a writer of elegance and skill and audacity. *Montenegro* (Farrar, Straus) is an example of historical fiction at its best and most relevant. In a year of fascinating first novels, this one stands out as a superior and delightful work of fiction, in every way worth a grown-up's time.

–George Garrett

Dictionary of Literary Biography Yearbook Award for a Distinguished Volume of Short Stories Published in 1997

Dust jacket for the winner of the 1997 Dictionary of Literary Biography *award to a volume of short stories*

Though there were many fine collections of short stories published in 1997 (a fact which, in a sense, testifies to the example and influence of our award winner) nothing came close to competing seriously with *Bernard Malamud: The Complete Stories* (Farrar, Straus). The fifty-five stories, written between the early 1940s and the 1980s, gathered here from his eight previously published collections, with a few stories which have not until now been collected, are demonstrable proof that this is the work of a master of the form constantly changing and refining his art. In a wise and thorough introduction to the book his longtime editor, Robert Giroux, says of the stories: "They reveal an astonishing development over forty years, from the realism of the grocery-store and Brooklyn background stories to the fantasy and freedom of stories like 'The Jewbird,' 'Talking Horse,' 'Angel Levine,' and 'The Magic Barrel.'" Honoring this book, we celebrate a major writer who greatly influenced (and continues to influence) younger American writers.

–George Garrett

The Year in Poetry

John E. Lane
Wofford College

It is "late in the millennium," as the poet Deborah Digges noted almost a decade ago. There is a sense, no matter whether or not one believes the cults, the kooks, and the prognosticators, that we are near the end of something, or, at least, we whisper among our cohorts, something else seems about to begin. Alvin Kernan in *The Death of Literature* (1990) says the rise of literary theory and the postmodern sensibility has infused much of our art and poetry. He sees the last apocalyptic phase "of an old literary order collapsing in on itself." I don't think many would argue that theory has taken its toll on "the old order." The poet and critic David Lehman has noted that Ezra Pound's optimistic modernist "Make it new" has been replaced. Lehman quotes postmodern poet Andre Codrescu: "Get it used." But Lehman suggests in his essay "The Questions of Postmodernism" (1995) that it's possible we aren't "postanything. We are, miserably or splendidly, ourselves, living now, living here."

If Kernan is right about the cultural crack-up, and the literary *Titanic* (modernism and its hold) is about to dip below the millennium's waves, then a yearly conspectus of the sort I'm taking on for 1997 becomes a form of cultural beachcombing. If Lehman is right, then this essay is no island at all, and literature no sinking ocean liner; it is instead only part of a long, complex, continuing conversation. I need to say up front that I believe in the conversation. I am on Lehman's side, hopeful about the future of poetry, excited about its present, though reflective and critical about its past.

So, onward, into what Gary Snyder calls "the big flow." First, I would like to offer a wide overview of sorts, and then make some observations more specific to this calendar year. If I have one grand conclusion to draw about what's happening in poetry-at-large, it is that we live in a time of abundance, of rich poetry production. Poetry is everywhere. There are probably a thousand poetry volumes published and available every year, if one is willing to include self-published work. There are more than three hundred writing programs at colleges and universities. Record labels release spo-

ken-word albums with regularity. There are probably more coffeehouses in America than there are bars, and many of those coffeehouses have an open-mike poetry night. The neighborhood Barnes and Noble superstore (with one in almost every town of any size) stocks poetry in impressive quantity, and even in Spartanburg, South Carolina, where I live, I have seen patrons, both young and old, sitting in overstuffed chairs reading a poem or two.

Maybe Stanley Kunitz was right twenty years ago in *A Kind of Order, A Kind of Folly* when he said that we in America have a "democratization of poetry" underway. The king is dead. King Eliot. King Pound. King Joyce. (If not King Elvis.) Even the midcentury princes and princesses are dead as the century (and the millennium) draws to a close: Robert Lowell, John Berryman, and Elizabeth Bishop, though Kunitz himself–friend to Theodore Roethke, friend to Lowell–continues to publish well into his nineties. Long live the people's poetry! one might cry from some open microphone deep in the Barnes and Noble boonies.

Some with a more cynical, elitist, or claustrophobic bent of mind might side with William Butler Yeats's proclamation near the turn of this fading century, as he glanced around the Rhymers Club: "There are too many of us." Others might feel that, when perusing a year's worth of poetry volumes (much less the two decades since the Kunitz proclamation, or the ten decades since Yeats), "it is not a pretty sight." But instead of ugliness, I see abundance. I don't feel overrun by the unwashed hordes.

Now the observations more specific to this calendar year: first of all, 1997 was a year that will be noted for the deaths of four major figures: James Dickey, Allen Ginsberg, Denise Levertov, and the poet-publisher James Laughlin. There were other literary losses–William Matthews, David Ignatow, James Michener (the novelist whose generous gift once helped fund the National Poetry Series), William S. Burroughs (Beat novelist among Beat poets), among them–but the passing of Dickey, Ginsberg,

Levertov, and Laughlin is of primary importance to those interested in poetry.

Ginsberg will be remembered as one of the major literary figures of the twentieth century, not so much because he was a great poet, but because he was a great presence and had a shrewd business sense. Like Pound in the 1910s and 1920s, Ginsberg in the 1950s and 1960s helped broaden poetry's reach; and like William Carlos Williams, he helped shift the focus of contemporary poetry from an elite English model to one attending to a poetry closer to immediate speech. (Even when Ginsberg dipped in the English well, he preferred the visionary working-class William Blake to upper-class John Milton.) Ginsberg pioneered the long rant through the best-selling "Howl," and his later poems continued the Beats' "first thought, best thought" journal style, a quotidian verse steady as his Buddhist breathing. Today, that Ginsberg-franchised immediacy of utterance can be found everywhere in contemporary poetry. He will be missed, and as poetry raconteur and popular performer his passing will be widely noted.

Denise Levertov died in late December. Levertov, the poet Kenneth Rexroth once called "probably America's best post-war poet," and "completely a poet of married love, motherhood, daughterhood and the problems of transfigured domesticity," was long associated with the Black Mountain poets. There is no doubt that the English-born Levertov will be remembered as a powerful and committed poet, and she will possibly emerge as a major voice once the entire arc of her work is considered. One thing, I think, is certain: she will also be remembered for her political conscience, leading poets against the war in Vietnam.

James Laughlin, the editor, poet, and publisher of New Directions, was probably the most important poetry publisher of the twentieth century in English. Pound's advice in 1934 to Laughlin, then a twenty-year-old poet "enrolled" in "Ezuversity," was to use his family money and begin a publishing venture. Laughlin took Pound's advice and began New Directions, which, in over sixty years, published many of the great writers of the twentieth century, including Pound, Levertov, Rexroth, William Carlos Williams, Dylan Thomas, H.D., Henry Miller, Thomas Merton, Lawrence Ferlinghetti, Hayden Carruth, Gary Snyder, Tennessee Williams, Delmore Schwartz, and Kenneth Patchen.

The most remarkable thing about Laughlin's publishing venture was his ability to distribute and sell his books worldwide. New Directions is the great success story of poetry publishing, and I wonder if anyone will ever be able to match it. It was a labor of love, subsidized with Laughlin's family money. In an age when people say "poetry doesn't sell," Laughlin consistently published volumes of verse with sales in the tens of thousands—Pound, Snyder, and Ferlinghetti chief among them. It should be noted that Laughlin also published a final volume of his own poetry this year, bringing to an end over a half century of work as a poet.

Since I am discussing New Directions, the first book I would like to consider for 1997 is the new collection by Lawrence Ferlinghetti, *A Far Rockaway of the Heart* (New Directions), which wins the award for the best title of the year. Ferlinghetti's collection is a bookend to his best-selling 1958 collection *A Coney Island of the Mind* but unfortunately lacks the immediacy, power, and passion of that early collection. It is a swan song but does not trumpet. In *A Far Rockaway* Ferlinghetti creates a loose sequence of 101 related poems which reads like a journal; he utilizes a stairstep composition meant to pull the reader down the page. I'm left, unfortunately, at the top of many of the breezy poems. Here is the entry (number 3) from which the collection's title is taken:

A native-born New Yorker
  I was from the Lower Inside
    a part of town much favored by
      addicts of the subjective
        (a subversive group always being investigated)
    as well as buddhists
      and their lower chakras
        and others seeking salvations
          from various realities
                      virtual or actual
And losing track of where I was coming from
                  with amnesia of an immigrant
        I traveled over
              the extrovert face
                          of America
  But no matter where I wandered
                    off the chart
    I still would love to find again
                that lost locality
  Where I might catch once more
          a Sunday subway for
              some Far Rockaway of the heart

Though this passage lacks much of what made Ferlinghetti a household name in the 1950s and 1960s (humor, revolutionary impact), my interest in the Beats and what they were able to accomplish makes me want to follow Ferlinghetti's career out to the bitter end. He is now approaching eighty, and I'm hoping that a future collection will break new trails into feeling and intensity.

In what could seem a strange transition, I move from Ferlinghetti's poems to Reynolds Price's *The Collected Poems* (Scribners). Price, a celebrated novelist, offers this hefty tome (464 pages) as a collection written mostly since a grave illness nearly took his life (and left him with no use of his legs) in the early 1980s. In his introduction to the volume, Price describes many of his collected poems as "meant to preserve some small incident which seemed in imminent danger of vanishing if not reproduced quickly in the most precise sentences available." Price does this beautifully in places. The book has a real feel of an intellectual's daybook: recorded dreams ("The Dream of Food," "The Dream of a House"); translations and versions from poems in other languages; memories of past encounters with the literary rich and famous such as W. H. Auden, Lowell, and Stephen Spender; and lyrical memories of travel with old friends and lovers.

Sometimes Price's language seems overly elevated, poetic, and hyperliterary, and it suggests that the novelist sits down and writes poems in a way he would never write novels, taking as models the masters of the past for his atmosphere and diction. But when the poems are successful (and they are often, especially the recent poems), they share much in common with Ferlinghetti's best poems: humor, deep feeling, and a lightness of diction. Here is one called "Mere Fact" I like a great deal from near the end of this hefty collection, from the section called "The Unaccountable Worth of the World":

This quiet life secretes these quiet poems—
Friends sicken, die, pets vanish, love rekindles,
Dreams witness mutely to impending doom—
And in the silent waits, I roll past time
So uneventful I could balance eggs
Safe on both my thighs through average days.
  Weekend, before and after lavish naps,
I half permit myself to search the wall
Of loaded photos from my distant past
And reply thunder, lightning, sleepless nights
When my limbs braided with stupendous others—
Torsos, calves, necks, napes, assorted thickets—
And watched the muffled dawn declare itself
Eight or nine times in a single dark:
That frequently the miracle recurred.
  So *quiet*–right. Earned quiet. Sounding silence.

Another major tome made this year's list of releases, *The Collected Poems of John Ciardi* (University of Arkansas Press). It includes 450 poems. This is "over 62 percent of the verse" that appeared in collections published between 1940 and 1993, according to editor Edward M. Cifelli. (Ciardi's children's poetry is not included here, though it is probably what the poet is best remembered for outside of university circles.) Ciardi is an old-school poet of line and meter, and he is hard for me to assess. But if, at some point, I really want to close this gap, the University of Arkansas has made an industry of John Ciardi, including Ciardi's war diary (1988), *Ciardi Himself: Fifteen Essays in the Reading, Writing, and Teaching of Poetry* (1989), a 497-page selected letters (1991), and a 448-page biography

(1997). Here, from Ciardi's 1961 collection *In the Stone Works,* is his clever "Epitaph":

Here, time concurring (and it does),
Lies Ciardi. If no kingdom come,
A kingdom was. Such as it was,
This one, beside it, is a slum.

At the other end of the poetry spectrum from John Ciardi, I find James Galvin's metaphysical-surreal *Resurrection Update* (Copper Canyon Press) an odd release. A "collected poems," this volume from the Iowa-Wyoming poet gathers Galvin's poetry from 1975 though 1997, a twenty-year period. Why not release a "selected poems" by this still-young poet with only twenty years of publishing?

Copper Canyon, a press that early on published many significant first collections by unknown poets, has in the past ten years moved toward "definitive" collections–selected and collected poems by U.S. and world poets. This year's catalogue includes Rexroth's collected love poems; Thomas McGrath's complete long poem, *Letter to an Imaginary Friend;* a "new and selected poems" by Eleanor Wilner; Odysseas Elytis's selected and last poems; the aforementioned Galvin; and finally forty years of "versions" by Stephen Berg. I guess as a marketing-niche move (libraries probably purchase more compilations than first collections) it can be understood, but for me it lends a funereal air to the press catalogue, a sense that one of the best poetry publishers in America feels we are, indeed, toward the end of things.

One final collected poems of note for 1997 is the 471-page *The Collected Poems of Amy Clampitt* (Knopf). Clampitt got a late start (her first book, *The Kingfisher,* did not appear until she was over sixty). Her collected poems pulls together an admirable harvest of poetry, though some of the later poems lack the intensity of her earlier work. Clampitt, along with Jack Gilbert, have seemed to me for years the standard-bearers for the old modernist rules of battle: be deliberate, avoid the universities, look to Europe for cultural models. Now Gilbert (who has published three gemlike collections in nearly fifty years) is the only one remaining, keeping old Ez's faith of exquisite image and diamond-hard diction.

Here's "Palm Sunday," an early poem, which plays out its fine sentiment and observation in one long sentence:

Neither the wild tulip, poignant
and sanguinary, nor the dandelion
blowsily unbuttoning, answers
the gardener's imperative, if need be,
to maim and hamper in the name of order,
or the taste for rendering adorable

*Dust jacket for a volume in the Louisiana State University Press
poetry series*

the torturer's implements—never mind
what entrails, not yet trampled under
by the feet of choirboys (sing,
my tongue, the glorious battle),
mulch the olive groves, the flowering
of apple and almond, the boxwood
corridor, the churchyard yew,
the gallows tree.

Though not quite as definitive as collected
poems, we now have an onslaught of new and selected
poems as well: Louisiana State University Press alone
published five in 1997, almost half of their published
volumes, and at my count at least fifteen others have
landed on my study floor. It seems that the four-
to-five-book plateau is the time to bring out one of
these, with the poet reaching fifty, twenty to twenty-
five years into "the career."

Thomas Lux's *New and Selected Poems* (Houghton
Mifflin) leads the list of this year's crop of compilations. Lux is steady and powerful. He is a poet known
for his sense of satire and love of the dividends paid
on 1960s and 1970s neosurrealism. But his lightness is
deceptive. As the dust-jacket copy says, "Who else

would write a poem about an unopened jar of mara-
schino cherries in a refrigerator, or feel himself able
to speak for today's commercial leech farmer?" His
poems are deadly serious in their way, though. His
way is often to puncture like an ice pick punctures: a
small hole pushed deep through images, voice, and
wit. What I like most about these poems are their titles: "Pecked to Death by Swans," "It Must Be the
Monk in Me," "After a Few Whiffs of Another
World," or "Walt Whitman's Brain Dropped on the
Laboratory Floor." What I like second best is Lux's
strong purpose and dark message underlying all his
poems. Lux has his speaker in "Old Man Shoveling
Snow" confirm: "Bend your back to it, sir: for it will
snow all night." It is the same message another poet,
Robert Creeley, reported forty years ago, "The
darkness sur- / rounds us, what // can we do against /
it."

Another of my favorites, released this year in paperback, is the late Jane Kenyon's *Otherwise: New and
Selected Poems* (Graywolf). Kenyon's life and poetry
production, tragically shortened by leukemia, offers a
model such as Keats presented in the nineteenth century: if we look to Kenyon's intense lyrical clarity, we
learn to live in service of an attentive mind, no matter
how short a life we are given. This is enough for a
poet. Here is a brief lyric called "Biscuit," the type
Kenyon is widely admired for:

The dog has cleaned his bowl
and his reward is a biscuit,
which I put in his mouth
like a priest offering the host.
I can't bear that trusting face!
He asks for bread, expects
bread, and I in my power
might have given him a stone.

Among the other notable volumes of new and
selected poems this year are Kathlene Fraser's *Selected
Poems* (Wesleyan Poetry Series/University Press of
New England) and all five from Louisiana State University Press: Marilyn Nelson's *The Fields of Praise,*
Brenda Marie Osbey's *All Saints,* Margaret Gibson's
Earth Elegy, Reginald Gibbons's *Sparrow,* and James
Seay's *Open Field, Understory.* Louisiana State University Press has made a substantial commitment to contemporary poetry, one unsurpassed I believe by any
other publisher in the country, and the quality of their
selections is always high. This year it is no differ-
ent.The National Book Award finalists this year include two "new and selected" poems: John Balaban's
Locusts at the Edge of Summer (Copper Canyon Press)
and Marilyn Nelson's *The Fields of Praise* (Louisiana
State University Press). Nelson's collection has a
beautiful cover—a linear wrap-around repetition of the

same shot of horses grazing in an autumn field—and the fine cover announces the poems to follow, a good selection from her five previous collections and a generous group of new poems. Nelson is a poet of strong voices, interior landscapes, and personal history. Here are a few stanzas from "Tuskegee Airfield," her poem about the black airmen of World War II:

> These men,
> these proud black men:
> our first to touch
> their fingers to the sky.
>
> The Germans learned to call them
> *Die Schwarzen Vogelmenschen.*
> They called themselves
> *The Spookwaffe.*
>
> Laughing.
> And marching to class under officers
> whose thin-lipped ambition
> was to *wash the niggers out.*

When I read Nelson's strong poems, I am reminded of Rexroth's contention (from an essay similar to this one written in 1965) that "the significant advances in American literature in the next decade" would be made by African American writers. Nelson's poetry shows that Rexroth could have extended his prediction to the end of the century.

All Saints, Brenda Marie Osbey's new and selected poems, is a book highly place-specific—so much so that the volume demands a glossary at the rear, explaining "New Orleans Ethnic Expressions, Place Names, and Characters." Obscure words are defined, such as *bamboula,* which we are told is "a ring dance of African origin danced by slaves and free Blacks in eighteenth- and nineteenth-century New Orleans," and the not-so-helpful *back-a-town* is elucidated. "Back-a-town," Osbey tells us, is "literally 'in back of the town.'" Could we not figure that one out?

There is a strong narrative sense to Osbey's poems, and a powerful sense of New Orleans; here is a passage describing a crazy conjuring woman named "Elvena":

> there is a house down on old roman street
> all the women pass through.
> one stands outside the gate
> bare feet
> broad skirts gathered loosely
> about her hips.
> *have you lost anything today?*
> *tell me neighbor*
> *what have you lost today?*
> and her madness is a conju
> slung like rope about her heart.

> i said i feel her madness like a conju
> like a rope
> slung round my heart.

For those who could not figure it out from context, Osbey tells us in the glossary that a *conju* is "the practice of conjuring or other spiritual trade and practice associated with Hoodoo."

The poems of Margaret Gibson, as selected in *Earth Elegy,* offer a similar sense of place as Osbey's. I did not know Gibson's poetry very well before encountering this collection but have now become an admirer of her quiet, specific vision. She is meditative and inclusive of many of what the Buddhists call "the ten thousand things." This mention of Asia is not flippant. Gibson shows an interest in things Buddhist with poems like the earlier "Doing Nothing," "Beginner's Mind," and "Making Salad," written after reading the Japanese master poet Eihei Dogen. Here is the first stanza from "Making Salad":

> I rub the dark hollow of the bowl
> with garlic, near to the fire enough
> so that fire reflects on the wood,
> a reverie that holds emptiness
> in high regard. I enter the complete
> absence of any indicative event,
> following the swirl of the grain,
> following zero formal and imminent
> in the wood, bringing right to
> the surface of the bowl the nothing
> out of which nothing springs.

I really enjoy the pace and music of this poem, the detail and the attention. Gibson is able to take something daily and simple—the making of a salad—and turn it into a meditation on the universe. *Earth Elegy* is full of this sort of meditation, and it is a book I plan to return to once this essay is put to bed.

In *Sparrow* the poet, fiction writer, translator, editor and critic Reginald Gibbons has selected poems from four previous collections. The book is beautifully designed, in blue and white, with a jacket illustration by the author showing a comic bird landing on a tiny house. Gibbons's book is part of a special Louisiana State University Press imprint edited by Dave Smith, *The Southern Messenger Poets,* but it is difficult to tell what makes these poems "Southern," though there is no doubt they are messengers. Maybe it's that Gibbons was born in Texas, but his poems do not speak of Texasness, and he now teaches at Northwestern University in Illinois.

The message Gibbons's poems give us is that reading is a primary source of poetry. The poems in *Sparrow* are beautifully literary in this way, with epigraphs from Tu Fu, Mazisi Kunene, Allen Tate, and George Herbert, and there are many poems in the collection that were written "after" reading, in the style or tone of another poet. These include poems in the wake of Chang K'o-Chiu, Carlos, Drummond de Andrade, Hugo (Victor, I presume, not Richard), Ezra Pound, Eugenio Montale, and many more. Here the elegant "In Memoriam Ezra Loomis Pound," the last poem in the collection, from near the beginning of Gibbons's career, offers these first seven lines, which could have been written by Pound:

A midland
          peninsular light
"Mediterranean"
                    hugs the white stucco

          and heat
rises, rearing up from cool dawn and earth
into its midday passion

My favorite of the Louisiana State University Press selected poems this year is the North Carolina poet James Seay's *Open Field, Understory*. This is another collection from the Southern Messenger series, and there is no doubt these poems are clearly Southern. A Mississippi native, Seay has lived much of his life in North Carolina, and his poems show it. They are full of light, trees, weather, talk, memory, and the coastal water of the Carolinas. Seay's sensibility finds his way into places, the way water finds its way around rocks. When you read many of Seay's poems you feel you are in the presence of the world, as in these lines from "Natural Growth":

Plant your eyes in the solid bank of trees
in the room where the pines are counting their long green.
Let your vision grow into the other kingdom.

Another fine new and selected poems is that of Dick Allen. His *Ode to the Cold War* (Sarabande Books) is a book that ranges more than most through much of the cultural change of the late twentieth century. These are not personal lyrics; instead Allen writes poems with an eye toward the zeitgeist. There is "Ode to the Cold War" ("You organized our lives. You made our sacrifices / Possible."), "At the Photocopy Machine" ("Another miracle. How many can he stand?"), "The Spaceship on its Gantry" ("is instantly primitive / as if the earth had never existed / without the means for getting off it"). If Allen has one major theme, it seems to be flight, with many of the poems exploring the many ways we have devised to free ourselves from the confines of the earth. This from "The Coming of the First Aeroplanes":

The coming of the first aeroplanes
out across America

obsesses me,
as other men are obsessed
by the President's face,

bi-sexual wives,
and I think *throttle, stick, loop,
barnstorm, goggles, dive,*
shade my eyes
and all the doors
of all the houses open, and upon the small
lawns of 1920, people stand
praising God.

It should be noted that Sarabande Books, Allen's publisher, is a relatively new small press from Louisville, Kentucky. This year's selection of four or five volumes is very attractive. I will watch their progress with interest.

The University of South Carolina Press continues its fine James Dickey Poetry Series (edited by Richard Howard) with four new volumes: *The Threshold of the New,* by Henry Sloss; *Error and Angels,* by Maureen Bloomfield; *Growing Back Poems 1972–1992,* by Rika Lesser; and *Portrait in a Spoon,* by James Cummins. Bloomfield and Sloss have both published solid first collections, and Lesser, a well-known translator, has gathered together fine poems from two decades.

In "Pages Toward the Turn of the Year" Lesser offers these lines: "*Men are /* largely absent from this book." Then Lesser goes on to explore the "why" of that question, calling past lovers "An alphabet soup of lower flames that burned." Her poems as well seem casual, a sort of "lower flame." If they burn, it is only through the entirety of the collection. Maybe that's why the collection was twenty years in the making, gathering enough kindling to start a bigger flame.

James Cummins is making his mark in poetry as the contemporary master of the sestina form. His first collection, *The Whole Truth,* was made up entirely of sestinas about Perry Mason. Though *Portrait in a Spoon* contains many poems which are not sestinas, I find myself paying closer attention to the ones that are. Cummins has a New York School sensibility (Kenneth Koch, Frank O'Hara, John Ashbery), and his whimsical flights are always entertaining. This, the first stanza from the sestina "Fling":

He wanted to tell her the weekend idea was "neat,"
But he kept hearing himself repeat the word "funny."
She named the names of trees, flowers: *sycamore, tulip.*
He asked her who did she think she was, Gary Snyder?
Above the car, then over the hotel, the spring moon
Was full, orange. "This isn't just another fling."

It's impressive to watch Cummins work his way out of this particular sestina hole, the machine of repeating stanzas set in motion with its pattern of line-ending words. How could Gary Snyder work his way through this romp? Cummins is a master of fulfilling such expectations. This is one of my favorite collections of the year.

Making another associative leap, I'd like to note that Snyder's long poem *Mountains and River Without End* (Counterpoint) was released in paperback in 1997. I admire Snyder's ongoing life of poetry and activism in service of wilderness and language, and I hope the long poem, when more people have a chance to study Snyder's achievement, will give him the recognition he deserves.

I will use place as a transition vehicle for several comments about Janet Sylvester's second book of poems, *The Mark of Flesh* (Norton). Sylvester's poems, like Snyder's long poem, are dense with history, both personal and cultural. In the collection's title poem (and the first), the speaker and a lover sprawl "wet and famished, across the sheets / of the Grant and Lee Motel in Appomattox." In this poem, as in many others to follow, history is filtered through the commonplace, to become script and metaphor for unfulfilled personal longing. Last battles are lost. Desire is surrendered. The entire collection has this sense of loss, and I look forward to seeing where Sylvester goes after this. "My heart aches," her poems say quite convincingly.

Jane Hirshfield's fifth collection, *The Lives of the Heart* (HarperPerennial), offers a serving of attentive, Buddhist-influenced, precise, celebratory poetry. The cover of the collection shows a pewter bowl of ripe blackberries, and reading Hirshfield's seductive poems often feels like eating blackberries. Each poem is an infusion of sweetness and seed. Hirshfield contributes a fine millennial poem in "Jasmine":

> "Almost the twenty-first century"–
> how quickly the thought will grow dated,
> even quaint.
>
> Our hopes, our future,
> will pass like the hopes and futures of others.
> And all our anxieties and terrors,
> nights of sleeplessness,
> griefs,
> will appear then as they truly are–
>
> Stumbling, delirious bees in the tea scent of jasmine.

A poet who does not take "all our anxieties and terrors" lightly is Paul Allen, College of Charleston professor and director of the Charleston Writers Conference. His first collection, *American Crawl,* which won the Vassar Miller Prize in Poetry from the University of North Texas Press, is full of struggle, of verbal terror. If Hirshfield is Zen quiet, Allen is western Jere-

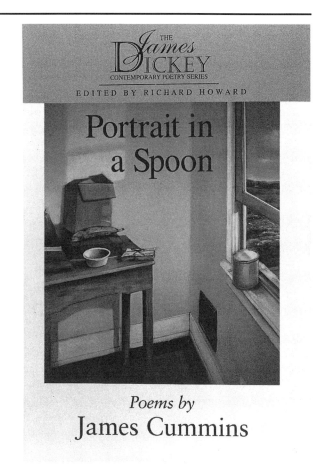

Dust jacket for a volume in the University of South Carolina Press poetry series named for the university's poet and teacher

miah, announcing to the world how hard things are to get *over* and *through* late in this American century. In the collection's title poem, "American Crawl," the speaker explains: "I learn now that giving up is not a matter of giving up. / There is a paddling slowly for all I am worth, / tossing whichever arm wills toward air, dropping it, / kicking one leg, letting the other leg drag to a state, / to a kind of dream of paddling, of trees over my arm." I like Allen's struggle and energy. I'm willing to swim with him, no matter how much strength it takes.

Homer's *Iliad,* Virgil's *Aeneid, The Song of Roland,* Milton's *Paradise Lost,* and now, Michael Lind's *The Alamo: An Epic* (Houghton Mifflin). Lind's poem, 281 pages and 6,006 lines in length, comes complete with glossary, chronology, and the 32-page essay at the back called "On Epic," just in case, dear reader, you don't know exactly what you've just hefted into your lap.

If *The Alamo* had been written in the mock-epic style of Kenneth Koch's *Ko, or a Season on Earth,* it might just make for more interesting reading, but the book is humorless; we are meant to take it quite seriously in spite of blurbs on the back from Dan Rather and Larry McMurtry. The pentameter lines and thudding rhymes—"The fog unravels. But this is no fog, / this blear amalgam of a scumbled dust / and stinging fumes. An isolated leg, / wrapped like a maize ear in a tattered husk. / A headless soldier bows; the freckling paint / has made his gulping pal a stigmaed saint." I fear that some Santa Anna of reviewing will overrun these stanzas and take no prisoners in the near future. Poetry, I'm afraid, may not remember *The Alamo* for long.

Released in 1997, though mentioned briefly in last year's review, Talvikki Ansel's *My Shining Archipelago* (Yale University Press) was James Dickey's last selection as judge of the Younger Poets series. It's easy to see how Dickey was drawn to Ansel's poems. These poems echo some of the recently deceased Dickey's deepest themes: how the civilized enters "the wild" (there is an eighteen-sonnet sequence on the Amazon River basin), the power of animals as encountered through hunting ("She won't look / when the boys kill the ducks / until her cousin twirls / the drake's head, left, right,") and even the slight echo of Dickey's "Into Stone" in Ansel's poem "From Stone."

Maybe it's because of these strong echoes of Dickey, still the master of many territories, that I think this collection is one of the strongest of recent Yale volumes. Ansel knows the world she writes about, whether it's the distant Amazon or the "adolescent rabbit in the county dump, among cans, / bedsprings and other rusting oxidizing elements."

James Ragan's *Lusions* (Grove Press) ranges far and wide, and like Yeats's *A Vision* or Jim Morrison's *American Prayer,* in the end it is hard to make straightout sense of it all. Ragan accompanies us on a clever poetic journey through a series of "lusions": Allusion, Delusion, Illusion, Collusion, Exclusion, Occlusion, and finally, nearing the millennium, Seclusion. The book moves historically, that much is sure, from prehistory with "The Birth of God" and "The Reindeer Age" to present-day "occlusion" in the Age of Communication. The poems, the jacket copy says, are about "change" and "cultural evolution," and it will take more than this brief review to figure out Ragan's complex scheme.

Poet, businessman, board chairman of Bennington College, president of the Poetry Society of America, John Barr is a man with a rack full of hats. Barr is a gracious and talented poet, and when he wears his poetry hat he looks more like a Wall Street banker than Walt Whitman in his rustic crusher. His fourth collection of poems, *The Hundred Fathom Curve* (Story Line Press), is crafted and sharp. His sensibility is observant and cultured (sort of Mary Oliver crossed with T. S. Eliot), and there are two or three poems in this collection I have reread several times. It was Barr, as board chairman, who helped pull Bennington College back from the edge of higher education oblivion in the mid 1990s, and in one of his poems called "Restoration" the speaker explains, "I love to recover the quality / of things in decline."

Danielle Truscott's *anthems of an uncut field* (New Native Press) is the first collection from a poet associated with the lively literary scene of Asheville, North Carolina. New Native Press only releases one or two collections a year, but like Jonathan William's Jargon Society (from the same area of the mountains), the books are worth the wait.

A journalist who has worked with various alternative newspapers up and down the East Coast, Truscott is constantly trying to live up to one of the epigraphs leading the book, Mina Loy's "Who says two plus two equals four?" Her poems fly in the face of logic and expectation, substituting these for rhapsody and rhythm: "Take / the tabernacles, / temples, and cathedrals, / take every desperate coquette / plagiarizing love / with regret's archival ken." These poems are pure lyric, and it will be interesting to see where Truscott goes from here.

The Errancy (Ecco) is Jorie Graham's first full collection since *Materialism* came out in 1993. It is a longish collection (almost one hundred pages) and slightly wider than the traditional six-by-nine-inch poetry book to accommodate Graham's occasionally long lines. Graham's poems demand two minds: one, like a flint point, willing to cut deep and clean; the other, like a swallow, quick to flutter away into a poet's enforced intellectual distances. Her poems defy easy explanation and quotation, but here, as an example of Graham's style, are some lines from the middle of "The Guardian Angel of the Little Utopia," the lead poem in the collection:

The party is so loud downstairs, bristling with souvenirs.
It's a philosophy of life, of course,
drinks fluorescent, whips of syntax in the air
above the heads—how small they seem from here,
the bobbing universal heads, stuffing the void with eloquence,
and also tiny merciless darts
of truth. It's pulled on tight, the air they breathe and rip.

Against Distances (BOA Editions Limited), by Peter Makuck, is as accessible as Graham's work is difficult. This collection, Makuck's sixth, is full of direct observation and storytelling. It is place-specific and water-bound. Most of the water is on the coast of North Carolina, not far from where Makuck teaches at East Carolina University and edits *Tar River Poetry*. If there is a ghost behind this book it is not Martin Heidegger; it is James Wright instead. There is even a poem written in the style of Wright's "Lying in a

Hammock at William Duffy's Farm in Pine Island, Minnesota." Makuck calls his "Leaning Against the Bar at Wrong-Way Corrigan's in Greenville, North Carolina," and it goes like this:

> Over my head, I see the green toucan,
> taunted into squawking, "Go for it!"
> by a red-faced juicer with jesus hair and a pool cue.
> Down two smoky stairs by the jukebox
> pool balls follow one another
> from the table's green field into long dark tunnels.
> To my right,
> on her bare shoulder, behind the scrim
> of long bleached hair, a tattooed butterfly,
> the color of crankcase oil, sleeps on and on.
> I lean back, as the late news comes on overhead.
> A drunk staggers out the door, blind for home.
> I have wasted my cash.

It's an easy parody, and it's not going to push the envelope of contemporary poetry, or give Jorie Graham a run for the Pulitzer, but it's funny, and there's a need for more humor in poetry.

Mary Leader's *red signature* (Graywolf Press), the National Poetry Series volume selected by Deborah Digges, is one of the most unusual collections of the year. Leader's poems are often collages of recipes, notes, overheard dialogue, and scored tunes. At times the poetry seems a domestic version of John Ashbery's audacious 1962 *The Tennis Court Oath*. There's even a poem, called "Girls' Names," near the end of the collection that is wonderfully impossible to read, and even impossible to describe. It's a typographic poem made shapely by underlining and a frame of brackets. All over the page a reader's eye is drawn to girls' names—Sarah, Susan, Mary, and many more. There are also phrases that make sense—"Dear Rebecca," and "North Carolina," and "The whippoorwill is surer of her name / than we are sure of anything." What does it all mean? I keep returning to this "poem," trying to make sense of it all.

Daylight and Starlight (Louisiana State University Press), James Applewhite's eighth volume of poetry, strikes an elegiac stance. Applewhite writes often of a vanishing way of life—piedmont and coastal plain Southern farm culture—with elegance and care. In "The Absence of New Graves in Fields" he describes driving past old farms between Stantonsburg and Greenville, North Carolina: "Sent packing, the dead gods // of this soil look from their burial at an easier ugliness: / ranch-style homes, azalea blooms, production-line rooms / as in a train. The hardship of a homemade beauty / has been voted away by money." Applewhite is often overshadowed at Duke University, where he teaches, by novelist Reynolds Price and the "reader response" theory crowd such as Stanley Fish, but his poems are always well

crafted. With this collection Applewhite continues to spin out his dreams of a time-present and time-past, where the moon shines on "the old stones' ghostliness."

When a new collection of Mary Oliver's poems appears, I always wonder what she will *see* and *hear* this time. In *West Wind* (Houghton Mifflin), Oliver's ninth volume (a mixture of prose poems and lined poetry), she watches as her dogs run a deer, as the sun rises over the housetops, as the ocean "empties its pockets," as the fields are "thickening . . . every morning"; she listens as "language / keeps making its tiny noises," and approaching wild turkeys sound like "the patter of rain, then rapid rain." This collection is my choice for the *Dictionary of Literary Biography* Award for the year's best volume of poetry. Why this book and not one of five or six others I really enjoyed this year, such as James Cummins's *Portrait in a Spoon*, or Marilyn Nelson's *Fields of Praise?* Oliver's poetry makes me want to get up out of my chair and walk around. She also makes me want to write a poem or two about what I see out there beyond the computer screen. She makes me feel deeply for landscape and question my relationship to place. She confirms for me the hope that poetry survives if our senses survive.

Mark Gewanter's first collection, *In the Belly* (University of Chicago Press), is tightly wrapped. The poems are often stanzaic—tercets and quatrains abound—and give the collection a sense of deep feeling under dangerous control. The title poem, concerns a dark "lesson" in the art of sailing. The speaker, a young boy, imagines at the beginning "*Dad pays him to teach me,*" and we see the boy's teacher, an old man "*older than Grandpa; he'll die soon,*" awash in his own incontinent piss. The poem winds through its course in eight three-line stanzas, leaving the boy on the dock, so to speak, staring into an ancient whale rendering kettle to sort out "the stink left in the belly." There are ghosts of Robert Lowell in these poems. For Gewanter, who teaches at Harvard, I can only hope he finds his own tack.

Tracy Philpot, a domestic violence counselor from Alaska, has produced one of the most unsettling collections of the year in *Incorrect Distances* (University of Georgia Press). The title comes from Jacques Lacan's reference to incest as "an incorrect distance from loved ones." Philpot writes in a sort of code, as if the "incorrect distance" is metaphoric and what is to be avoided in these poems is what the theory crowd calls the "signified," the "real" world. This from "News from Czechoslovakia":

> Married to a collection of individuals,
> A summer of excuses.

How long can you waithuman
Behind the cottages?
Tell her everyone resigns.

The remainder of the poem (and much of the collection) offers phrases which have been rearranged (made "incorrect?"), and the syntax has been troubled to the edge of nonsense. Each time I feel close to understanding, I'm pushed away. Still, I find the book intriguing.

A few collections that I received late but wanted to be sure to mention: Jim Daniels's *Blessing the House,* which leads a strong University of Pittsburgh Press Poetry Series. This year Pitt's series also includes books from David Wojahn, Toi Derricotte, and Allison Joseph. Frank Bidart's *Desire* (Farrar, Straus and Giroux) was nominated for the National Book Award this year. Bidart's poems are what poet-critic Liam Rector has called "the primary of voices" and always make me rethink my own vision of what a poem could be.

Alan Shapiro published a memoir about the death of his sister from breast cancer: *Vigil* (University of Chicago Press). Though primarily prose, the book includes a suite of powerful poems at the rear. One of the best is "Scree," a three-page meditation on climbing the "steep slope" of a loved one dying. It's encouraging to see publishers beginning to allow for mixed-genre publications. The University of Chicago should be applauded for this.

Many anthologies appeared in 1997. Two that require special note are *Reinventing the Enemy's Language: Contemporary Native Women's Writings of North America* (Norton), edited by Joy Harjo and Gloria Bird, and *Writing the Wind: A Celtic Resurgence/The New Celtic Poetry* (New Native Press), edited by Thomas Rain Crowe with Gwendal Denez and Tom Hubbard.

The Harjo/Bird anthology brings together many voices not yet heard from Native American writing and adds a valuable collection to the 1990s "diversity" push. The introduction, written as a dialogue between Harjo and Bird, is thoughtful and provocative.

Writing the Wind brings into English (with a lyric introduction and good biographies) a world of poetry so far mostly unknown to American readers: the Celtic-language poets of Wales, Brittany, Ireland, Scotland, Cornwall, and the Isle of Man. Crowe's anthology may do for these poets what Robert Bly did for the Spanish and Latin Americans in the 1960s. Some of the poems are reprinted in the original on facing pages if you want to try your hand at pronouncing these ancient languages. So far very few copies are available in the United States. The anthology's initial

printing sold out in Wales, Scotland, England, and Ireland well before the official publication date.

Finally, *The Bunker in the Parsley Fields* is Gary Gildner's new collection and the winner of the 1996 Iowa Poetry Prize from the University of Iowa Press. Gildner lives in Idaho, but his country is often his memory. He oscillates between childhood memories of baseball ("I learned to scoop up grounders on the cinders") and the immediate connection between weather and clothing ("On certain cold days / I wear a wool shirt / that belonged to my father").

Maybe in some future collection a sensibility more akin to Mary Oliver will win out. The wild world surrounding Gildner is constantly competing for his attention: in this collection there is an encounter with a wild cougar ("The cougar who prowls my mountain came down / close today and looked at me in my corral") and an owl constantly bashing into the house ("Ever since our cat Oshkosh disappeared / a great horned owl, *Bubo virginianus,* / has been slamming into our house"). Gildner is happy in Idaho. In "Collecting Cowpies" the speaker says:

We can't wipe off
a goofy grin, feeling lucky,
feeling connected to the genius
who or which keeps
turning everything over–

Well, to steal a metaphor from Gary Gildner, this reviewer has collected his final cowpies for the year. There are close to a hundred books pushed to the side now, ready to enter the great compost heap of my poetry shelf. Is there a better way to do this? Probably. Will I discover it? Probably not. Here's a possibility though: this morning, as I read, annotated, ignored, and reread a final time, a local radio station was running a contest: "Send in your list of the top ten albums of 1997 on a postcard, and if your card is selected as the grand prize winner, you will receive WNCW's 'top 100 albums' of the year as voted by our listeners."

As I close down this essay, I wonder if contemporary poetry could assess the calendar year in this way? At the moment it seems so sane, orderly, and civilized. The method would fall somewhere between the elitism of Harold Bloom presenting his "Western Canon" and the crude democratic impulse of the poetry slam.

What do you think? You, out there in Poetry Land? Send in your postcards for 1998.

Dictionary of Literary Biography Yearbook Award for Distinguished Volume of Poetry Published in 1997

Attention to the details of consciousness, the details of perception, marks the greatest poetry for me. This attentiveness is what marks Emily Dickinson, Theodore Roethke, Matsuo Basho, John Donne, *and* Robert Creeley. If some ambitious god wants to re-create our world after greed and pollution have done it in, all I can hope is that some Mary Oliver poetry survives as the blueprint.

Oliver's *West Wind* (Houghton Mifflin) is as attentive as it gets. The table of contents presents what we call "nature" (the titles read like a field guide: "Seven White Butterflies," "At Round Pond," "Black Oaks," "Pilot Snake," "Maples") and "culture" ("Shelly," "That Sweet Flute John Clare," "Late Summer Poem Touching the Subject of Faith").

This book is my favorite of the year because I discover so much I have missed when I read Oliver. Somehow Oliver has managed to keep paying attention in spite of all the hype about diminished time and concentration. Here is "Black Oaks," a poem very much about what is important and what falls away:

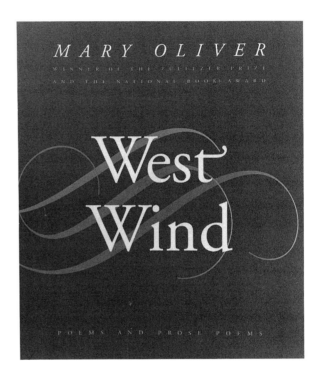

Dust jacket for the volume that received the 1997 Dictionary of Literary Biography *poetry award*

Okay, not one can write a symphony, or a dictionary,
or even a letter to an old friend, full of remembrance
and comfort.

Not one can manage a single sound, though the blue jays
carp and whistle all day in the branches, without
the push of the wind.

But to tell the truth after a while I'm pale with longing
for their thick bodies ruckled with lichen

and you can't keep me from the woods, from the tonnage
of their shoulders, and their shining green hair.

Today is a day like any other: twenty-four hours, a
little sunshine, a little rain.

Listen, says ambition, nervously shifting her weight from
one boot to another—why don't you get going?

For there I am, in the mossy shadows, under the trees.

And to tell the truth I don't want to let go of the wrists
of idleness, I don't want to sell my life for money,
I don't even want to come in out of the rain.

I love the specificity of this poem. Oliver's tree is not just a tree; it is not even just an oak; it is a "black oak," a specific being with specific needs of climate and soil. We can look it up in a field guide and know it intimately. Theodore Roethke said in "The Waking," "What falls away is always. And is near." Mary Oliver shows in her ninth collection that she has discovered the truth of "look around, call things by their right names, and get out in the rain."

—John E. Lane

The Year in Children's Literature

Caroline C. Hunt
College of Charleston

The children's-book world survived another year of confusion in 1997: grim financial news continued; some fine new publishing projects began while others ended prematurely; and censorship went on as usual, with a few new twists. Public response to the deaths of two very different authors, Michael Dorris and Marguerite Henry, symbolized the confusion.

Marketing continued its downward spiral. *Publishers Weekly* reported on 3 November that the top fifteen juvenile publishers had experienced a decline in sales of nearly 8 percent for the most recently available full year (1996, fiscal in some cases and calendar in others); even the industry giant, Golden Books, posted a poor year, while Random House and Putnam and Grosset reported flat sales; HarperCollins, Houghton Mifflin, and Harcourt Brace had slight gains; and Scholastic fell 25 percent after the popularity of the Goosebumps series waned. Only Landoll's and Candlewick surpassed the industry average (for all divisions, not merely juvenile) of an 11.5 percent gain. In Britain events paralleled those in the United States, with a slight time lag, as the erosion of library and school orders over nearly a decade forced publishers to prune their lists heavily. The British Random House Children's Books, as well as the previously quality-oriented Collins, offered a narrowed list in 1997 with an emphasis on old favorites and paperbacks. (Random House Children's Books also went through a series of management changes in 1997.) Meanwhile, Puffin (Penguin) acquired the Gollancz list, and Reed Children's Books was said to be up for sale. On the critical front, Dorothy Broderick retired as editor of VOYA (Voice of Youth Advocates), the uncompromising journal focusing on young-adult books. Fortunately, Broderick remained active with trenchant postings to E-mail lists.

Meanwhile, new ventures bucked the trend. Parachute Press and Golden agreed to copublish an ambitious new sixty-five-book series by R. L. Stine, the author of the Fear Street (Archway) and Goosebumps (Scholastic) horror series. Scholastic also brought out Stine's autobiography, engagingly titled

Michael Dorris (photograph by Louise Erdrich)

It Came from Ohio: My Life as a Writer. Two other houses also signed star authors for new series: Holiday House acquired a stable of experienced writers (including Cynthia Voigt and Marion Dane Bauer) for its Holiday Readers, and Cartwheel (Scholastic) launched Bill Cosby's Little Bill series. Cosby appeared on the Oprah Winfrey show to promote three of the titles—*The Meanest Thing to Say, The Best Way to Play,* and *The Treasure Hunt.* New chapter-book series were Puffin Chapters from Puffin Books and Harcourt Brace Young Classics, begun promisingly with the Mary Poppins books. HarperCollins announced a new line, Growing Tree, targeting preschoolers, and Sterling planned a line of Belgian imports, Balloon Books. Candlewick launched Candlewick Treasury, a series of reissued works by nineteenth- and early-twentieth-century authors. Dorling Kindersley announced the launch of DKInk, specializing in high-quality fiction and innovative ventures such as Chief Lelooska's *Echos of the Elders,* a collection of Kwakiutl legends illustrated by woodcut-style paintings and accompanied by a compact disc.

Bantam Doubleday Dell launched its new website (http://www.bdd.com/), which includes a Teachers' Resource Center. Another online entry was that of Dorling Kindersley (http://www.dk.com), which carried over its trademark clean appearance, clarity of language, and information-packed content to the web format. Random House opened a subpage especially for young readers (http://www.randomkids.com), joining those of HarperCollins and Houghton Mifflin.

The usual objections to the Goosebumps series books continued, sometimes successfully but more often not. Information books about adolescence again attracted complaints; *It's Perfectly Normal,* by Robie Harris, withstood a challenge in Albemarle County, Virginia, but an AIDS book was temporarily removed from schools in Jackson County, Kentucky, along with several other titles. In the absence of a complaint policy, the board held all but one of the books pending further review. The single book banned without further hearing was Alice Walker's Pulitzer Prize–winning novel *The Color Purple.* Admitting that he had not read it, a board member declaimed, "What it said on the first page was all I needed to hear." Similarly, parents in Champaign/Urbana, Illinois, objected to bad language in Richard Wright's *Native Son* and in several books by Toni Morrison. Fort Dodge, Iowa, also had its quota of vigilant parents, this time objecting to *YM* magazine and leading the school board to overturn the internal committee's recommendation to retain the magazine. Terre Haute, Indiana, produced perhaps the first-ever parental World Wide Web site (http://www.thnet.com/~thompsbk/) promoting the removal of a book, Brock Cole's *The Goats.*

In addition to new technologies, new kinds of revisionism surfaced. Peggy J. Miller's article in the May/June *Horn Book Magazine,* "Peter Rabbit and Mr. McGregor Reconciled, Charlotte Loves: Preschoolers Re-create the Classics," describes the author's experiences with her own children "role-playing" these stories. Initially frightened by Beatrix Potter's classic, Miller's son, Kurt, reworked it on his own, culminating in a startling scene: "Mr. McGregor, former enemy of the rabbit family, joins

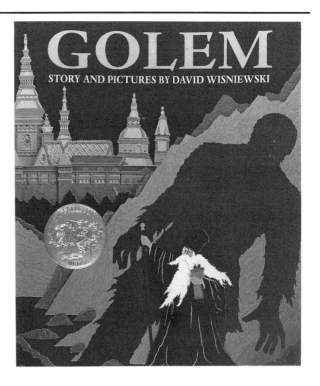

Dust jacket for the winner of the Caldecott Medal for the Best Children's Picture Book of the Year in 1997

the rabbits in planting parsley in the garden." Similarly, Miller's daughter, Kathleen, conquered her distress at the ending of *Charlotte's Web* by rewriting the text so that "Charlotte lived happily ever after with her baby spiders and Wilbur."

Also in the feel-good category, the online bookstore Amazon.com produced a "Children's Books Top 10" that avoided any whiff of controversy. The Amazon editors pulled off this amazing feat by concentrating on books for the very young: *Chuck Murphy's Color Surprises: A Pop-Up Book,* for instance, and Judy Sierra's *Counting Crocodiles,* illustrated by Will Hillenbrand. Two others on the list were new collections of old favorites: *George and Martha: The Complete Stories of Two Best Friends,* a compilation of James Marshall's beloved hippo stories; and *The Roald Dahl Treasury.* With the exception of the Dahl treasury, all were picture books. Though the quality of the list was indeed high, it certainly does not represent the range of books published for children in 1997 (or any other year). Lists from *The New York Times,* the American Library Association, and *Publishers Weekly,* among others, showed more balance between the traditional and the innovative, between the safe and the controversial.

When it came to awards, the situation changed, and disagreements grew heated. Most controversial was the Carnegie Medal, Britain's most prestigious award for a children's book, which went

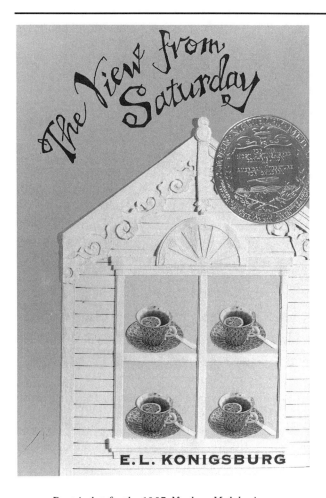

Dust jacket for the 1997 Newbery Medal winner

to *Junk,* by Melvin Burgess (Andersen); many critics disliked the choice of a young-adult novel about heroin use. The Greenaway, Britain's award for illustration, went to the less controversial bedtime story *The Baby Who Wouldn't Go to Bed,* by Helen Cooper (Doubleday).

The split between the traditional and the daring mirrored that in the United States. David Wisniewski's *Golem* (Clarion) took the Caldecott Medal for illustration, while E. L. Konigsburg's *The View from Saturday* (Jean Karl/Atheneum) received the Newbery Medal for best U.S. children's book of the previous year. This time the picture-book piqued debate; some considered the Golem figure too frightening for preschoolers. Konigsburg's story of gifted students on an academic team attracted less criticism. Gary Paulsen, author of the classics *Hatchet* and *Dogsong*—but also of the harrowing *Nightjohn*—received the Margaret A. Edwards Award for lifetime achievement in authorship for young adults. Coretta Scott King Awards went to Walter Dean Myers for *Slam!* and to Jerry Pinkney for

Minty: A Story of Young Harriet Tubman. Myers and Pinkney, as well as Patricia C. and Frederick L. McKissack, who as usual collected a King Honor Book designation, are all known for refusing to sanitize their subject matter; in 1997 this was most evident in the McKissacks' *Rebels Against Slavery: American Slave Revolts.*

In other ALA awards, *Parrot in the Oven: mi vida,* by Victor Martinez (HarperCollins), easily took the Pura Belpre award after receiving the National Book Award for a children's book the previous year. Gary Soto's *Snapshots from the Wedding,* illustrated by Stephanie Garcia (Putnam), won the illustration award. Both Belpre awards are for "a Latino/Latina writer and illustrator whose work best portrays, affirms, and celebrates the Latino cultural experience in an outstanding work of literature for children and youth." Presented for the first time in 1996, they will now become biennial. *The Friends,* by Kazumi Yumoto (Farrar, Straus and Giroux), won the Mildred L. Batchelder award for 1997; translated by Cathy Hirao, the story was originally published in 1992 in Japan.

Outside of the American Library Association, *The Friends* won another prestigious award, the Boston Globe–Horn Book. The Scott O'Dell Award for Historical Fiction went to Katherine Paterson for *Jip: His Story* (Lodestar); the Abby (selected by booksellers) was given to *Lilly's Purple Plastic Purse,* by Kevin Henkes. The National Book Award recipient, Han Nolan's *Dancing on the Edge,* was more controversial than most because of disagreement over its quality (not its subject matter).

The Newbery Medal itself came in for reappraisal at the end of its seventy-fifth-anniversary year. Zena Sutherland gave an excellent overview in "The Newbery at 75: Changing with the Times," which was the cover story of *American Libraries* in March. Michael Cart suggested a change in the medal graphic, which shows an alert-looking boy on his feet while a rather passive girl reclines on the ground. (The familiar sticker issued for award books does not show the children at all.) Other anniversaries also stimulated reexamination. *Charlotte's Web* turned forty-five; in its year of publication it received no Newbery, not even a Newbery Honor. Indeed, the influential Annie Carroll Moore disliked E. B. White's earlier *Stuart Little* (1945) so much that she tried to influence first White's wife, then his editor, to prevent publication of the new work. *The Cat in the Hat* observed its fortieth anniversary, and an adaptation premiered on Nickelodeon. Most of Dr. Seuss's millions of fans were unaware of the book's genesis: its author accepted a bet that he could write a story using only 225 words. In a half-page ad in the children's books supplement to *The New York Times Book Review* (16 November), "Thanks for the 65,000 birthday cards," Random House acknowledged fans' recognition of the renowned cat's anniversary and announced that it would give 65,000 books to the National Center for Family Literacy.

The Outsiders, S. E. Hinton's groundbreaking story of teenage gangs, turned thirty. Judy Blume's *Tales of a Fourth Grade Nothing* was twenty-five years old; less frequently censored and hence less notorious than two of Blume's earlier books (*Are You There, God? It's Me, Margaret* and *Then Again, Maybe I Won't*), *Tales* probably has had the widest readership. Moving with the times, Blume began a website (http://www.judyblume.com).

Some undisputed classics also observed anniversaries, led by that perennial favorite, Margaret Wise Brown's *Goodnight Moon.* A special fiftieth-anniversary edition, on sale for much of the year, included details about the making of the book. Turning forty along with *The Cat in the Hat* were Elsie Holmelund Minarik's *Little Bear* and Betty MacDonald's *Mrs. Piggle-Wiggle.*

Random House published an "anniversary treasury" of stories by Leo Lionni, *Frederick's Fables,* to celebrate the poetic mouse's thirtieth birthday; three new tales were included in addition to thirteen existing ones. At the twenty-year mark was Katherine Paterson's *Bridge to Terabithia;* marking ten years were Brian Jacques's *Redwal,* Cynthia Rylant's *Henry and Mudge,* and Gary Paulsen's *Hatchet.*

An important phenomenon was the continued output of high-quality nonfiction for young readers. As critics and nonfiction authors have long complained, nonfiction has not received the attention it deserves. Exacerbating this problem is the fact that libraries, schools, and some bookstores classify as "nonfiction" anything that is not straightforward "fiction": poetry, for instance, and folktales. The situation is confusing at best. A common result is that biographies become separated from the rest of "nonfiction" and are often housed in a separate section, while other information-oriented books languish in odd corners. All that is changing, in the marketplace if not in the library, with the success of aggressively promoted nonfiction titles for young people. The publisher Dorling Kindersley has led the way with its instantly recognizable visuals (lots of white space, detailed drawings, matching formats for many volumes), and small presses have joined the trend. Dorling Kindersley's recent offerings include *Stephen Biesty's Incredible Everything;* an ambitious *Junior Chronicle of the 20th Century;* a complicated *Kid's Art Pack* with "pop-ups, color wheel, 3-D models, and a separate activity book"; and *Celebrations,* a

successor to the highly successful *Children Just Like Me* (1995). Older children (including many teens) responded well to such titles as *Classic American Cars,* by Quentin Willson, and Bruce Fogle's *Encyclopedia of the Cat.* Fogle also worked on a series of dog-breed books for Dorling Kindersley; *Dachshunds* and *Poodles,* both 1997 titles, were well received by readers of all ages.

Subjects for nonfiction books continued to grow more varied. *Stone Age Farmers Beside the Sea: Scotland's Prehistoric Village of Skara Brae* (Clarion), by Caroline Arnold with photographs by Arthur P. Arnold, provides a detailed look at a Neolithic site in the Orkney Islands. Immaculately researched, beautifully photographed, and lucidly explained, Skara Brae comes to life in this fine presentation. Though less than fifty pages, the book has both a useful glossary and an excellent index (rare in juvenile nonfiction).

In more recent history, Russell Freedman presented a moving story in his usual lucid prose: *Out of Darkness: The Story of Louis Braille* (Houghton Mifflin), with Kate Kiesler's restrained black-and-white illustrations. David Adler's *Lou Gehrig: The Luckiest Man* (Harcourt Brace), illustrated by Terry Widener, profiles a hero on and off the field. Two aviators are indirectly contrasted in Corinne Szabo's *Sky Pioneer: A Photobiography of Amelia Earhart* (National Geographic) and James Cross Giblin's *Charles Lindbergh: A Human Hero* (Clarion)—one rich in visual appeal but not very critical, the other cautiously objective. Alison Leslie Gold provided further context for World War II's most famous diary with *Memories of Anne Frank: Reflections of a Childhood Friend* (Scholastic), which chronicles the parallel story of Anne's neighbor and friend, Hannah Goslar. Haunting photographs of the two girls add to the spare narrative. Gold's earlier contribution was *Anne Frank Remembered: The Story of the Woman Who Helped to Hide the Frank Family* (1987). A neglected episode of World War II history came to light in *Passage to Freedom: the Sugihara Story* (Lee and Low), by Ken Mochizuki and illustrated by Dom Lee: the story of a Japanese diplomat who, against government orders, saved Lithuanian Jews. Closer to the present, Ji-Li Jiang's *Red Scarf Girl: A Memoir of the Cultural Revolution* (HarperCollins) recalls that turbulent and frightening period in China.

Even the predictable sports stories showed competence. *Michelle Kwan: Heart of a Champion. An Autobiography,* by Kwan and Laura M. James (Scholastic), was one of the better ones. Three other Kwan bios—by Edward Epstein, Sam Wellman, and Richard Rambeck—appeared in 1997, and several more were scheduled for 1998. *Oksana: My Own*

Story, by Oksana Baiul ("as told to Heather Alexander") presents the figure-skater's life up to her 1994 Olympic victory. Somewhat sanitized, the book omits Baiul's many problems since then and closes by hoping that readers will "remember me as just a normal girl who loved to skate to *Swan Lake.*" Books about Tara Lipinski and other potential Olympians also abounded in the lead-in to the 1998 Winter Olympics in Nagano, Japan.

American history inspired some fine books. Michael L. Cooper's *Hellfighters: African American Soldiers in World War I* (Lodestar) presents its subject clearly and thoroughly and has excellent photographs from archival collections as well as a nicely chosen bibliography. Another excellent new title was Virginia Schomp's *He Fought for Freedom: Frederick Douglass* (Benchmark Books/Marshall Cavendish), with well-chosen illustrations and a useful bibliography. Also from Benchmark, Nancy Plain's *The Man Who Painted Indians: George Catlin* (Benchmark) details the life of a little-known nineteenth-century artist.

Several new series for readers in lower grades offer excellent information in attractive formats. Patrick Cone's *Wildfire* (Carolrhoda), for instance, with photographs by the author, covers the nature of fire itself, the cause of wildfires, their ecological effects, and methods of fighting and preventing them. The book is the ninth in the Nature in Action series. Seymour Simon, the author of more than 150 juvenile science titles, scored again with *Lightning* (Morrow), a lucid account illustrated with striking photographs; companion titles *Mountains* and *Oceans* also came out in 1997.

The Heritage Library of African Peoples (Rosen) offered introductions to cultural groups: Philip Burnham's *Gbaya* and Rebecca L. Green's *Merina* inaugurated this series. From Blackbirch Press in Connecticut comes the sometimes wrenching Children in Crisis series, represented for 1997 by *Rwanda: Fierce Clashes in Central Africa,* by United Nations staff photographer John Isaac. Also from Blackbirch, Edward R. Ricciuti's *What on Earth Is a Hyrax?,* illustrated with photographs from a variety of sources (documented), describes the nature and habitat of this unfamiliar mammal of Africa and the Middle East for the What on Earth series.

The mother-daughter team of Kathy and Tara Darling added to their On Location series with *Komodo Dragon on Location* (Lothrop, Lee and Shepard). The stunning photographs from the Indonesian island of Komodo pair well with straightforward descriptions of these rare reptiles. Another reptile book, for somewhat younger readers, is Rebecca Stefoff's *Chameleon* in the Living Things series from Benchmark Books (Marshall Cavendish). True to her environmental background, Stefoff concentrates on chameleons in the wild and discourages keeping them as pets.

Series offerings, though prominent, did not entirely dominate the nonfiction field; individual books showed a fine range of topics and approaches. *HIV Positive,* written and photographed by Bernard Wolf (Dutton), presents a sensitive topic clearly yet tactfully. The photo essay follows the daily life of a twenty-nine-year-old mother of two who has tested positive for the AIDS virus. A very different mother starred in a book about picture-making, *The Picture That Mom Drew* (Walker), written by Kathy Mallat and Bruch McMillan with illustrations by Mallat and photographs by McMillan. Modeled on "the house that Jack built," the book progresses from colors to textures, finally revealing the actual picture drawn by "Mom" (Mallat).

Transportation books have come a long way since this-is-a-dump-truck days. Steve Otfinoski's *Behind the Wheel: Cars Then and Now* (Benchmark Books/Marshall Cavendish) lovingly presents more than a century of automotive history, emphasizing American cars; David Weitzman's *Old Ironsides: Americans Build a Fighting Ship* (Houghton Mifflin) combines a detailed text with a series of black-and-white drawings.

Not all nonfiction offerings were distinguished. *Gertrude Chandler Warner and The Boxcar Children,* by Mary Ellen Ellsworth (Albert Whitman), is an earnest but pedestrian biography. One would expect an editor to slice preliminaries that sound more like an application to the DAR than a juvenile biography:

> Gertrude's mother's and father's families had lived in eastern Connecticut for a long time. Her father, Judge Edgar Warner, was a descendant of Ichabod Warner, one of the early settlers of Windham County, and of John Avery of Groton, who fought in the Revolutionary War. Her mother, Jane Elizabeth Carpenter Warner, was a descendant of the Chandlers, who had come to nearby Woodstock, Connecticut, in 1686, ninety years before the American Revolution.

There are pleasant, old-fashioned pictures by Marie DeJohn.

In the picture-book field as in nonfiction, 1997 produced a distinguished crop. At the apex were books from some well-known writers: Jack Prelutsky, Walter Dean Myers, and Paul Zielinsky. *The Beauty of the Beast,* edited by Prelutsky and illustrated by Meilo So (Knopf), includes more than two hundred short poems arranged "in five zoological classifications," each section headed by a new Prelutsky poem. Walter Dean Myers's poem *Harlem* appears in an oversize picture book with paintings by his son, Christopher Myers. Everyday activities are portrayed in bright and dark colors; "A weary blues that Langston knew / And Countee sung / A river of blues where Du Bois waded / And Baldwin preached." Zelinsky's *Rapunzel* (Dutton) was an instant hit with reviewers and librarians for its lush Renaissance-style paintings and its exploration of Rapunzel's sexuality.

Zelinsky's was not the only distinguished retelling with fine illustrations. Robert San Souci and Jerry Pinkney teamed up again for *The Hired Hand: An African American Folktale* (Dial); Aaron Shepard reworked *The Sea King's Daughter: A Russian Legend* (Atheneum); and Gennady Spirin provided splendid illustrations in more-muted tones than his usual palette. *Mr. Semolina-Semolinus*, a Greek folktale retold by Anthony L. Manna and Christodoula Mitakidou (Anne Schwartz/Atheneum), shadows the fortunes of a man "five times beautiful and ten times kind," made by the princess Areti from semolina wheat, almonds, and sugar. Despite the academic background of both authors, there is nothing pedantic about this tale of an inanimate object brought to life. The narrative is well paced and the prose musical, and whimsical colored ink-and-pencil drawings by Giselle Potter complement the telling perfectly. Simms Taback retold and illustrated *There Was an Old Lady Who Swallowed a Fly* (Viking), using the inspired device of a hole through which readers can see an accumulation of swallowed animals inside the old lady. *Hosni the Dreamer: an Arabian Tale,* retold by Ehud Ben-Ezer with pictures by Uri Shulevitz, was widely reviewed, even rating mention by Christopher Lehmann-Haupt in *The New York Times;* so was *The Hunterman and the Crocodile: A West African Folktale,* by Baba Wague Kiakite.

Others built on folklore tradition without actually retelling specific tales. Katya Arnold paid homage to Vladimir Grigorievich Suteev, the filmmaker often known as Russia's Walt Disney, in *Duck, Duck, Goose?* (Holiday House). This folklore-like tale describes a disagreeable goose's efforts to better herself by exchanging her neck with a swan, her beak with a pelican, and so on. Arnold's unusual artwork recalls animation effects by superimposing an overlay of heavy black lines over a baseplate of acrylic and watercolor. *Perfect Pancakes—If You Please* by William Wise, illustrated by Richard Egielski (Dial), tells of greedy King Felix, who promises his daughter to anyone who can make the perfect pancake.

The year's picture books included a gratifying number of titles "for all ages," a phrase used in the industry to suggest appeal to grownups. (Some publishers resort to marketing clichés like "for children from three to eighty-three" to emphasize the obvious.) Janell Cannon's *Verdi* (Harcourt Brace) almost recaptures the magic of her 1993 favorite, *Stellaluna*. Verdi is a small, lively yellow snake who is determined not to turn green, fat, and lazy like other adult pythons. How he changes while still remaining essentially himself is a charming tale, brought to life by Cannon's acrylic-and-pencil illustrations. *The Gardener,* by Sarah Stewart with illustrations by David Small, is set in the Depression but exudes hope. Its subtle tones, its beautifully evocative letters from a homesick country girl in the city, and its wonderful flowers (described as "Dufy-like" by one reviewer) lift this title over the team's previous offering, *The Library,* which was well received but not widely read. A retelling of *Noah's Ark* by Heinz Janisch, illustrated by Lisbeth Swerger, also found favor with critics and buyers alike.

Ann Turner's *Shaker Hearts* (HarperCollins), with paintings by Wendell Minor, is a quite different but equally impressive book. After a brief factual introduction, the text is in verse. On each left page is a four-line stanza describing one activity or facet of Shaker life, for example:

> Shakers bend to gardens neat,
> hands to work, hearts to God,
> herbs to knit and mend our bones,
> heal them as they grow.

The second line, based on a saying of the Shakers' founder, is the same in each verse. Facing the verse, a simple, luminous painting illustrates the activity.

Roxane Orgill's first book for children was one of the year's finest picture books "for all ages." *If I Only Had a Horn: Young Louis Armstrong* (Houghton Mifflin) follows the boy Louis from the grimy streets of New Orleans to the Colored Waifs' Home, where, improbably, he meets the man who will give him his first instrument. Meticulously researched, *If I Only* avoids the twin perils of sentimentality and exploitative sociology. Leonard Jenkins's illustrations combine collage, acrylics, and even spray paint in a disturbing but appropriate color palette. Coincidentally, another all-ages picture-book also focused on a jazz great: Chris Raschka's *Mysterious Thelonious* (Orchard) inventively portrays Thelonious Monk's music through color equivalents of his scale.

Art Spiegelman, not generally thought of as a juvenile author, also brought out a picture book for all ages. *Open Me—I'm a Dog* (Joanna Cotler) tells of a dog turned into a book by a wizard's curse; a leash and other gimmicks are included. *Rome Antics,* by

David Macaulay (Houghton Mifflin), lovingly portrays that city in the artist's trademark black-and-white drawings. Also for all ages, Jules Feiffer's *Meanwhile* (HarperCollins/di Capua) follows young Raymond's adventures from one escapist fantasy to another using the cartoon transition "meanwhile." In the tradition of classics such as Crockett Johnson's *Harold and the Purple Crayon* (1955) and Maurice Sendak's *Where the Wild Things Are* (1963), Feiffer's young hero comes willingly back to reality at the end. The same satisfying full circle anchors Eric Rohmann's stunning 1997 title, *The Cinder-Eyed Cats* (Crown), another imaginary journey. Less satisfying to some adults was Catherine Cowan's adaptation of Octavio Paz, *My Life with the Wave,* handsomely illustrated by Mark Buehner. The fact that Cowan changed Paz's ending offended some critics.

British imports made a strong showing. Rudyard Kipling's mongoose story *Rikki-Tikki-Tavi* (Morrow) appeared with lush new watercolors by Jerry Pinkney. Brian Wildsmith's *Amazing World of Words* (Millbrook Press) is organized by locale: Space, Desert, Ocean, and so on, down to School Play and Playground. Projecting tabs make navigation easy. Dick King-Smith's *The Spotty Pig,* with pictures by Mary Wormell (Farrar, Straus and Giroux), concerns a pig who hates his spots and tries various ways to get rid of them. Only as an adult, with spotted piglets of his own, does he accept his markings. The book was published simultaneously in Britain by Victor Gollancz. Another favorite British author, Pat Hutchins, returns with the tale *Shrinking Mouse* (Greenwillow), a charming essay on perspective. One by one the animal characters get smaller as they disappear into the distance—to the dismay of their friends left behind; one by one they regain their normal size as they return. The virtuoso play of language that characterizes William Mayne's books for over-twelves appears, amazingly, adapted for preschoolers in *Lady Muck* (Houghton Mifflin), illustrated by Jonathan Heale.

As usual, family life was at the center of many picture books. *The Great Frog Race and Other Poems,* by Kristine O'Connell George (Clarion), with paintings by Kate Kiesler, evokes life on a Western farm through simple things like a metal bucket, an egg (with an egg-shaped text), and an old black dog. Susan Campbell Bartoletti's *Dancing with Dziadziu* (Harcourt Brace) presents warm memories of a Polish grandmother's early years as told to her granddaughter, Gabriella. Annika Nelson's folk-art style illustrations fit perfectly.

The number of good picture books with appealing Asian characters continued to increase. *Chinatown,* written and illustrated by William Low

(Henry Holt), evokes the sights, sounds, and smells of Chinatown through the eyes of a small boy taking a walk with his grandmother on the Chinese New Year. Low's rich oil-on-board paintings more than compensate for the book's lack of plot. Chinatown of an earlier day–1914–appears in *Nim and the War Effort,* by Milly Lee (Farrar, Straus and Giroux), with pictures by Yangsook Chi. Allen Say played a new variation on his theme of East-meets-West with a poignant story of interracial adoption, *Allison* (Houghton Mifflin), in which a preschool girl first realizes that she is unlike her Caucasian parents. Laura Krauss Melmed's *Little Oh,* illustrated by Jim LaMarche (Lothrop, Lee and Shepard) and set in Japan, is a charming frame story about a toy coming to life.

Three appealing picture books (two of them about families) take place in northern settings. In *Arctic Son* (Hyperion), written by Jean Craighead George and illustrated by Wendell Minor, George's real-life grandson, Luke, acquires the Inupiat name Kupaaq and learns the Inupiat culture. Also from Jean Craighead George, *Look to the North: Diary of a Wolf Pup* (HarperCollins), with illustrations by Lucia Washburn, follows a young cub and his two littermates to adulthood. Kathryn Lasky's *Marven of the Great North Woods* (Harcourt Brace), illustrated by Kevin Hawkes, is about the author's grandfather. During the influenza epidemic of 1918, Marven is sent to a logging camp to escape contagion. Barely ten, with a strict Jewish upbringing and no command of French, he must adapt to new surroundings, to immense lumberjacks, and to being a bookkeeper. The protagonist of Robert Blake's *Akiak: A Tale of the Iditarod* (Philomel) is a ten-year-old sled dog. Blake's thickly textured oil paintings, done from sketches taken at the race venue, thoroughly suit the plot which, while predictable, is sparely told and satisfying.

Two collections of Inuit stories rounded out the northern offerings. In a review in the 16 November *New York Times Book Review,* Natalie Kusz contrasted the Americanized presentations in Howard Norman's *The Girl Who Dreamed Only Geese* (Harcourt Brace) to the more scholarly approach of John Bierhorst's *The Dancing Fox* (Morrow). Leo and Diane Dillon's illustrations put *Geese* on several best-books lists, though some reviewers, including Barbara Bader in *Horn Book,* especially admired Mary Okheena's black-and-white drawings for *Fox* to be more authentic.

In the hands of experts a winning formula can be repeated successfully. Virginia Hamilton's collection *A Ring of Tricksters* (Scholastic), with exuberant paintings by Barry Moser, was up to her usual standard. *Starring Mirette and Bellini,* by Emily Arnold McCully (Putnam), followed the intrepid pair last seen in McCully's Caldecott winner. Rosemary Wells and Susan Jeffers, previously teamed for *Lassie Come-Home* (1995), used their own West Highland White terriers as the inspiration for *McDuff Moves In* (Hyperion) and two other McDuff books. In *Alice Ramsey's Grand Adventure* (Houghton Mifflin) Don Brown recounts the first cross-country automobile venture by a woman driver, in the summer of 1909. Brown's earlier book was *Ruth Law Thrills a Nation* (1993). Donald Hall's charmer *The Milkman's Boy* (Walker), with nostalgic paintings by Greg Shed, re-creates a dairy farm circa 1900 as successfully as his *Ox-cart Man* (1979) did for an early-nineteenth-century farm family. Denise Fleming's trademark "pulp painting," developed through earlier successes like *In the Tall, Tall Grass* (1992), *In the Small, Small Pond* (1993), and *Where Once There Was a Wood* (1996), proved as effective as ever in *Time to Sleep* (Reed), a story about animals preparing to hibernate. David Kirk carried his seductive arachnid's adventures into a third volume with *Miss Spider's New Car* (Scholastic); he also signed a six-year exclusive contract with Scholastic and was working on a Miss Spider movie for Universal as part of that contract.

Every year some picture books refuse to be pigeonholed; one such was *Leon and Bob,* by Simon James (Candlewick), which follows a boy who exchanges an imaginary friend for a real one. Fans of the 1963 film *Blow-Up* (not, of course, a film for children) will appreciate the final scene. An ocean away from lonesome young Leon is Candace Fleming's Gabriella, moving through the sights, sounds, and smells of Venice in *Gabriella's Song* (Simon and Schuster/Atheneum/Schwartz). If it's possible to portray music visually, Giselle Potter's illustrations do it. A picture book for somewhat older children, Eve Bunting's *I Am the Mummy Heb-Nefert* (Harcourt Brace), with pictures by David Christiana, combines elegiac prose with an impressive arsenal of facts about Egypt.

Beginning reading texts have progressed a long way from Dick and Jane. For the preschool and kindergarten set, *Big Egg* by Molly Coxe (Random House's Early Step into Reading Series) tells of a mother hen who fosters a strange egg, with wonderful results. From the HarperCollins I Can Read Books series for lower-elementary grades, Barbara Bottner's *Bootsie Barker, Ballerina* provides a satisfying comeuppance to bully Bootsie (widely known from *Bootsie Barker Bites*); the illustrations by G. Brian Karas are hilarious, especially those depicting the ballet teacher as a bird and a frog. *First Flight:*

The Story of Tom Tate and the Wright Brothers, by George Shea with pictures by Don Bolognese, is a fine addition to the more advanced I Can Read Chapter Books series (also from HarperCollins). From Simon and Schuster's Ready-to-Read series, Level 2 ("reading with help"), comes *The Story Snail,* by Anne Rockwell, a 1974 folktale adaptation with new illustrations by Theresa Smith. The artist's fusion of folk-art elements with dreamy Chagall-like effects is most unusual.

Some books that fit the easy-reader category also transcend it. *Ant Plays Bear,* by Betsy Byars with illustrations by Marc Simont, was one; the latest entry in Viking's Easy to Read series, *Ant* appeared as a contender on nearly every best-books list. Not technically a series reader but ideal for this stage is Cynthia Rylant's *Blue Hill Meadows* (Harcourt Brace), a quiet story with one chapter for each season of the year. A recent entry is Delacorte, with the Yearling First Choice chapter book series. Sook Nyul Choi's *The Best Older Sister,* with pictures by the husband-wife team of Cornelius Van Wright and Ying-Wha Hu, presents the familiar story of a girl who feels abandoned when her baby brother arrives—a narrative given warmth and freshness by the introduction of believable Korean-American culture.

Unlike the generally high standard set by nonfiction, readers, and picture books, middle-grades fiction for 1997 was mixed in quality. With the downward spiral of Goosebumps sales, publishers scrambled to find new formulas that would appeal—resulting, predictably, in a rash of unnecessary sequels and ill-conceived series. Phyllis Reynolds Naylor's *Saving Shiloh* (Atheneum) continued the story of the boring beagle into a third volume. Like the first sequel, *Shiloh Season* (1996), the book focuses on the rehabilitation of Shiloh's former owner, Judd Travers. Can readers expect to see *The Courage of Shiloh, Shiloh Returns,* perhaps even *Son of Shiloh*? Another Newbery winner followed suit: Jean Craighead George's latest, *Julie's Wolf Pack* (HarperCollins), illustrated by Wendell Minor, played further variations on the survival tale begun in *Julie of the Wolves* and continued in *Julie*. Even Gary Paulsen produced a sequel, *Sarny: A Life Remembered* (Delacorte), which continues the story begun in *Nightjohn* (1993). Susan Cooper brought out a "companion volume" (not a sequel, but with the same characters) to her 1993 hit *The Boggart;* in *The Boggart and the Monster* (Margaret K. McElderry) the invisible creature sets out to save the Loch Ness monster, a distant relative. And Robin McKinley actually rewrote her most popular book, *Beauty* (1978), as *The Rose Daughter* (Greenwillow).

Rumer Godden, now in her sixth decade of writing for children, offered *Premlata and the Festival of Lights* (Greenwillow), illustrated by Ian Andrew. A book more satisfying in the details than in the plot, *Premlata* chronicles a poor Indian family's restoration to happiness through the adventures, or rather misadventures, of a seven-year-old girl. Though as competent as ever, Godden seems to be falling back on old motifs and power of description to sustain a story that lacks invention. Another master storyteller, Lloyd Alexander, used an Indian setting for an adventure loosely adapted from Indian myths, *The Iron Ring* (Dutton); again, some readers felt that the details were more satisfying than the whole.

Exploring American history was the purpose of a new series from Minstrel Books (an imprint of Pocket Books), White House Ghosthunters, "a new educational mystery series for middle-graders featuring historical information on America's past Presidents." Written by Gibbs Davis, the series opened with *Money Madness* (Lincoln), *Nest Egg Nightmare* (Jefferson), and *Dolley's Detectives* (Dolley Madison). Some existing series changed character, presumably to mirror changing taste. The fifth book in the Dorothy series by Judith Caseley, *Dorothy's Darkest Days* (Greenwillow), takes a more serious turn than its comic predecessors when Andrea Marino, a classmate whom Dorothy finds intensely irritating, is suddenly killed in an accident, and all her friends have difficulty adjusting. Caseley does comedy better than problem-of-the-week.

Another formulaic failure was Dian Curtis Regan's *Monsters in Cyberspace,* illustrated by Melissa Sweet (Holt); the old ploy of stuffed toys that come alive for their owner has been better done before. Rilla's adventures through E-mail do not compel interest, and her search for her missing father doesn't either, in spite of the intrinsic pull of the topic. One bright spot is the portrait of Rilla's environmentally oriented family–Sparrow Harmony Earth, her mother, and Poppy Harmony Earth, her aunt–along with a group of home-schooled children.

Honus and Me, by Dan Gutman (Avon), is billed as a "Baseball Card Adventure." Awkward Joey's job cleaning out Amanda Young's attic leads to his discovery of a potentially valuable card–a discovery that pales before his realization that he can communicate directly with Honus Wagner in 1909. Another baseball story is Steven Schnur's *The Koufax Dilemma,* illustrated by Meryl Treatner (Morrow). Danny's resentment at having to miss an important baseball game during Passover gradually gives way to a better understanding of his divided family, his

coach, and his own abilities, both on the field and off.

At the other end of the spectrum, some new authors with real promise appeared. Gail Carson Levine's debut novel was a Cinderella variant, *Ella Enchanted* (HarperCollins). Reviewers loved its inventiveness and whimsy, though reactions from librarians and young readers were mixed. Meanwhile, some established authors experimented with new moods, subjects, and audiences. Paul Fleischman's *Seedfolks* (Joanna Cotler/HarperCollins) begins with a Vietnamese girl planting beans in an empty Cleveland lot; soon neighbors of all imaginable backgrounds are involved in turning the lot into a garden. Each chapter is told from a different character's point of view; the only thing they have in common is the garden. One of the most widely discussed books of the year was Jerry Spinelli's uncharacteristically dark *Wringer* (Joanna Cotler/HarperCollins), a tale of a nine-year-old boy who dreads turning ten. In Palmer LaRue's town ten-year-olds become "wringers," putting wounded birds "out of their misery" on Pigeon Day. Palmer's efforts to reconcile his horror with his need to conform gain urgency when a pigeon adopts him.

Several authors better known for their work in other fields turned to the middle-grade audience. Julian F. Thompson, noted for young-adult books, made his debut with *Ghost Story* (Henry Holt); crammed with Thompson's usual excitement and good dialogue, *Ghost Story,* refreshingly, lacks the increasingly paranoid tone that had begun to dominate his young-adult books. Paula Fox, also better known for her young-adult books, produced a subtle story for middle readers, *Radiance Descending* (DK Ink/Richard Jackson). The resentment of an eleven-year-old boy for his brother with Down's syndrome is examined in detail, with a command of language that has become uncommon in juvenile fiction. Coming from the other end of the age scale, the award-winning picture-book author and illustrator Kevin Henkes offered *Sun and Spoon* (Greenwillow), his third work of fiction, which follows a ten-year-old boy's attempts to adjust to his much-loved grandmother's death.

Historical fiction accounted for a surprising number of titles in 1997. *A Pony for Jeremiah,* by Robert H. Miller with illustrations by Nneka Bennet (Silver Burdett), depicts an African American family's journey from slavery in Mississippi to farming in Nebraska. Ann Rinaldi's 1997 title was *The Second Bend in the River* (Scholastic), about a young pioneer girl in Ohio who befriends the Shawnee chief Tecumseh and nearly marries him. An excellent author's note describes the interweaving of fact and fiction, and there is a good bibliography. *Danger along the Ohio,* by Patricia Willis (Clarion), also concerns Ohio pioneers and Shawnees—in this case three children who become separated from their father and rescue an injured Indian boy. *My Brother, My Enemy,* by Madge Harrah (Simon and Schuster), covers the same ground of ambivalent native/settler friendship, but this time from an earlier period (it chronicles Bacon's Rebellion of 1676) and a different tribe (Susquehannock, in Harrah's chosen spelling; more commonly, Susquehanna). *Soldier Boy,* by Brian Burks (Harcourt Brace), follows an orphan who joins the army and is sent to locate General Custer. Moving forward to 1900, in *The Last Rainmaker* (Harcourt Brace), Sherry Garland depicts a young woman, Caroline Long, who discovers that she is half Indian.

Not all of the year's historical fiction dealt with Indians. Frances M. Wood's *Becoming Rosemary* (Delacorte), set on a North Carolina farm in 1790, explores the issue of conformity and nonconformity—with a touch of magic. *Ghost Canoe,* by Will Hobbs (Morrow), is a straightforward adventure taking place in 1874.

Though 1997 saw fewer European settings than were common a few decades ago, there were outstanding exceptions. The import *The Robber and Me,* by Josef Holub (Holt), translated by Elizabeth Crawford, transports young readers to a small German town in 1867. Other fine historical fiction was set half a world away from young American readers. Lensey Namioka's *Den of the White Fox* (Browndeer/Harcourt Brace) continues the adventures of two sixteenth-century Japanese Ronin, Konishi Zenta and Ishihara Matsuzo. Mical Schneider's debut juvenile title, *Between the Dragon and the Eagle* (Carolrhoda Books), illustrates Asian-European trade in the first century by following a single bolt of blue silk from China to Rome. The book is the latest in Carolrhoda's Adventures in Time series.

Books about World War II continue to be published, though markedly different from those published in the late 1960s and the 1970s. Those books recalled the authors' childhoods; the more recent ones are clearly historical novels. *Under the Shadow of Wings,* by Sara Harrell Banks (Anne Schwartz/Atheneum), brings back the feeling of the Alabama home front—streaky margarine and all. Banks's appeal to the senses (this book takes place before air conditioning), especially her evocations of southern home cooking, are splendid, recalling Robbie Branscum. The main plot, concerning a girl's mixed feelings about her retarded cousin, is less successful than the background—partly because it has been done so well before, in a line stretching from Sue Ellen Bridgers

back, ultimately, to William Faulkner. Another excellent home-front book was *Lily's Crossing,* by Patricia Reilly Giff (Delacorte), though the details of wartime life are more satisfying than the coincidence-laden plot.

Donna Jo Napoli's *Stones in Water* (Dutton) plunges readers into the world of children at war. A Venetian gondolier's son bounces from one work camp to another, accompanied by a friend who, unknown to their German "allies," is Jewish. Napoli shows the grimness of their situation unflinchingly, in the tradition of Ian Seraillier's *The Silver Sword* (1959) and Erik Christian Haugaard's *The Little Fishes* (1967). Tatjana Wassiljewa recalls her childhood experience in *Hostage to War: A True Story* (Scholastic), which reads less well than Napoli's fiction because of its artificial diary format and its double translation (Russian to German to English). A Canadian import, *The Garden,* by Carol Matas (Simon and Schuster), is a sequel to *After the War* (1996; here, Ruth Mendolson finds herself caught in a clash between rival Zionist organizations.

The 1960s are now "history" to young readers, and two very different offerings recalled key figures of that era. Candlewick brought out *Kennedy Assassinated!* (awkwardly subtitled *The World Mourns: a Reporter's Story*), which recounts the experiences of Wilborn Hampton when, as a cub reporter, he covered the assassination for UPI in Dallas; Scholastic offered a "gift edition" of Martin Luther King's *I Have a Dream,* with illustrations by fifteen distinguished artists and an introduction by Coretta Scott King. More recent still is the period of Marybeth Lorbiecki's *My Palace of Leaves in Sarajevo,* with pictures by Herbert Tauss (Dial). Based on published accounts (including *Zlata's Diary* among others), Nadja's story recounts the daily experiences of a young girl during the Bosnian conflict. Sources, both published and unpublished, are scrupulously acknowledged, and there is a bibliography. A portion of the proceeds will go to Bosnian relief.

Many contemporary stories focused on family problems. Originally a short story in *Ebony,* Sharon M. Draper's *Forged by Fire* (Atheneum/Simon and Schuster) portrays an admirable young boy, Gerald, who perseveres despite a dysfunctional family. In *Alias,* by Mary Elizabeth Ryan (Simon and Schuster), young Toby Chase is constantly on the move with his mother, a Vietnam-era radical. The past also pervades *Yesterday's Child,* by Sonia Levitin (Simon and Schuster), in which Laura must try to find out the truth about her recently deceased mother. Edward Bloor broke new ground with *Tangerine* (Harcourt Brace), in which legally blind Paul Fisher is determined to play goalie for his new soccer team in Tangerine, Florida. More than just a "handicap" story, *Tangerine* explores family dynamics compellingly.

Some family books were far grimmer. Adele Griffin's *Sons of Liberty* (Hyperion) dissects the anatomy of abuse and consequences when a right-wing father imposes rigid discipline at home. One son admires his efforts; the other resents them. The plight of a mistreated friend forces the climax. Reviewers were split on Griffin's book, assigning grades from A to D. The British import *The Tulip Touch,* by Anne Fine (Little, Brown; originally published in 1996), was more favorably reviewed, though equally lacking in hope. In Fine's book a girl who lives in a hotel develops a friendship with a disturbed girl on a farm; eventually, through the unwillingness of nearly every adult to intervene in any way, an inevitable tragedy occurs.

Natalie Kinsey-Warnok's *Sweet Memories Still,* a cross-generational charmer with pictures by Laurie Harden (Cobblehill), follows shy, artistically gifted Shelby as she comes to know her grandmother better in the wake of a catastrophic fire. Carolyn J. Gold's *Dragonfly Secret* (Atheneum) concerns a brother and sister whose widowed mother feels pressured to institutionalize her father. Amazingly, the slender plot device of a rescued dragonfly holds this tale together, and the resolution is satisfying for all.

Also family-centered, C. S. Adler's *More than a Horse* (Clarion) is more than its title suggests: a story of a girl uprooted from North Carolina to Arizona when her mother's second husband leaves her penniless. Leeann's attempts to fit in at a new school and to win over a crusty wrangler are standard fare, but the addition of a homely boyfriend, a classmate with a religious-fanatic grandmother, and a project for special-needs children make this a good read. A similar theme runs through Deborah Savage's *Under a Different Sky* (Houghton Mifflin), in which a boy and horse help a maladjusted girl recover emotional health.

One family-story-with-animals defied classification. Tor Seidler's *Mean Margaret* (HarperCollins/Michael di Capua) combines a dysfunctional woodchuck couple—one ultra-neat, one longing for children—with a horrific two-year-old called Nine because she is the ninth child of an even more dysfunctional human family. Renamed Margaret by her woodchuck foster mother, the toddler spreads chaos and destruction in her new home and soon forces the woodchucks to relocate. Nearly every character develops convincingly in a witty, warm book that slyly undercuts dozens of sentimental clichés about family, animals, and cooperation. Jon Agee's sketches complement the text perfectly.

Good short stories for middle-grade readers are uncommon. Gayle Pearson's *The Secret Box* (Jean Karl/Atheneum) continues exploring the family territory begun in her earlier *One Potato, Tu: Seven Stories* (1992). The five stories, each involving a secret, center on two brother-sister pairs; the mood ranges from the hilarity of a sentimental canine funeral to the sadness of a friendship betrayed. Peter Dickinson reached for a younger-than-usual audience with *The Lion Tamer's Daughter and Other Stories* (Delacorte), which received mediocre reviews. Harry Mazer, better known for young-adult novels, edited *Twelve Shots—Outstanding Stories about Guns* (Delacorte).

The young-adult field in 1997 was as uneven as that for middle grades. Two long-awaited young-adult novels attracted most of the attention in early 1997: Robert Cormier's controversial *Tenderness* (Delacorte); and Philip Pullman's *The Subtle Knife* (Knopf/Random House), a sequel to *The Golden Compass*. The Pullman book received raves all around—unusual for a sequel. *Tenderness,* which received a rare 5/5 rating from *Voice of Youth Advocates* (meaning tops for quality, tops for appeal), tells the grim story of a serial killer and the teenage girl who falls in love with him. *Tenderness* was issued with a "Reader's Companion," a pamphlet with an introduction and discussion questions. Although many publishers have provided these pamphlets for teachers since the mid 1970s, it is unusual to see one issued with the book to a general readership. Pullman's book continued the story of Lyra, her daemon, and their search for her friend Will's father. Another Pullman title, *Clockwork* (published in Britain in 1996), was scheduled for early 1998 release.

Other well-known young-adult authors produced more-predictable books. In Lois Duncan's *Gallows Hill* (Delacorte) a glass paperweight starts a series of strange happenings in a small town in the Ozarks. Duncan's handling of the eerie remains expert, but the book is slight. Another book set in a similar town was more ambitious. *Chasing Redbird* (Joanna Cotler/HarperCollins), Sharon Creech's latest, is a maddening blend of deft, sure touches and overall lack of focus. Thirteen-year-old Zinnia Taylor of Bybanks, Kentucky, finds an overgrown trail and begins clearing it as she seeks also to clarify her own identity in her large family. Admirer Jake's thefts on her behalf and Aunt Jessie's recent death complicate her search. Short, choppy chapters and uneven development mar a fine idea and interesting main character.

Gay and lesbian issues appeared in several young-adult titles. M. E. Kerr's *"Hello," I Lied* (HarperCollins), a parallel to her powerful 1994 *Deliver Us from Evie,* follows a homosexual boy's efforts to tell his family he is gay. Kerr also deals nicely with her hero's almost-romantic relationship with a French girl. Roger Larsom's *What I Know Now* (Henry Holt) covers the same ground, as a young boy confronts his own sexuality. In *Whistle Me Home,* by Barbara Wersba (Henry Holt), the main character, Noli, has to deal with the possibility that her new boyfriend is in fact gay. In *Blue Coyote,* a sequel to her 1993 success *Twelve Days in August,* Liza Ketchum follows Alex in a search for his missing friend Tito; not only does Tito turn out to be gay but Alex realizes that he is, too. None of the 1997 books on this topic equalled Nancy Garden's 1996 title, *Good Moon Rising* (Farrar, Straus and Giroux), a sensitive story of a high-school girl's realization that she is a lesbian.

A clutch of ambitious books dealt with a range of psychological problems in adolescent girls. *The Woman in the Wall,* by Patrice Kindl, portrays extreme, crippling shyness—a topic not often seen in contemporary young-adult fiction but well treated in this story of a teenage recluse. James Howe's *The Watcher* (Atheneum) also depicts a lonesome young woman, this time one who projects her own fantasies onto those she watches. An ambitious effort was Han Nolan's *Dancing on the Edge,* which mirrors sixteen-year-old Miracle McCloy's confused mental processes; sometimes she believes that she doesn't exist at all. Reviewers differed sharply in their estimates of Nolan's book. More widely accepted was *Out of the Dust,* by Karen Hesse, also the story of an adolescent trying to make sense of present misery by understanding the past. Hesse's wizardry with language (seen spectacularly in her 1996 title, *The Language of Dolphins*) combined with a convincing Depression setting to lift this book above the rest of the pack. Randall Beth Platt's *Honor Bright* (Delacorte) chronicles a summer in 1944 when a mother and fourteen-year-old twins take refuge with grandmother. Teddy, the girl twin, has severely scarred hands (like Hesse's protagonist) and a lifetime of unanswered questions; during the summer, puzzles are resolved, and the family begins to heal. Em Thurkill of Norma Fox Mazer's *When She Was Good* (Scholastic) must come to terms with a more recent past after her abusive older sister dies.

Brock Cole's new novel, *The Facts Speak for Themselves* (Front Street), explored another troubled young woman's struggles, but with a difference: thirteen-year-old Linda tells her story to a series of listeners after her middle-aged lover's murder. Cole admitted in a 17 February interview with *Publishers Weekly* that one problem with the narrative was Linda's lack of awareness: "She has no perspective. Whatsoever. She has no irony." (Some reviewers

found this a serious flaw.) Other excellent young-adult novels concerned crime in a more direct way. Shelley Stoehr's *Wannabe* (Delacorte) shows young Italian Americans tempted by, and succumbing to, organized crime in New York; in *Babylon Boyz,* by Jeff Mowry (Simon and Schuster), Oakland teens find a suitcase full of cocaine and must decide what to do with it.

Supernatural and mystery stories play a steady if not major role in the young-adult canon, and Annette Klause's *Blood and Chocolate* (Delacorte) was eagerly awaited after the success of her vampire book *The Silver Kiss* (1990). Most readers felt that Klause's werewolf story was sensationalistic and contrived, though a good summer read. Alan Dean Foster combined the macabre and the humorous in *Jed the Dead* (Ace), recounting Ross Ed's travels with a dead alien in the front seat of his car. A promising entry in the young-adult mystery field was *Murder in Perspective,* by Keith Miles (Walker), in which a boy sets out to study with Frank Lloyd Wright and becomes involved in a mystery.

The publishing year ends; children's books end; and, sadly, children's authors come to an end also. Michael Dorris, fifty-two, author of *Morning Girl* and other children's books about indigenous peoples, died in April; after attempting suicide on Good Friday, he succeeded in a second attempt on the night of 10 April. Soon after, news broke that he had been under investigation for molesting one or possibly two children in his family. Considered a model of new-style parenting (first as a single adoptive parent, then in a blended family with his wife, the novelist Louise Erdrich), Dorris was best known as the author of *The Broken Cord* (1989), a harrowing account of fetal alcohol syndrome. The book, which won a National Book Award and became a television movie, was based on his adopted Native American son Abel (who died in 1991). Two other adopted children also suffered from fetal alcohol syndrome, though less severely; both broke away from Dorris in young adulthood, and one was later charged, unsuccessfully, with trying to extort money from him. By 1996 separation from Erdrich led to divorce proceedings, followed by the sexual assault allegations. After Dorris's death Erdrich requested that the records of the court proceedings be sealed.

Reaction among friends and colleagues ranged from shock to disbelief, and children's-literature professionals faced some awkward questions. What judgment could they make if the facts might never be known? In the absence of proof, should they assume that Dorris was innocent? The issue of the flawed author who writes good books has been a cliché–most recently in the case of Roald Dahl, whose personal shortcoming and violent anti-Semitism were well known. Previous character flaws of juvenile authors, however, have not extended to child abuse, alleged or real. Questions and answers buzzed around E-mail lists for weeks, inconclusively. Meanwhile, Dorris's 1997 title, *Cloud Chamber,* received good reviews; a prequel to *Yellow Raft in Blue Water,* it profiles three generations of women. Like its predecessor, *Cloud Chamber* was published by Scribners for the adult market; unlike *Yellow Raft,* it is not likely to become a fixture on high-school recommended lists, at least until the fuss dies down.

A different reputation came in for reappraisal when Marguerite Henry died at the age of ninety-five. Coincidentally, 1997 marked the fiftieth anniversary of her most enduring book, *Misty of Chincoteague,* a horse story set on Virginia's barrier islands. Henry and her books represented, to most critics and parents, an old-fashioned America; a prolific writer who was first published at eleven, Henry was known for responding graciously to her young readers through the decades. In critical circles most thought that her early work outshone the increasingly formulaic books that followed; some considered her values too traditional and objected to the "patriarchal" family structures in her books. Animal activists criticized "pony penning," the roundup of wild horses depicted in *Misty.* Somewhat ironically, Henry has received credit recently for giving center stage to a handicapped character: the most important human in *King of the Wind* (1948), which won the Newbery Medal for 1949, is a mute Arab boy.

Dorris and Henry were not the year's only losses. Edith Thacher Hurd died 25 January in Walnut Creek, California. Author or co-author of more than seventy-five children's books, many done in collaboration with her husband, Clement Hurd, she was versatile as well as prolific: Hurd's output included science books (*Rain and the Valley* [1968], *The Mother Whale* [1973]), fiction (*Five Little Firemen* [1948], *The Little Fat Policeman* [1950]–both with Margaret Wise Brown, under the pseudonym Juniper Sage), and several books in the I Can Read series from Harper (now HarperCollins). Omar Castaneda died 11 January; he was the author of two well-received young-adult novels set in Guatemala. And the prolific Matt Christopher died at eighty in September. A largely self-educated writer who at one point combined a full-time day job, a semiprofessional baseball career, and writing detective stories, Christopher eventually produced over 120 sports novels for young adults and children. Most of his books deal with baseball, though he also wrote juvenile mysteries. Overcoming obstacles and fighting prejudice were Christopher's lifelong themes.

By midyear most analysts agreed that Goosebumps and its imitators were history, in spite of temporary revivals caused, unintentionally, by censorship efforts here and there. Among more "serious" topics, it was also clear that multiculturalism was receiving less critical discussion than in the previous three years. As the year ended, hot topics among children's literature people included Internet access for children in schools and libraries, continuing censorship efforts (especially in schools), and rapid changes in the merchandising scene. Those appear likely to remain important topics through the first half of 1998–unless, of course, a Goosebumps successor miraculously springs up out of the ashes of that series.

Dictionary of Literary Biography Yearbook Award for a Distinguished Children's Book Published in 1997

In less than sixty pages, Paul Fleischman again proves his versatility with *Seedfolks* (Joanna Cotler/HarperCollins). Fleischman received the Newbery Medal for *Joyful Noise: Poems for Two Voices* (1988) and the Scott O'Dell Award for historical fiction for *Bull Run* (1993); he has also written picture books, nonfiction, and short stories.

In *Seedfolks* residents of a run-down Cleveland neighborhood take turns describing their gradual involvement in a makeshift garden; by the end of the story, they have become a community. The story begins with the voice of Kim, a nine-year-old Vietnamese girl whose father died before her birth. In his honor, Kim secretly plants six dried beans in a vacant lot. Ana, a Rumanian woman who has lived in the area most of her life, takes up the story; with Wendell ("We're the only white people left in the building"), she rescues the plants as they nearly dry up. The voices of Gonzalo from Guatemala, Leona from Atlanta, and Sam, a retired professional, take up the tale. Soon the garden is covered with little plots. Sae Young, a Korean woman with severe agoraphobia because of a robbery, and Nora, a British nurse who cares for elderly Mr. Myles, are drawn in, like Amir from India and Maricela ("I'm a Mexican, pregnant sixteen-year-old. So shoot me and get it over with"). The book ends as it began, as "a little Oriental girl with a trowel and a plastic bag of lima beans" starts digging after the last April snow.

Though the idea of a large group of people drawn together by geographical accident is not new, it rarely occurs in books for children; Fleischman's achievement is to have combined this device with another traditional motif, the garden that brings life to humans as well as to plants. Most impressive of all is the range of voices as a different person relates each of the thirteen short chapters. Some are slangy, such as Curtis: "Deltoids—awesome. Pecs—check 'em out." Others struggle with English, such as Sae Young: "We save all for children's college, so they can have easier life. But no children come. Very

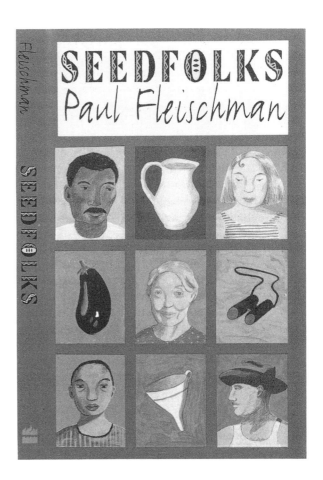

Dust jacket for the volume that received the 1997 Dictionary of Literary Biography *award for children's literature*

many years we hope, but still alone. Then my husband die."

The physical appearance of the volume supports Fleischman's careful craftsmanship. A dull green cover and springlike yellow endpapers enfold narrow pages of heavy, creamy paper; Judy Pedersen's effective black-and-white sketches and Christine Kettner's imaginative typographic design match nicely.

–Caroline C. Hunt

The Year in Drama

Howard Kissel
New York Daily News

There was a time when a survey of the year in drama would include information about new plays or revivals of works by America's best-known playwrights, some assessments of productions of European classics, and some notes about new voices who seemed promising. Looking back at 1997, one sees a few major revivals of plays by one of the most respected of American playwrights, Arthur Miller; largely depressing productions of the English classics; and plays by the generation of writers who have come into prominence in the last decade, none of whom has yet achieved the stature of the postwar playwrights (and none of whose current efforts lead one to imagine they will).

If the year in theater was not notable for the quality of its writing, it was memorable in New York for its effect on real estate. That may not seem a point worth discussing, except as a refutation of an assertion by Jean-Jacques Rousseau. In his famous letter to Jean d'Alembert, Rousseau charged that theater invariably has a negative effect on the surrounding community, bringing with it low morals and squalor. Like many of the puritanical Rousseau's ideas, which time has helped refute, this one has been undercut quite dramatically on, of all places, Forty-second Street. Only a few years ago Forty-second Street was a nationwide symbol of urban decay and degeneracy. In barely three years it has transformed itself completely and has done so, amazingly enough, in the service of the theater. On a corner that has been occupied for many years by porno shops now stands a Disney store. Next to it is the New Amsterdam Theater, a turn-of-the-century architectural masterpiece, which has been returned to its original splendor, sparking the revival of the neighborhood as a whole.

The restoration of the New Amsterdam was paid for by $24 million from the citizens of New York City and state and $8 million from the Disney organization. Its first attraction is a stage version of the hit movie *The Lion King,* adapted for the stage by McArthur Grant recipient Julie Taymor, who is known for her highly imaginative use of puppets and masks. She has deepened the coming-of-age story by emphasizing its African setting and giving it the quality of a folktale. Taymor has commissioned a score that uses the exhilarating harmonies of African music, which has the amusing effect of overshadowing the simplistic, sometimes shabby songs by Elton John and Tim Rice that constitute one of the production's most potent "draws." More important, Taymor has created a series of animal costumes that are so inventive and poetic that one comes away convinced she deserved the "genius" grant. Each costume is a work of art, a free-form interpretation of animal shapes, full of structural daring. The costumes dictate the way the actors inside them must move. Part of their artfulness is that they do not attempt to disguise that there are people inside—the way those people move is as interesting as the animal hulls they wear. They are as "animated" and riveting as the screen images on which they are based.

It may seem odd to begin a serious article about the year in theater by discussing Disney, but *The Lion King* was easily the most-talked-about theater event of the year, if only because it seemed remarkable that the Disney organization, not noted for its devotion to aesthetics, gave free range to Taymor, a serious artist. Mammon and Art have seldom functioned so harmoniously. (Taymor, perhaps alarmed by her commercial success, gave the press assurances that her next work would be more characteristic—an examination of the hard underbelly of the American Revolution. Judging by the runaway success of *The Lion King,* she will not need to apply for grants to finance it.)

Across from the New Amsterdam, two run-down theaters were gutted and remade into one beautifully designed new theater, the Ford Center for the Performing Arts, whose first production was a musical version of the E. L. Doctorow novel *Ragtime.* The overall effect has been to make Times Square and Forty-second Street an enormously promising site for real estate development. Among the new buildings going up on Forty-second Street is the corporate headquarters of Condé Nast, the publisher of the magazines *Vanity Fair* and *The New*

Yorker, which brings the discussion effortlessly back to literary concerns.

No Pulitzer Prize for Drama was awarded in 1997. Given what has won the Pulitzer over the years, this is by itself not a significant gauge of the current literary level of the theater. Very few plays even generate much public discussion. The thunder has clearly been stolen by musicals, a surprising number of which opened on and off Broadway both in the spring and fall. There was a great range in subject matter: *Titanic,* a musicalization of the endlessly fascinating 1912 disaster; *The Life,* a dramatization of pimps, whores, and drug addicts on pre-Disney Forty-second Street; *Side Show,* which was about Siamese twins in a carnival; *Steel Pier,* a show about marathon dancers during the Depression; and *The Triumph of Love,* based roughly–very roughly–on a play by Marivaux. There were also musical versions of *Dr. Jekyll and Mr. Hyde* and *The Scarlet Pimpernel.*

Although the subject matters of these shows were often promising, none realized its potential. The only musical that had actual content was a little show that played briefly at the Off-Off-Broadway Playwrights Horizons, opening there 11 March, *Violet,* based on Doris Betts's novel *The Ugliest Pilgrim.* Set in 1964, on the eve of Vietnam, *Violet* is about a young woman whose face was disfigured in a childhood accident. On a bus trip from North Carolina to Tulsa, where she hopes a televangelist can remove her scar, she befriends two soldiers, one white, one black. Her growing relationship with them reflects the country's changing ideas on race. The story was compellingly dramatized by librettist Brian Crawley and composer Jeanine Tesori. Tesori's music was an amalgam of country, rhythm and blues, and gospel. These are all American idioms that have had little impact on the musical theater because they have generally been the province of musicians with neither theatrical interests nor acumen. Tesori, however, has a deep understanding of how to infuse these genres, which often yield little beyond laid-back charm, with dramatic momentum.

It has been a long time since the volume of new musicals was this high. There were only a few noteworthy revivals. For twenty-four years Harold Prince has been staging Leonard Bernstein's brilliant *Candide* as a circus. The latest–and, it is to be hoped, the last–opened on Broadway at the Gershwin on 30 April. Despite elegant lyrics by Richard Wilbur and John Latouche, the original production of *Candide* was accounted a failure in 1957, largely because of Lillian Hellman's heavy-handed adaptation of Voltaire. In 1973 Prince had Stephen

Sondheim rewrite some of the lyrics. He staged the musical in an experimental space at the Brooklyn Academy of Music. Instead of a full orchestra there was a small band. Instead of operatic voices there were performers who acted the songs rather than giving them full musical value. There were a lot of sight gags. Having the performers engage in hijinks all around the audience undercut what had always been perceived as the work's musical seriousness. This approach gave *Candide* a new lease on life theatrically if not musically. In 1974 the production was mounted on Broadway, where it ran far longer than the original.

In 1982 Prince used the same approach for the New York City Opera. The hijinks no longer seemed useful when you had proper musical resources. Nevertheless this approach was appealing to regional opera companies, which saw Prince's circuslike staging as a way to attract new audiences. Canadian producer Garth Drabinsky saw Prince's staging of *Candide* for the Lyric Opera of Chicago and decided to mount it on Broadway. The staging is so busy it often interferes with the proper execution of the music. In "Glitter and Be Gay," a dazzling parody of nineteenth-century coloratura arias, soprano Harolyn Blackwell was so preoccupied with stage business she missed some of the notes. The production was greeted with notices even more dismal than those in 1957 and had almost as short a run.

Bernstein's first musical, the 1943 *On the Town,* which he wrote with Betty Comden and Adolph Green, was given a lavish and loving revival, which ran through the month of August at the Delacorte Theater in Central Park. The Roundabout mounted an impressive revival of the Peter Stone–Sherman Edwards *1776,* which opened 17 August and transferred in November to the Gershwin. An anomaly when it first opened on Broadway in 1969, only six months after *Hair* and in the midst of the antipatriotic mood of the Vietnam War, *1776* has aged with surprising grace. Stone has trimmed the book somewhat, modifying the leering humor of the first act, in which poor Tom Jefferson is pining for Martha and thus unable to write the Declaration of Independence. Benjamin Franklin sends for her, and, Bingo!, the next morning the quill is flying: "When, in the course of human events. . . ." The second act has always been a marvel, dramatizing as skillfully as a thriller the compromises necessary to getting all thirteen colonies to ratify the declaration. Scott Ellis's production, with Brent Spiner as John Adams and Pat Hingle as Franklin, conveyed the drama powerfully.

Program for the play by the Pulitzer Prize–winner David Mamet

The sheer amount of musical production over the course of the year suggests that the musical is a field no longer dominated by the British, as it was throughout the 1980s. They have not sent one of their blockbuster musicals in several years, though the ones they sent in the 1980s continue to run: *Les Miserables* celebrated its tenth anniversary in March, and *Cats,* which has been running for fifteen years, became the longest-running show in Broadway history in June. The lingering effect of this dependence on the British was apparent in the often appalling level of lyric writing in the new shows. Alan Jay Lerner once remarked that lyricists were the custodians of the English language. Nowadays their efforts are often so primitive it would hardly be correct even to consider them the janitors of the language.

When Americans were considered the masters of the form, the level of lyric writing was quite high–you can at this point provide your own examples from the work of Cole Porter or Ira Gershwin or Lorenz Hart, not to mention Lerner. The British shows, apart from *Cats,* which was based on the poems of T. S. Eliot, presented work that was subliterate. In the case of "Les Miz" the words were translations from the French of Alain Boublil. (I am unacquainted with the original French text, but my suspicion is that Boublil's verse will not qualify him for the Académie Française; nevertheless, the translations are stunningly primitive.)

The result is that young American lyricists do not take a very lofty view of their task. *Side Show,* for example, opened with a sideshow barker snarling, "Come look at the freaks. / Come gaze at the geeks." In the lyrics for *The Scarlet Pimpernel,* the chorus sings, "Oh, every Judas once loved a Jesus! / But fin'lly treason will seize us!" There was a time when the theater, especially musical theater, which was not hemmed in by the demands of realism, offered a literacy far above that of the language of the street. Now musical theater is barely more literate than the street.

Language, happily, does play a key role in some of the nonmusical works that opened this year. The most admired new play was Paula Vogel's *How I Learned to Drive,* which opened at the Off-Off-Broadway Vineyard Theater on 16 March, partly because it dealt with that most fashionable of topics, child abuse. What was interesting about the ninety-minute play was the tone of the narrator, a woman who had been abused by her uncle from a very early age. (Just *how* early we discover as the play moves farther and farther backward in time.) Her voice is cool and even. There is no shock or outrage as she remembers what her uncle has done, no sense that her life has been unalterably ruined by his actions. If anything, she regards him with an almost poignant sympathy.

The young woman's name is L'il Bit, and if that sounds provocative, it's intentional. As L'il Bit explains to the audience, "In my family, if we call someone 'Big Papa,' it's not because he's tall. In my family folks tend to get nicknamed for their genitalia. Uncle Peck, for example. My Mama's adage was 'the titless wonder,' and my cousin Bobby got branded for life as 'B.B.'" (for "Blue Balls"). In explaining this cognomen she is joined by what Vogel calls a "Greek Chorus." Lest you imagine a group in togas at the side of the stage, Vogel's chorus consists of a handful of actors who play all the other parts, all white-trash southerners. This family is as committed to alcohol as it is to sex. It is drinking rather than his penchant for young people that leads to Uncle Peck's downfall. By employing a fragmented narrative style and the

Greek Chorus, Vogel keeps us at an emotional distance from Uncle Peck. This prevents us from looking at him in a conventional judgmental manner, but it also undercuts her attempts, late in the game, to give his story a mythical component. She wants us to see him as a contemporary equivalent of the Flying Dutchman. Even as irony, it doesn't work.

The most interesting thing about the play is the elegant indirection of Vogel's language. One of its high points is a monologue Uncle Peck delivers on the joys of fishing. "We're going to aim for some Pompano today—and I have to tell you, they're a very shy, mercurial fish. Takes patience and psychology. You have to believe it doesn't matter if you catch one or not." The feigned indifference toward the fish is also essential to Uncle Peck's strategies toward his other catch—his "student" in this case is L'il Bit's cousin B.B. In the middle of the monologue in which Uncle Peck instructs him on how to catch the pompano there is a lovely moment when Cousin Bobby takes pity on the fish:

What? Well, I don't know how much pain a fish feels—you can't think of that. Oh, no. Don't cry. Come on now. It's just a fish—the other guys are going to see you. No, no, you're just sensitive, and I think that's wonderful at your age—look, do you want me to cut it free? You do? . . . I don't want you to feel ashamed about crying. I'm not going to tell anyone, okay? I can keep secrets. You know, men cry all the time. They just don't tell anybody, and they don't let anybody catch them. There's nothing you could do that would make me feel ashamed of you. Do you know that?

This is a prelude to Uncle Peck inviting Bobby to visit a nearby tree house: "It's a secret plac—eyou can't tell anybody we've gone there—least of all your mom or your sister—sthis is something special just between you and me." Had the play been less impeccably mounted, the essential seaminess of its material might have been more apparent. David Morse's dignified, graceful portrayal of Uncle Peck and Mary Louise-Parker's saucy Li'l Bit gave the characters strength.

David Mamet was represented by *In the Neighborhood*, three short plays written in the early 1980s but apparently revised. They had not been produced in New York before and were presented on Broadway at the Booth Theater on 19 November. The cast included Peter Riegert and Patti LuPone. It was Mamet's first production on Broadway since the Pulitzer Prize-winning *Glengarry Glen Ross* in 1984.

The first of the three is about two middle-aged Jews having a reunion in Chicago, where they both

Program for the play by Wendy Wasserstein. The cast included Hal Holbrook and Kate Nelligan.

grew up, reminiscing about their youth, their remarks constantly laced with an awareness of how their perceptions of their Jewish identity have changed over the years. It is a lighthearted mood piece and has the characteristically jumpy Mamet rhythms—sentence fragments created as the characters constantly interrupt each other or engage in quizzical editing of their own remarks.

An early such exchange goes like this:

JOEY: How's Laurie?
BOBBY: Fine.
JOEY: Yeah, but how is she, though . . . ?
BOBBY: She's fine. What did I say?
JOEY: You said that she was fine. (Pause)
BOBBY: Alright. (Pause)
JOEY: So? (Pause)
BOBBY: So what?
JOEY: Yeah. So what, so how is she, you give me this shit all the time. . . . you never fuckin' changed you

know that, Bob. "Fuck you, I don't need anyone, fuck you."

For a while this is amusing, but it quickly becomes self-parody.

The second sketch, in which a brother and sister rehash their childhood, constantly harping on the petty tyrannies of their late mother, seems even more protracted and self-parodying. Both pieces benefited from the work of Riegert and LuPone, who can deliver the dialogue with the cocky assurance it requires. The third and least successful of the sketches seemed tacked on, as if to make the evening long enough to justify a fifty-five-dollar ticket. (As it was, the evening only lasted eighty minutes, though it seemed interminable.) It was hard to get an accurate reading of the last sketch's merit because the chief role in it was performed by Mamet's wife, Rebecca Pidgeon, whose acting talent seems severely limited.

Wendy Wasserstein, who won the Pulitzer in 1989 for *The Heidi Chronicles,* was represented by a highly tendentious play called *An American Daughter,* which opened at the Cort Theater on Broadway 13 April. The title character is Lyssa, an extremely ambitious, successful doctor who has been nominated for surgeon general. Her fairly standard views on abortion are at odds with those of her father, a respected conservative senator, and her closest male friend, who is Waspish, gay, and also extremely conservative. The friend, presumably because of their differing views on this crucial subject, reveals to a television reporter that Lyssa once evaded jury duty. Suddenly her seemingly assured confirmation by the Senate becomes a national scandal. That her evasion of jury duty rather than her opinions should set off the controversy is supposed to be satiric, but it isn't really funny or pointed enough to achieve its goal.

Wasserstein uses her characters to make points about many current topics, but the people and their dilemmas never really engage us. Its only moments that go beyond the topical concern Lyssa's father, who, late in the play, reads a letter from their forebear, Ulysses S. Grant, written in 1862, when the South appeared to be winning the Civil War.

The letter, written to Grant's daughter, was infused with his indomitable spirit. It was read by Hal Holbrook, who played the father. Holbrook's voice, perhaps because of its long-term associations with Grant's friend Mark Twain, has the quality of vintage Americana. Holbrook gave the moment deep resonance. Lyssa was played by Kate Nelligan, who brought great passion and vitality to the role.

Horton Foote's *The Young Man from Atlanta* received the Pulitzer Prize when it was presented Off-Off-Broadway in 1995. The play seemed slight at that time, perhaps because the casting was not as effective as it was in its Broadway reincarnation in the spring of 1997 at the Brooks Atkinson. In the hands of Rip Torn, the main character, a successful Texas businessman forced into retirement by the son of the man with whom he founded his company, took on a quasi-tragic aura. The play is set in Dallas in the 1950s. A few months before the curtain rises the thirty-seven-year-old son of the businessman committed suicide in Atlanta. There is some ambiguity about the details, and it is possible to imagine that the untimely death may not have been suicide, but we know it was. The boy's mother, a delicate relic of a time when women were not expected to be much more than genteel and decorative, is in deep mourning, so much so that she is not fully able to acknowledge her husband's fresh distress. The title character is their son's friend, who has preyed on both mother and son financially. We have some inkling about the precise relationship of the son and his friend and that it may be the reason for his suicide. We also know that the friend is a huckster—that makes it easier for the parents to lament their son's bad judgment.

What raised *The Young Man from Atlanta* beyond its seemingly mundane, almost soap-operaish concerns was Torn's portrait of the father, whose dynamic energy, directed for so many years into his business, is now more and more merely fueling self-pity. Torn conveyed a powerful sense of an old warrior adrift in a diminished arena, where his prowess no longer matters. Shirley Knight had deep poignance as his wife, clinging to habits and manners long outmoded. Throughout the play there is a sense of the breakdown of venerable American values such as loyalty and trust, a collapse that leaves the couple painfully defenseless in an alien, hostile world.

In February another Foote play, *The Death of Papa,* was produced at Playmakers Repertory Company in Chapel Hill, N.C. Like other Foote plays, many of which are set in rural Texas just after World War I, *The Death of Papa* has among its charms a quality of stillness that makes you think it was set in some foreign country. Rural Texas in 1928 is indeed a foreign country. One of the things about its now rare and alluring climate is that the least action registers clearly—as it might not have in a noisier and more distracted world.

The Death of Papa concerns a well-to-do family whose father, a kindly businessman, dies just as the region enters a recession. His widow wants to help her son-in-law, a beleaguered cotton merchant, but he won't let her. That makes it easier for her to continue offering financial help to her ne'er-do-well son, an alcoholic who accidentally kills someone while on a binge. When a jury acquits him, his mother decides to sell the family farm to help him begin a new life in another town. Part of the "foreignness" of the place and time is the dignity its characters maintain, regardless of what they do. As the mother, Ellen Burstyn did a wonderful job preserving an air of judiciousness and aloofness when you knew she was being torn apart by her son's profligacy. The son was played by Matthew Broderick, who may have overplayed his character's reserve, though the understatement of his performance helped to explain his mother's misplaced loyalty.

Alfred Uhry, whose *Driving Miss Daisy* won the 1987 Pulitzer, offered another seriocomic portrait of wealthy Southern Jews in *The Last Night of Ballyhoo*, which opened 27 February at the Helen Hayes Theater on Broadway. The play is set in Atlanta in December 1939, when the movie version of *Gone with the Wind* is about to open. It concerns one of Atlanta's leading Jewish families. As the play begins, they are arguing, almost Talmudically, about what ornaments are acceptable on a Jewish Christmas tree. Ballyhoo is an annual event during the holiday season given by the Atlanta Jewish elite and attended by their counterparts from other Southern cities. It culminates in a dance, an obvious imitation of the exclusive balls their Gentile neighbors give to introduce young women to society, from which Jews are pointedly excluded. The most poignant moment in the play is a monologue in which a young woman recollects being asked to leave a swimming pool at a Gentile country club, where she has come as the guest of a close friend. It was her first intimation of what it really meant to be Jewish. A point that Uhry makes throughout the play is that his upper-class characters, descended from the better-heeled German Jews, are every bit as condescending to their Eastern European cousins—in this case a young Jew from Brooklyn—as their Gentile neighbors are to them. Uhry's ear for the absurdities and affectations of his characters is perfect. What was less satisfying was the plot—in the last twenty minutes of the play a crisis was concocted and almost immediately resolved.

Tony Kushner, whose *Angels in America* received the Pulitzer Prize in 1993, adapted S. Ansky's venerable play about a Jewish girl in an Eastern European shtetl at the turn of the century who is possessed by a demon. The title is normally given as *The Dybbuk*. In an unexpectedly diffident gesture,

Kushner titled his version *A Dybbuk*. It opened Off-Off-Broadway at the Joseph Papp Theater 16 November. Among the touches Kushner added was that at one point some of the characters travel by train and remark at what a miraculous invention the train is, one that can only bode well for the future. Lest the irony be missed, the car in which they traveled, starker than any conventional passenger car, evocative of the cattle cars in which millions of Jews traveled toward the Final Solution, remained on view throughout the second act. Neither the adaptation nor the production conveyed the emotional power of Ansky's material.

Lanford Wilson, who won a Pulitzer in 1979 for *Talley's Folly,* was represented by *Sympathetic Magic,* which opened Off-Off-Broadway at Second Stage on 16 April. *Sympathetic Magic* had the most arresting opening of any play in recent years. An astronomer walks onto the stage and asks us to imagine that the theater in which we are sitting is the universe. He then places a grain of sand on his fingertip, tells us that it represents "the visible universe," and declares: "We're legally blind."

The play that follows seldom achieves the magic of the opening, and its most powerful moment—when a husband assaults his wife—is explained less by the psychology of the character than by a scientific analogy, an event in outer space totally unpredictable and inexplicable, which changes scientific understanding irrevocably. There may come a time when the laws of physics will govern how we watch a play, but for those of us who still expect a playwright to guide us subtly, artfully, and logically to understand his characters and how they behave, the idea that a play hinges on unexpected and inexplicable behavior will seem a cop-out.

The last of the Pulitzer winners to offer new work in 1997 was Neil Simon. (He won the prize in 1992 for *Lost in Yonkers*.) His play, *Proposals,* which opened on Broadway at the Broadhurst on 6 November, is an autumnal piece about a summer forty years ago when a group of people gathered at a summer house in rural New Jersey. The house belongs to an upper-middle-class Jewish man who has made his money through a chain of stores that sell television sets. He is divorced from his wife, who now lives in Paris with a recently acquired husband. His daughter, who is spending the summer with him, has just broken off her engagement and takes an interest in his friend, who is a writer. Among the other characters are a young Italian with Mafia connections who met the daughter in Florida and a girlfriend of hers from New York who is beginning a career as a model.

The most endearing character is the black housekeeper who acts as narrator. One of the subplots is her reconciliation with her errant former husband. But her best material came in things she said directly to the audience. She is allowed to address us directly because she is dead. The play takes place in her memory. In her first monologue she tells us, "This all goes back some forty, fifty years ago . . . countin' time the way living folks do. . . . The world was different then. . . . Some ways better, some ways worse. . . . At the time I was a Negro. . . . Could have been Colored. Don' remember. . . . Don' know *what* they'd call me today." *Proposals* is full of characteristic Simon humor, leavened by the impending melancholy of the father's death. What was sad about it was that it was not presented as well as it might have been. There has always been a great polish about the way Simon's plays are mounted. Perhaps to indicate, rather late in his career, that he endorses the raw-edged style of younger theater, he had *Proposals* directed by Joe Mantello, who a few years ago directed another play set in a summer house, Terrence McNally's *Love! Valour! Compassion!* Mantello showed no affinity with Simon's characters—the only ones not cast against type were Dick Latessa as the father and L. Scott Caldwell as the housekeeper. Most of the other actors had an astringency that seemed out of sync with Simon's humor. *Proposals* is a play that may fare better in regional theaters that have no desire to present it as if it were cutting-edge material.

A much-heralded event was *Gross Indecency,* a play about the trials, literal and figurative, of Oscar Wilde. It was notable for the manner in which it is narrated. *Gross Indecency* is novel for being a play with footnotes. As the pathetic events leading to his courtroom appearances are detailed, the actors describe them directly and quite unself-consciously to the audience, holding up the books—courtroom transcripts, scholarly articles—from which the descriptions are drawn. There is a bald-faced artlessness about this quasi-scholarly approach that is, in its own way, breathtaking. Nevertheless, *Gross Indecency,* which opened Off-Off-Broadway at the Greenwich House Theater on 28 February and later moved Off-Broadway to the Minetta Lane, was effective in dramatizing the lamentable episode in Wilde's life because of the great intensity of the performances. The events themselves have a great sadness. They led to his imprisonment, his exile, his early death, and, most tragic, his inability ever again to write in the brilliant manner of his best work—especially the two plays he produced in the six months before his ordeal began, *An Ideal Husband* and *The Importance of Being Earnest.*

Richard Greenberg is a perennially promising playwright. A dozen years ago he had several one-acts presented Off-Off-Broadway (*The Author's Voice* and *Life Under Water*) that suggested an unusually literate, witty, thoughtful sensibility. His first major full-length effort, the disappointing 1989 *Eastern Standard,* had the quality of a sketch despite its two-act structure. There have been several interesting plays since then, but *Three Days of Rain,* which opened 11 November Off-Broadway at the Manhattan Theater Club, is in many ways his most successful work to date. In the first act a brother and sister, Walker and Nan, who have come to New York to hear their father's will read, meet Pip, the son of their parents' closest friend and architectural partner, Theo. The three conjecture what their parents' lives were like before they were born. Their only clue is a diary Walker and Nan's father, Ned, kept, which turns out to be of almost no use.

"It really is the most extraordinary document," Walker says. "The first thing you notice when you start reading is the style: It doesn't have one. And it manages to sustain that for hundreds of pages." Walker is most astonished at how his father treats the death of the man to whom he had been so close, Theo (who would have been only in his thirties when he died).

> Listen to our father's rendering: "January 3–Theo is dying." "January 5–Theo is dying." "January 18"–(I'll skip a little)–"Theo dead." I mean! His partner. Best and oldest friend: "Theo dying, Theo dying, Theo dead." You could sing it to the tune of "O'bla'di." . . . You know, the thing is with people who never talk, the thing is you always suppose they're harboring some enormous secret. But, just possibly, the secret is, they have *absolutely nothing to say.*

The writing throughout is very evocative, as when Pip describes his mother's arrival in New York in 1960.

> She would stay up till dawn debating Abstract Expressionism and "Krapp's Last Tape," and then she'd sneak out to a matinee of one of those plays you could never remember the plot of where the girl got caught in the rain and had to put on the man's bathrobe and they sort of did a little dance around each other and fell in love. And there wasn't even a single good joke, but my mother would walk out after and the city seemed dizzy with this absolutely random happiness, and that's how she met my father.

The second act jumps back thirty years and reveals that none of the clues the parents have left really tell their children anything about the actual nature of their lives and friendships. Ned, whose diary Walker has found so inadequate, is not without poetry in his soul. He tells Lina, who will eventually be the mother of Walker and Nan, that he wants to be a flaneur–

> someone who . . . idles through the streets. And lingers when it, when it . . . pleases him. . . . He just . . . walks, you see. His life has no pattern. . . . Just traffic . . . and no hope–Because he has no n-need of hope! The only thing he wants from life is . . . the day at hand. And when he's old . . . his memories aren't of Triumphs and Tragedies. He remembers . . . certain defunct cafes where he shared cups of coffee with . . . odd, scary strangers. And people he's known for years and years. Slightly.

It is a pregnant theme, and Greenberg has dealt with it with great vivacity and charm. It was performed with enormous vitality by Patricia Clarkson, John Slattery, and Bradley Whitford as the young people and, thirty years earlier, their parents.

Donald Margulies is another writer whose work always commands respect but has not yet reached the level one wants it to. *Collected Stories,* which opened Off-Broadway at the Manhattan Theater Club on 21 May, is about two women writers, one older, deeply repeated but surprisingly diffident, the other her protégée, a graduate student eager to follow in her mentor's footsteps. She is so eager, in fact, that she appropriates some material from the older woman's life that her teacher has never been able to use. The acclaim the younger woman wins from an act the older woman regards as a form of plagiarism ends their long friendship.

The play is conventional but full of insights and sharp humor. The conversation between the two is constantly amusing. Gossip, the older woman declares, is "our new literature." As for the chief subjects of it–movie stars–she says, "They misbehave all the time. That's why we wanted them–to act out for us." Occasionally they make shop talk, but even that is elegant, as when the older writer observes, "There is so much arbitrariness in the world–we mustn't let it seep into our stories." Alas, the opening and closing of the play both had a forced quality, but everything in the middle had great verbal and emotional richness. Debra Messing conveyed the younger writer's transition from a creature of jagged edges to one of polished poise very skillfully. It would be easy to make her a villain, but Messing never lost our sympathy for her. Maria Tucci was especially strong as the older writer.

William Luce's *Barrymore,* which opened at the Music Box on Broadway on 25 March, was about

Program for Richard Greenburg's play in which three adults speculate about their parents' past

John Barrymore in his final months. It seldom went beyond the limitations of one-person shows based on the lives of famous people. (Technically this was not a one-person show since it had an unseen actor in the wings asking Barrymore questions.) Whatever its shortcomings, it afforded Christopher Plummer the chance to give an astounding performance in the title role.

Plummer had two fabulous entrances. As the first act began, his makeup perfectly re-creating "The Great Profile," Plummer swaggered on in a dazzling blue, double-breasted, pinstriped suit that reeked of showbiz success. He was not strolling grandly down Broadway, alas, but dragging a rack of costumes, singing "I've Got a Gal in Kalamazoo," a fitting prelude to an evening of poignantly comic reminiscence. This Barrymore, with the smile of an aging but zestful vaudeville hoofer, has rented a theater to prepare for a comeback.

Program for Tina Howe's play about an elderly woman who had been a record-setting Channel swimmer

His second-act entrance occurred on a murkily lit set, a brilliant evocation of a theatrical backstage before everything was computerized. The shadow of Barrymore as the hunchback Richard III loomed large against a curtain, and Plummer clumped ominously forward. Wearing a maroon costume that perfectly parodied the grandiose style of the last century, he ascended a throne. The menace he managed to project was undercut by the effort required to hoist himself into place, but it made you yearn to hear him say, "Now is the winter of our discontent. . . ." Instead Plummer intoned, "Winken, Blinken and Nod," a sadly perfect image for Barrymore's career, his plummet from the most acclaimed actor on either side of the Atlantic to an alcoholic capable of little but self-parody. It was a bravura evening, aided immeasurably by the superbly evocative costume and scenic designs of Santo Loquasto, but you kept wishing Luce had given Plummer a greater palette to work with.

The other noteworthy one-person play was Roger Guenveur Smith's *A Huey P. Newton Story,* which opened Off-Off-Broadway at the Joseph Papp Public Theater 12 February. What made Smith's piece about the Black Panther leader refreshing was that it presented Newton as a complex and ultimately broken human being.

When we first see Smith's Newton he is surprisingly witty and sharp, but—equally surprisingly—shy and ill at ease, his legs twitching as he speaks. Responding to the charge that the Black Panthers are violent, he says, "Hey, existence is violent. I exist, therefore I am violent. It's hypocritical to try to claim otherwise . . . in the same way that these vegetarians are hypocritical when they tell you they're not harming anything. A carrot screams also." The tone is gentle, almost tentative, a man finding his voice, not yet a man who modifies his voice to suit the needs of the media. As the evening progresses, Smith becomes more confident, more cocky. Even when Newton mouths slogans (like a declaration while he is in prison that "this is just a little prison, the big prison is on the outside"), he follows it with an elegant quote from John Dryden to undercut the rhetoric.

In the course of the evening we see Newton lose control. The mind that understood how to seduce the public no longer seems capable of making challenging assertions. By the end Newton is no longer intellectualizing. He's telling us about Black Orpheus and, at the very end, when he's less and less coherent, he's reciting the lines from *Macbeth* about "a tale told by an idiot." Written with impressive complexity, the piece depends greatly on the talents of Smith. He has a musical voice and a body that communicates powerfully. He takes a life that might have lent itself to facile commentary or controversy and makes it deeply poetic and moving.

Mention should be made of two stylized comedies. Douglas Carter Beane's *As Bees in Honey Drown* is a fable about one of the most active and relentless industries in a consumer society, the creation of not celebrities (a complex process) but rather "hot" young things, which the media have learned to mass-produce with efficiency and zeal. In Beane's play, which opened Off-Off-Broadway at the Greenwich House Theater on 19 June, a young writer is "taken up" by a seemingly wealthy woman who has seen his photograph in a magazine. He sees her as the next step in his progress from a struggling novelist to someone enjoying a life of privilege. She skillfully exploits his assumption that a creative person should be able to live luxuriously. He assumes she is picking up the tab, but she eventually disappears, leaving him with monstrous bills.

Among the things Beane plays with are the ways people in the arts fashion their identities ("You're not the person you were born—who wonderful is?") and the way their self-creation increases their power. If the play has a weakness, it is that because virtually everyone in it is newly minted, virtually no one has any human depth. It was flawlessly performed.

The other stylized comedy was John Patrick Shanley's *Psychopathia Sexualis,* which opened Off-Broadway at the Manhattan Theater Club on 26 February. The dazzling farce by the screenwriter of the Oscar-winning *Moonstruck* reaches its climax in a replay of the gunfight at the O.K. Corral in which the combatants duke it out in a psychiatrist's office. The shrink is an outright bully who does not disguise the fact that he is in competition with his patients. Thus it's no surprise that the only client who can beat him at his own game is someone with an unabashed admiration for John Wayne. The patient whose crisis leads to this psychiatric showdown is Arthur, a young man with a sock fetish. Without a pair of his father's argyles in easy reach, Arthur is impotent. His psychiatrist, trying to help him perform without this "crutch," impounds the socks, leaving him helpless on the eve of his marriage. First Arthur enlists the help of his friend Howard, a retired stockbroker and neophyte Jungian, whom the shrink vanquishes handily. Arthur must then resort to, so to speak, the big guns: his fiancée Lucille, a determined Texan who says of herself, "I'm not one of those New York girls—I like to be happy." This kind of silliness requires enormous skill to sustain, and, with the help of an expert cast, especially Edward Herrmann as the hostile therapist, Shanley achieved an Offenbachian verve.

Tina Howe, the author of *Painting Churches,* had a new play, *Pride's Crossing,* which opened Off-Broadway at the Mitzi E. Newhouse Theater in Lincoln Center on 7 December. The story of a ninety-year-old New England WASP looking back on her life—particularly her youth as a woman who swam the English Channel—the play was notable largely as a vehicle for the radiant Cherry Jones, who played the woman from youth to painful old age. None of the other characters had any depth, reducing the play to a kind of monologue with extraneous chorus.

Normally New York is the recipient of many plays from England. This year there were fewer than usual. The one that was supposed to make a big splash was Pam Gems's *Stanley,* which opened on Broadway at Circle in the Square on 20 February. It was anticipated that the play might save the

venerable but perennially troubled institution; alas, it pushed the theater into unsalvageable insolvency.

Stanley is about Stanley Spencer, an English painter, an eccentric of childlike naiveté. Gems, best known here for her equally flat 1982 *Piaf,* focuses on Spencer's odd marital career. Late in the second act Spencer declares, "The whole of my life in art has been a slow realization of the mystery of sex." He leaves his frumpy but devoted wife and two children for a lesbian, who openly boasts that her association with him will help her own artistic career. They never have sex, which makes him want to sleep again with his former wife; she points out that this will now be adultery. All this might matter more if Spencer's art were better known to American audiences. The play was presented in a theater in which the audience is on three sides of the set. Much of the area above the set (into which the actors sometimes climbed) was filled with reproductions of his paintings. The play marked the American debut of the distinguished British actor Antony Sher, who made his mark in London in 1985 with a justifiably acclaimed *Richard III.* He has described how he developed his interpretation of Shakespeare's character in a valuable book, *The Year of the King.* Anyone lucky enough to have seen him in the Shakespeare or to have read the book can appreciate his acting better than anyone who might have had the mischance to see *Stanley.*

A more interesting British import was Patrick Marber's *Dealer's Choice,* which opened 22 May Off-Broadway at the Manhattan Theater Club. The play is set in the kitchen and basement of a London restaurant, where the owner, his staff, and assorted friends play a weekly game of poker. Marber uses both the restaurant and the game to bring out the pretensions and vulnerabilities of the male ego. The play was given a beautiful ensemble production.

Another superbly mounted British ensemble piece was Mike Leigh's *Goosepimples,* which was presented Off-Off-Broadway by The New Group, which produced an equally powerful production of Leigh's *Ectasy* two years ago. *Goosepimples,* an earlier play, is about a group of hard-edged middle-class Brits. A young woman has moved in with a car dealer for reasons of convenience rather than romance. It is Saturday night, and he is entertaining a fellow dealer and his wife, both of whom have fairly coarse senses of humor. When problems arise cooking dinner, he takes them to a restaurant. Just as they have left, his roommate comes home, bringing with her a wealthy Arab she has picked up in a bar. She imagines he is smitten with her. He imagines she is a prostitute. He speaks absolutely no English, and their essential misunderstanding is compounded when the others return from dinner, drunk. It is easy for him to mistake them for carousers in a brothel. Their condescension toward him and his incomprehension of them grow repetitive, but their mutual inability to communicate becomes increasingly, harrowingly painful.

Certainly the most audacious play of the year was Jonathan Reynolds's *Stonewall Jackson's House,* which opened on 17 February Off-Off-Broadway at the American Place Theater. The play begins with what appears to be a skit as a black woman guides cantankerous white tourists through the home of the Confederate general. The skit is, in fact, an entry in a playwriting contest run by a theater company whose dramaturge is Tracy, a young black woman the aging liberal founders, Oz and his wife Gaby, are grooming to take over when they retire. At first the play seems to have been written by a white cracker, but, to their horror, they discover that *Stonewall Jackson's House,* which charges that the welfare state enslaves blacks anew, was written by Tracy. Oz and Gaby are aghast. Nor are they mollified by Tracy's declaration: "I got so sick of reading all those self-pitying mea culpas we get over the transom about how we been wronged. I mean, we *have* been wronged, but it's over, folks. Or worse, all those fake 'I am a proud lesbian of color and some kind of indomitable.' Isn't there anything else to say about us? Are we forever to be defined by slavery and Jim Crow? That just makes us look wretched, like a permanent class of psychiatric patients. 'Hey, we went through slavery, we went through Jim Crow, we gotta be dysfunctional.' I want to change that, give us an identity! I want to change this theater, change the culture, change the world . . . [I want this theater to be] a place that makes people think!" Tracy refuses to back down. She reminds Oz of what he said only a few nights earlier when they had drinks together in a bar: "'If Marx were alive today in America, he'd say it's not religion that's the opiate of the people, it's the arts!' Don't you remember saying that? 'The chief responsibility of the artist has become to not hurt anyone's feelings.' And you weren't drunk. Our audience needs to be stirred up—that's what you said!" Tracy's recollection of Oz's remarks precipitates a battle between Oz and Gaby. Quickly Oz backs down and hides behind his wife, who declares he is now back on "the right side." Tracy won't stop. "You've never been on the right side of anything, either of you, just the comfortable one! . . . Sentimental, self-centered old lefties whose well-meaning, stubborn politics have wrecked this century—trying to stuff real, complicated anguish into simplistic theories!" For the next few minutes

Tracy is relentless. She upbraids Oz and Gaby for their unwillingness to acknowledge the evil of Stalin. "While he murdered and tortured more of his own citizens than Hitler and Pol Pot and Idi Amin combined, you protected yourself with lies so you wouldn't have to admit you were wrong—and instead focused on a bunch of mediocre movie writers martyred by a blacklist!"

"They were not mediocre writers!" Gaby responds.

"Well, mediocre martyrs then. I mean, what was your response to finding out about the gulags? To turn Solzhenitsyn into a crackpot for exposing them and ruining your lives?"

"He is a crackpot," Gaby says.

Tracy goes on to disparage the increasingly politicized definition of black: "You can't be black, if you date somebody white; can't be black if you don't blame all your problems on racism; can't be if you think some of our brothers in jail actually belong there; and you can't *no way* be black if you don't see that Clarence Thomas has two heads." She also attacks Black Studies: "Spend hours lecturing about the greed of your slave traders—and not at all about the greed of our homey chieftains so eager to sell us. And in the end if you have the nerve to praise Booker T. Washington instead of W. E. B. Du Bois, they give you an F." She goes on to decry the way black politicians capitalized on the Los Angeles riots and white women benefited from affirmative action.

Finally Oz and Gaby strike back in the only way they can—they threaten not to give her the artistic directorship they have promised her. Tracy realizes how much of her identity and financial security are based on her assumptions that she would have the job. She has no choice but to rewrite her play. The new politically correct version, *The House of Mary Anna Morrison-Jackson, Survivor,* is about a feminist martyr who murdered her abusive husband. It wins the Pulitzer Prize. It inspires a bidding war by the major Hollywood studios. Tracy appears on the cover of *Time.* Tracy, Oz, and Gaby all enjoy tremendous financial success. Tracy has become "the New Voice of the American Theater. Of all the arts, really." Reynolds's play may spend more time than is dramatically defensible in the "J'accuse" mode. Nevertheless anyone who has been exposed to the political cant that characterizes much of the American theater in the 1990s will understand the validity of its attacks. Surprisingly, given how corrosive and uncomfortable the play is, its run was extended several times.

In London the weaknesses of contemporary theater are often offset by brilliant productions of the classics. That has rarely been the case in New York. The situation has gotten worse as directors see the classics as vehicles to comment on fashionable topics. It is hard to imagine, for example, why Dostoyevsky, who is highly *un*-fashionable these days, given his reactionary politics, should have been trotted out, especially *The Demons* (the novel that used to be translated as *The Possessed*), his sardonic attack on revolutionaries. A version of *The Demons* opened 22 May at the Off-Off-Broadway New York Theater Workshop.

As soon as Elizabeth Egloff's nearly four-hour adaptation began, I understood why the material was suddenly "relevant." The first image we see is that of Stavrogin, the most contemptible of the revolutionaries, molesting a teenage girl. Aha! I thought. Dostoyevsky might have imagined he was writing about the diabolical influence of secular Western ideas on Holy Mother Russia, but he really was addressing the issue of child abuse. When Dostoyevsky first published the book, this element had to be suppressed. It appears in the chapter called "Stavrogin's confession," which only came to light fifty years later, in 1922, among the papers of Dostoyevsky's recently deceased widow. In other words, the novel attained its reputation without it, but in this dramatization it has been placed at the work's very core. The image of Stavrogin abusing a child is repeated several times and reinforced at the end of the play in an ugly rape scene. Dostoyevsky, we can see, was a feminist a century early.

Egloff tells the story of revolutionaries wreaking havoc in a provincial Russian town in a style that is often jarringly contemporary. Toward the end there are images that reflect a genuine understanding of the novel—especially when one of the radicals uses revolutionary jargon to justify fascistic brutality—but seldom does the play suggest Dostoyevsky wrote a novel of ideas. You could easily come away from this adaptation imagining *The Demons* was a crude and dated melodrama.

The rarely done Thomas Middleton–William Rowley *The Changeling* was given an unusually grotesque production by the celebrated Chicago director Robert Woodruff. It opened Off-Off-Broadway at Saint Clement's Church on 3 March. Woodruff filled the production with startling visual images. Many scenes took place, for example, in an insane asylum, the inhabitants of which are all women (or, in one case, a man dressed like one). We first saw them on gurneys, their legs in stirrups upstage, their bodies covered by sheets, their heads looking at us, whimpering as each underwent an abortion. They were then confined to telephone booths in which, from time to time, they writhed, again a silent

chorus agony. The acting that took place in front of them was largely overshadowed by striking lighting and sound effects. The play got lost in the shuffle.

The British sent over a much acclaimed production of Henrik Ibsen's *A Doll's House* starring Janet McTeer as Nora. It opened on Broadway at the Belasco on 7 April. McTeer, a tall, striking woman, was busy, busy, busy as Nora. Her frenetic energy helped us understand how exhausting it must have been for Nora to maintain her facade as her husband's plaything, but it could easily be construed as an actress doing a "star turn." McTeer made Nora sexier than usual, but this made it hard to believe she had spent her whole life knuckling under to convention. Nevertheless it made the play, which often seems stale, extremely lively.

Shakespeare is so routinely travestied in New York that it seldom seems worth noting, but when the miscreant is Vanessa Redgrave it cannot be ignored. Near the end of *Antony and Cleopatra,* as the queen of Egypt contemplates suicide, she imagines at some future date she and her lover will be mocked by vulgar actors: "The quick comedians extemporally will stage us." Redgrave seems to have taken Cleopatra's words as a guideline. It would be hard to imagine "quick comedians" could improve on what she did. Her production of the play opened at the Joseph Papp Public Theater on 13 March.

We know, of course, that Shakespeare's women were originally played by boys, which may be why much of the time Redgrave played Cleopatra as a tomboy, the shock of red hair atop her makeup-free face an homage to either David Bowie or Tom Sawyer. She made her first entrance wearing black jodhpurs, cavorting with her Antony more like kids on the playground than adults in the throes of love. Later, when someone brought her bad news, she kicked him in the groin. Redgrave played it more as a romp than a tragedy.

Arthur Miller, a somewhat easier playwright, fared little better. Some of his lesser-known plays were mounted by the Signature Company, which devotes each season to an American playwright. (Last year it was Sam Shepard. The year before it was Horton Foote.) Such plays as *An American Clock* and *The Last Yankee* were given in commendable productions.

There were two major Miller revivals, *A View From the Bridge* and *All My Sons,* both presented on Broadway at the Roundabout. *All My Sons,* which opened 4 May, starred John Cullum as the airplane-parts manufacturer whose dishonest business practices may have resulted in the death of his own son during World War II. *A View From the Bridge,* which opened 20 December, had Anthony LaPaglia as Eddie Carbone, the Brooklyn dockworker bewildered by a changing world. Like Miller's most famous father figure, Willy Loman, neither of these men is a character likely to win the audience's sympathy by anything that happens in the course of the play. Unless they capture that sympathy as soon as they appear, the plays seem futile exercises in trying to understand someone who may not be worth the trouble.

Eddie is a man who is deeply troubled. He is obviously enamored of Catherine, the niece he and his wife Bea have raised since childhood, who is just coming into womanhood. He is deeply jealous of the fact that Catherine is smitten with Rudolpho, one of the two Italian immigrants he and his wife are harboring illegally. His hatred of Rudolpho is based in part on his conviction that the good-looking Italian must be homosexual because he sings, cooks, and knows how to sew. His fears and animosities come to a boil when Catherine announces she will marry Rudolpho, thus making him an American citizen. Eddie makes an anonymous call to the Immigration Service to inform them about the presence of Rudolpho and Marco.

When the play was first produced in 1955, Eddie's act of "informing" was the play's central theme. (Miller refused to allow Elia Kazan, who had directed *Death of a Salesman,* to direct *A View From the Bridge* because Kazan had "named names" to the House Un-American Activities Committee.) Today the play's focus is homophobia. One of its dramatic high points comes when Eddie, in a rage at finding Catherine and Rudolpho alone in a state of undress, kisses Rudolpho on the mouth. In this production, staged by Michael Mayer, Eddie throws Rudolpho on a table and practically mounts him to deliver the kiss.

LaPaglia is an actor of considerable charm, but his physical presence is that of a working-class goon. If the play is to achieve the aura of Italian opera, which is inherent in its often lush language, Eddie must have a haunted, quasi-tragic aura, which La-Paglia lacks. The production was aided immeasurably by Allison Janney as his wife Bea but deeply undercut by Brittany Murphy as Catherine. Murphy, best known for the movie *Clueless,* played Catherine as a kind of Brooklyn Betty Boop, a caricature that marred every scene in which she appeared. Mayer's strongest achievement was the use of a large "chorus" of neighbors and fellow workers who filled the small theater and conveyed powerfully the sense of a community threatened by Eddie's actions.

The 1947 *All My Sons* was Miller's first Broadway success but has always seemed his most conventional, mechanical work. John Cullum is a powerful actor with a rich, musical voice, but what he projects is an angry cracker. Moreover, the production, directed by Barry Edelstein, had a cerebral, deconstructionist tone that minimized the play's emotional impact.

Even in these unsatisfactory productions, however, you came away with a sense of the ambitions of Miller. His criticisms of the American character at midcentury may not be as profound as they once seemed, but they still exercise a hold on our imaginations. That cannot be said of much of the new work on view as the century nears its close.

The Year in Literary Biography

William Foltz
University of Hawaii

This year's biographies cover a great sweep of time–two millennia, from the era of a Roman poet to that of a living South African–and place–a hemisphere and a half, from frozen and besieged Moscow to the tropical and relaxed Marquesas. Novelists predominate as subjects: there are fourteen, including all the Brontës and their first biographer, Mrs. Gaskell; Jane Austen, in two biographies; and Evelyn Waugh. Robert Penn Warren and Herman Melville are the American subjects. Four others whose appeal was primarily popular are presented with varying degrees of success: the evangelical Hannah More, Ilya Ehrenburg, Jules Verne, and Julia Peterkin, the American southerner. There are only two poets–Horace and George Gordon, Lord Byron–this year, unless one includes the early work of Jorge Luis Borges. Doris Lessing has continued her memoirs, and Isaac Babel's widow, Antonina Pirozhkova, laments her martyred husband. There are also brief lives of Mary Lamb, Sarah Disraeli, and Dorothy Wordsworth. This leaves two international figures, Isaac Bashevis Singer in Yiddish and Archbishop Thomas Cranmer.

When Eduard Fraenkel was preparing his long *Horace* in 1957, Peter Levi was his student. More than forty years later Levi has written a succinct appreciation of the poet and defense of a mentor who defended Horace from scholarly fantasies. One great advantage of *Horace: A Life* (Duckworth) is that its 270 pages reduce Horace (65–8 B.C.) to a manageable size for the Latinless and Greekless reader. This is an elegiac book, lamenting the passing of a sensibility that was central to an educated European culture (in the United States 0.07 percent of all degrees are in classics or religion). But if this biography is written for the modern barbarian, Levi's remarks on blue pubic hair, the quantity of "Apulia," and the textual crux in *Odes* I, 23 will seem labored. (The last is surely more than a "lovely little poem.")

Levi relies heavily on the life of Horace by Suetonius (A.D. 70) but extrapolates other details from the poems themselves. Horace was a short, fat man who died in middle age and commented hon-

estly and ironically on himself. His moral philosophy is really common sense, his desire for *otium* lettered ease, and his poetry inimitable. It is nearly impossible to summarize the events from Caesar's death (when Horace was age twenty-one) to Augustus's triumphs, but a biographer must since Horace comments on the major events even though his poetry takes a private focus. This provides an index with more than 120 of the poet's literary and political contemporaries who are introduced in the text.

Horace was the son of a "slave"–that is, a loser in the social wars. His father made good money and sent his son off to Athens for a gentleman's education to assure his social rise. Levi provides a good overview of the problems attendant on Caesar's death. Horace joined Brutus's party as a military tribune and was lucky to escape Philippi alive, fortunate enough to be forgiven and wealthy enough to purchase the sinecure of a treasury secretaryship. Through Virgil's good offices he met Maecenas, the great literary patron of Rome, in 39 or 38 B.C., the year of political amnesty. Maecenas bought Horace a farm, perhaps the most solid form of tenure for a Distinguished Writer. Horace declined to be Augustus's private secretary–perhaps, as Levi acutely suggests, because the emperor's immediate civil servants were slaves.

This biography is the result of reading and rereading: it offers more literary analysis than life and more than a hundred pages on the *Odes,* but its criticism is sane and lucid. Levi treats the first three books of *Odes* all at once: this obscures their already obscure chronology; the fourth book marks Horace's recovery from Virgil's death.

The chestnuts, the poems we had to know (now anthologized in vapid anthologies of classical literature in translation), are all here. Some are dismissed rather quickly, perhaps because they are too famous–for example, "Integer vitae" (I, 22) and "Postume . . . " (II, 14). Levi devotes little space to the latter, worrying more about the vintage of Caecuban wine than about Death. Apparently a biography of Horace can fail to include the phrase "seize the day"–but should it? Maps are also excluded.

But in compensating for these curious faults Levi calls attention to fine poems one has forgotten (or never read). He did the same in his recent and successful biography of Alfred Tennyson.

There is less on the (late) *Ars Poetica* than one might expect, but Brink's recent two-volume commentary fills this gap. Levi is modern in disliking the poems of Empire: he avoids the "serpentine manacles of theorists" by refusing to see these poems as ironically subverting the Roman Principate, as some have claimed for the *Aeneid* and Lucan's *Pharsalia*. His praise of Horace's *Carmen Saeculare* as the most successful commissioned poem in history is temperate.

Though Levi finds some poems to be too gruesome for his generation, his explanation of how the alternate pyrrhics and spondees of *Odes* III, 12 "put a small worm in an ell-pie or a cow pat" borders on the gruesome. The poet's unashamed bisexuality is simply accepted. The biographer pulls the images of Horace into our times, or at least into this century: he records the last date on which sheep were driven through Rome, snow could be seen on Mount Soracte, and nightingales could be heard near the Truglia's waterfalls. That the rail terminal in Milan now has as many toilets as Nero's golden palace had is an interesting detail, but when the formality of *Odes* I, 35 is compared to the ironwork of a palace near the Tretyakov Museum, we admire Levi's traveling eyes more than his analysis.

The biographer's own curiously punctuated translations look a bit surprising at first, but a glance at the Latin shows their freshness in this book, which Levi has written with lighthearted erudition. His claim that these are not poetry but merely attempts to explain what he is talking about is too modest. He also provides the famous English translations of Horace: of the *Odes,* those by John Milton, Samuel Johnson, and A. E. Housman, but also of less familiar versions by Sir Richard Fanshawe and Thomas Creech; Abraham Cowley translated the *Satires.*

The educated of the last two centuries read the poetry of Horace; those of the last four centuries still have the works of Thomas Cranmer, the archbishop of Canterbury, whose English, as Jonathan Swift wrote, possesses "as great strains of true sublime eloquence as are anywhere to be found in our language." Some seventy million still hear and repeat weekly the strains of the Collects and liturgy of the *Book of Common Prayer* (1549, 1552), a work that contributed to the formal rhythms of modern English. Consequently, the three hundred million who regard English as their language will welcome *Thomas Cranmer: A Life* (Yale), Diarmaid MacCulloch's

seven-hundred-page study of the compiler of the *Book of Common Prayer* (*BCP*). With its five-hundred-item bibliography (including dissertations), MacCulloch's work modifies J. G. Ridley's 1962 biography of Cranmer; the forty-four illustrations, from Cranmer's early marginalia on Martin Luther to his later antipapal beard, are apt and interesting.

Life is not entirely dispassionate. MacCulloch's archbishop is a hero—muddled, confused, and confusing to others—but still a hero. The biographer's use of *conservative* and *evangelical,* rather than *Roman* and *Anglican* or *Papist* and *Protestant,* works to clear the *odium theologicum.* But MacCulloch doesn't absolve Cranmer, who, like his master, Henry VIII, burned both evangelicals and conservatives in order to keep the Church inclusive.

The general knowledge about Cranmer is that he helped Henry VIII with annulments and divorces, wrote the *BCP,* and was burned. MacCulloch expands on these topics and adds much more, especially on Cranmer as a reformer during the reign of Edward VI. But what he cannot provide are details of Cranmer's private life; of the archbishop's surviving one hundred letters, only one refers to his wife and family. In fact, his first forty years are covered in as many pages.

MacCulloch emphasizes that Henry knew of Cranmer's skill as a diplomat as early as 1527, two years before the annulment controversy of 1529. Hence, it was not unusual that Cranmer would be sent abroad to canvas theological support for the king's separation from Catherine of Aragon. Twenty-three universities deliberated ("the single most lucrative source of consultancy fees for academics during the whole of the sixteenth century") and concluded that Henry had a point, so Cranmer took a second wife in 1532. MacCulloch argues that the revolutionary liturgical change apparent in the 1549 *BCP,* which adopted a view that marriage could be fun, followed Cranmer's sixteen years of happy marriage.

That marriage, like Henry's initial marriage to Anne Boleyn, had to be kept secret. In any event Cranmer became archbishop in 1532 and began his royal career of annulment, marriage, and divorce. Rather than presenting Cranmer as the craven toady to his master that earlier biographers have seen, MacCulloch presents a man who provides pastoral advice about Boleyn's faithlessness and realizes that Henry will be happier with Catherine Howard than with Anne of Cleves. Yet Cranmer arranged for both Boleyn and Howard to die. If not toadying, this is highly Erastian. He seems not to have wished for Sir Thomas More's execution, but he watched friars burn; he continued Erasmus's pension, but he had nothing to do with the spoliation of monasteries, nunneries, or friaries. Cranmer believed that the fault of the Apostolic Church was its lack of princes to correct it.

Cranmer's gradual movement from holding a view of a transsubstantial or a real presence in the Eucharist to holding memorialist position was, to MacCulloch's delight, the "greatest wastershed in his theological pilgrimage." Cranmer made the Mass "Communion" in the *BCP* and his *Defence* of 1550. Though the revisers of 1662 changed that, the devotional vacuum left by Cranmer's revision of the mass brought about a new emphasis on morning and evening prayer.

Cranmer was more consistent, theologically and liturgically, than his king, whose grammar he corrected and whose "liturgical antics" could include creeping to the cross in order to attract the political support of European and English conservatives. The archbishop's skills were considerable: in 1548 he secured assent to an English liturgy by avoiding the use of convocation. More important for literary purposes was his immediate insistence that Scripture be preached in its literal and not typological sense. The extended religious and political discussions in the *Life* allow readers to put the literary merits of Cranmer in the theological context of the mid 1500s. The evolution of the *BCP* can be found in this biography, but readers must jump around and skip pages to do so. Cranmer's nascent abilities begin with his 1531 *Determinations* in support of Henry's annulment. The archbishop's use of two English words for one Latin term enlivened theological debate and added new words to the language (MacCulloch corrects the dates of the *OED*). A man who believes that there is no poetry of devotion in the Early Fathers and that images exist for theology rather than for imaginative pleasure will not write good poetry. Cranmer knew that he could not write poetry, and he kept it out of the *BCP*.

MacCulloch quickly and expertly summarizes the sources of the *BCP:* much from Miles Coverdale, Cardinal Quiñones's breviary of 1535, Protestant texts from Germany and central Europe, and liturgies of Mozarabic Spain (but not the Eastern Fathers). Of equal value is MacCulloch's reconstruction of Cranmer's English collaborators: Cranmer, he concludes, is responsible for the seasonal Collects that combined ancient examples, his own translations from the Sarum rite, contemporary texts, and, to a lesser extent, his own compositions. In examining Cranmer's felicitous ear and ability to adapt, MacCulloch presents him as a gourmet of language, one who avoided the excesses of Latinate humanism. In his last one hundred pages MacCul-

loch carefully and cautiously follows Foxe's account of Cranmer's death under Mary I: Cranmer dies, thrusting the hand that signed his recantation into the fire, affirming his beliefs about communion, and condemning the Pope as the Antichrist.

The exhaustive scholarship of this work is relieved by current wit and an agreeable tolerance. It is not primarily a literary biography, but it is the life of a commemorated ecclesiastical functionary whose prose has helped shape English-speaking culture.

Hannah More (1745–1833), if not a good late-eighteenth-century writer, was certainly prolific; she died as the Mother of Victorianism and as the butt of jokes from Samuel Taylor Coleridge, Thomas De Quincey, and George Gordon, Lord Byron, who objected to her politics, her style, her sex, and her lack of this last. One reader used a nineteen-volume edition as mulch; a recent scholar finds her plays "droopy." In 1952 Mary Jones's *Hannah More* began her revival, but much has happened since then, and Charles Ford's *Hannah More: A Critical Biography* (Peter Lang) defends a writer of whom many have heard but few have read with pleasure. Ford's work is admirable and thorough in scholarship; he demonstrates a mastery of primary and immense secondary literature on feminism and politics of the last twenty years. Alas, recent jargon intrudes: references to "strategies," "coded passages," "cultural outsiders," and "marginality" occur within three pages, and the Duc d'Orléans is described as "radically chic." But whether one agrees with Ford or not, his documentation is massive and learned: the footnotes alone are worth the stiff price of $54.99.

Her biographer must defend a writer who adjured readers not to tip the servants, attend oratorios or get their hair dressed on Sunday, read female novelists (because they corrupt the young), or attend plays (because they promote adultery)–but to tolerate the double standard, vote Tory, and for God's sake act like Milton's Eve.

Despite all this, the new More looks better than the More of earlier biographers. Ford treats More's life and career as a writer, examining her publications–plays, tracts, bad verse, and her notorious novel, *Coelebs in Search of a Wife* (1808)–in their historical context, and this approach keeps one from getting any interior view of More. The biography presents the older men, starting with her father and ending with the reactionary prime minister, Lord Liverpool, who encouraged her, as well as her middle-aged Bristol fiancé who, having jilted her three times at the church door, settled on her a yearly sum of fifty thousand dollars, an amount that led to later scandal. Samuel Johnson found her flattery a bit thick, but she held her own in debate.

David Garrick encouraged her dramatic abilities: *The Inflexible Captive* (1774) received an "undeservedly warm" reception, and her next play, *Percy* (1777), made a fortune. Her poetry, *Sir Eldred of the Bower* and *The Bleeding Rock* (both 1775), were also successes. Readers will be grateful that Ford has provided plot summaries and analyses of these dreadful works in which virtuous maidens remain faithful to high ideals. Yet to prevent More from seeming to toady to patriarchal values, Ford insists that More merely "parrots" the views of her times and that underneath the "veneer" one finds a proleptic feminist.

The death of Garrick and accusations of plagiarism forced More to rethink her life and to emerge as the subtle Valkyrie of evangelicalism. Plays were replaced by biblical skits about Old Testament evangelicals such as Daniel. The evangelicalism Ford shrewdly examines in her works was not the namby-pamby kind later condemned by Victorians: it was vigorous, incisive, and theologically sloppy but socially skilled. The biographer is adept with relationships of the Clapham Sect, all those Wilberforces, Macaulays, and Thorntons.

More wore big hair, made friends of the right bishops, and, to convert Horace Walpole, wrote the bad Hudibrastics of *Florio* (1784), the hero of which anticipates the preternaturally middle-aged god of *Coelebs in Search of a Wife*. Her real indignation, however, was directed at the politics of the upper-middle classes rather than at their ethics, and this led to later accusations of hypocrisy. Ford argues that *The Slave Trade* (1788) marked the end of her accommodation with Britain's elite, yet he admits that she had to publish her attacks on Sunday fun anonymously.

Aristocratic dissipation could, and did, lead to revolution. The worse the French became, the higher More's reputation as a prophetess rose—and the more she published. Funded by William Wilberforce and William Pitt from 1795 to 1798, two million copies of ballads, allegories, and short stories of *The Cheap Repository* brought tears to the eyes of the literate and deserving poor and laughter to later generations. Readers will be grateful for Ford's plot summaries of works that were designed to destroy male conviviality while increasing the number of deserving and deferential poor.

Part of our present scorn for the earnest but intolerant paternalism of her tracts is our ignorance of their social, religious, and political background. Ford fills us in, and, although we may not like More and her evangelical adherents, we understand her background. The debates over Poor Law reform in the eighteenth century have their melancholy parallels today.

Ford comes closest to her personal life in a lively chapter on what has become known as the Blagdon Controversy of 1798, when More insinuated her own clerical candidate into the Anglican establishment. This eventually successful attempt at founding Sunday schools can be seen as either the success of lay leadership or the failure of parish government. Hannah and Patty More ("the Weird Sisters") were either crafty plotters or astute controversialists, bishops in petticoats or victims of Erastianism; her opponents venal prelates, low-born Welshmen, and reptilian pluralists or worse (Methodists).

The clear winner, More then turned to educational reform for girls in general and Charlotte, the Princess of Wales, in particular. More's reforms would have averted an Amelia Osborne, but not a Becky Sharp or Mme. de Staël, whose novel *Corinne* (1807) More adopted a year later in her famous *Coelebs in Search of a Wife,* More's only work still read. She made more money on this than Scott did on *Waverley* (1841). Ford is wise enough not to justify its literary merits—it has few—but acute enough to place it in the context of earlier educational programs.

More's *Practical Piety* (1811) was her most successful book commercially—but even Ford doesn't like it: "Her age here had both dulled and deluded her muse." Next year was worse: eleven editions and ten thousand copies of *Christian Morals* (1812). Her *An Essay on the Character and Practical Writings of Saint Paul* (1815) tells us more about More than the martyr: both were friends of the people, respected the government, allowed women to preach, and defused the learned by sincerity. As her politics became increasingly conservative, she recycled her early works into reactionary politics: bad harvests are God's judgment on a sinful nation, especially on the sinful poor. More's feminism, which figures highly in the first chapter, peters out in the succeeding three. Her biographer seems to despair of her social views and politics after her sixties.

By 1817 her reputation had slipped. She never recognized the Regency, and she died after being robbed by her servants and rescued by Zachary Macaulay, an eighteenth-century evangelical marooned in the Romantic movement with a style too diffuse for meaning.

Michael Plowetzky's brief *Prominent Sisters* (Praiger) brings conveniently together the sisters of two Romantics and one late Romantic: Dorothy Wordsworth (1771–1855), Mary Lamb (1763[?]–1847), and Sara Disraeli (1802–1859). All receive about fifty pages. Documentation is light; the scholarship is not current, and though the brothers of all three must figure large in their sisters' lives, it is

Coleridge–the later Coleridge, rheumatic, drug addicted, and paranoid–who often eclipses the other brothers, William Wordsworth and Charles Lamb.

Of these three brief lives, Mary Lamb's is the most interesting. We have her Wednesday literary dinners she began with her brother when she was thirty-six, some three years after her first attack of madness, when she knifed their mother. Her pathetic madness is gathered from the letters of her brother and others. By the age of fifty she was lucid only half the year.

Polowetzky is concise and scrupulous with the Lambs' joint *Tales of Shakespeare* (1807), but even better with her now-forgotten *Mrs. Leicester's School* (1807) and its criticism of class position. Whether it still has any literary merit remains to be determined. Mary's name could not appear on the title page of either book because she was both an occasional lunatic and a woman. More appealing to a modern reader will be her 1814 essay "Needlework" and her occupation, which she saw as the objective correlative of economic oppression. Polowetzky's analysis supports his claim that Mary was one of the first to stake out a vocational claim to a job of one's own. Mary sewed, from 9:00 A.M. to 11:00 P.M.

The friendship between Mary Lamb and Dorothy Wordsworth is secured by the poem Mary sent to console her when John Wordsworth and his boat foundered in 1802. Unfortunately we have only a few of Dorothy's replies to Mary's letters. The biographer wishes to bring out some prominent aspects of her personality that are still overlooked. To do so he uses both Wordsworth's Alfoxden and Grasmere journals, not to establish what her brother took from them for his poems–this has been common knowledge for some years–but to demonstrate that, at least at the turn of the century, it is Dorothy who provides the fullest and most sympathetic account of the rural poor. The journals show Dorothy as more sympathetic than her brother toward the rural poor. But whether she is initially as radical as the author makes her out is not clear. The puzzling dynamic between the sister and the brother remains an uninvestigated enigma. Dorothy spent twenty years slowly slipping away in mental darkness.

Of the three, Sarah Disraeli will most interest readers, but she remains the most shadowy. Polowetzky wishes to show that Sarah Disraeli affected Benjamin as Mary did William. There doesn't seem to be much to know. The few letters that survive are gleaned for life but are often lifeless. So also are the abstracts from her brother's grand tour: hyper postcard prose. This lack of primary material can lead to unproven though reasonable as-

sertions. Did she hope to attain emotional and intellectual fulfillment through her brother's success in politics and literature? Did she think a new party could transform Britain into a just society? Apparently she did.

Hers was an unhappy life. Like Dorothy Wordsworth and Mary Lamb, the young Sarah suffered from poverty. Dorothy was content to be her brother's amanuensis, critic, and sourcebook; Sarah was kept at home looking after her father, with no time to exercise her imagination in journals. Once she tried her hand at half a novel; her brother finished it disastrously.

Sarah wanted marriage (Dorothy didn't; Mary couldn't): after a wait of ten years, her fiancé died of typhus in Egypt. She never expected that her brother's marriage would separate them, but it did, and his letters recede into social anecdotes.

There is one important exception to this unhappy, quiet life: her brother's *Tancred–or, The New Crusade* (1847). Though Sarah was not a "terribly spiritual individual to begin with," in 1833 she began a never-published book of religious instruction for children that would demonstrate Christianity's debt to Judaism. Publishers turned her down, but her brother did not. He dedicated *Tancred* and his earlier *Coningsby* (1844) to Sarah. Both novels helped Victorian Britain tolerate, if not accept, the ideals of Zionism by the end of the century.

Jane Austen (1775–1817) and her family have two biographies this year: David Nokes's *Jane Austen: A Life* (Farrer, Straus and Giroux) and Valerie Grosvenor Myer's *Jane Austen, Obstinate Heart: A Biography* (Arcade). The latter is half the length of Nokes's clearly superior 577-page work. But length doesn't determine the merit of Nokes's *Life;* even if Myer's study had documentation, which it doesn't, it fails because it doesn't provide necessary background information for American readers.

Myer's audience consists of those who have seen the recent films but never read the novels, those who have not been and never will get to London. And to retain their interest Myer adds far-fetched spice: a clumsy Byron gives the bride away to Lord Portsmouth, the pupil of Jane's father and a necrophiliac (no documentation) and sadist who is then abused by his wife and her lover's children. These are the tabloid equivalents of recent scholarly yet smarmy speculations about Jane and her sister.

Nokes assumes we've read the novels and earlier biographies. He takes on the latter: the early family hagiographies, David Cecil's *A Portrait* (1978), Park Honan's *Jane Austen* (1987), and Deirdre Le Faye's even more recent *Jane Austen: A Family Record* (1989). He brings his encyclopedic knowledge of the eighteenth century to the times without sounding like an encyclopedia.

Myer, however, is better with domestic details: rural seats, the number of bedrooms in Godmersham, Jane's brother's place in Kent. Some of her facts appear irrelevant and odd: most details (on knickers, stays, dancing, and the invention of the mangle) fill in the physical picture of Austen's times.

Both are good with figures (and Nokes has more): prize money, dress money, rates for fashionable rooms by the week. If we are to believe Myer's conversion figures and use Nokes's numbers, Jane Austen made the equivalent of forty-eight thousand dollars from *Sense and Sensibility* (1811), but Ann Radcliffe had made six hundred thousand dollars from *The Mysteries of Udolpho* thirty-five years earlier. Austen's brother Frank cleared half a million in private China trade. Jane spent forty-seven hundred dollars on clothes and pocket money but gave thirteen hundred dollars to charitable causes.

Both biographies have too many family members and details—of alliances, of cousins' bankruptcies, of visits. This is especially true of Nokes's *Life*, which gives us a Jane who is one, but not the major, member of a Hampshire family with extensive connections: we get Austen's times rather than Austen.

The twenty-three-year-old Jane explains a Mrs. Hall's miscarriage: "owing to a fright—I suppose she happened unawares to look at her husband." Nokes lets his reader judge Austen. Not Myer: "Dead babies are not funny," for Myer feels she has to apologize if her heroine is not saintly. Nokes uses distasteful material carefully. His Jane's maternal uncle was an idiot and was kept in a private asylum. When she was six years old, her own brother joined him, and both were forgotten. It is also true that opium profits assisted her father. These events, slighted if not ignored by Myer, show us that Nokes is not revisionist, but honest. His placement of the retarded brother and uncle at the beginning and end of his *Life* frames his presentation of the occasionally disinterested if not cool charity of the Austen family. Myer's Austen is more sour than pointed: a witty remark becomes a "sneer," and a trenchant one becomes bitter.

The longer and more convincing portrait that Nokes presents is not of the stay-at-home clergyman's daughter but of a connection of the duke of Chandos and the cousin of Warren Hastings's bastard daughter, Elizabeth. The daughter became first the Countess de Feuillide and finally Jane's sister-in-law when, widowed, she married Austen's brother Henry. Jane's childhood was spent not in the Arcadia of earlier biographies but in a noisy rectory with muddy roads, noisy because of her six brothers and

sister. We follow the various brothers around the world, trying to remember their wives, their children, and their finances.

Nokes's *Life* reads forward like a novel. Initially this is confusing because it opens in Bengal, two years before his subject's birth. There her maternal uncle's early worries about tigers and opium are followed by those about the fondness that Philadelphia, his wife, has for the twenty-seven-year-old Warren Hastings, who fathered her illegitimate child, later Hastings's godchild. Jane herself isn't born—and then in a clause and only as "another girl"—until fifty pages later.

At times, direct narration stops, and the biographer becomes a novelist as we enter the limited consciousness of Cassandra, opium smugglers, Elizabeth, and Jane. These interior visions re-create what should have happened or what probably happened to Jane. For the periods when there are few documents, especially for the years at Bath, 1801–1806, Nokes revises the accepted accounts of Jane's misery. Austen was not miserable, and she didn't faint when she learned they had to move. If anything, she looked forward to the move: this differs completely from Honan and Le Faye and from Myer's chapter "Exile."

Also at Bath, Nokes must fashion the mysterious clergyman who dies suddenly, like Cassandra's beau, Tom Fowle. Nokes's suggestion that Cassandra read her own story into her sister's encounter with a secret, romantic, and soon-to-die lover is convincing: a nonromanticized Jane with a nonexistent lover. His additional account of Jane's twelve-hour engagement to a bumbling landowner is dramatic. The brevity of her engagement, Nokes argues from Austen's fragmentary *The Watsons* (1923), was due to Cassandra's interference and Jane's sense of art rather than prudence. We also have a rather sad if not self-deceived Jane, when she was almost forty years old, falling for her niece's apothecary.

After the death of Cassandra's fiancé, neither sister saw herself as the other's rival. This was the basis of their friendship. Recent suggestions of an irregular emotional attraction between Jane and Cassandra are firmly ignored.

The high wit, style, and sensibility of Jane Austen proceeded from her early exposure to her maternal uncle's family; his wife, Philadelphia; and later Elizabeth, Jane's cousin. Trying unconvincingly to keep Jane firmly in Hampshire, Myer plays this down. Austen's world, as Nokes ably demonstrates, was wider than a parsonage. Elizabeth marries a comte and names their eldest child "Hastings"; the comte is arrested by the Committee of Public Safety, denounced by his mistress, and later guillotined.

His wife flees to Calais, where her newborn dies, and then escapes to England. Jane's dislike of republics and of France becomes understandable.

At Elizabeth's house in London, Jane, too rational for romance and too confined by Hampshire, learns "the racy idioms of society flirtations" and the "dangerous excitement of sexual deceit." And the comte's relic sounds like an independent Austen heroine: soon after her widowhood she concludes that "independence and the homage of half a dozen are preferable to subjection and the attachment of a single individual." Yet at thirty-six she will marry Jane's brother Henry, her junior by ten years. Given the priggishness of some of Jane's brothers and their wives, Elizabeth came as a relief to Jane, and given Cassandra's dullness, she comes as a relief in Nokes's biography, which makes it clear that it was Cassandra, the letter burner, who made Jane a sainted mystery.

Nokes argues and establishes—sometimes in tedious detail—that Jane was not just a novelist. He is good on Jane's early, unpublished fiction: she wrote to shock. Her comic history of England, written when she was fifteen years old, shatters historical myth as her novels attack social pretense. She can even joke about James I's awareness of the "keener penetration" of male friendship. Young Jane is widely read in Henry Fielding's *Tom Jones* (1749), Matthew Gregory Lewis's *The Monk* (1796), and obscure lady novelists of the late eighteenth century, and so is Nokes. Consequently, he sees Austen satirizing Richardson's *Sir Charles Grandison* (1753–1754), not being enamored of it, as Myer insists. Further, Austen held a fine contempt for Hannah More's *Coelebs in Search of a Wife*.

Nokes's literary criticism is light: he defends *Mansfield Park* (1814) but is best on *Persuasion* (1818). A sign of a good biography is to increase not simply the reader's knowledge but his enjoyment of the text. Nokes's readers will reread her novels.

Jonathan Keates, a music critic and novelist, follows Stendhal's final words, "lived, loved, wrote," in his fine biography *Stendhal* (Carroll and Graf). Stendhal wrote his epitaph in Italian some twenty years before his death. Keates's work records the career of Marie Henri Beyle (1783–1842), a man of humane curiosity. This Stendhal is a European figure whose journalism was English, whose sensibility was eighteenth-century French, and whose emotional homeland was Italy.

Eschewing ponderous documentation, Keates has wisely used the masses of material published since 1979, but he can't refuse funny footnotes: a paste of olive oil and tarantula ashes rubbed on the big toe of the right foot will maintain a permanent erection. A novelist writing a biography of another biographer has an immediate advantage: he goes for coherent narrative and judges the value of the work as a fellow practitioner. Keates's biography reads like a civilized novel. It is not a psychological biography; the women that may underlie the novels are not excessively investigated. Nor is it properly literary: Stendhal's two most-read works, *The Red and the Black* (1831) and *The Charterhouse of Parma* (1839), do not appear until the last sixth of this *Life*.

Keates maintains that English readers are still puzzled by novels in which romanticism remains equivocal and a novelist whose life doesn't fit over his works as well as many would desire. Stendhal remained indifferent to theories of the novel and other novelists; he wrote well because he read widely in history, social sciences, art, and philosophy—but not, fortunately, Keates implies—in other novelists.

To explain Stendhal, the biographer has given us his childhood in provincial Grenoble, a frugal if not cheap father, a sympathetic sister, a loathsome religious aunt who replaced his mother and then died before she could do more harm. But his grandfather encouraged his intellectual curiosity so that his early reading in the works of John Locke, Thomas Hobbes, and Helvétius later precluded extreme romanticism. Throughout Stendhal's life he kept his distance from the cult of sensibility even when he encountered it, in bed, in Silesia, where he seems to have sired a bastard girl. As a ten-year-old he rejoices at King Louis XVI's execution but invariably found revolutionaries dull and grubby.

Stendhal's first affair, when he was fourteen, was with an actress and singer. Keates sees that this merging of aesthetics and erotics at an early age anticipates Stendhal's later concerns. When he was twenty-five, he spent twice as much on "entertainments, books, and girls" than on housing. At age sixteen he fled to Paris in 1799 and became the protégé of his cousin, Noël Daru, Napoleon's secretary for war. Six years later Stendhal would idealistically but unsuccessfully woo Daru's wife, who figures vitally in his journals for 1810–1811. The Daru connection helped his career and got him stationed in Milan all too briefly. Stendhal's Italy became a land of eroticized aesthetics: love and music, affairs, and La Scala. The Milan of the early 1800s was, and would remain during his second visit ten years later, an intellectually hospitable and artistically alive city—perhaps the most exciting in Europe, Keates claims.

Taking a commission, Stendhal left Milan for Vienna, fought in the 1809 Bavarian campaign, and contracted syphilis, which may have hastened his death at the age of fifty. The horrors of the retreat from Moscow show a Stendhal of understated courage and dignity who provided for his men. A third of the way through this biography Napoleon falls, and Stendhal, back in Milan, is about to publish his first work: undistinguished and plagiarized lives of Joseph Haydn and Wolfgang Amadeus Mozart. Yet his early works reveal what Henry James valued in him, "the restlessness of a superior mind." James meant sensibility. Keates demonstrates that Stendhal can think as well as feel. The biographer locates the first appearance of analytic superiority in Stendhal's *On Love* (1822), a work marked by honesty, diffidence, and self-reproach and the book that best prepares readers for the novels. It also documents a three-year unconsummated passion for the marmoreal Matilde Visconti Dembowski.

Keates has conscientiously located his subject's liaisons as far as he can and as many as he can—often a shadowy list of single mothers, provincial actresses, and London whores. But he refrains from identifying the idealized lovers, surrogate mothers, and substitute sisters of Stendhal's novels with the appropriate Euro-mistress, whether she be a Gina Pietragrua, Mina von Griesheim, or Mélanie Guilbert. By the time Stendhal is twenty-seven years old he acts out a love affair as though it were part of a novel. Stendhal survives the "perpetual ambiguities of adult relationships." When he falls in love for the last time, he knows it's the last time. But unlike Horace, who looked back, Stendhal wished to re-create his love of twenty years earlier with Matilde.

Appointed to the consular corps by Louis Philippe in 1830, he was posted to Trieste, where Austrian authorities objected to his politics. He was permanently banned from his beloved Milan, where he often fell in love and once met Byron. Bored and fat, he spent most of his last years as consul at Civitavecchia before dying in Paris. Readers will be disappointed that this work has no pictures of him, his lovers, or the places he lived.

Did Byron (1788–1824) ever seek a wife? Two years after his birth, his paternal aunt and uncle consummated an incestuous passion; when he was twenty-six years old, his half sister, a "narcissistic projection" of himself, bore his child—who would have three children by her own brother-in-law. And in between there were young men from Harrow, gondoliers from Venice, and swains in Albania.

This is the stuff of sensation, and the natural temptation is to treat it sensationally. Phyllis Grosskurth does so in her *Byron: The Flawed Angel* (Houghton Mifflin) from the very beginning. Her prologue introduces Lord Clare, a friend from Harrow whom Byron meets and then ambiguously embraces in October 1821 as he travels to Bologna. But when we see the two again, almost four hundred pages later

and after a brief look at Harrow in 1814, it wasn't worth the wait.

Documentation for some of Grosskurth's assertions can be garnered from that in Louis Marchand's three-volume *Life* (1957). The publication of twelve volumes of Byron's letters has given her almost too much material. Too often Grosskurth's scandalous assertions are simply that, as she presents a series of young men from Harrow to Missolonghi, his mother's infatuation with twenty-three-year-old Lord Grey (who may have tried to sodomize him), the certainty of the affair with his half sister Ada, and their resulting child. Then we're told that Byron wasn't even highly sexed; his debaucheries were sporadic; and were he living today he could have had bisexual affairs to fill "the emptiness of an aching heart."

The biographer plumbs Byron's early psyche and finds that his passion for boys re-creates ideal father-son relationships and that his tantrums with his lovers (of either sex) reenact his relationship with his mother, from whose fatness he could separate himself only by dieting. Her death, more than those of four beautiful young men who also die when he returned to England, created the Byronic persona of the Man of Sorrows. This might be convincing, except the Byronic persona exists, before Byron's return, in the first cantos of *Childe Harold* (1812).

Grosskurth also presents another scholar's medical reason for all this: manic depression rather than schizophrenia. She also maintains that the influence of his nanny, Mary Grey, has been exaggerated: she didn't sexually corrupt the preteen and didn't introduce him to Calvinism. Yet we learn that, two decades later, Byron is beset with Mary Grey's Calvinist notions when he sleeps with his sister after his marriage, and in 1821 *Cain* allowed him an outlet against Mary's cruel Calvinistic God.

Byron's courtship of Annabella Millbanke is the best feature of this *Life*. The "flaw" to Byron implicit in this book's title first occurs here: the marriage was miserable. As Grosskurth did with the material at the London Library in her earlier biography of John Addington Symonds, she has found new information on Byron that, from months of reading the Lovelace material at the Bodleian Library, she turns into one hundred pages and seventy-five footnotes.

These chapters are the best in the biography. This Annabella, doomed and dithering, pursued Byron, but her list of what she wanted in a husband defines what Byron was not. Byron, a mixture of panic and insouciance, married for money, companionship, and salvation; his sister Augusta encouraged him in order to protect their reputations; Lady Melbourne encouraged her niece's marriage, for it would calm the fires of incest. By November 1815 Annabella could list her husband's chief marital fault: ennui.

The biographer's shocking account suggests—rather unconvincingly since Grosskurth has to rely on Annabella's vindictive depositions (as long as they're "vivid" and have "the ring of truth to them")—that Annabella began to suspect the incest the night after their nuptials, that the first three weeks of their honeymoon reveal a man tortured by his homosexuality and his incest, and that Augusta admitted to incest in September 1816. The consequence? Annabella's aim in life was now to humiliate and destroy Augusta. The alliance between Augusta and Annabella seems odd, and the alliance between Augusta and Byron probably incestuous. After the birth of this supposititious child Grosskurth says Byron put Augusta out of his mind, but two chapters later he admits that the child is his daughter. (Byron was probably being Byronic.) This new information about the marriage is valuable; readers may draw different conclusions.

After this the *Life* becomes rushed, as Byron scurried from England. Grosskurth presents him at his honest worst with Allegra, his daughter by Claire Claremont, the stepsister of Shelley's Mary and a woman who, "avid for excitement," had approached Byron. He eventually stored the child in a convent so that he could pursue Countess Teresa Guiccioli, another woman who was to save him from himself. Grosskurth's Teresa is not the sentimental woman of her memoirs but a manipulative, jealous, deceitful—yet devoted—one. Byron's last years in Venice ("he went native with a vengeance"), Ravenna, Pisa, and Genoa are crowded: Allegra dies; Shelley, who has been reading Plato's *Ion* and *Phaedo* and perhaps become homosexually attracted to Byron, dies; and Byron dies.

Grosskurth is good with the early Byron abroad: initially he preferred the Turk to the Greek; his attitude toward Lord Elgin would change; *Childe Harold* finds its context. Byron's timing was perfect: Albania was a hot topic when his first cantos appeared. *Don Juan* (1819–1824), however, is shortchanged, and that a poet is more magnanimous in his persona than in his life should not come as a surprise to a biographer. Byron's life will remain sensational, but there is little reason to natter about the "droit de seigneur" when it comes to a servant girl. It is inaccurate to speak of the "enormity" of his debts, redundant to call Lord and Lady Byron "self-absorbed narcissists," pretentious to correct a harm-

less citation to Horace, and silly to have two boys who are both "nubile."

Much is known about Byron's youth, but as John Chapple admits in his *Elizabeth Gaskell: The Early Years* (Manchester University Press), the first twenty-two years of the life of Elizabeth Cleghorn Stevenson (1810–1865) before she married the Reverend William Gaskell will remain dark. She left no early letters, and her later ones that Chapple co-edited say little about her youth. If she kept a travel journal as her cousins did, it hasn't survived; her own daughters knew little of their mother's premarital life.

So how has Chapple turned what doesn't exist into nearly five hundred pages? Perhaps one-fifth of this work is the life of Mrs. Gaskell; the rest is a "study of *race, milieu,* and *moment.*" This gives the reader not the life she had, but the life she probably lived in the larger context of late-eighteenth- and early-nineteenth-century Britain, and specifically the Britain of upper-middle-class Unitarians. What we never see is Gaskell the writer who, twelve years after she "dwindled into" her husband's life, arose to become the author of *Mary Barton* (1848) and *North and South* (1855), the contributor to Charles Dickens's *Household Words,* and the biographer of Charlotte Brontë in 1857. To re-create Gaskell's life the biographer must "deliberately refrain from using her creative works." His index has only six main references for the ostensible subject of the biography, but twenty-two for members of the Stevenson family; eighteen for her maternal family, the Hollands; eight for her father's in-laws, the Thomsons; and twenty-three for her husband's family.

The events of her young life are unexceptional. William, her father and a former Unitarian minister, after the death of his wife sends his one-year-old daughter from London to live with her maternal aunt in Knutsford. She receives a liberal education; her father's remarriage creates problems; and her brother vanishes at sea. She remains with her father until his death in 1829, returns to Knutsford, and marries in 1832.

But for each of these events we have exceptionally massive contexts. Wills, letters of relations, unknown novels, parish registers, reforms in the apothecary trade—all accumulate in this detailed history of Gaskell's times. William Stevenson's Unitarian career leads to a discussion of Socinianism, a discourse on the beliefs of Samuel Taylor Coleridge, and an analysis of compensation for clergy. After Stevenson left the ministry and settled briefly in Edinburgh, we have the Scottish Enlightenment and the foundation of the *Edinburgh Review.* His patron, Lord Lauderdale, disappointed by not being appointed governor general of India, nevertheless rewards the faithful William with the post of keeper of records at the treasury in London. All this means politics.

Every event has its associative context, but often the context is inchoate: Elizabeth can vanish for seventy pages at a stretch. What surfaces occasionally is a young, well-connected, and intelligent woman widely traveled in Britain and about to experience the suffering of nineteenth-century Manchester, a metropolis that was, incredibly, only twelve miles from eighteenth-century Knutsford.

The lives of a compassionate clergyman, his three famous daughters, and his unfortunate son are also done, but it took just over one thousand pages in Juliet Barker's *The Brontës* (St. Martin's Press). Readers can now return to the extraordinary novels and remarkable poems and no longer feel obligated to infest Yorkshire with paid tours of "Brontë Country" in order to see where Barker spent six years as the curator of the Parsonage Museum in Haworth, a remarkable town intellectually and industrially. It was not some Byronic moor with bad sewers, bad weather, and worse people; its parsonage was austere but not poor.

Had the Irish-born Patrick accepted a chaplaincy in Martinique, English literary history would not have been the same. Instead, this hardworking man with connections to the evangelical Clapham Sect, a liberal who supported the Reform Bill of 1831 and opposed the Poor Laws, buried three children in nine months, settled in a decent-sized town to raise six children, and shortly became a widower. The childhood of the Brontës, even with a dead mother, was normal; that their forty-seven-year-old father would send them to a boarding school was not peculiar. True, they read a lot, but they weren't child prodigies, and what they read the most was *Blackwoods* and children's works. Their father played with them, and he and his wife encouraged them to write. His own poems would influence his son's and daughters'.

All this is not the accepted picture, as a quick perusal of standard reference works shows, works that now must be radically revised. To grasp the extent of Barker's revisions, scan her text for the word *tradition* or look for references to Elizabeth Gaskell in the index. Gaskell's *Life of Charlotte Brontë* (1857) distorted the life of Charlotte (1816–1855) and distressed those of her surviving father (who knew Gaskell's other novels) and her husband. Barker gives an emotionally compact family but refuses to discover deep, psychic, or weird autobiographical truths in their fiction. She has read local newspapers

of the time and consulted the manuscripts in over eighty archives whenever possible.

And not just those newspapers. Branwell (1817–1848) left one tutoring position after six months—not to follow Coleridge's advice to pursue literary efforts, not because he was discovered drunk on the job, but because he sired a child by one of three possible servants. The servant and any legendary issue are thoroughly pursued through registers and census returns.

Barker has delved, perhaps at too great a length, into her subjects' juvenilia, especially Branwell's. Much has been made of Charlotte and Emily's early secret plays, but they were confidential because they excluded Branwell and Anne from joint composition—not because they contain pubescent sexual matter. Barker's new Brontës are not a dysfunctional family, but a loving one of sometime unlovable members. Anne (1829–1849), about whom we know the least and whose unorthodox *Agnes Grey* is prophetic of woman's rights, is merely dull in Gaskell's *Life,* but here she is practical and devoted. Emily (1818–1848), about whom we know a little more, now obsessively rereads her adolescent poems and is terrified of leaving a home where she is tenderly loved by her father. Her poetry is not that of a mystic, and her emotions are not exhausted in writing *Wuthering Heights.* Nor did the reviews of that novel discourage her from planning a second novel, one whose (incomplete?) manuscript Charlotte destroyed.

Charlotte is no longer the martyr who sacrificed her literary career but too often a flirt possessed of an acerbic and cruel sense of humor. She failed to see the merits of Anne's *The Tenant of Wildfell Hall* (1848). The Lowood School of her *Jane Eyre* (1847) is grim but representatively grim, as Barker shows from comparisons with other schools. But to Charlotte, away from home for the first time since her mother's death, the school became in her perception a prison that deliberately killed her two elder sisters and once again orphaned her, Emily, and Branwell (but not Anne, the youngest and most sensible daughter). To excuse Charlotte's *écriture* to Victorian readers, Gaskell blamed them on her father.

This biography puts the men back on the pedestal where they belong although Branwell takes a dive. Barker demonstrates that the male Brontës are not the pistol-shooting, drunken wild men of Gaskell's grim and deserted landscape. Nor was Charlotte the martyr to domestic toil. The twenty-eight-year-old Branwell, as Barker shows from new evidence, was not dismissed from yet another tutoring post at the Robinsons', where Anne also taught, because he forged his employer's signature or, worse, corrupted one of his charges, but because for two years he had a not-quite-unrequited passion for the forty-three-year-old mother of his pupils.

Branwell encouraged his sisters' writing, and he was, if not the cause, at least the catalyst in the printing of their novels and poetry. He thought of publication first, and Charlotte "accidentally" (the word is hers) came across Emily's poetry. The rest is history, but now a revised history expertly present in this essential study.

In 1850 an American novelist, having made a brief tour of Europe and England and being aware that he needed to save money for his wife and child, decided to return to New York not on a fast steamer but by sail. During this voyage of five and one-half weeks Herman Melville (1819–1891) decided on his next book, one that would be as informative as his successful *White-Jacket* (1850) and as literary as his misunderstood *Mardi* (1849). Hershel Parker asserts this convincingly in the first of two volumes, *Herman Melville: A Biography, 1819–1851* (Johns Hopkins University Press). This one ends with Nathaniel Hawthorne scanning the author's dedication to him on the title page of that new novel, *Moby-Dick; or, The Whale* (1851). Parker tells a story adroitly, with a mastery of scholarship unprecedented in Melville studies. He surpasses what Livingston Lowes did for Coleridge; he presents not just the reading or the sources but the life of an American writer and his country in the first half of the nineteenth century.

Two essential genealogical charts help the reader to keep Melville's family straight. Parker emphasizes their fall from a heroic colonial past in which one grandmother still spoke Dutch and a grandfather helped dump the tea in Boston harbor. Financially the family crashed three times and moved as often. The last twenty-five years have brought masses of family letters to light, and Parker has used them all—sometimes overused them, for example, in his hunt for a spurious illegitimate half sister.

Melville remembered his father for the elegance of his language, but his financial incompetence meant that Herman had little formal schooling. After his father died in 1832, his elder brother, Gansevoort, became head of the family and Melville's intellectual mentor; as secretary to the American legation in London, Gansevoort found him an English publisher for *Typee* in 1846. These family details, along with Melville's experience in what were then the hinterlands, show the novelist as an American aware of his heroic past, searching for a heroic future, and all the while trying to support his family.

Dust jacket for the first volume of the biography, published by Johns Hopkins University Press

English reviewers accused Melville of exaggerating or even faking his South Seas adventures in *Typee* and *Omoo* (1847). But Parker's immersion in primary sources (ships' logs, letters, and contemporary accounts) validates his subject's strictures on the political and sexual intrusions of missionaries. American reviewers agreed with the English about the missionaries, but they were not initially outraged by Melville's dalliance with Fayaway. By 1847 Melville had become, in Parker's words, "the first American author to become a sex symbol," damned for the licentiousness of his book, which hinted at the author's sexual depravity. And all this just before his wedding to the daughter of the chief justice of the Massachusetts Supreme Court.

Worried about the publicity, Elizabeth Shaw, his fiancée, avoided a public church wedding. The second volume of this *Life* is already written, and readers can anticipate learning how Elizabeth stood in Fayaway's shadow both before and after her marriage and why she thought her husband to be mad.

Readers who cavil at the cetological chapters of *Moby-Dick* may feel (insofar as they confuse the unity of art with the untidiness of life) that Parker is opulent with information: ten pages of the manuscript changes in *Typee,* letters that were concerned with the failed marriage of a Rensselaer cousin and eventually inherited by the consort of Edith Wharton, smoked salmon for an exorbitant fifteen cents a pound. These facts delay rather than impede the narrative. The same is true of the extensive lists of what Melville borrowed from libraries ashore and read aboard ship.

Exactly how such reading shaped what he wrote remains unclear in this biography, but Melville's reaction to his audience is clear: he honed his narrative skills by telling yarns to fellow sailors after his enlistment in the U.S. Navy. The skepticism that greeted the facts of *Typee* and *Omoo* convinced him he might as well write a romance, and he did–the difficult *Mardi.*

When that failed to please, he reverted to the quasi-autobiographical *Redburn* (1849). Again disappointed, he left New York City's literary feuds and moved to the Berkshires, where, mulling a new sort of novel, he met Nathaniel Hawthorne. The meticulous chronology of these final one hundred pages documents Hawthorne as the catalyst who, surprised at Melville's praise in *Mosses from an Old Manse,* was further surprised to read an American novel like nothing else to that time.

Melville gave readers the middle oceans of his time; George Eliot (1819–1880) gave them the Midlands of an earlier generation; and Rosemary Ashton's *George Eliot: A Life* (Penguin) is best at chronicling the voyage of a mind trapped, as her characters were, between two worlds. Eliot was caught between the radicalism of her ideas, her nontraditional private life, and her need to be accepted in London society.

This biography will almost replace Gordon Haight's 1968 work. Ashton has written an admirable, fat, and indulgent biography. She assumes, correctly, that her readers are interested in her subject's writings and the life that created them; Eliot's life, works, and letters (lots) intertwine. Ashton implies that Eliot is the best novelist of her nation and her century. She was certainly one of the most intellectually acute, and Ashton's recent biography of Eliot's consort, George Henry Lewes, has served her well. At least this Eliot is not last year's prophetess of Modernism.

Ashton postpones discussion of Eliot's publishing career until halfway through her biography, and this allows for a gradual development of Eliot's intellectual growth. Ashton's summaries of Eliot's early and continuing articles for the *Westminster Review* are succinct, her analyses astute. Eliot's famili-

arity with English and Continental scholarship of the times is wide ranging. When she decides not to go to church in 1842, we see it as the product of friendship and vast reading. In 1838 Charles Hennell's theological conclusions in his *Inquiry* matched those of Strauss's earlier *Das leben Jesu.* But the Germanless Hennell had done it on his own and was the brother-in-law of Charles Bray, who was Eliot's first intellectual mentor and through whom she met Ralph Waldo Emerson, J. A. Froude, Herbert Spencer, and Harriet Martineau.

The biographer has a surer hand with her subject's intellectual than with her emotional life. Charles Bray, like Lewes, her later companion, also had an irregular erotic life. Ashton has established that the unconventionality of Eliot's life began, intellectually and socially, before her move to London in 1851. This is an important point and is better treated than the confused ménage with her publisher, John Chapman, the same year.

Ashton treats the affair with excessive sympathy for Eliot but none for Chapman. She has decoded and restored those entries in his diary that record his erotic confusion. A few years later when she ran away with the unhappily married George Henry Lewes, her early friends and many London intellectuals took what the biographer calls the "high moral line" and cut her. Ashton is as indignant at their disapproval as they were of Lewes and Eliot's open adultery. She further argues that Eliot's later odd marriage to a man more than twenty years younger than she would not look so peculiar had we more of her new husband's letters. Ashton's treatment of this is not convincing.

Eliot came to vindicate the "special circumstances" of her alliance with Lewes in her subsequent novels and essays, but some Victorian readers became more aware of her sanctimoniousness than her fellow feeling. Her novels did sell, and while Ashton is good with details of publishing history, reception, and finances (Lewes became her agent), she doesn't investigate the extent to which Eliot's radical ideas could sell her fiction. The biography's thirty-one illustrations are an agreeable surprise: they include one commissioned by Victoria herself–of a simpering Hetty and a nonthreatening, almost epicene Captain Donnithorne.

Melville once wrote that the best places are not on any maps; Jules Verne (1828–1905) would agree but add that they're also the most profitable. Yet as Herbert R. Lottman makes clear in the epilogue to his *Jules Verne: An Exploratory Biography* (St. Martin's Press), Verne was more than a successful writer. He was a cultural force that guided Richard Byrd to the North Pole (*The Adventures of Captain Hatteras,* 1864), put William Beebe in a bathysphere (*Twenty Thousand Leagues Under the Sea,* 1869), and bemused James Lovell aboard *Apollo 8 (From the Earth to the Moon,* 1865). Both Werner von Braun and Michel Foucault read him attentively. His novels—on the big screen—also enriched Hollywood. In 1994 a rediscovered novel, *Paris in the Twentieth Century,* became a best-seller in France and has been published by Random House in the United States.

This popular biography brings Verne from the dark side of the moon, where he has his own crater, to English readers. Many letters to his publisher survive, but not so many to his family. The consequence was that the family biographer, Marguerite Allote de la Fuÿe, assembled, invented, and reworked events of her ancestor's life in her 1953 biography. These apocryphal stories are repeated here but corrected, as are the wilder psychological speculations of French biographers.

Verne grew up in Nantes, was admitted to the Paris bar, and wrote five dreadful early plays and some librettos for ten years while speculating as a stockbroker. In 1857 he married a widow worth eight hundred thousand dollars. His first literary success, *Five Weeks in a Balloon,* sold seventy-six thousand copies in 1862. In that same year he met his publisher, Pierre-Jules Hetzel, and they became a "perfect symbiosis." Hetzel could edit and insist on the right mixture of erudition; Verne would listen. Hetzel wanted three books a year for six years and control of the copyright; Verne signed. Hetzel even changed plots: the original Nemo was a Pole wanting vengeance on France's ally, Russia—and that would have to go. Verne complied. Hetzel marketed him well but, giving him perhaps no more than fifty thousand dollars a year, also underpaid him.

Verne hit upon a formula that worked: the imaginative hero, his skeptical double, the clever manservant—but no romance: the very word *love* frightened him in writing: Phineas Fogg is proposed to by Mrs. Aouda. The anti-Semitic passages that disfigure his later works, Lottman argues, are unfortunately typical of Verne's time.

The novelist's timing was perfect. Major discoveries of the nineteenth century could be explained in family magazines like those in which Verne's novels serially appeared. The books—typical nineteenth-century faux luxury books with bindings of pressed cloth pretending to be morocco, gilt, and good pictures—were what an uncle would give a favorite nephew. Of the thirty plates in Lottman's work, fifteen are of these illustrations.

Verne turned out his best work between 1862 and 1872, and, like Dickens, he could write two novels at once. Verne had his science checked by outside experts, and the sources for his novels are varied but rarely include personal experience: he never got farther north than Norway, farther south than the Riviera (too sunny for him). James Fenimore Cooper provided narrative frames. Then there was Poe's influence. George Sand suggested the setting of *Twenty Thousand Leagues Under the Sea* (1870), but Verne's brief trip to America aboard the luxurious *Great Eastern* in 1867 gave him ideas for the indulgent comforts of Captain Nemo. Is the fictional Nemo the increasingly reclusive and unhappily married Verne, as some have speculated? Lottman refuses to speculate. *Twenty Thousand Leagues Under the Sea* sold fifty thousand copies; his earlier *Illustrated Geography of France and Its Colonies* (1868) and a history of explorers from Hanno to Columbus were equally successful.

By 1870 Verne was alienated from his wife and kept an apartment in Paris. Turning forty-two, the beginning of middle age, and being prosperous and French, he seems to have had a series of affairs with exotic women. This may be, the biographer suggests, reading the works back into the man. Verne is more passionate in his anger at his unstable son, whom he later sent off to sea and whose first wife he paid off.

His 1871 move to Amiens isolated him from Paris, yet there he wrote his biggest seller, *Around the World in Eighty Days* (one hundred thousand copies). Again like Dickens, he turned the novel into a play and made twenty-five thousand dollars. The American performances added one of P. T. Barnum's elephants. In this decade peculiar allegations, quickly dismissed by Lottman, begin to surface: he fell in love with the teenage Aristide Briand, a future prime minister. And peculiar events: his nephew shot him in the leg. The conclusion of later critics (that it was a crime of gay passion) is rejected. The nephew was unstable—that's it.

Lottman recounts the plots of those novels that we probably will never read: *The Jangada* (codes and the Amazon), *Kereban the Inflexible* (the Bosporus), and *Dick Sands, a Fifteen-Year-Hero.* But others might engage a modern reader. Verne turned *Michael Strogoff* (1876), a modern odyssey set in czarist Russia as Tartars invade Siberia, into a play that brought him six hundred thousand dollars in 1881. Indiana Jones and Captain Kirk may have replaced Nemo, but the *Nautilus* travels to better places than the *Enterprise* does.

In 1929 the best-sellers in America were Sinclair Lewis's *Dodsworth* and Erich Maria Remarque's *All Quiet on the Western Front.* The Pulitzer, however, went to Julia Mood Peterkin's *Scarlet Sister Mary,* which won because it was one of the first to show the culture of plantation blacks, a culture not only in decline, but separate from whites. This makes Peterkin (1880–1961) more than a regional novelist. The title of Susan Millar Williams's *A Devil and a Good Woman, Too: The Lives of Julia Peterkin* (University of Georgia Press) is from Peterkin's judgment of a favorite black servant, Mary Weeks, whose life provided the basis for the novel.

Peterkin tended to elaborate on, if not lie about, her life. But Williams, who grew up in South Carolina, has mastered her subject by examining all Peterkin's works—novels, sketches, lectures, interviews with survivors, new caches of letters.

The biography begins awkwardly with Peterkin brooding about her marriage in 1903. Only later do we have her split family: some fled Sherman; others, the Moods, were Methodists and were opposed to slavery. Williams arranges the biography this way to demonstrate how Peterkin, attentive to the stories of her one hundred servants and field hands, decided to be more than the mistress of a decaying, weevily plantation. She was forty and decided to write.

The itinerant Carl Sandburg encouraged the sketches of this "Turgenev of the plantation niggers." She pushed for his assistance and then flattered H. L. Mencken, who found her Gullah difficult and her plots gruesome (a rooster pecks out a child's eye; a child inadvertently gives his grandfather caustic soda). But Mencken approved of anything that might outrage the South, so the *Richmond Reviewer* published her first story in 1921 and then his *Smart Set* published another.

By 1925 Knopf had issued a small volume of her short stories, *Green Thursday,* and readers couldn't tell whether she was black or white. Williams sees "A Baby's Mouth," in which a newborn black child must have his mouth cut open, as freeing Peterkin. This was her first narrative from a black point of view, and this was her métier. She switched to Bobbs-Merrill for her first novel, *Black April,* in 1926. David Davidson, a founder of *The Fugitive,* regarded it as "the first genuine in English novel of the Negro as a human being."

By 1927 Peterkin was famous and an expert whose inconsistent advice to blacks ("I am black, all except my skin") was to foster their racial pride. Peterkin doesn't deal with the anxieties of the middle-class black, as did writers of the Harlem Renaissance, but with plantation hands. The received writers dealt with Southern blacks only when those characters were black professionals. Williams also proves that Peterkin relied on research, not just oral history, for this and her novel *Scarlet Sister Mary* (1928).

Scarlet Mary has nine children by nine different fathers—and doesn't repent. This Mary was based on Peterkin's gardener and washerwoman, who was sexy, independent, and outspoken; she became even more so in the novel. In addition, the servant Mary bore two children to the brothers of Peterkin's husband, a fact excluded in the novel. Debating, but not deciding, whether the servant was raped, paid, or simply curious about sex, Williams is fair here. In any event, the servant left Peterkin's plantation, which, like other plantations, was disappearing as a social institution.

Scarlet Sister Mary was banned in Boston, and Peterkin's popular stories soon became proper and sentimental. She took a lover, Irving Fineman—an obscure, struggling, and younger novelist whom she had met on a cultural pilgrimage to Europe in 1927. Williams calls Fineman "callow, second-rate, and self-centered," and Peterkin's affair with him may have inspired the theme of escape in her next novel, *Bright Skin* (1932).

Bright Skin is a novel of "rejection, depression and exile"—and family connections too complicated by incest, abortions, and stillbirths to summarize. Hands flee the plantation culture for Harlem and then the homeland. Peterkin, Williams claims, was the first novelist to chronicle the gradual dissolution of the plantation. Preaching hatred, the most interesting hand returns from Africa via Marcus Garvey, and this offended many. Leftists saw her treatment of blacks who remained on the plantation as too sympathetic and not involved enough in the class struggle. Peterkin pays some scores against members of her family, but she lost not only money but also readers with this, her last novel.

Had she died in 1932, she would not have been so forgotten. The little that she wrote thereafter celebrated the good ol' days of the plantation. Williams's assessment of Peterkin's abilities may be too high; her insistence that Peterkin's fiction reflects her hatred of fathers, husbands, and sons is perhaps exaggerated. That she was gradually shut out from the African American community that had given her life "structure, language, and meaning" is arguable. But Williams does an excellent job in presenting a voice not heard in the Southern Literary Renaissance of Robert Penn Warren and Allen Tate.

A wealthy, upper-class anti-Semite escapes her family, joins the Church of Rome, and moves in with an older, successful lover who introduces her to London's literary set. But after writing some good volumes of minor verse, she deserts him for a younger lover. They live together for twenty years, both of them maltreating a child from the new partner's first marriage. Then, after having written a controversial novel at the age of fifty-four, she takes up with a virgin almost half her age, pays the rent, and buys the clothes. All the while her longtime partner remains faithful: after the novelist dies, he even disperses funds to the younger lover, as the will requires. This is the engendered life of Radclyffe Hall (1880–1943). Sally Kline's *Radclyffe Hall: A Woman Called John* (John Murray) comes close to success in her major biography.

She has located new letters from the participants, superbly used secondary material, and deftly drawn on current scholarship. Hall, aside from some letters to her last lover, Evgenia Souline, left little personal material. Until recently readers had to rely on the one-hundred-page memoir of a previous lover, Una Troubridge. Yet Kline succeeds in presenting Hall from the perspective of others and almost succeeds in persuading us that we should read her subject's other works.

The biography is organized by the years Hall spent with three major lovers: ten years with her mentor, Mabel "Ladye" Batten; twenty-eight with Una Troubridge (the last eight miserable), and four with Souline. Published drafts and fragments of short stories fill in an unhappy childhood. Hall was an "incest survivor" who seems to have been sexually abused at the age of eleven by her stepfather. She fled her "disturbed family" when she came of age and inherited her grandfather's fortune. She visited relatives in America, a grandmother serving as chaperon, and perhaps had a brief affair with a cousin. But her first serious liaison, when she was twenty-five, was with Violet Hunt, eighteen years her senior and the then syphilitic future lover of Ford Madox Ford. For Hunt it was an experiment; for Hall it was liberating.

Hall's income allowed her to subsidize her first long-term affair with Ladye, a fashionable singer who, at age fifty-one, was the first to return the twenty-seven-year-old Hall's passion and provide enough maternal and intellectual direction that the lost child became the "writer-woman." The death of Ladye's husband in 1910 allowed them to live together. But after six years, some stops in between, and initial literary successes Hall deserted Ladye for her first cousin, Una Troubridge. Hall may seem heartless, but Una's "was a younger mouth." Una's diaries are primary documents, and she destroyed some of the early ones. Kline has cut through Una's point of view and used Hall's fictions, especially *The Unlit Lamp* (1924), to provide, if not facts, at least cogent interpretations of their relationship.

Kline argues that this novel is her subject's best, and in examining Hall's early work she notes the influence of Robert Bridges and Robert Browning on her poetry. One poem, "The Blind Ploughman" from her fourth book of poetry (1913), became famous. By the end of World War I, Hall was an established literary figure among those who were once important—such as the novelist May Sinclair, who encouraged Hall to write fiction.

Most readers will focus on the sixty pages of "Crusade and Martyrdom, 1928–1933" to understand the furor over the muted lesbianism of *The Well of Loneliness*. Kline's presentation of the trial is clear and succinct. In three weeks *The Sunday Express* judged the novel as justifying "unutterable putrefaction" that was "more poisonous than prussic acid for a healthy boy or girl." Hall welcomed the storm. But her publisher, Jonathan Cape, called the government's bluff. Without telling Hall, he wrote to the home office and offered to withdraw the novel if officials there found it offensive. They did, and he had to.

Hall was furious. Though Cape had made earlier arrangements to print copies in Paris, his deviousness injured the subsequent court case. Kline's list of fainthearted litterateurs is sobering, as is the inclusion of the South Wales Miners' Federation among her supporters. The multifaceted sexualities of the Bloomsbury group prevented members of that contingent from supporting Hall publicly, and her intransigence irritated those still closeted. The biographer neglects Hall's confusion of inversion with freedom of the press and fails to see that *The Sunday Express* was attacking male homosexuality as much as female. In the United States, Knopf tried to insist that Hall be held personally responsible for any legal action.

Stephen, Hall's heroine in *The Well of Loneliness,* is born lesbian, but Hall believed that one can choose lesbianism "as an expression of feminism." Kline further argues that the presence of the born lesbian in Hall's novels was really a ruse to gain sympathy for the cause. The biographer sees *The Well of Loneliness* as more than "the lesbian novel" as its modern readers are "inheritors of her vision."

Hall saw events more in ethical than political terms: she pleaded for the beleaguered lesbian but had little sympathy for liberal causes. English ladies do not regulate their conduct in conformity with that of miners, she wrote as a "former suffragist" (during 1912) to the *Pall Mall Gazette,* and in 1939 she insisted that the Jews wanted to destroy Europe.

A biography like this, meticulously researched and sympathetic, has been needed for some years. Leonard Woolf's review of *The Well of Loneliness* faulted the novel for some of its propagandistic flaws. Some readers will think the same of this biography, and those interested in Souline and Hall will wish to read *Your John: The Love Letters of Radclyffe Hall* (New York University Press), edited by Joanne Glasgow as part of the series The Cutting Edge: Lesbian Life and Literature. Glasgow has admirably edited and annotated some 133 of Hall's 576 letters at the University of Texas.

The useful chronology in Joshua Rubenstein's *Tangled Loyalties: The Life and Times of Ilya Ehrenburg* (Basic Books) almost obscures the complexities of Ehrenburg (1891–1967) and his times. Rubenstein admits his problem: many Western and Soviet critics see Ehrenburg as Joseph Stalin's collaborator, the Jew who betrayed his people, a propagandist who distorted the truth, and a European expatriate rather than a great Russian. But to see this, his biographer argues, is to ignore the consistency with which Ehrenburg met the cataclysm of his country's history. Often he was independent of Stalin. He tried to record the anguish of the Holocaust. From abroad in *Izvestia* and on the front in *The Red Star* his words unified his people.

Rubenstein is to be praised for making the labors of recent Russian scholars available to English speakers. Chief among them is Boris Frezinsky, who has provided a commentary on Ehrenburg's memoirs, written a chronology of his life, and with Irina Ehrenburg is editing a new edition of her father's works. The biographer has interviewed many survivors, including the writer's daughter. The Hoover Institution, archives in Geneva, and unpublished memoirs contributed to the scholarship used in this biography.

Ehrenburg's memoirs, which he began to publish in 1960, are obviously apologetic and should be treated with due caution. The final volume wasn't allowed to be printed until 1990. Rubenstein notes that Ehrenburg's 1958 private statement that he would consider himself a Jew "as long as racists walk the earth" became, in the later memoirs, "as long as there was a single anti-Semite left on earth." But would he have written either during the Doctors' Plot of 1952? Wasn't he silent during the venomous attack on "Zionists" in 1948? These and similar questions raise doubts that will always remain, but Rubenstein has provided as many answers as possible in a comprehensive, tactful biography.

The public events of Ehrenburg's life—his early radicalism (he mocked, quit, and rejoined the Bolsheviks twice); his childhood friendship with Nikolai Bukharin; his being in bohemian Paris before the war with Amadeo Modigliani, Pablo Picasso, and Diego Rivera—are not in question. From 1924 to 1940 he lived mostly in Paris, covered Europe for *Izvestia,* supported the Non-Aggression Pact between Germany and the Soviet Union, but escaped Paris after the Nazi invasion to cover the war for *The Red Star.* At the end of the war he supported Stalin once again, wrote *The Thaw* (1954) after Stalin's death, and pushed for liberalization under Nikita Khrushchev and his successors. This is a biography that is sensitive to the winds of doctrine.

In Spain he reported a war George Orwell, Ernest Hemingway, and Simone Weil never saw; during the Purge he kept silent about the fate of his friend and mentor, Bukharin. But his later memoirs record his private tensions and assistance to Isaac Babel's widow. As the conduit for introducing Soviet literature to the West, the friend of the censured Zamyatin and others, he escorted André Malraux to the Writers' Conference of 1935, yet he excluded the Surrealists, whom he called "masturbators" and "sodomites." However, under some prodding, he made sure that Babel and Boris Pasternak would attend.

During the war he joined the Jewish Anti-Fascist Committee and somehow, unlike most members, escaped execution. In more than two thousand dispatches he taught the Russian soldier how to hate, even in defeat; then at the war's end he was rebuked for being too vengeful. He waffled on the establishment of Israel, yet his 1946 poem commemorating the massacre at Babi Yar anticipated Yevtushenko's more famous one of 1961. He defended the Soviet takeover of Eastern Europe and joined in Stalin's cult of personality. These are distasteful years to recall, and Rubenstein is mournfully dispassionate. But he also shows that Ehrenburg continued a dangerous friendship with the slandered Anna Akhmatova.

Only after Stalin's death did he publish *The Thaw,* but the novel anticipated Boris Pasternak and Aleksandr Solzhenitsyn. The early editions of his memoirs are more than circumspect about politics. His novels from the 1930s and later about automobile and shoe magnates are industrial soap operas; yet soldiers revered him, and Adolf Hitler vowed to hang him.

Ehrenburg's loyalties were always tangled, and his private life was equally tangled: as a husband he was not unfaithful but rather "never monogamous." Like a picky Frenchman, he despised the food of America during his postwar tour but hustled to acquire a Buick, a refrigerator, and a washing machine. Back in the Soviet Union he denounced "Deutschland-America." Rubenstein's Ehrenburg, however much he may have waffled out of "personal and professional necessity," remains an ambiguous hero who won the Stalin Prize for Literature.

"He believed in progress, in everything getting better. And look, they murdered the man," Ehrenburg remarked in 1964 of Babel (1894–1941) at the commemoration of his seventieth birthday, as Antonina Pirozhkova, Babel's widow, writes in her *At His Side: The Last Years of Isaac Babel* (Steerforth Press), a poignant, short recollection of her husband during 1932–1939. The last third of this slim, touching volume of 170 pages austerely records her painful attempts to unearth the date of his death and the cruelty of a government that, surely sadistically, pretended that Babel was still "alive in camps." Government officials even got someone to claim that he had seen Babel in reasonably comfortable circumstances in prison some twelve years after his death.

First published in censored form in 1972, this volume—a translation by Anne Frydman and Robert Busch of the full 1989 version—reads well. The Babel whose short stories have become models of ironic brevity doesn't appear here, but we can glimpse an intimate side of the writer working with others, his humane curiosity about farmworkers, his generosity, his pleasure in racing (reflecting his *Red Cavalry* stories), his devotion to writing, his love of mimicry. And there is his omnipresent merry irony: arrested at five o'clock in the morning, Babel asked one of his captors, "So, I guess you don't get much sleep, do you?"

Ehrenburg, who met Babel in Paris five years before his arrest, was one of the few who stood by Pirozhkova afterward. As usual, he sent money via his secretary rather than directly, but he did send money and helped to publish Babel's works. Pirozhkova was responsible for the collected edition of her husband's work in 1990, some twenty-five years after his "rehabilitation." Told repeatedly that there was a paper shortage, she retrieved what manuscripts survived (the ones taken by the NKVD vanished), tracked down family members from her husband's earlier marriages, and succeeded in forcing the authorities to publish.

Going upstairs (or downstairs) to escort a young woman (or he may have been going alone) to lunch (or perhaps dinner), Jorge Luis Borges (1899–1986) one Christmas Eve walked into a staircase window, cut his head, and suffered an aphasic septicemia so severe that he doubted his sanity. Only then did narrative writing take its midcentury revolutionary turn: he awoke, and realized that fiction is truth. This is James Woodall's argument in *Borges: A Life* (Basic Books). But it was also around the time that Borges's father died and he got his first

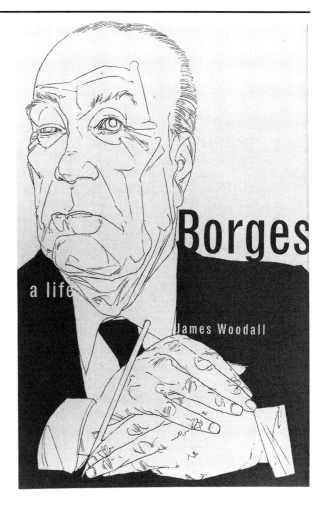

Dust jacket for the well-received biography of the Argentinian author

job: these last two facts, unlike his reconstruction of the accident on the way to a meal (Borges's account, his fiction of it, and his mother's report disagree), are not emphasized in this, the first biography written of Borges in English.

Woodall was impeded by copyright problems and missing or hidden caches of letters, but this is not, nor did he intend it to be, an official biography. It is a sympathetic working account that almost retains Borges's dignity as he became a cult figure in the 1960s.

From an Argentine family with an English overlay, nonaristocratic and mercantile, Borges after an isolated childhood spent the war years in Switzerland, where his ailing father had sought treatment for a blindness that would eventually afflict Borges. His father also inflicted sexual trauma on the seventeen-year-old Borges by insisting that the boy become a man by having sex with the father's mistress in a Geneva brothel. This "error of paternal judgment" prevented Borges's marital happiness—or so Woodall argues for thirty interesting pages that have a political twist.

Woodall convincingly argues that President Juan Perón, in addition to being an affront to Borges's imagination, stood for that emigrant gaucho class that murdered his heroic grandfather. Woodall's tepid explanation for Borges's later conservatism in the 1960s and 1970s is that he was "simply out of touch." He never liked Pablo Neruda but deplored García Lorca's murder during the Spanish civil war.

Borges's internationalism, which created his later fame, began when his family moved to Spain in the early 1920s and continued when they returned to Buenos Aires, where in 1934, amid a confusing welter of futurists, ultraists, and locals, Borges found his voice. Those early 1930s were difficult for him: his father died; he contemplated suicide; he got a civil-service job as a cataloguer; and he walked into that window. He also wrote journalism and began an early series of stories that became famous: *The Garden of the Forking Paths* (1939), which confused readers, and *Ficciones* (1944), which confused readers a little less. For most of his stories Woodall supplies brief plot summaries, insofar as they have plots. He praises Borges's prescience in realizing the inefficacy of the written word as early as 1939, some twenty years before the "1960s toiling campus critic" promoted deconstruction.

Except for a brief, unsuccessful marriage in 1967 to a woman he had met forty years earlier, Borges lived with his mother until her death. We get a better picture of him from Estela Canto, his unsatisfied companion of the 1940s. Woodall interviewed her some fifty years later and treats her recollections with a certain degree of skepticism. He also corrects an earlier psychoanalytic biography of a "camp follower," Emir Rodriguez Monegal.

By the 1940s Borges had a strong following in France; he had met his French translator in 1928, and when *El Aleph* (1949) along with his earlier *Ficciones* won the then-obscure Prix Formentor in 1960, his literary reputation grew quickly. The prize, sort of an alternative Nobel and almost a publisher's gimmick, secured his international reputation for what he had written during the previous thirty years. After 1954, Woodall admits, Borges wrote little of merit.

Sinecures followed his increasing fame. Perón's regime had promoted him to chief poultry inspector, surely a surreal transfer within the civil service, and the dictator's successors made Borges, nearly blind, the director of the national library, which he described as another surreal appointment:

"they handed me at one time 800,000 books and darkness." Then there was world travel and world translation. Borges made the cover of *Time* and in 1971 challenged an insulting Puerto Rican student at Columbia to a duel, but he never received the Nobel Prize (his politics were too conservative, Woodall suggests). Until the health of Borges's mother declined, she accompanied him on the lecture circuit; María Kodoma, his junior by half a century, later accompanied him, and shortly before his death Borges married her. Kodoma seems not to have been as helpful as Woodall would desire, but to call her "inscrutable" seems reductively insulting.

The end of Borges's life is one of diminished creativity ("sub-Borgean" is Woodall's euphemism) and international adulation. He died in Geneva: we get his polyglot epitaph on a tomb that could also record the title of doctor (honoris causa) fourteen times.

The early career of Evelyn Waugh (1903–1966) is treated tersely but thoroughly in the two hundred pages of John Howard Wilson's *Evelyn Waugh: A Literary Biography, 1903–1924* (Fairleigh Dickinson University Press). Wilson concedes that other lives are fuller, but he wishes to show how an understanding of what Waugh experienced at public school and Oxford became *Vile Bodies* (1930), *Black Mischief* (1932), and especially *Brideshead Revisited* (1928). In the last novel Waugh comes to terms with his Oxford experiences, both aesthetic and sexual. Wilson's arguments are dense; Waugh's diaries, which he revised, are judiciously corrected by appeal to contemporary accounts and archival material at the University of Texas. This can lead to overcitation as Wilson patches together the diaries and excerpts from *A Little Learning* (1964): forty-two quotation marks on one page make for an awkward narrative.

By age eight Waugh was a paranoid child, and he later came to see himself as a victim whose overdeveloped ego allowed him to overcome the physical, emotional, and intellectual difficulties of public school and college. We get much on his rebellious years at Lancing, a public school that appears only fitfully in his fiction but extensively in a posthumously published fragment that his publisher called "Charles Ryder's Schooldays" (1982). Insofar as they illuminate *Brideshead Revisited,* the Lancing years deserve the two chapters Wilson gives them: he argues convincingly that Waugh's classics master taught him the power of language and performance, and his classmate Francis Crease proved that the artist must work in dedicated isolation.

Waugh learned about sex, drink, and entertaining at Oxford. He hated his tutor, Cruttwell;

while Waugh was a student, he told vicious jokes against him, and as a novelist he slandered him. Wilson is almost just: Cruttwell was doing his job, but Waugh always needed a target, a pattern the biographer locates earlier at Lancing. Waugh's odious behavior was a way of praising and excusing himself. He became an ultra-Tory to scandalize others.

Waugh's vicious portrait of Oxford in *Decline and Fall* (1928) shows a university that failed to recognize his ability, and his Oxford journalism should not be dismissed as ephemeral: it prepares us for the later novels' exaggerated portrait of barbarians, philistines, and snobbish dons. Part of Waugh's skill is in the concrete details that create the painful nostalgia of his novels, and, unfortunately, Wilson slights Waugh's ability as a draftsman (for which he was recognized) at Oxford, an ability that led to one of his earlier works, a study of Dante Gabriel Rossetti (1928).

Having learned about the inadequacies of homosexuality (he never gave up drink and parties), Waugh left Oxford. Wilson corrects earlier biographies that downplay Waugh's homosexuality, especially Martin Stannard's 1987 volume. Waugh destroyed the diary he had kept at Oxford and never admitted having any homosexual affairs in his autobiography, but he wrote about these later in private letters. Waugh had two love affairs (not three as earlier thought), but Wilson sees these as acts of rebellion rather than evidence of male exclusivity. Wilson sees *Brideshead Revisited* resolving aesthetic and erotic tensions of Waugh's Oxford years, and his chronology presents this outline of Waugh's sexuality: 1922–1924, homosexual at Oxford; 1924–1926, bisexual; 1927, marriage (but tenuous because Waugh was still ambiguous). Wilson's analysis will confirm what readers have suspected, but the affair between Charles and Sebastian was less serious, less dangerous than Waugh's affair with Alastair Graham.

Isaac Bashevis Singer (1904–1991), who received the Nobel Prize in 1978 for writing in Yiddish, a language without a country, is treated affectionately in Dvorah Telushkin's often sorrowful *Master of Dreams: A Memoir of Isaac Bashevis Singer* (Morrow). From 1975 until his death Telushkin was Singer's secretary, answering letters, driving him about, and trying to run interference as kooks showed up. By the time she became his secretary Singer's major works had been written although these would be later translated by the biographer and her subject and published in English.

Telushkin does not cover Singer's early years in Poland, his arrival in America in 1935, or his infidelities and marriage. We do get flashbacks as

Dust jacket for the book about Nobel laureate Singer by his secretary

Singer reminisces to Telushkin, and these are quickly if reductively linked to his writings. He ran from both love and death when he left the threat of Hitler and the affection of his Polish lover, his cousin Esther. Perhaps to compensate, his stories reveal an indestructible rage and fierce bitterness against the promiscuous female.

The emotional immediacy of this biography is both its strong point and its weakness. Telushkin's chapters are short, well-told, three- to five-page anecdotes: a proper Barbra Streisand and *Yentl* (1983), Menachem Begin belittling Yiddish culture just before Camp David in 1978. Telushkin keeps his accent: Ve, as readers, vill not object. But we will object to clichés and overwriting that falls toward the mawkish.

Initially Singer comes across as a grandfather, a funny, acerbic grandfather who wrote stories that treated sadomasochism, and a vegetarian: "For the animals, everyday is Treblinka." This early portrait changes, as did Singer. His acerbic temperament became cruel; idiosyncrasy became mental confusion;

and almost indiscriminate goodwill became bitter suspicion. From 1976 to 1978 he got six hundred dollars a lecture; by 1986 he got six thousand dollars. His fame, as Telushkin shows, began to erode his existence: he read flattering reviews to all who would listen. The biographer, grieved by these painful changes, cannot record them dispassionately. The book begins and ends with the disposal of his effects: the manuscripts of the shtetl are now at Austin, Texas.

Joseph Blotner, the biographer and editor of William Faulkner, has given us a sympathetic if not benevolent life of another Southerner in *Robert Penn Warren: A Biography* (Random House). For this work Blotner uses extensive interviews with Warren (1905-1989), who was then in his seventies, and with his family, friends, and colleagues.

After Warren's brother put out the future writer's left eye with a piece of coal, there was to be no Annapolis for Warren, whose eyes always bothered him and kept him out of World War II. Instead of an admiral, the United States got a man of letters, a writer of novels, poetry, criticism, and drama. Only in the last could he be said not to have succeeded. And he did succeed: a Pulitzer Prize for *All the King's Men* in 1947, another in 1958 for *Promises* (poetry, 1954-1956), and yet a third in 1979 for *Now and Then* (poetry, 1976-1978). He was twice Consultant in Poetry to the Library of Congress, and his other recognitions include a Rhodes scholarship, two Guggenheim Fellowships, membership in the American Academy of Arts and Sciences, and a National Book Award. At the age of forty-four he got, in today's money, six hundred thousand dollars for the movie rights to *All the King's Men,* nearly as much for *Band of Angels* (1955) when he was fifty-one, and then the MacArthur Prize (three hundred thousand dollars) when he was seventy-six. It would be interesting to know the royalties that he shared with Cleanth Brooks for the various editions of their textbooks, including *Understanding Poetry,* which undergraduates, if they are lucky, are required to use. Blotner's biography is that of the almost-too-successful man of letters.

Obviously the South formed Warren. This becomes immediately apparent at Vanderbilt University, where he was taught by John Crowe Ransom, met the future poet Allen Tate, the future critic Cleanth Brooks, and discovered the poetics of T. S. Eliot's *The Waste Land* (1922). Vanderbilt inspired a sudden flowering of Warren's poetic abilities. The result was the literary circle and its journal, *The Fugitive,* that same year; the next year Warren attempted suicide, for obscure reasons.

California gave him an M.A. and a fiancée; New College gave him a B. Litt. His sense of region next appeared in the agrarian manifesto of 1930, *I'll Take My Stand.* That Blotner fails to comment on Tate's suggested title, "Tracts Against Communism," illustrates one of the faults of this work: a general unwillingness to comment on his subject's politics.

An appointment at Huey Long's Louisiana State University in 1935 led Warren and Brooks to found the influential *The Southern Review* (1935-1942), which ended in a contrived budget cut. But in collaboration with Brooks, Warren changed the teaching of English. Students then had no idea how to read. (They still may not: Warren walked out of his last class at Yale in 1973 when no one in his graduate seminar could recite a poem.)

Much of this biography, especially the second half, is taken up with quick critical comments on Warren's poetry and novels. Blotner is especially perceptive with *Brother to Dragons* (1953), which established his popular reputation as a poet just as *All the Kings Men* had established him as a novelist six years earlier. Contemporary critics see Warren's finest achievement in his later poetry, which they compare even to the late work of William Butler Yeats. Blotner, however much he might wish to agree, correctly sees that Warren's greatest success remains *All the King's Men,* the best of his ten novels.

Doris Lessing's *The Golden Notebook* (1962) has become almost the bible of the women's movement, but this was not the author's intention: such a reading is, in her words, "hysterical," for it focuses only on the female and the womb. "It's fascinating, reading about all those old times," Lessing was recently told. The second volume of her autobiography, *Walking in the Shade* (HarperCollins), gives us those times selectively from her arrival as a twice-divorced single mother in England in late 1949, when she was thirty, until 1962. It will be of more interest than her first volume: London is more interesting than the former Salisbury, Southern Rhodesia; disillusion with communism is more interesting than conversion to it; and *The Golden Notebook* is more interesting than her earlier works, which she covers very briefly. It will also provide an important and salutary outrage to currently fashionable beliefs.

The event that shaped her life began a year before her birth in 1919: World War I destroyed respect for government and provided the political milieu for fascism, national socialism, and, in Lessing's case, communism. The communists were the only sensitive, compassionate, socially concerned people she knew. They also, ignorantly or willfully, connived at Stalin's horrors, horrors that surpassed Hitler's. She admits that "the most neurotic act of my life" was in joining the party even when she had torments of doubt. Expanding on Arthur Koestler's 1941 *Darkness at Noon,* she concludes that the party was her church: a desacralized ideology of heaven, hell, the redeemed, and purgatory (the postwar purges). Hungary in 1956, the exposure of Stalin in 1956, and a new emotional focus in the mid 1950s were catalysts in her recantation of communism.

The Golden Notebook, then, is better seen as being not about women but about humanity. In writing it Lessing escaped from a package of false, sentimentally wrapped beliefs that include shreds of Jean-Jacques Rousseau, orts of Oliver Cromwell, and articles of faith from Karl Marx and Lenin. But the package is still, in 1997, sold and bought: the complacent beliefs in "God-is-dead, Science-is-king materialism," in deconstruction as more than an "intellectual game," and in the writer as someone caught in her times and not, in fact, inspired. If John Henry Newman's *Apologia pro Vita Sua* (1864), upon which this autobiography is probably modeled, is a "History of My Religious Opinions," Lessing's is one of her Material Opinions.

Thrice in her autobiography she interrupts her narrative to present Newman's equivalently changing creeds: these are, in italics, "Zeitgeist" sections, the climate of political opinions of her then co-religionists. This can seem arid, but she aims to record outward events as a framework into which she can fit her emotional life. Some readers may get less of her internal life than they think they deserve. Her sexual activities, yes; they figure as a required coda to this book—which, like a competent essay by an active, and (I hope) prudent sophomore, compares and contrasts men by nationality and ethnicity. Given what is important in her memoirs, this sec-

tion can come across as a men's smoker monologue rather than proof that she had sex with blacks and even Americans.

All this happens against the social and intellectual background of postwar English poverty (today's poor, we learn, are materially better off than the prewar middle class) and movement from flat to flat (the ostensible divisions of the book demonstrate the continuing incompetence of the Housing Authority). In the early 1950s the Angry Young Men (a media invention, Lessing insists) and the Royal Court Theatre emerge: they're all here briefly—for example, Tony Richardson, Colin Wilson, and John Osborne, often with their spouses and, in the case of Kenneth Tynan with his *sjambok* (a rhinoceros-hide whip), "always irresistible to a sadomasochist"—but they talk of politics and sentimentality.

Others appear fitfully: Christine Keeler's pimp and an official Soviet poet, a colleague of Ehrenburg. Mikhail Sholokhov wants to flog her (she saw through his plagiarism); Paul Robeson bores her; American refugees from Sen. Joseph McCarthy accept her hospitality. The saddest portrait is of the manipulated Bertrand Russell during the Ban the Bomb movement. There is, unfortunately, no index.

Literature paid Lessing £20 a week in 1958. From this follows her tirade on postwar publishers and commercialization. One consequence of the Cold War's poison was that publishing houses became toys for rich men as writers changed into interviewees. Best-sellers are never real books, she explains twice in an Arnoldian mode: real books, setting a standard or tone for the country or culture, have always been for a "serious minority." This would seem to exclude Dickens and, ironically, some of the thirty works the author has written. Her title, the errata slip informs us, is from "The Sunny Side of the Street." And except for the ending, she has moved from the shade.

William Faulkner Centenary Celebrations

Mary Jo Tate

The twenty-fourth annual Faulkner and Yok-napatawpha Conference, "Faulkner at 100: Retrospect and Prospect," was held at the University of Mississippi in Oxford, 27 July–1 August. The conference was sponsored by the Department of English and the Center for the Study of Southern Culture and coordinated by the Center for Public Service and Continuing Studies. A record audience of more than three hundred attended this centennial conference; participants came from thirty-nine states and ten countries. The Faulkner and Yoknapatawpha Conference is believed to be the longest-running formal conference devoted to the works of a single author.

Donald M. Kartiganer, the William Howry Professor of Faulkner Studies at the University of Mississippi and the director of the Faulkner Conference, explained that the usual conference format had been altered to accommodate more speakers. For the longer presentations Faulkner scholars were chosen whose work had contributed to a significant shift in Faulkner criticism since the 1960s. All presentations were followed by question-and-answer sessions. All of the conference papers will be published by the University Press of Mississippi in 1999.

The conference began on 27 July with an afternoon reception at the University Museums, featuring an exhibit titled *Faulkner's World: The Photographs of Martin J. Dain*. Also on display at the University Museums was the exhibit *The Paintings of Maud Butler Faulkner*, William Faulkner's mother, from the collection of Larry and Dean Faulkner Wells.

University of Mississippi Chancellor Robert C. Khayat welcomed conference participants at the opening session. William Ferris, director of the Center for the Study of Southern Culture, presented the Eudora Welty Awards in Creative Writing. Nelson Eddy of the Jack Daniel's Distillery announced the winner of the annual "Faux Faulkner" contest, sponsored by the Center for the Study of Southern Culture, Yoknapatawpha Press, *The Faulkner Newsletter*, and the Jack Daniel's Distillery. Wendy Goldberg of Boston, a professor at Stanford University and the

Front cover of the program for the University of Mississippi centenary conference

first woman to win the contest, read her entry, "Dyin' to Lie Down," a tale of Quentin Compson being overtaken by and caught up in the Boston Marathon of 1910 on the last day of his life.

Evans Harrington, professor emeritus of English at the University of Mississippi, who directed the Faulkner and Yoknapatawpha Conference from its founding in 1974 through 1993, introduced "Voices from Yoknapatawpha," dramatic readings from Faulkner's fiction that Harrington selected and arranged.

The evening conference session featured an opening lecture by Michael Millgate (University of Toronto), "Defining Moment: *The Portable Faulkner* Revisited." Millgate explored Malcolm Cowley's contribution to Faulkner studies through the publication of *The Portable Faulkner* in 1946, questioning assumptions about the extent of Cowley's influence in shaping Faulkner's career and reputation.

The second day of the conference began with a panel titled "Who Was William Faulkner?" Kenneth Holditch (University of New Orleans), whose great-grandfather enlisted in Colonel Falkner's Second Regiment in 1861, presented personal recollections of the influence of Faulkner's writings on him and "an impressionistic portrait of the man" in "Growing Up in Faulkner's Shadow." Lothar Hönnighausen (University of Bonn) discussed "Faulkner: The Role Player," an exploration of masks and metaphors, of Faulkner's various personae and his imagery. Noel Polk (University of Southern Mississippi) presented "Was Not Was Who Was Not Was Since Philoprogenitive," an exploration of the difficulty of attempting to define or "fix" Faulkner. The panel was followed by André Bleikasten's (University of Strasbourg) presentation, "Faulkner in the Singular." Bleikasten criticized the predominance of cultural theory in Faulkner criticism and called for more attention to the literature itself.

The afternoon session began with Joseph L. Fant (major general, U.S. Army, ret.), coeditor with Robert Ashley of *Faulkner at West Point*, discussing Faulkner's April 1962 visit to West Point, reading excerpts from Faulkner's answers to questions from the press, and playing recordings of Faulkner's question-and-answer sessions with the cadets. Faulkner's nephew J. M. Faulkner and his daughter, Meg Faulkner DuChaine, presented a slide lecture, "Knowing William Faulkner." The evening session began with Joseph Blotner's "Some Brief Recollections of Then—For Now," reminiscences of past Yoknapatawpha conferences and his memories of Faulkner. A panel considered the topic "Why Faulkner?" Richard Moreland (Louisiana State University) presented "Faulkner as an Education," focusing on Faulkner's critique of modern life and the way his irony sometimes turns against itself, with special reference to *Intruder in the Dust*. In "Faulkner's Playful Bestiary: Seeing Gender Through Ovidian Eyes," Gail Mortimer (University of Texas, El Paso) explored Faulkner's technique—similar to that of Ovid's *Metamorphoses*—of using animals to express various aspects of his characters, particularly in *The Hamlet*. Philip Weinstein (Swarthmore College) presented "'A Sight-Draft Dated Yesterday': Faulkner's Uninsured Immortality," focusing on temporality as a major issue in modernism and as the core of Faulkner's appeal today.

The next day, 29 July, featured guided tours of North Mississippi areas associated with Faulkner, including Oxford and Lafayette County, Columbus, Holly Springs, New Albany and Ripley, Pontotoc, and the Mississippi Delta. Journalists covering the conference—including reporters from *The New York Times*, *The Washington Post*, *The Times* (London), Spain's *El Pais*, and *The Los Angeles Times*—had lunch at Faulkner's home, Rowan Oak, and listened to Jimmy Faulkner's stories about his uncle. The evening conference session featured novelist and critic Albert Murray's "Me, Uncle Billy, and the American Mythosphere," a recounting of his introduction to Faulkner's work and the evolution of his impressions of Faulkner.

The following day began with two sessions on teaching Faulkner: *The Sound and the Fury* with James B. Carothers (University of Kansas) and Robert W. Hamblin (Southeast Missouri State University), and "Whose Text Is It and What Shall We Do With It?" by Charles A. Peek. Next was a panel titled "The Career of William Faulkner." In "Faulkner Before Faulkner: The Early Career as a Construction in Retrospect," Hans Skei (University of Oslo) explored the problematic concept of career and focused on the evolution of the Snopes material from *Father Abraham* to *The Hamlet*. Judith Wittenberg (Simmons College) considered "*Absalom, Absalom!* and the Challenges of Career Design." In "Faulkner's Career: Concept and Practice" Karl Zender (University of California at Davis) traced Faulkner's use of the incest motif as a way to understand "one of the central transitions in Faulkner's career—his shift from an early fiction of self, libido, and family to a later fiction of history, race, and region."

The afternoon session featured John T. Matthews's (Boston University) presentation, "Whose America? Faulkner, Modernism, and National Identity," in which he identified *The Sound and the Fury* as Faulkner's most thoroughly modernist novel, "in part because it realizes the relation between literary language and a Southern dialect." Next was a panel titled "Faulkner in Oxford," including M. C. ("Chooky") Falkner, Faulkner's nephew; Dr. Charles M. Murry, whose grandfather was Faulkner's great-grandfather; and Patricia Brown Young, whose parents were friends of Faulkner. The evening session featured a panel titled "Faulkner and America." Doreen Fowler (University of Kansas) discussed "'The Eggshell Shibboleth of Caste and Color': Race and Culture in Faulkner's *Absalom, Absalom!*," exploring strategies used by the novel's narrators to "foster a myth of racial otherness." In "Not the Having but the Wanting: Faulkner's Lost

A Faulkner 100:
THE CENTENNIAL EXHIBITION

Detail from photograph of William Faulkner and William Evans Stone V ("Jack"), Pascagoula, Mississippi, 1925 or 1926. Catalogue number 12.

JULY 28-DECEMBER 22, 1997

A selection of 100 items from the Faulkner Collection. The exhibition catalogue, written by
Thomas M. Verich, University Archivist, includes a contribution from Gabriel García Márquez,
and several unpublished Faulkner manuscripts and photographs.

THE UNIVERSITY OF MISSISSIPPI LIBRARIES
SPECIAL COLLECTIONS

Poster for the Faulkner exhibition

Loves" John Irwin (Johns Hopkins University) discussed Faulkner's affinity for "troubadouresque" romantic attachments. In "The Strange, Double-Edged Gift of Faulkner's Fiction," David Minter (Rice University) considered Faulkner's interest in creating "texts that drew readers into active, re-creative roles," as well as two contradictory views of American history–one Northern and one Southern–which Faulkner explored in his fiction.

A panel titled "Untapped Faulkner" began the sessions on 31 July. Arthur Kinney (University of Massachusetts) presented "Faulkner's Other Others," a discussion of Indians as a critically neglected aspect of Faulkner's work. In "Untapped Faulkner: What Faulkner Read at the P. O.," Thomas McHaney (Georgia State University) speculated on Faulkner's reading during his tenure at the university post office. In "Faulkner and Love: The Question of Collaboration" Judith L. Sensibar (Arizona State University) explored the complex relationship of Faulkner and Estelle Oldham, focusing on the centrality of their "erotic and intellectual relation-

ship to Faulkner's creative development." Thadious M. Davis (Vanderbilt University) then presented "Race Cards: Trumping and Troping in Constructing Whiteness"; she investigated what happens to *Go Down, Moses* when she locates Tomey's Turl as the center of the novel. In the evening novelist and short-story writer Randall Kenan read from his work-in-progress.

The final day of the conference, 1 August, began with two more sessions on teaching Faulkner: an open discussion with Carothers and Hamblin, and "Teaching the Short Story" with Arlie E. Herron (University of Tennessee at Chattanooga). Carolyn Porter (University of California at Berkeley) then presented "Faulkner's Grim Sires," a study of Faulkner's representation of "dynastic fatherhood," particularly in *Absalom, Absalom!*

The afternoon panel featured "Whose Faulkner Is It, Anyway?," responses to the entire week's presentations. Susan Donaldson (College of William and Mary) suggested that the "conversation held this week . . . is as much about ourselves as readers of Faulkner and about the politics and pleasures of reading Faulkner as it is about the work and multiple personae of the master himself." Minrose Gwin (University of New Mexico) emphasized the "intensely personal experience" of reading Faulkner and elaborated on Donaldson's suggestion: "This conference is not now, nor has it ever been just about reading the novels. It is also about who we are as readers, and more crucially, about who we may become by the reading." Warwick Wadlington (University of Texas, Austin) emphasized that because Faulkner is dead, "he exists only in the collaboration that we award him . . . he only speaks if we give him a voice." The question-and-answer session following this final panel focused primarily on the controversy over the role of race, gender, and cultural studies as opposed to New Critical–style close reading of the text.

The Department of Archives and Special Collections at the university's John Davis Williams Library featured an exhibit accompanied by a catalogue by university archivist Thomas M. Verich, *A Faulkner 100: The Centennial Exhibition* (University of Mississippi Libraries Special Collections, 1997). The catalogue, which features "Faulkner, a Caribbean Writer," an original contribution by Gabriel García Márquez, is available for twenty dollars from the John Davis Williams Library, Archives and Special Collections, University, MS 38677; phone 601-232-7408. Verich has obtained Faulkner items not included in other collections, such as a manuscript including the first mention of the Snopes family. In his introduction to the exhibit catalogue, Verich explained his rationale for selecting the one hundred items: "One goal of the exhibition was to select printed materials unique to the University of Mississippi's collections. Another aim was to choose pieces that relate to the city of Oxford, to the extended Faulkner family, and especially to Faulkner's association with The University of Mississippi. Since an exhibition is a visual experience, we have chosen photographs, original artwork, signed documents, and illustrated ephemera that are graphically appealing as well as intrinsically interesting."

The exhibit, which was displayed through 22 December, included the manuscript for *Pylon;* Cowley's letter proposing the Viking *Portable Faulkner;* a copy of *The Marble Faun* inscribed to the postal inspector who recommended Faulkner's resignation as postmaster; and Faulkner's Nobel Prize medal and certificate.

Photographs of Faulkner by Col. J. R. Cofield and his son, Jack, were displayed at Barnard Observatory 1 July–30 September and were then available for touring. Patti Carr Black, former director of the Old Capitol Museum in Jackson, assembled the original exhibit, which was later given to the Center for the Study of Southern Culture.

Oxford, Mississippi

The town of Oxford, Mississippi, began a celebration of William Faulkner's centennial on 25 September with a program on the Courthouse Square for the dedication and unveiling of a controversial statue of Faulkner, commissioned by John O. Leslie, Mayor of Oxford for twenty-four years, and Chester McLarty, a retired physician who treated Faulkner. Faulkner's family had asserted that Faulkner's home, Rowan Oak, was a more proper location for the statue than a public place such as the square; some family members had suggested the statue be placed in the cemetery where Faulkner is buried. In January 1997 the conflict escalated when a magnolia tree was cut down in front of City Hall to make room for the statue. Two days later twenty-five people held a memorial service for the tree; the next night Faulkner's nephew Jimmy described the tree-cutting as the sort of thing a Snopes would do. The controversy impacted local elections and raised concerns about Faulkner's being promoted as a tourist attraction. Faulkner's family, who celebrated the centennial privately, were absent from the September ceremony.

Faulkner's birthday dawned cold and drizzly; author Willie Morris, who served as master of ceremonies, commented, "This is Faulkner weather. I think it means that he's really with us today." Donald M. Kartiganer, the Howry Professor of Faulkner Studies at the University of Mississippi, welcomed the crowd estimated at 750 to 1,000 people. Kartiganer suggested what Faulkner's reaction to the centennial fanfare might have been: "He probably would have accepted it so long as he didn't have to be here."

Novelist and historian Shelby Foote, a friend of Faulkner, commented that *Light in August* was the first modern American novel he ever read. Noting the microphone malfunction caused by the rain, he said, "Mr. Faulkner would be pleased with the breakdown of the sound system. He was mostly opposed to modern mechanisms anyhow, except for airplanes." Foote recalled Faulkner's funeral, which he attended.

U.S. District judge Neal B. Biggers Jr. of the Fifth Circuit District introduced keynote speaker the Honorable John Brademas, formerly a congressman from Indiana, president emeritus of New York University, and chairman of the President's Committee on the Arts and the Humanities. Brademas addressed issues in education, the arts and humanities, democracy, and racism. He quoted Faulkner's "prescient counsel" about racism at a 1955 meeting of the Southern Historical Association, concluding, "William Faulkner is speaking to us still. Will we listen?"

Sculptor William N. Beckwith's five-year-old son, Christopher Clay Beckwith, unveiled the slightly larger-than-life-size bronze statue of Faulkner seated with crossed legs on a park bench, wearing a jacket and tie and fedora, holding his pipe, lost in thought. The statue is on the southwest corner lawn of City Hall, a nineteenth-century building which served as the federal courthouse and post office during Faulkner's lifetime. Local filmmakers Kent Moorhead and Elizabeth Dollarhide are making a documentary, "Motion Arrested: William Faulkner and the Oxford Stories," for which the statue controversy serves as a narrative focus.

The University of Mississippi sponsored an afternoon program in Fulton Chapel on the university campus. Mississippi senator Gray Tollison presented a gubernatorial proclamation of William Faulkner Week in Mississippi. The Right Reverend Duncan Montgomery Gray Jr., bishop emeritus of the Episcopal Diocese of Mississippi and former chancellor of the University of the South, who officiated at Faulkner's funeral in 1962, presented a sermon which he felt he "owed" to Faulkner since there was no sermon at the funeral. Gray explored theological themes in Faulkner's writings, including a

William Beckwith's disputed statue of Faulkner in the Oxford Courthouse Square

strong belief in original sin, doom and damnation, and human dignity.

Kartiganer; Richard Howorth, the proprietor of Square Books in Oxford; and author Larry Brown offered testimonials to Faulkner's work. Kartiganer noted that Faulkner chose to stand apart from the world or relate to it only through masquerades and discussed Faulkner's "staggering" devotion to his work. He recounted an anecdote in which a woman in Oxford was offended by Faulkner not speaking to her little girl when he passed her on the street. The woman called Faulkner's mother to say, "Maud, you've got to do something about that son of yours." (Faulkner was in his fifties and had already won the Nobel Prize.) Maud Faulkner said, "I will talk to Billy" and urged the woman to tell her daughter that he meant no harm. "He just didn't see her. . . . He was writing."

Brown described the Oxford of his youth as "a magical place" and recalled his first experience of reading Faulkner's "The Bear" when he was sixteen: "I had never seen anything like it. There was so much in there that touched me." The experience compelled Brown to read more of Faulkner's writing, and he commented that Faulkner's books later became not just good books to read but tools for learning how to write.

Following the program, guests headed to the student union for the cutting of a birthday cake featuring a reproduction of Faulkner's map of Yoknapatawpha County. The university post office, where Faulkner was once employed, offered a one-day Faulkner centennial postal cancellation featuring an ink drawing of Faulkner's Underwood typewriter, designed by Oxford artist Deborah Freeland.

As part of the centennial the University Press of Mississippi published *Faulkner's World: The Photo-*graphs of Martin J. Dain, a reprinting of Dain's *Faulkner's County: Yoknapatawpha* (1963) with the addition of previously unpublished Dain photographs; the volume includes photographs of Faulkner and Oxford. Dain's collection of photographs and more than eight thousand negatives was acquired by the Center for the Study of Southern Culture in 1992.

Precentennial events in Oxford included John Maxwell's performance of his one-man show, *Oh, Mr. Faulkner, Do You Write?* on 16 September; a lecture by J. M. Faulkner titled "Maud Faulkner: Her Boys and Family" on 18 September; and a panel discussion titled "Faulkner Centennial Celebration" with University of Mississippi professors Kartiganer, Evans Harrington, Katie McKee, and Jay Watson on 24 September.

University of Mississippi English department scholars launched an outreach program to make Faulkner resources available to Mississippi educators; information packets included biographical sketches, information about Oxford, ideas for teaching "A Rose for Emily" and "Barn Burning," and suggestions for locating inexpensive Faulkner paperbacks. A graduate student is available to travel to schools to speak to teachers and students about Faulkner and his works, and a seminar for high-school teachers was held on 15 November at Rowan Oak.

New Albany, Mississippi

New Albany, Mississippi, where William Faulkner's birthplace at the corner of Jefferson and Cleveland Streets is indicated by a small green historical marker, held a William Faulkner Centennial Celebration 25–27 September. Robert W. Hamblin, professor of English and director of the Center for Faulkner Studies at Southeast Missouri State University, led a "Teaching Faulkner" workshop on 25 September. A Community Birthday Concert featuring Mac McAnally, a singer-songwriter who grew up in Belmont, Mississippi, was followed by a Faulkner Birthday Party.

Friday, 26 September was designated Faulkner Education Day. Guided tours of the "Faulkner Family Loop" included New Albany, Greenfield Farm, Ripley, and Oxford. E. O. Hawkins, professor emeritus at Mississippi State University, presented "Mr. Faulkner's Friends," a discussion of various people who may have served as models for some of Faulkner's characters. Hawkins focused on people Faulkner met during his visits to Charleston, Mississippi, in 1917–1923 and on the family stories of Faulkner's wife, Estelle Franklin. Faulkner's nephew J. M. Faulkner presented a slide lecture program, "Knowing William Faulkner," with the assistance of his daughter, Meg Faulkner DuChaine. William Ferris, director of the Center for the Study of Southern Culture at the University of Mississippi, moderated a lunchtime session on the lawn of the Union County Courthouse featuring comments by Faulkner family and friends, including M. C. (Chooky) Falkner, Faulkner's nephew; Charles M. Murry, whose grandfather was Faulkner's great-grandfather; Martha Glenn Stephens Cofield, the widow of photographer Jack Cofield; and Catherine Smallwood Spragens.

Keith Fudge, former assistant curator of Rowan Oak, conducted a student workshop on *Go Down, Moses*. Fran Polek, professor of English emeritus, presented "Tick Tocks, Whirs, and Broken Gears: Time and Identity in Faulkner." Polek noted that the concept of success or failure in some characters is connected to the way they perceive time: a small group of successful or prevailing characters accept a natural, circular view of time; while less fortunate characters tend to hold a mechanical or linear view of time.

Ferris presented "Mules and Him" at the New Albany stockyard, where a mock mule auction and a drawing for a mule were held. He described the mule as "the symbol of the American South" and noted that Faulkner saw in the mule a "wisdom and ability to survive that all people can learn from." John Maxwell, the artistic director of New Stage Theatre in Jackson, Mississippi, presented his one-man play *"Oh, Mr. Faulkner, Do You Write?"* on Friday evening, as well as a special morning performance for area students.

On Saturday, William Dunlap, the award-winning artist commissioned by the Union County Historical Society to paint *Postage Stamp of Native Soil* for the centennial, served as master of ceremonies at a morning birthday ceremony held on the Union County Library lawn. Sen. Thad Cochran commented on Faulkner's speeches and presented excerpts from Faulkner's 1952 speech to the annual meeting of the Delta Council and from Faulkner's April 1962 appearance at West Point.

Polek recalled meeting Faulkner's mother and his first visit to Oxford, and he presented a "Ten Birthday Thank-Yous to William Faulkner." Robert W. Hamblin presented the keynote address, focusing on Faulkner's story "Shall Not Perish" as the source of some of Faulkner's most serious reflections on the nature of art and the artist.

On Saturday afternoon storyteller Rebecca Jernigan of Oxford, Mississippi, presented "A Rose for Emily" and other selections from Faulkner's

short stories. Centennial festivities concluded with the evening presentation of "As I Lay Dying," a song cycle of folk, country, blues, and gospel by David Olney, Tom House, Karren Pell, and Tommy Goldsmith.

The Union County Library offered Faulkner-related events throughout September, beginning with a 7 September reception at the opening of a traveling exhibit of the photographs by Martin J. Dain. Novelist Joan Williams spoke at Lunching with Books on 16 September; Jenny Odle and Alice Berry of Playhouse on the Square in Memphis presented their award-winning show, *Twenty Will Not Come Again,* written by Williams, on 18 September.

Southeast Missouri State University

Southeast Missouri State University in Cape Girardeau, Missouri, home of the Center for Faulkner Studies, hosted "A Faulkner Centennial Celebration" throughout September.

Max Cordonnier, emeritus professor of English, Southeast Missouri State University, presented "Faulkner and the Visual Arts" on 4 September. He discussed William Faulkner's early interest in painting and traced that interest in Faulkner's mature prose style.

The formal opening and awards ceremony of the art contest and exhibit *The Faulkner Centennial: A Visual Arts Exhibition* was held at the University Museum on 7 September. The exhibit featured thirty juried pieces of original art based on Faulkner's life and career, created by painters, photographers, and sculptors from eight states. The ceremony was followed by the dedication of a Faulkner mural by Grant Lund in the Kent Library. The ten-foot-by-eight-foot color painting superimposes a portrait of Faulkner on a background of Rowan Oak and an adaptation of Faulkner's map of Yoknapatawpha County. A limited-edition booklet about the mural features preliminary sketches of Faulkner at different stages of his life, based on photographs of him, as well as Lund's comments about the mural.

On 10 September, Willie Morris, the former editor of *Harper's* and author of *North Toward Home,* gave the keynote presentation. Morris discussed Faulkner's influence on Southern literature and then read excerpts from his own work, including portions of *Faulkner's Mississippi.* Charles A. Peek, associate professor of English, University of Nebraska, lectured on 18 September about *As I Lay Dying* in relation to its historical, sociological, and theological contexts.

On 23 September, Robert W. Hamblin, professor of English and director of the Center for Faulkner Studies, showed a 1952 television documentary, "William Faulkner of Oxford," and presented "Faulkner at 100," identifying some of the reasons why Faulkner is currently considered the greatest of the twentieth-century American novelists.

Material from the Brodsky Collection was exhibited in the Kent Library Rare Book Room throughout September. A catalogue, *The Brodsky Faulkner Collection: The Collector's 101 Favorites,* by Louis Daniel Brodsky and Hamblin (Center for Faulkner Studies, Southeast Missouri State University, 1989), is available from the Center for Faulkner Studies, One University Plaza, Cape Girardeau, MO 63701-4799; phone 573-986-6155.

New Orleans

"Words & Music: A Literary Feast in New Orleans," held 25–28 September, was designed to honor William Faulkner's centennial and to acknowledge the role of New Orleans in the lives of many literary artists and musicians.

The first day featured "The music went on in the dusk softly . . . ," an evening of music and readings from Faulkner's work. Odetta read the lines from *Sartoris* that gave the title to the program. S. Frederick Starr, musician and author of a biography of composer Louis Moreau Gottschalk, delivered the prologue, a musical salute to Gottschalk and to New Orleans. James Watson (University of Tulsa), editor of *Thinking of Home,* a collection of Faulkner's letters, discussed the letters; and actor Harry Shearer read a letter from the volume. Novelist A. J. Verdelle (Princeton University) read from *Soldiers' Pay.* Actress Lolita Davidovich read from *Mosquitoes;* and actress, singer, and songwriter Judith Owen read from "The Priest," one of Faulkner's *New Orleans Sketches.* Yevgeny Yevtushenko read Faulkner's poem "The Portrait." Novelist Joan Williams read Faulkner's poem "If There Be Grief" as a birthday toast to her friend. W. Kenneth Holditch (professor emeritus, University of New Orleans) delivered the epilogue, "100 Candles." This event was followed by "100 Candles!," a gala supper party hosted by Ronald and Anne Simms Pincus at the Hotel Monteleone.

On 28 September the Pirate's Alley Faulkner Society sponsored "Happy 100th, Mr. Faulkner!" as its eighth annual meeting at Le Petit Théâtre du Vieux Carré. Odetta opened the program by singing "Go Down Moses," and Shearer served as master of ceremonies. Gold medals were presented to the winners of the annual William Faulkner Creative Writing Competition in six categories: Rita Ciresi, novel; Lynn Stegner, novella; K. Jennings Hancock, short story; Katherine Clark, personal essay; Ralph Adamo, poetry; and Eve Kidd, high-school short story. The Marble Faun Award for poetry was added during this centennial year. Shearer introduced Holditch, who set the stage for dramatic readings from Faulkner's work. Actor Gerald McRaney read his favorite passage from *A Fable;* actress-producer Myriam Cyr and actor Tony Crane read from *The Wild Palms;* actress-producer Maryam d'Abo, Gerald McRaney, and Odetta read from *Requiem for a Nun;* and actress-producer Delta Burke read from "The Tourist." The festival ended with a block party in Pirate's Alley and Saint Anthony's Garden with music by Fred Starr and the Louisiana Repertory Jazz Ensemble.

"Words & Music" included Perfect Words, a four-day writer's conference at the Hotel Monteleone, featuring sixteen panel discussions on new trends in creative writing and contemporary culture led by authors, editors, publishers, and agents; workshops on various genres and markets; and manuscript critique sessions. Speakers included Howard Leslie Bahr, John Barry, Fredrick Barton, James Gordon Bennett, Jason Berry, Roy Blount Jr., Sheila Bosworth, Graham Boynton, Douglas Brinkley, Poppy Z. Brite, John Gregory Brown, William Craft Brumfield, Bethany Bultman, Jack Butler, Robert Olen Butler, Betty Werlein Carter, Chris Champagne, Beverly Church, Matt Clark, Andrei Codrescu, Peter John Cooley, Elizabeth Cox, Moira Crone, C. Michael Curtis, Arthur Q. Davis, Jack Davis, Randolph Delehanty, Tom Dent, Elizabeth Dewberry, Susan Dodd, Dale Edmonds, Louis Edwards, Lolis Eric Elie, Lucy Ferriss, Gary L. Fisketjon, Robert Florence, Shelby Foote, Tim Gautreaux, Barry Gifford, Bill and Diana Gleasner, Arturo F. Gonzalez Jr., Shirley Ann Grau, Roy F. Guste Jr., Ernest James Hill, W. Kenneth Holditch, Tom Huey, M. Thomas Inge, Wendy Jacobs, Rosemary James, Gregory Jaynes, Rodger Kamenetz, Iris Kelso, Ruth Moon Kempher, Randall Kenan, Mari Kornhauser, Michael Llewellyn, Bret Lott, Mark Mayfield, Skye Kathleen Moody, James Nolan, Stewart O'Nan, Molly O'Neill, Brenda Marie Osbey, Judy Conner Palmer, Katherine Pearson, David Pelton, Tom Piazza, Noel Polk, Robert S. Robins, Mary Robison, Peter Rodger, Mary Rohrberger, Arthur Samuelson, the Reverend Patrick H. Samway, S.J., Henri Schindler, Fatima Shaik, Ron Shelton, Edward F. Sherman, Joann Sherman, Julie Smith, Lee Smith, Patricia Burkhart Smith, Jessie Tirsch, A. J. Verdelle, James Watson, Curtis Wilkie, Joan Williams, Yevgeny Yevtushenko, and Marion Young.

University of Michigan

The University of Michigan Library hosted *William Faulkner: The First Hundred Years,* on 7–8 November. It was sponsored by Irwin T. and Shirley Holtzman, who donated their extensive Faulkner collection to the library in 1989.

Panel participants were Irwin T. Holtzman; William Boozer, editor of *The Faulkner Newsletter and Yoknapatawpha Review;* Robert W. Hamblin, director of the Center for Faulkner Studies, Southeast Missouri State University; Engelsina Pereslegina, librarian of the Gorky Institute of World Literature, Moscow; Julia Urnov, professor of English at Nassau Community College; Lyall Powers, professor emeritus of English at the University of Michigan; Richard Candida Smith, director of the Program in American Culture at the University of Michigan; and Katherine Beam, curator of the Humanities Collection, University of Michigan Special Collections Library. Panel discussions included "A Southern Life" and "Genius at Work."

An extensive exhibit of Faulkner's work, drawing on the Holtzman collection, was on view 25 September–22 November. The catalogue, *William Faulkner: The First Hundred Years* (Special Collections Library, University of Michigan, 1997), is available for five dollars from Special Collections Library, 711 Hatcher Library, University of Michigan, Ann Arbor, MI 48109-1205; phone 313-764-9377.

University of Nottingham

On 12 July the University of Nottingham hosted "Faulkner and Modernism: 100 Years On," as the second in a series of Southern Culture Conferences. R. J. Ellis of the Nottingham Trent University and Richard King of the University of Nottingham organized the conference, which was partly sponsored by the British Association of American Studies.

Two morning sessions included the following lectures: Beatriz Vegh (Montevideo), "A Dreamer's Hallucinatory Tale: Carcassone, Cordoba, and Rincon as Modernist Topographical Variations from Dunsany to Faulkner"; Helen Oakley (Nottingham), "The Influence of *As I Lay Dying* on Maria Luisa Bombal's *The Shrouded Woman*"; Barry Atkins (Leeds), "The Principle of Bayardly Behavior: The

Self-Confidence of Ignorance and Problematics of Telling It How It Was"; Evy Varsamopolou (Cardiff), "The Crisis of Masculinity and Action in *The Sound and the Fury:* Quentin Compson's Modernist Oedipus"; and Carl Dimitri (Essex), "Faulkner and the Project of Modernity." The afternoon session began with Charles Joyner (Coastal Carolina University) reading his long poem "Sartoris Resartus." David Rogers (Kingston) presented "The Perversity of Water: Faulkner and the Aesthetics of Modernism"; Susan Bell (Lampeter) presented "Faulkner, Nietzsche, and Literary Modernism." Richard Gray (Essex) delivered the keynote address, "They Worship Death There: Faulkner, *Sanctuary,* and Hollywood."

Tbilisi State University, Republic of Georgia

Tbilisi Ilia Chavchavadze State Institute of Western Languages and Cultures at Tbilisi State University in the Republic of Georgia held a conference on 25 September celebrating William Faulkner's centennial. The program, which was held in Georgia, included the following lectures: Ts. Topuridze, "Faulkner: 'Native Soil' and the Concept of History"; L. Khvitharia, "The Narrative Technique in Faulkner's 'The Town'"; K. Gogolashvili, "Faulkner's 'Red Leaves': The Legend and Reality"; M. Jaoshvili, "J. P. Sartre's Interpretation of Faulkner's Poetics in 'The Sound and the Fury'"; N. Macharashvili, "Faulkner on A. Camus's Conception of God"; M. Gelashvili, "Faulkner: Minute Frozen"; K. Mskhiladze, "Faulkner's 'Beyond's The Principle of Cycle'"; N. Thevdoradze, "'Stream of Consciousness' as Text in Faulkner's Novels"; N. Gubeladze, "The Synthesis of Modernistic and Realistic Trends in Faulkner's 'The Sound and the Fury'"; N. Tlashadze, "Simile in Faulkner's 'Absalom, Absalom!'"; L. Samniashvili, "Faulkner's Early Poetry"; and E. Chialashvili, "Georgian Translation of Faulkner's 'An Odor of Verbena.'"

Moscow, Russia

"William Faulkner's Centenary" was celebrated 2–4 December at the Gorky Institute of World Literature, Russian Academy of Sciences, in Moscow as part of the annual conference of the Russian Association for the Study of American Literature and Culture.

On 2 December, Yassen Zassoursky (Moscow State University) conducted the opening ceremony and chaired the first session. Ann Abadie (University of Mississippi) discussed "William Faulkner: From Mississippi to the World"; Maya Koreneva (Gorky Institute of World Literature, RAS) considered "Faulkner: The Art of Creation"; Donald M. Kartiganer (University of Mississippi) discussed "Faulkner vs. The Reader"; and Peter Palievsky (Gorky Institute of World Literature, RAS) considered "Faulkner as a Prophet." Robert Haws (University of Mississippi) chaired the second session, which featured Charles Reagan Wilson (University of Mississippi) exploring "The Southern Cult of Death in Faulkner" and a discussion including Peter Palievsky, Nikolai Anastasiev, Sergei Chakovsky, and others.

On 3 December, Kartiganer chaired a session that included Tamara Denissova (T. G. Shevchenko Institute of Literature, Ukrainian Academy of Sciences, Kiev), who presented "The Epic on Faulkner's Work," and Robert G. Brinkmeyer Jr. (University of Mississippi), who contributed "Faulkner and the World at War." The second session of the day was chaired by Maya Koreneva. Ekaterina Stetsenko (Gorky Institute of World Literature, RAS) discussed "Faulkner and the Literary Tradition"; Robert Haws considered "Faulkner and the Historical Context"; and Ludmila Tatarinova (Kuban' State University, Krasnodar) discussed "William Faulkner's 'The Bear' and European Religious Philosophy."

Ann Abadie chaired the session on 4 December, featuring Thomas Rankin (University of Mississippi), who presented "Evoking William Faulkner: Martin J. Dain and Yoknapatawpha," and Chris LaLonde (North Carolina Wesleyan College; Fulbright Professor, University of Turku), who contributed "Language and 'Barer' Bonds in *Light in August*."

Other Celebrations of William Faulkner's Centennial

Randolph-Macon College in Ashland, Virginia, hosted The Achievement of William Faulkner: A Centennial Conference, 3–6 March. The conference, which was organized by Thomas Inge, Blackwell Professor of Humanities, included a performance of *Oh, Mr. Faulkner, Do You Write?* by John Maxwell, a showing of the films *The Reivers* and *Tomorrow,* and a discussion by panelists Joseph Blotner, Thadious M. Davis, and Lothar Hönnighausen.

The University of Delaware in Newark sponsored an exhibition, *William Faulkner: A Centenary Celebration,* 17 March–20 June. A web version is accessible at http://www.lib.udel.edu/ud/spec/exhibits.faulkner/.

Fondation William Faulkner at Rennes 2 University sponsored a Centennial Symposium on 22–25 September, with literary seminars and workshops, readings, concerts, award presentations, and exhibitions. On 25 September the program moved to Paris for an official ceremony, a visit to the Luxembourg Gardens, and the installation of a commemorative plaque. Papers on the topic "Faulkner's Birth and Rebirth(s)" that were presented at the symposium will be published in Homage to William Faulkner, the second volume of the Etudes Faulknériennes series.

Peking University in Beijing, China, sponsored a four-day international conference on William Faulkner in celebration of his centennial in November.

Faulkner Centennial Addresses

Defining Moment: *The Portable Faulkner* Revisited

Michael Millgate

Michael Millgate presented the opening lecture of the Faulkner and Yoknapatawpha Conference, an examination of Malcolm Cowley's contribution to Faulkner studies with the publication of The Portable Faulkner *in 1946. Millgate explored the extent of Cowley's role in bringing Faulkner to national and international prominence and whether Cowley in fact "rescued" Faulkner, as one of Cowley's obituaries claimed.*

Absolutely central to all aspects of *The Portable* was Cowley's pre-existing perception of Faulkner's work as integrated in terms of a single cohesive design—a "living pattern" that manifested itself narratively in the "story" of the "mythical kingdom" of Yoknapatawpha County, and conceptually in a reading of that story as "the Yoknapatawpha saga," "a parable or legend of all the deep South" (*Portable Faulkner,* 2, 8). That terminological salvo (myth, saga, parable, legend) is indicative of both the strength and the weakness of Cowley's scheme—the fact that it was, precisely, a scheme, a theory in search of a practice: not a personal or consensual selection of Faulkner's finest or most powerful or best-known writings but the projection of an abstractable pattern perceived as pervasive and potentially repeatable throughout an entire corpus—an attempt, as it were, to make Faulkner portable through essentialization.

Millgate noted that Faulkner objected to Cowley's emphasis on his southerness, as well as to biographical portions of the draft of the introduction he first saw; Faulkner insisted that the South was not very important to him, but just what he happened to know. Nevertheless Faulkner demonstrated his commitment to the project by contributing a specially written "Compson Appendix" and by drawing a new map of Yoknapatawpha for the volume. Millgate then considered what impact The Portable *has had on the development of the Faulkner canon.*

If Cowley can be said to have defined the canon for his particular moment, he can scarcely be said to have determined it for the future. In this respect, at least, he was not so much an originator as a shrewd assessor and transmitter, playing at a crucial time and on an almost empty stage a crystallizing role that no single critic or editor could dream of playing today.

. . . .

The most impressive endorsement of *The Portable's* organization and arguments—as Cowley quietly notes in a footnote to his expanded introduction of 1967—was Faulkner's own deployment of specifically Yoknapatawphan settings, characters, and narrative strands in all but one of his post-*Portable* volumes.

Millgate detailed Faulkner's American audience and reputation in 1945 and concluded that he "had not in fact been deeply in need of The Portable*'s assistance" and that his American reputation at any rate had little impact on his selection for the Nobel Prize, an award more attributable to his high reputation outside the United States, particularly in France, where he was praised for his modernist experimentalism. Millgate commented on the differences between national and international criticism of Faulkner and noted his agreement with André Bleikasten's recent description of North American Faulkner criticism as limited by a parochial or provincial obsession with Faulkner's southerness. Millgate explored Faulkner's own attitude toward his southerness, noting:*

Faulkner himself always insisted on his regional roots, preoccupations, and way of life, and it is, I think, clear that the entire post-*Portable* course of his career virtually demands interpretation as showing either that Cowley was right from the start about the importance, if not perhaps the role, of Yoknapatawpha in Faulkner's imagination or that Cowley's work was at least partly responsible for Faulkner's reassessing and reinstating that importance.

William Faulkner
1897-1962

Oxford, Mississippi

Honoring His 100th Birthday
September 25, 1997

Front cover for program of the Oxford centenary events

Millgate likened Faulkner to Thomas Hardy in evoking a kind of "nationally conditioned response" from his own countrymen.

The Portable Faulkner in 1946 was already demanding some such response, its coordinated act of critical and textual conceptualization simultaneously challenging and enabling American critics and readers to think again about Faulkner, and to contemplate his work in its entirety virtually for the first time. Cowley had a thesis to advance and substantiate, and he was neither the first critic nor the last to choose occasional adaptation of evidence over impairment of the beauty of his original idea. It was precisely *The Portable*'s consistency and integration—map, introduction, texts, appendix, map, each in its ordered place—that gave ballast to the thesis and thrust it out, so to speak, into the mainstream of literary history. Designed for and accepted by a general readership, it nonetheless set the terms for criti-

cal debate, its projection of a sharply defined position, so persuasive in the short-term, generating over time a whole series of revisionist and rejectionist positions by successive critical generations.

As judged from this particular late twentieth-century moment, Cowley seems to have been sometimes right, if not always for the right reasons, and sometimes wrong, if not always for the wrong reasons. But he was right to celebrate Faulkner's achievement, right to demand that Faulkner's work be read, and right to offer his own understanding of how it might best be approached. By so emphasizing Yoknapatawpha and Yoknapatawphan texts he may even have contributed to Faulkner's deliberate shaping of the final stages of his career. And I submit, as a persistent if lonely admirer of those late novels, that it is a rare critic whose writings can lay claim to such momentous consequences.

Faulkner in the Singular

André Bleikasten

André Bleikasten presented what was, judging by the question-and-answer session following his talk, easily the most controversial paper of the 1997 Faulkner and Yoknapatawpha Conference. He began by invoking the centennial observance as a time to ask "what valid insights have been gained" in the hundreds of books and thousands of articles on Faulkner that have been written in the past decades, noting how faithfully Faulkner criticism has followed critical fashion. He traced the formalistic methodology that prevailed—with significant exceptions—up to the early Seventies before the critical landscape was "shattered out of recognition" by the dominance of theory, particularly that loosely categorized as "poststructuralism."

Bleikasten hailed John T. Matthews's The Play of Faulkner's Language *(1982) as the "first systematic venture into poststructuralism," after which Faulkner criticism became "increasingly theory-oriented," moving from "sloppy underconceptualization" to "compulsive overconceptualization." However, Matthews's book was less indicative of subsequent trends than* Faulkner: The House Divided *(1983) by Eric J. Sundquist: "Sundquist was the first critic to assess Faulkner's achievement and to reorder the Faulkner canon according to extra-literary criteria. Faulkner's importance, he argued, is not to be sought in his contribution to the art of the novel but in the seriousness with which he addresses social and historical themes; he only became a major American writer when he came to fully confront within his fictions the difficulty of being white, male, and from Mississippi. Nearly all recent Faulkner criticism starts from similar premises and resembles Sundquist's study in its insistence on cultural issues such as race, class, and gender."*

Bleikasten acknowledged that the emphasis on cultural concerns has shed some new light on Faulkner's work but that "not all of it is illuminating" and that it is easy to overemphasize these issues.

One unfortunate consequence of the current dominance of cultural criticism is that Faulkner finds himself once again imprisoned in his Southernness (no other great modern novelist has been as closely and as permanently tied to his region) and that his fictions are increasingly instrumentalized into documents for sociologists and historians of culture to exploit for their own ends. Another perverse by-effect is regression to a naively realistic conception of literature which not so long ago seemed irrevocably outdated. . . . From radical questionings of language and sophisticated explorations of textuality we have thus reverted to more or less traditional analyses of content, or, to put it more crisply, from poetics to mimetics. Faulkner's fiction is now read again in representational terms; attention focuses once more on characters, and all that seems to matter in a number of recent studies is how much they conform to or deviate from racist or sexist stereotypes.

Bleikasten argued that "Faulkner's novels should first of all be read as novels." He noted, "Even though theory is indispensable to any kind of criticism, it should not be allowed to take the upper hand in our examination of specific texts, and I am tempted to say that to read Faulkner only in the thin cold light of theory is not to read him at all." He complained that in current discourses about cultural issues, "no allowance is ever made for the possibility of dissent." He argued that the first duty of literary critics is to literature, not theory, and he explored the definition of literature, including its role as "an uncanny force of provocation and destabilization."

Faulkner's finest and fiercest fictions have acted and continue to act as rebukes and irritants to established ways of thinking and feeling, and as relentless reminders of the legacies and liabilities of history. . . . The scope of Faulkner's demythologizing goes well beyond the denunciation of the patriarchal culture of the South he knew and remembered: in enabling their readers to realize the horrendous costs of the iniquitous order that ruled the slaveholding antebellum South, novels like *Absalom, Absalom!* and *Go Down, Moses* awaken the suspicion that all established power is rooted in violence and injustice, that all social origins are fatally flawed.

Nevertheless, Bleikasten cautioned against reading Faulkner's work "as a systematic frontal critique of Southern society in the realist tradition," for its "moments of insight" cannot be isolated from its "moments of blindness."

But it is equally important to acknowledge the fertility of Faulkner's formal inventions, the sharpness and depth of his historical sense, his complex awareness of genealogies and inheritances, his keen sensitivity to the violent innocence of the downtrodden, and the capaciousness of imagination that allowed this particular neurotic white Southern male to create characters as much removed from the range of his own experience and background as Benjy and Vardaman, Darl and Addie, Joe Christmas or Rider in "Pantaloon in Black." I cannot think of any novelist of our century who showed more courage in taking on the challenges thrown up by his particular heritage, more daring in venturing into the labyrinths of time and guilt and into the taboo territories of otherness, more willingness to take risks and to accept failure. Since Melville, there has probably not been a more adventurous, more heroic figure in American literature. Faulkner is a most singular writer, and more than anything else it is his startling singularity, the unique strangeness of his work, that needs to be probed and defined.

Bleikasten described the tributes to Faulkner's achievement and acknowledgments of his influence by important writers from all over the world as a more significant indicator of the "undiminished vitality" of his work than the steadily increasing attention of academics to his work. He described his hopes for the future of Faulkner studies:

I would wish for a lighter touch, a more flexible and more graceful manner, with a greater readiness for nuance, a greater willingness for discrimination and qualification. Less priggishness and arrogance would be welcome too. In reading what has been written about Faulkner in recent years, one gets all too often the impression that, literature being a poor relation to theory, there can be no valid interchange between his novels and their audience without the merciful intercession of the academy, that reading Faulkner as he should be read requires the expert services of the professional critic. . . . Faulkner, after all, though he was ignorant of deconstruction and had little knowledge of Marx and Freud, knew more about the riddles of selfhood and the ruses of language than any of his critics. He was a gigantic writer and, compared to him, we—teachers, critics, scholars—are all just scribbling dwarfs.

Bleikasten called for a shift from "macro-criticism" to "micro-analyses" and predicted that current emphasis on cultural relevance and historicity will not endure. Even now, he pointed out, "at least to a non-American reader, the Civil War seems almost as remote and exotic as the Trojan War in *The Iliad*." However, readers a century or two from now "will respond to the prodigious energy and restless inventiveness of Faulkner's language, and listen to the scandalous wisdom of his tales, and the more astute will recognize his signature at every turn, as unmistakable and as vibrant as a brushstroke by Van Gogh."

"A Sight-Draft Dated Yesterday": Faulkner's Uninsured Immortality

Philip Weinstein

Philip Weinstein chose Will Varner's comment in The Hamlet *(1931) that "breathing is a sight-draft dated yesterday" to focus on temporality as a central concern of the Faulkner centennial conference, as a major issue in modernism itself and in Faulkner's modernist practice, and as the core of Faulkner's appeal today. Weinstein characterized modernism as "an understanding that human life, because it is in time and destined for death, is radically groundless" and noted its use of linguistic innovations that shatter grammatical conventions. "When modernism repudiates its culture's various models for domesticating temporality, it declares its alienation."*

He noted that in Faulkner time manifests itself as a consciousness that "Something is going to happen to me," as in the case of Temple Drake, Joe Christmas, and Harry Wilbourne. He identified Benjy Compson as the character in whom Faulkner "first fully releases the poetry of irreparable deracination," a character whose core is "nonadaptation, the rebuke of all schemes of maturation and empowerment." In Faulkner's earlier works, he noted, "Scandalous encounter between self and circumstances seems metaphysical," as in As I Lay Dying *(1930). However:*

In later novels the unraveling of subjectivity—the hallmark of Faulknerian plot—becomes less metaphysical and more cultural. Joe Christmas, Thomas Sutpen, Charles Etienne St. Valery Bon: when these figures shatter, they reveal—in the disarray that radiates into and out of them—an incoherence in the scheme of things that is man-made, not natural or metaphysical, indeed normative, not aberrant. At his diagnostic best Faulkner shows the madness of the normative—shows, patiently and dizzyingly, how long-sustained cultural structures of recognition and empowerment for some folks are simultaneously—for other folks—structures of non-acknowledgment and abuse. In Thomas Sutpen—he who is first the child abused, he who is later the adult abusing—it comes together as one: we end by seeing *Absalom, Absalom!* as an unbearable mapping of differential cultural positions (where you are on that map determines your fate)—a map that only a Southerner both outsider and insider could delineate in all its absurd and poignant contrariness.

Weinstein situated Faulkner's greatness in his refusal to judge and his decision to record language and culture in all their contradictions.

A modernist sense of incapacitation holds him in its grip: time does not behave, the same event "abrupts" anew and "repercusses" again, people and things become uncanny, go awry.

The grip I speak of is trauma itself, and it registers insistently upon the Faulknerian body. "Breathing" is of the body, yet its being figured as a "sight-draft dated yesterday" places it in the social. Faulkner's drama is of breathing gone wrong because of social arrangements gone wrong. His achievement is less to summarize this disaster than to dramatize its "abruption" within the body and from body to body. He knew early on that his culture's most intractable contradictions operated within or beneath language, that language was a tool provided by culture, co-opted by the psyche's defenses, and eloquent mainly for its evasions. Faulkner's greatness lodges in his decision not to judge but to cite this language in all its variety, pathos, and offensiveness. He thus gives us, in an unparalleled manner, an entire social text. Rather than attempt to master his culture's contradictions and indict them through his own voice or that of a delegated narrator, he arranges his memorable fictions architectonically, letting voice play against voice, no voice reliably his own. The benefit of this move is a capacity to say even the most outrageous things fearlessly, freshly, so long as they remain true to character. . . .

The Faulkner I summon to answer the question "why Faulkner?" is a writer who never pretended to domesticate time. In his great tragic work he writes of wounds that do not heal, encounters that repercuss rather than resolve. He is our supreme writer of the culturally unworkable. His fiction is not pedagogic: in the presence of can't matter and must matter he knows that both are true and that they cannot coherently exist. He is our American witness who knows he is also witnessed—knows he is in history's gaze—but he does not pretend to know what he looks like witnessed, as on this day in 1997 when we are gazing at him. His work gathers an unparalleled authority in its generating of narrative structures that call authority into question: who better than Faulkner has shown us how men invent and enforce authority in the absence of authority's grounding? In short, he is the writer of pain radiated by the failure of culture's defenses rather than of wisdom garnered from the visibility of culture's platitudes. The candor with which he accepts his own not-knowing—a not-knowing he turns into the most intricate fictional structures of delay and revision and reversal rather than temporal mastery—makes me think that the risk figured in a "sight-draft dated yesterday" is exactly how he would want his work's future to be viewed. . . . Faulkner's immortality is not only uninsured but ininsurable—a mark that "is" and therefore at perpetual risk of becoming "was"—why would we defend it otherwise?

Me and Old Uncle Billy and the American Mythosphere

Albert Murray

Albert Murray recalled his first reading of Faulkner's work as a freshman at Tuskegee in fall 1935: "I will always remember the faded red print on the blue and beige binding of the Jonathan Cape-Harrison Smith edition of These Thirteen *(1931) that was right there on the tilted display tray at your elbow on the checkout counter in the main reading room on the second floor of the Hollis Burke Frissell Library." Next were* Light in August *(1932) and* Absalom, Absalom! *(1936), which "were like tunes you keep humming to yourself because you like them for yourself regardless of what anybody else thinks." What impressed him about Faulkner's fiction from the first was "his stylization of the idiomatic particulars of the deep south," the way that he transformed "all too familiar everyday down home environmental and demographic details into the stuff of poetry."*

Murray described how although the impression Faulkner originally made on him was not as yet avuncular, "he had become old Faulkner almost as fast as Little Louis Armstrong had Old Louis and the handsome young Duke Ellington had become Old Duke," because he was "already on his way to becoming an elder" and was obviously "headed for the status of legendary and who knows, perhaps eventually the status of a classic."

As a graduate Murray returned to reading Faulkner with the publication of The Hamlet *and* Go Down, Moses *(1942).*

My image of the idiomatic dimension of him as a deep south elder became that of a book oriented corn whiskey drinking cracker barrel lie swapper and hot stove yarn spinner, whose cosmopolitan literary awareness was as natural to him as was his comprehensive courthouse square awareness of local, regional, national and global affairs. None of which seemed to have very much if anything to do with drawing room chic but was clearly of a piece with the nuts and bolts stuff of local politics and ever so confidential inside gossip. And thus perhaps not little to do with motives underlying narrative action.

It was when he became more and more involved with the Snopes people and the Varners that I realized that along with everything else that had made him Old Faulkner there was also something that made him Old Uncle Billy as far as I was personally concerned. My having grown up in the deep south as I had he was my own personal very special big house equivalent to and literary extension of my traditional brownskin fireside, barbershop and storefront loafers rest bench Uncles Bud, Doc, Ned, Pete, and Remus (with pipe whether sometimes alternating with cigar or not).

Because just as it was as if old Uncles Bud, Doc, Ned, Pete, and Remus existed to make you aware of attitudes, acts and implications that you were not yet old enough to come by on your own for all your ever alert and even ingenious curiosity, so were old Uncle Billy's books there to pull you aside and provide you with inside insights not readily available to you as an everyday matter of course because you were neither white nor a personal servant.

. . . .

I assume that the role of the serious literary artist is to provide mythic prefigurations that are adequate to the complexities and possibilities of the circumstances in which we live. In other words, to the storyteller actuality is a combination of facts, figures, and legend. The goal of the serious storyteller is to fabricate a truly functional legend, one that meets the so-called scientific tests of validity, reliability and comprehensiveness. Is its applicability predictable? Are the storyteller's anecdotes truly representative? Do his "once-upon-a-time" instances and episodes imply time and again? I have found that in old Uncle Billy's case they mostly do.

Murray concluded with a reading of his poem about Faulkner, "Noun, Place and Verb."

"Faulkner before Faulkner": The Early Career as a Construction in Retrospect

Hans H. Skei

Hans Skei explored the problematic concept of career and warned against "all kinds of teleological thinking, of cause and effect, of historical or other types of contextualization which have as their aim to explain Faulkner's early or late work." He disagreed with the tendency of critics, literary historians, and biographers to explain Faulkner's transformation into the author of The Sound and the Fury *by "searching for the child of the father in his early and formative years." Instead, he suggested, "the promises we find in the early career are only there because Faulkner later kept them."*

The early texts are significant and worthy of detailed study, Skei noted, "because they were written by the young and uncertain hand of one who became a great storyteller." While acknowledging the importance of the New Orleans sketches as "good writing practice," Skei pointed out that "the most important 'discovery' of the early years is that of Yoknapatawpha itself."

To focus on "the question of what can be achieved by searching for similarities and sources and even early indications of later mastery in texts from the twenties which were re-used in later works," Skei focused on Father Abraham (1983) *and* The Hamlet. *He noted that although he was not "trying to establish a continuous line of development," he wished to explore the "textual connections that warrant an evolutionary study of the Snopes material."*

Father Abraham shows that the basic outline of the whole trilogy was there at a very early point, since Flem's position as a Jefferson banker is described briefly before the story moves backwards to its central concern: the auction of the spotted horses. The quality of this text proves that Faulkner was on the right track, having found "his" people and his kind of stories, whereas the awkwardness of parts of the early manuscript story proves that he was still not quite ready for the big leap into the chronicle of the Snopeses. The strength of the story material itself lends narrative power to the text, and is clearly what makes this an efficient and convincing story, more so than the narrative voice, point of view, juxtaposition of character, etc. In other words: *Father Abraham* is an accomplished and entertaining and skillful story primarily because of a happy idea (the Snopes clan and

the horse auction) and a material too rich for the limits of a short story, not because of the narrative handling. In order to move from *Father Abraham* to *The Hamlet,* Faulkner had to go far beyond the historical and sociological reasons behind this new class of people. He had to make his transition from self-involvement to the dialogic use of voice and character, and in the long period between the early Snopes material and the first Snopes novel, Faulkner reached levels of formal mastery, rhetorical forcefulness and thematic complexities unparalleled in American literature of the 20th century.

Skei briefly considered the question of why Faulkner did not write the full Snopes novel at the time of Father Abraham, *including his writing and revision of* Flags in the Dust *(first published as* Sartoris, 1929) *and* The Sound and the Fury, *the possibility that he "was not yet quite the craftsman his abundant material required," or that he had too many ideas at one time to concentrate his efforts on this project. He concluded:*

The facts of a writer's life and career cannot explain how the works were written or what made it possible to write them, yet knowledge of the career aspects may be of great help in understanding individual works better. And this is, after all, what is important: We study Faulkner's career because of the literature he wrote, and we should always concentrate more on the books he wrote than on his life and career. His writing may not always be for the uplifting of people's hearts, and it does little to brighten our everyday life. But in the intricacies of the narrative patterns, in the incessant murmuring of almost inaudible sounds and silences, in the pervasive and traumatic darkness of his tales, there are magical and profound moments of beauty and wisdom, reminding us of that which we did not know we had lost or forgotten. The study of a writer's career must help us understand the literary works better. After all, art, as Schopenhauer said, "has always reached its goal."

Absalom, Absalom! and the Challenges of Career Design

Judith Wittenberg

Judith Wittenberg explored the problematic concepts of the author and of authorial career design and considered Absalom, Absalom! *as a work that "rather explicitly dramatizes an unresolved struggle with both the concept and* the implementation of career design." Prior to this novel Faulkner had rarely used the word design and had never used the word career. But design appears at least thirty times in Absalom, Absalom! (added at least three times in Faulkner's manuscript revision), and "the career of Thomas Sutpen" is mentioned.

In terms of authoriality, if you will, Sutpen could well have functioned as an important tutelary figure for Faulkner, embodying both the hazards and the splendors of visionary planning and intense commitment at a pivotal moment in his own career as a writer. Just why he might have chosen that particular time in the mid 1930s for such a consideration remains a matter of sheer speculation; its origin may have been, on the one hand, his "astonishment" to discover, not long after the publication of *Sanctuary,* that to at least some New Yorkers "I am now the most important figure in American letters" (*Selected Letters,* 53), and, on the other, his awareness that he remained a minority writer notorious for his "difficulty" and fondness for "violence," and hence likely always to generate only a modest literary income.

Wittenberg noted similarities between Sutpen's career and Faulkner's.

Faulkner spoke at times of wishing to be, as a private individual, "abolished and voided from history" (*The Faulkner-Cowley File,* 126), but he expressed eagerness at other times to be recognized for his artistic accomplishments, particularly after another American war had interrupted his work and the vagaries of critical reception and book publishing had almost eradicated him from the literary domain. Faulkner's difficulties with "fate" diverged sharply from those of Sutpen, to be sure, but in the period just before Malcolm Cowley's "rescue" of him in the 1940s, Sutpen must have seemed like a prophetic creation. Faulkner wrote somewhat plaintively to Cowley in 1944 that "I have worked too hard at my (elected or doomed, I don't know which) trade, with pride but I believe not vanity, with plenty of ego but with humility too . . . to leave no better mark on this our pointless chronicle than I seem to be about to leave" (*The Faulkner-Cowley File,* 7), and one thinks of Sutpen, whose ultimate legacy is a burned-out shell of a house and a retarded great-grandson whose whereabouts are unknown.

The observers who relate Sutpen's story, Wittenberg pointed out, "tantalizingly evoke, at least in some of their rhetoric, the phrasing of certain of Faulkner's reviewers in the years preceding his completion of Absalom, Absalom!"

In addition, "the thematizing of language and communication in the novel enhances the authorial implication of the depictions," and "Sutpen's status as an author-surrogate is further suggested by the way he talks compulsively to his rare listeners."

Wittenberg described the map that Faulkner prepared for the first edition of Absalom, Absalom! as "almost Sutpenesque."

Thus the apparatus external to *Absalom, Absalom!* evinces Faulkner's proprietary pride in his fictional oeuvre as well as a growing sense of his potential consumers, both perhaps signs of a consciousness that he was fashioning a career, not simply discrete literary works, a career, moreover, that he was attempting with some success to move in the right direction. In addition, the narrative itself highlights the process of artistic creation in a celebratory way. Much has already been written by Faulkner critics about *Absalom*'s status as perhaps the most important metafiction in his corpus.

Wittenberg noted aspects of the novel that highlight its metafictional nature, "from actual artifacts—such as the lawyer's ledger, the letters by Charles Bon and Mr. Compson, Sutpen's stone monuments, Rosa's odes to Confederate soldiers and Bon's portrait—to suggestive elements such as the motif of architecture and the role of the French architect." She drew a parallel between Thomas Sutpen's design for Sutpen's Hundred and Faulkner's acquisition of land in the Oxford area during the 1930s.

Although Sutpen is finally defeated, in part by his own deficiencies, commentators inside the text testify to his "courage and shrewdness," and Faulkner himself later spoke rather approvingly of Sutpen's "grand design" and of the fact that he not only "dreamed so high," but "had the force and strength to have failed so grandly" (*The Faulkner-Cowley File,* 15; *Faulkner in the University,* 97). These latter phrases bear echoes of Faulkner's subsequent comments on other writers, whom he rated "on the basis of their splendid failure to do the impossible," and on his own work, which was impelled by the desire to write "one perfect book" but which "never matched[d] the dream of perfection" (*Lion in the Garden,* 81; *Faulkner in the University,* 65). However much *Absalom* may have allowed him to contemplate the "demon-driven" necessity of his writing career and to consider proleptically its risks, within ten years he was able to look back with pride and proprietorship and say, "By God, I didn't know myself what I had tried to do, and how much I had succeeded" (*The Faulkner-Cowley File,* 91).

"The Eggshell Shibboleth of Caste and Color": Race and Culture in Faulkner's *Absalom, Absalom!*

Doreen Fowler

Doreen Fowler began with Quentin Compson's observation in The Sound and the Fury *that the African American is "a sort of obverse reflection of the white people he lives among." From this starting point and from Toni Morrison's reflections on race in* Playing in the Dark *(1992), she explored how "black has been constructed as what white is not, the other that makes possible the normative."*

In Absalom, Absalom!, *Fowler noted, "Faulkner negotiates the insidious myth of racial otherness by focusing on the mythmakers and their articulation of racial identity." She examined the "strategy employed to foster a myth of racial otherness—a cultural erasure of the visible signs that white inheres within black and black within white," noting the antebellum accounts of Harriet Jacobs and Mary Chesnut that documented how culture either hid or ignored racial mixing. She explored evidence of possible interracial alliances among Faulkner's ancestors, noting the difficulty of verifying the relationships, which have not been acknowledged by the Faulkner family.*

Fowler invoked Toni Morrison's observation in a 1993 interview in The Paris Review *that* Absalom, Absalom! *is characterized by "a form of racial censorship," which, Fowler explained, is due to the narrative being "informed by a racial ideology that mandates black-white separation."*

. . . [W]hen an Africanist presence threatens racial binary oppositions, when a link between black and white surfaces, that link is buried. Accordingly, Henry kills Bon; and the narratives of Miss Rosa, Mr. Compson, and, for a time, Quentin and Shreve are censored. Charles Bon's murder is rehearsed over and over again in *Absalom,* but the reason why he must die is not explained until the final pages of the novel because the narrators conform to the same racial code that dictates Bon's death. Like Thomas Sutpen who will not say "my son" to Charles Bon, the narrators, until just before the novel's conclusion, withhold that Charles Bon bridges the distance between white Sutpen and black other.

Fowler focused on Miss Rosa's strict adherence to the code of racial separation in her narrative: "Miss Rosa unconsciously erases all traces of a connection between Bon and those whom she constructs as the other. In this way, by exclusion, otherness is fabricated." Fowler examined Miss Rosa's

comment to Jim Bond at the end of the novel that "You aint any Sutpen" in light of Freud's writings on repression and negation: "We can utter a repressed meaning so long as we simultaneously disavow it by negating it."

Fowler likewise sees "forbidden subliminal meanings . . . in a disguised form" in Mr. Compson's acknowledgment of the failure of his account to explain: "'Yes, Judith, Bon, Henry, Sutpen: all of them. They are there, yet something is missing.'"

With these words Mr. Compson strikes on precisely the problem with not only his narration but also Miss Rosa's and, until nearly the end of the novel, Quentin and Shreve's. "Something is missing" from these versions of the Sutpen story because the narrators unconsciously censor their accounts. "Something is missing" because they have wrenched apart black from white and opened up a gap. It is noteworthy, I think, that as Mr. Compson continues to reflect on the shortcomings of his interpretation, he repeatedly underscores the word, "nothing": "they are like a chemical formula exhumed along with the letters from that forgotten chest . . .; you bring them together in the proportions called for, but nothing happens; you re-read, tedious and intent, poring, making sure that you have forgotten nothing . . . ; you bring them together again and again nothing happens" (80). Compson's emphatic reiteration of the word "nothing" is a clue, a disguised meaning out of the unconscious mind. "Nothing" is what the narrators introduce into the narrative as they erase evidence of racial fusion. "Nothing" is what they make of Charles Bon. Bon is a "shadowy, almost substanceless" (74) figure in the narrative because they have rendered him so. Because what he is cannot be accounted for within their racial ideology, because in him black and white fuse, they blot him out. Like Thomas Sutpen who will not acknowledge Bon, and Henry who kills him, the narrators make a cipher of Charles Bon and censor his story.

This essay has traced a pattern of unconscious racial repression. In conclusion, I want to make clear that I am not accusing Faulkner of racial censorship. Rather, I contend that, like Harriet Jacobs and Mary Chesnut, Faulkner, through a different medium, is challenging and exposing racial censorship. Faulkner represented a world that held as its first principle that black must be separate from white, for, if black is not separate from white, then whiteness itself is undermined. Faulkner accurately renders this world, but even as he transcribes the perspectives of those who cling to notions of racial difference, he reveals that racial identity, like all identity, is constructed through language. Faulkner structures *Absalom, Absalom!* so that the reader struggles through wave after wave of language to reach a long withheld denouement. When that denouement finally arrives, it is all the more powerfully evoked because it so so hard won. At the novel's conclusion Quentin and Shreve at last disclose that Charles Bon resolves notions of racial difference, that he effaces the difference between white Sutpen and racial other; and this revelation opens upon another—that it is not race but social prohibition, as enforced by language, that separates father from son and brother from brother.

Not the Having but the Wanting: Faulkner's Lost Loves

John T. Irwin

John T. Irwin focused his presentation on a recurring aspect of Faulkner's life and art, namely, his affinity for a type of romantic attachment best characterized as "troubadouresque," an attachment in which the love-object is idealized and often unattainable, or is ultimately denied to the lover (because he is rejected), an amorous involvement in which the lover's devotion is absolute, the measure of his love the suffering it causes, and the ultimate form of this love a consummation that is death, a liebestod.

Irwin mentioned Faulkner's own failed courtships of Estelle Oldham and Helen Baird and explored the influence of Faulkner's love for Helen Baird on five of his works: Mayday *(1976),* Helen: A Courtship *(1981),* Mosquitoes *(1927),* The Sound and the Fury *(1929), and* The Wild Palms *(1939). In* Mayday *Sir Galwyn learns "that it is not the thing itself that man wants, so much as the wanting of it." The theme of* Mayday, *Irwin explained, "is that the possession of the beloved is the death of love, and that the true romantic must find a way to keep desire always in a state of wanting, never of having." He discussed the flame imagery of the poems in* Helen: A Courtship *and noted Helen Baird's scars from a massive burn, a feature that Faulkner gave to Charlotte Rittenmeyer in* The Wild Palms. *In addition,* Mosquitoes *is dedicated to Baird, and the character of Patricia Robyn is modeled on her.*

Now consider the number of structures and images that, by the time of *The Sound and the Fury*'s publication in 1929, had become associated in Faulkner's mind with the "troubadouresque," unattainable love-object: first, an incestuous attraction, usually between brother and sister; second, the structure or imagery of narcissism, sometimes involving twinning, always involving doubling, and probably relying on the classical story of Narcissus

as told by Pausanias in which Narcissus has a dead, beloved twin sister of whom he is reminded whenever he looks at his own image in the pool, a detail that accounts for the gender-difference that cuts across Faulkner's narcissistic pairs; third, the fact that this gender difference, annexed to the structure of narcissism, involves as well a blurring or reversal of gender, in Faulkner's words in *Mosquitoes,* a kind of "emotional bisexuality" or hermaphroditism; fourth, a sense of the narcissistic love-object as potentially death-dealing because suicide-inducing; and fifth, a sense of art as a means of creating a substitute, narcissistic love-object in the work, a work that captures and holds forever the otherwise unattainable beloved in the artist's life.

Irwin suggested that Faulkner "was primarily operating in an American gothic tradition, a tradition whose major nineteenth-century exponent, Edgar Allan Poe, had experienced the same interplay between real-life love objects and his own fiction-writing that Faulkner was to experience later." He then turned to the relationship between Charlotte Rittenmeyer and Harry Wilbourne in The Wild Palms. *He discussed Faulkner's love affair with Meta Carpenter at the time he was writing the novel and noted that Faulkner suffered third-degree burns on his back when he passed out against a radiator steam pipe in his hotel after encountering Meta and her new husband, Wolfgang Rebner, in fall 1937. Faulkner's burn, he suggested, brought back memories of Helen Baird, and the character of Charlotte Rittenmeyer merges Helen and Meta. Faulkner once noted that he worked on* The Wild Palms *to stave off heartbreak at losing Meta; Irwin suggested that it also served "as an examination or expression of his own feelings about her and about marriage"—which he had come to believe "spelled the inevitable death of love."*

Irwin further proposed that Faulkner's exploration of the negative effects of marriage on love in The Wild Palms *reflects his relationship with Estelle Oldham. He pointed out that the Mississippi Gulf Coast beach in the novel resembles Pascagoula, Mississippi, a setting which has "a dual resonance." Faulkner courted Helen Baird in Pascagoula in 1926, and he took his wife Estelle there on their honeymoon in 1929, when she tried to drown herself by walking into the Gulf of Mexico.*

If the Stanislavsky method of acting involves using emotions associated with events in one's own life to understand and portray the emotions of a character one is playing, even though events in that character's life may bear little resemblance to events in one's own, then we could say that Faulkner practiced something like the Stanislavsky method of writing, using recurring incidents and emotions in his own life not just to create characters in his fiction but also to fuel the writing of various works from gift booklets to novels, and none of the recurring scenarios in Faulkner's life seems to have been more productive, and dare one say, more sought after, than that type of troubadouresque attachment that sprang from his being rejected by an idealized woman. This scenario of an unfulfilled love, of an unattainable or lost love-object, entered into Faulkner's fiction again and again, wearing, I would suggest, always the same mask, that of a forbidden, incestuous attachment between brother and sister–Josh and Pat Robyn, Narcissa and Horace Benbow, Quentin and Candace Compson, Darl and Dewey Dell Bundren, Charles Bon and Judith Sutpen, Charlotte Rittenmeyer and her oldest brother, Gavin Stevens and his sister Margaret.

Irwin discussed Meta Carpenter's account of her affair with Faulkner in A Loving Gentleman: The Love Story of William Faulkner and Meta Carpenter *(1976), focusing on her explanation for Faulkner's refusal to divorce Estelle. Carpenter reports that Estelle had threatened not only to seek custody of their daughter but also to seek a large financial settlement which, Carpenter says, would have required him to support himself through scriptwriting and exhaust his talent.*

On one occasion after Meta's marriage to Wolfgang Rebner, Faulkner, in describing his emotional situation to her, had quoted what he said was a line spoken by one of his characters: "Between grief and nothing I will take grief " (*Carpenter*, 230). Perhaps Faulkner would have been more truthful if he had said that between art and love he would always take art. Indeed, almost from the first, there was never any real contest between them, and if on the odd occasion Faulkner did choose love, he preferred the kind that was unattainable, hopeless, irrecoverably lost, the kind that broke the heart but fueled the imagination, the kind of love that always turned back into art.

The Strange, Double-Edged Gift of Faulkner's Fiction

David Minter

David Minter examined two scenes in Faulkner's fiction in light of two quotations. He first quoted from M. M. Bakhtin's The Dialogic Imagination *(1981) a passage about the equal participation in the creation of the text by reality, authors, performers, and listeners or readers. He then quoted W. H. Auden's distinction between the sacred and*

the profane in The Dyer's Hand *(1962): "The value of a profane thing lies in what it usefully does, the value of a sacred thing lies in what it is; a sacred thing may also have a function but it does not have to."*

With these quotations in mind, I want to state the central contentions of this paper–first, that without his ever having put it to himself in these terms, Faulkner somehow recognized (or sensed so deeply as to make it tantamount to imaginative recognition) that the kinds of texts he was most interested in and had the most talent for creating were texts that drew readers into active, re-creative roles of the kind that Bakhtin delineates; second, that one of the things that he drew his readers into was the process of understanding and imaginatively revising two contradictory views of American history, one allied with the North, the other with the South, both of which redefined both its status and that of the other by surreptitiously redrawing the line between the "sacred" and the "profane," each implicitly claiming for itself the traits associated with the "sacred" while assigning to the other traits associated with the "profane"; and third, that he also drew his readers into the process of recognizing that the traditional cultural authority of these terms and the claims based on them were changing.

Minter reviewed C. Vann Woodward's observations in The Burden of Southern History *(1960) regarding two conflicting views of American history that were common during the time Faulkner was emerging as a writer. The North viewed the South as backward and decadent, while the South criticized the North's abandonment of the land and pursuit of industrialism and money. Minter suggested that despite Faulkner's "limited and even strained relations with the Southern Agrarians," he shared with them "the need for a sense of aesthetic form that seemed somehow allied, if not with a sense of the sacred, at least with considerable nostalgia for it" but that Faulkner's solution had more in common with poet Wallace Stevens and with literary modernism in general than with Southern Agrarianism.*

By way of further clarifying the implications of the interrelated contentions that I have stated as a thesis, let me suggest, first, that one of Faulkner's hopes had to do, not with redrawing of the line between the sacred and the profane, but rather with finding new ways of coping with the continuing diminishment and corruption of these terms as interpretive and even foundational concepts. For it is at least in part his re-visionary stance in these matters that accounts both for the complexities of his fiction and for the resistance that his fiction initially provoked, including, to take three very different examples, the *New York Times'* editorial [responding to the Nobel Prize award], the early silence and neglect of most of the Southern Agrarians, and, more surprisingly, what we might call the taming efforts of the "New Critics" and their heirs, some of whom were, of course, also Southern Agrarians.

Minter focused on the seventh chapter of Absalom, Absalom!, *in which when young Thomas Sutpen's family moves from a simple mountain community into Tidewater Virginia, he encounters in the Southern plantation system the institution of private property ("a country all divided and fixed and neat") and a caste system of slaves as property and wealthy landowners who exploited poor white families ("a people living on it all divided and fixed and neat because of what color their skins happened to be and what they happened to own"). He then considered the trial scene in chapters 27–29 of* Sanctuary.

Minter suggested that these two scenes "represent Faulkner's angry, conflicted, iconoclastic imagination at its most daring" and that they interrogate "several treasured assumptions about both the United States and the American South."

[The scene from *Absalom, Absalom!*] not only revises, it explodes the South's favored version of the plantation system as based on a supportive, caring form of paternalism rather than the remote and callous ownership of northern capitalism. It thus calls into question the South's sense of itself as made more humane, gentle, and caring, indeed, more "natural," by virtue of its agricultural economy and way of life. . . . Furthermore, by bringing both the class system introduced by the plantation system and the caste system introduced by the institution of slavery under the aspect of the institution of private property, and thus under the aspect of modern capitalism, Faulkner created scenes that, read with care, were virtually certain to disturb and even offend Northerners and Southerners alike. The scene from *Sanctuary* presents legal institutions in general and courts in particular, not as institutions dedicated to ensuring justice by punishing the guilty and protecting the innocent, but as institutions cynically committed to serving the interests, shoring up the egos, and protecting and even enlarging the power of rich, arrogant men whose overriding concern is with themselves and their status. Together, in one way or another, scenes such as these challenge all of us. "Whose myths and whose history?" they seem to ask in all but words, as they draw us into perilous versions of what Bakhtin calls active participation and, indeed, complicity "in the creation of the represented world of the text."

By looking back into the past in novels like *Absalom, Absalom!* and out into the world around him in novels like *Sanctuary,* Faulkner was able to create participatory texts that remind us that the human need for community is born of a need for order as well as a need for relatedness, and further, that the writing and reading of novels are, among other things, expressions of both of those needs. At the same time, however, and in the same motion, he also reminds us that people fully drawn into such ventures—whether they begin with little fear of order or much fear of it—soon find themselves moving in harm's way. For there is no sanctuary in any active relationship with the worlds of either of these novels. Once the reader's role is raised to an active pitch, it becomes not only challenging but also perilous. That, as it turns out, is Faulkner's strange, double-edged gift to all of us, even now, one hundred years after his birth. To adapt a line borrowed from another great writer, the texts that constitute that gift might well be marked with some such warning as this: "Beware, ye who enter here."

Untapped Faulkner: What Faulkner Read at the P. O.

Thomas McHaney

Thomas McHaney suggested that one of the major untapped areas of Faulkner studies is "his intellectual life, especially the development of Faulkner's mind as he made his way into the culture of writing" and speculated on Faulkner's reading during his nearly three-year tenure at the university post office (December 1921–October 1924). McHaney characterized the job as "the kind of undemanding position Poe, Hawthorne, and Melville would have killed for in their own time" but noted Faulkner's relief at losing the job: "Now I won't have to be at the beck and call of every son of a bitch who has two cents for a stamp."

Faulkner was accused of holding back some of his customers' magazines in order to read them himself. McHaney noted that among his customers were not only students but also university professors and the university library; he suggested various periodicals that likely came through the P.O. during Faulkner's tenure and noted that they "carried material about nineteenth- and early twentieth-century writers who were as attractive and important to Faulkner as were the avant garde of the twenties, but they also often promoted the avant garde." The magazines may have included The Dial, Time *magazine, the* Atlantic, The American Mercury, The Nation, North American Review, *the* Yale Review, *and* The New Republic. *McHaney pointed out that these magazines published "the writing of his acquaintances collected with essays and reviews about other writers in whom he was taking increasing artistic interest: Balzac, Bergson, Conrad, Dostoyevsky, Flaubert, James G. Frazer, Freud, Joyce, Thomas Mann, Nietzsche, and Proust."*

It was Faulkner's good fortune, then, I think, to have this position in the period when he had the greatest need, and probably the greatest receptivity, to explore and absorb the information, the language, and the recommendations for further reading that came in so many American magazines of his day. It was likewise good fortune for this to occur not in some far and alien place but in a world he took for granted, surrounded by family and friends. Education, we know, is unpredictable. It doesn't always happen when or where or how we expect it to. Three years of reading other people's mail, and borrowing other people's books, on a university campus was, after all, for a man who'd trained in an RAF ground school, done some college work, and undergone a personal tutorial with a man who had four college degrees and a splendid library, enough to complete a post-graduate program. We might be reminded of Ishmael's remark in *Moby-Dick* (a book Phil Stone bought Faulkner in 1922) that a whaling ship was his Yale College and his Harvard. Much later, in *Go Down, Moses* (1942), Faulkner has the past-haunted Isaac McCaslin think that, in turn, the woods have been his kindergarten and the great bear his alma mater. Faulkner himself might have said with justice that Phil Stone was his Yale College, and the Post Office his Harvard.

Several years after Faulkner published *The Sound and the Fury*, he was invited to write a preface for a new limited edition of the novel. This 1933 project never came off, and the drafts of a preface Faulkner wrote for the volume did not surface for another two decades. In one draft preface written in 1933, he says that the writing of *The Sound and the Fury* changed his own consciousness, and "without heeding to open another book and in a series of delayed repercussions like summer thunder, I discovered the Flauberts and Dostoievskys [*sic*] and Conrads whose books I read ten years ago." Faulkner was notoriously casual about dates, but I am tempted to interpret "ten years ago," penned in 1933, as applying to the post office years: that is, specifically to 1923 and '24, the culmination of Faulkner's three years of habitual reading and study on the Ole Miss campus, not as a registered student but as a member of the staff.

The postmaster who read his patrons' or the university's magazines, experiencing what the art critic Robert Hughes has called "the shock of the new," also read the novels by writers who were repeatedly featured, reviewed, explicated, and recommended in those magazines.

After he came into his own as a writer and mastered the influences and techniques that he had absorbed during his apprenticeship, after he had created a fictional cosmos that put him on a world stage in Stockholm, Faulkner in Lion in the Garden called Yoknapatawpha County "my own little postage stamp of native soil." For all his jokes about being postmaster, I do not think he had forgotten what the responsibility of selling a few stamps to a few sons of bitches had allowed him to achieve.

Faulkner and Love: The Question of Collaboration

Judith L. Sensibar

Judith L. Sensibar discussed her work in progress on the complex relationship between Estelle Oldham and William Faulkner during 1921–1925, focusing on "the centrality of William's and Estelle's erotic and intellectual relationship to Faulkner's creative development." She noted the common portrayal of Estelle as "a stupid, spoiled, hysterical Southern Belle" and as a "millstone around the great author's neck," as well as the lack of explorations of her fiction and Faulkner's use of it. She suggests that Estelle had a "shaping effect" on Faulkner's "creative vision, especially in regard to the erotics of human desire in the context of those historically bound terms, race and gender."

On 17 November 1924, Sensibar recounted, Estelle Oldham Franklin with her two children left Shanghai for Oxford, Mississippi, evidently with no plans to return to her husband, Cornell Franklin. She took with her manuscripts of a novel and short stories she had written in the past three years, including "Star Spangled Banner Stuff."

Estelle's stories are comparable to contemporaneous popular colonial romance stories published in the Shanghai English language newspapers, short story collections, and mass circulation magazines like *Scribner's, The Saturday Evening Post, McCall's,* and *Freeman.* "Star Spangled Banner Stuff " is, in a sense, a period piece. Stylistically Estelle was no modernist revolutionary. It was her sensibility that was subversive. While her contemporaries wrote about their host country's barbaric practice of buying and selling its women and children, she wrote about her contemporaries' marketing of their own women.

The narcissism of her bratty heroine, her sly portrayals of her fellow colonials' sexism, and her exposure of the shallowness of their devotion to democratic ideals, highlighted in her title "Star Spangled Banner Stuff," gives her story an edge not found in most east-west encounter fiction then appearing in the popular press. Her often campy tone mocks the very genre she has chosen.

Sensibar suggested that the importance of Oldham's fiction lies in its importance to Faulkner at a "crucial turning point in his career." During Oldham's three-year stay in Shanghai, Faulkner wrote little that was new.

In early December 1924 when Estelle first showed William the fiction she had completed during their three-year separation, he was still writing poetry almost exclusively, the same poetry he had been writing when she left. Yet shortly after her return—in the space of weeks—Faulkner moves first from poetry to prose sketches which were published almost as soon as he wrote them. And then, remarkably, in early March, Faulkner begins his first novel, which he finishes by mid-May 1925. What internal and external circumstances help to account for the massive and almost instantaneous paradigm shift in Faulkner's imaginative development at this particular point in time?

. . . All previous accounts have given Faulkner's brief and intense friendship and his tutorial with Sherwood Anderson that began in March 1925 as the immediate impetus for Faulkner's extraordinary burst of creativity during the first six months of 1925 and, most importantly for his sudden and so seemingly magical transformation from poet to novelist. I suggest, a rather less dramatic, more obvious, and simpler explanation; one much closer to home and deeply rooted in Faulkner's own history. Estelle's return to Oxford where she and William could resume their relationship which included their comfortable intellectual exchange was probably a more significant factor than his new and short-lived friendship with Anderson.

Sensibar noted that Estelle had long commented on Faulkner's writing at his request, even when they were children. She also discussed his interest in imitating Estelle's appearance during their adolescence.

William's inclusion of Estelle's voice in his writing process, his fascination with clothes and with altering his body image to mirror hers had taken many permutations during the course of what was already a long relationship by December of 1924 when Estelle returned to Oxford from Shang-

hai. But, by then, collaboration with her (and others) and masking as a form of collaboration was clearly part of Faulkner's creative process. Yet until this point, as far as is known, William identified himself as a poet, not a fiction writer. As a poet he had made no recognizable advance since 1921.

One can only speculate about Faulkner's response to Estelle Oldham's fiction. But informed speculation based on prior history suggests that it would have been profound. Especially as her extant stories show that, while they originated in her own imagination and experiences, they often responded to and offered alternative readings of major themes and characters in the books of poems he had given and dedicated to her. In short, by effecting a role and gender reversal—she as writer and he as reader—her stories expanded the terms of a dialogue in which both had participated since childhood. I suggest that when Estelle arrived in Oxford in December 1924, showed William her work and he offered to type it for her, the act of taking over her words, entering and assuming the mask of her imagination—of becoming in this way a fiction writer rather than a poet—was a defining moment in his transformation from poet to novelist. Typing her novel and her stories, entering and merging with her voice in the very physical way in which typing and perhaps, at times, editing or revising another's words permits, gave him access to a voice and identity or self he had never reached before.

In October 1926 Faulkner would offer Estelle Franklin a private commemoration marking the moment of his transformation from poet into novelist. Like other hand-made books he had given her, he dated and dedicated *Royal Street,* a hand-printed "slightly revised" collection of all but one of the eleven short sketches he had published in the January–February 1925 issue of the New Orleans *Double Dealer,* to Estelle. But he added an additional sketch called "Hong-Li," his extension of their continuing literary dialogue and tribute to the wealth of imaginative material present for him in the fictional voices Estelle brought home from Shanghai. We might also speculate that Faulkner again commemorated this moment in 1935 when he imagined the transaction between the poet laureate of Jefferson County, Rosa Coldfield, and Quentin Compson, the might-be short story writer in his opening chapter of *Absalom, Absalom!* Here fiction triumphs over life as it always did for Faulkner and identity as man or woman becomes indeterminate: the failed and ridiculed poet is a woman but her overwrought and hyperbolic language is the constant touchstone for the incredible tale that Quentin and other men will then attempt to tell.

"Star Spangled Banner Stuff," with "Writing for Faulkner, Writing for Herself: Estelle Oldham's Anticolonial Fiction," an essay by Sensibar, was published in Prospects: An Annual of American Cultural Studies, *22 (December 1997), 357–378, story 379–417.*

"Like a Big Soft Fading Wheel": The Triumph of Faulkner's Art

Robert W. Hamblin

Robert W. Hamblin began the keynote address for the New Albany Centennial Celebration by considering Faulkner's celebration of both art and the artist in his Nobel Prize acceptance speech, particularly Faulkner's emphasis on the "anguish and travail" and "the agony and sweat of the human spirit" through which much art is achieved. To accomplish his goal of celebrating both Faulkner and his work, "not only the monumental work that survives to delight and instruct its readers but also the dedicated artist who struggled and sacrificed and suffered to create that work," Hamblin focused on Faulkner's 1942 story "Shall Not Perish" as the source of "some of Faulkner's most serious reflections on the nature of art and the artist."

In "Shall Not Perish," Hamblin noted, "Faulkner pays homage to the capacity of art to both record and transcend the life it captures and, as a result, to inspire its participants to a greater awareness and understanding of the human condition." He pointed out the World War II context of the story and Faulkner's linking of art and death. A nine-year-old boy's mother takes him to the town museum after visiting Major De Spain, whose son has been killed in the war, as has the boy's older brother.

Not insignificantly, Faulkner's text identifies the museum as "a house like a church," an altogether appropriate description since in the museum the young boy experiences something very like a religious epiphany, a rush of sudden insight in which he comes to understand his kinship with human beings from other places and times. Thus, we note, Faulkner encapsulates a tribute to art, and the humanizing effect of that art, within a text that treats the personal and communal tragedies of war, death, and grief.

This merging of art and death is hardly coincidental. In numerous interviews and public statements, Faulkner expressed his belief that all artistic endeavors are ways of "saying No to death," of "scratch[ing] 'Kilroy was here' on the last wall of the universe," or, as he expressed it in *Absalom, Absalom!,* of leaving "an undying mark on the blank face of the oblivion to which we are all doomed." But art is not

only the artist's personal protest against time and death; it is also, as Faulkner noted in his Nobel Prize Acceptance Speech, "one of the props, the pillars to help [man] endure and prevail." It accomplishes that goal, as do the paintings in "Shall Not Perish," "by lifting [man's] heart, by reminding him of the courage and honor and hope and pride and compassion and pity and sacrifice which have been the glory of his past."

Hamblin also explained that Faulkner wrote the story not only during the national crisis of war but also during a time of "extreme artistic, financial, and personal distress." Faulkner's letters to his agent and editors reveal his financial desperation and his doubts about his own work.

Looking back on Faulkner's doleful situation in the early '40s from our perspective over a half-century later, with our knowledge of his eventual triumph over both critical neglect and financial difficulty, his Nobel Prize award, his ever-expanding international fame and reputation, his now-familiar picture adorning a commemorative stamp, and this month his centennial birthday being celebrated by events like this all around the world, we are struck with amazement and incredulity that this writer, the one who is unquestionably the greatest American novelist of the twentieth century, the one who has been called "the American Shakespeare," should, at age forty-five, with his greatest work already accomplished, have found himself largely unread, unappreciated, unmarketable, and unrewarded.

Hamblin traced the history of Faulkner's achievement from The Sound and the Fury *in 1929 through* Go Down, Moses *in 1942, labeling this period "a magical run of creativity that, in the aggregate, is unmatched in the annals of American, and perhaps world, literature." He then returned to "Shall Not Perish" to examine "what it reveals about Faulkner's ideas concerning his own artistic creation."*

First of all, it seems quite evident that Faulkner, whether consciously or unconsciously, is paralleling the descriptions of the paintings that the young Grier boy views in the Jefferson museum to his own fiction. The wheel metaphor alluded to earlier is one that Faulkner often applied to his artistic creation, most notably in *Requiem for a Nun, The Mansion,* and the maps he drew of Yoknapatawpha County—the "hub" being the courthouse and Jefferson square, the "spokes" being the roads and rivers leading outward, as he put it, "from Jefferson to the world." Moreover, all of the paintings are characterized by their particularity, by their relation to specific places, that is, the homes of the individual artists, "the houses and streets and cities and the woods and fields and streams where they worked or lived or pleasured." The same observation, of course, may be made of Faulkner's Yoknapatawpha novels and stories. Indeed, like Thomas Hardy's Wessex or James Joyce's Dublin or Nathaniel Hawthorne's New England, Faulkner's Yoknapatawpha County is inextricably rooted in the actual landscape and history of its creator's native region.

Hamblin explored Faulkner's use of the South.

In considering the close ties of Faulkner's fiction to the region of his birth and residence, we cannot ignore, even on this day of celebration and triumph, the negative characterizations that Faulkner sometimes presents of the South. As a realist, of course, Faulkner well understood that an honest and accurate depiction of life—anywhere, anytime, not merely in the twentieth-century South—must include the ugly and the ignoble as well as the beautiful and the admirable. But many of Faulkner's contemporaries were not inclined to view his work from such a detached philosophical perspective, and they responded to his incidents of violence, murder, racism, incest, sodomy, and fanaticism with the same question that Shreve asks Quentin at the end of *Absalom, Absalom!*: "Why do you hate the South?" Today, I think, readers, even loyal Southerners, are more prepared, more willing to view Faulkner's work in the context he intended, that is, as a critical reassessment of Southern mores and traditions, the bad as well as the good. In this regard it is helpful to recall that such fellow Southerners as Hodding Carter and Robert Penn Warren defended Faulkner from charges of perversity and cruelty and, indeed, quite to the contrary, saw in his novels and stories the striving of a moral conscience under siege by the forces of darkness. In this regard, too, we should recall Faulkner's own words at the end of his loving tribute to Mississippi, published in *Holiday* magazine in 1954: "Loving all of it even while he had to hate some of it because he knows now that you dont love because: you love despite; not for the virtues, but despite the faults."

Hamblin noted that it was the universality, rather than merely the regionalism, of Faulkner's art by which it must ultimately be judged. He explored Faulkner's use of

"the mythical method" of interweaving ancient stories with tales of contemporary life:

Faulkner seems clearly intent on reminding his readers that human nature has not changed a great deal down through the centuries, that humanity's deepest needs and desires, what he called "the old verities and truths of the heart," are the same in the modern world as they have been from the beginning. And as Faulkner well knew, it is only a literature that treats these universal concerns that deserves to "endure and prevail." In the paintings in "Shall Not Perish" the people live in different kinds of houses, and build different types of barns, and grow different crops; but they are still "the same people" because they all share a common humanity that, even as it confronts the ravages of war, injustice, suffering, grief, and death, nevertheless longs and quests for identity, peace, love, and community. And, in Faulkner's view, it is only an art that expresses these universal conflicts and values that can ever possess the power to truly move its viewers and readers. Faulkner's choosing to emphasize that point through the responses of a nine-year-old boy, I would submit, merely demonstrates just how fundamental, indeed how elementary, he considers that point to be.

Hamblin considered Faulkner's "blending of pathos and comedy" as another element of his universal appeal. He noted Faulkner's repeated use of the motif of the fortunate fall "not only because he recognized it as a central myth of human desire and history but also because he lived out that recurring story in his own personal life and career."

And this week, here and at similar events being held around the world, we and readers like us are reminded that we have received from Faulkner's hands a double legacy—an impressive number of literary masterpieces that rank among the best the world has ever produced, and the inspirational example of a dedicated writer who demonstrated that a life devoted to imagination and creativity is well worth the "anguish and travail," all the "agony and sweat." And both of these legacies, we can be quite sure, "shall not perish," because, to rephrase the ending of that story, "North and South and East and West, . . . the name of [who he was and what he did] became just one single word, louder than any thunder. It was [Faulkner], and it covered all the . . . earth."

"Faulkner 100–Celebrating the Work," University of South Carolina, Columbia

Tracy Simmons Bitonti

An international group of scholars convened at the University of South Carolina on 4–5 September 1997 for *Faulkner 100–Celebrating the Work: A Centennial Celebration of the Works of William Faulkner*. The conference was sponsored by the Institute for Southern Studies, the Department of English, and the University Provost's Office. Discussions and presentations ranged over many aspects of Faulkner's life and works, with special attention paid to "The Bear," a long story that was part of Faulkner's 1942 book, *Go Down, Moses and Other Stories,* and had first appeared in a commercial version in *The Saturday Evening Post* and in a shorter form in Faulkner's 1955 collection of hunting stories, *Big Woods.* "The Bear" was chosen as the work for the USC 1997 First-Year Reading Experience: on the Monday before fall semester classes began, between 650 and 750 incoming freshmen who had read the *Big Woods* version spent about four hours discussing it in small groups led by some seventy participating faculty members, including university president John Palms. According to Interim Provost Donald J. Greiner, "The Bear" was chosen in conjunction with the Faulkner centenary and for its moderate length and relative accessibility. The conference organizers and presenters intended the gathering to be useful for students. The Department of Rare Books and Special Collections at Thomas Cooper Library marked the occasion with "William Faulkner and 'The Bear': A Centenary Exhibit," which featured photographs and memorabilia from Faulkner's entire career but focused on "The Bear."

Hans H. Skei of the Department of Scandinavian Studies and Comparative Literature at the University of Oslo, Norway, one of the cocreators of the conference, made the first presentation, "The Legacy of William Faulkner." He reminded his listeners of Faulkner's 1950 Nobel Prize Address, when Faulkner spoke of the ways in which the writer can "help man endure." Assessing Faulkner's achievement, Skei first suggested that Faulkner's "most decisive discovery as a writer was of his own local area as 'a cosmos of my own.'" Concomitant with that discovery was the reali-

Poster for the University of South Carolina centenary symposium

zation of the need to control self-conscious involvement in his texts in order to create his transcendent narrative patterns. Skei emphasized that the legacy is in the writing, and described various manifestations:

> The legacy of William Faulkner has been a living and vital force in the literature of the American South after his time. Writers have either embraced him,

critically and creatively, like Eudora Welty, or they have tried to free themselves from his influence by actively using his texts in their books. Indeed, some of them even used the biographical person or characters resembling him in their novels. . . . And less obviously he is present everywhere, since he set a standard against which perhaps no one but himself should be measured, yet others inevitably are.

Less obviously, but true in a general sense, is the influence of Faulkner for writers in other countries all over the world. The legacy of William Faulkner is, for instance, strongly felt and openly admitted in the works of Gabriel García Márquez, and seems to have been particularly strong in Latin-American or Spanish literatures. . . .

The rich and intricate texture of Faulkner's texts, in addition to the problematic nature of his stories of blacks and whites and Indians, of injustice and sin and oppression and inequality, have contributed significantly not only to American literary scholarship but to the direction and development of this scholarship. I am not thinking only of Faulkner studies in a limited sense, but of the use of Faulkner's texts in more general studies of narratology, style, thematic criticism, etc. We call ourselves Faulkner scholars or even "Faulknerians"—maybe he is the father of us all, and he certainly is a major reason for what many of us have been doing professionally and seem to continue doing as long as we live.

Skei then turned to discussion of Faulkner the short-story writer, another important aspect of his legacy. He concluded that, although readers cannot turn to Faulkner "to brighten our day or sustain whatever belief we may have in our fellow men. . . . despite influences, sources, intertextual dependency, internal interrelatedness, Faulkner's writing has one source, a rare one, seldom acknowledged, seldom understood: the generosity of the human spirit at its best and fullest."

The evening session on 4 September was devoted to a panel discussion of "The Bear." Participants included Skei; Thadious Davis of the Department of English, Vanderbilt University; Pat Robertson, the outdoor writer for *The State* (Columbia, S.C.); Tom Brown of the Institute for Southern Studies, University of South Carolina; and moderator Jim Miller, African American Studies, University of South Carolina. The audience participated actively as the discussion ranged over many different approaches to "The Bear."

* *

Miller: I do have a question, an observation that really derives from some of the observations that Professor Skei made in his very illuminating and rich lecture this afternoon. He said that the Faulkner that we hear about, read about, and talk about today is the one kept alive by teachers, students, and critics; and I'm very interested in the idea that we in the academy have assumed the primary responsibility of circulating a certain notion of Faulkner and his texts. And as I listened to that comment, it made me wonder whether there are other Faulkners and other Faulkner texts that those of us who guard this legacy are neglecting. And that's one of the reasons that I am particularly happy that Pat Robertson from *The State* newspaper is here, because it occurred to me that his presence gives us the opportunity of asking someone who is not directly involved in the academy which Faulkner it is that you honor, and which "Bear" is it that you honor, because it seems to me that one of the questions that we need to establish at the beginning is which text we're talking about, not only which Faulkner we're talking about but which "Bear" that we're talking about. So I invite any comments that you may have, Pat.

Robertson: I had not read "The Bear," or reread "The Bear," in quite a long time; it's been thirty, over thirty-five years since I was on this campus as a student. . . . So in re-reading the story, I was struck by the fact first of all that it definitely is a story about rites of passage—not only about a young boy becoming a man on several levels, but also about an old man passing on at another level, passing on to the great divide at the end, there; and also about the passing of the bear. Now, from a hunter's standpoint, "The Bear" is a classic tale of the competition that exists between the person who hunts and the animal that he hunts. And it's tied in, I think, to this thing that happens to us as we begin to mature when we're very, very young and we have this gnawing fear inside of the unknown, of what's going to happen to us, and we try to find ways to push that fear aside, to hide it, or to conquer it. And with a hunter, the hunter does not go out and hunt just to kill something. If he's hunting for sustenance, then he's hunting to put meat on the table. But on another level, if he's hunting for this conquering of the fear that lives within him, it's tied into this male bravado thing. . . I think this is what happens here with the bear. The bear symbolizes that fear, and the hunter goes after the biggest and the best. And the bear, on the other hand, is there because he *is* the biggest and the best—he's survived all of the other bears, all of the challenges. . . .

Miller: I'm going to do something that's probably obvious for literary scholars and critics and simply ask whether Mr. Robertson's "Bear" is the same "Bear" that you read. Anyone else on the panel?

Skei: It's clearly in my story too, because "The Bear" is among other things one of the great hunting stories in literature. But your opening question about which text do we read, and which text do we discuss, is to a nonhunter, or an academic scholar, not to say a textual scholar, a very intriguing question. Because what I suppose we're going to do here is to discuss "The Bear" on the basis of that chapter in *Go Down Moses,* with all its five sections the way it is; which is perfectly all right, of course, and deserves an extensive discussion. But the short story "The Bear" may well be something totally different, and there are very interesting and intriguing questions around that problem. But I suppose that's not what we're going to discuss, because there is the short-story version, or two if you like—one only about Lion the dog, and basically with the hunting story in it, ending with Boon Hogganbeck and the squirrels, back from 1935. Then there is the *Saturday Evening Post* story, printed two days before the publication of the book in 1941, which is interesting in a strange way, because Faulkner revised material from his book chapter on the basis of the chapter and memories as himself to suit the needs of the *Saturday Evening Post.* So the *Post* text of "The Bear," without section four, is really Faulkner's latest version of that text. . . . I think we can learn, and perhaps explain a few things, by using textual criticism, but I'm perfectly willing to say, let's not haggle about this, let's use the chapter from the book, that's the text, and it's good. . . .

Davis: Well, there's also, after 1942, then there is 1955 and *Big Woods,* so during Faulkner's lifetime there is yet another version. But I think what's interesting about this question is not just what text are we using, but how are we, as readers, reading. And I as a reader locate myself as a Southerner, from New Orleans, as an African-American, and as a woman. And when I read "The Bear," I'm very interested in all five of the parts. I have an interest in each section. And I see it as a text that has largely to do with issues of race and also issues of gender—in particular, masculinity. For me, it's a text about how someone becomes acclimated, acculturated, into white Southern male culture at a particular time. And what's interesting for me about that is that I have not a lot of windows through which I can look and observe how in a particular time and place young white boys became young white men, particularly in the South in a segregated society. So the text that I read is complicated by understanding

what the heritage is that Faulkner represents for an Ike McCaslin, what the heritage is for the descendants of Carothers McCaslin, old Carothers—all of them, the black ones and the white ones—and how those interconnections speak to issues that have to do with not simply initiation, as far as I'm concerned, but with masculinity. . . . And I just want to say one more thing about this text for me: it's never been a hunting story, because somehow I always felt that the bear was not being hunted.

Miller: Can you elaborate on that?

Davis: It just never seemed to me to be the story of a hunt. When you think about it, they are in fact having a sort of a game in which they are all equal participants, equal players; what I know of hunting, hunting doesn't quite work that way. And at the moment when several of the players are too old, including the bear, to play anymore, then it's time for the game to end; and it becomes very important not to get the right rifle, or the right gun, but to get a player who is strong and fresh and young who can enter into the contest—and that's Lion, the dog—and change the dynamics that have been established previously. And so then it becomes something else: it becomes a way in which, at least in my reading, not of hunting but of exiting from life. That is, how can one as man—and the bear, as we remember in the section, is described repeatedly as "he," "the man," so on—how can the bear, Sam Fathers, and all of the old men begin that process of exiting from life, entering into the realm that has been defined as mythic but also is the realm that we can define as the afterlife, somehow. . . .

* *

Brown: Well, I suppose I come to it in terms of locating the reader, as Thad so helpfully put it, from a somewhat different point of view. . . .[I]t's the particularity of the place and time that is most striking to me, as a historian. Hans said this afternoon that one reads Faulkner not as an abstract philosophical writer, but as someone who appreciated the potentialities in the historical specifics of his situation. What seems most immediately striking to me in "The Bear" is this interpretation of some of those potentialities: the story as an interpretation of the post-Emancipation South; the story as an interpretation of the evolution of the South towards industrialization, and how so much of the story is built around the destruction of the forest—the rise of the lumber industry and the taking down of the forest. So in some ways, I said this is a historical approach, but I guess you would say maybe a more social and political one in some ways.

* *

Miller: . . . I do not want to suggest that all points of view are equally valid; I do want to suggest that we need to continue to create space for those of us who have assumed the responsibility of guardianship of the various Faulkners floating around, and that there is more work to be done. . . .

* *

Thomas McHaney of the Department of English, Georgia State University, led the first session on 5 September with his presentation, "Faulkner's Legacy to Youth." He showed pictures of young Faulkner and some of Faulkner's boyhood friends in order to give the audience a sense of Faulkner the man. He acknowledged that, for students especially, Faulkner may seem like a difficult writer whose concerns are alien to modern readers:

> Not many of us grow up any more on isolated farms where we have to discover the family's tainted heritage by poring over the ledgers in the old commissary; few of us hunt deer, much less bear; and we are all far more apt to change our lives by learning a profession different from our parents' and setting out for a new city at home or abroad instead of repudiating an inheritance of family land that signifies not just a complex history but the startling ambiguity of the past.

McHaney asserted, however, that Faulkner cared especially about the lives and fortunes of young people, and that his work encompasses "those passionate generalizations great writers can give us that touch on matters that we *are* likely to do and know, to recoil from or anguish over. If you read through all of Faulkner's work, . . . you will find that he explores the problems of being human more often than not through the eyes and minds of youth." *The Sound and the Fury* (1929) was Faulkner's "*first* most startling experiment with the consciousness of youth," and from then until his death he returned to young people in his work:

> Sometimes, like Twain and many modern writers who followed Hemingway in regarding *The Adventures of Huckleberry Finn* as the beginning of a distinctly American literature, Faulkner used young people for the pure unprejudiced point of view they provide upon adult folly, mock-heroics, hypocrisy, and inhumanity. Point of view aside, however, often he simply found that he had to use a young person—that is, someone under twenty-one—as the central figure for at least part

of the novel. Sometimes, within Faulkner's tragic vision of humanity, the young are his heroes—the characters who get things done when others spout abstractions—or at least foils to his villains: Caddy Compson of *The Sound and the Fury,* Bayard Sartoris of *The Unvanquished,* Chick Mallison of *Intruder in the Dust,* Linda Snopes of *The Town* and *The Mansion,* Lucius Priest of *The Reivers.* Certainly the shaping and misshaping of many poignant and memorable characters begins, and is dramatized in the novels, by scenes that occur when they are very young: Quentin Compson and his siblings in *The Sound and the Fury,* the Bundrens in *As I Lay Dying,* Joe Christmas and Lena Grove in *Light in August,* Thomas Sutpen and his children and the obsessed laureate Rosa Coldfield of *Absalom, Absalom!,* and, of course, Ike McCaslin in "The Bear," to name a few, are shaped as adults by their lives as children and youths.

McHaney suggested that youth in Faulkner "is a presence that signifies this problem: how do we keep faith with the promise and the idealism of our relatively innocent days as human beings and still accept our own growing up—the changes, the responsibilities, the inevitable discovery of contradictions and betrayals and complex significances of which we had never dreamed." Faulkner's legacy to future generations is the way in which he captured the struggles of youth and made them representative of the struggles of humankind.

The first speaker of the afternoon session was Thadious Davis, whose presentation, "Bear Facts: Race and Gender Signatures," dealt with "the silent spaces and the palpable fragments" within the text of *Go Down, Moses.* Davis focused especially on the character of Tomey's Turl:

> It seems to me an appropriate name because it retains his social history, positioning him outside white McCaslin domination and figuring his mother, Tomasina, called Tomey, who died giving birth to him. His genesis is bodily in a game of running that culminates in a game of hide-and-seek; materially, in an enactment of property ownership; and textually, in a word game analogous to the Sphinx's riddle that Oedipus solves.

Davis also discussed Faulkner's legacy in more general terms, delineating "four particularly noteworthy areas":

> 1) his location of history and memory as major sites in American fiction. . . . Faulkner's achievement in this regard is like Proust's in France, because he is our first major American novelist of memory. 2) Faulkner's construction of race as central to his representation of characters, specifically his construction of whiteness. His achievement is remarkable for its insistent race consciousness and for its amazing discourses on race

and racial taboos in the United States. 3) Faulkner's creation of a language of loss, longing and desire as the articulation of a modern American sensibility—a practical language of poetry and prose. His achievement is the painful beauty and the lasting richness of his writing style over the course of his entire career. 4) Faulkner's positioning of environment, both ecological and social, as the center of his fiction—in particular, his Yoknapatawpha landscape of Mississippi and the South as natural world and social world, but in general, his world view as manifested in his concern about the destructive potential of the Second World War and the atom bomb and their aftermath in the nuclear age.

Davis posited these qualities as "Faulkner's primary assets for the next century and a new generation of readers," and she suggested they are linked to "the ethical humanism that Faulkner increasingly articulated late in his career" as well as to "the matter of race and its importance in Faulkner's canon."

The second speaker of the afternoon was Peter Nicolaisen of the Department of English at Pädagogische Hochschule Flensburg, in Germany. His presentation, "The Sins of the Fathers: Reading 'The Bear' in Post–World War II Germany," traced the influence of Faulkner's work on the postwar generation of German readers and writers, most notably on Uwe Johnson, whose novel *Jahrestage (Anniversaries)* was published in four volumes between 1970 and 1983. *Jahrestage* demonstrates the extent to which Faulkner's concerns in "The Bear" and other works mirrored issues with which Johnson struggled:

> At its center is a young German woman—clearly the alter ego of the author—who is living and working in New York City in 1967 and 1968. She wants to know how she, born in 1934 in Jerichow, a fictional town in the province of Mecklenburg, is implicated in what happened during the time of the National Socialists, what her father's—reluctant—involvement in war-time activities in Germany meant and, above all, what her moral and spiritual obligations are, as someone who feels that she has inherited a guilty past. By searching acts of memory, and often with the help of older friends, neighbors, and acquaintances she tries to reconstruct her own and her family's past, parts of which she passes on to her young daughter. This reconstructed past is held against, and interwoven with, the daily experience of the heroine's life as an employee in a bank in Manhattan and, more importantly, against the flow of daily news as they are recorded in the *New York Times*, of the war in Vietnam, the racial conflicts of the late 1960s, the Soviet invasion of Czechoslovakia, local events like robberies, Mafia killings, traffic accidents, plane crashes.

Nicolaisen acknowledged that Faulkner's first impact on German writers was technical: "he opened new ways of telling a story, of handling the problem of consciousness in fiction and subjectifying the world to be portrayed, narrative methods that were felt to be at once revolutionary and liberating." But another important effect was Faulkner's imagination of the past:

> I believe that the specific vision of history Faulkner created in his novels spoke to Johnson—and other German readers after the war—with a sense of immediacy, of urgency even, as here they at once recognized a form of painful questioning that strongly resembled their own. For the most pressing question for any sensitive German after the war was how to cope with a burdened past; how to go on living with the knowledge of what had happened; and how to deal with a heritage that was deeply tainted. Lest I be misunderstood, let me say that I do not mean to draw an analogy between Germany's past and that of the South. I am talking about the problem of coming to terms with an inheritance that you feel is corrupt, of bitter legacies that are yours, but that you do not want to accept.

Ike McCaslin's sense of guilt, his desire to do something to set things right, and his need to preserve some sense of hope and believe "that among all the crimes committed in the past there must have been virtue, too, a kind of saving grace," were all emotions that would have registered with postwar German readers. Nicolaisen concluded that while *Jahrestage* "is written in a language all of its own, and is truly the work of a great and powerful imagination," it nevertheless owes a debt: "When Johnson read Faulkner in the 1950s, he learned to look at the past of his country—of my country—in a new and different way."

Richard Gray of the Department of Literature at the University of Essex in Colchester, England, was the first speaker of the evening session with his presentation, "'They Worship Death Here': Faulkner, *Sanctuary* and Hollywood." Faulkner spent a total of four years of his writing career in Hollywood; and although there were some good aspects, such as his friendship with director Howard Hawks, his affair with Meta Carpenter, and his talent for improving scripts, Gray said, "there can be little doubt that Faulkner hated Hollywood." Faulkner's 1931 novel *Sanctuary* was the work that kindled Hollywood executives' interest in Faulkner, and Gray described one of the writer's first film projects, a synopsis that is closely related to that novel: "Called 'Night Bird,' it traced the career of the daughter of a professor in a small southern college." This woman, who is never named, encounters a mysterious, strange, older man; her reaction to their liaison is to run off and marry a former suitor, becoming pregnant with his child. The stranger, who is insane, hunts her down in her new home, but as he attacks, the woman's husband kills him. After that, the woman's husband rejects her on the basis of her past; she suffers a miscarriage; and she returns to her hometown as a "night bird," lonely and wandering the nightclubs and "bachelor hotels." One night, she sees her former husband and his pregnant new bride: "And the final line of the synopsis is the one line of dialogue in the entire piece. Raising her glass, the heroine of 'Night Bird' offers a toast—at once gay and bitter—to the woman who has replaced her. 'To the mother of my child,' she says."

Gray pointed out the parallels between this synopsis and *Sanctuary,* and posited that "both the book and the synopsis—and the preoccupations they dramatise—were woven into the fabric of the times," and that they illustrate "the *noir* narrative." Faulkner turned the synopsis into a story outline titled "College Widow," which was rejected by a reader for M-G-M in 1934:

> *Sanctuary* had been Faulkner's ticket of entry into the money machine of Hollywood. But, ironically, any attempt to repeat the obsessions of that novel in the form of a movie—to translate the patterns of feeling that haunt the written text into cinematic terms—was evidently forbidden. The *noir* novel was possible in the early 1930s. *Sanctuary* showed that. So, for that matter, did books like *The Postman Always Rings Twice* and *Double Indemnity* by James M. Cain. But *film noir* had to wait another ten years.

Gray also discussed the ways in which *The Story of Temple Drake,* the 1933 movie version of *Sanctuary,* provides "intriguing examples of what happens when scriptwriters—in this case, Oliver Garrett and Stephen Roberts—have to keep one eye on the original narrative and one eye on contemporary taste—and, besides, have an emotional and financial attachment to the formulaic." But *The Story of Temple Drake* was still "regarded as pretty strong meat at the time," and contributed to the development of the Production Code which, ironically, helped to prevent Faulkner "from replicating his vision, repeating his success in depicting the darker side of American life on the screen." Finally, Gray described some of the ways in which *Sanctuary* followed, or presented variations on, characteristics of the noir narrative, such as the disposition of the protagonist lured to the dark world by an intriguing but frightening stranger; the feeling on the part of the audience of sharing the characters' plight or their sensation of helplessness; and the fundamental point "that no one, not even the evidently innocent, can expect to escape the spider's web of fear, suspicion and guilt."

The final presentation of the conference was "Faulkner and Mississippi," given by Noel Polk of the Department of English at the University of Southern Mississippi. Polk is "particularly interested in the power of fiction and film and other media to create images so powerful that they often *create* the reality," and he discussed the reactions of himself and others to the images created by Faulkner. Polk went on to show how Faulkner's 1953 essay "Mississippi" is the author's "eloquent and moving record of his own attempts to grapple with the problems and pressures his native land had caused for him, and of his reconciliation with her."

Skei concluded the proceedings by remarking that Faulkner knew he wrote for the ages, and as the variety of viewpoints presented at this gathering illustrated, there are plenty of rewarding avenues of exploration for future papers and conferences celebrating his work.

Impressions of William Faulkner: Donald S. Klopfer

This interview with Donald S. Klopfer was conducted by S. Chodes in New York City on 19 July 1962 at Random House. Published by permission of the Estate of Donald S. Klopfer and the Columbia University Oral History Research Office.

Klopfer: Bill Faulkner was a very close friend of mine, and on Friday, July 6th, I got to the office at about nine o'clock in the morning and was informed by CBS television or radio news that they had bad news for me, that William Faulkner had died at 2:30 in the morning. This was a great blow and a great shock, because I had dinner with Bill when he came up here to get the American Institute of Arts and Letters Gold Medal last May. He was in fine shape; in fact, physically he seemed better than he had in a long time, and I expected that he would live for many and many a year.

I immediately got in touch with my partner, Bennett Cerf, who was up at Mount Kisco, and we decided to go right down to Oxford, Mississippi, to attend the funeral, as Bill had been a very, very close friend of both of us.

Q: Had you visited him in Oxford before?

Klopfer: Neither Bennett nor I had ever been in Oxford before. We flew down to Memphis that afternoon, getting to Memphis in the evening. I had not been able to get in touch with Jill Sommers, Bill's daughter, because she was flying to Oxford at the time I was trying to communicate with her. And then we were informed by *Life* magazine that they were sending William Styron down to cover the funeral for *Life*. Styron is a close friend of ours, and we were delighted that they had picked a Southerner, a man of sensitivity, to do this job, and a great, great admirer of Mr. Faulkner's.

We got to Memphis and picked up Bill. I communicated with Jill in Oxford, and she asked us surely to come down to the funeral tomorrow, to the private funeral, which was before the public one. We spent the night in Memphis and then drove down to Oxford, and we were shown around the town by the editor of the local newspaper. And at about half past eleven or a quarter of twelve Bennett and I and Bill Styron went to the Faulkner house.

We walked down the lane of trees, pictures of which I had seen many, many times. And at the doorway to the house itself, we met the whole Faulkner family. I was informed that every member of the family was there, and standing in the entryway was John Faulkner, Bill Faulkner's brother, who from twenty feet away was the spitting image of him, but when you got close you could see that he was a little whiter and a little thinner than Bill had been.

We were introduced to all of these people, nephews, nieces, stepchildren, brother, and the whole Faulkner clan.

Q: Were there any other outsiders?

Klopfer: At the family funeral, the private funeral in the Faulkner house, there were only six people outside of the family, and of the six Styron, Cerf, and myself were three, and Shelby Foote, who lived in Memphis and who is a fine writer and a good friend of Faulkner's, was there; and two other friends of his from Charlottesville, Virginia, the Masseys, who had come down from Lake Placid that morning and who had used every method of conveyance to get there in time.

We were taken into the living room. The gray coffin was there, closed, not a single flower at Jill's orders. All flowers were to be out at the public funeral, at the cemetery. And we were taken into the kitchen to see the great mass of food that had been brought by all the members of the family. This is evidently a standard operating procedure in Southern families—hams, turkeys, cakes, a great spread.

I was taken up to see Estelle, Mr. Faulkner's wife, and I spent a half hour with her, talking about Bill. She was composed and sensible, shocked, unhappy, but in complete possession of all her faculties. And we chatted and talked a great deal.

Q: Had you had personal contact with her previously?

Klopfer: Oh, yes. I had known her. Mrs. Faulkner had spent a night at my house in the country, and she felt that we were good friends. My wife and I were very close friends of Mr. Faulkner's daughter Jill and her husband, Paul Sommers, and both of

The hearse carrying William Faulkner's body through Oxford; from
Faulkner's World: The Photographs of Martin J. Dain,
*edited by Tom Rankin (Jackson: University Press
of Mississippi, 1997)*

them seemed genuinely glad to have us there. In fact, they *were* genuinely glad to have us there. I think the rest of the Faulkner clan figured we were Yankees, interlopers, and this was an invasion of Mr. Faulkner's privacy. But we frankly didn't care because we had been asked by Jill, and we were greeted so warmly and effusively by Estelle that we knew that we were really welcome by the people who counted.

Q: What made you feel that the others were somewhat hostile?

Klopfer: This was just a feeling. Bill Faulkner had always been most meticulous about the privacy of his personal life, and he guarded it jealously. He

never read reviews of his books, didn't care; wrote what he had to write, wrote brilliantly, and wrote because he was that unique writer that crops up once in a generation.

Well, we were then asked down to have lunch, and we had a sandwich and made some use of the food that was on display there, together with the rest of the family in the dining room. You could see the coffin in the living room, through the open door. And then I went out on the lawn. Jill took me around a little bit and showed me the gardens where Pappy used to sit, and we spent about a half hour with her and then were told that the funeral was to take place at two o'clock.

The family was sitting and standing in both the living room and dining room. Mrs. Faulkner, who had come down, escorted by her son by a previous marriage, Malcolm, was visibly shaken at the time, was terribly distressed. And she sat there and was kind enough to beckon to Bill Styron and welcome him, saying that she had read his books and she was glad that he was the person who was going to write about this if anyone was to write about it. She was a most gracious hostess even in her grief.

The Episcopalian minister gave a ten-minute abbreviated service without one word of eulogy, and that was exactly what Jill had wanted and I'm sure what Bill Faulkner would have wanted. He hated funerals, I know that.

We were then told to go out and get into the cars and a procession would form. There was no funeral cortege of separate cars but the cars we drove up in. The first six went out, back of the hearse, down through the line of trees, and on through the main street of the town, and this was most impressive because the whole town had closed down during the time of the procession and funeral. Every store had a printed notice on its window, that in respect to the memory of William Faulkner, they would be closed from 2:00 to 2:15 or 2:00 to 2:30, I don't know just what the times were. But the whole town was obviously closed down.

And as the procession—six cars with family coming first and then Bennett and myself and Linton Massey and his wife, who were the other strangers who were there, came in the car following the family. We went slowly around to the right of the courthouse, which figures in so many of Faulkner's stories as the courthouse of Jefferson. And everybody was obviously deeply respectful and deeply interested. The policemen stood there with their hats over their hearts. Everybody was interested and mournful. Photographers all over the place, of course.

And we slowly wended our way a couple of blocks further on down the main street and turned to the right, and there we were at the cemetery. There was a little tent on the side of a hill; the coffin was put under the tent. There were probably twelve or fifteen chairs there for the family to sit on. The rest of us stood around. And the minister gave, again, the ten-minute Episcopalian service for the dead with no eulogy whatsoever.

Q: Was Faulkner very religious personally? Would he even have objected to this kind of ceremony?

Klopfer: No, he would not have objected to this kind of a ceremony. I think he was a deeply religious man but not a churchgoing man. After all, he

wrote a book called *A Fable,* which was a religious book.

And there, of course, all the photographers with their telephoto lenses were on the hillside snapping pictures all over the place.

And we said good-bye to Estelle. We said good-bye to Jill. And we went back to Memphis by prearrangement with them, because I tried to get back to New York that night.

Q: Had there been many Negroes out in the town watching the procession?

Klopfer: I think it was about two-thirds white, one-third Negro, I would guess. There were black faces all around.

Q: In a recent book James Baldwin suggested that Faulkner was, in effect, kind of a comfortable liberal who really wasn't very engaged in the problems of the Negro.

Klopfer: I don't think that's completely unjustified on Mr. Baldwin's part, but I do know that Bill had a deep love for the Negro, a real understanding for him, a deep sympathy for him, and just the sure knowledge within himself, having been born and raised in Oxford, Mississippi, that this wasn't going to happen overnight and that it would take a long time for true integration to happen in the State of Mississippi, or Alabama, or the Deep South.

Q: Did he ever express himself about the Freedom Rides or . . .

Klopfer: I never heard him say a word about them, no.

But the funeral was a most impressive thing and really what Bill would have wanted. It seemed to me to be just right for the man. He was hated in the town; he was loved in the town. My own feeling about this, and this is pure conjecture, is that they couldn't quite cotton up to the fact that a man could scribble words on paper and get paid for it and make a decent living. This wasn't working, to Oxford, Mississippi, and consequently Bill was sort of an outsider, although he was as much a part of the town as anyone could be.

Q: He had a reputation of being somewhat unsocial. Did he show this in your relationship?

Klopfer: He was a very quiet man. Bill was a quiet man; he was a moody man. He would come down to our farm in New Jersey and spend the weekend with us. In the evening he would sit and talk in his quiet way. He was a man who never said anything until he thought about it. He was not a garrulous man at all. He thought when he spoke.

He loved my wife, I know that. I think he liked me. And he liked Bennett and Phyllis very much too. He felt comfortable in our house. I knew that he did because he came down and would sit around and not talk sometimes, but it wasn't the kind of enforced silence that was embarrassing or bothersome.

Q: What did he talk about when he did talk? Some writer claimed that he mostly talked about hunting and fishing.

Klopfer: He talked about horses; he loved horses, and mules, more than humans, I think. He would talk about his farm in Oxford, which is not the place from which he was buried; he was buried from the town house. He had—his family owns a three-hundred-odd-acre farm in Oxford. And he would talk about sitting on a log and watching the birds and animals, and about hunting, and above all else about riding. He was crazy about horses. In fact, he had been thrown by a horse just two weeks before he died, on this very farm in Oxford, and was rather seriously shaken up. His family said that he'd never recovered from that, that he really hadn't gotten his appetite back, that he was, they said, in bad shape from this fall.

Q: Did he have much of an interest in music—folk music or jazz?

Klopfer: I don't know. I don't think he had any interest in music or jazz, and he had little interest in the so-called cultural arts. I mean, when you took Bill to the theater in New York, at the end of the first act he was just likely to say, "I can't stand this, take me out of here." It was a claustrophobic sort of thing. I doubt if he ever watched television, but I don't know.

He was an extraordinary man. He was a gentle man, too. He was soft-spoken, gentle and thoughtful, introspective, and, well, he was the last of the giants in American literature, until some new ones come along. Hemingway, Wolfe, Fitzgerald, and now Faulkner gone; there they are. Of course, this dates me, too.

Q: Were you disappointed when he didn't accept President Kennedy's invitation to go to the Nobel Prize dinner?

Klopfer: I really just couldn't understand it. He was sitting in this chair when he came to New York for the dinner, and I said, "Bill, why didn't you go there?" and he said, "Well, a hundred miles is too far to go for a meal." He was in Charlottesville at the time, not in Oxford.

I was rather surprised because since he had gotten the Nobel Prize, I felt that he liked the honors and the attention that was shown to a Nobel Prize winner, a fine writer—in a very modest way. I don't mean that he would ever gloat or boast or anything like that. Before that he was really almost a recluse as far as seeing critics or seeing anybody was concerned—about his work, not with his friends.

Q: Did he ever talk about his teaching experience at the University of Virginia? I wonder if he enjoyed that or found it kind of burdensome.

Klopfer: I think he enjoyed it at the beginning, and then I think he got rather bored by it, which I guess is par for the course. He'd enjoyed it. He'd been up at West Point a couple of months ago, and he said it was a most interesting experience, and he said, "And, oh my, were they drilled what to ask me! They knew what to ask, and this was not an off-the-cuff thing." And he said, "Those boys knew what they wanted to know, and they had been told beforehand." He was very realistic about this and very cute about it actually. He had a very good time there too, he said.

James Dickey

(2 February 1923 – 19 January 1997)

James Dickey's love affair with literature came to a close on 19 January 1997, when, after a fierce and prolonged battle with lung and liver ailments, he died of a pulmonary infection in Columbia, South Carolina. With the help of a tank of oxygen, he taught his last class on 14 January, the day before he entered the hospital, an act emblematic of the stubborn, willful joy he held for life and poetry.

Several weeks prior to his death I visited Dickey in his classroom at the University of South Carolina, the school he had taught at since 1969. Standing in the hallway, I tuned into his voice, the strong, passionate conviction he brought to his subjects. I couldn't help but smile, a gesture that was difficult to maintain as I entered the room. Dickey was sunk into a chair at the head of a large table, with students gathered to hear him. He had withered. I remembered teasing him that he had the constitution of an ox, that the hard drinking and hard living would take down any other human in a month. I remembered Matt Bruccoli telling him that his first act as executor after Jim's death would be to send the poet's liver to the Harvard Medical School to be studied as a natural wonder. Matt had been joking, of course, but that final moment seemed much closer. Matt had taken Jim to a specialist at the Medical School in Charleston. He had let me know that Jim wasn't looking too well. But I was shocked to see that the hale and hearty fellow with whom I had spent afternoons throwing a football when he was in his mid sixties looked like the wind could toss and turn him.

Dickey seemed mildly surprised to see me. He thought that I'd be coming into town the next day. I stood at the back of the room; it was almost the end of class. His voice boomed, demanding that the students pay attention to the craft of poetry and never settle for less than the "necessary" word and cadence; it was the teaching style that had won him awards and that compelled his former student Pat Conroy to say that studying poetry with Dickey made him want to "eat" poems. As class ended and the students slowly detached themselves, he waved me forward, and with a motion both sincere and histrionic, he held out his arms and said, "My old friend, let me hear your heartbeat." As he pressed

his ear against my chest, I kissed the top of the head of one of American literature's most spectacular and controversial poetic geniuses.

Jim asked about my kids. I continued to be struck by the quality of his voice: the strong southern accent, cultivated in the Atlanta suburb of Buckhead, where he was born on 2 February 1923 and lived until he departed to play football at Clemson College in 1942; the tone and timbre of his speech, radiating the sense that something important was happening, that the conversation would eventually push to the point where, as he wrote in *The Eagle's Mile* (1990), the world would "stretch and tell" a deep secret.

The pursuit of the remarkable was Dickey's singular obsession, one that often resulted in extraordinary poetry, personal excess, and an insatiable desire to consume experience. Dickey's letters home from 1943 to 1946, his years in the U.S. Army Air Corps, show him reading voraciously, studying navigation, and soaking up the disparate experiences that traveling to new places and meeting new people afforded. Thirty years later in *Sorties* (1971) he displayed much the same attitude, insisting that "The longer I live, the longer and better the whole perspective of possibility becomes, and the more I see how necessary it is to *throw* one's self open to the least chance impulse or stimulus coming from anywhere."

This attitude kept Dickey teaching and writing at age seventy-three, despite the severity of his illness. Getting from the second-floor classroom to the van the university provided to chauffeur him to and from his home took the better part of an hour. Wincing at the effort to hoist himself out of the chair, Dickey gauntly lumbered to a bench just outside the classroom, where he sat gulping for air, leaning forward, his forearms resting on his thighs. I sat by him. He must have noticed the look of concern on my face. He tried to force a smile, mumbling "I'll be all right in a minute." After about ten minutes, we began to talk about his children, a topic of which he never tired. His oldest son, Christopher, born in 1951, was the chief Middle East correspondent for *Newsweek*. I recalled the pride and concern that Jim had displayed when Chris covered the front lines of the Gulf War with Iraq. Kevin was living in New Haven, Connecticut. Seven years younger than Chris, he had studied urology in medical school. Dickey remarked that Kevin had picked that particular specialty because "Kevin likes to see his patients' pain eased immediately. A urologist sees more of this than most doctors." Bronwen was the apple of his eye. Dickey had married Bronwen's mother, Deborah Dodson, in 1976 after Maxine Syerson, his wife of twenty-eight years, died. Born in 1981, Bronwen was, according to her father, thriving as a dancer, writer, and student. Her visits home from the New England prep school she attended were the highlights of Dickey's life. They would sit up and read to each other hours into the night. When away, she called daily. Talking about the children seemed to restore him. He asked me to push the button for the elevator.

In the elevator, he leaned against the panel by the floor numbers, his hair sparse and disheveled, his eyes focused on the floor, as he prepared for the effort to get out of the elevator and to the bench immediately outside of it on the first floor. Once there, he again leaned forward, gasping. After a few minutes Dickey said "They're trying to make me use a wheelchair, but I've got to keep moving." Dickey had long described himself as a "survivor." He had survived World War II, when he served as a navigator for the 418th Night Fighters in the South Pacific. After running track and graduating magna cum laude with a B.A. from Vanderbilt University in 1949, he earned an M.A. in English a year later but was summoned after one semester of teaching at Rice University for air force service in Korea. His military experiences had a profound impact on his work. His earliest poems, not collected until the publication of *The Whole Motion: Collected Poems 1945–1992* (1994), describe a young soldier juggling war and literature. In "The Place of the Skull" the narrator wakes to "pick up the poetry books"

> And walk through the area, out,
> Over the rise with the crumbled machine-gun pit,
> In the licked, light, chalky dazzle
> Kicking the laces of my shoes along,
> Until sea blue from under my belt
>
> Trembled up, as down
> To a bench in the stillest side
> Of height, I came, to meet my holy masters in the Word
> Above the gauze- and powder-burning bay.

Dickey amassed more than five hundred hours of air duty during the war, flying at night while spending the day poring over books that he requested and that his mother sent. His early note-books, published as *Striking In* (1996), show that after the war he remained obsessed with literature, drawing up weekly schedules crammed with hours of reading, writing fiction, and, most of all, mastering poetic forms. He felt lucky to be alive and pursuing his passion, an attitude he never relinquished. I remembered that in 1989, when I first met Dickey, he greeted me at the doorway of his home on Lake Katherine in Columbia and asserted, "There is so much I can write, if life will give me the time."

He was still wrestling for time, telling me of his plans for a new novel, "Crux," a sequel to *Alnilam* (1987). Dickey put his hand on my shoulder and shoved himself up, aiming for the glass door that led to the courtyard. I opened the door for him. Dickey went through the passage, turned right, and made his way to a concrete bench ten yards away. He had been going through the same routine all semester. He puffed, squinting out over the sunny campus. We were waiting for the university van to pull up on the sidewalk. A pack of ROTC students jogged over the bridge to our left, chanting in unison. Dickey listened until we could no longer hear them. "There's nothing that attracts and horrifies me more than people marching and chanting. The rhythm is extraordinary; it makes you want to be part of it, to get up and join them. But for all that we know they're the next Hitler Youth."

Like many soldiers who served during World War II, Dickey's attitudes toward subsequent experience were shaped by the war. From the powerful poems of his first books—*Into the Stone* (1960), *Drowning with Others* (1962), and *Helmets* (1964)—to his final two novels—*Alnilam* and *To the White Sea* (1993)—World War II influenced Dickey's subject matter and, more importantly, his approach to writing. Dickey's characters often combat and court danger through action, resulting in a volcanic eruption of psychological tensions. Most often, he creates differing characters and situations in order to explore the positive and negative dimensions of the elemental in order to assess what varying mixtures generate. However, his emphasis on the contradictory and his resistance to presenting easily discernible moral conclusions troubled critics attempting to assess Dickey's "ideology," particularly after Robert Bly labeled him a warmonger.

The mention of Dickey's one-time friend and publisher Robert Bly would instantly anger Dickey, and for good reason. "The Fire Bombing," the centerpiece of National Book Award–winner *Buckdancer's Choice* (1965), set off a storm of controversy in 1967 after Bly published "The Collapse of James Dickey." Bly interpreted the poem as if it were about Vietnam, rather than World War II, using the

James Dickey in World War II

term *Asians,* instead of distinguishing between the Japanese and the Vietnamese. Bly also declared that Dickey was "a toady to the government" because of his position as consultant in poetry to the Library of Congress and claimed that Dickey supported the Vietnam War despite Dickey's work for presidential candidate Eugene McCarthy. Bly's attack triggered a series of vicious assaults over the next several years by Ralph J. Mills, Michael Mesic, Norman Silverstein, Fredric Jameson, Anthony Thwaite, Martin Dodsworth, and others, whose denunciations of Dickey's use of violence were informed by their dissatisfaction with the war. The situation was further complicated by Dickey's public image as a "macho" poet and his self-advertisements. Dickey refused to alter his themes or his way of living, displaying the same intractability toward his critics as he later did toward his illness.

We could see the van coming down the street. Dickey spoke about *Alnilam,* "Crux," and the fine line between discipline and fanaticism. He continued to be fascinated by the themes—survival, an individual's relationship to nature, humanity's pro-

pensity for violence, the relationship between power and the imagination—that had preoccupied his creative life. Dickey headed for the front passenger-side door, which his secretary held open. I slid open the side door and sat in the couchlike seat behind Dickey and the driver. Dickey started telling the driver that I looked like a beatnik but that I was actually the chairman of an English department and a pretty good writer for a descendant of Fidel Castro. Then he said that I had come down from Washington, D.C., to work out a plan to assassinate Castro, who had betrayed my father. Dickey asked me what I had come up with so far. I presented a scenario. The man had been driving Dickey all semester. He offered to commandeer the submarine.

Once home, Dickey sank into a worn cushion chair surrounded by stacks and stacks of books. Except for the books and the tanks of oxygen, the room looked exactly like it did when I first stepped into it in 1989. Pictures of family members were perched on top of the piano. Awards, citations, a letter from Jimmy Carter thanking Dickey for reading at the Presidential Inaugural Gala in 1977, crossbows, and other memorabilia hung on the walls. A fireplace with more books stacked around it and a large TV dominated each end of the room. Dickey had long loved to watch ball games, wildlife shows, and movies.

Mary, his longtime housekeeper, brought out his lunch, vanilla pudding and chocolate milk. For years he had been having trouble swallowing, severely limiting his diet. In the early 1980s he had almost died from esophageal and abdominal complications. "I'd offer you a beer but I'm selfish. Since I can't drink, I don't keep anything around," Dickey explained between spoonfuls of pudding.

The screenplay for the movie version of *To the White Sea* was on his mind. Jodie Foster, Clint Eastwood, and the Coen brothers were the possible directors. Dickey picked up the script.

We're working on how to present [the ending] in the movie. As of right now, the script has it this way. A voice-over says, 'And then it was there, too. A red wall blazed. For a second there was terrible heat. It could have burned up the whole entire world, and I was sure I was gone.' Then there is a shot of swirling snow obscuring the scene as the shot pans skyward, and the only sounds are the rushing wind and the faint inkling of the wail of a hawk, barely audible. The voice-over says: 'But the bird, snow and the cold came back. The wind mixed the flakes and I knew I had it. I was in it and part of it and I would be in it from now on.' Close in on hawk. And Muldrow's voice says: 'Everywhere in it from the first time and the last as soon as I close my eyes.' And we show him close his eyes and the hawk fades off into the snow and everything is white, when we hear the wail. Then the screen goes to black. That's the way we're going to do it as of right now. We'll see what happens. I have some other touches I want to make.

Sick as he was, Dickey still yearned for excitement. The prospect of being involved in another movie clearly appealed to him. He was disappointed that *Alnilam,* which he thought was his best novel, had never been filmed, though he wrote a screenplay and had sold the movie rights. When he talked about the movie version of his best-seller *Deliverance* (1970), he alternated between pride and pleasure and keen disappointment. He loved the river scenes, Jon Voight's and Ned Beatty's performances, and the commercial and critical acclaim the film reaped, but he wanted more character development, finally protesting so vehemently that he was asked to leave the movie set.

I knew that Dickey could be difficult. As a courtesy I would show him things that I had written before they appeared in print. On more than one occasion he had become angered by my opinions and telephoned, once in the middle of the night, insisting that I make changes. After I'd refuse, we'd argue and not speak for a few days. Then we'd talk, and he wouldn't want to discuss the disagreement at all, but veer the conversation toward other matters. He hated the articles and parts of my book that dealt with vicissitudes of his literary reputation. As one would expect, he didn't want attention called to the negative things that critics, often unfairly, had written about him and his work.

I told him that he'd better hope for a director who wouldn't throw him off the set this time. Someone else had done the script for *To the White Sea,* with Dickey serving as a consultant. But he had strong ideas about how he wanted the film made:

Muldrow wants the perfect camouflage. He believes that the perfect camouflage will enable him to cease to exist and merge with the landscape. The only thing that will give him away is his eyes. When he closes them, he thinks he can become the place. He is covered with his own blood and swan feathers when he goes out into the snow and attempts to become a landscape of snow and cold and desolation, an environment that he's always loved so much. . . . I want them to show, through the thick and swirling snow, intermittent glimpses of the posse shooting at Muldrow. I want the posse to come up to where he is standing, and for nothing to be there. Then the camera could pull back to a longer shot and show the posse walking around aimlessly, confused. They don't know where he is. They don't know what's happened. What's happened is that he's a place. One of the posse picks up Muldrow's red knife out of the snow and looks at it uncomprehendingly, and then they go on

walking around, as the camera pulls back, and that's the end.

We spent the rest of the afternoon talking about his poetry. His mind remained sharp, as evidenced by his ability to quote long passages of prose or poetry verbatim. During the 1960s Dickey had experienced an extraordinary streak of literary accomplishment, for which he won a Guggenheim Fellowship, the Melville Cane Award, and other prizes. But as he remarked, he didn't want to keep "repeating" himself, so he turned away from narrative by creating still pieces with complex sonic patterns. He was particularly proud of *Puella* (1982), a book in which the masculine, two-fisted poet had reinvented himself, exploring the consciousness of a young girl emerging into womanhood.

As night settled in, we tuned in to the University of South Carolina football game. He told me that he loved the university, that he loved his students, his children, and his friends, particularly Ward Briggs and Matt Bruccoli. He fingered T. R. Hummer's book *Walt Whitman in Hell* (1996), read a selection aloud, and then exclaimed, "Isn't that good? Poetry *can* make things happen." Picking up a pen with his long wrinkled fingers, he opened up a folder of papers. "I've been working on this poem for fifteen years; it's called 'Two Poems of the Body.' I don't know if I'll finish it."

He continued to write as I watched the game. Occasionally he looked up and read a few lines. He had enjoyed a long and prolific career. In 1988 he had been inducted into the fifty-member American Academy of Arts and Letters and assigned chair number 15, previously held by the scholar Wilbur Cross, the painter Raphael Soyer, and the novelist John Steinbeck. Good company. But despite his accomplishments and the physical agony he endured, the last time I saw James Dickey he was still struggling to write. Like the dying old man in "Gamecock," Dickey was "doomed," but "demanding, unreasonably / Battling to the death for what is his."

         –Ernest Suarez

Tributes
(Edited by Judith Baughman)

Betty Adcock

I first saw James Dickey when I attended a reading at North Carolina State University the year before he won the National Book Award. I was a housewife-mother in my twenties, unable yet to take classes. I hung around literary events like this reading, keeping quiet, learning. I had been reading this man's poems for years, watching for them in magazines, and I was trying for my own versions of the kind of verbal magic I had seen in his lines. The reading was wonderful. He was sober. He wore a suit and tie. He was not overly dramatic, but he gave the words their real weight. He neither preened nor showed off. He seemed very dignified. Of course I did not speak to him.

Sometime in the early 1970s, I think it must have been 1971 or 1972, I was working for a small advertising agency—in those days if you could write you could work for these, no degrees required, and I had none. I'd worked up from minimum-wage receptionist to copywriter-producer. I had also written my first book of poems, and the manuscript had been rejected on my first try. I was asked to interview for a job with a large ad agency, one that would pay what seemed to me an astronomical salary but would require all my energy—as such jobs always do. No one wanted my poetry, I felt. No poet whose work I admired deeply had read my work. Except for acceptances from the editors of some good magazines, I had had no responses in any sort of depth. Could I become a poet? I would write poems because I had to, but was there any point in the effort to make that activity the center of my life? I was in my thirties by then; my daughter would be entering college before long. I had decisions to make.

One day I simply picked up the phone in my office at the ad agency and called James Dickey at his home in South Carolina. I knew nothing about him beyond his poems. I cannot imagine how I came to make such an uncharacteristically impulsive call. He was gracious, kind enough not to voice what must have been his suspicions that I was some kind of crank or groupie or worse. He invited me to send him my work. He suggested I come to Columbia, and I did. I spent part of an afternoon at his home. Maxine and their younger son were there.

Of course I had to listen to much talk about the upcoming movie of *Deliverance* (1970). Dickey was very aware of his powerful personality. He liked showing off, scaring a beginner with wild pronouncements and strange observations, then looking sidelong to see how I might react to what he'd said. He was putting me on, as he did everyone much of the time. But when he spoke about my poems, which he had indeed read carefully, he was very serious. He told me to keep writing, that I was already a poet and had no choice in the matter. He pointed out lines he found strong and compared me

to older poets I admired. I left with renewed confidence and firmer intentions.

I didn't stop trying to make poetry the center of my life. Perhaps I'd have been as stubborn without James Dickey's encouragement, but I was isolated in the business world, lacking a formal literary education, and it *is* possible for the spirit to be starved out of anything, even poetry.

I did not communicate with Dickey again for many years. After my second book was published, he wrote me a letter I treasure. It was full of praise for the poems of a stranger. He had no memory of having met me or of having read my early work.

I can't know how much any event has influenced my life or my writing. I do know this: I stayed poor and kept writing poems. I never even went to the interview at the big ad agency.

Michael Allin

Jim taught me two great things—one a small technical secret, the other real big.

The secret is to sit down every day and not write, but just get started by copying out what you're working on. Something might cause you to put in a comma that wasn't there, then you might argue with it and decide to take it out . . . and you're working. Never mind about finishing. It isn't about finishing. It's about that comma. This singing-with-procedure concentration on detail was the navigator in Jim—"If you get it right, celestial navigation *demands* the universe to tell you where you are. *It has to!* "—and it was the navigator who evolved into the teacher who had you seeing poems in that unlikeliest of all places, your own life.

The other thing, the big thing that everyone got from Jim, was to take things on—writers, ideas, problems, illness, lack of aptitude or whatever else is wrong even more than what's right with you, and especially places—and find your own relationship with them in what he always called "this one human life." Not to triumph, but simply to come away with something, anything that makes the experience your own and, above all, to develop an admiring but unintimidated mind. (When I faced being drafted in the worst of the 1960s, Jim suggested that I join up!)

Jim was passion itself, but more than anything he enjoyed the human mind wherever he found it. Serious or silly, he turned the world into chronic mental fun. The summer Neil Armstrong walked on the moon, I swam across Lake Katherine every day—there were more nipping critters in it then than trash—and once as I emerged Jim pointed out a leech on my leg, which took us to his Britannica where we were hilariously fascinated to learn that the leech re-

Dickey engaged in one of his principal interests: playing bluegrass and country music

produces by "reciprocal copulation." *Leech* became one of the many, many triggering code words that were Jim's own personal navigational tables. From that day for the next twenty-eight years, we laughed whenever I used it so he could say, "Because: if you tell a leech to go fuck itself, it *will!*"

Places. The first time I ever saw the words *Jardin des Plantes* was in Jim's poem "Goodbye to Serpents." I loved the poem for its snakes in my imagined paradise of Paris, and for the little son in it, and for its searching irony that is quintessential Jim: that the poet's disconnection with what he's seeing dogs him and drives him to "God damn you, Dickey, *dig*" something out of it—to do what Jim called the hardest thing in the world, "Make a mountain out of a molehill."

So, years later, my first morning finally in Paris, I dragged my wife into that sad old art nouveau "serpentarium" off the rue Cuvier. Oh, Jim, was evil dying tired that day. The place was pathetic. The snakes were pathetic. My pilgrimage was pathetic. The dial tone was more dangerously alive than this place where my Eve said to me, "God damn you, I'm missing *Paris!*" Until a zookeeper ran through yelling, "On ferme! On ferme!" and ordered us outside and around to a big window looking into the cage of the python.

The python was as thick around as my thigh and had climbed vertically most of its fifteen feet up

a corner of the window. Its head was up out of sight and we didn't realize at first that it was a snake because its body was so big and gleaming dark like a wet tree. But it moved.

A three- or four-inch slit in the snake, perfectly positioned for us to see, widened, and out of it we watched eggs slowly appear, one by one, as asymmetrical and irregular as stones, no two alike. At the inside door of the python's cage two khaki-uniformed keepers and a blond woman wearing a white smock over a yellow dress were beside themselves with excitement. I have no idea how much time went by, but when we had counted seventeen eggs, they stopped coming. Then, after an animated consultation, the two nervous keepers climbed through the door into the cage, one with a gunny sack that he held up at full arms' length around the python's head, struggling to hold it as the snake began to writhe, while the other man handed the eggs out to the blond woman, who gathered them in her smock like a farmer's wife in her apron. When she had them all in her standing lap, both keepers bailed out of the cage. The two men and the woman disappeared until we saw them hurrying in a tight group, their six hands all carrying her smock full of eggs, out of the serpentarium and across the gravel and into another building.

The snake came down off the window, huge-headed and even more awesome in its horizontal length as it searched around the cage. My wife looked at me very seriously and said, "Take me anywhere, Michael." As we left, I crossed my fists over my heart and said to the Jardin des Plantes, "Thank you, Jim."

James Applewhite

James Dickey: A Brief Recollection

James Dickey's public persona did not much help his readers understand the heart of his vision. The shy sheep child, sacrificed on the duality between the human and the animal, is more essentially Dickey than the former Clemson halfback, firebombing aviator, or bow-hunting woodsman. Like Whitman's, Dickey's imagination entered more possibilities than most of us can be comfortable with: stewardess falling to her death, undressing, voyeur in his tree, truck driver homing in on a signal of children's cries from the heart of a city. The other, macho poses fail to prepare us for the passionate, far-reaching tenderness and empathy that grasped, from so many "Faces, Seen Once," the nearly anonymous, divine humanity all had in common.

Dickey's poems show us both winners and losers but tend to be read as praising only the former category. But even "The Firebombing" significantly records the horrors underneath the beautiful skin of fire this aviator sees, in his aesthetic detachment; and in Dickey's greatest poems, there is at least equal sympathy for those who do not prevail. The first aviator we remember from Dickey's *Poems: 1957–1967* (1967) is Donald Armstrong, who succeeded only in playing magnificent tricks for his captors (and for the reader) before "he toppled his head off" at the feet of the Japanese swordsman.

Dickey incorporated great vulnerabilities, mastered great war-related insecurities, and was honest enough in his poetry to report his frequent identifications with the deviant or socially reprehensible. Even his seemingly dominating narrators, as in "The Shark's Parlor," may exaggerate in memory, wondering, like Whitman, if what was so, was so, hardly able to credit the crazy impulse which led two kids to haul a shark into a house. Thus, even his most macho characters, in the poems, undercut themselves by the extremity of their claims. They invite us, by implication, to see, deeper down, the struggle against oblivion that drove both the original action and the often misleading reconstruction of it, in the poet's language.

The stone Dickey bruised his breast against was the world, and time and again his personae try as they may to change it—stewardess struggling to learn to fly as she falls, failed lifeguard imagining himself walking on water—winning against their defeats only in the expression of their supreme, shining efforts. So the sheep child faded from his hybrid existence beyond the human, but looks at us still, from his glass house, in our collective memory. So will Dickey's poems continue to gaze out at us from their hellish mild corners, challenging our normalcy, our inattention, our failures of empathy, our suburban boredom and lack of passion. The legendary size of Jim Dickey was founded not really in his own large frame, or in his physical appetites, but in the fierce dimension of his emotive imagination. He was able to envision, and to embody, in appropriate spectrums of words, a vast range of possibilities, from the bestial to the angelic. Within his naturalistic-seeming tales there resides the ambition and scope of the epic poet and the agonized, idealizing vision of the philosopher of the bone. His poems will endure.

I recall now two personal glimpses: driving him to a poetry reading in eastern North Carolina in the early 1960s, the failing recap of my old Buick beating out, under the fender, what he good-humoredly called "a new American prosody." And him sitting in my graduate student living room, watching the Masters on my black-and-white Sears TV, holding my three-year-old daughter on his lap. I remember from these moments, and from others like them, what many did not see: his essential humanity, his humor, his often-obscured kindnesses. The last letter he ever wrote me, addressed care of the American Academy in Rome in May of 1996, asks me to find for him a copy of Géricault's Byron, in the Keats-Shelley Museum. That is *my* Byron, he insisted. The Dickey who had room in his heart for failing recaps, for golf on TV and my young daughter and my beginning ambition and insecurity as a poet, as well for his crying children and war survivors and glorious losers, is *my* Dickey. May he remain with us.

Richard Bausch

But Not Die Out: An Appreciation, a Gratitude

The first time I ever saw James Dickey's name was on the shiny page of an *Atlantic Monthly,* circa 1966. Spring, I believe it was. Anyway, I remember sun outside; I was inside, sitting at a desk, wearing air force fatigues, waiting for students of mine to finish answering the questions of what was called a "block" exam. This was the Survival and Survival Equipment School of Chanute Air Force Base. Vietnam was heating up. We were working six days a week, round-the-clock shifts, training others like us for work in the field, which mostly meant work in Vietnam. I was half convinced that I might be a poet, or at least some kind of writer—I was doing it all the time back in the barracks, imitations mostly, and of course I'd commenced with the poets easiest to imitate: the Beats, so many of whom wrote from a kind of attitudinal effusion, rife with exclamations of studied ecstasy, a sort of *us* versus *them* stridency I found, at twenty-one, rather alluring. (Who doesn't find that sort of thing alluring at twenty-one?)

So I was waiting for my students to finish answering their objective questions about how many pounds of pressure was oxygen kept at in the tanks which accompanied the MD-1 Survival Kit with its one-man raft, and what procedures were necessary in order to procure food while floating on such a raft in the middle of the ocean, and here on the long green table was an *Atlantic Monthly,* part of a group of magazines lying there. I paged through it, thinking about one day publishing. Why not? It was pleasant enough to contemplate. And there were plenty of things I could be studiedly ecstatic about. I opened to the poem and looked at the poet's name. James Dickey. The poem was "For the Last Wolverine."

> They will soon be down
>
> To one, but he still will be
> For a little while still will be stopping
>
> The flakes in the air with a look.

I remember being impressed with the punctuation—the fact that the first line stood alone, and changed your sense of the word *down* as you got to the second line. I was impressed more by tricks of the appearance of words on a page, then. I didn't know nearly enough to bring more than that to a poem, any poem. But I liked this poem and marked the name, and later, when I made my usual ride into Urbana and the University of Illinois bookstore, I bought *Drowning with Others* (1962).

I read it with some appreciation for its difference from the Beats. There were no attitudes in it; the lines were arranged in a cadenced, musical way I could hear without quite understanding. There were no rhymes (I had learned from the Beats that rhyme was out, though Gregory Corso had some very good and funny rhymed poems in his book *The Happy Birthday of Death* [1960], which, by the way, is still a pleasure to read, as opposed to almost everything else the Beat poets did); there were no rhymes in the Dickey poems, and yet many of them were set in verse and *were* verse. You could hear it. Even being unlearned and fairly out of my element, as I then

was. At that time I had read almost nothing else of literature. I had read a smattering of Shakespeare and was reading *War and Peace.* Most of my other reading had been history and religion.

Yet I liked the poems in *Drowning with Others.* And when, a year later—after much more reading (there wasn't much else to do in that part of the world if you were stranded on an air base, without a car)—I bought *Poems 1957–1967,* I pored over it and tried to imitate it (I was reading Faulkner then, too, and trying to imitate him as well). I had come to be able to hear more of the subtle and various music in Dickey's lines, and I had found poems which I would carry with me into my middle age, and on, and I knew this then, too: "Falling" and "The Fiend" and "The Leap" and "The Performance." "Drinking From a Helmet" and "Angina" and "Pursuit From Under," and so many others.

I learned, sometime late in spring, that Dickey had come to the University of Illinois to give a reading and that I'd missed him. It seemed strange to me that a living writer would actually come to a university to read. I had thought writers lived off in some exclusive other world: Fitzgerald's Left Bank, or Hemingway's Spain. New York, or Provincetown. Key West.

I was twenty-two.

If someone had told me back then that one day I would know James Dickey, that he would give me the title of my first novel, that I would publish a story in *The Atlantic* and put a wolverine in that story in honor of Dickey's poem, that I would point this out to him and we would have a laugh over it—if someone had told me that knowing James Dickey would lead me to knowing George Garrett, and Mary Lee Settle and Fred Chappell, too, that I would one day call these people my friends, I would of course never have believed it. Even now, it sounds like a kid's daydreaming. This past April, I was inducted into the Fellowship of Southern Writers, and on a bronze plaque fixed to the back of a chair I found my name engraved under this: *James Dickey, 1923–1997.* That, too, is going far past daydreaming.

The last time I saw him, I almost didn't recognize him. He was sitting in a wheelchair, with oxygen tanks in his lap. I sat next to him and waited to say something—it had been six years since I'd seen him. He was attending to several people who wanted to talk to him—two women, librarians, and a couple of students. Finally he looked my way. Without the slightest hesitation, he reached across his frail chest and offered me his good right hand.

"Hello, Dick," he said. His grip was strong, solid.

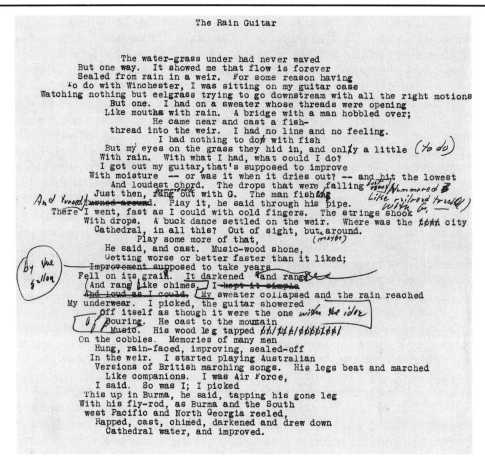

Dickey's revised typescript for his 1972 poem collected in Strength of Fields *(by permission of the Estate of James Dickey)*

"Been a long time, Jim," I said.

He nodded. "How's everything?"

"Pretty good," I said. I felt at a loss. He smiled, and then someone else was seeking his attention. I decided to get up and give him a little room. He had leaned one way to better hear what a woman was saying—something about the flowers in the garden where we all were. I went on to the other end of the place, thinking about how far we had all come. All the stories I had ever told about him—all the times I had performed him for others, clowning, giving my impression of his gestures and mannerism, his voice. He was Big Jim. Jimbo. A huge presence—physically and intellectually; a man capable of fantastic excess in all things, a prodigal talent, a generous and outrageous ego, a lover of every worthy thing ever said or written, and an inveterate trader of jokes, good and bad, dirty or clever, mindless or complex. A poet of the first rank—maybe one of the best we ever had—and a good novelist, too. A brilliant essayist, especially about poetry. And *poetry* was the word he used to wear emblazoned across the back of one of his leather jackets.

Once, when he was younger and I was young, we sat reading our poems to a group of my friends. This was in early 1978. He and I were teaching at George Mason University; I was part-time then, unpublished. Karen and I were living in a run-down old hunter's cabin, with a leaky roof, and no closets to speak of, and a dirt basement. But we had invited a dozen or so people, and Jim had come up from where he and Deborah were staying, a few blocks down the street. We got to reading poems. He read "In the Mountain Tent," I remember, to great effect. And then I read one of mine, called "Standing on Snow." Jim liked the poem, and said so. And I said the truth about it—that it wasn't nearly at the level of "In the Mountain Tent." He considered this a moment, then leaned back and said, "You know, I've never liked false modesty, Dick." He paused. Then seemed to consider again. "Or even *true* modesty, now that I think of it."

And then there was the time, years later, we spent a quiet morning in another of a long line of houses Karen and I rented in those hard times—this one considerably better appointed than the first. I was making poached eggs and toast, and Jim stood leaning on the counter, talking. We got onto the *Iliad,* and tragic Hector, how the *Iliad* is really Hector's story. We had been talking about it for some time, and then we were quiet. "Well, Dick," he said, abruptly, "we're both gonna die, and there's nothing we can do about it." And it was truly as if we had both been up all night trying to figure a way out of it:

"What if we—no, that wouldn't work."

"Well, what about—naw, hell, that won't work either."

I remember being glad and admiring of his vast knowledge. I remember soaking it up, listening to him, watching his eyes glitter with love of the good line, the thing said wonderfully and rightly, the delight of the poet in the *sound* of a phrase: "Only line of Edwin Arlington Robinson's that I remember is 'And Lingard, in his eerie joy.' Isn't that great?"

When I sold my novel, *Real Presence* ([1980], then called "The Vineyard Keeper"—it was a story about a frightened priest having trouble being a priest), I called to tell him about it. He said, "Now here's what you do. You're like the kid who comes to school thinking there's gonna be school, and somebody's just said school's out. School's out, good buddy, and it'll never happen again, just this way. You go out there and spoil yourself for a day. Just have a ball, okay?"

A couple of months later, after I'd told him that my editor didn't like the title of the novel, he asked to see it. I had my editor send a copy by express mail. Jim called two days later and said, "You know, I've been reading Gerard Manley Hopkins, to keep up with this Catholic wife of mine, and there's a line he said that gave me an idea for a title for this novel. Hopkins said, 'If I didn't believe in the Real Presence of Christ in the host, I would become an atheist the very next day.' And you know, the poor man went through terrible crises of spirit, in his life. Do you know the sonnets?"

I said I did. Jim went on: "He was wrestling with some bad angels, whud'n he? And he won, too. Hopkins's last words were 'I'm happy, so happy.' Anyway, Dick, I think you ought to call your novel Real Presence."

I said I'd try that on my editor (feeling a little dubious; I can't imagine another name for that book now).

Before Jim hung up, he said, "Well, remember what I told you that time in your living room, when you read me the first thing of yours that I ever heard."

I remembered. And, laughing, told him so.

What he had said was a flattering, kindly, flippant but greatly generous admonition, one that he bestowed on younger writers in whose work he found something to like; I knew this, and even so it was one of the best gestures of encouragement I've ever had as a writer. He had smiled and nodded with that look of shared understanding that was so like him, and he said, "My only advice to you as a writer is, don't die. Just don't die."

For Jim, Death was more than anything the enemy, Silence. The stilled word. The stopped possibility of expression, the end of voices, of the beautiful clamoring song, the glorious tragic continuing story of people in all the permutations of experience, brought alive through language shaped as Art. Say it: Poetry.

James Dickey has disappeared into his poems.

Rereading all of them, one senses that he will indeed fare quite well, there, and this work will have its place in the world. If I could address him directly, I would say: Jim, rest well, old son, you have won away from, you have won at home. Farewell.

David Bottoms

Jim Dickey on the Bank of Lake Katherine

In my study I have a wall of sectional bookcases, the old lawyer kind, somewhat beaten up but prized by me since they are almost all I salvaged from a fifteen-year marriage. Here I keep my small but select poetry collection, the books I care about and keep coming back to. On top of these bookcases I've propped a few important photos. One is a 1947 wedding picture of my mother and father, she wearing a wide-brimmed straw hat tilted back like a halo, he wearing a white suit and shoes, a perfect complement. A few more family photos keep them company, folks long gone or scattered; a photo of my friend Steve Belew, just back from Vietnam, playing the blues on his Gibson flattop; a funeral-home fan, the kind you used to see in country churches, with an illustration of Jesus as the Good Shepherd; and an eight-by-ten photo of my friend Jim Dickey.

Often when I'm working at my desk I'll look up at that picture and see his eyes gazing down at me. There's a softness in them that you don't typically see in other photos, those dramatic shots of him drawing a bow string or fretting a guitar, or just hamming it up. No theatrics here, rather a quietness, a tenderness in his eyes that suggests an understanding and acceptance of common failure. This is a picture taken late in his life, though before his fatal sickness, I would say. His face is serious, and he looks tired. In his hand he's holding some sort of navigational instrument as though he's trying to explain how to use it. His expression seems to be saying, "Look, I'll go through this one more time with you." He's wearing a dark polo shirt and khakis, a pendant or medal I can't make out, and of course, the CSA buckle found on some battlefield by his brother Tom. The waters of Lake Katherine stretch out behind him, only a few riffles on the surface. On the far bank rolls a dark wall of trees.

I work almost directly under this photo, so that when I look up from my desk, I catch him eye to eye. This, to me, recalls the gentle encouragement that characterized his friendship. "Listen," he says again with those eyes, "all writers fail. Good ones less often because they're willing to work through frustration." From the first moments of our friendship, he said similar things, prodding me on to do all I could with the word. Only after a few years did I begin to understand that he was trying also to encourage himself.

He said something like this to his graduate class only a few days before he died. The folks at the university taped that last class and replayed a portion over the public address system during his memorial service on the campus Horseshoe. Quoting Flaubert, Jim said, "The life of a writer is a dog's life." Then after a pause, "But it's the only life worth living. You suffer more, you're frustrated more, by things that don't bother other people." Only a moment earlier he'd mentioned Michelangelo's little adage about the angel in the stone. The shape of the angel was always there; the marble only needed to be chipped away. He wanted us to remember that the chipping was hard work. Too often we tend to think that a great writer simply spills the words onto the page, and there they lie, exhibiting genius. Jim wanted us to know that great writing requires great talent, certainly, but also great labor. He spent a lifetime learning that, and anyone doubting that he was a worker need only take a quick look through his papers, housed now at Emory University. A glance at the drafts of "May Day Sermon" will suffice.

Something else he said many times connects. In that last class he put it this way: "The world doesn't esteem the poet very much, but we are the masters of the superior secret, not they." During our last conversation, a long telephone conversation a few days before he died, he told me that the purpose of the poet was "to make the world available to the reader." He'd said this to me many times, but now he wanted to emphasize it. The world, he believed, held secrets it would only give up to the artist, and for the poet anything less than a revelation of those secrets was the sin of triviality. These cautions are what he wanted to leave to his students at South Carolina and to all of us who have been his students more informally. But those words, and his constant gaze from the top of my bookshelf, are not only counsel. They are also affirmations. The angel is, indeed, inside the stone. The talented who labor hard may watch it take shape. Not every time, of course, but the possibility is real.

I remember many things about the man and all with great pleasure: his outrageous jokes and stories, his funny imitations (Marlon Brando most impressive), his guitar playing and his love of the bluegrass flatpicking (even my own, especially a tune called "Jerusalem Ridge"), the personal kindnesses he showed me over our sixteen-year friendship. But when I struggle with my own poems, which is most always, his call to hard work and seriousness of purpose is my best medicine. I go back to his poems, and my amazement is renewed. He found the angel more often than I could ever hope to. Then I glance at the top of my bookcase, and his eyes catch me again with all their tenderness and gentle encouragement.

Hayden Carruth

The main personal memory I have of Jim is a phone call he made to me in, I think, 1969, which was a particularly bad year for me. He offered to send me money. I declined his offer, but I was genuinely touched by his concern. I think each of us had a good deal of respect for the other even though our lives didn't intersect much. His review of my first book was one of the best and was important to me.

R. V. Cassill

A poet is a poem too unruly to fit his page, and the crumpled life in his waste basket is the majestic gloss for the achievement of his finished books. To encounter him in those books is not quite the same as to encounter him in the "Cage Country" on the other side of the confining bars.

It seems a long time that I have known him, but in those three decades I was never sure I was his friend. I did know there was a fiercely profound recognition between us, whatever disguise of civilization might confine us to separate roles. A long time ago I settled on definitions of his merit that barely changed over the years when I saw nothing of him.

I saw him as preeminent among his peers, not for his versification but for his conceptions. His sheep child, his lifeguard, owl king, and stewardess on her long plunge through the "beast whistle of space" are not in my mind the blades drawn by authority from the primal stone but are the substance of the planetary stone itself.

Those who knew him longer and at closer range than I have brought me anecdotes of his life, not seldom hilarious. Hearing them I responded as I responded to his poems. "That's him! That's Jim!"

Leslie Fiedler

I have never forgotten the letter James Dickey wrote to me in 1960, praising my poetry for demonstrating "what the English language can do when it really tries." His hope that he "might someday hold a collection of those poems aloft" has never, alas, been fulfilled. Indeed, most who read me as a critic are unaware that I began my career as a poet. Somewhat similarly, Dickey is now likely to be remembered not for his poems but for his novel *Deliverance* and the film made of it. It seems to me, therefore, necessary to remind latterday readers that in his verses Dickey really did for our common language what he extravagantly attributed to mine.

George Garrett

I first met Jim Dickey in the late 1950s or early 1960s (certainly before 1961), and, needless to say, I had heard about him and had seen his poems in the magazines and, as well, his reviews of other people's poems (including my own) before that. So we are talking more than thirty years, maybe forty, of acquaintanceship. Never close friends—that wasn't possible for a lot of little reasons, mostly trivial; never enemies either. In fact, we were collaborators a number of times and places, at writers' conferences, especially the big and inimitable one at Hollins College in 1970. Shortly after that we worked together as a kind of team at the University of South Carolina, dividing up the chores of creative writing, sharing a lot of the same students along the way. Middle of the 1970s I moved on, he stayed. Stayed on to the end. I saw him for the last time at the Fitzgerald Centenary Celebration at South Carolina. While I was still there in Columbia I was often invited to his house, where we cooked up all kinds and receipts of mischief and laughter. Sometimes he and Maxine came to our apartment. Sometimes we went to the movies or, at Jim's generous invitation, to the Palmetto Club. Where we ran up some amazingly grand tabs.

Later, thanks to Cleanth Brooks, we were both charter members of the Fellowship of Southern Writers. We met and had some (believe it or not) wild and woolly times in Chattanooga. The whole fellowship will miss him.

Dickey as the sheriff confronting Jon Voight in the 1972 Warner Bros. production of Deliverance

Having said that much, I also have to say I did not know him well. Oh, yes, I knew of, heard about, contributed to the multitude of stories and anecdotes that followed him all his life. And not much without his approval. I know of no other literary figures, no contemporary at least, more cloaked and camouflaged in a mantle of myths. He said and did a lot of memorable things, things which were, in fact, remembered and retailed and modified and mythologized in the telling. I have collected them and passed a few along myself, in conversation or a couple or three times in writing. Some day, one of these days, before we are all gone, we need to gather up all the Dickey stories, real and apocryphal indifferently, and preserve them.

I think that would suit Jim just fine. I believe he understood exactly what was happening and that there was some design in it. And it was for a purpose. In one of the few perfectly straightforward and uncomplicated (and unmasked) conversations we ever had he told how he was fully aware of the impression he was creating and the myths that circulated about him, adding that, as he saw it, that was the least he could do to be worthy of the poems, the great ones, he had been given. It was not himself, he told me, who wanted celebrity and notoriety and public attention. But, as his experience, and especially his brief experience in the advertising world, had taught him, the American scene was (and is) too busy and self-concerned to pay attention to poetry, for example, good or bad or indifferent, without some means of capturing attention. If he had to dance a jig to do it, it was all right with him and, in the words of the old song, "nobody's business but my own."

Either before or after that conversation, which, as I recall, simply confirmed my own opinion as to why he was (almost) always "on," performing, I wrote a little "snapshot" to introduce his interview in a collection of interviews with nineteen writers who participated in the Hollins conference in 1970. Each of the writers, in the absence of a "real" photograph, was introduced with a verbal picture. His seems oddly appropriate now and, I hope, celebrates the life he lived and the poems that live on after him. Here is the "snapshot" from *The Writer's Voice* (1973). I meant it then and mean it now:

Legends, myths, fables and fabliaux, anecdotes, quotations from, hard and funny sayings, true and false, wheel and flock about him, a shrill invisible halo of birds explosively circling the edges of his wide-brimmed Warner Brothers sheriff's hat, the one he probably sleeps in (they say). No, not once upon a time an ad man for nothing at all, and he can *do* some splendid impersonations, best of all (I think) King Kong and Marlon Brando. Yes, more masks and costumes than a whole Halloween party, more hidden rabbits and aces than a magician. Something else! But . . . but behind all obvious shucks and colorful charades is the powerful dedicated poet and a complex man burning alive in pure intensity. Not even his big, strong, long-legged body can deny his curious gentleness, his clear vulnerability. His head-high easy swagger does not disguise his suffering. Jim can be like a carnival pitchman because the truth is so precious to him and always so threatened. To know him, the only way, look for him, truly tall and strong and all alive, in his poems.

Gordon Lish

Dickey the poet? Sometimes great, sometimes not great. Dickey the novelist? Sometimes greatish, sometimes not so greatish. Dickey the man? Great, great, great!—in every instance of my great luck in being in his company, greatness itself, that's what James Dickey was. Well, hell, this man was a man and a half—and I loved him and did all I could to keep clear of him, lest his presence remind me of the puniness of my soul. Tell you this one other thing: let Dickey take from my hands one of my babies once; let Dickey throw this baby up and up and up: hey, pay attention: it wasn't a thing I would have trusted even my father—or mother—to do. So how's that for, you know, for tribute?

Walt McDonald

If we could be even half as decent and brave as the heroes in James Dickey's poems—Mangham, for instance, or Donald Armstrong—we'd deserve the plaudits of our pals. His best men are not Charles Atlas but ordinary, with "spindle-shanked forearms." Those of us who love his poetry know that the best in Dickey was no braggart. "Only those who did could have done it," he wrote in "Between Two Prisoners." It's the normal trucker who against all odds slows down and goes in to "Them, Crying." Whatever fate such heroes face doesn't stop the best of them from trying to make the stand on the hands "perfect," does not "stop / Mangham for one freezing minute / of his death // From explaining" to us for "our good."

Whatever happens to us, his splendid poems—like Mr. Mangham the dying math teacher—teach us "dullards" more than blackboard math or prosody, teach more values about ourselves than any of us can grasp: "Identities! Identities!" "It is difficult to get the news from poetry," Dr. Williams said. But for me, so much of what James Dickey wrote is essential. Dead poets like Dickey, like dead coaches, "live in the air, son   live / In the ear / Like fathers, and *urge*   and *urge*. They want you better / Than you are."

In Dickey Country
for James Dickey

Jim said travel's a mean canoe trip
down a river about to be dammed,
home a bow and arrows ready,
a good dog sleeping at your feet.
Memory is Doris Holbrook's wrench
and a well-oiled Harley for a getaway.

Life is a trap and always short
and often ugly, if you're a lifeguard
and the boy drowns when you're not around.
We're all drowning with others
and all we can do is try to save someone
another hour, maybe by the highway,

your own boy maddened by bees.
Odd things happen, sleeping out at Easter
or in the mountain tent, hunting relics
at battlefields and finding *fathers,
fathers.* Always, in masks like armor
or in the common grave, they wait,

all living and long-gone heroes
and out-of-shape runners wildly connected,
only one leap to beyond-reason gold,
one sip from a helmet for the last brief hope
of another, who died as we all must come

to our last performance, having done

all we can do, kneeling down by our hacked,
glittering graves, under pressure,
or in amazing armor we put on
when we begin living forever, falling
in the dark without a parachute, calling
with our last few feet of breath for God.

Willie Morris

I am deeply saddened by the loss of my old comrade Jim. I always called him Jimbo. I've been thinking of him constantly these recent days. It breaks my heart that I couldn't be there today [at the University of South Carolina's memorial service]—a horrendous conflict involving writing that Jim would have understood. I'm soon to begin editing the "James Dickey Reader" drawn from his poems, fiction, and essays. I hope that will be my memorial of sorts to him and that I'm adequate to the task.

Jim was a towering literary presence, one of those truly great ones who achieved richly deserved immortality in his own lifetime. In American letters he was unmatched, among other things, for sheer *virtuosity:* poems, novels, and many of the finest literary essays of our day, an absolutely fabulous corpus of work. For that reason alone he has not really left us and never will. All we have to do is reach for the nearest bookshelf to have his imperishable spirit with us forever.

In this brief tribute I won't talk about his work but offer some snippets about Jim the man. The two really can't be separated, because he was in the highest order of artists whose words were such profound reflections and embodiments of his own character and personality. And what a character and personality! I could spend eight hours telling stories about Jim, as could all of us blessed enough to have known him, because he touched everyone within reach of him with his wonderful, indeed incredible, persona, gargantuan and life-giving.

I was with Jim over the years in many disparate American venues, from the treacherous stone canyons of Manhattan to the byzantine corridors of Washington, D.C., to the beacon of the New South, Atlanta, to the haunted alluvial flatland called the Mississippi Delta, where he went wild with his camera and sent me a portfolio of his Delta photographs which I cherish. He was one of the most generous people I ever knew. He was always wanting to *give* you things. He was intensely proud of and deeply loved his children. He talked often to me of the pride he had in Chris and Kevin. As for young Bronwen, I can recall at least two dozen times in various

Dickey on the grounds of the University of South Carolina, where he served as poet in residence from 1969 to his death (photo by Terry Park)

locales in which he withdrew his wallet and showed me his photographs of her.

I admired his keen sense of mischief. In a restaurant one day on Capital Hill, where he was serving as consultant in poetry to the Library of Congress, our equivalent of the national poet laureate, he got into a conversation with a couple at the next table. They wanted to know what line of work he was in. He told them he was a salesman for Dickey Business Machines. He became so eloquent in this discourse that after a time the man pulled out his checkbook and was about to purchase an order for the latest thing in cash registers. At this Jim became a little guilty and admitted he was not a gadgets salesman, only a poet, and by the way, had they ever read Rilke?

I can remember as vividly as yesterday the morning we were driving from my hometown of Yazoo City up to Ole Miss when he began talking to me about the phenomenon of terror, of the awful human experience of encountering unexpected and fortuitous terror, and what did one do about it? He went on and on in this brilliant, vivid monologue. Two years or so later, when he sent me one of the early copies of *Deliverance* and I started reading it, I recognized with sudden clarity that he was writing that book in his mind's eye that day, that he was actually trying it out on me.

I wish I had taken his courses at the university, for teaching was also part of his crown, of course, and others have told me what a superlative teacher he was, one who changed many lives. I think it was the writer Pat Conroy, who once took his courses, who told me that whenever he left Dickey's classes, he was so enthusiastic he not only wanted to *read* the book of verse under discussion that day, he wanted to *eat* it.

I can see, I guess, that I have a little memoir here someday. It would be immensely difficult to capture the whole essence of the man. He was a vital, elemental force. He was brave, brilliant, and outrageously funny. In his indwelling soul he felt the true nature of things, of the shadow behind the act, of the complexities and transgressions and passions of the human heart. He suffused the lives of many, many people in ways none of us will ever, ever forget. I was very lucky to have known him. I loved Jim Dickey. Godspeed, Jimbo!

John Simon

Jim Dickey was a force of nature, which is what a poet ought to be. When he came into a room, one could feel the temperature go up by several degrees. When one discussed the two topics most important to him, poetry and life, enthusiasm for or against his specific subject was like a fire lighted under one's chair. When he slapped your back in friendship or approbation, you felt one of the elect.

Dickey did the most ordinary, everyday things in the grand style. If he flirted with a waitress in a restaurant, it was not some lout trying to score with the hired help; it was a primal masculine principle responding to the allure of the eternal feminine. When he drank copiously at a party, it never seemed to dilute his intellect; if, as some say, he drank out of a hidden sadness, he gallantly kept it hidden. When he told an anecdote, it came out ready for Chaucer, Boccaccio, or Mark Twain to commit it to paper.

Being that he was big and bluff and, in the jolliest way, blustering, and being also that the South was commodiously ensconced in his speech, it was possible for someone who didn't know better to mistake him for a redneck in a suit. But in a trice, out would come a quotation from Dante or Mallarmé,

pointedly relevant and in the original language, uttered as casually as a "please" or a "thank you." He knew things that a smiling grizzly bear or a hunter with bow and arrow had no business knowing and shared his wisdom with us without stinting, affectation, or self-consciousness.

That he was a major poet I never doubted. Some of his poems thrilled me, some of them were beyond me. But even in the latter I found an authenticity that would not be denied; visualize a good suit of fine cloth with exquisite tailoring that happens not to be your size but that you handle with reverence. He wrote poems on many subjects, but what I always recognized in them was an archetypal American landscape looming within. Now the roles are reversed: James Dickey has become a perennial part of the American landscape.

Dave Smith

Dickey of the Tribe

People who knew Dickey the man invariably used the familiar Jim, and they thought of him as both looming and gentle, a sort of John Wayne. He encouraged this shortening of the distance between people, and he believed in intense relationships. I think he hugged me on the second occasion we met, in Saint Louis, Missouri, where he had come to read poems in 1968. He said to me once that he loved people more than others did, perhaps in contradistinction to Ezra Pound, who had written "the public is a jerk." Poets, I think, are loners by definition, so it was, even in my callow youth, a shock to see this self-proclaimed wilderness lover had a thing for his fellows. He was contradictory that way, as poets are. I never was able, in all the years I passionately admired him, to comfortably call him Jim. He was *James* to me, a hierarchical leader of the tribe, one whose eminence deserved every title and every honor.

Yet in what did that eminence consist? Dickey won only the National Book Award in Poetry (*Buckdancer's Choice,* 1965) and a handful of magazine prizes. He was far less belaureled than his senior Southern poet Robert Penn Warren, who held three Pulitzers, and less medaled by far than Allen Ginsberg, John Ashbery, or his longtime nemesis, Robert Bly. But I am willing to bet that among those who do read poetry, Dickey's are the memorable and readable poems. His *Poems 1957–1967* remains an icon of a decade notable for Vietnam, Mayor Daley, the political assassinations of Kennedys and King, Charles Manson, the Peace Corps, affirmative action, Ray Charles, James Brown, and the Beatles.

Dickey campaigned for Sen. Eugene McCarthy, the peace candidate, and he posed on national television with his bow and arrow for a feature presented at halftime of a University of South Carolina basketball game. He taught the novelist Pat Conroy. He wrote the best criticism of poetry published in his generation in *Babel to Byzantium: Poets and Poetry Now* (1968). He jumped out of airplanes and MGs, went to jail drunk, and was elected to the American Academy or whatever it is that honors one hundred writers, painters, musicians, and so forth.

Dickey's eminence lay in an imagination that was big, outrageous, independent, aggressive, and, finally, healthy. The usual word for this is *moral,* a word we now fear. He stood, when he could stand, for a tribe's values: courage under fire, a willingness to take fire, an appetite for sublime vision, manliness in big graces and big tendernesses, a passion for the quirky beauties that language can provide the ear. I don't think it is off the mark to say that he was a *lover,* even as he was a consumer, of the world. He had little use for the charlatan, the self-inflated noisemakers that poets so often are, but you had to hear his prissy, delicate way of saying *poetry* to know how much this arcane art mattered to him. In that, he linked us to a world of manners, concerns not defined by cash values, discriminating minds and intelligences not pushed around by the Boston–New York academic troops.

In late years Dickey's poetry was so out of fashion only the poets talked about it. He was the sheriff-actor who wrote *Deliverance*. He was the subject of boozy anecdotes that aligned him with behavior many wished they could bring off and few managed, for it always seemed only small by comparison. The poets noticed him for this and for his poems. I don't know what his one-time public noticed him for, if anything. Dickey connected us to roaring bards, Roethke, Dylan Thomas, the Russians. He made us believe the world need not be trivial, dull, unmeaning, and you could, if you were like me, think of him, sometimes, as a Beowulf. Who among us is like that now? Kinnell? Bly? Hall? Even Hugo and Wright didn't match him. The closest alive may be Carolyn Kizer. It's telling that he debunked Lowell and admired Berryman.

I heard he was in bad shape a year before his death and drove to Columbia to see him, staying only a little more than an hour. He was then attached to an oxygen cylinder; he'd lost so much weight he looked like a weak old tree and sat amid knee-high piles of books that surfed outward to fill a very large room. He said he was reading these. I noticed my last book in one of the quivery little towers but did not dare to ask what he thought of it.

This was the man who, upon hearing in 1968 that I'd been drafted, called me out of the blue to express his concern and goodwill. I'd met him twice for about twelve minutes total then. He was the man who in that same year, at then Webster College, in Saint Louis, peered through a drunken consciousness at an audience, good Lord, of nuns. That's what the college was about. He started with "Adultery." Then he read "The Sheep Child." And then, blinking over a great lectern he kept rocking, he saw my wife and I on the front row and stopped reading only to come sit and chat with us for a few moments. Only when I had nudged him and said the nuns were waiting did he grin and go back to his sex and poetry routine.

Jim Dickey treated me the way he would have treated anyone he actually recognized, reading audience or not. He extended his grace and his affection, his humor and his stumping for poetry in the face of what he must have thought a potentially philistine group. He read great that night. But then he always read great. He made you feel alive with words. In that last hour we covered a wide anthology of his personal favorites, most of them startling me in that I expected dislike (Berryman?). He thought James Wright and Richard Hugo were whiners, an opinion that disappointed me. He did not recant his admiration for Roethke, an admiration I do not entirely share. When I saw he was weary, I stood. I felt that I was somehow at attention for what he had meant to me as a young poet. He took my hand, turned it palm up and kissed my palm, saying "you won't see me again."

What melodramatic claptrap, I thought. And so like big Jim to pull off, the sly grin, the deep eyes watching, and for it all the sense of a ceremony with power. It certainly made me nervous, and I was glad to leave. But now I think of it as the moment of recognition of something substantial—friendship, apprenticeship finished, poetry carried on?—and I know only James Dickey could have brought me to the sense of gratitude I have. For him. For his poems. For his bigness. For his capacious and unyielding love that made him the tall tree under which the rest of us could rise a little.

It doesn't make a lot of sense to track those whom he influenced because he was, as the Brits say, a one-off. Those who know his poems know his was a world outside the now-urban grids. He liked to believe in the natural world, the deterministic, animal-ruled, and, by comparison, clean, if not pure, existence. For most of us that's a world as gone as the movies of the forties with their bungalows and smokers and fair cosmological operations. I think Dickey was naive in the way, oddly enough, those veterans of World War II who save the lovely future were naive. But that's only one side of a vision that is toughly human, that has at its heart a fear of being that only his big courage could face. Not many poets have ever had such an expansive, complex view—Whitman, Dickinson, Frost, Warren, Neruda, Mistral come to mind—and it is neither imitable nor much inheritable. When gone, it's gone, and that's the great shame.

James Dickey didn't doubt the durability of his poems, and I don't either. He appealed to our endless appetite for stories. He fed our hunger for conviction and courage. He made myths that answer our mysteries. We live in a time that believes it can legislate final solutions to bedeviling problems of the heart. We like to think we can outlaw racism, injustice, inability, hurt's memory, the urges to war and harm and action that assuage what we are. Dickey's poems did not much accept what our intellectual lives value. He wrote books, it must be said, for men. But the readers now are vastly women. Our tribe's character is dominantly feminine. Yet his poetry sings what transcends all that because at its best, as epic struggle, it is timeless. It is so, finally, for the singular reason that it is about freedom, and freedom can't be legislated unless it is already won by the body and soul of the man or woman who would keep it and honor it. Freedom is not the habit of a small life but the ambition of the largest lives, one by one, with a name and a rank and a place that is not given but is earned. James Dickey earned his place. Let the rest of us do as well.

William Styron

One of the most beautiful tributes ever made by one writer to another was that made by Jim Dickey upon the death of Truman Capote. It could only have been written by a man who, like Jim, knew firsthand of the hard work, anguish, but also of the final exaltation of the artist's calling. I wish I had the time, and also the gift, to be able to pay such homage to my friend Jim, but I hope these few words will in some way express my admiration for the poet who was the laureate of his generation. I come from the same generation—the generation of World War II—and Jim and I were both born in the South; our Southern upbringing in the years of the Great Depression, and our experience in uniform during the war, helped weld our long and enduring companionship.

Jim was Southern to his fingertips, but he was of that category of Southerner, richly endowed with humanity and learning, that always confounds Northerners. My Mississippi friend Willie Morris tells the story of a taxi ride he made with Jim and another Southerner from LaGuardia airport to Manhattan. The taxi was driven by a beetle-browed type who thought the Dixie accents from the backseat gave him the license to erupt into a tirade against black people. For a long while the three riders listened to this racist diatribe, until at last Jim, exasperated beyond endurance, leaned forward and said: "Shut up! If there's one thing I can't stand it's an amateur bigot."

What Jim had seen and suffered during the war was, like his Southernness, a determining element in much of what he wrote, and I began to understand this part of him back in the early 1970s, when he lived near me for a summer on Martha's Vineyard. It was the summer just before the release of that fine movie *Deliverance* (1972), and Jim was on a perpetual high, quite aware that he was on the verge of that rare happening: that of an author of an exceptional novel seeing an exceptional movie made of it. As everyone in the world knows, Jim loved the bottle—and so did I in those days—and I shudder to recall that we would hit the tennis court at 10:00 in the morning fortified by a pitcher of dry martinis. After these disastrous games we'd sit on my front porch, and it was there that he told me about his life in the air force. He spoke of fear and of the exquisite fragility and vulnerability of the men who flew those planes, and as he told me of these desperate matters, I began to see how *Deliverance,* which I had so admired as a novel, was, in a sense, an allegory of fear and survival: of innocent and well-meaning men, set upon by forces of inexplicable evil, who nonetheless triumph even if that triumph is by the skin of their teeth. An awareness of the nearly unbearable sweetness of life, which we cling to despite preposterous hazards, is at the heart of Jim's work.

Jim was rambunctiously and vigorously alive to a degree I've rarely known in anyone. His energy carried over into his prose and, perhaps more significantly, into the best of his poetry, which will surely live as long as that of any poet of his time. His personal excesses and abuses committed upon himself were the result of journeying to dark places that other people have shunned, and having the need to find the solace of forgetting. What one must remember about James Dickey are his words, words that will timelessly sing like these:

My green graceful bones fill the air
With sleeping birds. Alone, alone
And with them I move gently.
I move at the heart of the world.

Mona Van Duyn

James Dickey's poems excited me for the first time, on first hearing, at the YMHA in New York, where three of us "young" poets, strangers to each other, read together. I pounded my palms to pinkness after his reading and watched for further work when I went back home. His reputation rose like a meteor. Soon he was in manic demand for poetry readings all over the country and perhaps set a pioneer record of some sort for performances given per week. He came through Saint Louis (my hometown) fairly often, once bringing his first wife and two little boys, usually spending the evening, sometimes the night, with us, talking, singing hymns and strumming his guitar, downing impressive quantities of alcohol, radiating his conscious but completely compelling charm.

When Robert Lowell died, it seemed clear that James Dickey would receive the mantle of top American poet. Instead, he veered from poetry into writing a best-selling novel, and, with the equally popular movie version of it (in which he played a small part himself), entered a kind and degree of celebrity not available to a poet. (When I was in Spain on a Guggenheim-supported trip abroad, I was thrilled to see in Madrid the block-long lines of moviegoers waiting to buy tickets to the Spanish-titled version of *Deliverance*.)

After his further exploration into the novel form, Dickey returned to poetry. However, by this time the American poetry scene had changed, with dozens of qualified applicants for leading poet, a tremendous democratization of poetry publishing, an army of traveling poetry readers, and a semi-amnesia about his earlier work and reputation. Alcohol was not a friend to Dickey's writing, but his best work will *surely* always remain a landmark in American poetry.

Herman Wouk

James Dickey in person was much like his poetry: masculine, salty, original, beguiling, and utterly American. We met and became friends when he occupied the poetry chair at the Library of Congress, and I was working in Washington on my World War II novels. I admired his wide-ranging gifts and greatly enjoyed his humor and his zest for life and art.

Interview with Stanley Burnshaw

This interview was conducted in Stanley Burnshaw's apartment in New York City on 28 March 1997.

DLB: At lunch you started to talk about reviving Christina Stead. Let's start with that.

Burnshaw: I met Christina Stead in August 1935 when I was working as an editor of the weekly *New Masses*. She and her companion Bill Blake—an American Marxist ex-banker and novelist-to-be—had come over from England, and Michael Gold introduced us. They had met in Paris the summer before as delegates to the First International Congress of Writers for the Defence of Culture—1934, the year when writers from everywhere were trying to build an intellectual's front against fascism. Chris and Mike had become good friends, and Chris and Bill and I became close friends. After a year they sailed back to Europe but returned in '37. Christina's huge novel on banking, *The House of All Nations,* came out the following year to prestigious reviews that shocked her publishers, Simon and Schuster, and their "marketing experts." Two years later *The Man Who Loved Children* appeared, a "family novel" in the midst of World War II! It did remarkably well in view of the time and in spite of oddly mixed reviews: it confounded critics, though they sensed its power. Two more novels were published before she went back to Europe at the end of '46, and a third in '48, a fourth in '52—then no more. Publishers lost interest in her though Clifton Fadiman kept praising her in *The New Yorker* and Rebecca West had called her the finest novelist writing in English.

Through my correspondence with Chris and Bill, I came to learn of their grim financial plight. And in '59, when we met again, their "home" was a damp, dimly lighted one-time livery stable and coach house on the fringe of London. Something, I felt, had to be done—*soon.* In a wild moment I offered to publish a paperback of one of her novels. By then the Dryden Press, which I'd founded in 1939, had been merged with Henry Holt, where I bore the high-sounding title of vice president and editorial director. "Let's choose the book," I said. It was obviously *The Man Who Loved Children.* Elizabeth Hardwick's essay "The Neglected Novels of Christina Stead" had appeared some time before in *The New Republic.* And I knew that Christina's books had a loyal underground. I also knew I'd have problems with the financier-president of Holt. At a certain point I said to Frost, "Robert, did you ever hear of Christina Stead's *The Man Who Loved Children?* I may ask for your help—help with 'the Holts,' whom I'm hoping to rouse to reissue the work. It's a rare novel, quickly hailed and then ignored because of the war. She and her husband barely manage to survive. We can rescue the book and resuscitate a truly remarkable writer."—"I don't read novels these days—not many, that is; but send me the book. Stead? Where does she come from? What part of England?"—"Sydney, Australia," I said. "Her novel is based on her life there, but it's set near the Chesapeake."

I decided to speak with Randall Jarrell: some years before he had published a paean to Chris as a writer. "How would you like to write an introduction to *The Man Who Loved Children?*"—"I'd love to," he said. "It's the greatest family novel I know." I wrote to Robert Lowell, Peter Taylor, and others. They replied with comments for the jacket. I was doing all that I could to assure for the book the attention it deserved. Time passed, the ever unfortunate publishing delays. Then in April '64 I told the Holt president I was ready to proceed. He raised his hand. He had "given much thought to the project," he said, and it made "no sense—publishing a book that came out twenty years ago and hasn't been heard of since."—"I was sure," I said, "we had settled the matter when I guaranteed the munificent $750 advance that *you told me* to offer and which the author, under pressure from me, accepted. This book," I went on, "is important to me . . . very important. In fact so important that unless . . . unless." He glared at me, threw up his hands, and nodded.—Then Jarrell phoned: could he publish his introduction as an essay in the *Atlantic Monthly?*—"Publish it all over America," I said. One year later, April 18th, the book appeared—with superlative reviews.

This was a new generation of critics and readers. . . . My telephone kept ringing: calls from knowns and unknowns thanking me "for giving the great Stead novel back to the world." An instantaneous literary success. And for Christina Stead, a turning point in her life from the years of want and critical neglect. Suddenly she felt rich, with a $19,000 publisher's advance for her manuscripts that had gathered dust. Hard to believe, but true—and at her death she left an estate of $70,000, I was told. Five years ago her selected letters appeared (two volumes dedicated to me), and to date there are three biographies, the most comprehensive by Hazel Rowley, an Australian professor. I spent days and days correcting her manuscript, but errors remain. Christina died in 1983, having won great honor and acclaim. Three years later her executor published her unfinished novel *I'm Dying Laughing,* an astonishing portrait of her friend Ruth McKenney, author of *My Sister Eileen.*

DLB: This morning I went by Gotham Book Mart, and I picked up three volumes by Stanley Burnshaw. Perhaps you'd like to comment on how you feel about these volumes now.

Burnshaw: My first book of poems appeared in 1936. After I'd graduated from college in 1925, I went to work as a copywriter in a steel plant outside Pittsburgh, in a company town—Blawnox—named for the mill. My first two weeks were a shock and a revelation. Much as technology interested me—I'd always liked to work with my hands; I had handset the type for a book; I had built the walls of the rooms in my country house; and so forth—I realized what was happening: industrialism's excretions were destroying the earth. I wrote a poem: the first ecological poem, I believe, in America. It appeared in this book, this political book, *The Iron Land.* It tells the story of the steel mill—as the preface explained—seen with the eyes of a young middle-class white-collar worker. It records his personal growth through workday experiences (poems in roman type) as well as through personal doubts, deliberations, escapes (poems in italics) into a new-world directive. This was published during my communist days, you see.

I started to write it in 1925, and that particular ecological poem appeared with four others when I broke into print for the first time *importantly,* as it were, in the fall of 1927 in the first *American Caravan,* edited by Van Wyck Brooks, Alfred Kreymborg, and Lewis Mumford. I was in high company—Ernest Hemingway, Archibald MacLeish, Edmund Wilson,

Eugene O'Neill, Hart Crane, Allen Tate, and other well-knowns. I was probably the youngest contributor when that poem appeared. It's been fairly widely reprinted: "End of the Flower World." At the time, people didn't realize that the earth was being destroyed. Here's the poem.

Fear no longer for the lone gray birds
That fall beneath the world's last autumn sky,
Mourn no more the death of grass and tree.

These will be as they have ever been:
Substance of springtime; and when flower-world ends,
They will go back to earth, and wait, and be still,

Safe with the dust of birds long dead, with boughs
Turned ashes long ago, that still are straining
To leave their tombs and find the hills again,

Flourish again, mindless of the people—
The strange ones now on a leafless earth,
Who seem to have no care for things in blossom.

Fear no more for trees, but mourn instead
The children of these strange, sad men: their hearts
Will hear no music but the song of death.

By 1952 I had turned to other thoughts; my attitude toward the world, toward life, had matured, one could say. I was older, late forties. I decided to bring together all the poems I had done that I felt worth saving. They seemed to form an early and late testament, my name for the sequence—lyrics and meditations. One of these is the poem I just read. Another may surprise you. It says that the writing of poems—the creation of art—aspires to the cessation of the need to create. The poem is "Song Aspires to Silence." Shall I read it?

DLB: Please.

Burnshaw: I don't think people gave it much attention, yet it startled Louis Untermeyer when he read it. No matter. It's true for me, I assure you.

Song aspires to silence.
Men of defiant words
Look to the breaking moment
When blood will shed the fever,

Freed of the ceaseless striving
To fasten mountains and seas
And tame the resistless wills
Of hell and heaven defiant.

Song aspires to silence
The fear that drones above
The fury of all song,

Seeking its calm in driving

The blood to bury in words
The ever-unnameable love
That plunders the mind
        and storms the bewildered heart.

DLB: That was written when, roughly?

Burnshaw: I should say in the late forties. You feel that you're being driven to create, and you hope that the fever will pass, and it doesn't. But this book. . . .

DLB: Early and Late Testament.

Burnshaw: Yes. The book set forth what I felt was an early *and* a later testament. I kept thinking of Frost at times and wondering if I might send it to him and ask if he'd let me dedicate it to him, despite what I viewed as our "differences."

DLB: For the sake of the record, Stanley Burnshaw is consulting his book, *Robert Frost Himself,* which has a very useful annotated table of contents.

Burnshaw: It's here. Let's see what it says. There's a bit about Untermeyer's talking to me about the poem. Then I said that I'd thought of writing to Frost about it. He shook his head, then, jokingly, "What else is new?" I gave him a hasty sketch of an eight-part poem that would interweave parts of my steel-mill book with my personal verse of the last twelve years, to be ready, I said, in September. I had spoken too soon. Months passed before it was finished enough to show it to him, and four other men who were just as likely to say what they thought: MacLeish, Horace Gregory, Mark Van Doren, and Hiram Haydn, who tried to persuade the *American Scholar* to print it in full. The response gave me the courage to do what I shouldn't have otherwise dared: dedicate the work to Frost. In May I mailed it to Ripton with a letter saying I hoped he might grant permission in spite of the differences in our point of view. I probably added, "Some of your public statements that I've read since our last talk make me think that you put more trust in the strength of singleness than I am able to do. Which isn't to say that my trust is small but that you might not be quite ready to grant its limits." I had no way of knowing whether the package had reached him. I waited through June before giving up. Six weeks later his answer arrived.

Dear Stanley Burnshaw,

May, June, July, and half of August. What must you have decided to sentence me to for neglecting your letter all that time? I wince to think. And it isn't as if it were just any ordinary letter of the kind I let pile up against me without qualms—no, I would never have left yours unanswered if I had known I had it. But it got among a lot of things raked together from my two homes when I was in transition between them in the spring, and I just now found it. I might never have. I'm that bad. I'm not defending myself. Neither am I boasting of my badness. I'm sorry. That's all. Of course, I should be proud to have a poem like that dedicated to me if you haven't already given me up and dedicated it to someone else more deserving. At any rate, I am deeply moved that you should have thought of me—moved, but amused that you should think you knew the final idea in my writing well enough to tell how it differs from the final idea in your own. You aren't as young as when I first knew you, but you are still young. . . .

Isn't that nice? Well, I was very lucky to have spent those later days with Frost.

DLB: How many years did you work with him?

Burnshaw: I arrived at Holt in June 1958, my daughter's birthday. Frost died at the end of January 1963. We saw a great deal of each other.

DLB: This was when you were vice president at Holt. You were vice president in charge of Robert Frost.

Burnshaw: I was theoretically—and theoretically I was also in charge of all editorial projects, which of course was absurd. I knew nothing about children's books and almost nothing about *Field & Stream* or the other magazines that Holt published. I didn't know anything about high-school books or elementary-school books. But you know what can happen in publishing. The men at the helm of Holt were business people, not bookmen. And the president appointed me the editorial director of everything. And I wasn't, but I did what I could. I expected to stay six months, and I stayed nine years.

I had a most remarkable time with Frost, though. And it was because Frost was there that I decided to make the move to Holt instead of some other publisher.

DLB: You got to be this exalted personage at Holt because they acquired Dryden Press and more or less acquired you with Dryden Press. Did you found Dryden?

Burnshaw: Oh yeah. Yeah.

DLB: Was it independent when you started it, or . . .

Burnshaw: No, Dryden didn't exist. What had happened was curious. In my last year at the *New Masses* I'd meet all sorts of people who'd come in and waste time. One of them was connected with Macmillan's college department–a disarmingly persuasive man, older than I, who had taught French at Boston University some years before, till "for personal reasons" he decided to move into publishing as a "road representative" for Macmillan's college department. . . . Well, I'd become fed up with journalism–and besides, I hadn't done any work of my own. I had been at *New Masses* since the fall of '33, on a very arduous schedule. I left in July 1936, the day before the eruption of the Spanish civil war. I didn't know what I'd do to earn a living. I supposed that I'd have to return to advertising. And I did. I found a job in the fall and was working in an agency when this man I mentioned called on me. "I've read your splendid book on André Spire" and so forth. Then: "Could I interest you in becoming a publisher?" To make the long story short, he told me in very, very convincing terms that there were a number of people at the Macmillan Company who were very dissatisfied and who wanted to leave and start out on their own. I listened, asked questions, and after some months of talking–and my dependence on him was total since I knew nothing about that operation–we worked out a plan whereby four people would leave the Macmillan Company and form a company of our own. They would be the "traveling representatives," the men "on the road." I would be the inside man: I'd edit, design, produce, and arrange the distribution of books. But the project couldn't last. Two years later I started the Dryden Press, which I ran till it merged with Holt in '58.

DLB: I'm writing an introduction to a book about the American expatriates in Paris in the twenties, and I'm finding it hard to explain satisfactorily for today's students the pull of France, especially Paris, in the 1920s. You went over in '27.

Burnshaw: Yeah. In May. The first six weeks in England, then France. My *Wanderjahr.*

DLB: What were some of the forces that attracted you to France and Paris?

Burnshaw: Great question. I guess I never even asked myself why. Paris, of course, was the culture center of the world, unlike New York and America in the Roaring Twenties, with its heart on prosperity. Remember: this was the time of Sinclair Lewis's *Main Street,* the threat of Babbitry. There was, in some of us, a deep desire to get away from that world. One "naturally" gravitated toward Paris, the very center of the avant-garde: everything was going slightly crazy, extreme, in a charming way, and everybody knew it. Besides, one could live there for almost nothing–Americans, that is–because the franc had been depleted. I used to have a seven-course dinner with wine for seven francs, twenty-eight cents, served in a private apartment by White Russian émigrés. And I lived in a Left Bank hotel for a dollar a day. . . . But above all else: Paris was *exciting.* The very air seemed charged. . . . And, of course, we had heard all about American expatriates. . . .

DLB: Everybody else was there.

Burnshaw: Everyone was there–"including" Hemingway. The expatriate world had become a world of importance, and then I had also known that Frost had had his great success after years of neglect in America by being recognized in England, and that was a talisman of a sort. It was . . . but why? I can't explain it.

DLB: What did you get out of it? What can you point to and say, "If I hadn't gone to Paris, I wouldn't have learned this; I wouldn't have met him; I wouldn't have written that.

Burnshaw: Oh, boy. I went from London to Paris–or, rather, through Paris–and stayed till September in a beautiful city, Tours, in the heart of the chateaux country, the garden spot of France. And of all things, while living in this paradise I kept working on my steel-mill poem! One of the first things I did when I moved to Paris in the fall was to go to the Sorbonne to hear a great comparative literature scholar lecture on "Some Living French Poets." I entered the hall expecting to hear the usual things about the usual poets, that is, the ones well known. I was wrong. The speaker decided to talk about some poets who were not too widely known, and the first one was a man I'd scarcely heard of, named André Spire. I listened. I was so taken by the poems that I found myself making translations as he

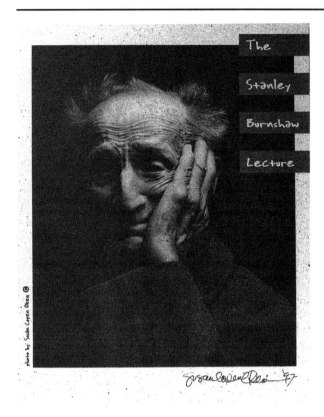

*Cover for program of the 1997 lecture sponsored by the
University of Texas–Austin*

talked. At the end of the hour I walked to a nearby bookstore in the hope– small hope–of finding some writings by Spire. This was 1927, and he hadn't published a book for years–or so I thought when I asked a clerk if by chance he had the works of André Spire. "I'm sorry," he apologized, "I don't have his 1923 volume, but I've this one that appeared in 1908." Nineteen years before! I dashed to my room on Monsieur le Prince and began translating some of the poems I'd heard the hour before. And the words seemed to fall almost naturally into place, phrase by phrase: into free-verse lines, though I had never written vers libre. . . . I'd been working for hours when my wife called out, "I hate to interrupt, but we're supposed to go to a party tonight. By the time we eat and walk to the Ile Saint Louis. . . ." I stopped reluctantly, but our hosts were the only people we knew in Paris. We were met at the door by Marvin Lowenthal, a literary critic and the editor at large in Europe of the *Menorah Journal,* one of the leading "intellectual" reviews. "I'm so glad you've come," he said, "but I have to warn you. There are two old friends here tonight, and they usually stay till eleven, so we'll have to be quite sober till then. Do you think you can behave yourselves?"–"No," I replied.–"Good, then come right in! Most of the

guests are Americans who happen to be in Paris. I don't know them well, so please introduce yourselves." He led us inside. Suddenly he turned to me, pointing to a small man with a large beard, "Why don't you speak with my old friend now? He's the man of the couple I mentioned. He *reads* English very well but can't speak a word of it. He's all alone there, as you see."

I walked up to his friend and introduced myself in French. Instantly he wheeled around, *"Moi, je suis André Spire."*–"André Spire, the poet?" I exclaimed.–"Yes, but why are you shouting?"–"I've just been translating some of your poems and . . ."–"You have, eh?" eyeing me sharply. "And where did you come across my poems?"–"At the Sorbonne this afternoon in a lecture on some living French poets by Professor Baldensperger."– *"Baldensperger!"* he cried. *"Impossible!"*–"Impossible, but also true," I replied.–"You say that you're translating some of my poems. Then tell me their titles." I reeled them off. His eyes moistened. Then quietly, "Baldensperger reading my poems at the Sorbonne! Hard to believe!"–"He also said that a book of yours had been issued in London." He nodded. . . . And by the time we finished talking, he had made a date for me to visit his home in Neuilly on the Bois de Boulogne. He'd read my translations and see if he could approve what I'd done. That was the start of a close relationship that lasted the rest of my life–the rest of *his* life. He died in the evening of his ninety-eighth birthday, July 1966.

Spire and Pound–"Ezra Poond," he called him–had been very good friends. Pound and Richard Aldington and F. S. Flint were responsible for the London publication by the Egoist Press of André's war poems, *Et j'ai voulu la paix,* in 1916.

Et j'ai voulu la paix–I favored peace–I hoped for peace–literally I wanted peace. As I say, he was very well known in England. Flint and Aldington were particular fans. Aldington, in a letter to Spire, called him the most important living French poet. And Guillaume Apollinaire, the "general" of the avant-garde, was a great admirer, as was the more conventional Romain Rolland. Spire had been published in Europe and South America. He was all but unknown in the States until Mark Van Doren included him in his 1928 *World Poetry.* By the way, it was at a party of Spire's that Joyce met his future publisher Sylvia Beach. Pound, who'd been invited, asked if he might bring along a talented Irish writer who'd just arrived in Paris. Chance, pure chance!

DLB: And your book on Spire was published . . . ?

Burnshaw: It appeared in 1933, I believe. Spring of 1933. I'm pretty sure. It was called *André Spire and His Poetry,* which is a critical biography and forty translations and an essay on vers libre that Harriet Monroe published in *Poetry.* Is it there?

DLB: Yes, sir. *André Spire and His Poetry.* Philadelphia: Centaur Press, 1933.

Burnshaw: Oh, I bumped into George Antheil one day, you know, the avant-garde composer. Also by chance, my brother-in-law Leo Robin—known for his Hollywood lyrics for Maurice Chevalier—came to Paris in the spring in the company of his friends the Gershwins. And so, by chance, I was able to meet George Gershwin and to have an afternoon when he devoted himself to playing for me in his hotel room. It was really quite an interesting afternoon. And we had a good time together. He couldn't believe that the serious French composers who were seeking him out really admired him as a serious composer. I assured him that French composers didn't waste their time flattering people. They had too many more-important things to do.

I met James Stephens, you know, the *Crock of Gold* man, and you remember the story that was current at the time? Joyce was presumably going blind—wasn't able to finish his work, and writers were being asked if they'd care to complete it. Stephens was one of them. "Yes," he said. "I'd be glad to, but on one condition: that I don't have to read what he's written so far."

There were all sorts of interesting things that went on in Paris. You never knew whom you might meet—on the streets, in cafés, in the Sylvia Beach bookshop. Who knows whom I met? I had published a poem in *Transition* and an essay on translation in *This Quarter.* It was all a great experience, just *being* in Paris at that time.

DLB: Pound was gone by the time you arrived. 1927.

Burnshaw: He had gone pretty early, yes. But he maintained a very close relationship with André Spire, and that's a very interesting thing because André Spire was a Zionist, and Pound, as you know, became very anti-Semitic. As the French say, "Figurez-vous."

DLB: How crazy was Pound, in your judgment? Always crazy, became crazy, never crazy?

Burnshaw: Oh, something must have gone wrong. Certainly after he'd left America and re-

turned to Italy and performed the Fascist salute. Incredible, don't you think? Eliot told Frost that Pound was pretty "nutty." There's no doubt about it. But think of Eliot's debt to Pound. Without Pound would there have been *The Waste Land?* Certainly not *The Waste Land* as we know it.

DLB: Crazy or not, he was a brilliant editor.

Burnshaw: Of everybody's work but his own. He always managed to spoil things of his own. As Malcolm Cowley once wrote, he had a failure of taste in his own work, but not with others'. Strange, isn't it? I don't understand it. And I'm no great admirer of Pound's poetry, because I get lost in the *Cantos* and I don't want to spend my life looking up references. And I don't think Eliot helped very much with a lot of his footnotes to *The Waste Land.* The most important one is missing. The best line in *The Waste Land,* in my opinion, is "I will show you fear in a handful of dust," which comes from Donne's *Meditations.* And it's always credited to Eliot. But Eliot never said, "No." So the reader assumes it was Eliot's. For example, Louis Untermeyer did.

DLB: After the twenties you wrote for the *New Masses;* you edited the *New Masses*—you were a man of the Left.

Burnshaw: I was a man of the Left from the time of my steel-mill job. I felt that the Earth was being destroyed, and, as I said before, industrialism was the enemy. I became what I thought was a communist in my first two weeks because—I reasoned "logically"—that if the Earth belonged to the people, the people would take care of it. Which of course, is the opposite of what happened, when you think about what the Soviets did: Lake Baikal, for example. Think of "socialist" Sweden, of its failure to preserve its lands. For me the "mortal" issue facing humanity was saving the Earth. It still is.

DLB: Were you under party discipline?

Burnshaw: I never was a member of the party. I was approached at times to join. I always explained: "It may be a personality failure, but if I *have* to do something, I often feel disinclined to do it. A problem of compulsion for me." Nobody ever pressed me to join the party.

DLB: But obviously on the *New Masses* you worked with and associated with members of the party. Hard-liners.

Burnshaw: Oh, yes. They were all party members. And the business manager of the *New Masses* was the brother of Earl Browder, who was the head of the party. Oh no, nobody ever questioned my political loyalty, though we had disagreements. The *New Masses,* I felt, could be all wrong about Roosevelt, and I said so.

DLB: As someone who was born in 1931, I cannot understand how it was possible for communists, fellow travelers, admirers of Russia to be willfully blind to all the horrors and the terrors and the executions that were going on under Stalin. Were you all stupid? Did you just not want to know?

Burnshaw: No, I'll tell you how I reacted to the Moscow trials. I assumed that here were a bunch of dissidents, people who were opposed to Stalin, who honestly believed that he was ruining everything that they had fought for—these were the old Bolsheviks, whom he was executing—and that these people *did* try to get rid of him, because they believed he had been a traitor to the Revolution. I assumed they believed that they had every right to get rid of him—*if* they were sure he was guilty. And Stalin had every right, *if* he was sure they were guilty—not to kill them, but to silence them.

DLB: But you had no inkling about the Gulag . . .

Burnshaw: No. We didn't know any of that.

DLB: . . . about the deliberate starvation of the farmers?

Burnshaw: Nothing. It was all hushed up. And whenever there was something in *The New York Times* that would in a sense reveal some horrors in Russia, we'd say "Oh, well, that's the capitalist press." But there was one man, one of the editors of the *New Masses* by the name of Joshua Kunitz, who had attended the first of the Moscow trials. When he came back he told a few friends that there was something very fishy about it. And he was not allowed to attend any subsequent trials. But he didn't say anything in public, of course: there was "a higher goal" involved. I personally never had any desire to go to the Soviet Union. It didn't interest me very much. I didn't read through any of the Soviet novels that the Left was praising. I was interested in saving the situation of Americans who were suffering. Starvation here. Apples on the streets. You remember that.

DLB: I remember the Hoovervilles, too. I saw them.

Burnshaw: You saw them; I almost slept in one in East Saint Louis. It was terrible. I'm going to write about a lot of this in my literary autobiography.

DLB: Tell me about your associates on the *New Masses.*

Burnshaw: You want to know who they were?

DLB: Yeah, you've mentioned Mike Gold.

Burnshaw: Mike had been the editor—on and off—of the *New Masses* monthly. A charming man, and, I think, a highly gifted writer when he was good, but not so good when he was hasty. A most disorganized person, who depended on others to see that the monthly appeared on time—which it rarely did. But all that changed in '33 when the party decided to make the *New Masses* a weekly to compete with the "liberal-radical" *Nation* and the *New Republic,* and come out every week on time and be just as efficiently run as the others. The man the party chose to be the managing editor was Herman Michaelson, formerly editor of the *Call,* a socialist daily, then Sunday editor of the Pulitzer *New York World.* A seasoned professional. All I learned about journalism I learned from him. My technical past in layout, design, and typography came in handy. I did the makeup and designed almost all the covers of the weekly. But my main role was that of reviewer of poetry and drama.

DLB: Was Dos Passos writing for the *New Masses* when you were there?

Burnshaw: Not at that particular time. He was beginning to turn to the Right at that time. I'm sure I never met him, but I met a great many others who visited our offices. People were gravitating there: we were "the hope, the answer." And not only writers but other artists—painters, musicians, photographers, filmmakers, architects. . . . You remember the election in 1932 when some fifty-two well-known writers and others signed a public endorsement of the Communists' platform for the presidency. There was no other program, no other concrete action, that one could align with. Especially for writers. And I was one of them. I had written some then-called proletarian poems about a steel mill which the monthly *New Masses* had published. When the weekly began, I felt at home.

DLB: You walked away in '36.

Burnshaw: I had worked there since the fall of '33. In January '34, when the weekly appeared, there were four full-time editors, but now I was the only one of the four who remained. By then, as I said, I'd become fed up with the task. It was work, very hard work.

DLB: Fed up with the work or fed up with the "political correctness"?

Burnshaw: No, it wasn't the political correctness; that didn't bother me at all. I just assumed that the party line was what it had to be at the time, and when I had reservations, I said so. But remember: everything changed in May 1935 in the wake of the Soviet arms pact with France. World revolution was shelved—pro tem—and replaced by a United Front against the fascists. People we used to call "Social Fascists" were now our comrades in our common fight. Hitler was the great cohesive force. Middle-class housewives gave money-raising parties for the League Against War and Fascism. People began to feel they were *doing* something for themselves and the world.

Norman Thomas, with his more-or-less ministerial background, the perennial socialist candidate, was an impressive, charming figure, but for him, as for his party, violence was not the way. They put their faith in the ballot box—which the communists disdained: "To gain power, you have to seize it . . . Now!" I recall what Professor Prescott said about politics when I went to Cornell for a year to learn poetics: "The difference between a radical and a liberal? A radical is just a liberal in a hurry."

DLB: Did the *New Masses* during your term on the staff develop any major literary talents?

Burnshaw: I don't think so.

DLB: Were first-rate writers coming out of the proletariat?

Burnshaw: The proletariat? First-rate? From the vantage point of 1997? What do we mean by proletariat? Was Mike Gold a proletarian, or Richard Wright, or Henry Roth? First-rate writing can be done without regard to movements or journals. On the other hand, Mike Gold was always involved with a magazine: the *Liberator,* the old *Masses* and the *New.* And Richard Wright: I met him at the John Reed Club in Chicago in 1934, an unknown writer. I urged him to move to New York,

Stanley Burnshaw at the time of The Refusers *(photograph by Ken Browning)*

where he would meet with fellow writers and have a chance to be recognized. Before too long, he came, and you know the rest of his story. But Henry Roth was wholly independent. His *Call It Sleep* was misunderstood by communist critics yet hailed by freelance leftist writers, then lost to the world for thirty years. Some of its pages, by the way, were done when he stayed in a cabin I had in Maine.

DLB: You were drama critic; you were poetry reviewer; you were book reviewer. Were you told, ever, which plays, which books were deserving of laudatory reviews because of their political content? How much party line was there in the editorial policy?

Burnshaw: None. Nobody ever told me to do anything, and nobody ever tried to change a line of anything I had written. I had complete freedom to do what I wanted—which was also a great responsibility. My best-known—most notorious—review involved a book by Wallace Stevens, *Ideas of Order.* No one at the *New Masses*—except the man who handled the book reviews—knew what I had said. My review came out in October 1935. It raised a kind of storm a year later when a poem by Stevens—"Mr. Burnshaw and the Statue"—appeared in *The New Caravan.* My review had addressed the

161

author with a plain question: How today can you write the beautiful verse you published in 1923–now in 1935, in the depths of the Great Depression?

DLB: You charged him, then, with irrelevance?

Burnshaw: I said that he was closing his eyes to the world about him, a world of suffering.

DLB: And he responded.

Burnshaw: I published an essay in the *Sewanee Review* called "Wallace Stevens and the Statue." It was written twenty-five years after my review had appeared. It provides the background–the ideology, if you will. It also reprints the review.

Well, I reviewed two books in that issue, and it was called "Turmoil in the Middle Ground," that is, the ground of writers who weren't sure where they stood. And there was turmoil there. One of the books was by a poet who's scarcely mentioned today, though he should be remembered: Haniel Long.

DLB: Jim Dickey spoke very well of Long.

Burnshaw: Oh yeah, a very good writer. I introduced Jim to the *Pittsburgh Memoranda*–a very interesting book. And then there was *Ideas of Order* by Stevens. Let me just read this to you.

I say:

Confused as it is, *Pittsburgh Memoranda* is a marvel of order alongside Wallace Stevens' volume, and yet to many readers it is something of a miracle that Stevens has at all bothered to give us his ideas of order. When *Harmonium* appeared a dozen years ago Stevens was at once set down as an incomparable verbal musician, but nobody stopped to ask if he had any ideas. It was tacitly assumed that one read him for pure poetic sensation. If he had a message, it was carefully buried, and would take no end of labor to exhume. Yet he often comes out with flat judgments, and certain ideas weave through the book consistently.

And I quote three lines:

"The magnificent cause of being / The imagination / The one reality in this imagined world" underlies a number of poems. Realists have been bitter at the inanity of Pope's "Whatever is, is right," but Stevens plunges ahead to the final insolence: "For realists what is is what should be." And yet it is hard to know if such a line is not Stevens posing in self-mockery. One can rarely speak surely of Stevens' ideas.

But certain general convictions he admits in such a

poem as "To the One of Fictive Music." Bound up with the sovereignty of the imagination is his belief in an interfusion of music among the elements, and "music is feeling, not sound."

Harmonium, then, is mainly sense poetry, but not as Keats' is sense poetry, because the serener poet is not driven to suffuse sensuous imagery with powerful subjective emotions. This is scientific, objectified sensuousness, separated from its kernel of fire, and allowed to settle, cool off, and harden in the poet's mind until it emerges a strange amazing crystal. Reading this poetry becomes a venture in crystallography. It is remembered for its curious humor, its brightness, its words and phrases that one rolls on the tongue. It is the kind of verse that people concerned with the murderous world collapse can hardly swallow today, except in tiny doses.

And then it goes on to document. A number of people considered the review quite fair. I think it was, given the time and place.

DLB: How should poetry be properly taught? What's the right way, the best way to teach poetry?

Burnshaw: I think the important thing is for the reader to read aloud and the reader to feel the sound in his body. Because, as I try to make clear in my book *The Seamless Web,* poetry begins with the body and ends with the body, the entire organism. It is not the cortex that writes the poems; it is the totality of the organism.

DLB: We were talking about how to teach poetry.

Burnshaw: Well, have you ever seen my book, *The Seamless Web?* The most important act for a reader is to learn the poem by heart, if he can, and to read and reread. He has to look up the meanings of words because if he doesn't *know* the words, he isn't reading. And he has to know that they look at each other, that their interconnections create the poetic totality.

DLB: Say that again. "The words in a poem look at each other."

Burnshaw: They do. They look backward and forward. They almost touch each other–bells ring, as it were. There's a constant reverberation. It's not just a series of words but a series of words that talk to each other. It's a little bit like chamber music, you know? Conversation among the instruments: conversation among the words. But of course, as I wrote in *The Seamless Web,* the only way to describe a poem is to write one book-long sentence, because everything is totally involved—"intra-involved," to coin a barbarism.

One of my problems with present-day verse is that the language often is dead and soundless. The words are not heightened. Poetry is heightened speech, and the heightening comes from the emotion and from the interrelationships among the words.

DLB: What did Pound say: "language charged with meaning"?

Burnshaw: Quite so, but I'd rather say that it's words charging themselves with meanings.

DLB: Who's the most brilliant word man you ever knew? The master of putting words together, making words talk to each other, look at each other?

Burnshaw: I would say Shakespeare, wouldn't you?

DLB: I was thinking in terms of the people of the twentieth century you know and work with.

Burnshaw: There's Frost, for one. He can do things with words that make them so subtle, so fugitive, that you cannot contain them. They run off into a silence, as it were. Take "Nothing Gold Can Stay." It reads in different ways:

> Nature's first green is gold,
> Her hardest hue to hold.
> Her early leaf's a flower;
> But only so an hour.
> Then leaf subsides to leaf.

And then:

> So Eden sank to grief,
> So dawn goes down to day.

Nothing gold can stay.

Eleven years passed before he heard the last three lines. He waited. One has to. One cannot force them. They come or they never come. . . .

I wrote a poem about that picture up there, a picture of a man who knows he's going to die.

DLB: It's a man sitting on a bench by some trees, seems to be in a park.

Burnshaw: It's in the garden of his house, in the twilight—summertime. He had taken a dip in the pool, then made his way to a bench, and sat there brooding. A large, powerful man—gradually being eaten away by cancer. He knew it. He was sitting there, brooding, chin in his hand, legs splayed, sitting within a trinity of trees . . . the crepuscular light of the greensward. He knows he is going to die, to move upward into that darkness at the edge of the sward, where the planet slips off into seas of space, into blackness.

DLB: Did you know him?

Burnshaw: No, he was the father of my friend who took this photograph. One evening she showed it to me—it was as though I had experienced a wound. Within the next few days I found myself writing a poem. I saw the trinity of trees—and the indescribable feeling. . . .

I just don't believe in charging permissions fees. Anybody can reprint any poem of mine he or she wants to, because I don't think I'm anything more than a vehicle. And I don't think a vehicle must be paid for the privilege of bringing something new into the air, adding an object to the landscape. . . . A poem—as I wrote in *The Seamless Web*—is something that happens to a poet. I refer to the kind of poem that Juan Jiménez calls *necessaria* in contrast to the kind he calls *voluntaria*: a poem that demands to be born, that's created by the total organism. As John Donne said, "The body makes the minde."

The James Gould Cozzens Case Reopened

Cozzens's *Michael Scarlett*

George Garrett
University of Virginia

It may seem a passing strange way to celebrate the achievements of James Gould Cozzens by turning back to and focusing attention on one of his early novels, in this case the second novel he published at the outset of a long career–*Michael Scarlett,* written in the second half of 1924 and published in November 1925. All the more so since in due time he dropped that title, together with three other novels of his youth–*Confusion* (1924), *Cock Pit* (1928), and *The Son of Perdition* (1929)–from the list of his published works, not so much denying or disowning those books as simply announcing that in a real sense his career as a novelist may be taken as beginning with *S.S. San Pedro* (1931). Beginning with that novel and including all the works thereafter, he was willing to take his stand and to be judged. And, fully allowing for the ups and downs of literary reputation, the ins and outs of grace and favor in the fickle literary scene, in his works from *S.S. San Pedro* on, almost fifty productive years until his death in 1978, Cozzens created enough major works of fiction to be justly called one of the century's major writers.

He is probably best known and remembered by readers for his "professional" novels, novels that were not primarily *about* any of the professions he dealt with (though in almost every case living professionals credited Cozzens with having represented their work and lives better and more accurately than any other American writer) but, rather, novels in which many of the central figures are deeply involved and engaged in their respective professions: *The Last Adam* (medicine, 1933); *Men and Brethren* (the clergy, 1936); *The Just and the Unjust* (law, 1942); *Guard of Honor* (the military, 1948); *By Love Possessed* (law and all the others, 1957); and *Morning Noon and Night* (1968)–more "autobiographical" than "professional," but told in first person by a sixty-five-year-old management consultant. What is important here and as defining in his

Cozzens at the time of Men and Brethren *(photograph by Ben Pinchot)*

fiction as an artist's signature is not that he was able to imagine deeply, more than skin deep, the lives and beings of twentieth-century American professionals (though that in itself was a rare accomplishment in our time, almost unique), but that he was able to write fiction about that class, thus class in general, and at a time when most of our writers, even the best among them, studiously avoided the high risks of trying to portray the flexible and sometimes mysterious systems of class in our supposedly classless society. It is a fact that many professionals who did not often read much fiction, often for every good reason, found in the "professional" novels of Cozzens something worth their leisure time and energy, something worth a grownup's time. It ought to be said, though it seldom is and less and less so as we move into our era of assertive multiculturalism, that these professionals, the central characters in these novels by Cozzens, were, in fact, the managers and the makers of the nation (and, to the extent that the nation was, in peace and war, at the center of the world), for good and for ill, and that any vision of representation of life in the United States in the twentieth century that ignores them in favor of artists or outlaws or outcasts or "marginalized" groups and people, no matter how intense and interesting, is a distortion of reality. Only a few others among our leading novelists tried to deal seriously with these people—one thinks of John O'Hara, John P. Marquand, and a few others. But nobody cultivated this particular turf with the care and depth that Cozzens did. It was then, and remains, daring, risky. Even disregarding the ignorance of the felt hostility toward the professional classes demonstrated by the majority of literary critics (among others), it is aesthetically easier to write about outcasts and outlaws and other marginal figures than it is to write about the people, mostly men and mostly white, who kept the machinery of things running, who won the wars and tried to keep the peace. His professionals are not saints, far from it; and only a few enjoy moments of real heroism. They are not trying to be "role models." But they live and learn, are by turns admirable and reprehensible. The poetry is in the action and the pattern, in an Aristotelian sense, the "fable" of their stories. Cozzens does not, not much anyway, depend on the brilliance and fluency of language, all very evident in the early books, for his effects. Rather, the language is decorous in the eighteenth-century sense of that term, fitting and proper to its subjects and characters, appropriate and transparent.

It is usually to these books that we return now, those that seem most validly his own, written in a voice we came to know. And whenever (rarely) Cozzens is still taught in college classrooms, depending on the vagaries of what books are still in print and in stock at a given time, it is the teacher's habit to lead from strength—perhaps assigning *Guard of Honor*, which, besides being a wonderfully realized novel and one of the finest novels coming out of World War II, also carries the credentials of a Pulitzer Prize. Or maybe the difficult but magnificent *By Love Possessed*, which gives the teacher the escape hatch of dealing with the sociological significance at the time and/or the consequent literary up-

roar created by critics with their not-well-hidden agenda.

All of which is a roundabout way of saying: why on earth go back to the beginning? Why open a door that he closed long ago?

Of course, there are always reasons. As a writer, myself, I am endlessly interested in trying to discover (though knowing full well that it can't be done, still always hoping . . .) how other writers *did it*. Where were they coming from to get where they went? It is also sometimes helpful and reassuring to see how clumsy and inadequate, how *bad* were the very early works of very great writers. I have often sent my students on such search-and-destroy missions, keeping an ace up my sleeve to be played in class: "All right. We can agree that this Great Writer was not very good at the outset; that he here demonstrates not a great deal of talent or intelligence—you need not feel inferior to him, at that moment, on either count; that you, a beginner, can easily see how much can be accomplished with what appear to be limited gifts; that you can work hard and learn almost in spite of yourself, if you really want to . . . etc., etc., etc." And then dropping the one card—"How do you suppose this writer got from here to the first major works that established him as a major writer in a very few (two or three usually) years? It must have been magic, a miracle."

Most of the time one has to turn to originally unpublished materials, manuscripts, to see the given Great Writer's juvenilia. And it's interesting to consider that our latest age, the age of the computer, will allow many of our writers to escape that ex post facto scrutiny, just as it will deny students and would-be writers of the future the opportunity to see that, perhaps with the exception of some lyric poets, our best and brightest writers had to begin somewhere and very often with work that was not best or brightest by any standard.

The really unusual thing about the early Cozzens novels is that, even though they offer few hints and clues that they might be moving toward the achievements of his major novels, they are quite good in many ways. Allowing for all kinds of conventional reservations, one still has to consider that they were published and reviewed and even sold some copies on the market. Not everything he wrote at the time, from about nineteen through his early twenties, was published. But that is another story. Here our concern is that most of what he wrote was published and, by the standards of the time, he was an established "professional writer," albeit not yet a successful one, before he was thirty. He had a track record—spotty, sure, but undeniably there—and a first-rate agent. And when he married his first-rate agent, Bernice Baumgarten, he acquired a mentor who knew his basic strengths and weaknesses and was able to teach him how to be the writer he became, to be himself. (The story of this relationship is told in Matthew J. Bruccoli's *James Gould Cozzens: A Life Apart,* 1983.) If, as I think is true, Maxwell Perkins, recognizing the talent of Ernest Hemingway, also taught him how to be Hemingway, the writer we now know, Bernice Baumgarten taught her gifted and lucky young husband what he needed to know to be the writer he became, what habits he had already acquired, writing and publishing novels, that needed to be broken, cast aside, or modified, and what things were missing from his workshop that could be found and mastered.

All the more reason, you might justly say, to do exactly what Cozzens did. Write off the first four novels and call the career's beginning from when and where he started over. But I would reply, since the early books are there, even if only in the darkest niches of large libraries, why not take a look at them? What we have here is a very young writer who taught himself, who learned by doing. He had encouragement from friends and teachers, but they couldn't teach him much. He had to learn it the hard way, all on his own, at least until he found Bernice and she found him. He learned by writing novels that, remarkably perhaps, were published. It may well be that he wasn't "ready" for the experience and the exposure of publication, though several publishers were willing to bet money on him at the time. They lost the bet (in their terms anyway), but that's what they do most of the time to this day.

In my lifetime I have known a few, a very few, writers who learned their craft while actually playing the game. Their first work was somehow published and they had to learn how to write, which included coming to understand what they had already done, before they could continue, if they could continue. But this is less and less common. In 1997 it was easier to find a publisher for a first novel than for, say, a solid, midlist writer's third or fourth or fifth novel. True. But it was also very hard, chancy and unlikely, to place a first novel. That *Cold Mountain,* the literary success story of 1997, is a first novel adds a nice edge of irony to the current situation. One should keep in mind, however, that Charles Fraizer, author of *Cold Mountain,* was more than forty and pushing fifty when the book came out and caught on. More and more first novels are the works of writers of early middle age and are usually not by any means the first novel written by the given writer. Most often a first novelist will have several novels, unpublished and maybe unpublishable, stashed away in the filing cabinet. Most of what

young Cozzens wrote, and wrote easily and quickly by any standards, ended up in print and between hard covers.

It is true that in those years, the 1920s, following World War I, American publishers were looking for young writers to come forward. (The same thing was true in the first few years after World War II.) Young writers, on the whole, had a better chance, at least at the beginning, then than now. And it is thanks to that self-conscious search, a hunt for new young talent, that we have F. Scott Fitzgerald's *This Side of Paradise* (1920), Hemingway's *The Sun Also Rises* (1926), Faulkner's *Soldier's Pay* (1926). Of course none of these men knew enough yet to realize that their beginnings had been fairly easy and that soon enough it would be harder than they could imagine. Neither could the young Cozzens, younger than any of these others, imagine how it really was and would be. You write the book and they publish it. It is, in a sense, a knack like a game of tennis among friends. This innocence-ignorance gave them, Cozzens too, a casual confidence when they needed it most, a kind of self-confidence seldom seen before or since.

What about the early novels of James Gould Cozzens? In *James Gould Cozzens: A Life Apart* Bruccoli handles the apprentice novels in detail, and he is truthful in pointing out their unquestionable flaws and faults while at the same time recognizing strengths that would be valuable later on. Here, speaking of *Confusion,* he points out: "In publishing his first novel Cozzens had produced a false start. *Confusion* is pretentious and overwritten; the characters are unbelievable; the whole thing has a secondhand quality of a novel written from books, not from experience or observation." Elsewhere, taking note of Cozzens's "remarkable store of erudition," he adds an important observation: "What he did not know, he researched. He would always be able to assimilate information for the needs of his fiction, but he still had to learn how to use his research naturally." He also had to learn, and did, a much greater trick, how to engage his imagination, by and through the things he had learned from research of all kinds, so that he could present credible, dimensional characters for whom these things imagined were facts of life.

Which is one good reason to take a look at *Michael Scarlett.* Set in Elizabethan times, it involved a good deal of research, of course, and it required an active, awakened imagination. These people could not just be modern people in funny clothes, though that is often the case in historical fiction. To work well it also required a language, something accessible and acceptable to the modern reader, yet suggesting and evoking the grand (and very different) language of the time. Bruccoli notes that "the sixteenth-century setting permitted Cozzens to display his erudition without ostentation, and the Elizabethan speech concealed his stylistic indulgences." The latter point is important. His style, at the time, was already halfway there, fitting for the historical context. This is always a major problem in any historical novel. That Cozzens, so early on, saw the problem and then handled it well, consistently enough not to be merely a happy accident, tells us now that he was already challenging himself with narrative problems and trying to solve them. He was already *thinking* as a writer, thus somewhat independent already from the power and influence of his own habits and inhibitions. Put more simply and directly, this second novel shows that he was ready and willing to learn.

The creation of an effective "Elizabethan" language likewise must have helped him significantly as, later on, he learned to create a narrative language, third person in every book except *Morning Noon and Night,* which is appropriate to the story and its specific characters. Probably the finest, perhaps the most obvious, example is the narrative language of *By Love Possessed,* in which the narrator speaks to us as if it were Arthur Winner speaking on writing. This kind of narration is subtle and rare, very effective in creating the context of a credible world. A little risky, too. Incompetent critics and reviewers elected to argue that Arthur Winner's thoughts and feelings and words were those of the author, not of his perfectly realized character. They were dead wrong. But more to the point: creating a language for Elizabethan dialogue and for an Elizabethan world clearly demonstrated that Cozzens had a predilection and a talent for making the narrative language as much a part of the story as the things described and signified.

Michael Scarlett opens in the days immediately after God and the English defeated the Spanish Armada. Beginning at Gull House at Dunbury, where young Michael, future earl of same, is being carefully tutored to prepare him for service in the rough-and-tumble world. From the country he is sent to St. John's College, Cambridge, where he falls in with a rowdy literary set including Thomas Nashe and Christopher Marlowe and even the earl of Southampton. Troubles at Cambridge drive him to London, where the rest of the story plays out. There the central place is a literary hangout, *The Golden Asse,* where he is reunited with his Cambridge friends and manages to meet just about everybody else worth knowing or even heard of, including the earl of Essex

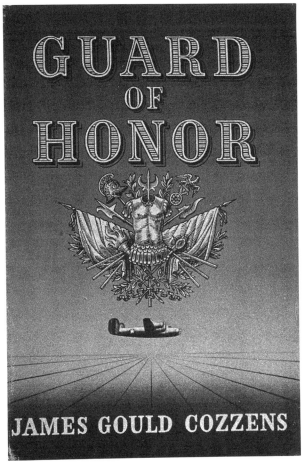

Dust jacket for the first edition of what is widely regarded as the best American novel of World War II

and even William Shakespeare. (Who is, amusingly and probably accurately, portrayed as a little less lively and more of a workaholic than the university wits.) There is plenty going on—true love, sex and violence, plenty of swordplay, and an operatic ending for the young earl. Maybe that was a problem, the downbeat ending, though it was the only logical and appropriate conclusion for this novel of doomed youth. The story covers a lot of ground and time quickly, and is built in a series of well-made scenes. Descriptive passages, brief and brisk, are excellent and give life and credibility to the action. It's a third-person omniscient narration in which the narrator is almost another character; indeed, in one or two places, the narrator eases in and out of a first-person voice: "Despite his admiration for Henry Wriothesley, and his respect for Sir Edward, I do not think Michael came prepared to like Cambridge." This device gives the otherwise omniscient narrator the opportunity to comment on and to qualify events and action in the story and even, as in this brief case, to create an ambiguity, an uncertainty on the part of the narrator. This is a pretty sophisticated game played with point of view by the gifted young novelist.

Michael Scarlett was not a critical success. Bruccoli reports that it sold 707 copies in the American edition, 269 in the slightly revised British version. Not good, but not so bad, either. The break-even point for a publisher at the time was roughly, give or take a few, 1,000 copies. *Michael Scarlett* lost a little money, then, but not a lot. That it wasn't widely reviewed was a piece of bad luck and, then as now, probably the publisher's fault. Though hit or miss like everything else, historical novels were still a popular genre in those days, ever since Mary Johnston's *To Have and To Hold* (1900), which sold in excess of 500,000 copies in a smaller world than ours and tempted every publisher and many writers to go for the gold of history. Years later they were still looking and found, among others, *Gone with the Wind* (1936) and, later, *Cold Mountain*. After *Michael Scarlett* Cozzens remained deeply interested in history, but evidently never felt a need to revisit the Elizabethans.

Part of my interest in *Michael Scarlett,* it might as well be said, is purely personal. I wrote three novels set in Elizabethan and Jacobean times, myself; and even though I don't plan to go there again in fiction, I remain interested in the subject of fiction about Elizabethan times, old and new. Of the factual world of Elizabethan England, much has been discovered and uncovered in the past fifty years or so; and the scholarship goes on, constantly changing and rearranging the shape and setting of things. Much that Cozzens presented to us in *Michael Scarlett* holds up well even in the bright glare of new information and insights. The literary scholarship devoted to Elizabethan England was quite good in the 1920s. Basic elements of social and cultural history were more rudimentary. Cozzens didn't have a lot

to work with, but he seems to have made the most of what he could find and to have fully activated his imagination. The Elizabethan world picture that he imagined and presents is, in general and in detail, closer to contemporary views than to what was accepted in the 1920s. What this tells me is that he had a powerful (and trustworthy) imagination. He couldn't have known that then or later. He didn't have time to worry much about sources or, for that matter, futures in Elizabethan research. The only Harvard course that might have helped him, History II (History of England during the Tudor and Stuart periods), taught by Professor Roger Merriman, Cozzens had dropped.

In short, to create the historical setting of *Michael Scarlett* Cozzens had to make up a lot on the basis of limited information. If he had been far off the mark, if he had wildly misimagined and misrepresented the Elizabethan world, few would have known it, fewer still would have cared one way or the other. That the Elizabethan world in *Michael Scarlett* has the authority of authenticity to this day and that in that sense, anyway, the book can stand and hold its own with the best of its kind shows the power of that writer's imagination, almost total immersion in the subject.

One of the things that Cozzens was criticized for in *Michael Scarlett* was a certain kind of factual inaccuracy, in chronology and in bringing together people who would not likely have joined each other in real life. This is true. The answer is, of course, that this is a novel, not a simple recapitulation of the known facts. But more to the point, there is this to be said. Sir Walter Scott's *Kennilworth* (1821) is chronologically impossible and free and easy with all the facts; but, in its way and in its own terms, it is a great Elizabethan novel, faithful to the spirit of the age. *Michael Scarlett* is not *Kennilworth*. It is apprentice work by a very young and inexperienced writer, but one who keeps the faith and is worthy.

James Gould Cozzens—A View from Afar

John Iggulden

For me, and I must suppose for many of my contemporaries, James Gould Cozzens was one of the great novelists of our times perhaps, for some, our own time's greatest. Reading through Cozzens again, with the fifty more years of experience and skepticism I've added since my first encounter, that remains my own view.

It outraged me at the time, and it still troubles me greatly as I enter my final years, that in a manner almost certainly unique in the annals of literature, a lasting shadow was thrown across the reputation of this dedicated literary giant by one of those venomous nonentities, haunted by their own lack of creative talent, who infest the margins of every art.

How could this deed be done with such crippling effect? Simply enough, had anyone thought of it before. Do not attack the writer or his work head on but, rather, mount a derisory campaign against those who have written favorable reviews of the author's most successful novel. So by condemning those reviewers, through them, condemn the author.

In this case, remarkably, as the spoiler himself wrote: "The only really hostile review I have been able to find was"—[by a Catholic critic who took exception to some mild critical discussion, in the subject novel, of his religion]. Even more remarkably, the editor of *Commentary* saw fit to devote twelve of its pages to this blatant job of demolition.

After this ingenious attack was publicized worldwide, it would have been a poor career move for any reviewer, anywhere, to give favorable attention to any of the works of James Gould Cozzens. For any writer, could a more devastating situation be imagined?

Those unprecedented events were in 1958. I had first read Cozzens many years before when I came across the English edition of *The Last Adam* (1933; rechristened for the English, *A Cure of Flesh*, 1934). Barely into my twenties and an insatiable reader, I absorbed this new literary experience. Here in a book were real people, acting like real people in real situations. Here in a book were moral attitudes and motivations viewed from a humane and staunchly upright authorial standpoint. Captivated and captured by this author, I realized that from my viewpoint this was how the novel should be.

It did not matter that soon after, I was frustrated by *Castaway*—by which, as he would one day tell me, Cozzens himself had been frustrated. And so through the sequence of the next five books over the next twenty years—through to *Guard of Honor* (1948), a faultless novel, which I have enjoyed the most—and on to *By Love Possessed* (1957), which I admired greatly and have enjoyed almost as much. Those years ago, as a personal choice, I would have listed those two books above any other novels written in English in my times, and now, my first impressions refreshed, I would do the same.

* * *

It surprises me now to note afresh that *By Love Possessed* was published two years before the publication of my own novel *Breakthrough* in 1959. Remembered now, my own modest career as novelist had its actual beginning when I plunged from the brash innocence of my first book's writing into the temperamental hell of the second novelist; that torment where no choice is left but to confront the big questions until now avoided; the toughest of those being: What the hell is it I am trying to do?

After a while of this, I came to a first conclusion: What I most wanted to do was write novels about people as they were in life, not as they were in books. This from a realization that what most readers and critics actually seek in novels, and what most novelists agree to provide, are characters whose motives, behavior, dialogue, and manner meet a complex of behavioral conventions complicitly agreed among writers, readers, and most critics.

I do not mean here the "conventions of the novel"—that tacit agreement by which writers are allowed to employ, but must keep within, an array of devices by which to tell and to illuminate their stories. Though these conventions change over time—and are opened out when a Hemingway or a Joyce or a Márquez leaps onto the stage with some successful new act of literary choreography—they are universally agreed and closely fixed, to a surprising degree, at any given time.

I believe that similar conventions also cover the attributes and behavior of the characters in novels, but I do not expect any great chorus of agreement that this applies to "serious" novels. It does very obviously apply of course at the subliterary level of the various "formula" genres. Yet I have always held to my stubborn view that this set of secondary conventions does exist, that every serious author should be required to spurn them, but that more than a few don't.

It is a hazardous business for a writer to challenge either of these conventions. To challenge both, as Cozzens did in *By Love Possessed*, was to bend down and shout, "Kick me!" And, no doubt not expecting to be kicked, kicked he was. For in that book, Cozzens challenged the "standard" conventions by his ideosyncratic syntax—his elaborately constructed sentences and paragraphs quite different from those of any other author—and by the rarity of many of the words he employed.

But Cozzens also challenged the implicit conventions covering the behavior of fictional characters by ascribing to his seemingly respectable and much-to-be-admired protagonist, Arthur Winner, thoughts, motives, and deeds unworthy of the expectations which those conventions would call for from such a character. Behaving like a character from real life instead of a character in a book, Arthur Winner was found guilty as charged—as was Cozzens, the author of that character's existence—by that one-man jury who, by savaging the author's receptive reviewers, sought from safe cover to ambush the author. Branded as politically incorrect within the terms of the literary conventions of those times, one of the great books of this century and its author were sidelined, perhaps never to be brought back into public favor again.

* * *

In 1963, having been chosen to fly for Australia in the World Gliding Championships in Argentina, I would be returning to Australia via New York. I wrote to Cozzens most respectfully seeking to visit him were that possible. A courteous note came back with his unlisted number, suggesting I should ring when I was in New York; that I would find it harder to get from New York to Williamstown, Massachusetts, than from Australia to Argentina; and that if we did meet we might talk about the weather over a few drinks, as he didn't like to talk about writing or books, his own or those of others.

I arrived by Greyhound at the Williamstown Inn late on a March afternoon and was met by Cozzens; we bought each other drinks, talked about such things as Hemingway's recent suicide, how we'd got through the contests in Argentina without actually killing anyone, and, on my part, how traveling by Greyhound was by no means the ordeal he considered it, but an interesting experience for an Australian who had never seen so much snow in all his life. Then we drove out to Shadowbrook in a red Thunderbird in which Cozzens took a shy pride as it swished and skidded through the deep snow. In the only reference he made to his books he said it was the best auto he had ever had, thanks to *By Love Possessed*. But he'd had big tax problems, too, he hastened to add.

Mrs. Cozzens and her sister, Mrs. Collins, received me with the relaxed hospitality I would have expected in my own country, but with the pleasantest nuance that I was something exotic come into their household. They were charming women, and I was charmed. There was a lightness about it all, and I took care to respect that lightness. But over brandy in another room Cozzens surprised me and left a standing question in my mind. I'd expressed admiration for President Kennedy's resolution in the then-recent Cuban missile crisis. Cozzens got quite shirty with me. "People can't know what happened at a time like that," he said rather angrily. "The only people who know what really happened are the people who know what happened." He saw how surprised I was and made a gesture with his hand to wipe it away, and left it at that.

Though I understood what he meant, I did not understand his strong feelings about it until years later when I read *A Time of War,* his Air Force Diaries, 1943–1945. The introduction to this work quotes comments by Cozzens to the publisher of the English edition of *Guard of Honor,* the great novel he based very directly on his war experience:

> as my so-called military service drew on I began slowly to realize that through no fault (or indeed merit) of my own I was being shown the Army Air Force on a scale and in a way that was really incredible. I was coming to know about, I had to know about, more of its innumerable phases than anyone with real command duties would ever have time to know. Not many officers, and I would guess not any, had reason or opportunity to fly into and look over such a number of air fields and installations of a variety quite unbelievable. With the exception of the CG himself, in whose office I was in the end working, I don't think anyone had occasion to sit down and listen to so many of the air generals. I know that no other person read, as I had to read each morning, yesterday's activity reports from all of the Air Staff sections along with the CG's in-and-out log, the messages from and to the commanders in all combat theaters.

Not only did that explain the flash of impatience from a courteous host at the naive expression of a view which had no foundation in direct experience, but it confirmed the enormous trust which in that time of war had been placed in him, and the evident self-certainty with which he accepted and discharged that trust, and I believe that says a great deal about the impressive qualities of Cozzens, the man.

Whether or not he was as great a writer as I and many others believe he was, there can be no question that here was a man of impressive presence, of great strength of character, of noble intentions and loyalties, and of fine intellect and extraordinary competence.

* * *

Homeward over the Pacific I wrote a note of appreciation to Mrs. Cozzens and expected that would conclude this episode, but a letter arrived from Cozzens almost as soon as I was home. He wrote kindly of my visit and of my two first novels which I had left with him, along with a couple of boomerangs I had made myself and carried around the world. For the first time but by no means the last, he referred to my regrettable enthusiasm for activities other than writing. His letter concluded: "A man who puts writing ahead of such interests certainly strikes me as crazy; but there you are. To write you have to be crazy. P.S. Your boomerangs hang on my study wall. We still have 3 feet of snow; but come spring I'll go into action with them."

After my adventurous months away, I settled back into my normal life in Melbourne—business stuff to be caught up with, a procedures manual needing to be edited for the Gliding Federation of Australia, to try to stop so many people from getting killed through lack of proper standards.

When I refused to let them cut large chunks out of my third novel, my London publishers and I had parted and, with my fourth novel finished, I had two novels floating around unpublished. That serious writing had lost some of its appeal for me was evident when I wrote back to Cozzens and said I was thinking of taking a break and writing "something that will only have to be like life in books, instead of being an attempt to be like life in Life, and I'll dodge the responsibility for doing such a shady thing by using a phony name."

This letter (which I read now with retrospective embarrassment), concluded: "Jim, remember this little thing about boomerangs. If you do it all dead right the boomerang will come back and hit you in the head, an obvious fact sometimes overlooked, applying also to people standing beside you, and believe me by no means as funny as it sounds."

Cozzens can't be blamed for letting a few weeks pass before coming back on that one. When he wrote, he was stern but helpful: "you must take the pledge and get rid of all dodges and devices at once. The one possible excuse for allowing or making yourself do work you aren't willing to sign is that you've found you can do tripe or crap that will sell and you need money to eat." He assumed we were both among those "rare ones among writing wretches who eat no matter what." He was a failure with the boomerangs: "I can make them go through the most engaging gyrations, including coming back on a hairpin-turn course fifty feet to my left (I guess because I'm right-handed); but I can't make them hit me on the head."

I hastened to answer because I'd just had news that my unlucky third novel, *The Clouded Sky* (1964), had been sold to Macmillan and I wanted to report that, before that news had arrived, I'd already decided to take a break from writing fiction by working full time on editing the gliding manual, and had resolved that after that "I was going to make a new start and I was going to see it through as far as I needed to go, even if that took years." Then I voiced concern that in writing to me he would be taking time from works that no other man then alive could produce, that he must not be distracted by irrelevancies and that I was an irrelevancy.

It never occurred to me that in those years Cozzens, taking on a style of life that was close to hermetic, had reduced his regular correspondents to the merest handful. It was twenty years later that I learned this from Matthew J. Bruccoli's Cozzens biography, and now I wish very much I had known this at the time, so that I would have written to him differently and more often. Certainly I would not have let this

correspondence die after 1969 when my life turned to other responsibilities and other activities that took me away from the writing of novels for many years. Out of a bastard kind of modesty, though I valued this friendship enormously, I misunderstood it; quite overlooking that I had become as much his friend as he had become mine, and believing that, being a novelist no longer, no longer could I claim his time and interest. That was foolish, and I am sorry, but all my life one of life's slow learners have I been.

But, back then, a card came back immediately. He was "delighted to hear about *The Clouded Sky* and also about your Good Conduct." Having studied my detailed instructions on the throwing of boomerangs in a previous letter, he now realized: "I was throwing the boomerang backward. Hope to hit myself on the head this very afternoon."

Nine months passed before I wrote again. I had reminded Macmillan to send Cozzens one of my author's copies of *The Clouded Sky,* and they said they'd sent him a proof copy in the hope he'd give the book a plug. I hastened to tell Cozzens that I'd like it if he told Macmillan: "Well, look, he's a nice chap, I rather like him but, honestly as a writer, he's a bastard." And, I said, I had been tempted to write before, "but a letter asks an answer, and an answer demands a degree of writing time and writing effort which, however slight, could be a loss to something vastly more important."

When a kindly answer came right back using most of a page to explain how and why Cozzens never gave quotes, I suffered the red-faced mortification of one who, having let a wing drop, has spun down right into the middle of a false position. For all that it was archetypal Cozzens:

By now it's perfectly understood in the trade that sending me stuff is a waste of substance since nobody ever yet got a quote from me. Today the ruling fact is that I can't give quotes. I've fixed it so that too many of my fellow workers have every right to say: why you son of a bitch; what do you mean by doing for anybody else what you got me to excuse you for doing for me? The business started as a callow piece of ingenuousness, not to say silly self-consciousness and self-conceit, well suited to my then-age (21). Taking my first look at the literary world, I noticed that the more active givers of quotes were cheap bastards bent on grabbing even such trifles of cheap publicity for themselves if they praised new writers. If they praised their established contemporaries, with me they couldn't win, either. I saw them as equally cheap log-rollers corruptly intent on a deal: I'll rave about your work; you'll rave about mine. Such goings-on I considered beneath me. Today, while I'm not sure I was altogether or absolutely wrong about the practice in some cases, starting from scratch I would, I hope, have the composure to say what I thought, and to hell with what may be made of it. But I'm

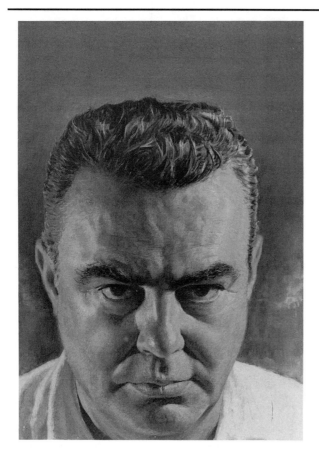

Time *cover portrait of James Gould Cozzens by James Chapin*
(Bruccoli Collection)

not starting from scratch; so I'm stuck with my pretentious little policy.

The good news was, he had followed my orders and was doing better with the boomerang "but not nearly well enough to leave a widow. Instead of missing my head by fifty feet I once or twice missed it by no more than ten feet."

So, in such fits and starts, did the written traffic of this friendship continue. At the end of 1964 he wrote that he had received a copy of *The Clouded Sky* but was most concerned that, while it had been published six months before, he had seen no sign that it had been advertised, promoted, or even stocked into bookstores. I saw no point in telling him that this unlucky book had been orphaned when Macmillan's brilliant editor, by then a personal friend, after some kind of ethical disagreement, had moved to another publisher where I planned to follow him with my next novel, *Dark Stranger* (1965).

Cozzens was very kind, I hoped without friendly bias, about much of *The Clouded Sky,* though he didn't think I wrote at all well about people getting laid, or men quarreling. "As a writer," he wrote,

you aren't let off that easily. Your job is to inveigle me . . . into that suspension of disbelief fiction has to work. When, once in a while, I find you're not doing this I'm driven to suggest to you, Dutch uncle style, that for those moments you're lying down on the job. You haven't required yourself to write to the point. You haven't tested, line by line and word by word, to see if you're really saying, and saying unmistakeably, what you mean, what you know to be true. This takes time; you've got to be ready to give it time. I don't mean I forbid you to go gliding or become champ again, but writing's a hell of a jealous mistress. You mustn't lose interest (while you) haggle about the next book; and you must see to it that the one after (everyone takes wrong turns; think nothing of that) gets blood and sweat enough–no; what the hell; all writers are sedentary softies, say, gets enough concentrated attention, to keep having the makings of a book.

True, I didn't write at all well about people getting laid, at finding that exact necessary point between the pornographic and the coldly factual, between brutal objectivity and tenderness. A few years later, reading in *Morning Noon and Night* (1968) that passage which Cozzens called "The Afternoon of Mrs. Van den Arend" I realized that with no chance at all of ever winning, this was a contest I didn't ever want to fly with him.

Two months later I reported I'd hit some power lines landing out after a seven-hour cross-country race in the 1964 National Gliding Championships, fracturing my spine; that I was wearing an elaborate spinal brace, but I became each day more mobile. I acknowledged his comments on *The Clouded Sky.* About my accident I said, "being alive is what impresses me most, even some weeks later. The strangeness of being spared and the humble wondering why. Four or five different ways you could be and should be dead. Clearly, I'm getting old. Almost old enough to bow my spirit before the workings of a will that is not my own. This is a crossroads, anyway. Always before I've been torn between the life of action and the life of reflection which must be lived if one's small spark of talent is to be developed. I see a bloody great, firm finger pointing at the crossroads and I'm almost reconciled to obedience; and there's only one other person in the world (who shares my bed) to whom I'd give expression to these thoughts."

An instant Cozzens card: "Dear Jack: mend your own back by all means but, damn it, never mind mending that shiny glider's back. I don't know how many glider drivers Australia grows but I do know that, as of so far, it grows hardly any writers of either promise or performance. For God, for Country, and for whatever your equivalent of Yale is just keep your eye on that bloody great firm finger. You owe it to the Commonwealth as well as Mrs. Iggulden and me. J."

My turn, but for whatever varied reasons I left that for seven months and then I said: "It seems that the bloody great firm finger, having writ, has moved on. I went for my first fly since the prang, last Sunday, and what it proved is I'm too old for reformation. Please, Jim, *must* I keep myself inviolate for writing and for nothing else? Can't I keep up those few harmless amusements that make my life as much worth living as it is? Maybe, if I were a genius, or thought I was, or even had enough talent to be sure I had it; maybe then I'd knuckle down—but that ain't the case as far as I can tell. I have a little gift or knack which, because I'm clever and pertinacious, I can learn to stretch as far as it will go. (Maybe) some day I'll make the first ten places in the Australian writing team (most of the candidates are pretty crook), but I'm too proud a man to think that a goal worth the utter dedication of a life. Guess I'm a World Comps man at heart, and the World Comps writers—you and a couple of others—all they do is make me discouraged." I reported on other matters: I'd finished with the spinal brace; I'd gone to McGraw-Hill with my next novel, *Dark Stranger,* and they'd be sending him a copy; I had problems with the book I was working on; and I enclosed a photograph of my repaired "aerial steed," the prototype of the fifteen-meter Schneider Boomerang.

Again Cozzens answered almost by return:

Indeed your steed's pretty (only perhaps you should remember you can't see how pretty it is unless you're outside watching it, not inside riding it). But if your back is *that* subject to repair, I agree that you're entitled to break it whenever you damn well please. So this might be the right moment to say all that 'dedication' stuff is eyewash, crap, or whatever (you) prefer to call it. I'm the most disciplineless bastard I ever met. I've never dreamed of doing anything just because I know I ought to do it; and if I want to do it, anything I know I ought not to do I've always done. I don't like to fly (it took the whole US Army Air Force, you might say, to make me do it for four years. Fortunately by then having come to be a major on the Commanding General's staff, I was in a position to wangle myself out a record-breaking 6 weeks after Japan quit, and I haven't been off the ground since) but if I liked to fly, be sure I'd be flying. You'll see the truth. Since I'd rather write than do anything else, I've thought up a number of high-sounding reasons for only doing what I'd rather do. To everyone, at every opportunity, I say, in effect: allow me to sell you a couple. Still and all (an Americanism and a down-east one to boot) I hear with relief that the back is OK—I twice dropped you a line, but pulled back. As a sexagenarian, I come to find that no news is the only good news about a friend. Just you wait. I'll be very glad to see *Dark Stranger.*

When I wrote back to thank him for letting me off the hook I told him what I had some time back realized:

that it doesn't matter much what anyone says about this thing; a man is going to be as dedicated as it's in his nature to be, and nothing much is going to alter it. What other people say or do will only have this effect: to make him a little more or a little less comfortable about the way he is by nature. In short, you had made me a little guilty and uncomfortable about the way I let myself be distracted from the main line and work of my life; and now I'm a good deal more comfortable about it. And not one whit more or less dedicated and single-minded than I've been all along. . . . 'Still and all' may be an Americanism, as you say, but it's occasionally heard out here. I suspect it is of English rural origin. It was a favorite phrase of an old fisherman I knew in my childhood holidays at Apollo Bay, Tony Fisk. Tony was awarded a medal for rushing into the surf without his pants on to save three people from a shipwreck. I was about 10 at the time and the fact that he didn't have his pants on always seemed more significant to me than the shipwreck or the medal. A lot of spinsters, schoolteachers on holiday, were standing around, I think that has something to do with it. He taught me how to fish for bream with maggots, and how and where to find maggots, and how to get a maggot on a fish-hook. Still and all, I don't think I could do it now.

Then came a letter which I accepted with some difficulty. His copy of *Dark Stranger* had come and from his reading came a rather hurtful misunderstanding:

I must suggest to you that what you here chose to do, and with that good-to-see exact control did do, isn't what you ought to choose to do. . . . To my mind . . . you are letting yourself be directed more than you have any reason to let yourself be by various literary fashions of the moment. All of them are bad—by which I mean not necessarily bad in themselves, but bad for anyone like you. You've come to write in a way that makes it clear you can, and so you must, go it on your own. Never mind about William Golding—never mind about anyone—and this includes, even if I don't sound that way—me. It is a use of the moment, and a moment now nearly a generation long, to be partial to that shock-effect trick of putting yourself behind a character who altogether plausibly, for often good, impressively well-presented reasons, doesn't know whether he's coming or going. But your right job as a novelist is to purvey "that new acquist of true experience" of Milton's. People who haven't all their wits about them, though as subjects or objects of observation allowable, must frustrate and stultify your purveying if you, the purveyor, sink yourself in one of them, confine yourself to saying what he would say, to seeing what he would see. You're electing to start with two strikes on you. When you do it as well as you've done it, some pity and terror is evoked, all right; but those are communications only of an instant. You have it in you to give something more lasting than that. Next time, get in there and do it.

William Golding? The one-great-book author? I had been influenced by an author who, but for that one book, I found pointlessly tedious? No. In the sec-

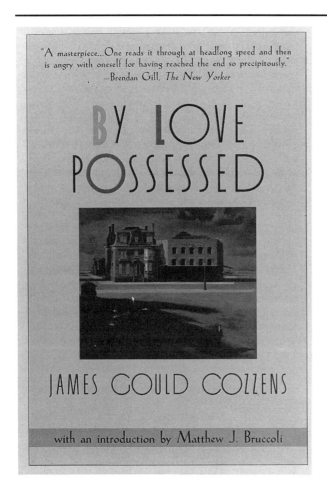

"A masterpiece...One reads it through at headlong speed and then is angry with oneself for having reached the end so precipitously."
—Brendan Gill, *The New Yorker*

BY LOVE POSSESSED

JAMES GOULD COZZENS

with an introduction by Matthew J. Bruccoli

Front cover of the current reprint published by Carroll and Graf

tion of my book (twelve pages) to which Cozzens referred, the actual influence indeed had been a "new acquist of true experience." My father had a bad accident in the family sailplane. I went with him to a big city hospital. In the next ward lay a young man, good-looking, unconscious, a police officer seated beside his bed. "What happened?" I asked the cop. "Crashed his getaway after a holdup." "Jesus," I said, "What's he going to wake up to!" The cop shook his head. It stayed with me, a new acquist of true experience indeed. In quite a different context, I used it.

Did I straightaway write and tell Jim Cozzens that? No. Why waste his time and energies? Why waste mine? I sent him a book I thought he would enjoy—*Camels and the Outback.* He sent back a card: "You're perfectly right. I would have guessed that if there were anything I was unlikely to care about (well; next to professional sports, flying, television, the theater, cinema, modern art, modern music, and betting on horses) it would be camels outback. Mr. Barker overcomes me. Many thanks."

We exchanged letters over the next few months, mainly about *Dark Stranger,* but they didn't take us far. I said in mine that I could make excuses: "But what's the use? The thing's written and fixed in print. In a sense, and you'll know what I mean, it's more other people's problem now than it is mine." But I did add: "You mightn't believe me, but I don't want to write like Mr. Golding, I never tried, and never will. I'd like to write like Mr. H. M. Barker only I just don't know enough about camels."

In his reply, after a page of further good advice, Cozzens said: "This is meant to hie you on, but the moment may be a good one to . . . advise you that, finger exercises done, and going as good as one ever will, the troubles won't by any means be over. One permanent discouragement in writing (and uniquely writing's, I think) is that the more you do of it, the better at least relatively you get at it, the tougher you may expect to find it. So, yes, I have a new book; but as the case must be under this law, doing it to suit me grows harder and takes longer. A couple of books ago I expect it would have looked fine to me. Now I just see it's not the book I meant to do. No; and no book ever will be. Hearten yourself with the thought. . . ."

After that, a card from Cozzens two years later thanking me for sending him a second book by Barker; and a year and a half after that I wrote, in part: "After this long time something urges me to write to you to express in a brief Christmas greeting at least some part of my continued respect and goodwill. I suspect that my total lapse as a correspondent stems from a mild form of suppressed guilt—you seem to figure in my thoughts as a literary taskmaster, and a hard one; with requirements so austere and dedicated that one so easily involved in the distractions of an active life, as I am, can't hope to meet them."

Cozzens answered immediately:

It was good to hear from you. I've reached the undesirable age when everyone I ever knew and liked is having every new month or each new year Something Happen to him. Why shouldn't that steed of yours however beautiful to see have duly compounded you with clay? So I'm glad to think you'll keep the hell out of it and stick to your right job. As the late Aldous Huxley (who, I nowadays ask myself, isn't *late?*) noted: in writing, there's no substitute for talent. You show the talent; but O miserable condition of humanity there's no substitute for wholetime work either. I judge you have no more need to earn your living some other way than I have. You're left without any good reason for not getting in there and doing what you could & ought to do. So do it.

There, now to my sadness—and to my failure fully to understand exactly why—our correspondence ended.

* * *

Someone—Randall Jarrell?—accurately defined a novel as "a large work of fiction which has something wrong with it." Perhaps most novelists might well be similarly defined. In this sense, I am fairly sure that one of the things that was wrong with James Gould Cozzens was that he was not at all what he seemed, nor was he at all what he purported to be, nor even what he thought he was. To me there is something entirely enigmatic—and self-defeating, too—in his obsessive requirement that writing should be the only thing in a writer's life. I have wondered whether this was not entirely his own obsession but, in whole or part, that of Bernice Baumgarten, that delightful and talented woman who was first his literary agent, and then his devoted wife.

But that is no business of mine. The obsession existed, and I guess the truth is that not only did I find it so oppressive that I could not hack it, but in all common sense I could not agree with it. I believe there is something wonderfully real and direct in the living complexity of the events and the people which make *Guard of Honor* (1948) a better novel than, and quite unlike, any of the others; and if ever a novel came from a direct involvement with a vivid part of life, separately lived from the writing part of the author's life, *Guard of Honor* was it.

Perhaps I should have said to Jim Cozzens (though, fourteen years younger, I never would have): "If one is to purvey 'that new acquist of true experience' of Milton's—doesn't one need to go out into the world and acquist the experience first?"

* * *

Now gladly I grant Cozzens the last word on the wrecker's job that was done on *By Love Possessed* and,

by that, on him. Never once over the time of our friendship did he say one word of this. One had to believe that it left him quite unaffected, either from an innate stoicism or from a sturdy conviction of his own superiority—as if, to this, he applied that great thought: "the dogs bark, but the caravan passes on."

He and the wrecker, one Dwight Macdonald, exchanged quite urbane letters; with Cozzens, I believe, in the end taking the game they were playing by leaving Macdonald no room to deny that at least one of the passages which he had held to ridicule was a quotation from Shakespeare.

But in *Morning Noon and Night* can be found what surely can be taken, moderate though it is, as Cozzens' own last word on this episode. The character, Knox Frothingham, is clearly intended to be seen as taken from life:

> Graduated, Knox had been able to find himself, starting in the fall, an editorial job on a New York weekly magazine . . . [he] has never become a noted writer. Joining his New York magazine and doing, to start, bits of editing and staff writing, he apparently, continuing with it, was able to find in the work adequate means of self expression, and as time passed and he grew very accomplished, moving up to the editorial top, also adequate means of livelihood. The great novel he had a youthful aim to write remains unwritten, and though finally . . . made a member of the National Institute of Arts and Letters, he enjoys no general literary reputation. Still, he has assured means and authority to write and to cause to be published whatever he wants to write in whatever way he wants to write it. Today I see him touched no more by sense of failure than he would have been by the abusive criticism he must almost certainly need to support had he produced his great novel and had luck made it a great success.

James Gould Cozzens: How to Read Him

R. H. W. Dillard
Hollins College

The fortieth anniversary of the publication of James Gould Cozzens's most widely known book, *By Love Possessed* (1957), and yet, aside from the new Carrol and Graf edition of the novel with an introduction by Matthew J. Bruccoli, I've come across only two references to the novel during that year and the first month of 1998. Those two references give a certain ironic insight into the current literary (or, at least,

popular) standing of that novel and its author. The first mention was in a story by Lee Smith ("Live Bottomless" in her collection, *News of the Spirit*); in the story, which takes place in 1958, a thirteen-year-old girl reports that "I was reading *By Love Possessed* (pretty hot stuff), which had just arrived in a package from the Book-of-the-Month Club. I kept it under my bed." The second mention was by Robert Osborne, introducing a showing of the movie *By Love Possessed* on Turner Classic Movies on 22 January 1998; he described the movie accurately enough as "unabashedly a soap opera," but he went on to say that it was based on a novel by Cozzens (which he carefully and incorrectly pronounced with a long *o*) and that the novel "although it stayed on the best seller list for months . . . was so long and so complicated that it became known as the best seller nobody ever finished reading." Both Smith's character and Mr. Osborne also related Cozzens's novel to *Peyton Place,* Grace Metalious's scandalous best-seller of 1956: the teenager in Smith's story also has a "dog-eared, hidden copy of *Peyton Place,*" and Osborne announced that the movie takes place in "a small town in New England [*sic*], a village not unlike Peyton Place." As one who did indeed finish reading *By Love Possessed,* who did not find it "hot stuff" (probably because I wasn't then and certainly am not now thirteen), and who can find only the most superficial parallels between it and Metalious's romantic tell-all tale, I found the ironies in these uses and misuses of Cozzens's great novel to be compound and complex, but, unfortunately, fairly typical of the critical disregard into which both this novel and Cozzens's work in general have fallen.

In the 2 September 1957 issue of *Time* magazine, in a cover story which was to mark both the high point and the beginning of the major downturn in the literary reputation of James Gould Cozzens, T. E. Kalem, the unsigned author of the piece, said that "After a writing span of more than three decades, during which he produced an even dozen novels, Cozzens is the least known and least discussed of major American novelists."

Kalem's assessment, like the rest of his article, was to some degree accurate; Cozzens was (and is) certainly a major novelist, and he was not as widely known or praised as many of his important contemporaries, especially William Faulkner and Ernest Hemingway, both winners of the Nobel Prize. But it was also far from entirely true at the time: Cozzens's novel *Guard of Honor* had won the Pulitzer Prize eight years before in 1949, and his work was widely known, respected, and read, with four of his earlier novels (*S.S. San Pedro, Castaway, The Just and the Unjust,* and, of course, *Guard of Honor*) readily available in inexpensive hardcover or paperback reprints. *By Love Possessed,* the publication of which generated the *Time* story, was a Book-of-the-Month Club Main Selection and would be on the best-seller list of *The New York Times* for thirty-four weeks (in first place for twenty-three of those weeks), and the movie based on that novel, an expensive Hollywood production, would be released in 1960. In the decade following, by 1968, four critical monographs (to use a word that Cozzens scorned) had

appeared about his work, and he had published a collection of stories and his last novel, *Morning Noon and Night.*

Along with the novel's popular reputation as "hot stuff" among those who never finished reading it, the *Time* cover story was one of the reasons for the great popular success of *By Love Possessed.* Ironically (or perhaps appropriately, for such a major ironist as Cozzens), the picture the story presented of Cozzens and his purported attitudes toward Catholics, Jews, Negroes, and women (along with the notorious attack on the novel by Dwight MacDonald which followed in *Commentary*) began a process which has led to Kalem's assessment's becoming more accurate forty years later than it was at the time. One other scholarly monograph (a volume in the Twayne series by Pierre Michel) was published in 1974, but, since then, the unstinting efforts of Matthew J. Bruccoli, both as publisher and as scholar, have been responsible almost single-handedly for the bulk of interest that remains in Cozzens's work. His bibliography of Cozzens was published in 1981; his *Just Representations: A James Gould Cozzens Reader,* in 1978; his collection of critical essays by various writers and scholars, *James Gould Cozzens: New Acquist of True Experience,* in 1979; and his full biography, *James Gould Cozzens: A Life Apart,* along with his two editions of selections from Cozzens's notebooks, in 1984. As of this writing, only six of Cozzens's thirteen novels are in print (including *Ask Me Tomorrow,* which is available only in the Cozzens reader), and his work is seldom represented in college curricula or in scholarly discussion. Certainly other important novelists have not been given their due, but it is surely arguable that in 1998, as the twentieth century nears its end, James Gould Cozzens is "the least known and least discussed of major American novelists," especially of the novelists of this century.

Cozzens himself knew that complaining himself about unfair critical treatment was absolutely futile, as he made clear in a note from *Selected Notebooks: 1960–1967:*

> *Why silence is golden.* The just complaint must always amount to a self-serving declaration: and the juster, the more cogent or reasonable, the complaint, the worse for you. Your obvious anxiety to do right by yourself can never be engaging. What complaint gets you is just the opposite of what you're making it in the hope of getting. With every word, you're not winning, you're alienating the average person's sympathies.

I suspect the same results accrue when the complaint is lodged by a writer's admirers as well, so rather than complain about the lack of interest in Cozzens, or attempt to answer the negative criticism he received when he was under severe critical attack in the late 1950s, I would like to honor Cozzens and *By Love Possessed* by suggesting some ways for readers to begin to approach that novel anew, to reexamine it, and all of Cozzens's work as well.

Although there have not been a great number of them, certainly not when compared with the volumes and volumes of critical writing about Faulkner, the serious interpretative analyses of *By Love Possessed* have been unusually thoughtful. Even Kalem's *Time* cover story, for all its inaccuracies and all the harm it did, gave Cozzens's work a careful and respectful reading. These studies have, for example, examined the structural complexity of the novel, in part a result of Cozzens's efforts (inspired by remarks of Aldous Huxley and his novel *Point Counterpoint*) to write a genuinely contrapuntal novel; they have noted the many varieties of love that Cozzens explores in the novel; and they have explored the subtleties, ironies, and complexities of Cozzens's view of the dual nature of humankind, the perpetual struggle between reason and the emotions. George Garrett, in particular, studied the necessity of Arthur Winner's having to give up the thing that meant most to him (his integrity) for moral reasons, a good man forced to do a bad thing for good reasons. Cozzens's complex syntax and his use of difficult vocabulary have been examined closely with results ranging from Bracher's conclusion that his "diction reflects his basically Pyrrhonistic temperament, his apoetic intelligence, and his troubled aloofness" to Bruccoli's argument that "Cozzens's effort with language aims at achieving greater precision of statement." There have also been less fruitful discussions of the sentiments and ideas about race, class, and gender in the novel and whether they are, as Harry John Mooney Jr. put it, direct expressions of "Cozzens's philosophy, which was now stated so plainly and pungently that it could no longer be overlooked."

As intelligent as the best of these readings of the novel are, even they suffer by standing so very much alone, by seeming to be the only approaches to the work, as though the recent critical silence were the result not of neglect but of all that need be said's having been said. Once "cultural studies" and "literary theory" soon crest and finally wane in academia, I hope that younger readers and scholars (to whom the Cozzens Wars of the 1950s and 1960s must seem as ancient as the eighteenth century's Battle of the Books) will read Cozzens anew, that they will discover the extraordinary artistry of this work and proclaim it to a new generation of readers and students (and per-

haps help their elders understand Cozzens better as well). To that end, I should like to suggest several areas of study or approaches to *By Love Possessed* that they might take.

1. *The Consistent Development of Cozzens as an Artist*

By Love Possessed does not stand alone in Cozzens's work in its concerns with the great difficulty of trying to live morally and well in a nexus of interwoven time and space, reason and emotion, clarity and confusion. From the epigraph of his significantly titled first novel, *Confusion* (1924), published while he was a sophomore at Harvard, to the final pages of his last novel, *Morning Noon and Night,* Cozzens was philosophically and aesthetically focused with great consistency on that central theme and human problem. The epigraph of *Confusion* was taken from Marcus Aurelius: "Wipe off all idle fancies and say unto thyself incessantly; now if I will it is in my power to keep out of this my soul all wickedness and lust, all concupiscences, all trouble and Confusion . . . ." Cozzens's world is certainly a world of wickedness and lust, concupiscence, trouble, and confusion, and although his characters struggle to attain both the rational clarity and the strength of will to protect themselves from that world, confusion nevertheless prevails. Cozzens, of course, uses the lines from Marcus Aurelius with as much irony as Edgar Allan Poe used the passage ostensibly from Joseph Glanvill with which he prefaced "Ligeia," for it is certainly no likelier that one may will oneself free of trouble and confusion in this world than that one may will oneself free of mortality. Cozzens built from this clash of human yearnings an art of irony and paradox, an art in which characters learn to deal with confusion rather than vainly attempt to overcome it. Or, as Arthur Winner learns at the end of *By Love Possessed,* "Victory is not in reaching certainties or solving mysteries; victory is in making do with uncertainties, in supporting mysteries."

While, with the single exception of the parabolic and Poe-like *Castaway,* Cozzens wrote novels in the realistic tradition, he never allowed himself the simple truths of realism; he always pressed the form and style of his work as well as his thinking into increasingly greater complexity. His work ranks, both because of its central concerns and the aesthetic inventiveness and complexity with which it expresses those concerns, with that of Herman Melville and Henry James rather than that of William Dean Howells, John O'Hara, and John P. Marquand. Ellen Glasgow once demanded a fiction of "blood and irony." Cozzens's novels meet that demand fully.

Much detailed and sophisticated critical examination has been given to Poe's work over the last quarter of a century (especially to his novel, *The Narrative of Arthur Gordon Pym*), as it was to Melville's work beginning a half century before that—to their ironies, to their uses of narrative point of view, to their rigorous examination of the confusions of reason and passion, to the difficulties of sorting out and separating objective and subjective understanding. The result of that thoughtful scrutiny was a positive reappraisal of both Melville's and Poe's standing as major literary figures, a giving to their work its due. A close reading of Cozzens's work in similar ways would, I predict, reveal him to be much more than an apoetically intelligent writer, but rather an artist of great aesthetic inventiveness, subtlety, and complexity. And one, as well, who developed as an artist throughout the entire range of his career, from the apprentice novels of his youth (which he disowned, but we needn't) through the solidly accomplished "professional" novels of his mid career to the major achievement of his last three novels.

2. Cozzens's Uses of Narrative Point of View

Perhaps the primary reason for the misreading of *By Love Possessed* as an anti-Semitic or anti-Catholic novel (aside from the literary politics that gave rise to conscious misreadings such as MacDonald's) is that readers simply overlooked how completely disciplined Cozzens's use of point of view is in the novel. In addition to his thoughts, everything in the novel, every description, every action is filtered through the consciousness of Arthur Winner; even the apparently objective (and authorial) description of Winner, "thoughtful in a pose of habit," in the second paragraph of the first chapter, when examined closely, reveals itself to be as much a description of his inner habit of mind as his outer habit of stance and behavior. The social and physical world through which Winner moves is described as he sees it, reflecting his biases as well as his intelligent perceptions.

Cozzens's creation of a man who is earnestly striving to be a good man but who is also a realistically rendered man, one who lives a life of position and responsibility in the town of Brocton, Pennsylvania, in America in the 1950s, requires that he allow the reader to share that man's prejudices and inner confusion as well as his moral concerns and inner clarity. It is a remarkable piece of work, one in which the author disappears as thoroughly as Henry James insisted he should (and far more completely than James himself ever managed). It is Winner, for example, not Cozzens, who, after thinking so carefully about the (probably repressed, certainly well-closeted) homosexual church organist Elmer Abbott, while trying to do absolutely the right thing by him, rails to himself about a man "so tame, so pridelessly relieved at the withdrawal of a false charge, at the permission to continue his namby-pamby round, keep his piffling post, his unpaid job's clung-to prerogative of inflicting on a captive audience his mediocre music." I have no idea at all what Cozzens's personal attitudes were toward homosexuals or even "sissies," nor do I particularly care, but I do know exactly what Winner thinks and how he acts, and the tension between those thoughts and acts is at the very heart of Winner's identity, his moral dilemma, and finally his resolution of that dilemma and discovery of himself. Political correctness, that spin-off from the tenets of socialist realism, would require that a good man must not have a bad thought, much less commit a bad deed; a mature and honest art requires exactly the opposite. As Henry Worthington, the narrator of *Morning Noon and Night,* puts it, "Our Lord long ago may have pronounced the final fact in this matter—'Why callest thou me good? none is good, save, one, that is, God.'" The victory Arthur Winner ultimately attains, he must earn; it is not his by any inherent goodness, by any right of class or moral certainty or commitment to any political position.

The rigorously controlled point of view of the novel is essential to its structure, its style, and ultimately its meaning. Both the complicated structure and the style of the novel are determined by the novel's being told from Winner's point of view. The events of the novel cover precisely forty-nine hours and occur in strictly linear order, but, at the same time, the novel also moves in the nonlinear pattern of Winner's thoughts. The linear structure is contrapuntally filled out by Winner's inner digressions, musings on the personal histories of those he meets, fragments of poetry (the touchstones of his understanding of the particulars of his daily life), and echoes of conversations and scenes from earlier in the day. An extension of some of the structural devices of Henry James, Cozzens's technique is not as radical or as stylized as that of James Joyce in *Ulysses,* nor is it as linear as that of Dorothy Richardson's *Pilgrimage.* It is, oddly enough, quite similar to some of the narrative techniques of another writer who, like Cozzens, has been accused of emotional distance—Alain Robbe-Grillet, especially in *The Erasers* and *The Voyeur.*

The syntax and diction which make up the novel's style are also a direct result of Cozzens's strict adherence to Arthur Winner's point of view. Winner's mind determines both the long, complicated sentences and the variegated diction (which ranges from the highest levels of unfamiliarity to the most familiar of colloquialisms) as thoroughly as it does the overall structure of the book. "I try hard," Cozzens told Frederick Bracher in 1958, "to fit the wording, the syntax and the structure to the material, so that the manner will vary as the matter varies." Winner reveals himself to the reader (and ultimately to himself) in every aspect of the way he thinks and speaks. The notorious sex scene, which has been parodied almost as often as it was marked and dog-eared by inquisitive teenagers, is as complicated in syntax and diction as it is, not because Cozzens was attempting to write a sex scene and didn't know how, but because he was quite explicitly writing about a sex act as experienced specifically by Arthur Winner. A close analysis of that scene (actually only one long paragraph) would reveal those facets of Winner's character which constitute both his strength and his weakness: his emotional intensity and his caring for his wife, as well as his detached rationality and analytical nature. It is a remarkable piece of writing as long as one keeps in mind that the point of view is fully that of Arthur Winner.

Even an elementary understanding of the book's richness of meaning depends directly upon the reader's awareness of the way in which point of view reveals and disguises truth simultaneously as it does continually in the confusion of even the most rational of human minds. The revelations that come to Winner at the end of the novel gain their force and their import directly from the way that they are arrived at. They are most often ascribed to Winner's law partner, Julian Penrose, who does persuade him in the closing section of the book that there is such a thing as "a wise lie" and that what he has long considered the truth (specifically in regard to Penrose's knowledge of his adultery with Penrose's wife) is not what he thought it was at all. However, the truth is not only given to him by Penrose, but, bit by bit, by all of the people with whom he has dealings during the forty-nine hours of the story.

Arthur Winner does what he can to help Elmer Abbott, despite his private scorn for the man, but, ironically, Elmer Abbott is one of many people who are necessary to Winner's own victory. The same holds true for Mrs. Pratt, the sentimental Catholic proselytizer, whose theological lecture collapses with the appearance of a snake in Winner's garden. The same holds true for Jerry Brophy, the upwardly mobile Irish prosecutor who seeks Winner's backing in his bid for a judgeship; for Alfred Revere, the elderly and seriously ill black sexton of Winner's church, who tells him about a cartoon in which a man falling from a tall building calls out to people in a window he is passing, "Don't worry! All right so far!"; for Mr. Woolf, the New York lawyer who leads Winner to look more closely into his partner Noah Tuttle's accounts; for Helen Detweiler, Winner's secretary for whose suicide he is at least in part responsible, and for her ne'er-do-well brother, Ralph; in fact, for everyone Winner comes across. Their situations trouble his thoughts, and many of their words echo with startling truth in his mind as the events of both days pass. Near the end of the novel, in a moment of helplessness and despair, Winner says aloud, "I am a man alone," but even at that moment he realizes that is "silly." These other people, most of them far less intelligent than he, many of them far less moral as well, nevertheless bring to him, providentially, all of them together, the lesson he must learn. Arthur Winner, for all his winning qualities, is, at the novel's beginning, a man caught in a trap of his own reliance on reason and his distrust of emotion (a condition caused in great part by the example set by his father, whom he, with some irony, calls "the Man of Reason"), a bleak view of God's presence (or absence) engendered in great part by the deaths of his first wife and his son, and an intense fear that all love is finally selfish, literally a love of self. The restricted point of view of the narrative allows Winner's self to be revealed in a way that he would never allow to those around him, even those he holds dearest, and it allows, especially by the device of repeated allusions and echoes of conversations, the learning process that saves Winner to develop naturally without imposed explanation or forced symbolic action. At the end of the novel, having lost the things he felt were most central to him (his sense of the truth, his total dependence on rationality, and, as Garrett said, his integrity, but also his unwarranted fears and guilt), he is possessed by love, shaken by it, and renewed by it. He surrenders his old self in order to protect those he loves and thereby finds a new self and can answer to the needs of others, as he does in the novel's last words: not "I am a man alone," but "I'm here."

The multiple-point-of-view technique of *Guard of Honor* enabled Cozzens to show best, as he put it in a letter to his English publisher, "the peculiar effects of the inter-action of innumerable individuals functioning in ways at once determined by and determining the function of innumerable others," the United States Army Air Force in a world at war. The first-person narrative of *Morning Noon and Night* allowed him to present the passage of time and human interaction from the point of view of a man consciously musing upon his life. But the restricted point of view of *By Love Possessed* places the developing consciousness of Arthur Winner at the very center of the fray; for all the plot happenings, which are many and complicated, the story of the novel is Arthur Winner's, and it is an interior story of a consciousness shaped by human interaction. A detailed analysis of the functioning of that point of view would lead to a much richer understanding of how the novel moves and means.

3. *Motifs as Keys to Meaning*

Among the more-intriguing notes in Cozzens's *Selected Notebooks* are his responses to his twice seeing the movie *By Love Possessed* (1961). The movie, directed by John Sturges and produced by Walter Mirisch, is, as Robert Osborne suggested, a very polished soap opera, ironically enough, a sort of offspring of Mark Robson's *Peyton Place* (1957) and Douglas Sirk's *Imitation of Life* (1959), complete with Lana Turner. The screenplay is credited to "John Dennis" because its original author, Charles Schnee, sued to have his name removed after script changes were rendered by other hands at the behest of the producer; the result is an amazingly garbled version of Cozzens's plot, complete with new characters cobbled together from those in the novel. Cozzens knew that "the job they undertook was impossible; the book defeated them at every turn and was indeed specifically intended to." But he was nevertheless able to praise the film, especially for its "small touches, often faithfully taken from the book," its "good careful small points," its "excellences of small detail."

I have felt for some time that Cozzens's critics have not paid proper attention (aside from some excellent analyses of the ornate clock on the opening and closing pages of the novel and the appearance of the snake in Arthur Winner's garden) to his careful and meaningful use of motifs in the novel. I have already suggested that future readers examine the words and phrases that recur in Arthur Winner's mind throughout the novel, but I would hope also for a close scrutiny of his other uses of motifs, particularly places, physical objects, and animals.

While watching the movie this year, with an eye to testing my theory, I noted the small touches that pleased Cozzens on his viewings of the movie. There were a number of them, none used to great effect: the church (both its tower and the steps leading to it), Winner's law office building (which seems to stand in for the courthouse with its clock which figures so importantly in the novel), the Union League

(although its painting of an event of local pride that never actually occurred in the Civil War has been replaced by the town Revolutionary War heroes' grave–now thought to contain the bones of pigs–which the movie has moved to a position under the club!), more than one grandfather clock, not the ancient tree at the Winners' lakeside lodge but at least the thunderstorm that breaks it, the room over the garage with its disused bed, a statue of Cupid and its shadow that appears twice by the staircase in Noah Tuttle's home (standing in for the cupid on the old gilt clock in the Winner family home), and once, just maybe, the gilt clock itself in the far background on the mantel in Arthur's house. Neither the snake in the garden nor the opossum on the road, both very important in the novel, make it into the movie.

A close reading, not of these echoes and whispers in the movie but of the novel itself and its motifs (such as and including the ones I've mentioned), will show clearly that Cozzens built the novel contrapuntally not only in its structure but also in its use of motifs, and that those motifs are keys to the novel's larger meanings. For example, the three buildings that dominate the town's center speak to the thematic concerns of the novel directly: all monuments to that which endures in a society but all caught in the flux of human confusion and change. The courthouse with its clock stands firm in the novel, but within its walls change is inevitable: the Jewish lawyer (but Episcopalian convert) Woolf's important presence and Jerry Brophy's ascendance toward the bench, despite his being a mere politician and an Irishman, mark that change most clearly. The Union League marks the change even more clearly, for it is the most prominent emblem of the old social order in the town. Although the building itself with its painting ("This was man's incurable willful wish to believe what he preferred to believe") stands firm, the club as a powerful social entity (and, as it turns out, as an ongoing institution) has reached the end of its days; the changing life of the community has rendered its presence untenable and useless. But the church, whose new pastor wishes to impose a number of changes in its ways and means (including bringing into check Elmer Abbott's tendency to play hymns on the carillon at unexpected times), does, however, have a continuing strength, like the oak beam supporting its bell, which "Ought to be here, no different, two-three hundred years when we're all gone." A thorough analysis of those and other motifs will, I believe, make much more clear than it has seemed to most critics a central theme of the novel, the ways of providence in a hard-luck world beset by human confusion.

4. *The Texture of Time in the Novel*

I have stolen my heading for this section from Vladimir Nabokov's *Ada,* in part because only Nabokov and William Faulkner among Cozzens's major American contemporaries have been so deeply concerned in their work (and in the form and style of their work) with the interrelationship of present, past, and future time as he (and he never more so than in *By Love Possessed*). As Gavin Stevens puts it in Faulkner's *Intruder in the Dust,* "It's all now you see. Yesterday won't be over until tomorrow and tomorrow began ten thousand years ago." Or as Nabokov's Van Veen puts it in *Ada,* "'To be' means to know one 'has been.'"

The uncertainties and mysteries of time, as Arthur Winner comes to see, are at the heart of human confusion, the past always present in time present, not as a completely determinant factor as he had earlier thought but as a living texture, the generative source of moral freedom and responsibility. When he says, "I'm here," at the end of the novel, he means that he is fully *here* at what Melville called the "vital centre," at one of those "turning-places and growing-places" which William James called "the workshop of being, where we catch fact in the making."

No wonder, then, that the structure of *By Love Possessed* is so complex, so contrapuntal, and that the syntax of the sentences that make up that structure is so complex. Each moment is the product of and the producer of other moments; no moment stands alone. It is this understanding that also produced the long syntactically complex sentences of Henry James's last novels, the complexities of both overall structure and syntax in Faulkner's novels (especially *The Sound and the Fury, Absalom, Absalom!,* and *A Fable*), and the synchronous "link-and-bobolink" textures of Nabokov's fictions (among which, for example, *Lolita* is as much about an obsession with time as it is about an obsession with little girls).

Cozzens's *Guard of Honor* is constructed in an equally contrapuntal way, but its concerns, for all the many flashbacks in the novel, are primarily horizontal, spreading out across the air base, the army, literally the world at war at a moment in time, rather than vertically down through and up into time; its sentences and paragraphs and chapters, though complex in structure, have none of the consistent, page-by-page temporal awareness and parenthetical syntactical complexity of *By Love Possessed.* The same is true of *Morning Noon and Night,* which, although it is very directly concerned with time, is a first-person

account of a life lived, a meditation on the passage of time, rather than a thorough and direct examination of that "workshop of being" itself. Its structural and syntactical rhythms are appropriately those of its narrator's reflective mind rather than the knotted complexities of Arthur Winner's very active mind, which is very much in time.

I suggest, then, that a close analysis of Cozzens's thinking about time and his uses of it in syntax and structure will reveal him to be a peer of both Faulkner and Nabokov in ways that have not yet been fully recognized.

I have only begun to suggest ways in which *By Love Possessed* and Cozzens's other fiction may be read, but I hope that I have at least encouraged new serious readers to begin a close examination of his work. The benefits, I guarantee you, will be many and profound.

Addenda:

1. Given the renewed critical interest in John Dos Passos's work after the publication of *U.S.A.* in the Library of America, I suspect that the single best way both to make Cozzens's work readily available to the audience it deserves and to renew serious interest in that work is to press for its inclusion in the Library of America as soon as possible. In fact, a full-court press by Cozzens's admirers is probably called for.

2. Although the *Time* cover story stated that Cozzens and his wife had not seen a movie in seventeen years (and I've seen nothing elsewhere to contradict that), I nevertheless find interesting certain odd similarities between the character of Arthur Bannister in Orson Welles's *The Lady from Shanghai* (1948) and that of Julius Penrose in Cozzens's novel, similarities that lead me to speculate that Cozzens may have seen that movie and may well have drawn from it, however consciously or unconsciously, when he first conceived and began to write *By Love Possessed* in 1949.

Both Bannister and Penrose are prominent lawyers; both are seriously crippled and walk only with the aid of great effort and a pair of canes; both have faithless wives whom they married in full knowledge; and both speak of life with a bitter cynicism (the tone of voice with which Bannister calls his wife "Lover" sums it all up). There, the similarities end; Arthur Bannister, in his deadly rage, is almost an antimatter version of Penrose, who, for all his cynicism, is Arthur Winner's last and best moral teacher. But, at the end of the movie, Michael O'Hara's decision literally to stand up, when challenged by the funhouse sign to "Stand Up or Give

Up," and face the truth of his own failings as well as those of others is very much akin to Winner's decision to say, "I'm here."

Those analogues at first struck me as mildly interesting but scarcely convincing, but when I saw the film based upon Cozzens's novel, I was surprised to see that coincidentally—or by one of those synchronicities ("links-and-bobolinks") that Nabokov took such delight in—Everett Sloane, the actor who played Arthur Bannister in *The Lady from Shanghai,* played Doctor Shaw in *By Love Possessed.* The pieces all came together when I then noticed

that Cozzens in his notes on the movie made specific reference to only one actor as well cast—Everett Sloane (whose name he did not know), "who in the trifling part allowed him was almost disconcerting, he was so exactly in face and manner what I was seeing as I wrote."

Make of that concatenation of events what you will. I find the evidence fairly compelling that Cozzens did see and was influenced in some way by Welles's movie, but I offer my surmise here only as a footnote to my serious reacquaintance with a major American novel.

Novels for Grown-Ups

Matthew J. Bruccoli
University of South Carolina

Writers who ask a good deal of the reader. I don't mean in the factitious guessing games about symbolism or levels of meaning of the little magazines but in point of adult experience and a grown-up mind. If, for reasons of partisan anger, or arbitrary doctrinaire critical concepts, he doesn't feel like giving a good deal; or if, in fact, he doesn't have much to give, he will naturally find the too-demanding work a bad one—those who were put off for various partisan reasons and so didn't feel like giving a good deal.

Notebooks, *13 April 1960*

James Gould Cozzens (1903-1978) published his fifteenth novel, *By Love Possessed,* in 1957. It was a best-seller and a bonanza. The initial critical reception that repositioned him among the major American novelists of the century elicited denunciations of Cozzens as an illiberal spokesman for aristocracy and condemnations of the novel's style as pretentious and unnecessarily difficult. The reviewers who had praised *By Love Possessed* ran when the attack began. Consequently all of Cozzens's novels—including his 1948 masterpiece *Guard of Honor*—fell into disrepute and are omitted from the official canon of American literature.

Despite his insistence that he didn't "give a damn about posterity's opinion" of himself and his books, it is obligatory to reopen the James Gould Cozzens case twenty years after his death. Not for his sake, for he truly had contempt for the critical establishment and the ways literary reputations are cultivated. For the benefit of readers who are missing some of the best novels in American literature: *The Last Adam* (1933), *Men and Brethren* (1936), *The Just and the Unjust* (1942), *Guard of Honor* (1948), *By Love Possessed,*

and *Morning Noon and Night* (1968). Most of these are in print—which means in the warehouse—and can be special-ordered by a competent bookseller, but they are not now stocked in bookstores. There are encouraging signs: in 1998 *Guard of Honor* will be added to the Modern Library, and *By Love Possessed* will be reprinted by Carroll and Graf.

After settling in rural Lambertville, New Jersey, in 1933, Cozzens stayed home and wrote—except for a stint on *Fortune* and his World War II Air Force service that provided the material for *Guard of Honor.* He wrote to satisfy his own requirements, which included clarity, accuracy of observation, and objectivity. The only other judgment of his writing that mattered to him was that of his wife-agent, Bernice Baumgarten. Apart from her successful daily involvement in the New York literary and publishing business, Cozzens had no direct contact with the envies, political agendas, and logrolling that operate in the society of letters. For twenty-five years he eschewed the activities embraced by many prominent admired writers. Cozzens was convinced that most writers have something wrong with them—which is why they are writers—and avoided them. He made no public appearance; he joined no literary organizations; he signed no manifestos; he gave five interviews; he divorced no wives; he drank at home; he made no noble declarations; he provided one blurb, for Walter Jackson Bate's *Samuel Johnson* (1977); he reviewed two books; he cultivated no tame critics; he attended no conferences. Cozzens's surely temporary disrepute may well be "condign punishment" for his failure to nurture his career except by writing well. Professional writers write to be published and read. Cozzens was not indifferent to success, but he believed that it was enough for a writer to write well. He understood that he made requirements on their attention and intelligence that some general readers were unable or unwilling to meet, and he was prepared to do without them. Yet his novels are not difficult. His intention was clarity of meaning; the complex structure of the later novels enables the reader to make connections and to comprehend the causality of events. Before *By Love Possessed* Cozzens's prose was unornamented, and his novels were notable for their inside knowledge of difficult subjects—the law in *The Just and the Unjust* and the vast organization of the Air Force in *Guard of Honor*. His purpose was to provide the reader with Milton's "new acquist of true experience."

Cozzens's principal tool is irony—irony of style and irony of action. Irony is a dicey tool: readers and reviewers often don't get it. The stylistic devices of *By Love Possessed* that elicited attention and protest were in certain cases intentionally self-mocking. Although Cozzens reminded himself that it is not the novelist's job to amuse himself, *By Love Possessed* is occasionally self-indulgent, with off-putting consequences. In this novel he relished unfamiliar words—which he insisted were the right words to convey his meaning—made unacknowledged references to the classics of English literature, and constructed formal periodic sentences. Readers were offended by what seemed to be Cozzens's indifference to their requirements. Yet compared to Faulkner he is clear and easy.

The voice or tone of Cozzens's prose is impersonal; he makes no effort to elicit the reader's approval; he maintains distance from his characters and his readers. Accordingly, he has been labeled as cold and deficient in sympathy. Cozzens knew that he was not a crowd-pleaser. Writing in his *Notebooks* about Richard Hughes's *The Fox in the Attic,* he observed:

> . . . this seems to be the kind of writing (my own is another) that must have some emotion-arousing quality that makes those who like it unable to see its faults; and those who don't like it, unable to see its merits. The result is no critical middle ground. The likers, in effect, love it and give it the highest praise: the dislikers are not just bored or indifferent. In effect, they hate it; actively and loudly they assert it's as bad as possible (30 January 1962).

By Love Possessed requires readers who know how to read a novel, but Cozzens's other novels are notably accessible. Six of them—including *By Love Possessed*—were Book-of-the-Month Club selections

(agent Baumgarten was good at her job); and the BOMC was in the business of meeting the requirements of the celebrated mythical general reader. *Children and Others*—his only short-story collection—and *Morning Noon and Night* were BOMC selections after the *By Love Possessed* debacle.

The only real literary influence exerted by professors of English is their power to assign books for required reading, thereby exposing the students who do their homework to works that may or may not take hold. Most of the current crop of English majors have never heard of Cozzens. Pedagogues who have read the novels—*By Love Possessed,* especially—are generally repelled by the antisentimental accounts of human behavior and outraged by the political incorrectness of the characters. Moreover, Cozzens is hard to teach because he leaves little for the teacher to explicate. There are no ambiguities, ambivalences, and obscurities. Critics who write for academic journals have the same difficulty. Cozzens does not provide them with opportunities for explication and deconstruction or for satisfying "the ambition of critical discovery"; therefore, they devote their attention to authors who afford promotion and tenure.

Cozzens relished the Johnsonian phrase "just representations of general nature." He insisted that his fiction was objective, but there is no such thing as purely objective fiction. He of course provided evidence for judging his characters, and his standards were not those of academe—particularly of the academicians who profess themselves humanists. Cozzens's novels demonstrate that people are what they do and how well they do it; that privilege—including intelligence, education, background, and superiority of character—requires duty and responsibility. His protagonists see life in terms of their professions; their attitudes toward society and individual conduct are determined by the success they have achieved in their professions. The recurring subject of Cozzens's novels is the examination of the chain of causality in life and how the responsible characters contend with the messes caused by the weak, foolish, sentimental, or self-deceived.

Cozzens's novels are about something: the professional men who are good at what they do. His characters are convincing because he understands their duties and standards. Cozzens's knowledge of the church or the law or medicine or business is never faked or cribbed. He really knows what he is writing about. F. Scott Fitzgerald observed that action is character; in Cozzens, vocational conduct is character. He stipulated this rule in *Morning Noon and Night:*

Just as you cannot live without the job you hold, you cannot live apart from it—and, indeed, to say a man holds a job is to misstate the fact. The job holds the man. The job. By "holding" it he gives his time to it, and what a man spends his time doing is what he is, and through what he is he sees things as he sees them.

Some other American novelists have understood this truth, but very few have been able to write about it. In most novels the protagonists are not seen practicing their professions; they are shown drinking, coupling, and suffering emotional crises. In Cozzens they work. His characters accept the responsibility of responsibility. Thus at the end of *The Just and the Unjust* Judge Coates instructs his lawyer son: "We just want you to do the impossible." Cozzens wrote for grown-ups about the actualities of American life: not for "adults of the infantile persuasion."

It is true that he mainly wrote about educated upper-middle-class white Protestant men. But he also admired the intelligent, sensible women who supported these men. That was the society that he knew and that ran America in his time. Like all serious writers, he wrote about what was meaningful to him. Even if the society of the Thirties, Forties, Fifties, and Sixties is now history—and very few other American writers published major novels over the course of four decades—it is superbly realized social history with permanent value as such.

A novelist's prime duty is to depict convincing characters. Enduring novels are remembered for their characters, who are often romantic or glamorous or heroic or doomed figures. In contrast, Cozzens's protagonists seem dull to outsiders; but they are the men and women who do the work that keeps their communities functioning day after day. Ernest Cudlipp, Abner Coates, Col. Ross, Arthur Winner Jr., and Julius Penrose do not provide the emotional stimulation of Jay Gatsby or Robert Jordan; but they are accurately observed and entirely believable. If they are not exciting, they are remembered by readers who have the intelligence and experience to recognize them.

James Gould Cozzens's force of mind was formidable; his veneration for truth was inflexible; his dedication to the craft of fiction was uncontaminated by fashions. His novels merit a permanent place among the sound achievements in American literature.

Mens Rea (or Something).

James Gould Cozzens

This previously unpublished essay was written at the time Cozzens was working on By Love Possessed, *for which he was observing trials in the Doylestown, Pennsylvania, courthouse (Bruccoli Collection, by permission of Harvard University, Office of the Recording Secretary).*

Commenting on that byword of the Attorneys Room: *you never know with a jury,* the late Judge Calvin Boyer remarked to me a number of years ago that it was true; he was indeed a rash man who would venture to predict in any given case what a retiring criminal trial jury *must* bring back. Against the aspersion of this uncertainty—no rational person could possibly hope to follow the processes of silly whim or vagarious impulse that determine a jury finding—he had come to feel, however, that in fairness he ought to set one striking consistency that he had observed in juries. His experience (and he believed it the experience of most trial judges) had prepared him to say with a good deal of confidence what a jury would *not* bring back. A finding of guilty, so much against the weight of evidence, and, by its rejection of testimony in itself not improbably nor at variance with proved or admitted facts, so arbitrary and unreasonable, that as the Court he could consider himself obliged to intervene for defendant and set the verdict aside had never been returned to him. It was not-guilty verdicts, where the Court could do nothing, that had from time to time surprised or even shocked him. Findings against the evidence, flatly and willfully wrong, impossible to agree with, were those that acquitted, never those that convicted.

From this truth of long courtroom experience it seems safe to conclude that, offensive to the order of the law's thought as jury action may sometimes be, and annoying as disgruntled attorneys may sometimes find it, the madness is not wholly without method. It is to be observed that on the point of innocence jurors are virtually always at one with the law. What constitutes innocence in the law's eyes—absence of evidence strong enough to destroy the presumption that defendant is innocent—is good enough for them. What is justice under law is here

the same as what is justice to a jury. Manifestly, the point of guilt, what constitutes guilt, is where the law and the jury may not be at one, where the law's justice and the jury's justice may find themselves in complete disagreement, where the jury may unpredictably be moved to disregard the evidence, ignore all statutes made and provided, and defy the Court.

The jury's motive is obvious. Just as the Court, seeing reason to, holds itself to have a duty to step in, save defendant from what it deems the injustice of a conviction against the evidence, the jury may see (and by its verdict against the evidence, declares it has seen) reason to do a duty it holds itself to have of stepping in, saving defendant from what it deems the injustice of a conviction *on* the evidence. Since, to the law's justice, such convictions can never be unjust, the justice of jurors is plainly a different article. What the mutinous jury means to say is that *that*—the law's case—may be all very well but it doesn't happen to be justice here. Here, the law's principles and procedures will not do. This matter is going to be heard and determined on principles of the jury's very own, and no others.

The nature of these principles of jury-justice is not far to seek. The law has shown beyond a reasonable doubt that this man did this thing. When that is the case, punishment can be nothing but condign. The jury, in effect, says: because of certain circumstances, the fact that this man did this thing has become immaterial. For punishment to be condign, he must be shown guilty of something more. What our duty tells us to determine is whether, everything relevant or irrelevant considered, this man is so bad and blamable a man that the law's appointed punishment for the crime with which he was charged would only serve him right. This determining we will do in our own way, without a lot of legal nonsense. The principle embodied—that "badness" is the issue, that guilt is a matter of character—is one at which the law in its wisdom has long looked askance.

In the last century, the eminent jurist Sir James Stephen, animadverting on the ancient maxim: *actus non facit reum nisi mens sit rea,* put the danger in such a principle perfectly. He wrote: "To the unlegal mind it suggests that by the law of England no act is a crime which is done from laudable motives; in other words, that immorality is essential to crime" (LR 23 QBD 186). The disastrous damage to the law's fabric of reason and order that must soon follow any such holding is apparent. That it would make for an impossible situation is now generally recognized. Corpus Juris Secundus still declares that "a crime is not committed if the mind of the person doing the act is innocent" (22 CJS 29); but modern statutes have everywhere taken care to prevent a practical application. Innocence of mind, like ignorance of the law, cannot in practice be allowed to excuse a man if his act is a crime in the contemplation of the legislators. If we are to realize our aim of equal justice under law, we may not conceive as justice anything that stultifies law.

What we encounter here, what the recalcitrant jurors have raised for us in their little way, is one of the grand antinomies, the hard antagonisms of principle, the standing dilemmas of practice, implicit, it is to be supposed, in our human nature. If we have true liberty, what will we do for that order without which there is no living? The justice of the law, and that different justice that a jury may elect to oppose to it, the justice of Sir James's "unlegal" mind, do not consist together. When they collide, there can be no outcome that absolute reason is likely to applaud. The collision can instruct us only in the puzzlements of human thinking manipulated by human feeling.

On the morning of July 17th 1951 at approximately five o'clock, the Eagle Fire Company of New Hope, responding to an alarm with promptness that did it credit, turned up at a house on Low Hill just beyond the Borough limits. The house was a made-over and remodeled farmhouse of small size used by its owner, who was absent, as a country place. The fire was–or, rather, had been, in the kitchen. When the firemen arrived, except for a mop and a broom found smoldering in a closet, it was out. The kitchen ceiling was slightly blackened by smoke and some paint had blistered. At the house were three people. Two were young men who lived there; the elder, in his late twenties, was caretaker for the absent owner; the younger, in his early twenties, was employed by the caretaker to help him. The third person was a woman of middle age who lived in the neighborhood. She was present as a guest.

Beyond bringing the broom and mop outside and extinguishing them, there was no work for the firemen to do. Apologizing, the caretaker explained

that he and his assistant had found themselves able to get the blaze under control with the garden hose. He believed, he said, that a short circuit started it. Hearing this, one of the volunteer firemen, who happened to be an electrician, checked all the wiring. There had been no short circuit. The caretaker's assistant then spoke up. He said he might as well tell them. He set the fire. He had taken a can of gasoline used for a power mower, poured a quantity on the kitchen floor, and put a match to it. He did it because of a quarrel with the caretaker. As a result of this admission, a warrant was procured and he was arrested. Somewhat oddly, it was the woman guest who swore the information on which the warrant issued.

At the Justice of the Peace's hearing, the caretaker's assistant was held for the Grand Jury; and the Commonwealth moved, in Bill Number 87 of the September Criminal Trial list, to indict him on a single count of arson. A True Bill being found, on September 25th 1951, defendant was put on trial in this Court before Hon. Edward Pope Little PJ of the 34th Judicial District, specially presiding, and a jury. The Commonwealth undertook to show that defendant "did wilfully and maliciously set fire to, burn, and cause to be burned" the "certain dwelling house" in question. Since defendant admitted starting the fire, the sum of the Commonwealth's burden was to prove that he did so in willfulness and malice. To this end, the District Attorney called the caretaker and the woman friend.

By the testimony of these two it appeared that on the afternoon of July 16th the woman friend gave, at her home, a cocktail party in honor of her dog. The circumstance deserves mention. As well as anything could, it establishes what might be called the milieu. These were people moving in the sort of set or circle that relishes such waggishness. To pay their respects to the dog, came the caretaker and the defendant. They may be judged to have found it great fun, for they outstayed all the other guests. Somewhat past dinner-time, it seemed to them a good idea to take their hostess and go up the river to an inn, where they would have a couple more drinks and eat. This they did; or, at least, they had the drinks, and went on having them until the inn, around eleven, closed its bar.

In the mood induced in them by then, the night could be considered young. What now? That was easy. Just across the river in New Jersey were bars still open. Even earlier than this a hardly surprising haziness about detail had appeared in the testimony. Neither witness had been sober enough to remember just where they went or even just how they got there. At any rate, they succeeded in fairly soon finding a New Jersey barkeep who took an indulgent view of their condition and served them freely.

Now it was past midnight. Through the early evening a more or less perfect alcoholic harmony had prevailed; but as the drinks kept coming, discord suddenly developed. Defendant took issue with his employer, the caretaker. The quarrel proceeded until the caretaker ordered his employee to stop drinking and go home. Defendant refused. He was informed that he was fired, that tomorrow he would have to get out. Much upset, defendant did leave then.

The time of his leaving was not fixed. That haziness previously noted in the testimony now approached total blankness. Some hours are unaccounted for. A definite course of events could not be recovered until it was somewhat after four o'clock. At about that time, the caretaker and the woman friend drove out to the farmhouse. Defendant was downstairs, apparently waiting for them, and he at once resumed the quarrel. Losing patience, the caretaker informed him that, yes, he was really fired, and he could get out right now; he couldn't live in this house any more. No one seemed to remember defendant's exact words, but his answer was some muttering to the effect that if he couldn't live there, nobody else could, either. The caretaker and the woman friend had not regarded the threat, if it was one, seriously. What defendant then did they could not say, for he was out of their sight. Soon, however, sounds of a commotion reached them from the kitchen; and, going there, the caretaker found the gasoline burning. He ran to call the fire company. Defendant, perhaps sobered by the furious blaze, ran for the garden hose. This was the story as the Commonwealth's witnesses developed it. They were in agreement on all principal points; and none of these points was denied by defendant.

Jurors could have no trouble in sizing the thing up; and they wouldn't like it much. Some people of an irresponsible sort had been on a drunken party which ended in a drunken quarrel. A drunken attempt to burn down a house followed. No reason could be found to doubt that defendant committed the act he was charged with. The Commonwealth's case, though so complete, had one possible weak point, however. If defendant's condition was what, from the evidence, it might very well be taken to have been, could he be thought able to form any deliberate intent, to perform any deliberately conceived action? To go to this point the Commonwealth had other evidence in its possession. The Commonwealth offered to show the cause of the

quarrel—that here was no simple, senseless difference of drunks; that defendant's anger sprang out of a very clear idea on his part of what was going on, of what he was doing, of what other people were doing. The move to introduce this evidence was met by defense with vehement objections. The Court was asked to rule.

After the trial, Judge Little was most helpful in his willingness to discuss the Court's view. Plain to be seen was a by-no-means-remote chance that if he admitted the evidence a higher Court might hold that he had erred. He himself could not deny that it was evidence highly prejudicial to defendant. On the other hand, the same could be said of any evidence that tended to show defendant guilty as charged. The proper question, as he saw it, was: Has this evidence so vital a bearing on willfulness and malice that it ought not to be withheld from a jury that has been joined to make a true deliverance on that point? In the Court's opinion, this evidence had such bearing and the jury was entitled to hear it. Judge Little ruled that it would be admitted.

The evidence the Commonwealth was now free to produce took the form of an affidavit made and signed by defendant in the office of the Justice of the Peace, and of conversations had by defendant with police officers. In his affidavit, defendant swore that he had set the fire "to get even with my husband (the caretaker), for having sex and other things with (the woman friend). . . . Please consider our marriage to be something as between you and your wives. I think we are both queer. We seem to find the same satisfaction as we might with a woman." In what seems explanation rather than excuse, he added: "(the woman friend)'s home has been a haven for gay people for the past couple of years, and without her this thing could never have been brought to Court." In the conversations to which the police officers testified, defendant described even more frankly the nature of his relations with the caretaker. He told them that what started the quarrel was the caretaker's declared intention to bring the woman friend (who was apparently quite willing) home with them, and to sleep with her, instead of with defendant. When those two actually arrived at the farmhouse, convincing him that it wasn't a joke, that his "husband" really purposed to be "unfaithful" to him, he was so hurt and angry that he wanted to injure the caretaker in any way he could. He decided that by burning the house he could get the caretaker into trouble with the owner. He at once attempted to do it.

If it is safe to guess that jurors will feel little sympathy with the stupid and dangerous antics of drunks, it is even safer to guess that the parading before them of a homosexual relationship will arouse no sympathy at all. The feeling to be expected in people of normal sexual impulse is of outrage and disgust. Those with religious views must hold such practices sheer gratuitous wickedness. That there should be a quarrel between these two young men because one of them purposed to have normal relations for a change introduced an element of obscene farce to which a jury might react with vindictive indignation. The Court was fully aware of this jeopardy the defendant had been put in by its ruling. In his charge, Judge Little was at particular pains to spell out the jury's duties here. Defendant was not on trial for anything but arson. The evidence of his relations with the caretaker had been admitted, and must be used, solely for the light it might throw on the question of willfulness and malice in the act. In any other connection it was to be excluded from their minds entirely. Thus instructed, the jury, all men, took the case. It was out over two hours, while the jurors (by credible report) debated many matters, not all of them (at least in the legal sense) germaine to the issue. They came back with a verdict of not guilty.

To most of those awaiting it, this verdict was an undoubted surprise. It was a fine example of what persuades the disgruntled Attorneys Room that you never know with a jury. On the face of it, defendant's position was hopeless. He admitted starting the fire, and himself stated that his motive was to "get even." Assume, if you wished, that jurors would find it possible to obey the judge and not try defendant for his irregular sex practices. Still, they knew of them; and they did not like them; and the possibility of any feeling that defendant was a "nice kid" who needed another chance seemed to rule itself out. For once, it would not be rash to predict the verdict—guilty. The play of factors, reported or easily deducible, some simple, some complicated, which balked so reasonable an expectation makes an interesting study.

A simple factor may be taken first. This was the fire itself. As fires go, it amounted to nothing. Discussing the case, Judge Little remarked that a setting-fire to any certain dwelling house seemed to him doubtfully established. The testimony as he heard it, showed a burning of some gasoline and of a broom and a mop. Had defense on this ground chosen to demur to the evidence he would have felt inclined to sustain it. The jury did not trouble with such technicalities; they simply noted that all the legal pother was over very little damage indeed. Associated with this, it seems that they also weighed something else—to the law really horrifying in its

irrelevance. The owner of the property, for whatever reasons, had not seen fit to appear at any point. If he took no more interest than that in his own interests, he certainly had a nerve, it was said in the juryroom, to expect *them* to take the interest for him. Speculation on possible reasons for this absence of his did nothing to make the jury any better disposed toward him.

More complicated, given more weight—indeed, it appeared in the end, decisive weight—were factors compounding themselves out of the jurors' estimate of the character of the Commonwealth's two principal witnesses. Neither made a favorable impression. The caretaker, though fairly presentable when quiet, had merely to speak to develop excessively those mannerisms with which normal men have no patience. On the stand, he lolled in the chair, contorting himself negligently. His answers, suggesting in content and form a languid chat with his examiners, conveyed well the forbearance he seemed to imagine he was showing toward these very stupid people. To help him bear it, he apparently needed and had a number of drinks for lunch; and the effect of them was noticeable. Genially unaware of any danger, he got, as it happened a better break than he realized or could be said to deserve. Judge Little hesitated—partly, he said later, because the fellow was so odd it was hard to tell if he were drunk to a definitely exceptionable degree; mostly, because he, the Judge, was sitting as a stranger. He did not like to disrupt a trial in another jurisdiction unless he absolutely had to. In his own Court, with, so to say, his own jail handy, he made no doubt that at several junctures of manifest slight befuddlement he would have cited witness for contempt and given him a few weeks to ponder the unwisdom of taking the stand in such a state. The jury could be seen to regard this lackadaisical, nearly insolent behavior in a person objectionable to them on sight with more and more hostility.

The woman friend, though comporting herself well enough, and in a way meant to be ingratiating, was not a person to please jurors, either. From her speech and manner, advantages of education and background could be inferred. To a jury, she had, then, still less excuse for behaving as the testimony, including her own, showed her as behaving. That she was divorced, that she was quite old enough to be the mother—a distasteful idea in the circumstances—of at least the younger of the young men, that her appearance hinted in small ways a long habit of dissipation, made attempts at ingratiation vain. The jury observed her coldly. The odd small point that *she*—none of whose business you might think it—had signed the information on which the warrant issued, though again irrelevant, was reported to have proved irritating.

Against these two, the jurors could balance defendant—slight; younger looking than in fact he was, with a boyish (or maybe even girlish) face and a weak expression of obvious pliancy; a person difficult to regard with anything but a distaste of pity and contempt. This weighing went, of course, not to the Commonwealth's issue, the starting of the insignificant fire—the jury would seem to have thrown that out almost at once as a trifle they would not be bothered with—but to that special issue of the jury that finds against the evidence, the issue of "badness." Here, everyone had been "bad"; but, of the three, was the boyish-girlish defendant the most blamable? Could they, the jury, in justice come down on him, send him to jail, while his impudent "husband" (a far more objectionable figure; far more guilty on that count of badness; surely the aggressor, very likely the instigator of the unnatural relationship) was left untouched; while the woman friend, the unprepossessing cause of all this mess, was returned free and clear to that "haven for gay people" of hers? They could not! The law offered them no opportunity to punish those they found most deserving of punishment. Very good; they would, in a kind of protest, punish nobody. Let them all go! Let them just leave, make themselves scarce! With them and their twisted disgraceful goings-on the jury wanted no more truck.

The legal mind cries out. Assuredly law is not this. This is not equal justice under law. This is not due process. More than unresponsive, the finding is dishonest; by a vagary of those "unlegal" minds, the jurors have conspired to cheat on their oaths, to quit on their jobs. The law's justice is insulted. Everyone of them should be ashamed of himself; the law is ashamed of them and for them.

So pronouncing, the irregular action censured, the principles dangerous to law deplored, all proper public duty done, the legal mind may retire to its chambers. I will not presume to follow; yet I must wonder if, hanging up its robe and falling into private cogitation, the legal mind may not find itself admitting, regretful, a little embarrassed, that, in such a case, this jury-justice, cockeyed as it is, works fairly well the final purpose of all the law's justice.

Afterword

George V. Higgins

While I don't quarrel with the "substantial-justice" explanation Judge Edward Pope Little and James Gould Cozzens developed to account for the outcome of the arson case, it puzzles me that the judge didn't advert to the underlying reason for the acquittal: The prosecutor was either inexperienced or incompetent. By persuading the grand jury to ratify the bad judgment of the Justice of the Peace—JPs are usually lay persons relying for compensation entirely on the fees they charge for officiating at weddings and notarizing documents—he brought a case that never should have come to court. Furthermore, he was an utter fool to introduce the affidavit. The verdict served him right.

At least until recently, generations of Massachusetts prosecutors instructed their novices to think of criminal charges as feces. "Juries do funny things, and our investigators don't always find everything, so naturally you're going to lose cases, no matter how good you are. But never get an indictment out of the grand jury unless you're *sure* you're going to win it. Some day it's going to get to court, and then the jury or the judge will make you or your opponent *eat* it. Never order anything you wouldn't want to eat." And: "Don't lose your own case" as the arson prosecutor did by offering the affidavit. "At least make the *other* guy beat you."

Reader's *Ulysses* Symposium

A Joyce (Con)Text: Danis Rose and the Remaking of *Ulysses*

A. Nicholas Fargnoli
Molloy College

James Joyce was one of this century's most resourceful writers and one of its most meticulous. Sylvia Beach, the first publisher of *Ulysses* (1922), recollects in *Shakespeare and Company* (1959) that Joyce "had to see his work as he shaped it word by word" (39). Even when he was involved in the translation of his works, he paid special attention to the nuance of words and the phrasing of sentences. In the fall of 1926, while assisting in the revision of a German translation of *Ulysses* that the publisher was hurrying into print, Joyce wrote to his brother Stanislaus that the text "is . . . full of the absurdest errors and with large gaps. Such is financial literature. If they do not give me a délai, I shall ask Miss Beach to circularize the German press with a disclaimer." A little more than seventy years later Joyce's grandson, Stephen Joyce, in a letter published in the *Times Literary Supplement* (27 June 1997), called for yet another disclaimer–the removal of James Joyce's name from Danis Rose's Reader's Edition of *Ulysses*."If this book is to continue to be sold, the name James Joyce must be eliminated, stricken from the dustjacket, cover and inside title-pages of this edition." A slightly different version of Stephen Joyce's letter, which appeared in *The Irish Times,* is reprinted in this collection of essays.

Even before Rose's edition was published on 16 June (Bloomsday) 1997, many prospective readers were skeptical; and since its publication reviewers have questioned seriously Rose's editorial decisions, especially because he fails to provide full disclosure of the methodological apparatus used to substantiate his judgments. Although Rose's main intent, as stated in the preface where he attempts to shift attention away from "the scholarship informing the edition" to aesthetic appeal, is "to maximize the pleasure of the reader" (vi), he unwittingly seems to have maximized the ire of his critics. Rose is a competent and reputable textual scholar, and to devise what he identifies as the "isotext" of *Ulysses* is

an admirable achievement, if not completely convincing. Also intended to help eliminate textual faults, the isotext, which Rose likens to the continuous manuscript text in *Ulysses: A Critical and Synoptic Edition* (1984), edited by Hans Walter Gabler, Wolfhard Steppe, and Claus Melchior, is an editorial construct, an ideal error-free text, that forms the basis of Rose's edition. "The isotext," Rose claims, "is literally '*Ulysses* as James Joyce wrote it'" (xiii). Unfortunately for the critical reader, the isotext is not adequately presented in the introduction, leaving Rose susceptible to the criticism that his decisions were in part based on personal aesthetic preferences. To *correct* a Joyce text is a formidable, if not a collective, task, and to do so without completely delineating the principles and apparatus governing the textual emendations makes it virtually impossible for the critical reader to distinguish between the legitimate restoration and the objectionable distortion of a text.

With conscious deliberation over a period of more than thirty years from the publication of his first book, *Chamber Music,* in 1907 to that of his last work, *Finnegans Wake,* in 1939, Joyce forged a literary universe marked by innovative technique and originality of style that has had a lasting influence on writers to this day. However many times Joyce revised passages, he always wrote with extreme care in fashioning the verbal "chaosmos" as he called it in *Finnegans Wake* of his works, which at once can contain clarity and uncertainty. Understandably, then, the impulse to modify or correct what are seen as mistakes in a published text and impediments to the interpretation of a passage can be aroused in the editor. But should it be resisted?

In November 1919, a little more than two years before the publication of *Ulysses* on 2 February 1922, Joyce explained in a letter to his London literary agent, James B. Pinker, that the American publisher B. W. Huebsch must not tamper with the text

Dust jacket for the controversial attempt to make Ulysses *more readable*

of the novel, a stipulation Joyce repeated to Pinker in May 1922. Earlier in August 1918, Harriet Shaw Weaver, Joyce's longtime patron and friend, wrote on Joyce's behalf to Huebsch, explaining that any altered passages of *Ulysses* that appeared in *The Little Review,* where the novel was then being serialized, were to be restored to their original condition before publication. In March 1920 Joyce again stressed in a letter to John Quinn, the American attorney who unsuccessfully defended *The Little Review,* that "There must be no alterations whatsoever of my text." In April 1921, two months after *The Little Review* was forced to cease its serial publication of *Ulysses* on grounds that the work was obscene, Joyce withdrew his novel from Huebsch because the publisher insisted that changes be made.

As evidenced by his correspondence here and throughout his literary career, Joyce was unambiguous about the way he wanted his texts to be treated: *No Tampering, Please!* Printer's mistakes are one thing, intentional alterations another. Dissatisfied by printer's errors in the first edition of *Ulysses,* Joyce in a March 1922 letter to Weaver complains, "In a second edition the mistakes must be corrected. Some of the blunders and omissions which disfigure

Ithaca especially are lamentable." Rose tries to tidy up what he sees as blunders in the Ithaca episode of the novel, but does he succeed? Not quite, according to Fritz Senn. In "*Ulysses,* Reader's Edition: First Reactions," printed in this collection of essays, Senn argues that the accuracy Rose imposes on Ithaca transforms the nature of the episode by making it less Bloomian. Skeptical of Rose's claims, Senn considers the consequences of Rose's editorial decisions and concludes that at best the advantages are minimal. He finds Rose's alterations throughout the edition ill advised and contrary to the "vitality" of the *Ulysses* he knows.

Joyce's concerns extended even to the appearance of the printed text. He was, according to Stuart Gilbert, the editor of the first volume of *Letters of James Joyce* (1957; revised, 1965; volumes two and three edited by Richard Ellmann, 1966) "characteristically intransigent in matters of typography." In February 1906, when arrangements were being made to publish *Dubliners* (1914), Joyce informed the London publisher Grant Richards: "On one point I would wish you to be careful. I would like the printer to follow the manuscript accurately in punctuation and arrangement. Inverted commas for instance, to enclose dialogue always seemed to me a great eyesore." Facing a similar problem in 1924, when Jonathan Cape published a new edition of *A Portrait of the Artist as a Young Man,* Joyce objected to what he called "perverted commas" and "insisted on their removal." In a July 1917 letter Joyce instructed Pinker to place the names of the speakers in his play *Exiles* in the center of the page and not on the side. In previous editions of *Ulysses* (1922, 1934, 1961, and 1984) the names of the speakers in the Circe episode (chapter 15) appear in the center of the page, but in Rose's they appear in boldface on the left side.

That Joyce would not succumb to alterations in the text of *Ulysses* has a precedent in the difficulties he endured in trying to publish *Dubliners.* In a May 1906 letter to Grant Richards, Joyce adamantly defended his stories, including their language and allusions that might be deemed offensive to others. Although in October 1906 Joyce showed a willingness to make some concessions to get *Dubliners* published, he held to the position that remained with him throughout his literary career: *unauthorized textual alterations were not to be part of the compositional history of his works.* Joyce wrote *Dubliners* in what he labeled "a style of scrupulous meanness and with the conviction that he is a very bold man who dares to alter in the presentment, still more to deform, whatever he has seen and heard." Joyce's mimetic presentation of Dublin and of its citizens and their behavior was not to be adulterated by someone else's sentiments and taste.

The meticulousness with which Joyce approached the composition of his works is attested to by others. Frank Budgen, Joyce's Zurich friend, records in *James Joyce and the Making of "Ulysses"* (1960) that when he inquired about the progress of the novel in 1918, Joyce commented that he had been working all day on two sentences. Thinking of Flaubert, Budgen asked, "'You have been seeking the *mot juste?*' 'No,' Joyce responded, and added, 'I have the words already. What I am seeking is the perfect order of the words in the sentence. There is an order in every way appropriate'" (20). In the ensuing conversation Joyce also revealed that he preferred "the reader to understand always through suggestion rather than direct statement" (21). It is not that Joyce spitefully imposed burdens on the readers of *Ulysses* but that he expected to engage his readers in the act of creation, demanding of them as much as

he did of himself. To simplify the process of reading *Ulysses* or to make that process less challenging for the reader by tampering with the text is not to read the *Ulysses* Joyce intended. To suggest, as Rose does, that the "first-time reader should perhaps skip [the Oxen of the Sun episode] rather than become bogged down, stop and thereby miss out on the more accessible pleasures of the final four episodes" (xliii) is patronizing.

The essays collected here offer a critique of Rose's "completely revised edition" (iv) of *Ulysses,* published in London by Picador. In 1991 the copyright protection of *Ulysses* expired in the United Kingdom, where the term at that time was an author's life plus fifty years. It was then that Rose and the publisher could proceed with plans for a new edition of Joyce's novel without the consent of the James Joyce Estate. But on 1 January 1996 copyright protection was extended to seventy years after the death of an author. In "Public Domain and the Violation of Texts" Matthew J. Bruccoli includes a discussion of copyright protection, the responsibilities of textual editors, and the larger question of the proper treatment of literary works that fall into public domain. Terence Killeen in "Whose *Ulysses?*: The Function of Editing" argues that the complaints against Rose's failure to produce the apparatus and isotext are misplaced because their presence would not necessarily guarantee wholehearted acceptance by scholars of the changes wrought by Rose in his edition of *Ulysses.* For Killeen, it is Rose's *Ulysses* and no longer Joyce's. In "Danis Rose and the Rendering of *Ulysses*" Michael Patrick Gillespie briefly surveys the initial criticism of the Rose edition and then turns his attention to a critique of Rose's editing process, concluding that Rose needs to offer a detailed account of his editorial methods. Fritz Senn's essay on Rose's changes to the Ithaca episode has already been mentioned. Michael Groden in "We See the Editor at Work" objects to the absence of a textual apparatus that would support Rose's rationale and editorial methodology. To assess Rose's editorial decisions and determine whether they spring from manuscript evidence or from his own editorial predilections, Groden compares six short passages from various sections of *Ulysses* as they appear in the 1922, Gabler, and Rose editions. Stephen Joyce's letter to *The Irish Times* completes this collection. Danis Rose was invited to contribute, but he did not respond.

Public Domain and the Violation of Texts

Matthew J. Bruccoli

The controversy generated by Danis Rose's "Reader's Edition" of *Ulysses* raises the larger issue of the proper treatment of literary masterpieces after they go into public domain: what is owed to dead geniuses and their works that are no longer protected by copyright? This concern intensifies as, year by year the great works of the 1920s lose American copyright protection under the publication-plus-seventy-five-years rule. (For British authors the term of copyright is the life of the author plus fifty years—or perhaps seventy years—the Brits have not clarified this matter yet.)

Ulysses was published by Sylvia Beach's Shakespeare and Company in 1922. That means that American copyright expired in 1997. The Joyce estate contends, however, that American copyright commenced with the 1933 Random House edition. Joyce died in 1941; accordingly, all of his published work went into the public domain in the United Kingdom in 1991—or perhaps it is protected in the U.K. and European Economic Community countries until 2011.

These are some of the classics that are already up for grabs or will soon be available for promiscuous reprinting in America, along with the years in which they lost, or will lose, copyright protection:

My Ántonia (1918)–1993
Winesburg, Ohio (1919)–1994
Main Street (1920)–1995
This Side of Paradise (1920)–1995
The Waste Land (1922)–1997
An American Tragedy (1925)–2000
The Great Gatsby (1925)–2000
In Our Time (1925)–2000
Manhattan Transfer (1925)–2000
Soldiers' Pay (1926)–2001
The Sun Also Rises (1926)–2001

The going into public domain of these works will have certain beneficial consequences. In addition to generating the quick, sloppy, and cheap reprints that will proliferate, the expiration of the copyrights will make it possible for responsible publishers and editors to provide accurate texts for works that have heretofore been available only in corrupt texts because the copyright holders—heirs and publishers—have been indifferent or hostile to correcting bad texts that are selling steadily.

Maxwell Perkins's stable of authors at Charles Scribner's Sons provides exemplary cases. The legendary editor was a bad proofreader; he was concerned with the literary quality of a work rather than with matters of detail. None of the other editors—except in certain cases John Hall Wheelock—was permitted to work with Perkins's geniuses. Some of the classic works of American fiction published by Scribners were not properly copyedited. Copyediting refers to the process of proofing and checking a work in typescript and/or galleys to correct authorial spelling or punctuation and typographical errors—as well as identifying factual details, stylistic infelicities, and inconsistencies. Copyediting combines proofing, checking, and editing. It is also called line-editing because it is performed line by line, with all recommended corrections and queries referred to the author. The work is slow and therefore expensive; many publishing houses now forego it, except for star authors.

The Scribners texts of Fitzgerald, Hemingway, and Wolfe were peppered with errors of punctuation and usage. A few spot-corrections of egregious errors were made in the plates for later printings, but there was no question of resetting the text for the sake of correctness. Hundreds of textual cruces remained in *Look Homeward, Angel;* the puzzle caused by Hemingway's apparent ignorance of the rules governing quotation marks in dialogue was allowed to stand in "A Clean, Well-Lighted Place"; and Fitzgerald has been ridiculed for his ignorance because Scribners did not notice the mistake of Dr. T. J. Eckleburg's retinas or the mislocation of Astoria in *The Great Gatsby*. Editors are supposed to catch authorial blunders. Scribners was not the only or even the worst culprit; nevertheless Scribners' sins seem egregious because of the stature of the books and authors they published during the Twenties and Thirties. But the publisher is not necessarily solely responsible for the printing of a bad text: there are authors who resist editorial help, even when required.

As the classics of twentieth-century literature go out of copyright, scholar-editors will be able to find publishers for accurate, reliable, corrected editions—what were called definitive editions before *definitive* became a junk-word—and which are now often designated "critical editions" or "established texts" because they utilize all the evidence and documents bearing on the composition, transmission, and publication of the text. Such an editorial procedure is what Fredson Bowers developed and applied to a range of authors from Thomas Dekker to Stephen Crane. The purpose of an established text is to correct correctable errors and to recover the author's intentions; to provide the editing that should have been performed at the time of initial publication; to publish the error-free text that could have or might have been published if the author had been a painstaking proofer and fully cooperative, if the copyeditor had known more than the author, if the typesetters and printers had made no mistakes, and if—the biggest if—the evidence for establishing the author's intentions survives.

Thus it is impossible to edit a perfect text of *Look Homeward, Angel* because the setting copy and proofs do not survive. The best that can be done now is a corrected text based on a super-proofing of the published edition and collations of the manuscript and carbon typescript to verify problematic book readings that may have resulted from misreadings (or mis-hearings) by the typist and from compositional errors. The proofing would be based on the list of hundreds of queries submitted by Louis N. Feipel in 1930. Wolfe reacted with a Gantian howl of dismay to editor John Hall Wheelock, who assured Wolfe that these blemishes did not injure the novel:

> I don't doubt that one of the tribe who make a profession of this sort of thing could find a great many errors, typographical and other, if he went over the book with a fine-tooth comb; but then this much could be said of any book, however carefully edited. Unless author and publisher are willing and prepared to devote the rest of their natural lives to the ideal of absolute letter-perfection as regards every semicolon and spacing, there must always be errors.

The "super-proofing" process referred to is not to be confused with Rose's "copyediting" of *Ulysses*. Rose seems to begin sensibly by stating that "the editor should replace the original production crew when copyreading"; he vaguely continues, "and the edition's publisher's typographers and designers should replace their counterparts." Rose: "Only in this way can one produce an edition that is of its own time and that can, intellectually and aesthetically, stand on its own two feet." What is "an edition of its own time"? Presumably it is an updating or modernizing or contemporizing or revising or rewriting of a work that was written by a certain author at a certain time and published for the readers of that time. Why is it required? And what does

"stand on its own two feet" mean? It is odd that someone who writes that way has undertaken to revise and rewrite James Joyce. Rose explains:

> The craft of copyediting, as I mean it (apart from decisions concerning design features of the text, such as the matter of hyphenation in compound words, or the use of italics in unemphasized words. . . .), involves the determination of what I term "textual faults." But a textual fault is not the same as an error: A textual fault (the straight errors, it will be remembered, have already been eliminated in preparing the isotext) can be suspected when one realizes that "there is something wrong" with a particular sentence in the isotext, not simply where a word is misspelled but more subtly where the sentence is saying something that it should not, where the logic of narrative is inexplicably broken.

. . . the sentence is saying something that it should not: This means that Rose knows better than Joyce what Joyce was trying to say and should have written. This thinking resulted in more than ten thousand silent emendations—by John Kidd's count—in the Danis Rose version of what was James Joyce's *Ulysses*. It is not James Joyce's book any more.

The book belongs to the author. A masterpiece—or merely an enduring work—resulted because a genius did something no one else could have done. Genius knows what it is doing. Masterpieces are to be cherished and protected. A textual editor—who is not a literary genius—has the responsibility of correcting what is correctable without rewriting. And he'd better be damned sure that a correctable error is an error. Textual editors can be harmful drudges when they tamper ignorantly or out of a conviction that there is "something wrong." Thus Fitzgerald wrote *orgastic future* in his *Gatsby* manuscript and retained it in the typescript. Perkins surprisingly queried it in proof, and Fitzgerald replied that the word expressed the precise meaning he intended: a sense of ecstasy. In 1941 Edmund Wilson—who believed that he was immeasurably superior to Fitzgerald—silently emended *orgastic* to *orgiastic,* and the corrupt reading proliferated. Does this one word matter? Yes. Everything is important in writing.

The book belongs to the author, whether it is in or out of copyright. The textual editor exists to serve the author, dead or alive.

An unintentional factual error—sometimes called a "positive error"—can distract a reader and undermine reader confidence in the writer. When a writer is describing actual people in actual places, he endeavors if he is any good to get real things right. *Ulysses* occurs in the real Dublin on a particular date. When Joyce misspells the name of an identifiable

Dubliner for no discernible purpose, the name should be corrected. When Joyce provides an incorrect address for an actual building and the mistake has no function, the address should be corrected. Joyce made a real effort to get it all right; therefore, the textual editor has a clear duty to finish the job.

Retention of factual errors because they have become "part of the fabric" of a classic work of fiction is simplistic and timid. The anti-emendation school argues that it is sufficient to report factual errors in the apparatus of an established text—in the back of the book. But a minuscule portion of the readers of any classic reads it in a scholarly edition of an established text. Virtually all readers and most teachers of literature are unaware that there are foul texts or emended texts. Civilians assume that all texts are equal. These nonspecialists require a properly corrected text. Textual apparatus is of no use to a reader who does not have access to it or does not even know that such a thing exists in another volume somewhere. An established text—especially for a widely read and taught classic—should be potentially useful to all serious readers. The current protocol for the publication of established texts or critical editions is to format them so that the text pages can be reprinted without apparatus in so-called clear texts. Consequently when the text is reprinted without editorial back matter, readers have no way of determining whether errors have been corrected or retained. The Rose "Reader's Edition" of *Ulysses* introduces some ten thousand alterations with no stipulation. Most of these alleged improvements are matters of punctuation, but the many word changes are also concealed.

Deliberate functional errors must be left alone: the author knew what he was doing. Integral inadvertent errors must be left alone: the author erred, but the error cannot be corrected without rewriting. Textual editors may correct or emend single words or obviously incorrect punctuation marks, but they must not rewrite or supply additional words. Corrections must be word-for-word substitutions.

Punctuation is not a trivial matter—especially not in *Ulysses*. It is meaningful. Punctuation—or the absence of it—is the means by which an author controls the rhythm of his writing and the structure of sentences and paragraphs. To delete or add thousands of punctuation marks in an edition of *Ulysses* is to alter the style and the meaning of the work—to make it non-Joycean. *Ulysses* was and remains the most influential modernist prose-fiction work in the English language. Joyce's intentional omission of punctuation and his compound words were emulated by William Faulkner and John Dos Passos, among many others. Joyce may or may not have invented the technique of stream of consciousness; but he taught a couple of generations of writers how to convey interior monologue, for which his methods of punctuation are crucial. Everything in a serious literary work should be under the control of the author. Yet an author rarely gets everything he wants in the printed text. Given authors' writing habits, the exigencies of book production, and the unofficial collaborative nature of publication, many first editions are flawed. Correctable errors should be corrected in such a way that the reader is aware that the corrections are editorial. Unidentified corrections—no matter how necessary—render the text, in the words of Bowers, "a little bit pregnant."

Vladimir Nabokov—a strong admirer of *Ulysses*—commented that ideally a book should be read as deliberately as the author wrote it. (His son, Dmitri, reports that Nabokov was opposed to any tampering with *Ulysses*.) To simplify *Ulysses* or any other work in the name of readability or accessibility is to spoil it for the reader. The argument that the Rose version will introduce *Ulysses* to readers who otherwise would not be able to read it is silly. There will always be people who find *Ulysses* too hard to read. Let them read something else. The only *Ulysses* worth reading is the one that preserves James Joyce's intentions. That, of course, applies to all masterpieces—as well as to any other serious literary work.

Whose *Ulysses?* The Function of Editing

Terence Killeen
The Irish Times

Whatever else one may think of the Danis Rose edition of *Ulysses,* it is hard not to be impressed by the strategic planning that lay behind it. It was produced in conditions of considerable secrecy, with few people aware that the project was under way; it seems to have been done with some speed, given that Rose's previous work, *The Textual Diaries of James Joyce,* appeared as recently as 1995, and he had been heavily engaged in an abortive edition of *Finnegans Wake* before that; it was announced to an unsuspecting public only shortly before its publication; and care seems to have been taken to ensure that potential legal obstacles would not prevent the book's appearance.

But perhaps the most effective stroke in this operation was Rose's decision not to supply the "isotext" lying behind his version or indeed any apparatus to justify the editorial decisions taken. The isotext was assembled by Rose as the direct "transcription of the author's words as written down by him or by a surrogate" (xii), insofar as these could be restored, prior to any editing process. As Rose rightly says, it is not possible to present this as a reading text of *Ulysses* due to the complexity of the history of the composition of the book and the many stages it went through. Some editorial process is unavoidable.

Rose then edited this isotext to provide the Reader's Edition but declared himself unable—on grounds of cost, mainly—to supply the isotext itself. While this may well be the case (though it must be noted that to supply some minimal editorial apparatus, say to note the emendations produced by Rose's "copyreading," by far the most controversial part of his procedure, should not have been beyond his abilities and those of his publishers), the outcome has been a fortunate one from Rose's point of view. The effect of the decision has been in large measure to disable criticism: even some scholarly reactions I have seen have been hedged around with nervous qualifications of the type: "Now it may be that Rose has manuscript or textual evidence for what he has done. . . ."

These reservations are surprising. For the fact is, of course, that there are *no* new Joyce manuscripts or documents of any kind to justify any of these alterations, nor is Rose claiming to have found any. The available documentation is virtually all in, and

I make bold to predict that no further extant documents of any great significance will now be found. What this means in practice is that, despite the absence of any apparatus, any change Rose has made can be checked against either the relevant sections of the *James Joyce Archive* or the facsimile of the Rosenbach manuscript (the important and controversial "handwritten copy of each of the eighteen episodes of Joyce's novel at an intermediate stage of development," as Rose accurately and succinctly defines it [xlvii]; it was acquired by the American rare-book dealer A. S. W. Rosenbach and was published in facsimile separately from the *James Joyce Archive*) to verify its textual basis, if any. With only minuscule exceptions—an occasional postcard, the occasional magazine variant—the evidence is all there.

Thus in Rose's discussion of what he calls "Textual faults arising through Joyce's omissions in creatively copying out a protodraft" (xxi ["protodraft" means "original version" but this entire title is highly tendentious and questionable, since it is by no means certain that all these are accidental omissions]), when he asserts that the inserted word *was* in the passage: "the big wind of last February a year that did havoc the land so pitifully was a small thing beside this barrenness" (page 378 of his edition) existed in a protodraft, anyone can check that statement against the evidence; it did. (It does not follow that its restoration in this edition is justified; I do not believe that it is.)

Similarly, in the one instance when Rose does provide a brief example of his procedures (pages lxxiii to lxxxiii of his introduction, referring to pages 369 to 370 of his edition), when he inserts the word *wist* to replace *nist* in the phrase "and his neighbour wist not of this wile," it is quite clear that at no point at any level of the composition did Joyce write the word *wist;* it is Rose's idea of what he should have written—or perhaps what the modern reader needs to have supplied.

Thus it seems to me the frequent plaints that if only Rose would supply the missing apparatus and isotext, many things which are now obscure would become clear are misplaced. His introduction does, in fact, contain a clear statement of his editorial principles; while it would obviously be helpful to have the apparatus (a great deal of tedious checking could be avoided), I do not think it would in most instances make the changes more palatable to those who now find them unpalatable.

Certainly if the textual discussion of the 1922 reading provided on page xx of the introduction: "Stark ruth of man his errand that him lone led till that house," which does not even advert to the possibility that *lone* might be an adjective qualifying *him,* is an example of what we are missing, I think it is safe to say that there would still be room for disagreement after the publication of the complete isotext and apparatus. (The changing in Rose's text of *till* to *to* [page 367], incidentally, is a good example of the crassness of the approach to literary allusions that characterises this edition: *till* is a perfectly valid Middle English form of *to,* and there are no grounds for its alteration.)

It seems to be characteristic of Rose's practice that he tends to withhold the evidence. The same procedure was adopted in the "Finn's Hotel" episode. In October 1992 Rose astonished the Joyce world, not for the last time, with the announcement that he had discovered seven hitherto unknown "short stories" by Joyce. On closer inspection it emerged that these were seven sketches generally believed to be the germ of *Finnegans Wake* and already well known in that capacity. What was new was Rose's view that these were, in fact, intended for a different, uncompleted work called "Finn's Hotel," which Joyce subsequently abandoned in favor of *Finnegans Wake.*

Unfortunately, Rose refuses to produce the evidence for this thesis except in conjunction with the sketches themselves (as edited by him–and I think in view of the *Ulysses* edition we can guess what that might mean) under the highly contentious title "Finn's Hotel," thus achieving a fait accompli. Not surprisingly, a standoff has developed between Rose and the James Joyce Estate over this issue, but in the meantime Rose, throughout his 1995 work, *The Textual Diaries of James Joyce,* writes as if the existence of "Finn's Hotel" were a given which required no further elucidation. So, as in the case of Rose's *Ulysses,* the claim for the authenticity of "Finn's Hotel" is based not on any new textual discovery–there is none to be made–but rather on a radically different interpretation of material that has long been in the public domain.

What is the effect of this radically different interpretation in the current instance? The answer can be–needs to be–put very clearly and unequivocally. This is no longer *Ulysses* by James Joyce. One can call it several other things–an innovative editorial enterprise, a contemporary "interpretation" of *Ulysses,* returning a hitherto obscure work to the general reader, a slap in the face for the academics (my own

preference would be "a dumbing down")–but not that. The reason is not accidental, but is integral to Rose's editorial procedures. It lies, of course, in the abandonment of text as the basis for editing and its replacement by the exigencies of something called "copyreading."

While there is much theoretical debate at present about the nature and purpose of editing, with the Anglo-American and Germanic schools taking markedly different approaches, it remains the case that up to now, editing has been textually based; the very word seems to require it by definition. Once text ceases to be the basis, the way is open for editorial anarchy: anyone's ideas are as good as anyone else's, including the author's. It is not a mere archaism that makes one feel that the author's words are sacrosanct, interpret them as one may; it is, rather, an essential basis for the continuation of literary studies in any meaningful form.

The theoretical basis for Rose's approach seems to run as follows: since, according to Jerome McGann's "social contract" theory of editing, the work of the text's original proofreaders, copyeditors and typesetters must be given due weight along with that of the author in the editing process, and since it is notoriously well known that the original team producing *Ulysses* did not make a very good job of it, there is no reason why Danis Rose should not now come along and with his superior textual resources, do the job as it should have been done. Anything less "social," or less historical, it is difficult to imagine.

Of course, editions of *Ulysses* may differ; a work whose textual history is as complex as this will allow for a large number of "judgment calls," as Gabler, in *The James Joyce Quarterly,* calls them in his important review of Philip Gaskell and Clive Hart's *"Ulysses": A Review of Three Texts. Proposals for Alterations to the Texts of 1922, 1961 and 1984* (Gerard's Cross, U.K.: Colin Smythe, 1989; Totowa, N.J.: Barnes and Noble, 1989). The text of *Ulysses* will probably always resist definitive fixing, will always retain a certain measure of inherent instability, and claims to have produced "corrected editions" will, one hopes, no longer be made. But these variations will be within acceptable limits of interpretive plausibility; they will be based on "judgment calls" and arguable from the evidence, like most editorial decisions. (The work of Stanley Fish on the authority of interpretive communities applies, passim.)

To give a swift instance of the difference between the two approaches–textual and nontextual–one can consider again Rose's restoration of the word *was* in the passage "the big wind of last February a year that did havoc the land so pitifully

James Joyce in Switzerland near the end of his life

was a small thing beside this barrenness" (378). The restoration is not, in my opinion, justified: I think Joyce deliberately dropped *was* in order to bring the sentence closer to the clipped, economical diary style of Pepys and Evelyn that he is parodying. But nevertheless, the change is textually based: Joyce did at one stage write *was,* and some kind of an argument can be made for its restoration.

On the other hand, the replacement of *nist* by *wist* in "and his neighbour wist not of this wile" is completely gratuitous, having no textual foundation. In fact, it actually undermines Joyce's artistic purpose in this parody. *Nist not* is a perfectly normal Middle English double negative, standard in texts such as the *Travels of Sir John Mandeville,* which Joyce is parodying, and there is not a shred of justification for its alteration. The essential issue is that no matter how desirable a particular alteration may seem, no matter how appropriate it may look, if it is de-

void of any textual justification a very strong case has to be made out for its acceptance—much stronger than any Rose presents in the course of this work.

In this connection, I may quote from Jeri Johnson's excellent edition of the 1922 *Ulysses,* (Oxford and New York: Oxford University Press, 1993), which I think sums up the position: "Just for the record, the fact that Thrift and Buller were real Dubliners is utterly irrelevant. The only thing that matters is what Joyce wrote" (liv). The point concerns the function of the textual editor: it is not to act as a tour guide to Joyce's Dublin, or as a historian of that city; it is to convey as faithfully as possible the words Joyce actually wrote, "errors" and all (but what is an error, in a literary text?), and to alter those words only in the very rare cases where there is overwhelming reason to believe that something has gone wrong. The question of the "correct" spelling of the names of Dubliners such as Buller and Thrift is a matter for the notes, not the text.

I think Joyce was in general in control of what he wrote and knew what he was doing. The fact that we do not fully understand everything he wrote does not mean that he was necessarily in error at those points. (Rose seems to think it does.) Joyce did not perhaps have all the advantages available to Danis Rose, but given that, he made a fair fist of it. The central principle of Rose's "copyreading" is that the editor must intervene whenever the text "is saying something that it should not" (xvii)—the most extraordinary editorial principle since that of the late Dr. Bowdler, to which it bears an unfortunate resemblance. Some other people, before Rose, also thought *Ulysses* was "saying something it should not" and wanted to emend it; he is not in their camp, but their example might have given him pause.

The answer to the question posed in my title has been implicit in all the foregoing, but it may be as well to spell it out. It is not Danis Roses's *Ulysses:* no editor can appropriate a text in that way. It is not the "Reader's" *Ulysses:* the category of "reader" is far too wide and diverse to make this a feasible formulation. There are as many types of reader as there are of people. It is James Joyce's *Ulysses,* and that in a fundamental way that precedes any act of editing or interpretation. Any editorial enterprise that does not start from that basic premise is bound to come to grief.

Danis Rose and the Rendering of *Ulysses*

Michael Patrick Gillespie
Marquette University

No one familiar with the complex textual history of James Joyce's *Ulysses* feels completely satisfied with any existing edition, and the obstacles to compiling a version acceptable to a majority of readers remain formidable. Indeed, the appearance in the spring of 1997 of Danis Rose's Reader's Edition of *Ulysses* has highlighted the kinds of intra- and extratextual problems that any editor must face. Initial responses to the Rose volume in particular have underscored how strongly scholars feel about the integrity of Joyce's book.

A selection of the earliest reactions to the Rose edition reflects the conflicted views that surround any attempt at emendation. The author's grandson, Stephen Joyce, has likened the Rose editorial process to an act of rape and has suggested that his grandfather's name should be removed from the edition's title page. More measured, but no less rigorous, opinions have come from Terence Killeen and Gerry Dukes. In "The Blue Book of Rose" in *The Irish Times* (14 June 1997) Dukes balances praise and censure, characterizing Rose's work as "audacious, challenging, welcome, readable, irritating and, occasionally, wrong." Killeen adopts a far less tolerant approach in "Every Book Has Some Mistakes" in the same issue of *The Irish Times,* summing up the changes as "unwarranted, gratuitous, and baseless." The complexity of the topic has led some to avoid serious engagement with textual issues and instead to focus on collateral topics. Eric Korn, to cite one example, has substituted flippancy for wit in "Words Known to All Men" in the *Times Literary Supplement* (5 September 1997), an overview of the volume that takes the safe approach of sneering at selected changes without engaging the reasons behind the revisions. Such a tone, however, does not inevitably accompany overviews, and Sarah Lyall, by way of contrast, deftly demonstrates in "*Ulysses* in Deep Trouble Again" in *The New York Times* (23 June 1997) how an account of the circumstances surrounding the publication can evaluate the process without sniping at the participants.

The most sustained early discussion has come from John Kidd, who gained attention through a series of attacks, begun in 1985 on Hans Walter Gabler, Wolfhard Steppe, and Claus Melchior's *Ulysses: A Critical and Synoptic Edition* (1984). In his article critiquing Rose's work—"Making the Wrong Joyce"

in *The New York Review of Books* (25 September 1997)—Kidd follows the pattern that he established in his approach to the Gabler edition. He begins with a retrospective and highly selective account of the critical reception accorded to the Gabler edition. He then offers misleading statements about Rose's role in that project, adroitly representing opinion as fact. And, while seeming to summarize scholarly opinions of Gabler's work, he suppresses any views that run contrary to his own. When he turns to Rose's edition of *Ulysses,* Kidd draws attention to changes in spelling, additions to Joyce's prose, and corrections of factual errors. Unfortunately, he fails to offer a rigorous analysis of the theoretical validity of Rose's assumptions behind the creation of a Reader's Edition. Kidd's omission, of course, does not validate Rose's approach, but it does relegate his own article to little more than a begrudger's carping.

An academic commonplace is the assumption that frank and open analyses of a scholar's work can only lead to a fuller understanding of its ultimate worth. While I wholeheartedly agree with that proposition, such analyses can only have value if critics bring to them the intellectual rigor and scholarly expertise necessary to produce valid results. If we learned nothing else from the controversies that arose in the mid 1980s after Gabler and his colleagues published their version of *Ulysses,* we did come to see that readers too often take for granted the constitution of a familiar piece of literature and that we learn much about our own process of interpretation when we begin to debate a work's makeup. One impedes this effort, however, by slandering specific critics—as Kidd does in his essay—through unsupported insinuations that they acted in concert to suppress right-minded scholarship and to forward inaccurate views. The blatant unfairness of such tactics only succeeds in provoking defenses of Rose (such as this one) that might otherwise have not occurred. Clearly, the more that we focus discussion upon the way that a book like *Ulysses* was, is, or should be constituted, the more clearly we will understand both its complexities and our responses to it.

One need not, however, attempt to judge the motives behind debates on the validity of either the Rose or the Gabler edition to see that much of the furor and all of the inappropriate criticisms could have been avoided if readers had consistently shown themselves willing to critique it according to the goals and the standards that the edition set for itself. This means, quite simply, showing less concern for individual changes made by an editor and rigorously examining the general principles governing the methods for making changes.

Of course, individual emendations stand out as a tempting topic for initial responses to a new edition. The specific changes which catch the eye of the casual reader and which, more significantly, threaten the comfortable interpretations that one has already established predictably act as an impetus for closer examination. Such a response is not inherently wrong as long as one takes the examination to the source—the overall editorial plan. However, debates that do not progress beyond the level of quibbles with specific modifications threaten to divert attention from what should be the scholar's central concern: the critical apparatus—with its theoretical assumptions and frame for emendation—stands as the centerpiece of any new edition, and scrutiny of it will determine the validity of any volume.

This is nowhere more true than in examinations of this new edition of *Ulysses*. To offer fair and useful assessments of the worth of Rose's efforts—what he labels a Reader's Edition—we must be willing to keep in mind the goals and methodology announced by the editor. To a degree this means judging the book on its own terms and not according to what we would have produced had we decided to edit *Ulysses*. This, of course, does not mean giving to Rose the final say in determining whether his editing efforts have succeeded or failed. We may quite legitimately question either the inherent logic of his fundamental editorial assumptions or the consistent application of his own criteria in the editing process, but we cannot fault him for failing to do things that he never claimed he would do—unless those omissions cannot be justified according to sound editing principles.

In his edition of *Ulysses* Rose rejects the traditional editorial goal of deriving "the fully determinate text"—that is, an edition free from ambiguities, with every editorial decision buttressed by objective evidence. He chooses instead to produce an edition that he believes will be more accessible to contemporary readers, and he does so through editorial techniques far more radical than any heretofore presented. Indeed, an inevitable result of discussing the Rose *Ulysses* will be the awareness that will come to many readers of just how conservative Gabler's editorial efforts actually were.

A crucial point to consider in examining this new edition of *Ulysses* and the issue from which all

subsequent criticism must emerge is Rose's unprecedented assumption about the aims of editing:

> It may even be that the hysteria surrounding the dispute over the Gabler edition of *Ulysses* was no more than the death rattle of that once potent idea, the fully determinate text. For many years now, since around the time of the publication of *Ulysses* in fact, the physicists have been telling us that we are in the era of inbuilt indeterminacy. With the passing away of the materialistic belief in certainties in favour of statistical probabilities, the contemporary but still widespread fallacy that the extirpation of mere printers' errors, important as it is, is the sole or even the primary function of a textual editor ought also to have passed away. (xi)

The passage, quoted in many reviews, neatly encapsulates the central issue of the Rose theoretical premises: the range of freedom and the extent of responsibility shaping the actions of an editor seeking to establish the text of a particular work. Rose is arguing that for books as complex as *Ulysses,* the interpretive aspect of textual criticism must be underscored. If one accepts that premise, there remains only a short step to endorsing the view that one can and indeed inevitably will derive multiple reading texts as variants of the original authorial manuscript—what Rose terms the isotext.

Rose elaborates upon this idea in the section of the volume's introductory material titled "The Rationale of the Reader's Edition." There, in speaking specifically of his editing goals, he distinguishes from "accurate editions of authors' manuscripts" those versions created for contemporary readers rather than for scholars: "the establishment of critical editions of works of literary art—books made for readers to be read for pleasure" (xii). That is not to say these latter versions are compiled in a haphazard fashion, for to create such works Rose advocates the application of the conjoined skills of textual scholars, publisher's copyreaders, and those experienced both with the specific work and the biography of the book's author. What distinguishes their efforts from the more conventional applications of textual scholarship is not intellectual rigor but the ends toward which they direct their efforts. Rose's team of experts would work to produce not the author's version of a work but a rendering that, in their combined wisdom, represents the most coherent construction of the text that the writer passed on to us.

Further, without in any way dismissing the value of his own efforts, Rose freely acknowledges their temporality. Indeed, he sees each version of a reader's edition as time bound, useful only as long as it "recaptures the 'flavour' of the first edition."

Advertising card for the publisher of Ulysses *(Bruccoli Collection)*

They would naturally give way to subsequent editions as "[r]eaders' expectations change with the passage of time" (xvi).

In fairness to Rose, I should note that he does maintain the importance of "accurate editions of the authors' manuscripts." They would serve as the basis of the isotext—"an error-free, 'naked' transcription of the author's words as written down by him or by a surrogate, positive faults and all, with their individual diachronic interrelationships defined" (xii). It is this isotext which would be periodically reedited to produce the reader's versions that conform to contemporary perspectives.

Rose's editorial position makes his *Ulysses* an organic, evolving work. If his methodology is followed to its logical conclusion, it would mean creating a new reader's edition for each new generation of readers. Over the next one hundred years the book titled *Ulysses* might evolve into something quite different from the one which we now have before us. In a conversation that I had with him shortly after the publication of his edition, Rose affirmed this concept: while the manuscript version of *Ulysses* might with sufficient scholarly work achieve some stability, the reading text will continue to change and require periodic reediting for as long as people examine it.

As noted above, most of the early responses to Rose's edition have not taken up this issue but rather have become fixated on its results. These concerns may be legitimate and completely understandable for a volume adhering to conventional rules for editing. Rose, however, has radically reconceived the role of the text, the functions of the editorial team, and the overall aims of editing. This makes disagreement with individual changes, even ones as far-reaching as the reconfiguration of whole chapters, irrelevant. The key issue to debate remains the validity of his conception of a continuously evolving *Ulysses*.

That does not, of course, mean that one should dismiss editorial details as unimportant. Any editor must base every emendation upon solid textual evidence, and in talking to Rose shortly before writing this essay, I became convinced that he could justify, according to the internal logic of his system, any change in the text that one would care to single out. For example, I had asked him why at the end of Wandering Rocks he had replaced "the Royal Canal bridge" (10.1273 in the Gabler edition) with "the Grand Canal Bridge" (243). He explained that the latter was geographically correct, for Joyce had forgotten that there were two posters of Eugene Stratton, one of which was next to the Grand Canal and on the route passed by the viceregal cavalcade, and so Rose merely rectified a factual error in the narrative. This sort of explanation, however, while fascinating in its own right, does not take up the larger question of the validity of making the changes in the first place.

What remained unclear to me after speaking with Rose, and what continues to remain unclear despite the sixty-page introduction to his edition, is the broad logical structure of his system. On this structure rests the validity of every specific change that he has made, and it is this foundation that needs elaboration if readers are to judge the validity of his approach. In its present form, however, Rose's explanation of the editorial process simply does not provide sufficient information for such a conclusion.

In the three subsections that make up Rose's introduction, the fundamental basis for his decision making never emerges. He speaks, for example, of preparing the isotext by correcting "errors"—mistakes made as the text is transmitted from one copy to another by someone other than the author—and of creating the reader's edition by removing from the isotext any "faults"—a mistake per se in the sense of a sentence (xvi–xvii). While a careful reading of this section may clarify the distinction that Rose seeks to make between the terms, the standards for judging the difference between errors and faults remain ambiguous. Rose in particular needs to outline what sort of evidence supports his designations and how in questionable cases he determines whether a variant is a fault or an error. Since the difference between the two stands as an informing element in the editorial process, one cannot come to a judgment of the worth of Rose's *Ulysses* until its editor elaborates upon those standards.

Likewise, one cannot critique the complicated process followed in the preparation of the Reader's Edition without much more detailed information on how the scope of different editorial functions are defined and then how they are put into practice. Too often Rose's truncated explanations fail to present in detail the logic supporting his conclusions and instead take for granted the reader's acceptance of their validity. One sees this, for instance, in the difference that Rose asserts as existing between two common terms in textual studies, *substantives* and *accidentals*. Substantives are elements which "affect the author's meaning or the essence of his expression." Accidentals, on the other hand, "mainly [affect] the text's form presentation"(xv–xvi). While this may very well be the case, his delineation here does not seem consistent with the indeterminacy that he seems to advocate in his opening remarks. Indeed,

the concept of indeterminacy makes his distinctions between substantives and accidentals extremely problematic. If, for example, he claims the apostrophes inserted in Penelope as accidentals, some readers may well respond that their inclusion profoundly affects the meaning of the chapter and so they should be classified as substantives. My point is not that Rose is wrong in this instance but rather that he has not offered enough information to assure me that his position is correct.

The problem is really larger than a conflict over the meaning of specific terms. Rose's erudition works against him. He seems to have forgotten that many readers will not have the textual background that he brings to the project of editing *Ulysses*. In consequence, his argument for the validity of his approach will require for others an elaboration of views that may seem self-evident to him. How, for example, can one either accept or dismiss the idea of an evolving reader's text without the opportunity to assess the evidence upon which Rose drew to come to his conclusions of its validity? A crucial element in support of this position comes from interpretation of the role of the holograph or Rosenbach manuscript version of *Ulysses* (the fair copy prepared by Joyce, purchased by John Quinn in 1922, and acquired at auction by A. S. W. Rosenbach in 1924). Rose, in a critique of Gabler's use of the Rosenbach manuscript (lv–lx), provides a most interesting thesis how the Rosenbach manuscript should be used in establishing the isotext of the novel, but it cries out for fuller documentation.

Like any reader of *Ulysses,* I have a history with the text, and I felt uneasy about many of the changes that Rose introduced into his edition. I cannot say, however, if this uneasiness is based upon legitimate textual concerns or simply on a paternal regard for the sanctity of meanings that I have already worked out. Unfortunately, none of us will be able to do more than make this sort of subjective, idiosyncratic response until Rose publishes much more information on the editing process. He has told me that he does not believe it would be financially feasible to bring out a copy of his isotext, and that may well be the case. I do, however, think that he must publish an essay of whatever length is necessary to make readers more aware of the details of the complex editorial methodology that he brought to bear on his version of *Ulysses*.

Ulysses, Reader's Edition: First Reactions

Fritz Senn
Zurich James Joyce Foundation

It is the new edition's stated claim "to maximise the pleasure of the reader"; its scholarship serves "the greater ends of clarifying the sense and sound of the individual sentences and freeing up the flow and the pace of the text as a whole" (preface, vi). The dust-jacket blurb promises the removal of "a plethora of small, yet not insignificant, obstructions between writer and reader that have hitherto marred the enjoyment" of the book. This boast has been taken up by the popular press: here, then, someone has saved the elitist book for the common reader, and already the scholars are up in arms to defend their territory against such sacrilege.

True, *Ulysses,* as we knew, studied, abandoned, or enjoyed it so far, is obstructive and hardly considered plain sailing (as its title indicates); it certainly does not go out of its rocky way to explain itself. But for all its undoubted complexities, it has proved accessible to many of us, whether we were instructed in class or whether we tackled the book, like myself, on our own, as long as we were sufficiently agile and attentive. However, if you do think that Joyce needs to be protected from himself, watch the result.

To take the claim seriously—*has* the book been purified for facile popular consumption? My contention is that no amount of surface-scratching (punctuation, hyphenating, spelling), which after all is all an editor is allowed to do (though this one goes beyond), can turn *Ulysses* into a book substantially easier to absorb. Just turn to the first few pages of the fourteenth episode (also referred to in Joyce's private Homeric terminology as Oxen of the Sun): in any edition, including the new one, we find "a plethora of obstacles" that we have to translate into our capacities. Editorial procedures simply cannot "clarify the sense." Reading is not essentially facilitated, though the book as an object and the look of its pages are remarkably appealing.

Some changes have cast their shadows before, and attention has focused on spelling, hyphenation, and punctuation. Joyce persistently wrote "jesuit, catholic, street, bridge" or "fortyfoot hole"; Rose overrides this usage with conventional upper-case letters: "Jesuit, Catholic, Street, Bridge," and so forth, or (slightly inconsistent) "Fortyfoot hole." Many of Joyce's compound words, mainly adjectives, are now clarified by hyphenation: we find

"sea-bedabbled, blood-boltered, ill-favoured, moony-crowned, myriad-minded," and so forth. Of course, the editor gratuitously had to choose between, say, "Glitter-eyed, green-capped, holy-eyed" (with hyphens) and "darkgreener, Gaptoothed" (all of these within a few lines on pages 176–177). The distinction follows a vague principle: some hyphens are thought "necessary"; "true Joycean neologisms," however, "are of course left stand" (lxi). Not everyone would draw the line, a self-imposed one, the same way. Compounds can also be taken apart: in "his eyes looked quickly, *ghostbright,* at his foe" (10.1052 in the Critical and Synoptic Edition edited by Hans Walter Gabler, Wolfhard Steppe, and Claus Melchior [1984]) the key word is split to *ghost bright* (237), which changes not only the visual appearance but also the intonation, the sound, the pauses.

The last chapter, Penelope, has always been known for its lack of punctuation (as well as its outspokenness). Rose does not introduce punctuation, but he puts in mandatory apostrophes (though an unapostrophied version is appended as well), so "its" is plainly distinguished from "it's" or "we'll" from "well," and we are spared some mental effort, an effort however, that hardly ever made anyone abandon the book at this late stage.

Rose again improves on the author by highlighting certain quotations that are buried in the text. Where before, faced with "he had a delicious glorious voice Phoebe dearest goodbye sweetheart *sweet*heart he always sang it" (18.1294), we had to figure out, with not too much ingenuity, that Molly Bloom remembers the words of a song, italics now proclaim it unmistakably: "glorious voice *Phoebe dearest goodbye sweetheart sweet*heart he always sang it" (681). We might be misled thereby to suppose that the Reader's Edition signals the presence of all or most quotations, but this it wisely does not do, nor could it, for in some essential way almost everything in *Ulysses* is quotation, secondhand, refraction, part of an intertextual network. Editorial nudges may be well meant, but they could never be dished out universally. Joyce himself, for that matter, was a notorious non-nudger.

The editor frankly, flagrantly, even proudly oversteps the traditional tactful boundaries of editing. He brazenly amends Joyce's ways, for all we know with best intentions. But many of us do not want, or have no need for, an ameliorated *Ulysses* (other than the weeding out of its abundant transmissional errors, though those are intrinsically hard to tell from intentional ones). Most of us trust that Joyce knew how to mastermind his manifold, variable rhythms. On occasion it may be hard to determine, from messy documents, just how Joyce wanted to punctuate, but beyond such text-critical judgments Rose often steps in to set Joyce's prose "right."

We now read "Everyone to his taste, as Morris said when he kissed the cow" or "Besides, they don't know" (363), where Joyce had put no comma. (On the other hand, the first sentence in the book, "Stately, plump Buck Mulligan came from the stairhead, bearing a bowl of lather," has lost its grammatical—as well as authorial—comma). Interventions seem most lumbering when they affect the interior monologue, as in Bloom's "Also a shop often noticed" (13.1239), which now becomes: "Also a shop, often noticed" (363), a version that is both clear and logical. Except that fleeting associations as Joyce evokes them are not characterized by logic or outward clarity. *Ulysses* abounds in thoughts that rapidly jostle each other, and, again in the view of some traditional readers, it might have been judicious to let the author decide on the orchestration of his own prose.

It is one of the editor's stated tasks to correct Joyce in externals, such as names or institutions that exist in the world without the fiction. In conformance with such facts *Callanan* becomes *Callinan; Rightaway-Thrale* becomes *Rightaway-Theale; Cuprani* is changed to *Caprani;* and *Tinnahinch* is rectified to *Tinnehinch.* Joyce's Hebrew is repaired: where Joyce had used transcriptions such as "Simchath Torah, Shira Shirim," we now find "Simhath Torah, Shira ha'Shirim." Such corrections may not temper our reading, but when, in a similar vein, *Agendath* is changed to *Agudath,* not just a foreign word but a dispersed motive is at stake. It is possible that Joyce simply misread a correct Hebrew *Agudath* as *Agendath* and then, with cavalier negligence, perpetuated his own error throughout the book; but it is also conceivable that Joyce made fallible (maybe not-too-attentive) Bloom misconstrue the name of a Zionist company as "Agendath Netaim" and let it ramify in the book's intricate network. I cannot tell whether the error is Joyce's or Bloom's, nor can any editor, but I prefer to be offered the choice to determine on my own. The Reader's Edition has rescued us from the possibility; it precludes our playing with the nonword: *Agendath* may be Bloom's specious equivalent to Stephen's antiquarian choice terms

Agenbite or *Agenbuyer,* or Bloom's faulty Hebrew may be seen in tune with his precarious Jewishness (he is and he isn't). Perhaps such speculations merely serve our urge to chart unintended profundities, but somehow *Ulysses* is the kind of book that, for better or worse, often does just that. Factual truth can blend into fictional clusters. In earlier editions Bloom's library contained the volume "Ellis's *Three Trips to Madagascar*" (17.1374), but now this has been rectified to "*Three Visits to Madagascar*" (619*),* an existing book whose spine and title page indeed spell *Visits,* not *Trips.* The book is described bibliographically, however, as "brown cloth, title obliterated," which at least allows for a guess that the obliteration of the title has caused confusion. Which links to the much more general question of the nature of chapter 17 ("Ithaca"). Does it strain to give objective facts, or does it include, in its apparently matter-of-fact diction, private, subjective, distortions and wrong notions? In this case: it is conceivable that Bloom, if he were pressed, might well have "Three Trips" on his memory, which is as imperfect as anyone else's. "Ithaca" raises this problem throughout. In Danis Rose's conviction Joyce wanted to get all facts right, and he does his best to adjust the wording so that in the imaginative relation of Bloom's and Stephen's ages the calculations are now mathematically correct, which before they were not. Bloom's budget is changed in accordance with bookkeeping standards, it newly includes expenses incurred in the brothel, "Mrs Cohen 0 11 0," and the former "Balance" of "0 - 16 - 6" now amounts to "0 6 3" (622). The implication must be that Joyce was so nonchalant in working out the book's actual economics that every cross-referring reader can do better. The "Ithaca" episode essentially changes its nature and becomes much more accurate and thereby much less psychological (or Bloomian).

The Reader's Edition does not display the extensive apparatus on which in fact it is based, so we can never tell which changes have their origin in documents and in the elaborate isotext that Rose meticulously prepared. So the edition has to be judged on aesthetic grounds. In this light many interferences appear ill advised. Stephen Dedalus, who shows off his erudition in the library scene, maintains that Shakespeare "dallied . . . between conjugial love and its chaste delights and scortatory love and its foul pleasures" (9.631); the odd form *conjugial* has been streamlined to a much more familiar *conjugal,* a word known to all men. The lexeme *conjugial* is limited to Emanuel Swedenborg's writings, and, as it happens, high-brow Stephen refers to Swedenborg's *The Delights of Wis-*

dom concerning Conjugial Love after which follows The Pleasures of Insanity concerning Scortatory Love (1794). The single intrusive but necessary letter *i* turns the word into something spiritual and highly specific.

External facts loom large behind the texture of the new *Ulysses*. Bloom notices a house as "still unlet" and then thinks "Valuation is only twentyeight" (4.235). Dublin houses had their valuations; they can be verified in Thom's *Dublin Directory*, which settles for "seventeen," and so does the Reader's Edition (59). This would hardly make much difference; still, coincidence or not, Bloom later remembers a "mistake in the valuation when I was in Thom's. Twentyeight it is" (13.1125). Here "valuation" appears linked to a mistake, and the number is again "Twentyeight"–not much, perhaps, but at least there is room for marginal wonder if the number may perhaps loom in Bloom's associations (there are other occurrences of *twentyeight* or *28* in *Ulysses*). The municipally correct valuation does not lead us into explorative bypaths, perhaps the floodgates of irresponsible numerology are sensibly closed, but as a reader I would prefer to have the opportunity to follow a stray potential lead and to roam afield.

Danis Rose makes choices for us, the readers, that have been authorized neither by Joyce nor by us. I have limited myself to samples that look easy to treat in isolation; others, of even more incisive interventions, would need extended contextual embedding.

We all read, assimilate, distort, and shape *Ulysses* in our own likeness. No one can tell, offhand, whose likeness is closer to what Joyce had in mind or whose comes closer to the whatness of the book. We, readers or editors, remain subjective. So, in fairness, I can only say that my likeness of *Ulysses* is not compatible with the one that is manifest in the new edition. I did express prospective trust in the editor's judgments (which I did not yet know) and would now be much more cautious. I find the edition's benefits (apart from the outward appearance, the type, and the visual readability) minimal, its vaunted clarification (if it *were,* indeed, desirable) superficial and most intrusions regrettable, reductive, and going against the vitality of *Ulysses* as I have come to feel it.

Readers might evaluate the Reader's Edition by comparing the traditional version (from 1922 to Gabler, 1984) with major changes that have been introduced. The passage is from Oxen of the Sun. For easy comparison it is broken into separate sections:

About that present time young Stephen filled all cups that stood empty	About that present time young Stephen filled all cups that stood **empty of their portion**
so as there remained but little mo if the prudenter	so as there remained but little mo, if **some of** the prudenter
had not shadowed their approach from him that still plied it very busily who, praying for the intentions of the sovereign pontiff,	had not **shrouded** their approach from him that still plied it very busily who, praying for the intention of the sovereign pontiff,
he gave them for a pledge the vicar of Christ	gave them for a pledge the vicar of Christ
which also as he said is vicar of Bray	which also, as he **judged, was by all signs and tokens,** vicar of Bray.
(*Ulysses: A Critical and Synoptic Edition*, 3 volumes, edited by Hans Walter Gabler, Wolfhard Steppe, and Claus Melchior, New York and London, Garland, 1984, 14.272	(Reader's Edition, 372)

Some departures look like excavations from earlier documents (not to be found on Gabler's Synoptic pages) while others ("shadowed">"shrouded"; "he gave">"gave") have the air of being emendations; but without an apparatus readers cannot tell and have to judge (as the Reader's Edition encourages them to do) on purely aesthetic grounds. It might be instructive to have the editor's rationale.

We See the Editor at Work

Michael Groden
University of Western Ontario

I reviewed Danis Rose's "Reader's Edition" of *Ulysses* for the *James Joyce Broadsheet,* and I wrote there that the edition "certainly offers serious contributions to our knowledge of Joyce's writing of *Ulysses* and of the manuscripts and their relationship to each other, but it grafts onto Joyce's text a willingness to intervene that completely flies in the face of two centuries of textual criticism and theory, which have attempted to prevent just such excesses." I argued that Rose's practice of "copyreading"–improving passages as a publisher's copyeditor would do for a work in the process of publication–counter to his claims in his introduction, does not logically extend Jerome McGann's "social theory" of editing, and I cited one of Rose's own examples as an unnecessary and also aesthetically inferior intervention. (Rose reorganizes Joyce's sentence "Mr Bloom ate his strips of sandwich, fresh clean bread, with relish of disgust, pungent mustard, the feety savour of green cheese." into "Mr Bloom ate his strips of sandwich with relish of disgust, fresh clean bread, pungent mustard, the feety savour of green cheese.") Largely because of Rose's copyreading, I called the edition "a project that has gone very badly wrong."

The Reader's Edition contains no textual apparatus, preventing a reader or reviewer from gaining a systematic sense of how Rose used the manuscript evidence or on what grounds he made decisions. Initial responses are therefore inevitably impressionistic, but in an attempt to learn more about Rose's practices, I arbitrarily chose six short sections from different parts of *Ulysses* and compared the 1922 (from the Oxford World's Classics reprint), Gabler, and Rose editions. I chose four sections for which drafts exist that precede the Rosenbach Manuscript (the fair copy, named after the collector who bought it and the Philadelphia museum that owns it), and also two short segments from Ithaca, the episode that Rose claims needed "more extensive and invasive surgery" but for which no pre-Rosenbach drafts survive. I wanted to see whether decisions seemed to come from the manuscript record or from copyreading. I looked for places where Rose differs from Gabler and in those cases how they each compare to 1922. I looked at words alone, ignoring Rose's changes in punctuation and his choice to split and or hyphen-

ULYSSES

by

JAMES JOYCE

SHAKESPEARE AND COMPANY
12, Rue de l'Odéon. 12
PARIS
1922

Title page of the first printing (Bruccoli Collection, Thomas Cooper Library, University of South Carolina)

ate words which Joyce wrote as compounds, most of which would presumably qualify as copyreading. The passages I chose were:

	Rose pages	Gabler line numbers	1922 pages
Proteus	37–45	3:1–335	38–45
Sirens	265–272	11:795–1096	266–273
Oxen of the Sun	377–382	14:434–656	377–382
Eumaeus	543–550	16:525–826	584–590
Ithaca	580–586	17:1–244	619–624
Ithaca	619–622	17:1345–1478	660–664

In the following passages, the words within brackets are the variants (R = Rose; G = Gabler; F = 1922 [first edition]; FR = 1922; and Rose, FG = 1922 and Gabler). The citations in parentheses give the location in Rose (R + page.line number), Gabler (G + episode:line number), and 1922 (F + page.line number). The sources that I could find for Rose's readings are indicated, along with pages from the sixty-three-volume *James Joyce Archive* (1978), edited by Gabler, Rose, Michael Groden, David Hayman, and A. Walton Litz (A + volume:page number). Readings for which I could not find a manuscript source are indicated as "copyreading."

Proteus

1) Will you be [R: wise] as gods? (R38.6; G3:38; F38.14)–Buffalo MS V.A.3 p. 2 (A12:240)

2) A hater of his kind [R: , he] ran (R39.39; G3:110; F40.8)–copyreading

3) ¶[R: You are a highly intellectual fellow, with your Oxford manner.] Reading two pages (R40.26; G3:136; F40.34)–Buffalo MS V.A.3 p. 6 (A12:244)

4) leaves, [so] deeply deep (R40.32; G3:154; F41.2)–Buffalo MS V.A.3 p. 6 (A12:244)

5) at the land [R: 's end] a maze (R41.6; G3:154; F41.13)–Buffalo MS V.A.3 p. 7 (A12:245)

6) punched [R: tram]tickets (R41.32; G3:180; F41.37)–Buffalo MS V.A.3 p. 7 (A12:245)

7) *Lui, c'est moi.* [R: Allee samee.] You seem (R41.35; G3:183; F41.3)–Buffalo MS V.A.3 p. 8 (A12:246)

8) Madeleine [R: , belated,] new-make (R42.27; G3:213; F42.32-33)–Buffalo MS V.A.8 p. 8 (A12:246)

9) between [R: his] hands (R43.18; G3:239; F43.23)–Buffalo MS V.A.3 p. 9 (A12:247)

10) The two Marys. (R45.1); The two maries. (G3:297; F45.6)–copyreading

11) any [R: more] of your medieval (R45.23; G3:319; F45.27)–Buffalo MS V.A.3 p. 12 (A12:250)

Sirens

1) thong. It buzzed. He drew and plucked. It twanged. While (R265.2); thong. He drew and plucked. It buzz, it twanged. While (G11:796; F266.10)–Buffalo MS V.A.5 p. 21 (A13:33)

2) a kind of retrospective arrangement (R265.4); a retrospective sort of arrangement (G11:798; F266.12)–Buffalo MS V.A.5 p. 21 (A13:33)

3) Street [R: jinglejingled.] (R265.18; G11:812; F266.25)–Buffalo MS V.A.5 p. 21 (A13:33)

4) by half [R:. Two] is twice (R265.37; G11:831; F267.7)–Buffalo MS V.A.5 p. 22 (A13:35)

5) flat pad ink [R: pen]. (R266.14; G11:847; F267.22)–Buffalo MS V.A.5 p. 22 (A13:35)

6) set [R: down] with (R266.14; G11:847; F267.22)–Buffalo MS V.A.5 p. 22 (A13:35)

7) knife fork [R: up]. (R266.15; G11:848; F267.23)–Buffalo MS V.A.5 p. 22 (A13:35)

8) Dignam, Patrick [R: A.] (R266.24; G11:857; F267.32)–Rosenbach MS, p. 29

9) Just [R: the ad] I was looking (R266.25; G11:858; F267.33)–Buffalo MS V.A.5 p. 22 (A13:35)

10) Accept my poor (R266.33; F268.3); Accep my poor (G11:865)–Buffalo MS V.A.5 p. 22 (A13:35)

11) lost the pin of her (R266.38; F268.8); lost the string of her (G11:870)–Buffalo TS V.B.9, p. 15 (A13:72)

12) driver James Barton (R267.7-8); driver Barton James (G11:878-79; F268.15-16)–copyreading

13) bright [R: with] tubes (R267.14; G11:884; F268.21)–Buffalo MS V.A.5 p. 23 (A13:37)

14) of Agudath [R: Netaim forcemeat] trotted (R267.14; G11:884; F268.21- FG = "Agudath")–Rosenbach MS, p. 31, but "Agendath" = copyreading

15) Dolphin's Barn Lane / City (R267.30); Dolphin's Barn Lane / Dublin (G11:900; F268.36)–Buffalo MS V.A.5 p. 23 (A13:37)

16) can't read. [G: There.] Right. (R267.31; G11:901; F269.1)–Buffalo TS V.B.9 p. 17 (A13:74)

17) ¶[R: Miss Douce, requested, served the same again.] Douce now. (R268.12; G11:920; F269.20)–Buffalo MS V.A.5 p. 24 (A13:39) and Rosenbach MS, p. 32

18) He did, [G: faith,] Sir Tom. (R268.22; G11:929; F269.28)–Buffalo TS V.B.9 p. 17 (A13:74)

19) more faintly [FG: that] that they heard (R268.28; G11:935; F269.35)–Buffalo MS V.A.5 p. 24 (A13:39)

20) sheet, a yashmak. (R268.36; F270.6); Sheet. Yashmak. (G11:943)–Buffalo TS V.B.9 p. 17 (A13:74)

21) clapper of a bell. (R269.29); clapper of a bellows. (G11:973; F270.34)–copyreading

22) Jigjog jogged, stopped. (R269.33); Jog jig jogged, stopped. (G11:977; F271.1)–Buffalo MS V.A.5 p. 25 (A1:41): Jigjog stopped.

23) talons gripped (R270.15); talons griped (G11:998; F271.21)–1932 Odyssey Press edition

24) of unlove, [R; of] earth's fatigue (R270.24; G11:1007; F271.29)–Buffalo MS V.A.5 p. 26 (A13:43): of fatigue.

25) best to sing it. (R270.28); best to say it. (G11:1011; F271.33)–Buffalo MS V.A.5 p. 26 (A13:43)

26) he had once. (R270.30); he did once. (G11:1013; F271.35)–Buffalo MS V.A.5 p. 26 (A13:43) and Rosenbach MS, p. 35

27) build [FG: them] cubicles. (R270.35; G11:1018; F272.3)–Buffalo MS V.A.5 p. 27 (A13:45)

28) play. [R: And] once. (R271.20; G11:1042; F272.26)–Buffalo MS V.A.5 p. 27 (A13:45)

29) boy. / [¶Deaf Pat held wider ajar the door.] / ¶Bronze, (R271.22; G11:1043-44; F272.28-29)–Buffalo MS V.A.5 p. 28 (A13:47)

30) music? [R: Music hath charms. Owls and birds.] Way (R271.28-29; G11:1049; F272.34)–Buffalo MS V.A.5 p. 28 (A13:47)

31) dibs. Moonlit walks by the sad sea waves. Want to keep your weather eye open. Those girls, those lovely. Chorus girl's (R272.18-19); dibs. Want to keep your weathereye open. Those girls, those lovely. By the sad sea waves. Chorusgirl's (G11:1076-77; F273.24.26)–Rosenbach MS, p. 37 (but "Chorusgirl's")

32) her lip and blow, (R272.30); her. Lip blow. (G11:1088; F273.36)–Buffalo MS V.A.5 verso of p. 28 (A13:48) (but "her. Lip and blow.")

Oxen of the Sun

1) hear [R: both of those things] unless (R377.3; G14:437; F377.19)–Buffalo MS V.A.12 p. 12 (A14:31)

2) grot [R: of shame] which (R377.20; G14:453; F377.34)–Buffalo MS V.A.15 p. 2 (A14:83) and Rosenbach MS, p. 20

3) learned [R: men also], Carnal (R377.21; G14:453; F377.35)–Buffalo MS V.A.12 p. 13 (A14:33)

4) he had [R: before] but (R378.38; G14:508; F379.12)–Buffalo MS V.A.12 p. 15 (A14:37)

5) for a [R:n omen of] change (R379.2; G14:510; F379.15)–Rosenbach MS, p. 22

6) scandal [R: in the town] he had (R379.28; G14:510; F379.15)–Buffalo MS V.A.12 p. 16 (A14:39) and Rosenbach MS, p. 23

7) purse [R: in any company] he could (R379.35-36; G14:542; F380.8)–Buffalo MS V.A.12 p. 16 (A14:39)

8) tongue [R: with] some (R379.36; G14:543; F380.9)–copyreading

9) moonlight, fecking (R380.18); moonlight or fecking (G14:562; F380.27)–copyreading

10) boat, says (R380.24); boats, says (G14:568; F380.33)–Rosenbach MS, p. 25

11) himself [R: soon] on (R380.35; G14:578; F381.6)–Buffalo MS V.A.16 p. 2 (A14:91)

12) Stephen, as he (R380.37); Stephen, and he (G14:580; F381.7)–Buffalo MS V.A.12 p. 17 (A14:41)

13) him [R: everywhere,] hanging (R381.6; G14:588; F381.15)–Buffalo MS V.A.16 p. 3 (A14:92)

14) his [FG: long] holy tongue (R381.16; G14:597; F381.23)–Rosenbach MS, p. 26

15) spermaceti oil (R381.20); spermacetic oil (G14:601; F381.27)–Buffalo MS V.A.16 p. 3 (A14:92)

16) all of [R: the] one mind (R382.21; G14:641; F382.28)–Buffalo MS V.A.12 p. 18 (A14:43)

Eumaeus

1) them Chinese does. (R544.11); the chinks does. (G16:573); the Chinese does. (F584.4)–Buffalo MS V.A.21 p. 2 (A15:325)

2) Mr Bloom and Stephen (R545.19; F584.25); Mr B and Stephen (G16:594)–Buffalo TS V.B.14.d p. 10 (A15:382)

3) Mr Bloom interrogated. (R545.19); Mr B interrogated. (G16:618); Mr Bloom interpolated. (F585.11)–Buffalo MS V.A.21 p. 3 (A15:327: "Mr Bloom") and Rosenbach MS, p. 16 ("interrogated")

4) sea [FG: on the wall], staring (R545.33; G16:631; F585.23)–Buffalo MS V.A.21 p. 3 (A15:327)

5) figures 6–16 (R546.38); figure 16 (G16:675; F586.27)–British Museum notesheet Eumaeus 1 (A12:65; Phillip F. Herring, *Joyce's "Ulysses" Notesheets in the British Museum* [Charlottesville: Published for the Bibliographical Society of the University of Virginia by the University Press of Virginia, 1972], p. 369)

6) bottom [R: of Stephen's cup,] and (R550.1; G16:791; F589.30)–Buffalo MS V.A.21 p. 7 (A15:335)

7) But [G: O] oblige me (R550.28; G16:815; F590.17)–Buffalo TS V.B.14.a p. 14 (A15:386)

8) removed [R: out of sight] the (R550.30; G16:817; F590.19)–Buffalo MS V.A.21 p. 7 (A15:335)

Ithaca

1) Temple Street North: then (R580.6); Temple street: then (G17:5); Temple street, north: then (F619.5)–Rosenbach MS, p. 1 Blue

2) son of Calpurnius (R581.2); son of Calpornus (G17:33; F620.7)–copyreading

3) and Donald Turnbull (R581.18); and Cecil Turnbull (G17:48; F620.22)–copyreading

4) the respectively premeditatedly and inadvertently (R582.13); the, premeditatedly (respectively) and inadvertently, (G17:80; F621.18)–copyreading

5) of his aunt Sara, wife of Richie (Richard Goulding), in the kitchen of their lodgings at

number 62 Clanbrassil Street; of his mother Mary in the kitchen of number 12 North (R584.4-6); of his aunt Sara, wife of Richie (Richard) Goulding, in the kitchen of their lodgings at 62 Clanbrassil street; of his mother Mary, wife of Simon Dedalus, in the kitchen of number twelve North (G17:141-143); of his mother Mary, wife of Simon Dedalus, in the kitchen of number twelve North (F623.11-13)–Rosenbach MS, p 3 Blue (but without *number* before *62* or *Mary* after *mother*)

6) numbers 84A–87 Stephen's (R584.8); 16 Stephen's (G17:145; F623.15)–copyreading

7) Green South: of (R584.9); Green, north: of (G17:146; F623.15)–copyreading

8) the Marianne Trench (R585.15); the Sundam trench (G17:187; F624.22)–copyreading

9) 6000 fathoms (R585.16); 8.000 fathoms (G17:187; F624.22)–copyreading

10) compassionate gaze (R619.2); compassionated gaze (G17:1346; F660.14)–copyreading

11) *Three Visits to* (R619.30); *Three Trips to* (G17:1374; F661.11)–copyreading

12) pectoral ribs, (R621.23); pectoral vertebrae, (G17:1441; F663.17)–copyreading

13) inflicted 3 weeks (R621.25); inflicted 2 weeks (G17:1448; F663.25)–copyreading

14) 17 November 1903 (R621.30); 17 October 1903 (G17:1454); 10 October 1903 (F663.29)–copyreading

[from the "Budget":]

15) Loan (Stephen Dedalus) 1 - 6 - 11 (R622.8); 1 - 7 - 0 (G17:1460; F664.7)–copyreading

16) Train fare 0 - 0 - 1 (R622.23; not in G or F)–copyreading

17) 1 Cake Fry's plain chocolate 0 - 0 - 1 (R622.25; F664.19); 0 - 1 - 0 (G17:1472)–first placards (A21:89)

18) Mrs Cohen 0 - 11 - 0 (R622.29; not in G or F)–copyreading

19) Balance 0 - 6 - 3 (R622.34); 0 - 16 - 6 (G17:1476; F664.24)–copyreading

20) Total [twice] 2 - 19 - 2 (R622.9 and 622.35); 2 - 19 - 3 (G17:1478; F664.25)–copyreading.

My samples, of course, may be unrepresentative; my manual collations almost certainly contain omissions or other errors; and some of my "copyreading" attributions probably have sources in the extant manuscripts. Nevertheless, I draw some conclusions from these examples. In the four episodes for which early manuscripts survive, far more of Rose's readings come from his interpretation of the manuscript evidence than from copyreading (but including punctuation and word forms such as compounds would change the proportion). Rose's interpretations and conclusions are debatable–he leans very strongly towards Joyce's earliest inscriptions rather than later ones–and the lack of an apparatus prevents him from providing any rationale for his choices, but his readings do offer a legitimate scholarly analysis of the available evidence. Had Rose stopped here, his edition would probably have been a valuable, but controversial, reconstruction of Joyce's writing with heavy emphasis on the earliest drafts and manuscripts. It is the copyreading, blatantly evident in the examples from Ithaca, that make the edition problematic and, ultimately, unacceptable. Unfortunately, some of the results of the copyreading (such as the changes in Bloom's budget) are so evident, and Rose has called so much attention to his practice in his introduction, that it is on these grounds alone and not on his scholarly use of the manuscripts that most people will probably respond to the edition. I, too, must highlight the copyreading and join the naysayers.

Stephen Joyce's Letter to the Editor of *The Irish Times*

Sir,

Readers of great literature, admirers of creative genius all over the world may well wonder why the Estate of James Joyce and I have to date remained silent on the newest ULYSSES controversy. The answer is simple. In spite of all our efforts since mid-March the London and Dublin Publishers of this so-called "Reader's edition" steadfastly refused to provide us with an advance copy of the text of this book.

It was finally pursuant to a court order on the afternoon of June 13, that five copies of the book were handed over to the Estate's representative. Since June 16, when those directly concerned received their copies, we have been looking carefully over this volume's contents. A number of eminent Joyceans have joined us in this examination.

To have had the audacity, the effrontery to put the name JAMES JOYCE on this "outrageous" misrepresentation of ULYSSES, my grandfather's unique masterpiece—often referred to as the novel of the century—is demeaning to his creative, imaginative genius. The integrity, the essence of James Joyce's novative writing has been obliterated, most notably but, alas, by no means exclusively from the *Penelope* closing sequence—the Molly Bloom Monologue—which represents the revolutionary, continuous stream of consciousness first used by Edouard Dujardin. The foregoing has been destroyed by the addition, where there were none, of well over seven hundred and fifty apostrophes, dozens of hyphens/tirets and italicized words and phrases—and this is merely "one" example of the many distortions.

One of the Joyceans who has gone through this volume has pointedly referred to it as "a blatant distortion of Joyce's artistic aims and achievement." In his view this so-called "Reader's edition" of ULYSSES "certainly shows no respect at all, to say the least, for the artistic integrity of James Joyce's whole literary creation."

If this book is to continue to be sold the name JAMES JOYCE must be eliminated, stricken from the dust jacket, cover and inside title pages of this edition. The Estate will spare no effort to achieve this aim.

Those who buy this book should realize that they are *not* purchasing James Joyce's ULYSSES. In the action the Estate has undertaken, we are in no sense trying to censor genuine "scholars" from expounding their theories but rather protecting a major work of art. It is our duty to protect readers from this type of charade; after all, over the years, this epic novel has become part of the heritage of the English language.

From something "génial" ULYSSES, which represents the highest standard of achievement in the World of Letters, has been transformed into something banal and run of the mill.

The year 1997 marks the seventy fifth anniversary of the publication by Sylvia Beach's Shakespeare and Company, Paris of ULYSSES. On this occasion it is necessary to recall the book's complex, tortured history—its travels, trials and tribulations. For fourteen long years this 20th century epic was banned de jure in Britain and de facto in Ireland. Early in 1923 four hundred and ninety eight copies were seized by customs at Folkestone and destroyed, not to mention what happened in the USA before Judge John M. Woolsey handed down his momentous decision on December 6, 1933. AND NOW THIS.

One can only wonder where all this will lead; who and what the likely next candidates and targets for this type of mutilation will be? Dramatists, poets, novelists, and short-story writers—not forgetting painters—past, present as well as future, BEWARE!

What the Estate and the literary world are faced with today is not another "Scandal of Ulysses"; but is this not "The Rape of ULYSSES"?!

Faithfully,

Stephen James Joyce
Paris, France
June 26, 1997

James Laughlin

(30 October 1914 – 12 November 1997)

See also the New Directions entry in *DLB 46, American Literary Publishing Houses, 1900–1980: Trade and Paperback.*

BOOKS: *The River* (Norfolk, Conn.: New Directions, 1938);
Some Natural Things (New York: New Directions, 1945);
Skiing East and West, text by Laughlin, photographs by Helen Fischer in collaboration with Emita Herran (New York: Hastings House, 1946);
Report on a Visit to Germany (Lausanne: Henri Held, 1948);
A Small Book of Poems (Milan & New York: Vanni Scheiwiller & New Directions, 1948);
The Wild Anemone & Other Poems (Norfolk, Conn.: New Directions, 1957);
Confidential Report, and Other Poems (London: Gaberboccus, 1959); republished as *Selected Poems* (Norfolk, Conn.: New Directions, 1959);
The Pig (Mount Horeb, Wis.: Perishable Press, 1970);
In Another Country: Poems 1935–1975; edited by Robert Fitzgerald (San Francisco: City Lights Books, 1978);
Gists & Piths: A Memoir of Ezra Pound (Iowa City: Windhover Press, 1982);
Stolen & Contaminated Poems (Isla Vista, Cal.: Turkey Press, 1985);
The Deconstructed Man (Iowa City: Windhover Press, 1985);
Selected Poems 1935–1985 (San Francisco: City Lights Press, 1986);
The House of Light (New York: Grenfell Press, 1986).

OTHER: *New Directions in Prose and Poetry,* numbers 1–55, edited by Laughlin (Cambridge, Mass., Norfolk, Conn. & New York: New Directions, 1936–1991);
Samuel Bernard Greenberg, *Poems from the Greenberg Manuscripts: A Selection from the Work of Samuel B. Greenberg,* edited, with a commentary, by Laughlin (Norfolk, Conn.: New Directions, 1939);

James Laughlin

The Fourth Eclogue of Virgil, translated by Laughlin (Windham, Conn.: Printed for J. Laughlin by Edmond Thompson, 1939);
A Wreath of Christmas Poems by Virgil, Dante, Chaucer and Others, edited by Laughlin and Alfred M. Hayes (Norfolk, Conn.: New Directions, 1942);
Alvin Lustig, *Bookjackets by Alvin Lustig for New Directions Books,* includes a statement by Laughlin and Lustig (New York: Gotham Book Mart, 1947);

Spearhead: Ten Year's Experimental Writing in America, edited by Laughlin (New York: New Directions, 1947);

Perspective of Burma, edited by Laughlin and U Myat Kyaw (New York: Intercultural Publications, 1958);

A New Directions Reader, edited by Laughlin and Hayden Carruth (New York: New Directions, 1964);

The Asian Journal of Thomas Merton, edited by Laughlin, Naomi Burton, and Patrick Hart (New York: New Directions, 1975).

Tributes

Michael L. Lazare

I met James Laughlin only once, less than two years before his death, yet when he died I felt I had lost a dear personal friend of long standing.

I don't think I even knew Laughlin's name when I was a Yale undergraduate in the early fifties, but of course I was familiar with the authors he published—Ezra Pound, Henry Miller, Dylan Thomas, Thomas Merton, Tennessee Williams, William Carlos Williams, Delmore Schwartz, Kay Boyle, Kenneth Rexroth, Vladimir Nabokov, Herman Hesse, dozens of others. The name "New Directions" was itself exciting, connoting talent, intellectual ferment, and passionate new voices.

Eventually my taste migrated to older authors, and I took a graduate degree in medieval literature. I abandoned my plans for an academic career and became a newspaper reporter. As my intellect matured and expanded, I seldom thought much about modern literature. Nonetheless the New Directions writers whom I had read and discussed passionately when I was young remained seminal in my intellectual development. So I was delighted when Matt Bruccoli, my Yale classmate, invited me to accompany him on a visit to Norfolk, Connecticut, in the spring of 1996.

We arrived at the Laughlins' house on a bright, sunny day and were met at the door by the gracious Gertrude Laughlin. James Laughlin—tall and white-haired, patrician in features and manners, courtly, unfailingly polite—joined us, and we sat down to a pleasant lunch, after which he led us into his study. Blessed with almost total recall, he talked for the next hour or so about his lack of interest in the family steel business, the publishing company he had founded in 1936, and the giants of literature he

had known—Ezra Pound above all others. He was reluctant to accept the title of tastemaker to generations of readers, yet who could consider him anything less? I listened with fascination to the man who had published more great literature than anyone in this century, whose intuition and ability to recognize talent had helped define American letters.

His conversation was memorable. At one point he noted that none of his own recent poems, written in pentastiches, a Greek form, had been published. "I find there's hesitancy," he noted. "The editors think there's something odd about the form. Well, that's good. All my life I've tried to make New Directions odd. Bill Corbett, who took on the job of writing a book about New Directions, asked what was my intention in starting publishing. I'd say it was to be odd and different and 'new directional.'" A bit later, talking about F. Scott's Fitzgerald *The Crack-Up,* he said, "It took me about two hours to see that this was a New Directions book. It was different. There was something odd and something serious. . . . There were other books of that kind. We came by E. M. Forster because Forster had been late for lunch with Alfred Knopf at the Ritz in London. . . . There were so many accidents in publishing, you know, so many accidents."

Near the end he said, "People ask me, 'What is the New Directions line? How do you know what you want to print?'" Laughlin's answer summed up his life's work as a publisher in twenty-four syllables: "I want to print something that I enjoy, that excites me to read, that seems to me new and different."

It was time to go. He gave us both a copy of *The Country Road,* a limited edition of his poems published by New Directions in 1995. On the fly-leaf of mine he inscribed, "To Michael Lazare, Ubi sunt qui ante nos in hoc mundo fuerunt, J. Laughlin, 4/20'96." I translated it aloud: "Where are those who lived in this world before us?" He smiled and nodded, but I felt I was missing something. It wasn't until a couple of hours after we had returned to my house that I suddenly realized why that quotation was so familiar: It is the first line of the second stanza of the medieval students' song, "Gaudeamus igitur, juvenes dum sumus"—Let us rejoice, for we are young. Certainly I had much cause for rejoicing that day. I had met a great man, eighty-two years old but with a mind as supple and stimulating as a youth's. I had listened to and lunched with one of the titans of modern literature.

Twenty months later I drove to New York on another bright, sunny day—in winter, this time, 9 January 1998—for a memorial service in the packed auditorium of the American Academy of Arts and Letters. A few of the tributes stayed with me. Herbert Leibowitz said, "To James Laughlin, civility was not just a part of the gentleman's role, but the nectar and ambrosia of human existence." Laurie Callahan told of his passion for butterflies and his hunts for rare specimens in the Wasatch Mountains of Utah with Vladimir Nabokov, which nearly cost their lives one day when they almost slid over a cliff, until they were able to grasp a tree and pull themselves back up. Eliot Weinberger noted that Octavio Paz had been discovered by Laughlin and commented, "Follow almost any path in modern literature, and there, at the beginning, is James Laughlin." Daniel Javitch read from Laughlin's letters to writers, including one to William Saroyan, who had requested page proofs. Laughlin refused to send any of his authors page proofs because the writers made too many expensive changes, and New Directions operated at a loss for many years. He wrote to Saroyan, "You don't know what writers are like, because you *are* one. . . . We can print you, but we can't humor you."

I left the academy thinking of the day I had met James Laughlin. The answer to the question "Ubi sunt qui ante nos in hoc mundo fuerunt" is obvious. He lives in our minds; he nourishes our intellects.

Peggy L. Fox

When James Laughlin died in November 1997, at the age of eighty-three, many obituaries focused on his early accomplishments: founding New Directions and developing the famous "List" that includes everyone from Pound to Bei Dao, from Nabokov to Antonio Tabucchi. Many of these tributes assumed that JL (or J as he was affectionately known both in and out of the New Directions office) had had little to do with running the corporation in the last decade. While it is true that J came to New York rarely in the last ten years, he was aware of every letter sent from the office (I sent copies of everything once or twice a week), and he exercised his oversight of all of our operations by the tyranny of the "little note." I've pulled out my current folder of miscellaneous "little notes"; most are typed or handwritten on pieces of carefully cut up scrap paper of about three by four inches. Longer messages would be typed on half a piece of paper, and occasionally an especially important communication would be dictated to J's part-time secretary. Notes about specific books or authors are filed accordingly, and I didn't consult them, but these random samples give the flavor and the range of J's involvement in the minutiae of New Directions and also show the per-

sonal touch that kept the ND staff devoted and committed to J's vision of publishing.

These notes begin in the eighties and continue until three weeks before J's death. All begin simply "Peggy":

Thanks for Dagmar's [Dagmar Henne, ND's agent in Germany] letter. I wrote the poem in German but needed her help to correct the genders and case endings, which I can never remember. J

That's a marvelous list of Pound books you made up for [John] Espey. THANKS. J

Brown was fun but the students sat like lumps and didn't laugh at my jokes. I hope they loosen up. J

Please do thank all for the lovely yellow roses—one of Ann's favorite flowers. J [During Ann Laughlin's illness, prior to her death in 1989.]

The new contract looks very good to me. Congratulations and thanks. J

Thanks for the account of your tour [to China in 1990 with a small group of American writers and publishers]. Very interesting. I wasn't aware they had no copyright system. J

The Limited Editions Club Pound *Cathay* came. Exquisite!!! J

That's a nice piece in PW [*Publishers Weekly*] about the Bibelots. As I've told you there are quite a few forgotten diamonds in the vault here when you get time to study over them. Not necessarily old ND books, but important ones from the modern tradition.

That's good that you were able to have Bei Dao out at your place. He sounds nice. J

THANK you for coping with the insurance. I never can understand these things. And also for dealing with the phone system. You are a blessing.

There are lengthy memos in 1994 about J's difficulties with a computer system set up by his son Henry, notes asking for more stationery of a particular kind, requests to have a certain book sent to someone, complaints about jacket or cover designs. But at about this time more comments begin to be made about his health. After a visit to Norfolk:

Thanks, those are VERY good pictures you took, especially of Gertrude. I look pretty decrepit—and am. J

My energy is diminishing and I find it hard to keep up with work and verse both. If I work for two hours then I have to lie down for a rest. So it goes. Best, J

*Note from James Laughlin to Peggy Fox about her impending visit to
Ezra Pound's daughter*

The Academy [of Arts and Letters] do was harrowing for me, except seeing [Jacques] Barzun. My legs have become very undependable. I was afraid I would waver and fall off the platform. Fortunately I had Jack Hawkes organized to get me out the back way to the car. J

E-mail what next? I can't read the top coding. For the archives I'd rather have regular letterheads. So if you want to Eat, please type some identification on the copy. J

That's great that you and Bob can visit Mary [de Rachewiltz, Ezra Pound's daughter] at Brunnenburg [in September of 1996]. It's so beautiful around there and she's a wonderful person. . . . I worry about her cooking big meals for guests and stray students. There are some charming little inns in Tyrol village. Why don't you ask her out for dinner one evening and charge it up to ND. Venison! J

When I returned from a trip to Spain in October 1997, I wrote J a series of memos about the status of the business and various projects. His last memo to me, of 22 October 1997, was a list of answers to specific queries, but I will reproduce parts of it as he typed it himself:

Dear Peggy—

Peggy—I'm glad you had such an interesting trip abroad.

Good for Rick [Taylor—editor of Pound's *Variorum Cantos* on CD-ROM].

I don't understand what [Christopher] MacGowan [editor of the William Carlos Williams / Denise Levertov correspondence] wants. So you can handle.

I'm too ill to travel to Brown. Thank them.

I'm sinking rapidly. J

Love to all.

Frederick Busch
Under J's Roof

James Laughlin brought me home, and he let me live in his house. Although by 1973 my first novel and volume of stories had been published in London, my second novel, *Manual Labor,* had been turned down by probably a dozen American houses. I was writing a book about the fiction of John Hawkes, a New Directions author from the start of his career and for many years thereafter. I wrote, to no one in particular at New Directions, asking for permission to quote from Jack's early novels—*The Beetle Leg, The Goose on the Grave*—and I was surprised to receive a letter from James Laughlin. He praised me for my interest in Hawkes, and he asked me whether I had something he could read with an eye toward publishing me.

That was how he worked in the early seventies, and it was how he had worked since 1936, when he brought out a magazine called *New Directions in Prose & Poetry,* "Edited by James Laughlin IV." His first issue included the work of Wallace Stevens, Gertrude Stein, Marianne Moore, Jean Cocteau, William Carlos Williams, E. E. Cummings, Kay Boyle, Elizabeth Bishop, Dudley Fitts, Henry Miller, Eugene Jolas, and that lifelong poet

James Laughlin IV. Many of those names were still on the New Directions list, and here he was offering me the possibility of joining them. I was thirty-two years old and had been sending novels out since I'd been twenty-two, but J made the wait seem like perfect timing. He told me he had learned from Ezra Pound that writers (and their publishers) must endure a twenty-year lag between the first appearance of significant writing and its acceptance by the reading public.

So there I was in a month or so, soon to be part of a list that was history, and somehow ordained as a genuine perpetrator of significance. I was also a married man, a father, and, in search of security, working on the Hawkes book in an effort to achieve tenure, and now, thanks to J, certain that I would. I blew my horn to the English department at Colgate, and I waited for great praise—not so much for what I had written as for being part of the most celebrated twenty-year lag in (according to my purview) all of literature.

I remember manufacturing a reason to telephone the offices of New Directions, which in those days were at 333 Sixth Avenue, in Greenwich Village. I introduced myself as a new ND author, and I waited for applause; instead, I was connected to the man who then ran day-to-day editorial operations for J. When I reminded this man that I was soon to be on the list he superintended, he allowed as how he hadn't at *all* decided that I would be published by New Directions—he would have to wait and see. And of course, I spent the day in shock, trying out phrases for casually telling my senior professors that, actually, I would *not,* after all, be publishing with New Directions. I didn't sleep that night, and at an early hour, perhaps seven-thirty, I rang J at his house in Norfolk, Connecticut.

He was casual and hospitable about the call and the hour. I heard him knocking dottle from his pipe, and I imagined that he struck it against the stone lintel of a fireplace. He said, "Well, well. Fred, do you have a New Directions book in your house?"

I said that, of course, I had many.

"Go bring one to the phone, if you would. I'll wait."

I ran and fetched.

"Please," he said, "read from the bottom of the page where the copyright appears. Read it out loud, if you would."

I read, "*New Directions Books are published for James Laughlin by New Directions Publishing Corporation.*"

"Exactly," he said. And I imagined him, chauffeuring Gertrude Stein and Alice B. Toklas

through France in the thirties, saying, "*Exacte.*" Then he said, unangrily, patiently, "When I tell you that New Directions will publish your book, New Directions will publish your book." It was his house; I was under his roof.

The rest of the conversation consisted of my verbal equivalents of the wagging of the tail, and J's modest fendings-off of my praise and my thanks. He never, to my knowledge, enjoyed public attention. And when, years later, tenured in no small part because of him, I asked him to Colgate for our inaugural Living Writers course, he was both embarrassed and pleased, and he gave what he declared to be his first college poetry reading as well as a superb lecture on the poetry and fiction of William Carlos Williams.

In 1977, after J had published *Manual Labor* and the story collection *Domestic Particulars*—each edited by Peter Glassgold, now my longtime friend who became J's editor in chief, a job he kept until he left the firm to write his own fiction—I brought in the manuscript of *The Mutual Friend,* a novel about Charles Dickens. J confessed that he was a little shaken by my taking on—by my reconstructing—one of the icons of fiction. It is possible that I derived more pleasure from knowing that I had gotten at the convictions of a great iconoclast than from further developments involving that novel. J said that, of course, he would publish it: he published authors, not individual books, as he saw it; he invested those twenty years of which he'd spoken. I asked whether I might not have a raise in pay; the advance for the other two books had been $1,000 each, and it seemed to me that for his sixth book overall, third with New Directions, a fellow might have a little more money.

"Oh," J said, relishing the parsimony behind every syllable—like many rich people, he was religious about paying (to his editors as well as his authors) as little as he could although he had virtually fed and clothed some of his neediest writers—"We only *have* two levels for our novelists. A very few, say someone like Jack Hawkes, might get as much as $5,000. But that's rare," he hurried to say. "You're not at Jack's level yet, I think you'll agree. We might go five hundred more for you—$1,500?"

I whined; I begged; I did not demand, for I was always intimidated by him—the clash of his heavy, long shoes against the floor; his sharpened pencil in his suitcoat pocket alongside a sheet of paper folded lengthwise in half, ready for notes: you interested him, you could tell, if he made a note while you spoke, and you worked to make him reach for his pencil; his bland expression, his large handsome face; the reach of his long fingers along the spine of a book about which he enthused; his portage of the literary past into the room in which you sat with him; his belief in the value of the work you did, and the pleasure he took (and gave) in making clear your importance in his immense and teeming experience of language made in Europe, South America, and the North American continent.

Finally, J said, "Look. Take the book to an uptown house. If they'll give you more money, you should publish with them. If they don't, bring it back down here, and I'll be honored to publish your version of Mr. Dickens."

Harper and Row paid the money, and I needed it. But I tried never to leave New Directions. They published several books of mine over the years and, until its awful death by slow sales in 1988, ran stories by me in their New Directions Annual. And in the early nineties, ND published a paperback edition of *The Mutual Friend,* the book I had taken uptown. I loved the house he admitted me to, and I tried to thank him—he hated expressions of gratitude—by dedicating my new and selected stories to him.

Until not too many years ago, royalties from New Directions arrived with an adding machine receipt, and a large green check written in J's precise, old-fashioned hand. He understood money as part of an important correspondence between the writer and the world—how it signified to the writer not only what you could use to live on, but how the world spoke when it acknowledged your work—and he showed, as he wrote out the amounts and inscribed your name, how he respected you and the money itself.

Often, a note, sometimes with a poem attached, came with the royalty check. I have a sheaf of spendid, pithy, funny letters from J, some accompanying those royalty checks. Even when he wrote to say that because of failing eyesight he would not be reading a new novel of mine I had sent, he referred to the "dimming" of his sight and then joked about whether it was not perhaps the dimming of his intellect. He promised that Gertrude—his wife, who had been his art director, and who had designed the jackets of so many of his authors' books, mine included—would read it for him. He talked self-deprecatingly about his long, autobiographical poem, saying that he'd started to write his autobiography in prose but found it—and this is typical of him—"so pompous and tiresome."

This final letter to which I refer was typed for him. But at the end, smaller than I recall it, and a little shaky perhaps, but indelibly etched over his name, is the letter *J.* In the world of letters, in the history of modern letters, in the lettered life he made possible for so many of us, and richer, and *better,* it is the most distinguished letter of all.

The Great War Exhibit and Symposium at the University of South Carolina, Columbia

This article was edited by Professor Patrick Scott and was excerpted from reports by University of South Carolina graduate students Park Bucker, Ellen Haggar, Brooke McLoughlin, Jason Pierce, Tom Powers, Todd Richardson, Aaron Shaheen, Staci Stone, Joanna Tapp, Jan Van Rosevelt, and Jason Vermillion.

From November 1997 through mid January 1998 the University of South Carolina's Thomas Cooper Library hosted a major loan exhibition on the Great War of 1914–1918. The exhibition was drawn from the Joseph M. Bruccoli Collection at the University of Virginia, with additional exhibits from Thomas Cooper Library's collections. On Armistice Day, Tuesday, 11 November 1997, a day-long symposium brought together British and American scholars to reexamine the historic and cultural legacy of the war. The exhibit attracted media interest and a steady stream of visitors right through to January, testifying to the imaginative hold the Great War still exerts on later generations.

The opening gathering on Monday evening, held in the hall of the Euphradian Literary Society, introduced both the collection that had inspired this event and the impact of the Great War at the university. In his welcome, Dr. George Terry, vice provost and dean of libraries and information systems, noted that eight Euphradian members had lost their lives in the war. Elizabeth Cassidy, assistant archivist, who had curated a special exhibit drawn from the university archives, sketched the lasting changes the war brought to students and faculty.

The Joseph M. Bruccoli Great War Collection

Also at the opening reception, Edmund C. Berkeley Jr. (University of Virginia) reported on the expansion of the Joseph M. Bruccoli Great War Collection since its founding in 1965. Joseph M. Bruccoli (1892?–1965) was a veteran of the Great War who served in eight major campaigns. He was severely wounded and was deeply patriotic. The col- lection was donated to the University of Virginia in his memory by his son Professor Matthew J. Bruc- coli. Berkeley described how the collection, initially focused on the fiction of war, now has over four thousand items, including "non-fiction, posters, sheet music, broadsides, manuscripts, ephemera, movies, photographs." The most recent addition has been the fifteen-hundred-item World War I col- lection formed by another Virginia alumnus, Dr. Charles E. Bailey, especially strong in contempo- rary pamphlets, reports, and official documents re- lating to the origins of the war.

The Exhibition

The main mezzanine exhibition drawn from the Bruccoli collection explored the story of the Great War in five segments. The first display island showed material about the outbreak of war in August 1914, recruiting and training, and the spirit of volunteer idealism. Items included glass lantern slides for war lectures, poems by Rupert Brooke and Julian Grenfell, and the marching song, *It's A Long Way to Tipperary*. A separate section had material about the Gallipoli landings in 1915, drawing on the collection's Australian holdings.

Island two featured first a group of books, col- lector cards, and toy blocks telling children about the war but gave most space to the actual development of trench warfare on the western front through books, maps, and photographs. Of especial note were the soldier's sketchbook from the Battle of Loos in 1915, the poster of John McCrae's poem "In Flanders Fields," (1915) and the programs for early movies about the battles of Ypres and the Somme.

Island three turned to the wartime experience of women and families during the war as women took over jobs in hospitals, munitions factories, and offices and as wives and parents coped with the news of death. Alongside the privately printed memorial editions of letters from the front were pictures from an album kept by a pub landlady with photos of her former customers now in uniform.

With island four the focus shifted to America's involvement in the war, first with Ivy League students driving ambulances and then, from 1917, with American military intervention on the side of the Allies. Here original sheet music for the songs *Over There* and *Oh, How I Hate to Get Up in the Morning!* was followed by Alan Seeger's poem "Rendezvous," battlefield photographs, guidebooks for American soldiers in Paris, and (in an adjacent upright case) the newspapers produced for the army in France. A separate case of material on the war in the air included jacketed copies of the photoplay editions for John Monk Saunders's *Wings* and *Dawn Patrol.*

Island five illustrated the legacy left by the Great War, in literary treatments such as *All Quiet on the Western Front* and *Journey's End,* in the formal remembrance of Armistice Day and the Unknown Soldier, and in the plight of unemployed veterans. The exhibit concluded with wartime memorabilia of Joseph M. Bruccoli and the corrected typescript for a statement about the war from the late James Dickey.

The main exhibition was supplemented by several smaller displays of other loan material and from the University of South Carolina's own collections. In the main lobby the university archives exhibit illustrated the local impact of the war. In the Graniteville Room the wall displays included the contemporary oil painting "The Recruit," by Margaret Law (1871–1956), showing an African American family's farewell to a departing soldier, loaned by Fred C. Holder, and original World War I posters loaned by Mr. Rex Sage. In the adjacent display cases were items about the war drawn from the Allen of Hurtwood Papers (on conscientious objection), the G. Ross Roy Collection (on Scottish war poetry), the Anthony P. Campanella Collection (on D'Annunzio and the war in Italy), and the Matthew J. and Arlyn Bruccoli Collection (on F. Scott Fitzgerald and the war). A catalogue describing all the exhibited materials has been issued by the University of South Carolina Libraries.

The Catalogue

In connection with the exhibition, and with private sponsorship, Thomas Cooper Library has published a catalogue of the South Carolina exhibition, *The Great War 1914–1918* (Columbia, S.C.: Thomas Cooper Library, 1997). In addition to listing the items displayed, the catalogue provides background on the aspects or events of the war that each item served to illustrate. There are brief essays on such topics as army pay scales, the machine gun, the Angel of Mons, safety razors, food policy, Thomas Cook's postwar tours of the battlefields, and much else, as well as capsule introductions to Great War writers. The catalogue as a whole forms a readable introduction both to the war itself and the range of the Joseph M. Bruccoli Collection. The cover illustrations of a trench near Loos and of an unemployed ex-serviceman's broadside poem are both from the Bruccoli collection.

The catalogue also prints details on the additional exhibit segments drawn from the University of South Carolina's own collections. The surprising depth of material on Scottish War poetry (pp. 39–44) and on F. Scott Fitzgerald's wartime experience (pp. 44–47) reflects two of the library's strengths: what other Great War library exhibition has shown not just Fitzgerald's writing about the war but also his army commission, his regimental collar-badge, and his stereopticon with glass slides of the western front? The segment on conscientious objection, while from a much smaller collection, lists and annotates printed ephemera apparently unavailable in any other North American library. The catalogue reflects the educational, visitor-friendly, museum-like quality of the exhibition, and it is also a useful reminder of unique research collections both at Virginia and at South Carolina.

Pre-symposium Discussion

Graduate-student participants prepared for the symposium itself with a preliminary debate on "Why the Great War matters now." Led by Mark Dollar and Andrew J. Kunka (both writing dissertations on war literature at Purdue University), students considered the relevance of the war to aesthetic theories, technological anxiety, and problems in defining postmodernism. Both in recent fiction and in literary scholarship the Great War has also become central to continuing debates for gender studies. For graduate students, Dollar and Kunka argued, it is through such current issues that the war retains its interest.

The Great War Symposium

On Tuesday morning, following a brief welcome by Professor Robert Newman (English Department chairman), the symposium's first session, with Patrick Scott (University of South Carolina) as chairman, explored changing American and Irish responses to what had started as a

"European" war. Professor Patrick Quinn (Nene University, U.K.) delivered the opening lecture on "The Conquering of America: German Invasion Novels of the Great War." Quinn described how, well before 1917, anti-German novels turned public opinion "in favor of military preparedness to confront the inevitable invasion of the dreaded Hun." Cleveland Moffett's *The Conquest of America* (1916) and Thomas Dixon's *The Fall of a Nation* (1916) used scare tactics to serve British propaganda purposes. In Moffett's novel Germans dynamite the Panama Canal and invade New York City, where the Kaiser's troops battle with Irish policemen, till after many defeats the Americans are rallied by the bravery of a Boy Scout pulling down a German flag and raising an American one. In Dixon's scenario Germany's defeat of Britain and the invasion of the United States lead to the revival of true American principles, turning female pacifists into ardent patriots. Both novels, gruesome in their detail of America's conquest, present a nation weakened by shortsighted politicians and foolish policies, yet both celebrate the strength and fighting spirit of the individual citizen. Despite a lone pro-German countereffort, pro-British writers overwhelmingly won the propaganda "war of words."

Two research presentations followed on the Irish response to the war. Mark Dollar (Purdue University) examined the role of the grotesque in Sean O'Casey's play *The Silver Tassie,* in his presentation "The Grotesque and the Great War in O'Casey's *The Silver Tassie,*" through the striking visual symbolism and "disjunctive impulses" of its haunting second act. James P. Haughey (Southern Wesleyan University) countered the "cultural preferentialism" of recent Irish critics of the soldier-poet Francis Ledwidge, aptly characterized as "our dead enigma." Haughey traced Ledwidge's shift from his initial defense of his enlistment against nationalist criticism to his increasing ambivalence about nationality and political allegiance. Ledwidge's war poetry, especially the late poem "Home," Haughey argued, expresses a "cultural codependence," combining nostalgia with a deep identity crisis.

The symposium's second morning session, "Recent Perspectives," chaired by Professor George L. Geckle (University of South Carolina), looked at the psychological and gender issues currently preoccupying much literary-critical discussion of the war. Jimmy Dean Smith (Newberry College) examined Siegfried Sassoon's "assault on motherhood." Sassoon depicted women as adhering to a defunct chivalric code that shut out any comprehension of the horrors of

modern warfare, part of his larger counterattack against several groups he accused of the blind encouragement of other people's sacrifice. Andrew Kunka (Purdue University) reported on his research into British shell-shock narratives. He contrasted two forms of rehabilitative treatment: Yealland's disciplinarist method, using electric-shock therapy to impose official values, and Rivers's psychoanalytic method, using one-on-one sessions to help patients reevaluate their experience to be acceptable in the military canon of heroism and achievement. The third presentation, "Modernism, Male Intimacy, and the Great War," by Sarah Cole (Ohio University), compared "comradeship" ("the ascendancy of group solidarity over individual preference") with "friendship" ("the privileging of individual intimacy"), using works by Hawkins, Nichols, and Sassoon to assert that, while the war "fostered comradeship as a replacement structure for nearly all civilian values and social forms, it relentlessly destroyed friendship." The fourth paper, read for Cheryl Mares (Sweetbriar College) by Staci L. Stone, examined the "ambiguities and complexities" in British novelist Pat Barker's recent Great War trilogy. In Mares's analysis Barker's trilogy epitomized many of the issues raised by earlier panelists, especially in depicting a "mystification of power relations" in Rivers's therapeutic relationship to Sassoon and Wilfred Owen at Craiglockhart Hospital.

The symposium's third session (chaired by Professor James Hardin, University of South Carolina) shifted focus toward more historical perspectives. Mark W. Van Wienen (Augustana College) explored African American experience in the Great War as represented in W. E. B. Du Bois's paper *The Crisis.* Du Bois called in 1918 for black Americans to "Close Ranks . . . shoulder to shoulder with our own white fellow citizens" while also depicting the war as fought by racist European powers. Some NAACP leaders wanted purer patriotism while many outside the leadership saw even Du Bois's conflicted icon of the black "martyr-soldier" as a "sell-out" to white America. Charles Bailey (Adirondack Community College) examined the process by which European Protestant theology, long German-dominated, was "torn asunder" by the German invasion of Belgium. French Protestants found an opportunity to prove their patriotism, while both French and English liberals could unite in condemning German war atrocities. Not until 1925 did rapprochement begin, with the Life and Work Conference in Stockholm. The third presentation,

Poster for the World War I Symposium and exhibition at the University of South Carolina

by David C. Dougherty (Loyola College, Maryland), charted the "triple dose of disillusionment" experienced by the American novelist John Dos Passos, who drew on service in France with the Norton-Harjes ambulance corps for such novels as *One Man's Initiation* and *Nineteen-nineteen*. Dougherty argued that, instead of battlefield gore, Dos Passos used satire against class injustice and dehumanizing bureaucracy to indict the war's challenge to individual autonomy.

Lectures by Peter Liddle and Hugh Cecil

The symposium culminated in major public lectures by two widely published British Great War

scholars, both from the University of Leeds. With Professor S. Paul Mackenzie (University of South Carolina) in the chair, the speakers described how firsthand research had altered their understanding of the war. Peter H. Liddle, the founder and keeper of the extensive Liddle Collection of First World War Archive Materials, took the title "Myths and Misunderstandings about Personal Experience in the First World War," presenting a corrective to simplistic literary-critical accounts based lopsidedly on Sassoon or Owen. The received account of senseless waste and bitter alienation was widely adopted, Liddle argued, not during the war itself but in the postwar world; Liddle recounted how, as a teacher thirty years ago, he had been moved by the memoirs of Great War participants and had "reorganized" his life to rescue their stories from oblivion. He offered "an abundance of evidence" from the resulting archive that both men and women spoke of the war as "a time more important than anything in their lives subsequently, a time when they had not put self first, . . . when they had felt called to put King, country and community" before their peacetime interests. "The men and women who experienced the First World War," Liddle concluded, "have . . . often been betrayed by their portrayal" in literature or academic commentary. Historians, too, would do well to consider less the retrospectives of writers and more the words and feelings of those who actually fought.

The second lecture, Hugh Cecil's "On the Track of Forgotten Great War Writers," also offered a correction to standard accounts. Cecil shared the excitement of discovery that underlay his 1995 study, *The Flower of Battle,* a quest for the now-unknown writers of World War I. In the book Cecil traced the war experience and postwar lives of twelve authors whose best-sellers reflected contemporary understanding of the war but who are on no modern reading list. Cecil wanted to put them back on the historical map. In his lecture he recounted his historical sleuthing of two of the twelve: Ronald Gurner, the schoolmaster-author of *Pass Guard at Ypres* (1930), "a brave, talented but ruined man" who killed himself in 1939; and Robert Keable, a former Anglo-Catholic priest whose shocker *Simon Called Peter* (1919) detailed a married padre's wartime affair with an army nurse. From his research, not just in the Bodleian or the Humanities Research Centre, but in school archives, government records, the *Dorking Advertiser,* the Cornish telephone book, and Tahiti, Cecil vividly evoked his aim, "to get closer to that generation and get a deeper understanding of their sensibilities." Unlike the canonical poets, these novelists were seldom guided in their interpretation by the national postwar mood; Cecil argued that instead they based their often positive image of the war "on what they had individually experienced" and that their varied reactions have "real value for the historian in showing how people felt and what people read about the War."

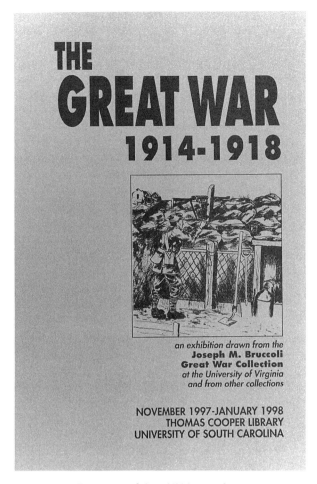

Front cover of the exhibition catalogue

recalled his father's participation in the Great War, recounted how the collection had been built, and concluded with F. Scott Fitzgerald's moving elegy on the war dead of Beaumont Hamel as the "last love battle," from *Tender Is the Night* (1934)—a passage also shown on the symposium keepsake poster. It was an appropriate ending, both in exemplifying the focus of the symposium on actual war experience and in conveying the excitement and impact of the loan items on display.

Conclusion and Exhibit Opening

Finally, the library's Thomas Cooper Society hosted a reception to mark the opening of the Great War exhibition. In his welcome, Dr. John Palms, president of the University of South Carolina, recalled the legacy of the war for his own birthplace in Holland. The last word, however, went to the donor of the University of Virginia collection, Professor Matthew J. Bruccoli, whose remarks

Excerpts from Matthew J. Bruccoli's Remarks at the Exhibit Opening

The Joseph M. Bruccoli Great War Collection was instituted because when I was a small boy my father took me to Armistice Day parades with his battle medal (Somme Defensive, Aisne, Montdidier-Noyon, Champagne-Marne, Aisne-Marne, Somme Offensive, Oise-Aisne, Defensive Sector)

pinned to my jacket. The Boss taught me these rules he had learned in France: "Always give to the Salvation Army. They were very good to the soldiers." And "Never light three cigarettes on a match." He fiercely loved America, and he was proud to have been severely wounded in the war.

Later I read the classic American and English novels of the war and developed an interest in less-than-classic aviation fiction: "You can't send that kid up in a crate like that!" When my father died in 1965, John Cook Wyllie–who had made me a bookman–encouraged me to build a World War I collection for the University of Virginia, where I had taken my graduate degree. My intention was to concentrate on fiction and the air war, using the books that I had already accumulated as the core.

I was not an amateur, having served my apprenticeship under Mr. Wyllie and in bookstores, and I had built notable collections of American authors. But I was unprepared for the stimulation and challenges of this new field. There was so much splendid material, particularly in Britain. My original narrow rationale had to be abandoned because it was impossible to leave many out-of-scope items that I found. Even so, I shamefully recall the things I stupidly declined. Trench diaries were abundant in the sixties; now they are virtually unprocurable.

There is a collecting rule that books are where you find them; they have no memory and can't tell you how they got to where you find them. Yet I was surprised to discover that once I started paying attention, Great War material was everywhere–not just in bookshops and often in the wrong shops. I don't mean to slight the British specialist booksellers whose catalogues provide irreplaceable reference tools: Paladour Books, Marrin and Sons, Charlotte Robinson, and Bertram Rota. But many of the most interesting finds came in American junk shops and what the Brits call jumble sales.

The Joseph M. Bruccoli Great War Collection provided my father's posthumous benefaction to me. I have learned so much from working on it, and it brought a new cadre of bibliographical friends–as always occurs when commencing work in a new field. All those trips to London may not have been mandatory, but I justified them by bringing back books for the collection. For years the London trips meant reunions with my cherished friend Jean Kennerley–daughter of General Sir Hugh Simpson-Baikie–who urged me to build a proper collection. Any excuse to see Freddie Zentner at the Cinema Bookshop is welcome. Sydney bookseller Nicholas Pounder donated superb Gallipoli material. Glenn Horowitz gave me more than he sold me. Charles Bailey shared in the acquisition of his extensive collection of material on the roots of the war.

After twenty-five years the Joseph M. Bruccoli Collection holds some four thousand items. Although there are smashing display items, it is a working collection for researchers. The collection cannot claim to be comprehensive because the subject is too large for one collector to embrace. But there are areas of strength, particularly literature. The Great War inspired moving fiction and verse. A generation of literary genius perished in the mud of France.

The Liddle Collection and First World War Research

Peter H. Liddle
University of Leeds

I am privileged to preside over the institutional development of what has in effect been a lifetime of academic work dedicated, as much as has been possible, to the rescue and interpretation principally of First but more recently of Second World War evidence of personal experience. In order to introduce you to the fruit of this work, undertaken over more than thirty years and now housed permanently in the Brotherton Library of the University of Leeds and bearing my name, I would like to focus, however briefly, on six aspects of the Liddle Collection.

First: what sort of material does it hold? Second: from what inspiration did the collection spring, and how has it been built up? Third: what is its particular character, and what are its strengths? Fourth: what does it tell us about British experience of the war? Fifth: whom does the collection serve? And sixth: what does it produce to give access from afar to its archival riches?

The material in the collection includes original letters and diaries; photographs; artwork; official papers; maps; newspapers; recollections in manuscript, typescript, and tape recording; elements of uniform; three-dimensional souvenirs; and, of course, books. There will be many items or series of items which at first thought might not be considered as included in such a list—sheet music and gramophone records, for example—but they are likely to be there. Well over six thousand men and women of the First World War are documented by one or more of the means indicated above, and there will be perhaps four thousand sound recordings (by interview) of their memories.

Every aspect of British personal experience is covered: soldiers, sailors, airmen, civilian workers, women in a whole range of war-related work, war resisters, and conscientious objectors. The collection is rich in Commonwealth experience, too, and useful for American, German, French, Belgian, and even Turkish experience. Choosing examples for a brief paper such as this one is easy, but it has to be said that on a different day a completely new list might be offered, and the well-informed independent observer browsing through the catalogues would almost certainly come up with his or her own list, including none of the names now to be mentioned: captain's clerk Keith Lawder's penciled notes made in the fighting top of a battleship during the battle of Jutland; Kenneth Brewster's heavy leather flying coat with its surprisingly insubstantial belt—the latter something which I had occasion to reflect upon when I listened, on the same day I collected it, to a former pilot, Hugo Ibbotson, explaining to me his problem when his flying coat caught fire and he could not get his belt undone to throw the coat off. Of other artifacts behind which there lay such stories, I am mindful of the diary and shell-fragment-damaged steel helmet of Gerald Brooks, a tank commander. He had evacuated his tank; he was then wounded in the head but kept his steel helmet and the diary into which he wrote an account of his experience.

Few artifacts as a pair, one for the First War and one for the Second, could match those associated with Charles Simpkin, a 1917 R.F.C. fitter who in 1940 was a civilian instructor, R.A.F.—a flying helmet belonging to the famous pilot ace Billy Bishop, and then the longbow made as a prototype on Air Ministry instructions in the spring of 1940 in the peril of a shortage of firearms against imminent threat of German invasion.

Returning to documentation by letter: could one better the emotional turbulence conveyed by this young officer's letter written in the immediate aftermath of the first days of the Third Battle of Ypres:

> Our three weeks away back from the line was not rest—it was hard detailed training for the coming battle. I entered into it very thoroughly and enjoyed it much. I quite felt fit for my allotted task when the time for the fight arrived.

> I am proud to say that this Brigade attained every objective exactly to the tick of each allotted time, that it gained more ground and took more prisoners than any other Brigade in the whole push. Moreover it never yielded a yard of ground despite withdrawals on right

and left. I think we are justly proud of ourselves and for a host of reasons I would not have missed it for anything. I am glad to have had a share in it—it was a great experience.

That puts the brighter side—the details are of heartbreaking fatigue, of stern physical hardships—of much toil, pain and death. But one is proud to think of the stoutheartedness and the grit and endurance shown.

By the end of the first day all objectives were taken and the hanging on process began. Unfortunately the rain began also and the next three days were a perfect nightmare. I went forward again on the 1st day to take charge of the guns in the line of resistance. Can you imagine anything more hopeless than having to hang on indefinitely to a waterlogged trench, without dugouts, without overcoats and without hot food of any description and *with* the Bosche shelling and the rain pouring at its worst? I think it was the worst experience I have had—in 48 hours everybody was about deadbeat, shivering all the time with the trenches ankle to waist deep in water.

There are many people associated in bringing potential donors to our attention, volunteers who collect and deliver such material, who tape-record men and women for us, who work on original papers to assist in cataloguing—students, men and women employed in all walks of life, and retired folk whose service is often exceptional for scholarship and enthusiasm.

From what inspiration and how has the collection been built up? More than three decades ago, as a schoolmaster stimulated by the fascination of history and attempting to implant this as a life-enhancing factor in my pupils, I used drama, mime, cookery, dance, singing, model-making, and, of course, facsimile original documents as teaching methods. In extending this approach, I began to explore memory and increasingly came to an awareness that memory represented an endangered area of our heritage. It was challenged by physical frailty and would be defeated by the oblivion of death. In a related way the artifacts associated with memory were always at the hazard of the dustbin through changed circumstance or loss of interest or identification. In fact, I had found what was to become the academic driving force in my life—a growing commitment to the rescue of evidence of personal experience in wartime.

This refocus was linked to career development but not, at that stage, the late 1960s, as a determinant. In a lectureship which evolved from teacher education into one with responsibility for war studies and international relations with the First World War as a special subject area, I found myself

additionally developing an archive, devising cataloguing and cross-referencing systems, widening my search for 1914–1918 veterans and then writing books to share with a wider community the evidence I was rescuing, setting it in an interpreted context. The story of the hurdles to be taken in the institutionalization of this growing archive is not for recounting here. Suffice it to say that it was achieved at the University of Leeds in northern England in 1988 with the establishment of the Liddle Collection in the University Library.

The building up of the collection from 1964 to 1987, and then from 1988 to date, has been through the commitment of countless hours with many people supportively involved. The pooling of inspirational ideas for reaching this or that group of men or women, mounting such an exhibition, and producing one or another article, book, tape, CD-ROM, or whatever, has been important in the work, but establishing contact with 1914–1918 and 1939–1945 men and women has been central. We have sought them as individuals and then in different "archival drives" as old comrades in the same unit or with kindred experience. By press and radio and also by letter after letter after letter we have been in pursuit of V.A.D. nurses, men in the Tank Corps, Socialist conscientious objectors, and now Battle of Britain pilots. Specialist gazetteers or magazines have been helpful in this, but I remember among the successes one hugely time-consuming campaign which was a conspicuous failure, an attempt to contact 1914–1918 dock workers, fishermen, and lifeboat men by publication of a letter in all of Britain's coastal newspapers.

The particular character and strength of the collection lies first in its comprehensive coverage of British experience with full representation, as has been indicated, of schoolchildren, women, workers, officers and men in the armed services with every front covered, and, as it happens, a particularly rich section on Friends' Ambulance Unit work and conscientious objection. Second is the unitary or integrated and not departmentalized method of cataloguing the holdings. By this means it is easy for us to make available if we were to have it the voice of a man, his uniform, his original letters, diaries, photographs, and written recollections, indeed everything which relates to his experience.

The third point to be made here is that in certain areas we have outstanding coverage. The Dardanelles/Gallipoli campaign is a good example, more than 900 men who have their papers or related material in the collection, and 450 of them tape-recorded too. Of the 34 conscientious objectors sentenced to death in June 1916 (but not in fact exe-

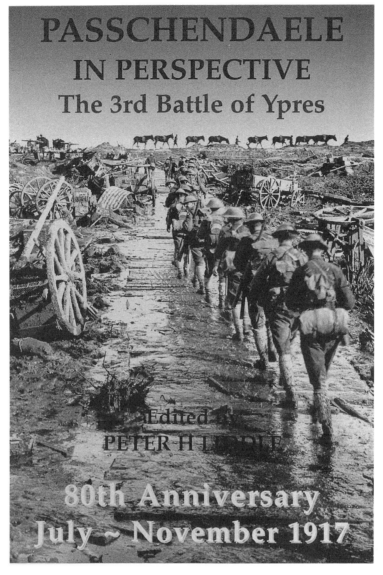

Poster for proceedings of the symposium at the University of Leeds

cuted), we have material for 8 or 9 of them, but there is too an exceptional body of documentation on the Mesopotamian campaign, on war hospital nursing, on certain R.F.C./R.N.A.S. squadrons, on Jutland, and on all the major battles for the British Expeditionary Force in France and Flanders.

The cataloguing and cross-referencing system is as distinctive a feature of the archive, however, as is the volume or the interest of the material. Topics such as sickness and health, entertainment, machine-gun tactics, vice and V.D., field punishment and courts-martial, the Battle of Loos, officer/man relations, these and many more are cross-referenced to help the researcher get directly into contemporary source material in specific areas. There is more

to this cross-referencing facility because an "attitudes and opinions" reference leads one directly to contemporary judgments, individual and subjective by definition, on, for example, the American troops, the French and Belgians, the Germans, striking munitions workers, the impact of war experience on a man's faith, and his political views, and a host of subjects.

What does research in this archive tell us about British experience in the war? I have written about this in books, and here I can only be brief. First, the trite unsubstantiated generalization will not do. It really is difficult to make soundly based overall judgments from single examples of subjective sources. I believe it can be reasonably stated, however, that the *Oh! What a Lovely War* or *Monocled Mutineer* perspective through which to judge a range of matters relating to command and service on the western front is thoroughly discredited. Much media-purveyed presentation of the reaction of Britons to their experience of war, especially soldiering on the western front, is woefully adrift, perhaps one ought to express it, willfully adrift, inappropriately tethered to the values of later generations. It seems proven by the rich evidence available that in general terms Britons responded resiliently to the prolonged stresses of the war. Even in the final years of the war, in every class of society, whatever evidence may be put forward of disaffection, it is swamped in significance numerically by that reflecting stern resolve.

Whom does the collection serve, and how does it help those who cannot come to research in its setting in the Brotherton Library of the University of Leeds? During any month in the collection, we will have students from the United States and the Commonwealth and from all over the U.K. There will be historians, authors, people with an interest in the two world wars, and media people. Theses, books, and radio and TV productions will all be advanced by research work carried out on the papers of men and women who lived through war experience.

Everything in the collection, including the tape recordings, is available for research consultation by appointment. An increasing percentage of the documentation can be examined through a microfilm reader. Researchers may use personal laptop computers, but it is not part of the service to offer photocopies. When photographs or documents in facsimile are requested for a publication, this can be arranged by discussion and on payment.

For those who cannot come to Leeds, there have been TV series and radio programs, CD-ROMs, videos, and tapes which may have provided some answers to general or specific questions, and may I recommend certain books that facilitate in fact a sort of inspection of the collection from afar. *The Worst Ordeal: Britons at Home and Abroad* (1994) is probably the best introduction to the collection as such; a serviceman's trilogy, *The Soldier's War 1914–18* (1988), *The Airman's War* (1987), and *The Sailor's War* (1985), would help, too. For those who would like to see personal experience material specifically dedicated to a particular battle, *The 1916 Battle of the Somme* (1992) and *Passchendaele in Perspective* (1997) are likely to be of assistance. Chapters in *Facing Armageddon* (1996) and *At the Eleventh Hour* (1998) might also be of interest.

Finally in this outline on the Liddle Collection, a few words on its next challenge. As would be expected we are well in advance in the development of a database, first on our Dardanelles/Gallipoli records, then on the Royal Navy. Progressively the whole collection will be entered on this database. (We are using "Idealist" Free Text to log both biographical and documentary data.) From the present to the future: it would be nice to concentrate on the collection's most attractive potential role as the core of a lottery-funded twentieth-century wartime family history museum in Leeds, but while the lengthy pathways toward this were being followed and the attendant problems tackled, what would be happening to the heritage of personal experience in the Second World War? The answer to that is that from Leeds there would consequentially be a diminished application of our endeavor toward the rescue of the threatened evidence of men and women who, in whatever capacity, lived through those years. It is our judgment that to lead or to inspire work in this area must be a higher priority than concentration upon the museum concept. We have in the last two years mounted drives to gather in Colditz, Arnhem, Bomber Command, Women's Service, and Battle of Britain experience. Time passes; the men and women of 1939–1945 are fading away from our reach. There is simply no time to lose. Of course there are problems of finance, archival space, and related resources, but the work must be done; it is infinitely worthwhile. No, that must be rephrased: it is totally compelling and calls us undeniably.

Interview with Norman Mailer

Kenneth Graham conducted this interview by phone on 23 June 1997, at the time of the publication of *The Gospel According to the Son*.

DLB: Mr. Mailer, you've been writing at least since you were twenty, perhaps earlier.

Mailer: I started at Harvard when I was seventeen.

DLB: I want to ask a question about the creative process. Do you think that your own creative process is something that you understand, or is it mostly a mystery to you?

Mailer: You know—I've thought about it, of course—it's analogous to a machine that you can drive without knowing how everything works in it. It's about equal to . . . you know how, when some kids learn to drive a car, they know the function of every last piece of the engine, and it's somebody just learning to drive a car? I belong to the second category when it comes to the creative instinct. I know what's bad for it; I know generally what's good for it; I know the disciplines I have to take on for each given book. They vary greatly. For instance, if you have a book that demands a huge amount of work, like *The Executioner's Song,* that's a different discipline than working on the last book, *The Gospel According to the Son,* and you work different hours as a result. But what I know always is the common denominators. There is always a specific discipline that you need for keeping on good terms with, let's say, what we call "the creative process."

DLB: Or the Muse, if we can personify it.

Mailer: Well, the Muse is really a poetic name for a process, and the only insight I have—although it might not be at all new—is that I think that we are not always on the best terms with our unconscious. There is the unconscious that prepares material when you're writing a novel. I can't speak for poets although I'm sure something of the same is true. In any event, if you are working on a novel day after day after day, it's as if, each night, the unconscious prepares the work for the following day, and you have to respect that unconscious work. If you tell yourself you are going to go to work on a given morning, unless you are really ill in the morning, you have to get up and go to work, even if you don't feel in the mood to do it.

DLB: So you obviously do find that your unconscious mind is primary and always has been in your work?

Mailer: My feeling is: don't get in the way of it, don't abuse it, don't play games with it. When I was younger, I'd have a good day at work, and I'd be so pleased with myself that I'd go out and get drunk that night, and then the next day I couldn't work. I started a lot of pieces I never finished, as a result, and I had a lot of trouble in writing. And over the years it sort of straightened out. I began to realize what my particular process was. I don't necessarily claim that it's that way for everyone. It's just very professional, that's all. It's not exciting, it's not glamorous. You show up for work every day.

DLB: Can you talk a little bit about *The Gospel According to the Son?* When you were in Columbia, you said that you did one draft, and then you did seven editings. Can you talk a little bit about the editing process, and specifically—

Mailer: The problem was one of, you see, I was trying to—I think they would understand what I was doing better if they—suppose I decided I wanted to rewrite *The Iliad* for the modern reader. Then I don't think there would be so much misunderstanding in the sense that, then, people wouldn't be that upset if I stayed very close to *The Iliad,* which is exactly what I was doing here. I wanted to stay very close to the story in the New Testament as one pieces it together from the synoptic Gospels. For that reason I wasn't interested in showing how much I could do in one direction or another. There are only three or four places in the book where I take a "flyer," so to speak, and those I felt were legitimate because, as is true of just about all Bible writing, it's very, very, very spare, and sometimes it's so spare that you're not sure exactly why

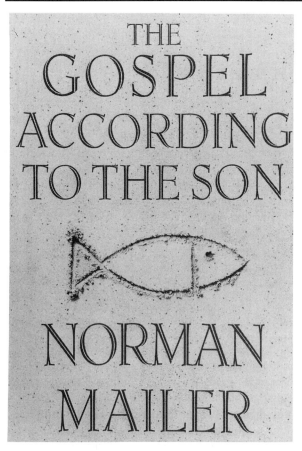

Dust jacket for Mailer's book of the New Testament as narrated by Jesus

one or another of the principals did something. I thought that was terribly true of Judas, that he needed some expansion. I thought it would be a help with Mary Magdalene and, of course, also with the Devil. I think those were the three places where I stepped out the most, if you will.

But generally I stayed pretty close to the Gospels. And because I did, the problem of writing it was not—you know, usually when you're writing, you have to find the continuation of your plot, and that can take an awfully long time. You can make terrible mistakes; you can have your protagonist go to the wrong country on a given day. You know you can make serious errors. You can have him or her get married, and then six months later you realize, no, no, no, they shouldn't have gotten married. And to tell you the truth, you may discover that you put them in interesting or uninteresting situations or that the situations you are putting them in do not express what you have in mind. So that makes it very tough.

But, since the story was there, it wasn't hard to write it. What then became important was, what style should be used? Because the first time I did it, I did it in a very biblical style, so it read almost like one more

Gospel. And then I thought, "No, it's too old-fashioned, and also people are going to question my right to write it in that form." And so I started simplifying it, but then it got terribly tricky because, in the act of simplifying it, you could flatten it terribly. So I kept working back and forth with simpler versions, more-complex versions, versus those closer to the Bible again. I probably took it through about seven editings before I felt, "This is about where I want it." And that took about a year and a half because I didn't work on it all the time. But you don't have to, with an editing. But I'd wait until it clicked in, and then I'd go back and edit it once more.

DLB: During that time when you were doing your editing, were you giving drafts to your editor, or to your wife, or to friends? Or is that editing pretty much, in its stages, a private process?

Mailer: No, this time it was. . . . I have a very good editor, Jason Epstein. Normally I don't like to work too closely with an editor, but Jason and I either agree or disagree. We disagree as often as we agree. He is a very good sounding board because his opinions are his opinions, and, you know, he's not afraid of me—put it that way. A young editor would say, "Gee, who am I? You know, he's been around all these years. I really shouldn't . . . I can't be convinced of my own opinion." Jason is always convinced of his own opinion. I often disagree with it. So it was very interesting. And always, finally, he'd say, "Oh, all right—you do what you want to do."

DLB: So it was during those seven editing stages that you were communicating with him, not at the end?

Mailer: Maybe three times, we went over it fairly seriously, and he'd look for changes, and invariably I didn't like his changes. But put it this way: essentially I did, I'd say, 95 percent of the editing.

DLB: On page 81 you were talking about Jesus and Matthew, whom you call Levi, one of the tax collectors who became a disciple. There is a passage that I was particularly intrigued by. Jesus says about Matthew, or about Levi, as you call him: "All the same, I had but one measure for a sinner. Was there some promise of happiness in this countenance? Even a man who cheated others . . . could reveal more of God to me than I would find in those who were sinless but downcast." I wonder if you could elaborate a little bit on the idea behind that passage?

Mailer: Well, one of the enigmas about Jesus is his great tolerance for sinners, and so I was trying to make that come real. I wouldn't put more into it than that. It doesn't represent . . . it would probably be in keeping with some of my own philosophy. There are very few of us who don't enjoy a rogue. You know, you don't have to trust someone completely to enjoy them. But I thought, in this situation, I felt what was very consistent in Jesus, even in the New Testament, where he isn't always that consistent, was that he really felt a certain animus against the pious. He felt they killed the spirit of God. And I happen to believe that, so it wasn't hard for me to come up with those thoughts.

DLB: One of the connotations I got out of that was the idea of humor. You used the word *merry* several times, and I thought it was engaging and intriguing to give Jesus a little bit more of a sense of joy, and perhaps a sense of humor, than one often finds in conceptions about him.

Mailer: Most of the people who teach young people about Jesus generally are fairly solemn, fairly serious. I felt that his ministry would never have worked at all if he didn't have a lively sense of paradox and humor. You know, if you're working that hard, you certainly want people around you who are merry.

DLB: I read an interview that you did with Christopher Hitchens in the *New Left Review* in March of this year. You were speaking about Salman Rushdie's experience of getting death threats because of his *Satanic Verses,* and you said that that "hit a nerve in every last writer."

Mailer: Well, it's what we start with. You know, a young writer . . . they're writing some things that are pretty far-reaching and pretty dangerous, and they expect a crowd to come to their door and knock the door down and beat them up. And then they learn that it is quite the opposite: no one ever pays attention to it.

DLB: That's what I wanted to get at. You went on to say, "but what you discover very quickly is no, nothing ever happens, you write books, you say powerful things, and then nobody ever knocks on your door and says, 'Hey, I've gotta talk to you, you're in trouble, you're going to bleed for this.'" So, did you think, in terms of *The Gospel According to the Son,* did you think that maybe somebody was going to knock on your door and say, "Mr. Mailer—you've really crossed the line here." Or, "You're going to bleed for this." Or did you not really think this book would stir up that kind of controversy?

Mailer: I felt that the odds had moved from one chance in a thousand to maybe one in one hundred. This is America, after all. I didn't feel that I was taking enormous chances. I felt the biggest chance I was taking was with my ego, which I knew was going to get some very, very bad reviews. One thing I knew about this book is that it's not the kind of book that's going to inspire a good many good reviews. It could have been twice as good as it is or half as good as it is: it still would have gotten the same kind of reviews. That I do feel. Mainly because, you know, you can't get a good review unless your book is read with a relatively relaxed mind, and the subject is so charged. Most people were going to approach it with preconceived notions. That you get used to. You get to the point where, as you get older, you just totally ignore reviews in every way except how they affect your income. People always think that books are better or worse than you think they are. And the same is true for what the reviewers do. Books are always better or worse than the reviewers think they are. So you just shrug. It's a way to keep going that's comfortable.

DLB: I think that [Rainer Maria] Rilke said in one of his letters that criticism is one of the hardest things, that the critics almost never touch the real parts of a work of art that you wish they would discuss, that somehow criticism, by its very nature, has a kind of a built-in limitation that is not very—I'm grossly overgeneralizing, but. . . .

Mailer: It's one of the few things that doesn't change. Actually, I had about three reviews on this book that came very close to what I felt were the virtues and faults of the book, where I learned something, too, because they pushed a little further. I liked Frank Kermode's review very much, although it was quite critical in places, because I learned something from it. I think I can say the same for Reynolds Price's review. And I liked a review—by someone whose name I don't know—very much in *Publishers Weekly* because it was three paragraphs: the first paragraph told about everything that was good in the book; the second paragraph was particularly severe, talked about everything that was bad in the book; the third paragraph came back and talked about what was finally very good in the book. I happened to agree with it. What it said, in effect, was that the parts that concerned Jesus as a man were—I won't repeat his praise, but it was high praise—but that the divine side of Jesus was not really achieved. And I thought, "Well, that is probably true." Actually, they're reprinting it on the back of the book now on the later printings—the entire review, unexpurgated, which has not been done in a number of years.

DLB: Where did Frank Kermode review your book?

Mailer: That was in the *New York Review of Books.*

DLB: I saw Reynolds Price's, but I didn't see Frank Kermode's.

Mailer: Yeah, that was in the *Sunday Times.*

DLB: I'd like to read Frank Kermode's, knowing that you had that kind of respect for it.

Mailer: Well, I think he may be the best critic alive writing in the English language.

DLB: Next year they're going to mark the fiftieth anniversary of the publication of *The Naked and the Dead.*

Mailer: Yes, it was in May '48.

DLB: So you've been on the literary scene for almost five decades now. Could you talk about what you think might be the most dramatic change you've seen in that time in terms of who the American writer is, or how he or she is received by the public?

Mailer: All right, I think I can answer that. I don't have a happy answer. Fifty years ago, when I started, those of us who wanted to be writers, major writers—you had that thought in your mind: I want to be a major writer—looked upon it as the happiest, highest achievement one could ever look for in one's life. The most depressing aspect of these fifty years is the way serious writing is just simply not taken as seriously now by the general public as it was then. There was a period back then when a new book, let's say, came out by Thomas Wolfe. The numbers were always smaller then, all over the place, because people had less money, but nonetheless—of course, the books cost a good deal less, too—but, you know, the people who wanted to read Wolfe would . . . you might have half the sales of the book come on the first day. The only small example of that that I have seen in our time is probably the reactions to [Thomas] Pynchon's new book, where a great many people immediately went out and bought it because they were waiting for a new Pynchon.

But, generally speaking, we have our constituencies, but it's just not the way it used to be. And my feeling is that, in another twenty years, if things go on as they have been (which is always dubious—usually things don't go on as they have been—but if they do), I think the average best-seller is going to be written by

computer. If a computer can play a great chess game, there is no reason why it can't write the average best-seller. Those writers who are serious are going to end up the equal of serious poets—which is, they won't try to make a living from writing serious novels; they'll do it because that has become their vocation. So in that sense I'm not too sanguine about the possibilities of the novel.

Also, there's the fact that we're getting so complex. In other words, you have to be an expert on so many matters, that it's harder to write a big novel now. You know, you couldn't do what [John] Dos Passos did back in the 1930s when he wrote his masterpiece, *U.S.A.,* because there are too many experts around who would know that you are weak on this subject, weak on that subject. It takes a long time to become cognizant of a subject now.

DLB: Would you still consider *U.S.A.* one of the major works of, say, the first half of this century in American literature?

Mailer: Well, it certainly was for me. I haven't re-read it in decades, so I might like it less, but then again, I might like it more.

DLB: But it did have a profound impact on you?

Mailer: Oh, absolutely—a tremendous impact.

DLB: I'm surprised more people don't know about it.

Mailer: Well, it takes so much time reading it! (laughs) That's the awful part of it. Everybody says, "Well, I got my options. I don't want to lose too many of them reading a long book."

DLB: Well, I did want to say, on a personal note, I did enjoy *The Gospel According to the Son.* I had underlined several passages in it. One of them, and I won't even ask you to elaborate, but I just had to tell you, even by phone, that I thought it was a remarkable statement when Jesus is with the Devil, before they actually begin their conversation, Jesus describes the Devil . . . or he says, "The Devil is the most beautiful creature that God ever made." I thought that was rather startling.

Mailer: You know, I wish I could take credit for that, but there credit must go to Paul Carroll, the poet, who said that to me about thirty years ago, and I never forgot it. And I've used it several times since in different books, in one way or another. I think it is a fundamental concept.

Oral History Interview with Donald S. Klopfer

Oral History Research Office
Columbia University

Interview conducted by Louis Sheaffer at Random House, New York City, 14 February 1975.

Q: This is an interview with Donald S. Klopfer, cofounder of Random House with Bennett Cerf. Mr. Klopfer is now Chairman of the Board at Random House.

Let's start with your childhood. In what part of the city were you born?

Klopfer: Well, my family had just moved from Syracuse to New York. My mother was pregnant with me, and I was born on the island of Manhattan, up near I think 117th Street between Lenox and Seventh Avenue.

Q: Oh, that's not too far from where. . . .

Klopfer: Bennett was born. That was a middle-class Jewish area, completely—on the same block where my family lived for a few years was Sigmund Freud's sister, Mrs. Bernays, Edward Bernays's mother, the public-relations fellow.

Q: What did your father do?

Klopfer: My father was in the shirtwaist business, and very unsuccessful.

Q: Nothing bookish there?

Klopfer: Nothing bookish whatsoever.

Q: Was your mother a great reader?

Klopfer: No, no, they were just normal readers. My father died when I was ten years old, and my mother then married a very old sweetheart from Syracuse who'd never gotten married. My father had gone into bankruptcy before he died, and we were really hard up.

Q: You must have been a great reader as a child.

Klopfer: I did read a lot. I read out of the public library at Sixty-ninth Street and Tenth Avenue. We lived on Seventy-fourth and West End at that time, and I was an omnivorous reader. I guess I read everything—G. A. Henty, Ralph Barbour, that sort of thing, and then went on to reading better stuff.

Q: You must have been pretty bright if you graduated from Williams at age eighteen.

Klopfer: I didn't graduate from Williams. I quit Williams. I quit Williams in my sophomore year. But I was reasonably—I graduated De Witt Clinton when I was about fourteen or something. I went to Andover for a year, before I went to Williams.

Q: Why did you drop out?

Klopfer: Oh, well. . . .

Q: If I ask improper questions, you can just say. . . .

Klopfer: There's nothing I don't want to answer, that's nonsense. I had the idea that I might want to be an engineer. Don't ask me why. I can't imagine my being an engineer. But I was doing very well in college. I probably would have been graduated in three or three and a half years. I was taking extra courses and it was all very easy, actually. College was easy in those days, you know.

My stepfather, who was a fine man, said, "Well, fine, if you want to do that then transfer to Yale Shef."

I said no, I wanted to be graduated from Williams, and then I wanted to go to MIT. And he said no soap. And I got mad and said, "Oh well, hell, I've had enough of college anyway, I'll come to work for you then," which I did. I think he was very pleased, frankly, that I did. Maybe it was lucky too.

Q: That's United Diamond.

Klopfer: United Diamond Works.

Q: Just what was that?

Klopfer: United Diamond Works was owned by two wholesale diamond merchants, Jacobson brothers—my stepfather was a partner in Jacobson Brothers—and Eichberg and Company. His name was Emanuel Jacobson. They conceived the idea some years before I moved in there of buying rough stones from the syndicate in London and doing their cutting and polishing over here, instead of just importing cut and polished stones from Antwerp and Amsterdam. So they set up United Diamond Works, which was a cutting and polishing plant, in Newark, New Jersey. I had to get over there at eight o'clock in the morning from Seventy-fourth Street and West End, and I didn't like that at all. But I did it.

Q: You did it for four years.

Klopfer: I did it for four years, that's right. And during that time, I had a couple of trips to England with my cousin Henry Jacobson, to teach me how to buy rough and procedures and what to look for and that sort of thing. He was breaking me into the business. And it was during that trip I bought my first first edition. I got interested. I was a great Conrad fan, and I bought probably what is the worst first edition of Conrad that's ever been sold, which I still have.

I gradually became interested in books, in collecting books, not just reading books. I have now accumulated what I think is a very fine small library. I have a very good Conrad collection. I have a really fine collection of press books, with all the really important ones in there: a lot of Ashenden, the Kelmscott *Chaucer,* the Doves Press *Bible,* and almost all of the Nonesuch Press.

Q: So you take both a sensuous and intellectual interest.

Klopfer: Exactly. I'm not a scholar—the intellectual thing is less than that. But I do like lovely books. Well, you get little hobbies like that and they influence your life.

Q: The *New Yorker* profile on Bennett said that you were his best friend.

Klopfer: I guess I was by the time we went into business together.

Q: How did you first meet?

Klopfer: Well, I met him around New York, when I just was graduated from Andover, 1918. And we were both taking out the same girl, and we got to be quite good friends, went to a couple of concerts together. He was four years older than I was, so there was some difference there. And the more we saw of each other, the better we liked each other. We went away together, summer vacations together and that sort of thing.

Q: He also loved books, I know.

Klopfer: Yes. Yes, we had similar tastes, the sensuous part, not so much in the literary part. But yes, we both did like them very much. Our interests were identical. The girl was one, you know. And actually what happened was that we started traveling in a whole social group. You must remember that in New York at that time there were various and sundry social groups which really don't exist anymore, amazingly enough.

Q: New York was a community of small villages.

Klopfer: Exactly. And Bennett and I were in the same community at that time. That's really how we first met, and then I went to work over in Newark—but it was quite good. I had no objection to that. Bennett and I, as a matter of fact, during the depression of 1921, worked down at the same Wall Street firm. Bennett got me a job there, so for about eight months we worked in the same back office of Sartorius, Smith and Loewi, and we got to be closer and closer friends, and. . . .

Q: Did you ever talk about going into publishing?

Klopfer: Not at that time, we never had. But then he got the opportunity of buying an interest in Boni and Liveright, and so he left Sartorius, Smith and Loewi. In the meantime, I'd gone back to the diamond business. They reopened the factory after the depression ended in 1922, and I went back to work there, and Bennett was at Boni and Liveright. So I used to see quite a bit of the shenanigans around Boni and Liveright, and believe me, there were shenanigans.

Q: I saw Anita Loos lately, who was a Horace Liveright author, and she said the place was just a regular house of assignation.

Klopfer: It was the damnedest thing. They spent more money for liquor in that place, I think, than they did for books. It was incredible. And what a marvelous list Horace had in 1925, the year we went into business. If you look at that list, that was by far, by far, the best list of any publishing list, including all the old-line houses, in the United States. It was an incredible group of people to come out of there.

Q: I heard that on *Gentlemen Prefer Blondes,* the production staff did not figure out the right cost, so that each copy that was sold cost Horace, instead of bringing him in money.

Klopfer: Could well have been.

Q: How did Horace strike you?

Klopfer: Oh, Horace was an incredibly attractive man. He fancied himself as another John Barrymore, something like that. He did look a little like him, too. And he was an extremely generous, extremely attractive man who had absolutely no character at all. He had no integrity whatsoever. And you got that feeling quite quickly, because I did not know Horace well. I knew him through Bennett. I met him when I was up at Boni and Liveright on Forty-eighth Street, seeing Bennett. But Horace was strange, generous, a very good publisher, actually. He never would have gone broke if he'd had any business ability whatsoever.

Q: If he'd stayed out of the stock market and the theatre.

Klopfer: And the theatre. I think the theatre. Yes, well, you see, Horace was a great operator, and then he was befriended to a certain extent by Otto Kahn, who did him nothing but harm, no good whatsoever. I suspect he lost money for him on the stock market, and he certainly murdered him by getting him into the theatre.

Q: Somebody said that if he had not sold the Modern Library, he could have weathered it.

Klopfer: He couldn't have, even though the Modern Library was very successful when Bennett and I took it over. He couldn't have weathered it, because he would just have thrown away more money. He had the seeds of his own destruction planted I guess at birth. I don't know, but they certainly were there, even with that brilliant list of

Bennett Cerf and Donald Klopfer at the time they formed their partnership to acquire the Modern Library

1925, the mid-Twenties. It wasn't just one list. He had a lot of them.

He was a man without integrity. Vain. A charlatan, to a certain extent. I don't know whether he ever read a book or not. I had the feeling he didn't, but I couldn't quite believe it, you know. But he had a feel—he had . . .

Q: As if he could smell a. . . .

Klopfer: That's the way it appeared to people, because everybody was convinced he couldn't read. Or he wouldn't read.

Q: When Bennett first approached you about buying—what was your. . . .

Klopfer: This was fantastic, because there I was, with a one-sixth interest in a diamond cutting and polishing plant. My stepfather had died and left me that one-sixth interest, which was his interest in it. Jacobson Brothers and Eichberg and Company decided what they were going to pay the United Diamond Works for their product. There was no formula for it. They owned the whole darned thing, and if they wanted to make money in the United Diamond Works, they paid them a little more. If they wanted to make money in their own firms, they paid less. Nobody had ever envisioned an outsider like myself owning any part of that factory.

So it was a pretty bad position to be in anyway. And then, my stepfather died. His older brother, whom I liked, died, and his younger brother was the boss man of the thing. It was rather written that I couldn't see very much future for me. His son Henry was running it, and it had a perfectly decent future, but I couldn't see making any great money over there, because why should United make it? All the money they made would be made for Jacobson Brothers.

So then Bennett struck up this deal with Horace, to buy the Modern Library. He told me he was going to try to get it, and succeeded in getting Horace's handshake, which was just as good as a written document, I assure you of that. That much—he had too much pride not to. . . .

He called me up and said, "Hey, I haven't got enough money to buy this thing myself. Can you raise money, and how about going into business together?" Which was the first time we ever seriously talked about anything like that.

I said, "Well, I haven't got a dime, unless I can sell my interest in United Diamond Works."

Bennett was going off to Europe, and I said, "All right, I'd like to do it, if I can, by the time you come back"—I think he was gone three weeks—"by the time you come back, I'll have a yes or a no for you."

So then I had to work through a quite good friend of my stepfather's who was in the pearl business, an allied business. I said, "What will I do?" He said, "Well, why don't you sell your interest there, go to Jacobson and Eichberg and say that you're unhappy and you want to get out. You have an opportunity of going into business for yourself some way or other. See what happens."

Well, the net result of quite a bit of palavering was that I sold my interest for 80 percent of the book value, and the book value was represented by U.S. Treasury Certificates at that moment. But I got enough money out to buy my. . . .

Q: How much money did you get, could you say?

Klopfer: Oh, sure—$100,000. Bennett and I put $200,000 in to purchase the Modern Library.

Q: He got some from an uncle of his, Herbert Wise.

Klopfer: Bennett had inherited a little more than $125,000, yes. He had the money—but that was the money to buy it—but we didn't have any money to run the business, so Herbert Wise loaned us—I remember very well—five hundred shares of Norfolk and Western stock, which was worth a great deal of money at that time, which was put up as collateral for a $50,000 bank loan, which we paid off in two years, we never called it—but he supplied the working capital for the Modern Library to start. He was a

very rich man at that time, and it didn't make any difference to him. It was awfully nice of him.

And that's the way we started. It was fantastic. We both worked very hard.

Q: I think it was you and Bennett and three secretaries and two shipping clerks.

Klopfer: There was Bennett and myself, and a bookkeeper, Emanuel Harper, who just retired a couple of years ago, a secretary, Helen Berlin, one other girl—I don't remember who it was—and two shipping clerks. Then we had an office about twice the size of this room, and a partition down the center, and all the books were on that side. We had two offices. Bennett and I shared an office, until after World War II, actually, with desks facing each other. Bennett and I shared an office, and the three of them were out in the other office. It was at 72 West Forty-fifth Street, which has now been torn down. It was a loft building. And it was great. We did everything. A small business. It was fun.

Q: The books of the beginning Modern Library smelled a bit —the imitation leather.

Klopfer: The imitation leather and the heat—the castor oil in it would get rancid, and they stank to high heaven. Awful. But we changed that very quickly because of this experience, having them right next to us.

I remember, we bought that imitation leather from the L. E. Carpenter & Company who still are in business on Fifty-eighth Street, still selling imitation leather—which doesn't smell anymore; they've really perfected it. But we just had a ball, working together, because we were splitting everything. We split the selling. One trip I would go north from New York with a bag of books, to Stamford, New Haven, New London, Providence, Boston, up as far as Portland, Maine, into Worcester and Northampton to get the Smith College trade, Springfield. . . .

Q: You and Bennett were the salesmen those first years?

Klopfer: On the East Coast, yes. Sure. Then he would go south. Next time I would go south and he would go north. We went as far as Richmond. From Richmond to Portland.

Q: How long did the two of you go out selling?

Klopfer: Selling? Oh, I would say, ten years. We did it for a long time. First of all, both of us enjoyed it.

Q: Well, to work at what you love. . . .

Klopfer: That's the whole thing. Of course it is. There's why my business career has been a ball. It's been absolutely wonderful.

And I know Bennett felt exactly the same way about it, although he attained so many outside interests, after World War II, that his loyalties were split a little bit. But publishing was the thing he really cared about.

Q: Did you ever have any desire to write as a child?

Klopfer: No. I write very badly. I bore the hell out of myself when I read what I write. That's all I can say. I really never have had any desire to, beyond writing an occasional. . . .

Q: I thought all critics were supposed to be frustrated writers so I thought maybe all publishers are frustrated. . . .

Klopfer: No. Never, I am (a) not sufficiently creative and (b) I cannot write well enough. My style is dreary.

Q: When the Depression struck, it eliminated the limited deluxe edition.

Klopfer: Yes, that was finished. That was great while it was going on too.

Q: You had a twenty-five-dollar *Adventures of Tom Sawyer,* and a Rockwell Kent *Candide.*

Klopfer: The Rockwell Kent *Candide.* We will reissue next August 1ˢᵗ a facsimile edition of it, to celebrate our 50ᵗʰ–for fifteen dollars. It's just a facsimile edition. There's nothing creative in it. Yes, but the Rockwell Kent *Candide* today, which we sold I think for twenty dollars. . . . It sells for forty or fifty dollars in the rare-book market, if you go around town and look, so I'm very pleased with that. That was the first book that bore the Random House trademark, published in 1928.

Q: The illustrations. . . ?

Klopfer: Rockwell? Oh, he was a good book illustrator. Then we did a trade edition of the big

Moby-Dick for the Lakeside Press. The first really big book that we did came out–I guess it was supposed to come out in early '29. It came out I guess either in late '30 or early '31, which was a $100 *Leaves of Grass,* which Ed Grabhorn of San Francisco printed for us, with Valenti Angelo illustrations, and there were four hundred copies at $100.

Q: That was your most expensive book.

Klopfer: That was the most expensive book we did, and believe me, we were very lucky to get rid of it by 1930 or '31. We had it oversubscribed three or four times, and we found ourselves with cancellations all along the line. But we did sell them all out. We never remaindered that.

Q: Did the Depression at any time threaten the firm?

Klopfer: No. It never did. This was interesting. Of course, we had the cheapest book in the market at that time. Don't forget, there were no paperbacks, and the ninety-five-cent Modern Library was an inexpensive book, and we went ahead every single year during the Depression. I don't mean we made a hell of a lot of money, but there was never a year that we didn't go ahead of the preceding year, with only that one thing too. And then in the Thirties, around '33, we began to go into general publishing, having had to give up the limited editions.

Q: It was '33 that you started with O'Neill.

Klopfer: That's when we started in the trade-book publishing. We started with O'Neill and Robinson Jeffers. Those two people. Then that same year or early the next year, we did the one thing that got us big publicity–the *Ulysses* case. That was, I think, the turnaround for us. It got us recognized as publishers, don't forget.

We always have done that. Right now, we're going to the Supreme Court with this Marchetti case, you know–that the CIA precensored. We threw everything as a last resort into the Supreme Court now. By God, we're going to do it.

Q: Do you remember how you came to the decision about *Ulysses,* about fighting it? Was this your idea?

Klopfer: No, it was joint. Nobody came along with a brilliant idea at the time. But both of us actually had met Joyce in Paris. I don't mean we knew him well, but we'd met him, and as the reputation of the book kept getting bigger and bigger, it seemed to us more and more disgraceful that this book shouldn't be published over here.

So Bennett wrote to–either wrote to, or once when he was over there I think said to Mr. Joyce that he'd pay him $1,500, nonreturnable, if we could fight the case. And if we won, we could have sole rights to publish. Joyce was absolutely delirious with joy, I assure you, and always was–well, I won't say was grateful, but he was very pleased with the whole relationship, with the whole way it was handled.

It was hilariously funny, actually, the case was–first of all, to get the Customs people to seize the book. Everybody was smuggling them in, you know, at that time. And we had one copy brought in, and we insisted on the–Morris Ernst and Bennett and I don't know how many people went down, when this man came through, and insisted that the Customs man seize–he wanted to put it through. It was a hot day, he didn't give a damn if they were bringing a copy of *Ulysses* in, you know. But we had a tough time getting this. And of course once they seized it, it was a case of the government of the United States against one copy of *Ulysses,* which we defended. It was a wonderful case.

Q: Well, you had a perfect judge, Woolsey.

Klopfer: Oh–and did we work to get that judge, too. Morris Ernst worked to get that judge. Sure. We didn't do anything, our lawyer did. Worked to get that judge.

But it was a very thrilling experience for me, who was reasonably young at that time, to go down to the courtroom. The trial was in June of 1933, in the Bar Association Building, which has a big oval room, very nice-looking room, and you come into a courtroom, and the judge saying, "It's hotter'n hell in here, gentlemen, take off your jackets if you like and smoke."

He got up on the dais, and there was Morris Ernst and his assistant, the U.S. attorney and his assistant. The only spectators were Bennett and myself. And we sat there all day long, and it was the only time–I've served on juries religiously and regularly, because I believe in it, to my seventieth year–the only time I've ever seen a judge really try to do justice and find out what the whole thing was about.

It was like a three-cornered conversation, with the judge, Morris, and the U.S. attorney. There were no objections. There was no trying to stop anybody talking. The judge asked just as many questions as they asked of each other. They talked. They

talked and had this three-cornered conversation, with a break for lunch, until about four o'clock in the afternoon.

And the judge said, "Gentlemen, you have anything more to say?" He gave them all the chance in the world. They said, "No." He said, "All right, then I'll read the book over the summer. You'll have my opinion in September."

Q: This was not a jury trial?

Klopfer: No. It was before Judge Woolsey, that's all. And it was really very encouraging, about the courts of the city.

It's a beautiful decision. That's a well-written decision, too. Of course, we put it in the book. It was in the public domain, so we could. All judicial decisions are. We used it in the introduction, not just because we thought it was such a good work of literature, but because any time any other state did anything about the book, it was in evidence at all times. You know, they couldn't not have it in evidence.

It worked out extremely well. Also, I have another funny little story to say about that. When we published the book, it was at a price of $3.50, as I remember, and we sent a complimentary copy to Judge Woolsey. It was his decision, after all. He sent it back to us. He didn't think it would be proper to take it. That's something.

A man like that was a great man. There were a lot of judges like that. Learned Hand, Gus Hand were cut out of the same cloth, too.

Q: I guess you would say that *Ulysses* was the house's finest hour.

Klopfer: I think so, yes. I think probably in the whole publishing career, the finest hour.

Q: This set a precedent.

Klopfer: It started–every porno shop on Forty-second Street derives from that!

As I say, all of a sudden, the name of Random House was known. Up 'til that time, what did we do? We distributed Frances Meynell's Nonesuch Press and any number of presses.

Q: Random House had glamour.

Klopfer: Well, that's true–of course, Bennett was influential. Bennett was a great public-relations man, you know. For a publishing house.

Q: What was the division of labor between the two of you?

Klopfer: Bennett took care of all publicity and advertising. I hate publicity and advertising. I took care of all the manufacturing and most of the office routine, office work, too. We split the editorial. Both of us did that and constantly consulted with each other.

Q: You were both in touch with authors.

Klopfer: Oh yes, we were both in touch with authors all the time. As I say, we split the editorial. Roughly it went that way: the advertising and publicity went to him, and the selling we both did ourselves, and both really supervised ourselves as we began to get a sales force together, until about 1936 or '37 when we got Lew Miller to come in to take care of the whole sales thing. Then we never paid any attention to selling, except to go out and sell ourselves sometimes.

Q: How many salesmen do you have today, would you say?

Klopfer: We have four completely separate sales forces. We have the trade sales force, which is what we had then, which represents Knopf, Pantheon, Modern Library. We have the college sales force. We have an el-high (elementary and high school) sales force, and we have the mass-market paperbacks, Ballantine, sales force. So I would say that we probably have one hundred people on the sales force today. I'm guessing at that. I could give you exact figures if they're ever important.

Q: Also you did books like, in 1933, John Strachey's *The Theory and Practice of Communism.* That took some courage too, didn't it?

Klopfer: Oh, not really. It doesn't take courage to publish books in this country. You're allowed to do it. And this is the great thing about the publishing industry—book publishing only, I'm talking about. There isn't a pressure. That's why we fight so hard against the C.I.A. on one book which is of no importance. But there's no pressure, there's no governmental pressure. There are no advertisers or businesses getting on your neck.

TV and newspapers are dependent on advertising, magazines are dependent on advertising, God knows TV is dependent on advertising. We are not dependent on that at all. That's why we're the last place where ideas can be handled back and forth.

And it doesn't take a lot of courage. People think it does, but it really doesn't.

Q: It might have taken a bit of courage, the Strachey book.

Klopfer: Oh no. John was a good friend of mine. I sat with John on Ellis Island when they didn't want to let him come into the country, for moral terpitude or something—I don't remember. He was held there for three days. I went out three days in a row. I went to Ellis Island just to keep him company, then took him down to my farm in New Jersey for the weekend to rest him up. We were friends until John died.

Q: You've seen great changes in publishing.

Klopfer: Enormous. Enormous changes. Look at Random House. Our first year, 1926, our volume on Modern Library, which was the only thing we had, was $256,000. We made a little money on that, too. Bennett and I never took big salaries. We never milked the business at all. We made the big killing when we sold it, but we never milked it.

Our volume—this is the same firm, after all, because Random House was started because we couldn't use the name Modern Library with press books. That was a ninety-five-cent item. And we had to have another name. So we took the name of Random House, which was Bennett's idea, incidentally. Well, this year we'll do over $100 million. Same firm. But the business has no relationship to the original business that we were in.

There's the Modern Library over on those shelves, over there, and it's almost finished, being phased out, because of paperbacks—perfectly sound, just as it should be. I regret it because I love it. After all, it's my baby. But the so-called egghead paperback has put us out of business. So we have our own. We have the Vintage line, which I think is the largest class paperback line in the country, and we're putting our Faulkner titles into paperback. We find out to our astonishment that for exactly the same price, we sell about eight times as many in paper as we do in that nice clothbound book. Because the fashion has changed, that's all. Young people aren't interested in clothbound books. Colleges, students of all sorts. There's been a fabulous change there, and then of course the enormous change with the mass-market paperback has been the greatest thing for publishing that we could have.

Q: I remember when they were twenty-five cents, the Pocket Books.

Klopfer: That was the original conception of it. It would be mysteries or Westerns and things like that, and they were all fairly short books, the quarter book. When Bob DeGraff started in with them, the Pocket Books—that's what it was. Now, it's a fabulous thriving industry that I think has done nothing but good.

It's done nothing but good for the whole industry because—you only realize it when you realize that your backlist is now going into paper—where you'd sell four hundred copies at $7.50 apiece, something like that, really first-rate books. Now you sell four thousand, at $1.95 or $2.45. They're not cheap either. But that means that they are getting around much more than they did before. Those four hundred are probably in the libraries anyway.

I think the mass-market paperback has been enormously important, for all of us, enormously helpful for all of us, because I assure you there are many more book readers now than there were twenty-five years ago. Absolutely sure. Of course, the war helped that, too. Those that Council for Books in Wartime put out—those Armed Services Editions—gee, they went out by the millions, to kids who never thought of a book before.

Q: When did Saxe Commins come in?

Klopfer: Saxe Commins came in with Gene O'Neill. He and Gene were very close friends, and he was Gene's editor. Gene would never have come to us if we hadn't taken Saxe, and Gene did us the biggest favor in the world. But he insisted on that. Saxe Commins dominated our editorial policy and everything about the editorial department until after World War II. He was very good, and, God, loyal and conscientious—had real integrity, too. He adored literature. He revered it. He was great, just great.

Q: You had some contact with the O'Neills, didn't you?

Klopfer: Oh, yes. I know Gene. Not well. I knew Carlotta, also not well, but I had some contact with her. Of course, I sort of worshipped at Gene's feet. I mean, after all, what the hell, he was the only first-rate playwright this country's ever developed, you know. And it's just being recognized now, especially in the last five years, I think.

Q: Since *Long Day's Journey into Night.*

Klopfer: That's right. That's right. So maybe Carlotta was right to release it. I just wish to hell we'd done *Long Day's Journey.* But we couldn't. Couldn't do it. Saxe and Bennett and I were the only people who had read that play, in our office. I think George Jean Nathan read it originally, and I think Russel Crouse did. But nobody in our place had read it except the three of us before we sealed it up, to be opened twenty-five years after Eugene O'Neill's death. But that was what he wanted.

Q: Did you feel that she dominated him?

Klopfer: Oh, terribly. Terribly. Certainly in the last years. I got a tremendous lot of this from Russel Crouse, who was a very close friend of mine. Anna (Crouse's widow) is still a very close friend of mine. Their two kids are friends of mine. We published Timmy Crouse too, *The Boys on the Bus,* very nice book that he did, for a first book.

Carlotta really really dominated him. She had a fatal attraction for him. My God, when he was here in New York, we had the lawyer getting the divorce papers together, and he was going to move down here. He was in the hospital. I think it was Doctors Hospital. I'm not sure which hospital here in New York. I wasn't in on this, but Bennett was reporting to me what was being done, and Buck Crouse was there, and our lawyer was going to attend to all the. . . . And all she had to do was come down from Boston, take him back, and he went. Just went.

Q: It was a very complex relationship.

Klopfer: Oh, it must have been. One of those terrific love-hate things.

Q: It was real Strindberg.

Klopfer: I would hate to have to live through it myself, is all I can say.

Q: But he wanted this.

Klopfer: Of course he did. Of course.

Q: Faulkner was a different kind.

Klopfer: Faulkner was a very close friend of mine.

Q: Dorothy Commins told me that she and Saxe used to call him Little Lord Fauntleroy because he was so polite.

Klopfer: Well, Faulkner was one of the greatest gentlemen that I've ever met. He was truly a gentle man. He always called my wife "Miss Pat." He always behaved himself when she was around. He was punctilious about manners and appearance, everything like that. He wasn't any character out of his own books. He was truly a Southern gentleman.

Q: But not down home when he drank.

Klopfer: Up here when he drank he wasn't either. I mean, he was an idiot when he drank. You wouldn't be able to understand him even. He talked sheer nonsense and passed out, and we had to dry him out any number of times. But as a human being, and in between these times, he was great—and these bouts were always caused by some emotional stress and so on.

And as he got older, there was less and less of that, too. The periods were greater between this compulsive drinking thing. He spent any number of weekends at our farm in Hunterdon County. We had a farm in New Jersey at that time, and the guest room was right next to the library, and the library had a regular bar table in it, you know, with three kinds of whiskey and gin and vermouth and everything, including Jack Daniel's, which he loved. I never put a bottle away. I never made any reference to it or anything like that. His room was right next to this, and he never, when he was down at our house in the country, he never got drunk. Ever. Always had his two drinks before dinner, and he would enjoy the best bottle of wine that I could get out, because he really appreciated it. He loved good wine. Then he would have a cognac after dinner. Never once did he get drunk. He went right past that bar to go into his room, and he could have come out into it: it was the other end of the house from Pat and myself. Never, never, never.

Oh, he was a marvelous man. Strange, involuted, but great, a great human being.

Q: Do you remember any specific things he said or anecdotes that would help to characterize him? Any incidents that stick in your mind?

Klopfer: Well, I do remember, one time—he had just had one of his slight affairs with a young girl. Whether these were physical affairs or not, I haven't the slightest idea, but he had been seeing a lot of one girl, who went off and got married, and he came down to the house. . . . He was walking with a cane—he wasn't hurt bad, but he was walking with a cane. But then he wrote to Pat, thanking her for the weekend, which he always did, absolutely punctili-

ous a thing like that. He had a wonderful line, I thought. He said, "You're always sympathetic to me, whether I've been thrown by a dame or a horse." Pat loved that letter.

I was devoted to Bill. I went down to his funeral with Bennett and Bill Styron. We got his daughter Jill to allow us to bring Bill Styron down from *Life* magazine. I said, "Somebody's going to write about him. You might as well have somebody write about him who liked Bill."

He was the only author I've ever known who didn't give a damn what anybody thought about his books, really. He didn't read the reviews. He knew what he wanted to do. Sometimes they came off, and sometimes they didn't. But he had to write. He was one of the really compulsive writers. And the way we treated him—oh well. His books were out of print, and we couldn't send him more money. We didn't have it. I feel ashamed of myself. But that was it.

Q: He never read his reviews?

Klopfer: Never.

Q: Did he discuss his books with you at all sometimes?

Klopfer: Very little. Very little. You'd say you liked some character, and he'd say, "Yeah. Nice fellow." Or "He was a bastard." But never in detail or anything. He lived them up here [pointing to head] and he never heard them here [pointing to ears]. I think that's the secret to Bill's prose, really. If you read it out loud, it sounds much better than if you're just reading, you know.

Difficult at times. I think some writers just do write the way they hear, the guy that's talking, and when you read it back it sounds fine. But as it goes through your mind and eyes it doesn't necessarily sound as good.

Q: In the literary marketplaces, like Wall Street, stocks go up and down. Is there anybody who's fallen as low as James Branch Cabell has, from the way he was regarded?

Klopfer: I don't think so. We had five or six Cabell books in the Modern Library in the Twenties, after we bought it. We shipped them as fast as we could get them from the publisher. And then they fell right out again. People don't even know, haven't heard of him, anymore. And yet, I sent a collection up to Chapin Library at Williams College because I was moving, and I wanted to get rid of some of my books, and I sent a collection of Cabell first editions, which they were damn glad to get, too.

Q: Of course, every publisher has surprise best-sellers. Can you think of some over the years, that really turned into sensational, like *Love Story* or *Jonathan Livingston Seagull?*

Klopfer: Sure. Alvin Toffler's *Future Shock.* *The Greening of America,* which we did as a favor to somebody else, printed five thousand copies, and ended up selling four hundred thousand in hardcover. Four hundred thousand of that book! How can you tell about that? And Toffler was in the same year, sold about three hundred thousand copies.

Well, of course, Truman Capote's big book *In Cold Blood*–it ran away. Just ran away. *Portnoy's Complaint* ran up to four hundred thousand in about six weeks, I think–just like that.

Q: But had you expected those?

Klopfer: We expected those to be best-sellers, yes, but not of the magnitude that they were. But the others, *Future Shock* and *Greening of America,* were complete surprises to us. Not by well-known people in the literary world, and they just came and–zoom.

Well, it was marvelous, yes, but my God. . . . We paid a $500 advance and printed five thousand copies of *The Greening of America,* as a favor to another author who was a friend of his. That's what I call stepping in it.

Q: What's the highest royalty you've ever paid, the highest advance?

Klopfer: Probably Jim Michener. I don't think anybody's gotten higher.

Michener really is the hardest working and really most dedicated writer I know. He really does most of his own research, not all, of course, most of his research, and keeps on turning out these tremendously well-researched books: *Hawaii, The Source, Centennial,* the smaller ones. A lot of other smaller ones are very good too, not as imposing as those blockbusters.

Macmillan published *Tales of the South Pacific.* It got a very good press. Then Saxe Commins came to me, and he said, "You know, Jim Michener wants us to publish his new novel."

I said, "Well, how about Macmillan?" He worked with Macmillan, Jim did, at that time. He said, "No, they want him to work in their educa-

tional department; they don't want to publish him if he's going to work there, and they want to keep him. Someday maybe he can head their college department or something.

So I called up George Brett at Macmillan because, after all, you don't do this. First of all, you want to be sure he's not under contract to somebody else. I called up George. I said, "This is the story, and Jim's up here with *The Fires of Spring,* a novel, and. . . ." George said, "Oh, no, it's absolutely true. Go ahead and publish it. I don't want to publish him. I don't think it's a very good novel anyway, but I don't want to publish him because I want him to work here. He's working in our educational department. I don't believe in publishing people who work in my office."

So we signed the contract for *Fires of Spring,* and about three weeks later the Pulitzer Prize came out, *Tales of the South Pacific.* We've had Jim ever since. We've made him a tremendous fortune, and he's made us a hell of a lot of money. He's been great. He loves Albert Erskine's editing. They get along just fine. And as I say, he's a prodigious worker.

He also is one awfully nice man, because one of the things he's doing with his money is buying contemporary art and giving it to the colleges throughout the country. That's pretty damn nice.

Q: Was Faulkner the last Nobel Prize winner the house has had?

Klopfer: Well, let's see. I guess so. I don't know. Knopf might have had some Nobel Prizes.

Q: At one time you thought of dropping Ezra Pound.

Klopfer: I was overseas. I was in the air force for four years, and I was overseas when that damn thing happened. They did, they cut Ezra Pound out of an American anthology, because of his Italian broadcasts and so forth and so on. And then they realized that they were wrong, because of the roar that was put up by everybody. Here we were talking about freedom. Well, they restored it, and Bennett acknowledged he was completely wrong about it. But he was outraged. He was an emotional person, Bennett was.

No, that was a very stupid thing to do. And I regret it, but as I say, I can't share in the blame for that because I was in the air force in England at that time.

Q: What did you do in the air force?

Klopfer: I was an intelligence officer with a combat bombardment group, the 445th group.

Q: Where were you stationed?

Klopfer: In a town called Tibenham in East Anglia.

Q: Do you find that writers are personally like what you'd expect from their writings? It's hard to generalize, but there must be some instances where they are.

Klopfer: Well, you could say that Gene was, to a certain extent, because Gene has written so much autobiographical stuff. I mean, *A Long Day's Journey.* . . .

Faulkner was, because Faulkner was a completely introspective, morose, silent man. You can imagine everything going on in that head. He would go down to the country, and he'd sit out in the field on a log, smoke his pipe most of the time, not say a word for a half hour. Said he was having a good time, afterwards. You'd take him to the theatre and he'd wake up at the end of the first act, say, "This is terrible, I can't stand it any longer." He did that several times.

Q: Is *The Random House Dictionary of the English Language* about your biggest seller?

Klopfer: No. It's not a very big money maker, actually, because it doesn't dominate the market. They cost a tremendous amount to produce. No. A good author will earn you more money than that. A man like Michener with consistent successes, and only that occasional flop that really doesn't cost you anything anyway because you sell enough to come out even on it.

Q: When you and Bennett took over the Modern Library, it had 109 titles.

Klopfer: 112, actually. Yes, we always used to argue about how many titles there were. Nobody's taken the trouble to go back and really look. It's not important.

Q: But you discarded fifty-five. Was this immediately?

Klopfer: No. Over a period of time.

Q: Can you recall some of the titles you dropped?

Klopfer: Yes, surely. When we first took over the Modern Library, there were, I think, four titles by Lord Dunsany. There were six or seven titles by Anatole France. There were five or six titles by James Branch Cabell, and a couple of H. G. Wells titles that we dropped out over a period of the next six or seven years. We didn't just go and massacre. As we dropped—and some titles were taken away from us, too. They were copyrighted books. The publishers decided they didn't want them in a reprint any more. But over a period of years, all through the history of the Modern Library, we've constantly been discarding titles. And adding others. And anybody who took the trouble to go through that would really have a fine inkling of how our taste in literature in the United States changed between 1925 and 1970.

Q: That's a good idea for an article.

Klopfer: There's a good one there, too, because there are some very famous books that we had to drop out.

The most famous one of all, the thing that really killed Bennett and myself, happened later than that. We got from Scribners the right to reprint *The Great Gatsby* in the Modern Library in 1934.

We got it, and we put it in, and we kept it in. We finally got down so we were selling about seven hundred copies a year of *Great Gatsby,* and we had to drop it out voluntarily. Scribners did not take it away from us, after two or three years of being able to sell only seven hundred copies. When I spoke to Charlie Scribner in 1955 or thereabouts—we served on the board of Grosset and Dunlap together—he told me he sold three hundred thousand copies a year of *The Great Gatsby* in paper at $1.45. We had it at ninety-five cents in cloth and couldn't give it away, to all intents and purposes. However, Bennett and I kept it so much longer than we should because we thought it was such a great book. It is a great book. Best business book that's ever been written, I think.

The best-sellers, when we took it over, were *South Wind* by Norman Douglas, *Green Mansions* by W. H. Hudson. They're still fine books. *Mlle. De Maupin,* which was supposed to be sort of a dirty book in those days, *Madame Bovary.* I think those were really the best-sellers.

Q: How about *Ulysses?* When the ban was first lifted, was there a big rush of sales?

Klopfer: Oh, we did very well with our publication, when the ban was lifted. We must have sold one hundred thousand copies, quickly. And it's been selling ever since, of course. We now have it both in cloth and in paper in the Vintage series.

Q: When you bought Modern Library from Liveright, I understand that you also agreed to pay him $5,000 for five years for nominal services. Did he give you those nominal services?

Klopfer: Five years. He didn't do anything, and we bought him out for $15,000 cash, and saved $10,000 that way. It was really just an afterthought and a racket, because he had us, and knew Bennett really wanted the series, and that was that. But he didn't do a damn thing for us, absolutely nothing.

Q: Doing my research on O'Neill, I came across a rather unattractive individual named Arthur Pell.

Klopfer: Oh God, he was the comptroller, treasurer, bookkeeper, whatever you want to call it, with Boni and Liveright. I've known Arthur Pell since those days.

Q: I got a feeling he was a kind of Uriah Heep.

Klopfer: Oh, indeed. Indeed he was, and he was constantly—well, to be perfectly honest, he was constantly falsifying the card, the daily card of cash balance, the sort of thing which almost every smallish publisher uses, because he would never let Horace know there was money in the bank. It wasn't for his own benefit, but because Horace would go out and spend it. Horace was the most extravagant man in the world and didn't know anything about business, and Pell was really trying to guard him, and he did some pretty shady things. I'm not sure for his own benefit, even. Maybe for the benefit of the firm of Boni and Liveright. He ended up, of course, owning the company. He was—I hate to say these nasty things, but he had an unpleasant personality, to say the least.

Q: I also had the feeling that he was nibbling away, getting shares of the firm for himself, until finally. . . .

Klopfer: I suspect he did. And I suspect that some of the money that was loaned to Boni and Liveright in those days at 12 percent, which was unheard-of then, of course, but not so unheard-of in today's market, was probably some of Pell's own money that he was making good money on, because he knew it was perfectly safe at that time. The secu-

rity was all right. I can't prove that, and I may be doing him a grave injustice, but he had a very unpleasant personality.

Q: What I find so hard to forgive was that when Liveright lost the firm, and he had no place to go, and he'd hang around the place, one day with a very loud voice in front of others, Pell told him, "Horace, it doesn't look good for the firm, your hanging around here."

Klopfer: Oh sure. Oh sure. Very callous individual. I'm sure that's true.

Q: During your ten years on the road, there must have been some incidents, tragical-humorous, as they say in *Hamlet*. . . .

Klopfer: Oh no. It was pretty cut and dried. I had my friends, the buyers that I liked and would have dinner with, as I went into a town. Both Bennett and I had a wonderful relationship with the booksellers, because it was our firm, and we were out selling them. We weren't just salesmen out selling them, although that's what we were doing. Which gave us a great advantage. For instance, both of us were completely devoted friends of Marion Dodd of the Hampshire Bookshop. She was the queen up there for very, very long, until she died, and it was a very kidding relationship, you know. She would come into the office and we'd smack her on the fanny, you know, kiss her hello. It was the bookstore of Smith College, the Hampshire Bookshop in Northampton, Mass., and a very good bookshop it is, too. The fellows that ran the Harvard Coop were friends of ours.

Q: You weren't selling groceries, you were selling. . . .

Klopfer: Exactly. Exactly. And we weren't just employees going out to sell; we were the men who helped create the books. That's why I say we had a tremendous advantage. They were mostly very nice people, and we took advantage of it, frankly, and made friends. Those who are alive, and there are very few of them alive, are still friends of ours. You know, the buyer for Marshal Field would never come into New York without coming to see Bennett and myself. It was the best kind of relationship that you could have, for merchandising your books. And of course, when we were selling the Nonesuch Press books, which were very heavily oversubscribed, until the panic of 1929, we were very sure that our friends were taken care of, and people who were nasty to us would get very few copies of these books. It was just doing a favor letting someone buy that book. That all changed in 1930, of course.

Q: What are the crises, emergencies you recall over the years?

Klopfer: No. There were never any crises. First of all, we didn't borrow money from the banks.

Q: Or personal. . . .

Klopfer: Personal, there were never any crises.

Q: Or with authors. How about plagiarism suits?

Klopfer: We were once sued. We, Metro-Goldwyn-Mayer, and Sidney Kingsley were sued, each for $5 million—which was the most complimentary thing that ever happened to us—by some lady who said that Sidney had stolen the idea for one of his plays, I forget which. That sort of thing has never bothered us at all, because we had a very good lawyer, Horace Manges of Weil, Gotshal and Manges, and he took care of those things, and we knew there was no merit in the case, actually.

Our legal experience was with the *Ulysses* case primarily. As I say, we grew very slowly between 1925 and 1941. Our volume increased from $256,000 in 1926, and we didn't grow to a million dollars until 1941, which is fifteen years. So you see. . . .

Q: Well, those were the Depression years.

Klopfer: Yes, they were, but we were going ahead a little bit every year, even though they were the Depression years. From 1941, when we did $1 million, to 1975, when we're going to do $100 million, it's not arithmetic, it's geometric now.

I'm sure it was more fun when we were getting to a million, frankly. Also we were younger, too. That's very important. That helps enormously.

Q: Did you do signed, limited editions of any other authors besides O'Neill and Robinson Jeffers?

Klopfer: Those were the only two we did it with, until well after the war, when we started doing it again. We still do it now, with O'Hara and Michener, people of that sort, who are collected to a certain degree. I think it pleases the author, and it also gives us some added revenue, yes. It's a very easy thing.

Klopfer and Cerf flanking the third partner, Robert Haas

The thing we haven't done is put out any beautiful books. Typographically beautiful books.

Q: When you took over Harrison Smith and Robert Haas, was that primarily because they had certain authors like Malraux?

Klopfer: We were delighted to get them, but we didn't think of it so much in those terms. It was the quickest way to become more-important publishers, because they were too small and we were too small to be really of consequence, and we got two very good things. We got some good authors, Malraux and Isak Dinesen and Faulkner, and Edgar Snow came with that, yes. But primarily, it was to give us more volume so that we could hire more salesmen and do a better job of publishing, and we also got Bob Haas as a partner for twenty years, and he was marvelous. He was older than either Bennett or myself.

Q: How did you divide your labors then, when it was three?

Klopfer: Oh, well, Bob was sort of in charge of the whole office. The management. The editorial thing, the three of us divided. I would oversee the selling, and Bennett would oversee the publicity and advertising. The rest of it Bob—the inside job, Bob took.

He was very valuable to us, because he was a man of the greatest integrity, and much more gentleman to the manor born than either Bennett or myself. But what I really mean is that Bob came from a very wealthy Western family from San Francisco.

He always was rich, and he'd been in several businesses. He also was one of the two founders of

243

the Book-of-the-Month Club, from which he retired, to write, and then found out he couldn't be happy trying to write, and then started with Harrison Smith the firm of Smith and Haas. And it was a good little firm, but it too was too small to really figure in things, so the combination was very good for us.

Hal Smith dropped out after the first year. We knew he would, because he was interested in magazine publishing, that sort of thing, more than books.

Q: If I'm not mistaken, all O'Neill's plays made money for you, except *Moon for the Misbegotten,* which I think was the last you published.

Klopfer: I believe it was the last we published. I think they all made money for us.

Q: Well, I found that one remaindered.

Klopfer: That doesn't mean it didn't make money for us, anyway, you know. You don't have to sell too many plays. First of all, the play advertises itself. You don't have to do a lot of newspaper advertising, that sort of thing, to get any attention. But we did literally dozens and dozens of plays. We published practically all the good playwrights during the late Thirties and Forties, even into the Fifities, because they were all friends of ours.

Q: In the mid 1930s about how long would it take from manuscript to published book?

Klopfer: Six months. Yes. That gave us plenty of time to do it right. Now, it has to be nine months.

Q: Then it's a bit of a rush, isn't it?

Klopfer: Then it's a bit of a rush, that's right. Well, it depends on the length of the manuscript and a lot of other things.

Q: Why did the cost of paper go up so much? What's happened to the cost of paper?

Klopfer: There's a much bigger demand than there is supply. In 1974 particularly. It is now leveled down, but it went up about 70 percent last year.

Q: Why was this?

Klopfer: Well, there was a shortage during the first hysteria, I think, of the energy crisis, and the blockade, or the shutting off of the oil supply from the Middle East. Paper manufacturing is enormously dependent on power.

Q: Somebody said, pollution and the ecologists.

Klopfer: There's no question about that, too, that over the past few years, that every state has become more finicky about what they do with the waste, and they're not going to have the rivers ruined by paper manufacturers. That equipment is very expensive, so the paper companies really had to make some capital investment in that. They hate to do that. But that has leveled off now, and I think we can get all the paper we want. And not pay any premium prices for it any more.

Q: Someone told me that Eliot Paul's *The Last Time I Saw Paris* was a monstrously large manuscript which Saxe Commins cut down, to about half the size.

Klopfer: Sure. Both of his books. *The Life and Death of a Spanish Town* was also a monstrous disorganized manuscript which Saxe just made a very successful publishable book, and a very good book. And the same thing happened with *The Last Time I Saw Paris.* Eliot was a slob, you see.

Q: He was another Thomas Wolfe.

Klopfer: Yes. He wasn't as good as Thomas Wolfe, and he wasn't quite as verbose as Thomas Wolfe, but he was as disorganized as Thomas Wolfe.

Q: So Saxe should have had costar billing with him.

Klopfer: He certainly should have. And with lots of other books too. He did more than just an editor's job. He was really marvelous in that way. And there are authors who resent it very deeply if an editor tries to do too much on his book.

Q: What are some of the other books besides the two Eliot Pauls that you can think of, where Saxe or some other editor carved out a viable book?

Klopfer: I think Budd Schulberg needed Saxe for his early books.

And other authors whom Saxe started with, and switched over to other people here, because they couldn't really take his emotional attitude toward their books and his complete involvement in it—well, I can see that. For a lot of our authors, Albert Erskine is a much better editor than Saxe would have been, much better, because he's competent and professional, doing his job. Saxe was an extremely emotional person, and got involved in everything he was doing, but—well, you could tell from his relationship with Gene O'Neill.

Q: Saxe didn't have a big enough ego. Most people suffer from insecurity, but he didn't think highly enough of himself.

Klopfer: He certainly did not. He was the most loyal person that—I don't know if I've said this before to you, but he was—he could have made twice his salary with other publishing houses. I know he got the offers from other publishing houses while he was working for Bennett and myself. He never would talk to them even. He liked what he was doing; he liked the people he was doing it with, and—there it is.

Q: Are there any books you specially regret, for one reason or another?

Klopfer: That I regret that we published? Oh, not really regret. I remember when I came home from the war, I screamed about a title of a book which I had never read and still haven't read, *Two Jills and a Jeep,* and I said, "What's a respectable publisher doing publishing a book with a title like that?"

Q: That became a movie.

Klopfer: Oh, yes, that's why we did it, I'm sure. I was away so I didn't know anything about it. Oh, certainly, on every list that you have, there's one book or two books that you think, oh gee, we really shouldn't have published that book.
I've regretted that we didn't get lots of books, don't forget.

Q: There must have been some big ones that got away.

Klopfer: Oh, there were big ones that got away. I should say there were.

Q: This happens with every publisher. Could you tell me some?

Klopfer: Oh, of course there were. I very much wanted to publish Solzhenitsyn and couldn't get him. I'd have given anything to get him. But I couldn't. And offered him more money than he finally accepted. But he was absolutely right to go where he did.

Q: Why was that? A personal thing?

Klopfer: It was—no, nothing personal, it was the fact that Farrar, Straus and Giroux had published the previous book of his, and they really should have got it, but we tried like the devil to get it.

Q: And you also offered more money.

Klopfer: Yes. Well, it never went directly to him. It went to his agent, that strange man in Switzerland. It was very complicated. But certainly we wanted that, because I think he's probably the great literary figure of the decade.

Q: Well, I'm thinking of manuscripts that came in that you turned down.

Klopfer: Oh, sure. I can't think of any one in particular. We certainly had. . . .

Q: Did you have a reverse Michener case, where you had somebody working here and. . . ?

Klopfer: Nobody who worked here. No, we haven't had that. As a matter of fact, we haven't lost any authors.

Q: You were saying that you published Irwin Shaw's *Bury the Dead,* Shaw's first work to see print.

Klopfer: Yes. Eight or nine years ago, we had a short story which he'd stretched out into a novella, that he insisted he wanted to have published that way, and a volume of short stories. We had done the editorial work on the novella and the volume of short stories they were working on, just copy editing. It was in our catalogue, and his agent, his movie agent, Irving Lazar, came in and said, "Irwin will not give you any of the paperback rights for this book."
We had a letter agreement with Irwin. We'd paid him $15,000 advance for the book and so forth and so on. You know, with Shaw like with Faulkner, we hadn't bothered about contracts. I have had bound books on my desk when Manny Harper would call up and say, "Hey, there's no contract for that book," and the next time Bill Faulkner came in, he simply signed the contract. That was that. Nobody paid much attention to that. We had nearly the same relationship with Irwin, and we'd never dealt through an agent before.
So we said we couldn't do that, because we'd have to do it with all of our authors if we did that.

We couldn't survive without getting a share of the subsidiary rights of all kinds.

Well, then he wouldn't let you publish the book. And Bennett got good and mad and told Lazar, "All right, I'll release him, but he's got to come in himself and ask me. I'm not going to do it through you."

So Irwin came in finally. He wouldn't see me, he'd see Bennett—because I was a closer friend of his than Bennett was, actually. He saw Bennett, and then he came clean with Bennett: he had an offer from George Delacorte—$250,000 advance for a three-book contract, two of the books which were in our place now, and the combined total sales of those two books was not going to be twenty thousand copies, I knew that. And he couldn't resist it; he needed the money. He didn't need the money, but he said he needed the money.

Bennett said, "Well, why weren't you man enough to come in and say that? Unless I was willing to give you the same thing, I'd never think of trying to hold a man away from making a fortune."

Bennett said, "All right, we'll release you from the contract, but not till we get a check for $15,000 for the advance we paid you." Well, about two weeks later the check came in from Irving Lazar.

And then about five or six years later, Irwin wrote a couple of novels for Delacorte which bailed Delacorte out. I think Delacorte came out all right on it.

In all the time that we published Irwin, his royalties and our profits did not amount to $250,000. We totaled it up afterwards to see if we were just being chintzy about the whole thing.

But that sort of thing happened.

Q: Also happened with Philip Roth, I think.

Klopfer: Philip left us because he would not allow us to have any share of the paperback rights. He went to Holt, Rinehart, and they didn't get any share of the paperback rights, and they took a terrible beating. You know, a publisher has to live, too.

I can see it from the writer's point of view on the thing. But I don't think there's ever been a case where the writer hasn't made more out of a book than the publisher has. In other words, if you give him a $2,500 advance, a very small advance, shall we say, for a book that you think is going to sell five thousand copies, something like that, but is well worth publishing, which we very often do, the writer will make $3,500 out of the whole damn thing. The publisher, I promise you, giving him his $3,500, will lose money on the book. He'll be on the minus side of it. Because he'd have to sell seventy-five thousand, ten thousand copies to break even. He'll come nowheres near breaking even.

When Mr. Michener's books sell three hundred thousand copies, he makes much more than we do out of it. Much more.

Q: Of course he has a high royalty rate.

Klopfer: Oh, sure. He has the top royalty rate.

Q: O'Neill was getting 20 percent.

Klopfer: Twenty percent, only author we ever did that with.

Q: I've seen the correspondence. How about great expectations that didn't quite come about? I imagine this happens quite often.

Klopfer: Oh yes. Those are the things that happen to every publisher.

Q: Yes, of course, but I was thinking of specific titles. Particularly ones that you had great hopes for that—you smile, so you're thinking of something.

Klopfer: Yes, I am thinking of a book. I'm thinking of a purely synthetic book we had great hopes for, and I was very glad we lost our shirts on it, frankly. We did a book called *No Time for Sergeants*—a very funny army book.

Q: Oh yes, Mac Hyman.

Klopfer: We did a book called *Don't Go Near the Water,* which was also a successful book about the navy. So we thought, what the hell, we can certainly do one about the marines and have it at least as good as *Don't Go Near the Water.*

So we got an author, sort of gave him a plot, and told him to give us something about the marines in wartime. I forget what we even called it, but we did put a lot of effort behind it. We thought, what smart merchants we are. It was cynical publishing of the worst sort. And it laid the biggest egg you've ever seen. We got exactly what we deserved.

Q: What was the title?

Klopfer: I can't think of it. I guess I've blocked it out.

Q: Have you had any books where the author is a couple of centuries late in delivering?

Klopfer: Well, we had a book with Irwin Shaw that he was twelve years writing that he never delivered to us, actually. We had a title for it and everything else. I'd see him in Paris every year, and he was going to get to work on it. He never wrote it. Started to write it and then switched off on a book he gave to George Delacorte.

Q: How about books a long time on the road, eight, ten years, can you think of any?

Klopfer: No, I can't think of anything that we waited for any extraordinary amount of time. Of course, Bill Faulkner would be irregular, but they'd always come in, every couple of years or something.

Q: Did you make any personal contacts, when you were in the air force in England, with writers that led to books?

Klopfer: No. None whatsoever.

Q: I'm sure you were very sad to move from Madison Avenue.

Klopfer: Oh, I was very sad. Not as sad as Bennett was. Bennett was in despair about moving, you know. But he was four years older than I was. No, but 457 Madison just didn't make any sense. We were a big publishing house by that time. We had five other locations in New York. Our production department was on East Forty-second Street. Our editorial office was on Fifty-first Street and Madison Avenue. You know the relationship between the production department and the editorial department. It made absolutely no sense. Our computer was over on West Sixtieth Street. Well, it made no sense at all. I hated to give it up, because that place had real class. It had style. This place has none. This is a perfectly nice publishing office. We lost a great deal, but my God, what we gained, in having the whole operation under one roof, the whole New York operation, at least. I spend more time on the eleventh floor than I do here. The editorial offices are all there, and the production offices down on the sixth floor, and we go down there. That takes thirty seconds to get to it. And it's available. And you know that damn thing, the telephone, isn't as good as getting down and talking to somebody.

We took a picture of Bennett in the office. He insisted that we do it. Do you remember the picture of Seward Avery being carried out of the Montgomery Ward building in his chair? We did a picture—Albert Erskine and I and a couple of other people picked Bennett up to carry him out of his office.

Gag photo of Cerf being carried out of 457 Madison Avenue by John Simon and Klopfer

He said, "That's the only way I'm going to go." So he had a record of it.

Q: Was that ever published?

Klopfer: No, I don't think so. I don't know where it is.

Q: Your relationship with Bennett seems to have been unusually harmonious.

Klopfer: It was. My temperament is completely different from Bennett's. I'm more of an introvert. Neither one of us was an intellectual, don't get me wrong, but I'm more of an introvert than Bennett. And Bennett was the biggest ham in the world. He would tell it to anybody to whom he spoke. I'm not talking behind his back. He begged me, in all seriousness he begged me, "For God's sake, why don't you go out and take credit for the things you've done? Why don't you go out and get some publicity for yourself?"

I said, "I hate it, I couldn't do it." I wouldn't do it. "I don't want to do it, and I hate it."

But the relationship was an unbelievable relationship. For forty-six years we were in business together. We were close personal friends, and in the forty-six years, we would argue about books, whether to publish a book or not, that sort of thing, but we never had one important business disagreement.

For instance, when there were three of us, when Bob Haas had an equal interest with Bennett and myself, as he did for twenty years, the business came up of buying 457 Madison Avenue. I had just gotten back from four years out of the office, and I was very much against it. Because I said I didn't think we had any business being in the real estate business and so forth and so on; we're publishers; we could publish just as well from a loft on Tenth Avenue. There was no space in midtown Manhattan. We couldn't get decent office space, because there hadn't been any new buildings since 1929, except for Radio City, in midtown Manhattan.

But they outvoted me two to one, and I went along with it, and they were right and I was wrong, because we got about eight times what we put into it when it was finally sold, and it was the best investment we ever made.

Q: Your being against it is also part of your not liking any ostentation.

Klopfer: Yes, that's true, and my belief that—you see, if I'd been running Random House completely, we would not be the publishing house we are today. We wouldn't be as big, and we wouldn't be as good, because I had the feeling that you are only judged by the books that you publish. And Bennett was much smarter than that. Bennett knew that you need the publicity; you need the ability to sell the books; you need all the things, the appurtenances that go with it, particularly television and that sort of thing, as that came into existence after we were publishing. It all became very important to us. I would have been terrible at that. He was brilliant at it.

He was—as I say, he was a terrible ham. He wanted everybody to love him.

Q: I was thinking that as an only child, used to being doted on by his parents. . . .

Klopfer: Worse than that. His mother died when he was quite young, so he was brought up by a father who doted on him, and who worked for us until he died, actually, his father did.

But yes, that's true. He wanted attention more than anything else—he loved those lecture tours that he went out on. Everybody else I know that goes out lecturing complains about the hardship and this, that, and the other thing. Bennett would come back with his batteries charged. He

loved the whole thing—particularly the colleges. "I talked to eight thousand students there," he would say. It was the most exciting thing he could imagine.

Bennett went out of his way to charm everybody. He wanted everybody to like him.

So you see, our temperaments were completely different. But we had no business arguments, and the main thing was that we trusted each other completely. Before we got so big and that sort of thing, he'd be away for six weeks at a time, and I would run the whole business, all the parts he did and the parts that were my own. Then the next year I would go away for six or seven weeks, and just left it to the other fellow, and never any—there was complete trust. There was scrupulous honesty, and trust in judgment too, of course, which is much more important actually. You expect people to be honest, but they don't always. . . .

Bennett has never been given the real credit for being as good a publisher as he was. He was a damned good publisher. He had an intuitive sense. He very seldom missed things, in books, and very seldom missed opportunities to merchandise them properly. He was much better at that than he was on television or on the lecture tour, any of those things. He was supposed to be very good at those things too.

Q: One thing that impressed me, that two-part profile in *The New Yorker*. . . .

Klopfer: He hated it.

Q: It told that when he was at Columbia, he was working on a paper, and he saw where the president said, "Anybody who volunteers (in the army, 1917) will get credit for all the courses he's taken," and the day before this was published, Bennett rushed to sign up for courses—half a dozen courses. . . .

Klopfer: Half a dozen courses that he never could have passed. That's where he got his degree. Oh, he had a kind of—he was quick, he was quick, sometimes shallow, but usually, he was also intuitive about things. After his disastrous few weeks with Sylvia Sidney, he married Phyllis. She made a marvelous wife. Marvelous wife. He wasn't easy.

Q: This new business, I'm sure you're against it, this business of libraries hooking up with others and transmitting books by Xerox—this seems quite unfair.

Klopfer: Well, it is unfair. There really should be legislation to protect the author. Just as the copyright law protected the author. It should be extended to forbid things. Of course, you get all the academics screaming bloody murder that you're interfering with their freedom of–I don't know what. Yes, I'm very much against that. It's very dangerous, too. Dangerous to our business. It's dangerous to the writing community.

Q: Did you see the Victor Navasky piece in the *Times Book Review* last Sunday? He always has some strictures about the publishing industry, and this time his point was, why can't the publishers pay the authors more than every six months? In this age it shouldn't take so long.

Klopfer: For royalties to be figured out? Well, look–if our computer worked perfectly, he's right. But we have to go over–more particularly on the royalties–and check and check. And we can't do that every month.

Q: He suggested every three months.

Klopfer: It could be done. It would be idiocy to say it couldn't be done. Of course it could be done. I don't know how much it would cost.

I don't mean the interest on the money; I just mean the sheer manpower. It would be silly to say that couldn't be done. Of course, anything could be done.

Q: Did you know the celebrated wits of the Twenties?

Klopfer: Franklin P. Adams was very witty, very sloppy. He and Heywood Broun were the two sloppiest men that I've ever met in my life. Broun came to my house for dinner one night. This was in the Thirties. Quite a good group there, I think. Jimmy Walker was there for dinner, and oh, William A. Brady, the theatrical producer. And my stepson was there, who was a little boy about eight or nine, and he was fascinated at meeting these people, and he sat with us for a little while, before we shunted him off to go do his homework. The next day he said to his mother, "And you say I have to be clean? You say I have to do this and that? Did you see Mr. Broun didn't have any shoelaces in his shoes?" Heywood didn't. He was a terrible influence around children.

I knew some of these people, so many of these people well, sïme of them just–Wystan Auden I knew reasonably well. Brilliant–I don't have any specific stories about him. His whole behavior was a story all the time. You know, he'd leave your house at nine o'clock. He'd never stay later than nine o'clock. He had his own schedule. When we gave him a party on his sixty-fifth birthday, the great thing he did was to stay 'til nine-thirty, then go back home.

Truman Capote, I've known since we first published him. Truman is a very, very, very talented person. But he either gets blocks about writing or he's too damned lazy or doing too many other things, being entertained too highly by royalty or richness. But when he really wants to write–he obviously doesn't want to write too much because he hasn't done anything in years but republish old stuff. I know he's working on two or three things, but he will never get down and finish them, at the present time. I think he will someday.

Whittaker Chambers was a very interesting person, whom I met when we published *Witness.* He was an extremely bright man and very convincing when you talked to him, too. We were soundly criticized by all of our liberal friends for publishing that book. But I think we should have. I have no feelings about that, that there was any betrayal of any liberal. . . . Somebody sent him to us. I think it was some conservative columnist who had respect for us anyway. Said, "It's much better if you're published by a house like that than if you're published by Doubleday or somebody, who has no convictions one way or the other." Doubleday's a good publisher, but they don't have the same range of publishing that we do. He came to us. We read the book, and it was a beautifully written book and a very convincing thing. Both Bennett and I talked to him quite a good deal, and we decided, yes, we were going to do it. Saxe Commins was upset about our publishing it, because, you know, he was Emma Goldman's nephew. He got over it though.

Ralph Ellison is a good friend of mine, who was at the house for dinner a couple of weeks ago, with his very pretty wife. We published *Invisible Man.* Albert Erskine's his editor, and he needs the editor, too. Albert doesn't rewrite anything in the way Saxe used to do, but Ralph's got that much manuscript of the next book already (indicating several thousand pages)–but Albert can't get him to cut down.

Edna Ferber–she and my wife were very good friends. She and I were good friends, but–Pat was one of the women she seemed to like. Oh, she was murderous, and she had a capacity for feuding with people. Before you could ask Edna over for dinner, you had to find out whom she wasn't talking to, that year, amongst her good friends. Oh, Edna was great. She was a great woman.

Samuel Goldwyn I knew only superficially. Moss Hart I knew very well, but I think Bennett was closer to Moss, liked Moss better than any other person. He was really devoted to him. Moss had the same kind of joy of living that Bennett had, you know.

Red Lewis was a person—there are stories and stories and stories about him that go on forever. He was asked to give a lecture up at Columbia, at the creative writing course, and of course when Sinclair Lewis came up there they had to have the auditorium, and they had about three hundred people there. I'll never forget, at the start of his lecture he gets up, he throws around his hands and he says, "What the hell are you doing here? Don't you know that if you want to become a writer, there's only one thing to do—you've got to write and write and write." And then he went on to give a very good talk. It was so marvelous to see these kids with their mouths open, and they'd sit there with Lewis saying, "All this stuff is nonsense, what you have to do is write."

Malraux I knew only superficially, because he would come into the office when he was in this country and swear he didn't speak any English, and my French is so lousy that Bob Haas took care of it as Bob was fluent in French. Sid Perelman I've known very well. George Jean Nathan I used to know.

Ayn Rand is a character, she's really something. She's quite a remarkable woman, you know. She's wacky as a fruit cake. I'd better stop this. . . . She really believes that she is the founder of a school of philosophy, which I think she calls Objectivism, which is more important than Aristotle, Plato, any of the others of the past, and these books that she writes, these big novels like *Atlas Shrugged* that we published, are simply to slam forth her whole philosophy, that the whole Judeo-Christian ethic is all wrong, and to the strong belong the spoils.

Well, we lost Ayn Rand because she handed us some nonfiction. We said we'd never try to edit any of her stuff out, her ideas, anything like that. She handed us a book of nonfiction which compared Franklin D. Roosevelt to Adolf Hitler, and we just couldn't take that. "You can get this published, but I'm not going to publish it. If you drop that essay out, we'll publish the book." She didn't. I think New American Library published it. They should have published it. It was all right, but I mean, I didn't want to, that's all. If nobody else had published it, I might have felt differently about it.

Q: Are there any phases of your history that you think of that I haven't covered?

Klopfer: The rest of it is pretty pedestrian. We started small. We kept getting bigger. We kept getting bigger, I think. We took a big step when we did a dictionary in 1947 which cost us a lot of money, *The Random House Dictionary of the English Language—College Edition,* and by that time we had really a very good reputation, and we began to attract authors to us, instead of having to go out looking for them. And we've kept that up, and we've enlarged our business by getting very big in the juvenile field, which is something I don't know anything about actually, but we are. We probably have the biggest juvenile line of any trade-book publisher today, and we have our good smallish college department, our pretty good smallish textbooks, elementary and high school department, and then we did the so-called *Unabridged Dictionary,* which was *The Random House Dictionary of the English Language,* which has been successful—hasn't budged Merriam Webster out of the first place or anything like that, but it's been successful. Two years ago we went into the mass-market paperback business with Ian Ballantine, Ballantine Books. And we hope to develop that into a first-rate mass-market publishing house. It is not yet, and was not when we took it over, but it's already much better than it was then. But that requires time and effort and money, and we're doing it because we feel that will give us a fully rounded business.

Q: You'll be in position to adapt to this. . . .

Klopfer: To this incursion of the mass-market paperback, into the hardcover field. I think it's important for a publisher to have that now. I didn't think so ten years ago. The mass-market paperback. We have a beautiful egghead paperback line, Vintage Books, which is really superb.

Q: Can you recall any writers ever becoming reminiscent, over some drinks, and you start talking about the past—can you think of any writers? I'm thinking of the important writers, who talk about their childhood or their parents, became confidential?

Klopfer: No, very little. Very little. I can't think of anything. I mean, Bill Faulkner, who was my best friend and the most prominent writer we've had, never—he wrote it in his books. He didn't talk about it at all. Talked about his mother occasionally, who was infuriated with *Life* magazine for something they wrote, canceled her subscription to *Life* magazine–she didn't like a review of one of Bill's books, which Bill had never read.

Moss Hart wrote all about his childhood in *Act I*. Jerry Weidman used his childhood for at least eight novels. No, I can't think of any case where there was any great insight shown, as to their childhood, formation of character, that sort of thing.

Q: Can you remember any idiosyncracies of the writers, especially the most prominent ones?

Klopfer: One of the authors who fascinated me was André Malraux, who was certainly one of the most important authors we published. Bob Haas always took care of Malraux, and I only saw Malraux a couple of times in the office, but I've never seen a more nervous man. He had a facial tic. You'd constantly think he was winking at you. He was thin and nervous, and very high strung, very high strung, it seemed to me. I'm absolutely convinced he understood English, too, although he would not speak it in the office.

And Bill Saroyan, when I first met Bill Saroyan in California in mid 1930s, I don't remember exactly what year it was, he was a very thin, wiry, charming, dark-haired Armenian boy. When I saw Bill Saroyan in London at the Savoy Bar during World War II, he was a big, fat, mustachioed American soldier. It was a tremendous contrast.

Q: You've anticipated a question I was going to ask, changes in authors over the years that you knew them.

Klopfer: Saroyan, I knew well at the time we published him, but you know, I'd only see him occasionally after that, so I don't know how much he changed. I doubt if he changed very much. He changed in appearance, but I don't think the inner man changed. I'm sure he still believes every word he ever wrote down on paper deserves to be preserved between cloth covers, which he did when we first started publishing him.

Certainly Bill (Faulkner) never changed at all. In appearance, he got handsomer and handsomer as he got gray. His figure didn't change. He didn't change at all.

Red Lewis got a little more crotchety as he got old and sick and disillusioned.

By and large, you know, the people that are inclined to be querulous and quarrelsome at times–a man like John O'Hara, who always had a chip on his shoulder, had it when we first started publishing him after World War II, and he had it till he died.

The great thing that happened to John that made him a much more pleasant person was when he had to stop drinking, or he would have killed himself, with his bleeding ulcers and things that he had. He did stop. He didn't drink at all. So his rages were not as great.

Q: Can you remember any particular rage which illustrates his unreasonableness or difficult behavior?

Klopfer: Yes. At a party at Bennett's one night, Faulkner was there and O'Hara was there. It was a large party. There were a lot of other people there. And O'Hara, who was devoted to Faulkner, admired him as a writer and said he was the only writer in America that might be better than he was–during the course of conversation, Bill admired a lighter, a lighter that Phil Barry, the playwright, had given O'Hara. And O'Hara, with a touch of generosity, said, "Well, I'd like to give this to you, Bill."

Bill took it and simply said, "Thank you very much," went and talked to somebody else.

O'Hara got up in a rage, went upstairs, called Belle, his wife, and said, "We're going home" and stormed out of Bennett's house, in a rage at Faulkner, who didn't know he'd offended him even. He didn't show the proper gratitude, according to O'Hara, the proper realization of the sentimental value, something that Phil Barry–it was a very generous gift. It's something that O'Hara really treasured, and he wanted to give it to another writer. But he stormed out of the house in a fury that night. That was a real rage, too.

Q: I imagine he was difficult for his editors also, cutting, revising?

Klopfer: He turned in the most perfect copy that any author ever turned in to Random House. His work was almost foolproof, and he was so outraged if anybody found a mistake in a date or something like that that at first he wouldn't believe them, you had to really–and you damn seldom found them. His copy was unbelievable, for an editor. No real need for copyediting, because–well, to prove that, I think *From the Terrace* was given us on the first of August, and he insisted on it being published on Thanksgiving Day. Those were his orders. Now, the first of August to Thanksgiving Day, for a 400- or 450-page book, 150,000-word novel–we didn't have time to copyedit.

So we sent it directly to the compositor, and then read the page proof, had it put in page proof very carefully. We didn't even have an abnormal alteration bill. The copy was perfect. He was an incredible craftsman.

Q: How about Faulkner?

Klopfer: Well, Faulkner also typed his manuscripts. He typed them in the office, he typed them anywhere.

Q: Did he type from the start, instead of longhand, when he wrote at home?

Klopfer: He typed from the start.

Q: He always typed?

Klopfer: I believe. I haven't seen the early manuscripts, so I don't really know that, but we always got them typed. Then, he'd chug along there, turn it in. Then Albert Erskine would go over it with him, and there was a great deal of changing around to do, because Bill really didn't give a damn if in the third volume of the Snopes trilogy Flem Snopes happened to be 179 years old. It didn't bother him at all. Albert would try to—we went back over the *Hamlet,* Albert went back over the *Hamlet, The Mansion, The Town,* the Snopes trilogy, trying to coordinate the dates, so that they weren't these ridiculous things—which Bill would allow you to change at will. He had no feeling about that. Character was not in the date of birth or anything like that. He would. . . .

Q: Eleanor Roosevelt?

Klopfer: Yes, I've met Mrs. Roosevelt several times. I had dinner with her several times. I thought she was the most wonderful woman in the world. But I don't know any real stories about her. I remember her telling about her experiences in the United Nations, when she was representing us there, and the fighting with the Russians, and how she would have to stay up until two or three in the morning, because otherwise they'd just outsit you and then outvote you—which indeed she did. How difficult that was.

I remember her saying once, "Franklin was absolutely convinced that he personally could get along beautifully with Stalin, and he might well have—but it's very difficult for all of us. He didn't realize the difficulties, although he felt that he personally could get along with Stalin."

We're publishing a great book on the subject this fall. Averell Harriman's book. From 1941 to 1946. It's a great great book. Elie Abel has written it, you know, dean of the School of Journalism at Columbia,

and he's done a brilliant job. But it gives all that inside story of what Roosevelt thought about Stalin, and what Stalin thought about Roosevelt, as conveyed to Harriman, or what Harriman thought, and Churchill. Averell was with them all the time. He was at every important conference with them.

He's worked like hell on this book, and he's been enormously helpful, because all of his records were available to Elie, and all the research that his people had done on his records. But the main thing that he got was from talking to Averell, and then when the first draft was written, Averell would write twenty pages of comment on, "No, it wasn't like this" or "Now that you say this, I remember it this way; it wasn't like this."

Q: What is the title?

Klopfer: Well, we're still fighting about that. The present title is—what was the damn thing called? Originally wanted to call it *Ambassador Extraordinaire,* which was sort of his official title, because he was appointed personal ambassador to Churchill originally. But we're calling it *Secret Envoy to Churchill and Stalin.* By Averell Harriman and Elie Abel.

Q: Can you remember any specifics about Harriman, incidents?

Klopfer: Well, I can remember a great deal about Harriman, which has nothing whatsoever to do with the publishing business. Oh, I think he's a great person. He has one of the best minds of anyone that I've ever met. He is a bad public speaker, very bad public speaker, but sitting around in this room talking with three or four of us, he is enormously effective and very straight thinking. And if you will look at his record and his reports and everything like that, they're right on the button, at least an awful lot of the time.

He's extremely intelligent. He's very devoted to the public good. He's a very rich man who really is interested in the welfare of the country, the country as a whole, not just for his own class, if you want to put it in those terms. And I think he's admirable in every way. He's an extraordinary man. And you know, starting out as an eight-goal polo player, leading a social life, then switching around to public service almost completely—which was never an ego trip with him, either. I could mention other names of very rich men who've gotten high political office, but that was to satisfy an ego, and I don't think this is true of Averell. I do think he wanted to make the name of Averell Harriman more important than that of E. H. Harriman, his father. I think he had that always. But after all, he was never off on the ego trip that some other men whose names I don't want to mention have been.

He thought Mr. Roosevelt was absolutely right. He was all for the New Deal. Not everything about it. He thought some of it was all screwed up but that the philosophy was right. He realized that rich people would have to give up some of their money to have the country go on. In fact, he once said to me that he thought a capital levy of 25 percent might be acceptable to the intelligent rich people, if they thought the money was going to be used for the betterment of the country. It was an impossible thing to get through–he never thought of it seriously as legislation. But just the idea that he would be willing to give up part of his fortune for his country. And I know he meant it too. This was in the depth of the Depression, don't forget.

No, I can't think of anything, except that all of his thinking was forward thinking, and God knows he worked like the very devil to get us into the war, to kill the isolationist movement. And his analyses, as you will see in this book, and quotations from reports and things like that. They're devastatingly right.

I really consider I'm privileged to have been a friend of his for all these years.

Q: Gertrude Stein?

Klopfer: Oh, Gertrude I knew well. She was great when she came over here. She was a tremendous success. She enchanted everybody, and had just a marvelous time. And in about two weeks became a well-known figure around New York. The cab drivers knew her. Everybody knew her. She was a great woman. When she came over here, she would sit in Bennett's living room at the Navarro Hotel and read to us from *Portraits and Prayers*. She had a page about Carl Van Vechten, and she read it to us, I remember, and read it very well and said, "Now, doesn't that suggest Carl to you?"

And Bennett and I both said, "Not one bit."

"Well, then you're just stupid, that's all."

She was charming.

Q: What made her so charming?

Klopfer: Because she was a woman who had a good mind and knew it, and she looked like a man, but had a wonderful–that picture out there of her is great. Look at it on your way out. She was a very cultivated woman, and a great conversationalist, and when she sat around with a group of people, she was irresistible.

We had lunch up at Bennett's, when she first came over with Alice Toklas. Alexander Woollcott

Alfred Knopf, Cerf, and Klopfer at the Random House trading post, New York Stock Exchange

wanted to meet her, and she started to dominate the conversation, and Woollcott couldn't get a word in edgewise during lunch. And I can remember, she was talking about the novels of Jane Austen, how marvelous they were, and everybody should read Jane Austen, and certainly Woollcott should read Jane Austen. You know, Woollcott was used to dominating a conversation, and he couldn't get in three sentences during the whole lunch.

Then when he got up from the table, he was very amusing–this, mind you, was about her second day here. He said to her, "Miss Stein, obviously you have not been in this country long enough to know that *nobody* tells Woollcott what to read!"

Delightful for everybody there–at which all of us burst out laughing, including Woollcott. And they became bosom companions. He loved her. They looked so funny together, both so small, fat.

Q: Adlai Stevenson?

Klopfer: I knew Adlai Stevenson. I wasn't a close friend of his, but I knew him. He was a really charming man, with an absolutely beautiful flow of English. It impressed you, when you were just talking to him. I remember, he was correcting the galleys on the speeches we published, and he was staying at, I think it's his sister's house at Sixty-first Street. I went up there and spent the morning with him, just going over the galleys in a rough way, and I was absolutely fascinated, the way he would put papers around on his desk–move them over here, then move them back, that sort of thing. And I thought: am I sure I want this man to be president of the United States?

I think he was rather indecisive. I just got that feeling that one day. Not in talking to him, just in the handling of these galleys, almost the physical handling of them, you know what I mean? When you have to push, you don't turn it over, you push it over here, then bring it back here, then look at it, then push it back there again. I was slightly dismayed by that. But he was an articulate, intelligent person.

But you see, I'm the quiet member of the firm. Bennett was always at the parties, and the sought-after person, so I don't have all the stories that he had. Anyway, he elaborated. He was such a good storyteller that you could never quite tell fact from fiction in his stories. That way, it's very difficult to get a book out of his oral history, which we're doing, of course [*At Random*, 1977].

Q: Who's working on that? What writer?

Klopfer: Albert Erskine. You couldn't get a stranger in on it because it just wouldn't work. Something very good's going to come out of it, I think. But it needs so much checking.

Q: Christopher Isherwood?

Klopfer: Well, I knew Christopher Isherwood back in the 1930s when we published W. H. Auden, Isherwood, Stephen Spender, Louis MacNeice, and Cecil Day Lewis. We published all of them in the Thirties, and a pretty good group they were, too. For that time, when we were young and—but I didn't know Isherwood well. I don't know any stories about him, no specific stories. Lots of stories about Auden, but that's not for this. Auden was the oddest character of them all, probably, and also our author until he died, so that I had much more contact with him than with any of the others.

Q: You once told me, his whole life was a story.

Klopfer: Oh, it is. But that's not for anything like this. That's for somebody to write. It's really a great story. I think it would be a great character study.

I liked, I was very fond of Auden. He was strange, craggy. He was enormously popular up at Bennington, on lectures, colleges, that sort of thing. But he was a very honest man. He never bothered to try and make himself well liked or anything like that.

Q: Clare Boothe Luce, did you know her?

Klopfer: Yes, I knew Clare, not well, but I knew her. She—we published her plays.

Q: You're smiling about something.

Klopfer: Well, I do remember a line that—I asked her to have lunch with me because we were publishing a play of hers. I think it was 1939 before we were in

the war. We were having lunch at 21, and she was—she had just been over to Germany, and she said, "You know, I know the Germans are convinced that they're going to win the war."

I said, "Why are you convinced that they're convinced?"

She said, "Because you know Mr. Hitler wouldn't have allowed me to see him if there was any chance that they weren't going to win the war," which I thought—my jaw dropped.

I said, "You mean, you think your seeing Hitler was indicative of his frame of mind, as far as winning or losing the war goes?"

"Oh yes." She was dead serious too, about that. I couldn't quite believe it. That's a story I know never has appeared anywhere. Well, she was a very talented woman actually, and a very able woman, hated by all women and liked by men, mostly. She's all right.

Q: How about Harold Ross?

Klopfer: Oh, I knew Ross well, sure.

Q: I still can't figure out why he was such a great editor.

Klopfer: Nobody else can figure it out, either. He just had something. Taste, maybe. God knows he didn't look it, and nothing that he did would indicate that—just the magazine he turned out was damn good.

Q: Was he much of a conversationalist?

Klopfer: Not really, no. He loved playing backgammon or gin, whatever people played in those days. He played for big stakes. He loved to gamble. He was a Puritan of the worst sort, hated bad language, no decolletage on women, nothing like that as far as he was concerned. Yet he was editing the most sophisticated magazine in the country. It was a strange combination. But I guess he was just a tough enough editor so that he was able to see whether something was right or wrong.

His appearance was idiosyncratic enough. You know, this fellow with the separated front teeth, that looked as though he could spit through them, which he never did, and the ruffled hair and the baggy pants, the clothes not fitting him—seemed so strange to be editing *the* most sophisticated magazine in the country, maybe in the world. And doing a very good job of it. And everybody loving to work for him, too. Hating the people who owned the magazine, from Raoul Fleischmann down, you know. It was a strange setup.

Responses to Ken Auletta

"The Impossible Years," Ken Auletta's New Yorker *article (6 October 1997), generated attention for its argument that American book publishing is in trouble—again—because of a decline in readership and because the industry does not pay editorial people enough at any level. Other problems are escalating returns ("Gone today; here tomorrow"), crapshooting advances, the power of book superstores, and the control of major houses by bookkeepers.*

I Wake Up Screaming

Irvin Faust

After reading Ken Auletta's piece in the *New Yorker*, I fell into a trance and had this daymare:

Herman Melville. Clutching his latest, he climbs on the future and hurtles eagerly into the present. He zips past a secretary who is making a personal call and faces an editor buried in the stock market pages. Editor finally looks up, turns on a smile after throwing drop-dead eyes at his secretary whom he can't fire because she reads and rejects all over-the-transom books.

"What can I do for you?" he says quite pleasantly.

"I'm Herman Melville."

"I see."

"I have a book."

"What else is new?" This with a disarming smile.

"I believe it has a chance at immortality."

Editor folds hands, sits back. "Humble is not your game, right?"

"Usually," says Melville, "I am rather humble. But not in the case of this manuscript." Taps very fat package.

"I see. Uh huh. Big baby."

"One says what one has to say."

"I can live with that. So okay, what's it about?"

"A whale."

"I see. Well, I listen. Unlike all the others. It's okay, Mel, I know you've had the brush from here to Timbuktu; it's okay. So what kind of whale? I mean a Willy or an Orca?"

"I beg your pardon?"

Sigh. "Willy: sympatico. Orca: a rat, a bum."

"I would say my whale fits into the latter category."

"He got a name? Or do you wait for a bolt from the blue?"

"I did not have to wait for anything. He identified himself from the outset."

"Oh, one of those. Hit me."

"Moby Dick."

"Mopy dick?"

"MOBY Dick."

"Is that some kind of dig at Mobil Oil?"

"No . . . it has nothing to do with oil, whale or otherwise."

"A play on words? A message about kinky sex in the ocean? A whale who screws real slow? A mopy dick?"

"MOBY. MO-BEE."

"Sure. Okay. Take it easy."

"That is his name."

"I hear you. Okay, let's punch him in." Editor zips up and down computer keyboard. "Whales. Whales. Gotcha, here we go. In 1987 *Our Friend, The Whale*. In '92 *Whales and Other Big Things*. Both kids' books, ages six to eleven and four to seven . . . *Friend* sold twelve hundred, *Big* eight ninety-seven." Looks up. "I'm sorry, Mel, whales are nowhere."

Melville crumples into a chair, lips trembling.

"Come on, Mel, it's reality, it's life in the trenches." He gazes at the forlorn figure. "Look, could he possibly be a gay whale?"

Melville straightens up. "He is very serious. Intense even. He has bitten off a captain's leg."

"Really?"

"Oh yes. The captain has pursued him ever since."

Editor stares at ceiling. Comes down. "He's hot for men?"

"I . . . there is a . . . that is to say. . . ."

"And this captain? He's got the hots for Mopy? Excuse me, Moby?"

"He is obsessed."

"Holy shit."

Silence. Then: "Is the . . . relationship . . . ever . . . consummated?" The editor leans across his desk.

"Moby Dick rams the ship and sinks it with everyone on board including the captain."

"That's all? Moby and the captain, they . . . don't . . . ever?"

"That's how it ends."

Editor swirls in his swivel chair, brakes. Gazes at the computer screen. Sighs. "Melvin, if you would like to play with that angle, well, come on back and we'll see, although I make no promises. Promises can kill you. But the way it stands you might have the biggest thing since *Valley of the Dolls,* but I wouldn't last five minutes with my sales manager if I told him I got a book about a whale who's lazy in the saddle. It's too risky. I'm really sorry, Mel, for a minute there you had me going."

"But. . . ."

"MONA. GETTHEHELLINHERE."

Herman Melville climbs on the past and hurtles gratefully back to 1851.

I wake up screaming.

Irvin Faust is the author of seven novels, including *Jim Dandy* (1994), and two volumes of short stories.

William Jovanovich

The essay by Mr. Auletta on contemporary book publishing is, on reading, rather too familiar; indeed, it could have been written, with small alteration, thirty years ago. As before, publishers complain of their own common practices. And most authors cannot be satisfied. And booksellers act as if each was a struggling shopkeeper—even when he's part of a large "chain."

The fact is that both the publishing and retailing of books are, at bottom, small businesses. The publisher owned by a large corporation still tends to approach each new book as if he'd never before edited or sold one. (Of course, a book should be unique in content.) Given this inclination, his overhead is large. Sixty years ago, the printer designed the page and copyedited the text for his publisher client; and selling to stores was conducted by travelers without requiring, back home, separate staffs for publicity and promotion.

There are, today, disproportionate financial effects from a publisher's dealing with agents who represent authors. As they have done in professional sports, agents have sharply driven up costs in trade (general books) publishing. Fifty years ago, even thirty years ago, the agent wasn't able to stir up publishers by playing the "greater fool" game, inciting competition with fanciful arguments on occasion. Further, the contemporary agent has a hand in driving up the number of

"returns" from bookstores by insisting contractually on large first printings that may prove unrealistic.

Sellers tend to return copies of a book quickly as its initial sales fall. Mr. Auletta quotes someone as saying that no publisher has dared (was "nervy enough") to go first in trying to end the practice of ruinously large returns. In fact, at Harcourt Brace Jovanovich in the 1970s I introduced the "Black Star" policy by which HBJ gave a much higher discount than usual to booksellers who would accept "no return" books (stamped on back endpaper with a black star). The presumption was that a bookstore can afford, as time goes by, to lower its price once or twice in "bargain" sales—as happens with goods in most forms of retailing. Today, as before, more books are found on the road in trucks than on shelves; and books in transit profit no one, least of all readers. What was the result? Not a single fellow publisher, not one agent, no author, not any jobber or retailer came forward by word or act to encourage HBJ. I gave it up because of losses.

Finally, there's no mention in this essay of the plain circumstance that too many new books are published each year. To cut a list is not necessarily a callous act by some chief executive. After forty-three years in publishing, I'm convinced that currently at least one in six books in the United States can simply not be produced, with no subsequent damage to our culture. Here, no truly deserving book goes unpublished, given the eagerness of so many good editors, but a lot of mainly unoriginal ones are published each year at great cost.

There will be, obviously, fewer publishing companies in 2000 than were at work thirty years ago. A trend toward monopoly has been evident in most industries since the 1960s, when mergers and acquisitions became common. (It's evident, by the way, in the publishing of textbooks, books in law and medicine, and academic journals.) In trade publishing the acquisition of several small companies by a large corporation has in fact brought few economies of scale and, worse, has not enabled anyone to neutralize the viruses that inflict the profession. We all decry these infections as we continue to feed them: high returns of unsold books, excessive money advances to authors against royalties, and the acceptance of too many manuscripts. Is there no hope of recovery?

Probably, technology will force a change in common practices. Reviewing of books can become common by electronic means. At present you can order a book on the Internet and soon will be able to preview it by using computer printouts. As production costs decrease and promotion becomes more varied, authors may become their own publishers. If there are losers in the coming technological age, these will probably be agents and "chain" booksellers.

For certain, books will be published.

William Jovanovich is a publisher, editor, and writer. He was for thirty-five years chief executive officer of Harcourt, Brace, which became Harcourt Brace Jovanovich in 1970. His works include essays and five books. He has just completed his memoir, *The Temper of the West,* part of which will appear in 1998 in a book titled *Serbdom.*

John F. Thornton

Now, however, some glimmerings of reason began to appear in my mind. I clung to certain numbers and chances, but soon abandoned them and began staking again almost without knowing what I was doing.

–from Fyodor Dostoyevsky, *The Gambler*

It isn't clear how good a book publisher Dostoyevsky might have made, but as a writer in thrall to a book publisher he had gotten himself into a pickle as pretty as any shared by his character *The Gambler.* It was September 1866, and if he didn't turn in an as-yet-unwritten novel by 1 November, he forfeited to his publisher the right thereafter to print any and all of his present or future works gratis.

High-stakes publishing in the consumer sector is the subject of Ken Auletta's article "The Impossible Business," and in it he wonders whether book-buying may have entered a period of irreversible decline. The Dracula dependence by publishers on new best-sellers–to the widespread neglect of more-modest titles offering backlist potential–has reached its bungee-cord limits of possibility. Now the back-snap has begun. The best example by the end of 1997 seemed to be the rumored advances totaling nearly $12 million paid by William Morrow to publish a book by actress-comedian Whoopi Goldberg and one by actor-comedian Paul Reiser, both of which lost their best-seller dice-rolling contests on the first throw. At quite respectably healthy advances of, say, $40,000 apiece, some three hundred promising new books by lesser-known men and women of letters and science might have been published instead. Who would deny that among their numbers not a few might have shown propulsion sufficient to orbit *The New York Times Book Review*'s "Best Sellers" list for months at a time?

The truth is that gambling and modesty have nothing in common when it comes to mass marketing. The consumer-book industry, after two decades of being tugged along behind the cart of mass distribution

via chain bookstores, has bought heavily into the related ideas that (1) it is a suburb of the entertainment business; and (2) it cannot support the marketing of new titles that don't come *presold* by having either celebrity authors, celebrity subjects, or content based on concepts as high as a new Spielberg release.

Such thinking amounts to cultural Darwinism and has driven from the lists of the top half-dozen conglomerate New York publishers countless projects of intrinsic worth. The consolidation of mainstream consumer publishing under the command structure of global media companies has produced much profit-taking by way of redundancy elimination. But on the editorial side the process has created a Hobbesian state of intramural competition, distrust, and unrealistic expectation supported by inadequate resources, duplicate products, and the reduction of traditional if quirky publisher vision to Mr. Magoo levels.

The solution? Since mass publishing famously follows the movie industry, usually at a lag of a decade or so, why not create the kind of symbiotic structure that lets Walt Disney Pictures, the blockbuster division, amicably coexist with its R&D division, Miramax Films? Both must make a profit, but the terms for doing it are well understood and accepted on both sides. Moreover, the chance a small movie might occasionally and satisfyingly provide the means of becoming a Big Movie remains a real promise.

In other words, after all the predatory acquisition of the 1980s and 1990s, does a book-industry giant, for example, Simon and Schuster, really need four or five dozen separate imprints to step on one another's toes in the rush to the new-release section at the superstore? Why not reprocess all these messy bits and pieces acquired and jammed together with their own tangled pasts into two clear streams of focused editorial activity, with appropriate sales/marketing support–one aimed unabashedly at maximum mass distribution and one at the traditional core reader interested in books whose value lies not in their obviousness but rather in their subtlety?

Surely we have learned enough in the last fifty years about creating and marketing High-, Middle-, and Lowbrow culture to permit books to find their audiences in the same way that film and TV have seemingly done without half the wasted effort and angst–or the Dostoyevskian addiction to Russian roulette.

John F. Thornton is a former book editor and book-club director and is currently practicing a hybrid profession of literary agenting and authorship. He is coediting a forthcoming anthology, *Tongues of Angels, Tongues of Men,* a book of the world's great sermons, for Doubleday Publishing.

The Art and Mystery of Publishing: Interviews

Three aspects of the contemporary publishing scene come together in the interviews that follow. The function of the editor is changing as the publishing business changes. *DLB Yearbook* sent *New Yorker* staffer Lauren McIntyre to interview two prominent editors, Samuel Vaughan and Daniel Menaker, both of Random House. Meanwhile, new directions include the new and serious player–the online Internet literary magazine. Katherine McNamara is founder and publisher of the international on-line magazine *Archipelago*. Representing *DLB Yearbook,* story writer and computer expert David McNair talked to McNamara about her new venture and its place in the publishing world.

Much discussed and argued about, in print and privately during 1997, was Carl Rollyson's unauthorized and forthcoming biography of a reluctant and vigorously resisting Susan Sontag. Kelli Rae Patton of the Ninety-second Street YMHA Poetry Center interviewed Rollyson on the subject of the place and purpose of the unauthorized biography in today's literary marketplace.

Carl Rollyson

This interview was conducted by Kelli Rae Patton on a rainy fall day in a bustling New York City coffee shop. The subject, Carl Rollyson, teaches film and literature at Baruch College of the City University of New York. He has written unauthorized biographies of Marilyn Monroe, Martha Gellhorn, Rebecca West, Norman Mailer, and Lillian Hellman. Rollyson has often been criticized for his renegade stance as a biographer and was one of several unauthorized biographers featured in an article in The New York Times *last year. Rollyson and his wife, Lisa Paddock, are currently at work on a biography of writer and cultural critic Susan Sontag, which will be published by W. W. Norton.*

DLB: How did you get started writing biographies?

Rollyson: In a sense by accident. I got my Ph.D. in literature from the University of Toronto. I had worked on Faulkner and wanted to work on the next generation of writers. I was always a fan of Norman Mailer and began reading his work seri-

Carl Rollyson

ously. I got very intrigued by his biography of Marilyn Monroe. He asks very interesting questions about biography, and I had never paid much attention to biography at all. He really asked fundamental questions about how you go about understanding someone else's life. And that aspect really intrigued me. About that time a friend of mine was doing a series of biographical bibliographies for Greenwood Press, and he asked me if I would do one on Marilyn Monroe. What I was supposed to do was write essentially a biographical essay and then a series of bibliographical sections about the other books and Monroe as a phenomenon and so on. But I got intrigued with the idea of biography, and I found myself incapable of following the Greenwood format. I began writing a biography. And I began interviewing people. I found I liked to interview people, that the subjects became much more alive to me. I had written an article about Mailer's biography of Monroe as well.

DLB: A review?

Rollyson: It was an article in a journal called *Biography.* In 1978. Once I started interviewing people, I began showing them the manuscript of the biography. Among them was Susan Strasberg, whose father had been Marilyn Monroe's acting teacher. And Strasberg, in the course of an interview said, "You know, you understand acting very well. Part of this reads like a treatise to impress your academic peers, and part of it sounds like the real book, a biography. Why don't you just trust your own voice?" And so she sort of gave me permission to do that. It took me some time to find my own voice. But once I started to do that, I realized that the only thing I wanted to do was write biography. My dissertation was about Faulkner's use of the past and his understanding of history, the way his narrators interpreted past events; essentially what they were engaging in was a biographical process. So then I realized I didn't want just to study this; I wanted to do it myself.

DLB: How do you begin your research? What's the starting point?

Rollyson: It's a kind of chain reaction. Each subject seems to lead me to the next subject. It's a number of things. I'm trying to reach not just an audience of academics but a general audience. Because I consider myself a professional biographer, I am looking for someone who I feel will have a broad appeal. There is a market consideration. I can't get trade-book publishers interested unless they think they can sell it. Just because a figure might be worth a book is not good enough. There is a pattern to my work. Beginning with Marilyn Monroe I am dealing with people who are in some particular fashion theatrical, self-invented (often they change their names). They're usually literary figures, though they don't have to be. Once I had wanted to be an actor. I had had contacts from the Marilyn Monroe book, so I thought I could use some of these to deal with Hellman and Hollywood. So there are usually both practical and literary or theoretical considerations. Often someone who is a minor character in one book becomes the major figure in the next book.

DLB: It's interesting that Mailer also wrote books about Picasso and Monroe.

Rollyson: Actually, I wrote my book about Picasso before Mailer wrote his. He had written essays, and I knew of his interest in Picasso when I was writing mine. And the Picasso book, which is a children's biography, was done with the Salem Press in California because an editor there knew of my interest in Picasso. He contacted me first. It usually works the other way around–I'm interested in the figure, and I have to get the publisher interested

in the biography. I used to joke that I wrote the biography of Mailer just to prove I could write about men.

DLB: I'm wondering about the fact that so many of your biographies are about women.

Rollyson: There are a lot of reasons for that. Again, to bring up a crass subject, there's the commercial aspect of it. Beginning in the late 1970s with the popularity and critical success of Nancy Milford's biography of Zelda Fitzgerald, publishers became increasingly interested in female figures. I have always been attracted to subjects in which there is in a sense a problem to be overcome, not just a person's story to tell. When I was an undergraduate, I did a senior honors thesis on *The Confessions of Nat Turner*. There was this book *Ten Black Writers Respond to Nat Turner* criticizing Styron as a white Southerner dealing with a black slave revolt. The book essentially argued that as a white Southerner he was almost disqualified from treating this subject. Whenever someone tries to put those kinds of limitations on literature, such as you have to be black to write about blacks or a woman to write about women, that's the signal for me to be the contrary. If literature is a work of the imagination, then why can't you? I think it is entirely possible that a man would miss things when writing about women, but to make it axiomatic and to disqualify people because of their race or their sex . . . With Lillian Hellman, the fact that she was a woman and that she had this incredible career as a playwright, a screenwriter, and then as a memoirist interested me. How many women have been as successful as Hellman?

DLB: There has been a boom in the publication of memoirs in the past few years. Has this affected your work and thinking?

Rollyson: I don't think that memoirs have affected the sale of my books. But memoirs are a type of book often called "life writing." It's such an accessible form. I'm not sure what accounts for this boom in memoir publication. Except that I think in a lot of ways the experimental novel, the modernist novel, has burned itself out. I have noticed that there are a lot of memoirs by academics these days, and I think that can be attributed to a desire to reach a broader audience, as I feel I have done with biography.

DLB: So the chief advantage to publishing your books with commercial/trade houses is that they reach a wider audience? Are there other advantages?

Rollyson: I spent a lot of my own money on the Marilyn Monroe book. Fortunately, because it was published here and in England, and got favorable reviews, I have made that money back. But it took ten years to do. When you write about Gellhorn, Hellman, Monroe, Mailer, and now Susan Sontag, you find that most of these people have traveled and have lived all over the world. It would bankrupt me to go everywhere my subjects have been. On the other hand, you need to go to as many places as you can. For the Rebecca West biography, I made nine trips to England and nine trips to the University of Tulsa because of their West collection. I can't do the books I want to do and be published by university presses. It is impossible. I need someone to pay for the work. I get an occasional grant–National Endowment for the Humanities or university support, for example–but it is just not enough.

DLB: Do you feel that your university affiliation has helped with your work? Do you have any sense of what your colleagues at Baruch think of this pursuit of yours?

Rollyson: Is there a tension? I think there is. And I would say not just at Baruch but in academic life in general. Biography is not held in very high regard. I've given talks on biography, and I can't tell you how many times graduate students have come up to me and said "I'd just love to do a biography, but my dissertation adviser tells me 'Don't do it.'" It's not considered scholarly. It is considered sort of popular. There are vestiges of a sort of New Critical bias against biography, that it's only the writer's work that counts. It's narrative and not analysis. I remember when I first came to Baruch almost twenty years ago, a faculty member in the department was surprised that I was getting grants for my books. Because, of course, it's not scholarship. There's a story about Lionel Trilling, who did an intellectual biography of Matthew Arnold for his dissertation at Columbia. At his Ph.D. defense one of the committee members said that it was brilliant and would pass but cautioned Trilling that it wasn't scholarship. I would never get a job somewhere other than Baruch on the strength of my biographies. One would be better served if one were simply interested in a spectacular academic career–to do one, two, three, four outstanding critical books–and then one could do a biography. But to begin as a biographer is sort of asking for trouble.

My university affiliation has helped in enormous amounts. There are some subjects about whom people have been interviewed over and over. In dealing with Europeans and people abroad, I

found it helpful to have letterhead and the university connection.

DLB: I found this book–the Marilyn Monroe book–to be very intellectual, academic. It was interesting to me that you focused so much on the *work* of film.

Rollyson: I felt like I was using all the tools I had learned in graduate school with that book. I found that once Mailer had gotten Monroe up on the screen in his book (which I admire very much), he didn't know what to do. He had no way of distinguishing between good and bad performance, no vocabulary for it. He didn't know anything about the vocabulary of an actor, how one would go about analyzing scenes and so on. So I decided to take a crack at it.

DLB: When I was initially approached about doing this interview, I was told you are an "unauthorized biographer." That's something that has stayed with me. I found it curious that most of your subjects are dead and wondered what that appellation meant. I know you've been taken to task by Sontag for the work you're doing on her biography, and I wanted to know if you would speak a bit about that.

Rollyson: Actually, I alternate between the live ones and the dead ones. All of the books about figures alive or dead would be called unauthorized. And that's important to me because authorization suggests that in some way the biographer has to get permission. But these are public figures. Their careers are built around their personalities. Susan Sontag is a big, big New York personality. She's a celebrity, not just a writer. There's no way that such a figure is likely to give you permission or authorize you. And if they did, you wouldn't want it, because then they'd be looking over your shoulder. Even if someone were to say "I authorize you, go ahead," it's like you've been blessed, tapped on the shoulder. Mailer used to call himself an "outlaw novelist." I like to call myself an "outlaw biographer." I believe very strongly that we are transgressing. There is an invasive aspect to biography. I think biographers kid themselves when they don't believe that is so. I often tell my students I believe in a conflict-of-interest theory of biography, by which I mean there is no way that my interest in doing a biography of Susan Sontag can be justified on her terms. It's her life. Of course she might be angry or nervous or upset about someone writing her biography. I don't blame her for it. I'm not surprised about it. It doesn't stop me. At the same time, I respect it, but not so much that I wouldn't write the book. Martha Gellhorn wrote me a letter when I proposed writing her biography and said, "Nothing personal, but I don't want a biography written." I say in the introduction I didn't take it personally; I went ahead and wrote the biography. No matter how good the book is, it is not really the sum of a person's life. I feel that there will be other biographies about all the figures I write about. I won't have the last word. You can't write a *Ulysses* of biography.

DLB: What sort of problems or obstacles have you encountered with Susan Sontag?

Rollyson: When you're dealing with fairly powerful literary figures, they essentially try to scare you or intimidate you. Essentially what they do is have a representative—often a law firm—write a letter to your publisher. They in a sense put the publisher on notice. In Sontag's case it's a brief letter saying that they feel we (my wife and I) are not qualified to write this biography, that we are interested in scandalous material. About three to four sentences to that effect. In many cases this will work remarkably well. Publishers will get scared and drop biographies. My Martha Gellhorn biography was supposed to be published by Doubleday and was instead published by St. Martin's Press. When Gellhorn threatened legal action when I finished my book, the manuscript went to the legal department at Doubleday, and it never got out of the legal department. Eventually my agent withdrew the book and sold it to St. Martin's Press.

DLB: Is St. Martin's going to publish the Sontag biography?

Rollyson: No, that's W. W. Norton. Publishing in New York is pretty much like free agenting in baseball now. Although there are authors and publishers who are loyal to each other, by and large that is not the case anymore. Every book is a separate entity. The publisher will look at the sales figures, and the editorial staff has to be interested. Scribners published my Rebecca West biography. The reviews were the best reviews I had ever had. They were not at all interested in Susan Sontag. Part of it was because the publisher was a friend of Sontag's and actually told my agent that Scribners did not want to be involved.

DLB: Norton is definitely a very respectable house.

Rollyson: A very good publisher. When my wife and I were submitting our proposals to publishing houses, people raised issues about unauthorized biographies, what happens if there are obstacles. We more or less expect there to be obstacles. This is not a book a publisher should take on if they don't expect there to be obstacles. Norton was the first publisher that actually thought through the problem from beginning to end, that understands it as well as I do as a biographer, and they stand behind the book. I find that rare in New York publishing. What I find is enormous enthusiasm because they like the figure, but as soon as there is any sort of problem, especially a legal one, they really run scared and pull out.

DLB: Who is your editor at Norton?

Rollyson: Gerry Howard. A wonderful editor.

DLB: What do you think about Kitty Kelley's book *The Royals?*

Rollyson: My first article on biography was published in the journal *Biography* in 1978. I just published almost twenty years later my second article for this journal, and the title of it is "God Bless Kitty Kelley." I belong to a biography seminar at New York University. I start the article with a provocative comment I made at one of the meetings. I said I didn't think there was much difference between Kitty Kelley and any other biographer, literary or otherwise. Everyone was absolutely aghast. They thought this was a shocking thing to say. I couldn't be serious. It couldn't be true. So I wrote this brief article talking about how biographers are nosy. Most of the things people don't like about Kitty Kelley most other biographers do in one way or another. When I made that comment, I had not read any of her books. In writing this article for *Biography,* I read her Frank Sinatra biography. I was impressed not with the style—she's a rather pedestrian writer. But what I was impressed with was all the voices in the book, how many people are on record talking about Frank Sinatra. People say she is fast and loose with the truth, but I have not seen any major source she interviewed for the biography contradict what she said. She interviewed some people who are very close to Sinatra. The virtue of her kind of biography is that you see so much of the biographer's evidence firsthand. The problem with it is that there's no discernible style, no elegance to it, or overall interpretive fabric. But she's done her homework.

DLB: Do you have favorite biographies that you go back to for inspiration?

Rollyson: I am really attracted to biographies that are a little quirky. There's an interesting biography by Elinor Langer about a thirties writer named Josephine Herbst. What is interesting to me is that Langer brings in her reactions to the subject. I find that interaction between biographer and subject interesting. Half of what biography is in a sense is a kind of autobiography. So when the biographer can work himself into the narrative in an elegant way, I appreciate that. I know how enormously difficult it is. I've only skirted it.

DLB: Who do you consider to be your target audience or reader?

Rollyson: I try to keep two things straight: that I am writing not just for my academic peers. Susan Strasberg cured me of that. At the same time I am trying to write for people who are familiar with the figure and those who aren't. I try to integrate the character with the incidents of their lives, to make it a story. I am not sure I am always successful, but I try to keep in mind that I am writing the story of someone's life. That may sound obvious or commonplace, but I don't believe all biographers do that. I can give you an example; some years ago I heard Michael Wrezin discussing his biography of the critic Dwight MacDonald. His theory of selection for the biography was that anything that might throw light on his work would be included. He said, for example, he learned that MacDonald had affairs with a couple of his students. He said, "But I'm not putting that in the book." I said that I would certainly put it in the book. Because it is the story of someone's life. It is not just an intellectual biography. Dwight MacDonald was a person who actually lived and breathed; he had a sex life; he wasn't all brains. For me Wrezin's basis of selection was far too narrow.

DLB: How do you decide what to leave out?

Rollyson: The story, as with novels, I believe, begins to take on a life of its own. I learn funny or interesting things, but they stick out; there's no way to incorporate them into the narrative. Or the book is already quite long, and my editor says that it is congested with detail. In my Rebecca West biography one of the major stories is about her very conflicted relationship with her son. There was a section in one of my chapters in which a young American showed up, and she sort of took him under her wing. He had no idea that the reason she did so was because he could serve as a kind of surrogate son without all the conflicts she had with her own son. Another biographer might have found a way to integrate that into the narrative, but my problem was here are all these tensions with Anthony and to stick this other situation into the narrative sort of broke things up. It never got told; it never got into the book.

DLB: Do you work closely with your editors?

Rollyson: Not very much. I've had one or two editors who told me that I could show them something early if I wanted. Most of the New York editors I have had are content to wait and get the whole book and then ask for revisions. For the Rebecca West book I had so many details to work with that fairly early on I sent drafts to editors. It was very helpful for them to say that something wasn't working.

DLB: Have you thought about writing in any other genres?

Rollyson: I've written a play, a one-woman play based on the writings of Rebecca West, which I would love to see produced. I haven't wanted to take time out from my other writing projects. I would love to write a novel, but if I could write a novel, I think I probably would already have written one. Every now and then I sit down and begin writing what I think will be a work of fiction, and to be honest I lose confidence. Even when I am wrong about my biographies, there is no lack of confidence. I don't want to write second-rate novels. I would like to be a contender. I feel as a biographer I am a contender. I don't think I would ever be a contender as a novelist.

DLB: Who are the novelists you admire?

Rollyson: Mailer, Faulkner, E. L. Doctorow. I have to be honest and say I do not read very much contemporary fiction. When I have, I have been very impressed with people like Toni Morrison. I like George Garrett. I reviewed his most recent novel, which I thought was just fantastic. And there's a Susan Sontag joke in it, too.

DLB: I wanted to circle back to a subject we touched on before. Can you explain what the categories of *authorized* versus *unauthorized* mean to you?

Rollyson: People have different definitions. Some people use words like *designated*. In my understanding, an authorized biographer has been given formal (written) permission by an estate. Sometimes people think they are authorized, and they write the book and show it to an estate, and the estate doesn't like it. They want it to be rewritten.

DLB: That's censorship, isn't it?

Rollyson: Well, it is. But there are copyright laws, and most biographers feel they can't write biographies without permission to quote from the author's work. The estate or the subject is going to be the copyright holder. One of the really awful things and a reason I feel quite negatively about authorized biographies is that literary figures in this country—and there are very few exceptions—have used the copyright law as a form of censorship. For example, one of the first things Martha Gellhorn did was to say that I would have no right to quote from her published or unpublished work. When I was working on the Norman Mailer biography, his agent tried to do that. They insisted on reading the biography. I told them that it was unauthorized and that I merely wanted permission to quote from his published work. They contended that some people might think that this permission indicated their approval. I said that that was silly and that anyone who thought that was dumb and naive, and I was not responsible. With authorized biographies, the biographer, depending on the written agreement, is either given carte blanche or sometimes is subject to review by the estate. In the case of Sylvia Plath's authorized biography, large portions were rewritten by the executors of the estate. I want to feel that I am completely independent. And the price I pay for it is that some people immediately assume that I am writing something scandalous.

DLB: How long have you been working on the Sontag biography?

Rollyson: Close to two years now, including the research and the proposal.

DLB: And how long do you think it will take you to complete the project?

Rollyson: About another eighteen months or so.

DLB: Do you give yourself a time line?

Rollyson: Yes. It varies from book to book, but I have a pretty strong sense of how long it will take me to write a book. I have publisher's deadlines, of course. The trade houses are fairly strict. They are increasingly strict about granting extensions to biographers. The Monroe book took six years, but I did not know what I was doing. The West book took about three-and-a-half years. The Sontag book, from the beginning to the end, will probably take about three-and-a-half years.

DLB: You have spoken a lot about Norman Mailer, so I would like to know what it is about him that so interests you.

Rollyson: What I find interesting is that he has done so many things; he's been a writer and a politician. He has been heavily criticized for spending too much time on politics. Not all his books are successful. My favorites are *Armies of the Night, The Executioner's Song.* I like *Why Are We in Vietnam?* His book on the Muhammed Ali and Joe Frazier fight is wonderful. What I also like about him is his honesty about literary competitiveness. I think he's very honest about how competitive things are. Not very many authors are really that honest. I like Mailer because he has stretched the idea of what a writer is. He has made it less religious, more a part of the marketplace, as weird as that sounds. His Marilyn Monroe book got some terrible reviews. He once called himself a semicommercial writer. He said he had to write for money, but it had to be someone he was interested in. The idea that money and one's career don't enter into one's thinking is preposterous.

DLB: Have you read the Adele Mailer book?

Rollyson: I reviewed it for Ebsco, an on-line outfit. Salem Press in Pasadena has a contract with them to do these three-hundred-word reviews. I write a couple of those a year. I found her book interesting. A lot of reviews complain about how poorly written it was. It was shocking because I thought I knew what happened between the two of them. But she presents an even cruder, egotistical figure than I thought could possibly exist. And though it could be dismissed as a revenge book, I think there is a lot of truth to it. What I think she does well is to demonstrate how demeaning and awful he was to her, and at the same time he was able to get people in New York to protect him. He knew how to manipulate the literary movers and shakers, and they covered for him. The man stabbed his wife, for God's sake.

DLB: The term *icon* has been thrown around a lot recently.

Rollyson: I do not think it is accidental that the term has come up now. I gave a talk in Las Vegas, which I think is so appropriate, on female icons from Marilyn Monroe to Susan Sontag. There are people like Sontag who consciously project themselves into the status of an icon. My wife and I have been enormously impressed and sort of taken aback when we have seen Sontag at readings in public at least a dozen times in the past year. She's treated like an icon. She comes in with an entourage. There's lots of kissing and hugging. There's a lot of flattery. The way she keeps her hair. By now it should be all gray. She dyes it so she still has the silver streak. All of that is a kind of iconic attempt to stamp yourself onto the consciousness of your time, as Mailer said. He wrote this book called *Advertisements for Myself.* Someone like Susan Sontag becomes an advertisement for herself by remaining true to type. She gave an interview to a journalist a few years ago in which she did say that she just picks it up and dyes it all around. There are some photographs of her without the streak. She says, "It wasn't me." It's like she's trademarked herself. Some years ago an interviewer asked her about her career and the marketing of her books. She said she didn't think of herself as having a career. That is probably the most disingenuous remark she has ever made. And the reporter was embarrassed for having asked the question.

DLB: Have you ever had to do slightly underhanded things to get the information you needed?

Rollyson: I hope I haven't lied to anyone. One of the reasons I am so public about being an unauthorized biographer is that I do not want people to be misled. I spoke with Nadine Gordimer about my Rebecca West biography, and she was helpful. When I decided to write the Sontag biography, I approached her again. She and Sontag are friends who once gave an interview together. She asked me if the book was being done with Susan's permission. I explained to her that it was an unauthorized biography. She then asked if Susan objected to it. I reiterated that the book was to be an unauthorized one. I suppose I could have told her that I received a letter from Sontag's lawyers. I would never pretend to have someone's confidence that I don't have. But to be honest, I think I work like a journalist in some ways, in the sense that I am certainly not going to volunteer such information. With someone like Gordimer, a seasoned and mature writer, I do not feel the need to spell things out. In fact, in her case, she had an assistant call a few days later to say that she wouldn't be available for comment.

DLB: Do you give readings from your biographies?

Rollyson: Occasionally I give readings. I haven't spoken at many writers conferences. When I look at the ads for such conferences, they usually have a nonfiction division. But they are not going to pick Carl Rollyson. They would pick a high-profile person, like Victoria Glendenning or Michael Holroyd, who has made a big splash.

DLB: You mentioned that you have written a play and that you are interested in writing a screenplay. What projects do you have in mind after the Sontag biography?

Rollyson: The next thing that my wife and I want to do is a biography of Joan Didion and John Gregory Dunne. A couple on a couple. So we can get into more trouble. The other thing I have just done is something that I think most biographers in New York would not do—I've told you what I'm thinking. Most would be terribly afraid that someone would steal the idea and do it first. At least three years before we signed the contract to do the Sontag biography, I was telling everybody in New York that I was going to do this book. That is how I get my sources and how I find out if anybody else is planning on doing a similar thing. What I found was that no one would dare to write a biography of Susan Sontag. Now I don't know what will happen with Didion and Dunne. Even if someone else is doing a biography of them, I won't be bothered because I am faster than most biographers. What I like about them is that they have worked as hacks. They are very good writers, but they have worked as hacks, and so have I. Dunne says that when they wrote that screenplay that turned into the awful Robert Redford movie, he was worried about his health benefits; he needed an operation. I just love that openness. I doubt he will be similarly open to me about a biography. I have just read *Slouching Towards Bethlehem.* What I find really interesting is that just as Didion was leaving New York, Susan Sontag was arriving. Everything that was sort of bothering Didion about New York is the stuff that Sontag was beginning to experience. Sontag was born in New York City, but she didn't come to live here for some time. She lived in Paris for quite a while.

DLB: What books by Sontag do you like best?

Rollyson: My all-time favorite is *On Photography,* which has had the most intellectual influence on me. Doing her biography is really paying an intellectual debt. She won't respond to it that way, but that is how I feel. I like *Illness as Metaphor*. I really like her last novel, *The Volcano Lover,* which was a best-seller for several weeks. Her early novels most people feel are not very good. There are some interesting essays in *Under the Sign of Saturn.*

DLB: So she is a character you admire?

Rollyson: Oh yes, very much so. And I don't feel at all angry at her for opposing the book. Maybe a little disappointed. My wife's fantasy was that she would co-opt us—rather than trying to scare us, that she might grant one interview. We did meet her once, in Poland in 1980, and we liked her enormously. Our first impression was very, very positive. I am also kind of thankful, enormously relieved, that we weren't granted permission because once you enter into any relationship with your subject, it changes the nature of the work. Suddenly the subject is responding to you. There is no question that becoming an acquaintance or friend of your subject would probably enhance your knowledge, but would you be able to write then?

DLB: You write in the Monroe book about viewing her life as camera setups. I'm wondering what you think of the recent controversy over the paparazzi's role in the death of Princess Diana. She was hounded by the press, but at the same time she seems to have used them to her advantage as well.

Rollyson: I'm certainly not angry at the paparazzi, and I would probably make the same argument for them that I did for Kitty Kelley. They're involved in the same process, this interest in celebrities. There's an awful lot of sentimentalizing of Diana. It is understandable and similar to the response to Marilyn Monroe, who was considered a victim of Hollywood. But she was a collaborator. All of the press has been about the driver, for example. I would like to know what the alcohol level in her blood was, what her judgment was like, why she got into that car. I don't want to be too hard on her. But it is so shortsighted to say that the problem is photographers. It is convenient, but it doesn't explain anything at all.

DLB: I read a Baruch College magazine piece that you wrote in which you said that acting was your initial passion. Have you acted? Why didn't you pursue an acting career?

Rollyson: I have acted. But essentially what happened is that at age eighteen I did a summer appren-

ticeship at a playhouse, and I saw what a tough life the theater was going to be. I saw many good actors who weren't getting jobs, and I was just too middle class for that. I also saw a fair bit of corruption. I was also developing at the same time a healthy interest in literature. And teaching is a kind of performance which brings in a steady paycheck. It took until the publication of my Monroe book that I realized that I wasn't an academic who would write, but rather a writer who just happened to be an academic.

DLB: You've written about Picasso. What art form is it that interests you aside from literature?

Rollyson: I think it's film. I got into writing about art and Picasso really by accident.

DLB: Do you admire Picasso as a man?

Rollyson: Not really. He made Mailer look like Little Lord Fauntleroy. He was a very mean and misogynistic person. There was this incredible scene with Francois Gillot in which he put a cigarette out on her cheek. The cruelty gets into his art. I think a lot of great writers have hated women. I am not saying such people shouldn't be criticized. I heard John Richardson talk about his Picasso biography, in which he said that Picasso could be excused for his chauvinist behavior because of his Spanish background. I wanted to get up and say that Picasso didn't live all his life in Spain. He is not someone who stayed in the village.

DLB: Since you mentioned that you and your wife are both working on the Sontag biography, I am interested in hearing about the process of cowriting. What is your wife's background? Does one of you do the research and the other write?

Rollyson: She has a Ph.D. in English from the University of Toronto. She had a career as a stockbroker as well. She has a University of Michigan law degree. It seems that every book I write gets me into legal trouble. So I have always consulted her. She has become an expert in copyright law. But she is also a fabulous editor. She has edited every major piece I've ever written. Both of us had a real interest in Sontag. To put it in a nutshell, she says that I am fast and she's thorough. So I can crank out a rough draft quite quickly, and then she goes over it. She is meticulous. All of my biographies have been dedicated to her and talked over with her. It always seemed a logical extension of that process, to do a

Daniel Menaker

Daniel Menaker (photograph by Sara Barrett)

project together. It has been a remarkably smooth process.

DLB: You're both writing?

Rollyson: Right now she's working on some other projects as well. I'm just starting to write the Sontag biography. It is sort of back and forth. That is one of the things I want to find out about Didion and Dunne—how they work together.

DLB: Is there anything else you want to add before we finish up?

Rollyson: I just want to mention a favorite film that I go back to over and over. *Citizen Kane.* It is one I've taught and thought about quite a bit. It is about the biographical process. I showed it to a class this summer, and there was a wonderful documentary on PBS about Orson Welles and his career and William Randolph Hearst's career. To show that documentary and *Citizen Kane* was just magnificent. I think part of the reason I like the film so much, even its film noir quality, is that it is very much like Faulkner's *Absalom! Absalom!,* which all seems to take place in the dark and has multiple narrators. Is there one key to character? Each narrator adds a layer to the narratiöe.

DLB: It is, then, in a sense about what is not revealed.
Rollyson: Yes.

Daniel Menaker joined the staff of The New Yorker *in 1969. For two decades he was one of the magazine's senior editors. In 1994 he was hired as a senior literary editor at Random House. His novel,* The Treatment, *is forthcoming from Knopf in 1998.*

DLB: In October *The New Yorker* ran a piece on the suspected death of book publishing. Do you think the industry really has one foot in the grave?

Menaker: First of all, I should mention that I am still a neophyte in book publishing. I've been here three years, which is nothing in comparison to people like Ann Godoff and Morgan Entrekin, who truly have this business in their blood. But I will say that even before I got into book publishing, I seem to remember having read that same piece—or something like it—a number of times. There was probably something to it each time, but the death knell is always being tolled for publishing, and for literary publishing, in particular. I suppose one could argue that it's harder to have literature of worth published—and published well and successfully—in this country than it used to be. On the other hand, the situation seems to be tidal: it seems harder at times and easier at others. I think that the last few years may have been a little easier than the *New Yorker* piece implied. Publishing a book is selectively difficult and selectively easy—and sometimes that selectiveness is arbitrary. Sometimes the right book will hit the right editor at the right time, and the publishing house will pay a lot of money for it and publish it well, and the book will succeed. It's like the weather. All the figuring in the world cannot predict a *Midnight in the Garden of Good and Evil,* or a *Snow Falling on Cedars.* There's no way to predict those books that come out of nowhere and do well. It's imponderable. So people will continue to take chances in the hope of finding such things. Generally, though, I think that literary publishing is in slightly better shape than that piece would have it.

DLB: Take a book like *Midnight in the Garden of Good and Evil.* Don't you think it would have done well, regardless? It had all the elements of a good story: a great sense of place, mystery and intrigue, the whole nine yards.

Menaker: It's hard to say. I don't know. I assume it would. I think the answer is yes, but I really don't know. Take something I do know a little bit more about: *Primary Colors* [which Menaker edited in 1995]. That book was, in many ways, a combination of extrinsic circumstance and internal value. One of the circumstances it had going for it was that Colin Powell decided not to run for the presidency. Clinton remained utterly central. Now, if Powell *had* run . . . first of all, of course, his book would've continued to do extremely well. It would have sold twice as many copies, perhaps, as it did. Secondly, it would have been extremely interesting to see what sort of impact his declaration would've had on the sales of *Primary Colors*. In fact, before we published it, I said, "I think this is going to be a number one best-seller if Colin Powell doesn't run for the presidency, and if he does I don't know what will happen." But surely he would have sopped up so much attention from the media, as a candidate, that the whole publication would have been a very different circumstance. Now, it could have done exactly the same; we'll never know. It's the road not taken. So you can see how totally arbitrary and unpredictable these things are. Look at *Into Thin Air*. It would have been a great seller, anyway, and I think it's a good book. But about two weeks after its publication something like seven *more* people were killed on Everest, and it just made it all the more urgent because everyone in the United States wanted to talk to Krakauer. It was a case of free publicity like you wouldn't believe for the book. And so, again, there are certain things that you just can't predict. Now, McCourt, on the other hand, the other great phenomenon of the year, would've done the same, I imagine.

DLB: All the books you've mentioned so far seem to me to be very good books.

Menaker: These days, I think, the good books tend to be on the nonfiction side. Although recently, in the last few months alone, there are certain exceptions, like DeLillo's book. The fiction side of the best-seller list has looked a little more appetizing from a literary point of view in the last year or so.

DLB: Why?

Menaker: Pynchon and DeLillo came out and made the list. Again, I think that it's a kind of coincidence that several big-time writers have all published books in the last year or so. I assume that 1998 will not have a Roth and a DeLillo and a Pynchon and an Updike all in the same six-month period.

DLB: I'm surprised you have time to read all these books.

Menaker: I don't. I don't read. I just read what I'm sent. Every now and then I'll pick up a book and race through it. I read *Deadly Feasts,* the Richard Rhodes book, and *The Perfect Storm,* by Sebastian Junger, which I absolutely loved. But, basically, outside of my work, I read maybe five or six books a year. A lot of what I'm turning down, I often see showing up elsewhere, which is something. But I'm not like my wife, who does all the reading for the *New York Times Book Review* and comes home and says, "I think I'll read a little." I can't believe it. I can't understand it. I say, "Where's the remote? Give me the remote! Don't show me a page."

DLB: Has *Primary Colors* been your favorite project so far?

Menaker: It certainly was a great bit of fun, and I think also in some ways it is a very worthwhile book. It was a ride, too. I haven't had a ride like that one since, and I doubt I will again. But it's impossible to compare that book to the modest success of Julie Hecht or Virginia Adair, which were equally gratifying in their own ways. It was a huge stroke of luck that I worked on *Primary Colors,* in that it was the first novel I ever published, and it gave me an instant credibility that might've taken ten or fifteen years—in my senility!—to establish. So it was enormously helpful to me—a great piece of luck. Also, I liked the book. I've always liked the idea of popular literary fiction. One of my great idols is Elmore Leonard. I think he's a fabulous writer. So I've never been a purely literary person, and this seemed to me to accomplish a lot of things at the same time.

DLB: Are there other books you've found especially rewarding?

Menaker: I've enjoyed working on all of them. *Journey to the Land of the Flies,* by Aldo Buzzi, which was translated from the Italian by Ann Goldstein, stands out in my mind. It's a wonderful book that didn't get the attention it deserved.

DLB: Was it jarring to jump from magazine to book publishing?

Menaker: Not at all. The important thing remains—and I don't care what anybody says—that at the heart of publishing, there is still the read. It is the essential act. And it's the same whether you're reading a short story for a magazine or a novel for book publication. The acquisition and your original conviction—the five or six or seven times a year you come to the edge of your seat because you feel that what you have in front of you is something of value—that's at the heart of this business. It doesn't matter which arm of the publishing business you're in.

DLB: The acquisition process in book publishing must be a bigger deal than it is in the magazine world, though. Have you gotten a feel for the deal-making aspects of the job?

Menaker: If I have it, I think I had it all along. So far, things have worked out pretty well. I trust my gut feeling when it comes to what to buy, when to buy it, how much to go for. I'm cheap. I sometimes get books for under the highest price. That's a risk on the part of the author. The author or the agent might say, "Well, X publisher is offering seventy-five thousand dollars. Random House is only offering sixty, but they already have good ideas about how to publish it, and it is, after all, just an advance against royalties. The money's going to be the same in the end. The only difference is what I'll see up front. So, I think I'll go over to Random House, even though they're offering less." Sonny [Mehta] got my book for five thousand dollars less than two other people offered because I wanted to be at Knopf.

DLB: Are you pleased to be a Knopf acquisition? How would you define the kinds of books they publish? High literary?

Menaker: High, yes, but also unexpected. As Bob Gottlieb used to say, "I like to publish things that are something." The idea being that no matter what you say about a given book, it's something—something you have to take into account. And that's what Knopf is good at literarily. I think one of the reasons Harry [Evans] offered me this job was to infiltrate some of that same sensibility at Random House.

DLB: How are you feeling in the midst of Evans's departure?

Menaker: I will never forget his spontaneity. He was always a kind of catalyst for good things coming together. After Harry hired me, however, Ann [Godoff, Evans's replacement] was the one who took me by the hand and taught me the nuts and bolts of the business. On the one hand, I'm sorry Harry's gone, and it will be interesting to see how the public aspect of this company does in the wake of his departure. But I know Random House is in good professional hands with Ann. There's no ques-

tion about that. As I said before, Ann has this business in her blood. She's been in book publishing for a long time, and she's relatively young. It's really part of her very being. After her promotion was announced, she said to the staff, "I'm you. If this is a triumph for me, it's a triumph for you. I came up through the ranks. I'm not someone somebody met at a cocktail party. I'm not somebody who rubbed elbows with the owner of the company last night. I'm somebody who worked in book publishing for fifteen years and, little by little, if I learned the trade, I learned it from the ground up. You don't necessarily have to have connections to come out on top." And I think it's true. I think it's a very old-fashioned appointment, actually.

DLB: You've published a collection of short stories, countless pieces for *The New Yorker,* a humor book, and now you have a novel coming out. You've written consistently throughout your career as an editor. How do you find the time to do it?

Menaker: I had some difficulty between '92 and '96, actually, because there was so much going on in my life personally and professionally. My mother died. I got a job offer. Tina [Brown] arrived at the magazine. But then, in the last year or so, I got back to the novel. I don't know the answer. I do believe that most people—even very busy people—waste a tremendous amount of time. Huge amounts of it. And I think you need to. I'm not being critical of this tendency. I think you need to be able not to do anything. But I find that after a short time, sometimes an hour or two, sometimes a day or two, I get kind of depressed if I'm not up to something or other.

DLB: But you would never say that your writing is a hobby?

Menaker: No, I just do it. I don't know when I do it. Who knows? Sometimes my wife and the kids want to stay in the city, and I go up to our house in Great Barrington, Massachusetts. I go up on Friday night and spend the first three or four hours on Saturday morning loathing the idea of working, hating everything and everyone, trying to fix the screens, et cetera. And then, little by little, I start to work. I work from ten or eleven in the morning till about six. The next morning I get up and do some more, and then I come home to New York, and that's how I did the novel. I hope I didn't shirk my family responsibilities too much. It's not so remarkable, though, when you think about how much time people waste. Some people need more down time than others. I could probably use some down time. I'm probably deranged from doing all these things. I think I am. I think I'm obsessed.

DLB: Obsessed with your work?

Menaker: Partially. I also think it's the way I am. I don't like to do things halfway. When I publish a book, I like to do everything I can for it. I think about it in the shower, what would be a good title. It's all in my mind. I hope it's not really truly obsessive, but it's probably somewhat close to it. And when I'm thinking about my own work, same thing. You could say I'm extremely focused, or you could say I'm obsessed.

DLB: How would you describe your novel?

Menaker: A sort of serious comic novel about an anxious young schoolteacher who's trying to figure out how to get a life. He has the help of a deranged analyst and also an entanglement with a very rich young widow.

DLB: Is the story something you've been living with for a while, or did it creep up on you?

Menaker: Both. The ending I had with me all the time. Some of the more intricate coincidental occurrences—or maybe I should call them noncoincidental occurrences—I stumbled on. One of the points of the book is that our lives really consist much more of happenstance than we like to believe. Jake, the main character, comes to terms with this as he tries to rationalize his mother's death. It's a philosophical conclusion, but it's also an emotional one, that things don't make sense and that things happen by brute luck. Our minds don't always want to accept this, and so we figure out how to tell stories in the hopes of making some sense of it all, and that's where fiction comes from.

Samuel Vaughan

Samuel Vaughan started his career in publishing in the rights department at Doubleday in 1952. He went on to serve as both the company's advertising manager and sales manager before joining the editorial department in the mid 1960s. Vaughan later became the president and publisher of Doubleday and eventually its editor in chief. Today he is an editor at large at Random House.

DLB: Do you find that writing itself is changing? I know that sounds like a ridiculous question, but it strikes me that some of the new fiction I've

Samuel Vaughan (photograph by Alex Gotfryd)

read lately feels different: quicker, grabbier, more movielike.

Vaughan: I think many writers today have an enormous fear of boring their readers, and some of them associate boredom with length. That's why a Don DeLillo or a Tom Wolfe is an exception, because many writers are unwilling to bite off that much to chew, in the fear that readers won't accept it. I think this is a classic mistake. Americans, until recently perhaps, have never been noticeably partial to the slim, well-made French novel, say. More often, we have tended to like the big, bulky novel that delivers a lot of bang.

DLB: I think of all those James Michener books that were on living-room bookshelves growing up. Do you tend to like meatier books?

Vaughan: I do. I like the achingly evocative, large-scale novel. The more excessive the better. I also like stylists. I like people whose style is absolutely apparent. I like writers like Updike, who you can't read without being conscious half the time of the style. I learned in publishing what I never thought I'd learn, too, which is an appreciation for the plainsong kind of writers—the writers who can write a clear English sentence.

DLB: What about short fiction?

Vaughan: The short story gets a lot of attention these days. There certainly seem to be many short-story writers whose books are selling better than they used to. If you read the *New York Times Book Review,* you'd think it was the "New York Times Review of the Short Story." As a reader, when I'm looking through the book reviews and I see a collection listed, I go on. I'm not looking to find tiny little epiphanies in books. If I give my time and attention—or even my money—to a reading experience, I want it to deliver a lot. There are, of course, some writers who can do that in a short space. But I like to curl up, not *with* a book, but inside it, and be with it for a while.

DLB: There's been a lot of talk this year about *Cold Mountain.* Have you read it?

Vaughan: I'm bustling to read it, but I haven't yet. I've heard the author interviewed, and I like the whole idea of it. I like the way it was published and the way it caught on.

DLB: I guess the memoir craze is starting to die down a bit?

Vaughan: That's a sort of a trend that isn't a trend. The memoir has always been around . . . it's just more noticeable now. Naturally, I'm sensitive, but I think fathers have had a particularly poor showing in memoirs recently. Those of us who are not child abusers are career obsessed or otherwise distracted. The father needs a rehabilitation.

DLB: Is there anything particular that you feel defines book publishing these days?

Vaughan: I think what you see today in publishing is a kind of journalistic recklessness. Ten years ago Harper or Doubleday, say, would never have published a book that made charges about a public figure or institution without rigorous checking and an absolute belief in the author's correctness—or, at least, fairness. Now we have what has been called the tabloidization of publishing. But nobody can resist the fuss these books create. It reminds me of a friend I once knew who read *The National Enquirer.* I asked her if she believed anything she read in it, and she told me, "I don't know whether I believe it, but I like it." So you have the Kitty Kelley school of so-called reporting. The books are untrustworthy, and yet they satisfy some appetite on the part of readers and publishers.

DLB: It reminds me of *The New Yorker* breakfast Tina Brown hosted for Dick Morris.

Vaughan: Dick Morris is a good example. It's funny, Harry Evans is a brilliant journalist and a damn good book publisher. I'm sure, though, that when he was at the London *Times* he made his reporters work longer and harder on individual news stories than some of our authors work on entire books.

DLB: Because he cared more about the newspaper business?

Vaughan: No, because he wanted to get the story right. He owed it to the paper and his readers, and he also had to contend with the tougher libel laws in England. So when they did stories on thalidomide or airline safety, they spent months on them.

DLB: Why did he change?

Vaughan: I think Harry got caught up in the excitement. He still bought books off the news wires, and those of us who surrounded him would say, "Don't buy so many." But he found them hard to resist. Sometimes he scored, and sometimes he didn't.

DLB: Now that he's left for *The Daily News,* is there a sense of unease—of "Where do we go now"?

Vaughan: It takes a while for a ship to change direction. It doesn't happen when one person walks out the door and another person takes their chair. I don't think Harry's effect on the imprint is going to disappear right away. At the same time, I don't think there's been a terrific sense of whither goest we because we have books, we have work to do.

DLB: I've heard that Random House got its name because its founders set out to publish at random. They didn't want to be tied down to any one genre. They just wanted to publish books they liked, regardless of whether the books were biographies or desk calendars or whatever. Is that true? And if so, does it still hold today?

Vaughan: Well, it's part of the Random House lore—or possibly its legend—that Bennet Cerf and Donald Klopfer, who founded the company, set out with the intention of publishing a few books at random. What they did first, though, was buy a line called The Modern Library. Any house that hopes to endure has got to have some kind of base—some kind of backlist—so they bought one, and they made a lot on it. On top of that, then, their idea was to publish a few books at random.

DLB: Do you like Random House?

Vaughan: It's like trying to love a dynamo. It's hard to cuddle up to. I grew up in publishing in a collegial, familiar atmosphere. So people trained me on purpose, and I trained other people. We were in and out of each others' offices all the time, reading for one another, et cetera. I don't find the same atmosphere at Random House. It's more internally competitive. But, on the other hand, to be fair, I'm somewhat in the margins. I don't come into the city every day. I don't carry as full a list as I used to although this coming year is fairly full.

DLB: Would you say the competitiveness is encouraged?

Vaughan: That's hard to say. I think it's encouraged on one hand and discouraged on the other. Every house within the house is encouraged to buy its own books and throw its own weight. But the chairman, on occasion, would like everyone to behave as if they were working for one company, all pulling the same kind of oar. So, there's a schizophrenic quality to it, in that regard.

DLB: I imagine there's a greater pull these days to get involved with the marketing of the books you're editing.

Vaughan: I think some of the really good editors and publishers have long been involved with marketing. They just didn't call it that then. A big part of publishing has always been to enhance an author's reputation. When Maxwell Perkins made sure that Hemingway and Fitzgerald were published in *Scribner's Magazine,* he didn't do it just so they could make some extra money.

DLB: Did you have a model when you started out as editor?

Vaughan: Early on, I read about Maxwell Perkins, who taught me—indirectly—the best and worst of editing. The best is to have a sort of devotion to what you're doing, and the worst is to try to make a silk purse out of something other than silk.

DLB: You must've known the Doubleday operation inside and out. Was it difficult to leave?

Vaughan: It was. But by the end of my tenure there, I felt disconnected from the house. I'd begun to feel that I no longer knew what kind of books they wanted, and that was very disorienting because I used to live and breathe the place.

DLB: Did they change the kinds of books they'd been doing before?

Vaughan: No. I think they lost their way. They lost their direction. I sometimes wonder whether most big publishing houses haven't experienced the same sort of shift. You asked about other trends in publishing. There's the disappearance of family names from the spines of books. Families don't necessarily make great publishers, and private companies aren't necessarily any better than public companies. But when a family name was on the book, there was a sense that somebody cared deeply about what was in the book—for better and worse. Now you see corporate names. Viacom, I think, owns Scribner now. And they're doing a good job of publishing. But the name Scribner used to have a much more profound relation to the books themselves than it does today.

DLB: It's sort of like the difference between buying a book at your corner bookstore versus ordering one from Amazon.com. There's something very remote about the transaction.

Vaughan: By the way, I'm not looking back to a time when publishing was pristine and full of values and standards and such.

DLB: I know what you're saying. But it seems like it's turned into a trading floor or something.

Vaughan: I'm supposed to write an introduction to a publishing memoir that appeared about twenty years ago. Part of it ran in *The New Yorker,* in fact. It was a book by an English publisher, and the title of the memoir was *An Occupation for Gentlemen.* The point I want to make in my introduction is that that title was used ironically, but people ever since have taken it to be a statement of fact. There's a certain amount of looking back to a time that never was that goes on in publishing. As far as I can tell, most book publishers in the English-speaking world arose out of two occupations: printing and bookselling. And neither of these were occupations for gentlemen. They were tradespeople. So the idea that publishing was once populated by extremely well-educated people of very high standards is a bit of a cartoon. There were always gentlemen and gentlewomen in publishing—and there is, of course, the obvious gentility that people associate with books—but that doesn't mean it was the norm.

DLB: What about today? Do you think there's gentility in publishing in the late nineties?

Vaughan: I think there are at least two layers of publishing—two levels. There's the frothy, newsy layer that bubbles up on the surface: the Dick Morrises and Jackie Collinses and Kitty Kelleys and Colin Powells. Books good and bad. These are the ones that get a lot of money and attention. Then there's a subterranean level of publishing where authors still write, editors still read and edit, books still get published.

DLB: It's ironic that what started out as the meat and bones of the business is now so buried.

Vaughan: It's buried because it doesn't attract attention, but it's how we really make our living. The big-money books are like money laundering. If you take $5 million for a book, you either get it back or you don't. You either lose three million, or two million—or you don't. But these books aren't really what support us. The books we publish on health and gardening, or massage, or running—these are still a large part of the business in any good publishing house. More than half of our annual revenue comes from the backlist—from books that are usually published some years ago. They may show signs of enduring, or they may not be all that distinguished at all, but instead fill a need.

DLB: What books that you've worked on over the course of your career have been your favorites?

Vaughan: I think I'll resist that question by saying that I'm working on a couple of books now that I expect to be my favorites. I've got a book coming out called *Laughing Matters* by Larry Gelbart, a memoir by Elizabeth Spencer, and I'm also working on an immense manuscript by Fanny Flagg—her first novel since *Fried Green Tomatoes.* I'd like to add, too, that one of the highlights of my editing life was being involved with George Garrett's first two Elizabethan novels. That really was a happy experience.

DLB: Who is Larry Gelbart?

Vaughan: He's the kind of writer who remains somewhat anonymous even though his work is very well known. He developed the *M*A*S*H* series for

television. He wrote *A Funny Thing Happened on the Way to the Forum* and the screenplays for *Oh, God* and *Tootsie.*

DLB: You must spend a lot of your time at work these days laughing.

Vaughan: It has tended to go that way. I have another book coming up which is not quite as light-hearted. It's an exposé of Sotheby's, and it's caused a lot of furrowed brows. I think it's a book that deserves to be published, but we're probably going to spend the rest of our lives in court.

DLB: Do you find you get to work with the same authors over and over?

Vaughan: I'm afraid the house author is a dying breed. It used to be when you took on an author, you did so with the rough understanding you were going to stay with that author for a while. You'd publish the off books as well as the on ones, until, finally, either the publisher or the author gave up. That's not the case as much today, partly on account of publicity—the buzz that gets generated when an author changes houses. Also, agents undoubtedly had a hand in the switch, as they tend to benefit when it happens.

DLB: There's the flip side, too, when a writer gets cast off after one or two books that are only modestly successful.

Vaughan: That's definitely true. It used to be harder to get a first book published than it is today. Now the real challenge is publishing a third or fourth one. I'm writing a piece right now on pseudonyms—how their function has changed in publishing. Rather than confusing the identity of an author for reasons of privacy or family or what have you, a pseudonym is now being used to conceal from the book trade that a given author had a book—or two, or three—that didn't sell very well.

DLB: I've read a lot about returns this year: how booksellers are able to send the books they don't sell back to the publisher after ninety days. Apparently, once the books are returned, they're tough to resell. A lot of them get damaged in transit, or they're worn out from being shifted around on bookstore shelves.

Vaughan: Returns have long been the bane of our existence.

DLB: I've heard that publishers are trying to come up with ways to get rid of the return policy–to tell bookstores they will no longer accept the books back, and, if the bookstores object, tell them, "Fine. We just won't send you any of the new John Grisham or Stephen King"–whatever authors are responsible for their biggest profits.

Vaughan: I got into a brawl with the chain stores back in the seventies, right when the chains were beginning to expand exponentially. I had been trained to know the law, which states that you're not supposed to favor one kind of bookseller over another. I found out that we were making side deals with the big buyers, giving them special favors that I didn't think were fair. There are lots of ways you can pressure a sales department, and our guys were getting the heat. So I said, "Knock it off." The big chains at that time were Walden and Dalton. And the mistake I made was not in telling them to knock it off but in doing it so abruptly. And so they both eventually stopped buying books from us.

DLB: How could they afford to do that?

Vaughan: They couldn't afford it. And neither could we. But they figured they'd put the maximum heat on us. We sweated it out jointly for more than a year. Eventually we worked out some terms we could live with publicly and went back to business. So it is possible for a publisher to cut off a chain. It's also possible for a chain to buy books indirectly. They can get them from wholesalers. It's less profitable for them, but they can do it. One thing I've learned about publishing is that it's a business of tremendous complexity and tremendous simplicity, with nothing in between.

DLB: Where does the simplicity come in?

Vaughan: In the elementals. People need to read–they want to read–and people need to write. And most of them will do it no matter what. If the writer is Manhattan and the reader is Chicago, then publishing is the Lincoln Tunnel. It's not all that important. It's important that the writer gets his book in front of the reader, and that's what we're supposed to be doing. But there's so much fuss and commotion about the way we do it. It used to be that nobody gave a damn about it, but as David Riesman said a long time ago that this has become the age of the insider, everybody wants to be backstage, so a lot of people are paying attention to the muddiness of our business.

DLB: I imagine one of the most frustrating parts of your job must come when you're trying to convey something to a writer who obviously doesn't understand what you're getting at.

Vaughan: I once edited a novel about a couple who were retired vaudevillians, living in upstate New York.

DLB: That's great in itself.

DLB: I thought so, too. When the manuscript arrived, it was done almost entirely as dialogue. There was no description of anything. At first, I gently suggested to the author that maybe he didn't need the whole book in dialogue. He ignored me. I tried again a little harder, and after three or four attempts to get through to him, I wrote him a letter that said, "Goddamn it. You're ruining your story by having it confined to dialogue alone. It doesn't do the whole job. I don't know what I can do to get you to pay attention. And I may be just a barber, but stop trying to cut your own hair." He wrote back and said that he could see what I was getting at. Why didn't I say so before? And he added, "P.S. I do cut my own hair."

Katherine McNamara

In the spring of 1997 writer, editor, and now publisher Katherine McNamara published the first issue of Archipelago: an International Journal on-line of Literature, the Arts, and Opinion. *Unlike other on-line publications or zines, as they're called,* Archipelago *reads and looks more like a serious literary journal that just* happens *to be on the Web rather than a website trying to be a serious literary journal. It's a distinction McNamara is quick to acknowledge and is proud of. Angered by recent and often radical changes in literary publishing that she witnessed firsthand through her own eyes and the eyes of her late husband, Atheneum editor Lee Goerner, as several distinguished literary publishing houses, including Atheneum, were either closed down or radically restructured after decades of operation, literally airbrushed off the cultural map in a matter of months by the conglomerates that owned them, McNamara went looking for a way to publish a serious literary journal without having to serve the almighty dollar. " . . . when Antheneum was closed down," McNamara has said, "I had a closer look at New York publishing than any writer should want to have." Ironically, perhaps, she found her way via the World Wide Web, that rogue by-product of our commercially driven Computer Age.*

Katherine McNamara (photograph by Lucy Gray)

Less interested in the Web as a fascinating new technology, McNamara saw it as a way to "distribute" good writing, art, and opinion without having to put up a lot of capital; therefore, without having to let the marketplace interfere with her freedom to publish what she wanted, or with her contributors' freedom to say what they pleased. One of the first things McNamara did was institute a series called "Institutional Memory: Conversations with legendary publishers of an older generation." According to McNamara, the art of publishing real books has been eclipsed by the conglomeration and restructuring of the industry. "It used to be that publishers loved books. Books were an absolute foundation of their lives. I wanted to find out what these distinguished publishers thought about the changes in the publishing industry."

One year and four issues later, Archipelago *has met and exceeded McNamara's expectations. Having already received positive reviews in* Bookwire, USA Today *online, and the* Times Literary Supplement *among others, it looks like* Archipelago, *particularly its in-depth and fascinating conversations with literary publishers such as Marion Boyers and Michael and Cornelia Bessie, has touched a nerve with literary-minded Web users who seem to have been waiting for a journal like* Archipelago, *a journal which McNamara has said "stands between the threshold of traditional print and cyberspace."*

The following is an interview conducted by David McNair (University of Virginia) with Katherine McNamara on 20 January 1998 at her home in Charlottesville, Virginia, where Archipelago *is published and where we talked a little bit about, as the title in her first editorial states, "Art and Capitalist relations and why publishing on the Web might be interesting."*

DLB: Archipelago *is called* An International Journal on-line of Literature, the Arts, and Opinion. *I find that interesting because, normally, given all the hype surrounding anything on-line, you would think it would be called "An International* On-line *Journal," but that's not emphasized. I wonder if you could comment on that.*

McNamara: For one thing, on-line is not an adjective. It's more of an adverb, I suppose. And it also had to do with the ear, how it sounds, you know. But more to, and also equally to the point, the Web was interesting to me not as a bit of technology but as a means of distribution. It made it possible for me to publish a literary journal without much capital. Entry and maintenance are relatively inexpensive. If you go to print you need a lot more start-up and continuation money. Of course, you still need money to start up something on the Web, but not nearly as much.

DLB: So, for you, publishing on the Web isn't so much about the Web as it is about a new means of distribution?

McNamara: Exactly. Around the time I started *Archipelago,* publishing journals and other documents on the Web had been done somewhat, but it was just beginning to happen. What interested me about the medium was not only being able to distribute the journal on-line but also being able to *deliver,* by means of downloading, a finished piece of work in a complete format. You see, I don't think anybody in their right mind reads seriously on-line. What I wanted to do with *Archipelago* was distribute good writing, which means that we start on the page, and I expect, then, that we end up on the page. Of course, it's not a beautifully bound book you're getting, but that wasn't my intention. The program we use is relatively simple, primitive, I guess, by web-page standards, but fortunately I found a Web designer who was interested in the "pageness," for lack of a better word, of *Archipelago.* Because I figured that most people who were going to read the journal, including most writers, didn't have state-of-the-art computer systems. In fact, more than half the writers I know don't even use computers. If they have access to the Internet at all, it's through a basic system, like this black-and-white desktop I use, and so I asked the designer to create something with that in mind. Because the people who read *Archipelago* grew up on print, and I didn't want to offend their sensibilities, or mine for that matter.

I like to think *Archipelago* is on the threshold between two rooms, one room being traditional print, the other being cyberspace. And we really do go back and forth between the two rooms.

DLB: You seem less enamored with the Web than most on-line publishers. What do you think about all the hype surrounding it? How it's going to revolutionize global communication and commerce, et cetera? Do you think we need to get over our fascination with it?

McNamara: Well, it's a standard American response. It's the new corn flakes, you know. Actually, I think it's very easy to develop things technically. We have that sort of mentality. We know how: *know-how,* it's a compound American word. We write technical manuals about everything, even technical manuals about heartache, which, of course, is what literature should be dealing with. The focus on the Internet is where the money is, and that's in technical development. That's beneficial to someone like me because it's incredibly easy to go online, to make something happen that isn't attentive to or focused on the technology. And besides, what's the technology doing? There seems to be this carnival-like Web aesthetic in place, all kinds of things spinning and popping up and flashing at you, particularly among deliberately commercial sites. For instance, the *Financial Times,* one of my favorite sites on-line, used to be very nice and dignified, accessible–not unduly friendly. It's British, after all–but now, even though they're a terrific site and have superb archives, the actual cover page is ugly, carnival-like. I don't know what happened.

DLB: That seems to be the overriding aesthetic on the Web. It's really become a visual medium.

McNamara: That's right. And the other thing that I think happens, and we see it everywhere, is group think. You see it in the media in New York, in book publishing, and certainly in the movies and in television. People don't take risks exactly, except technically. Actually, there's a marketing phrase called "thinking inside the box," the opposite of which is "thinking outside the box," trying to think of something different. Well, most people don't go too far outside the box, it seems.

DLB: Don't you think this situation is true of all new media? They start out with enormous potential and then get "boxed" into familiar formats?

McNamara: Sure. Absolutely. One of the ways it happened classically was with Apple computers,

and the other way it happened classically was with Microsoft. The Apple computer was invented in an attic by Steve Wozniak and Steve Jobs, and then Jobs went and turned it into a company. These were two young geniuses, and they made a brilliant, elegant "instrument," and they kept it that way–well, they were a little snobby about it, so it was thought–but they wanted to keep their instrument simple and pure, and in fact they kept it expensive and didn't market it. Then along comes Bill Gates and persuades IBM to adopt the little operating system they dream up. And they managed to do it because Gates is a salesman. It's a classic old story. The inventor has a different kind of mind than the salesman, and so the inventor thinks of the thing to be done, and the salesman gets it out there. Now, that's a neutral description; in fact, I have much stronger feelings about it. Who has the moral virtue here?

DLB: Ironically, I suppose, one by-product of all that has been the Internet, which seems even to be outside the control of a Bill Gates.

McNamara: Which is an interesting situation for journals like *Archipelago* because no one knows what the Web will be like in five years. For me, this is an interesting experiment–to see how long this medium can make possible and further what I have in mind for this publishing venture.

DLB: Do you think what's called Web literature, or writing on the Web, is different? And if it is, how is it different?

McNamara: The question, of course, is what is it different from. And that is, of course, print. If we're talking about what's called literature, what's roughly called literature, and the stuff that appears in zines, as they are called, I think it's a little like those small hand-stapled pamphlets that have been sold for decades, centuries perhaps, by poets printing their own material and selling it on the street–which is really the groundwork of poetry, when everybody's young. And there's plenty of that sort of thing on the Web because everybody's young.

I don't think we know yet if there are writers whose work has been altered in some way by the Web. My own experience, as I've said, is that many of the writers I've published don't even use computers. In fact, for most writers I know, it's not until you hand them the download version that they think there's something real to this journal, which I think is right and amusing. And it amuses me very much also that I can give them what they expect but also make it come about because of this experiment of mine. You see, *Archipelago* started with talk, talking to other writers—because I think of myself more as a writer than a publisher, or at least I like to think I am—and talking to friends and people who knew a little bit about the Web. So in a sense I tiptoed in, not so much interested in the technology as I was in the ability of the medium to distribute good writing. And this I find interesting: While the writing I collected was composed on the page, mostly by writers with little knowledge or interest in the Internet, it got translated into this stream of electrons, so it was as if it were paperless, as if it had been conjured—and that was fascinating to me because it really was a mind-body separation, in a way that making a book or a regular literary journal is not. And finally, it's the download that completes the cycle. Beginning with paper and ending with paper.

DLB: So, then, do you think the journal really exists in the middle there, when it's only a stream of electrons?

McNamara: If you're a writer, or if you're a literary person, that is, you think like a literary person, you know that there is, morally, a fundamental connection between words and things. Now, if you think you live in a postmodern era, or a highly commercial, global capitalistic era, you can very easily push that and say, yes, the words have become disconnected from the things. Rather as *Archipelago* exists in the ether. So there's a sort of analogue. Is it real if it exists in the ether?

DLB: Is it real?

McNamara: Is it? Sure.

DLB: It is?

McNamara: Well, because of the download it is.

DLB: So why should we have books? Why not have everything floating around in cyberspace, ready to be downloaded?

McNamara: There are a couple of answers to that. One is because people need books, physically. They want them; they love them. Also, something I've noticed very much, among writers at least, although who knows what they represent, is that people who use computers started using fountain pens again. Including myself. You see, some of us still want something to touch, to hold on to. Also, we

have a habit of publishing books, and that habit is not going to go away. One difficulty, though, has been that trade publishing, large publishing—and this is a roundabout way of answering the question of why we need books—has gone more and more to commercial books, Hollywood-friendly-type books, that sort of thing, and away from what we knew was literature, which has become a smaller point, a more specialized point. Also, the definition of what a book is has become wildly . . . metamorphosed, if you will. Anything that's loosely printed and bound is called a book. After all, look at all the technical manuals, technical manuals about computers, for instance. So there's always that as an ancillary to the question of why we need books—it's how we *know*.

DLB: What about book publishing and the Internet? How do you think these two might affect each other?

McNamara: I think small, serious publishers are going to turn more and more toward the Net and find it useful in ways that five or maybe fifty people are thinking of it now. For example, I think distribution is a very difficult problem for publishers. You need a distributor. Well, I think it's possible to reorganize the way we publish books by having printing centers where texts are downloaded and produced.

DLB: According to what's ordered?

McNamara: Yes, and I don't think it would be too difficult to implement. Of course, there'd be technical things to attend to, but that's a sort of entrepreneurial activity that somebody needs to look at. And what that would be is a sort of revival of, say, a seventeenth-, eighteenth-, early-nineteenth-century notion of the printer as publisher. That is, you could become a printer, producing texts from various sources. I think of how the French make their books, Gallimard, for example. Their Pleiade series, those simple, yellow-back books. It's not the cover that matters so much; it's the writer and the writing inside.

DLB: And yet it's an honor, and no small feat, for a writer to get underneath one of those simple covers. They have an integrity, despite their simplicity.

McNamara: Well, as you know, they are a literary culture. It's not just that they have one; they are one—in a way that we are not and can't imagine being. Anyway, this idea about the printer interests me a lot, and I'm a little surprised that small publishers haven't thought about it. I just think there must be another way to think about publishing. After all, if *I'm* thinking about it, there must be other people thinking the same thing. And there is no reason why books should be so expensive in this country because we have all the paper in the world. Of course, then there's the problem of book chains, who have, in large part, persuaded publishers to pay attention to flashy covers because that's what makes people buy books. In fact, during a conversation I had with the publisher Marion Boyars (*Archipelago,* volume 1, no. 3, Autumn 1997), she suggested that booksellers and publishers don't know how to sell books anymore. I've been thinking about that, and I think she's right. There is a standard line, in New York anyway, that there has always been the same number of serious readers. The numbers vary a little, but the highest I've ever heard is about sixty thousand. Big publishers no longer publish books for those readers in the old sense; that's not their purpose. Their purpose, in fact, is to please their masters, who are entertainment-based conglomerates. So, you see, their intentions have something to do with something other than what we call books. But if there are still people thinking about literature, and literature as it comes in books, the Internet is going to turn out to be wildly useful. But so far everyone's being very sluggish about thinking of a different way to do things.

DLB: Why do you think that is?

McNamara: People get into their habits; everybody's old now. Not old, but older than we were. We don't have as much money as we thought we would. Our joints ache. I'm talking about people I know, middle-aged people. For us the world has become bigger and more complicated than we thought it would; everyone's in debt. And also, getting back to those standard lines: "There are only a certain number of serious readers." "The book chains are killing us." The returns are doing in publishers–those are the more serious and real issues.

DLB: What motivated you to try something different?

McNamara: What I had, because I didn't have big capital, was a certain kind of energy . . . probably a little anger . . . and anger can be a very useful energizer. I was disgusted with what happened, and with what is continuing to happen, in trade publishing, and as part of that, what was happening to, if you want–I'll be grandiose–our national imagina-

tion. Something like what the movies did and then what TV did to the imagination is being done now by the big conglomerate publishers. They're turning toward more-formulaic books, repetitions of what they think is successful. Their job is to keep the conglomerate going, not to make interesting books, books to capture the attention of readers who don't already have their minds made up.

In a situation like that, where there is so much stratification and conformity, the answer is: do something else. Well, to do that it's very useful if you think you don't have to make a career of it and if you simply think it's work worth doing. In fact, what a publisher told me once was very useful, which was: "You need a little capital, and then you need to say: Fuck you, Money." Which means settling for just enough to do what you want without having to answer to some master. And if you can do that without worrying too much about your losses, then you can think about doing something else. And it's a good time for it.

DLB: There certainly are a lot of small presses out there.

McNamara: Yes, but small presses everywhere are strapped. They have distribution problems; the cost of printing has gone up. There isn't a small press out there that has enough money, unless they're privately backed. And this is another thing that ought to be remembered: James Laughlin just died. Laughlin was probably the most brilliant publisher of the century, certainly on this side of the Atlantic. The publisher Michael Bessie (*Archipelago,* volume 1, no. 4, Winter 1997–1998) said he was the best publisher of his generation, and that's saying something. Laughlin introduced America to modernist writing, consistently published essential writers, the writers who are the core and backbone of our twentieth-century literature, until, say, the 1950s. And he did that because he had money. He belonged to the Jones and Laughlin Steel family. He was given a certain sum of money and advised how best to invest it to keep New Directions going, and he used to say, as I understand, that, yes, they did make some money, but not a lot. As Michael Bessie has said, the margin of responsible literary publishing, the profit margin, is at the most 4 to 5 percent. Well, the conglomerates want at least 10 percent, if not 15 percent, from a book. More and more they're insisting that every book they publish has to make money. So they go with the safe bets, sell the movie rights, foreign rights . . . deals have become the marker. Now it's somehow prestigious . . . no, not prestigious but "cool," to get a big advance. I once heard of a young agent, under thirty-five that is—someone with not much experience. This young agent, who was supposed to be a hotshot, said that if his writer earned back the advance he felt that he hadn't done his job. This is bad economics, and bad economics runs publishing.

DLB: And just about everything else.

McNamara: That's true. But publishing has always been different. As Michael Bessie has said, publishing is countercyclical. So it's always out of step with the economy. And yet there are these people in the conglomerates who bought publishing houses, or what used to be known as "houses," thinking it was a way to synergize their holdings, meaning their movie companies could make movies out of their books, and their newspapers and TV stations could promote them. Well, publishing doesn't work that way, at least the kind of publishing we're talking about here. All three of the publishers I interviewed for *Archipelago*—and I'll talk about that a little later—have said that they didn't have a commercial instinct. What they do have is taste, acuity, informed intelligence, and they are deeply read. They had, as Cornelia Bessie has said, the habit of reading "clockwise around the library." Loving books. You see, this is the thing—the new publishers do not love books, and I think that's a radical change.

DLB: Another thing that's different about book publishing, or selling—and this may relate to the Internet and its usefulness in selling books, or rather, distributing literature—is that the general public seems to buy whatever it's told to buy. Books even more so than other things, it seems. Could you comment on this phenomenon?

McNamara: Odile Hellier, who owns the Village Voice bookstore in Paris, told me something interesting. In fact, let me read something she sent to me recently: "Over the years I have seen the reader change. Now, readers do not browse as they used to; instead, they come to me with the name of a book written on a slip of paper and ask for it, and if I don't have it, I order it. I can see why Amazon, Bookpost, and other Internet sources will do so well: because readers don't choose for themselves so much anymore, but the media decides for them. But there is always a place for a small bookstore like mine, where readers do come, and browse, and choose; because there will always be cultured people, people who are excited when they discover a good book, especially if that book becomes impor-

tant. It's a matter of getting to those people—they are people of my own age, not so many younger people these days. But I think they will always exist; it's a matter of letting them know that *we* still exist—that good books are here to be read."

Now that, I think, says a lot about why publishers don't know how to sell books. Partly, perhaps, because the verb *sell* is overused. Readers need to be persuaded, enticed, made to feel welcome . . . the more-gentler arts, the more formal arts. You see, it's not a matter of marketing techniques, per se. If you're going to be in this line of work, you're doing it because you're part of the literary culture, or you think you are, or you make yourself part of it; and that you know there are other people like you, and that you can find them, which is what I myself found interesting about publishing on the Web. I didn't know who I'd find, but I knew I'd find people interested in what I was interested in. What I learned from the old-time publishers is quite similar. I went and published what I thought was interesting, hoping others would find it interesting as well.

DLB: Given the current situation in literary publishing, do you think that, in order to sustain our literary culture, it will be necessary for writers, editors, and publishers interested in serious writing to walk away from publishing as it exists?

McNamara: What an interesting question. I bet you the answer is yes although it has to be a yes with a qualification. In *Archipelago* I've begun a series called "Institutional Memory," conversations with notable and often distinguished publishers of an older generation: publishers who loved books, who brought out important books and writers. Well, what they say about publishing is that, in a sense, it hasn't changed. Of course, it was always about commerce. What *was* different was when it was, along with making money, about publishing books, about the publishing of literature being their core responsibility.

DLB: At one time the two ways of thinking co-existed.

McNamara: That's right. And the commercial side made the other side possible. But also, that's what those people were made of, that desire to bring works of the mind into the world.

DLB: So do you think writers need to walk away from publishing as it exists?

McNamara: Young writers, perhaps. If you're older and established, there's really no reason to walk away. But if you're a young writer, just starting to play the game, you might want to consider alternate routes. Today, even if you're lucky enough to publish a book, odds are you'll get little loyalty from your publisher, little or no editorial guidance, and when the book is published, you'll be expected to go out and flog it. That's not the writer's job. The writer's job is to write the book. It's the publisher's job to sell it. So yes, I think it would be nice to see younger writers trying to do things differently.

DLB: So what do you think the advantages of publishing on the Web might be? Could this be one of those alternate routes?

McNamara: Well, it has been an interesting way to distribute what I've published. Even though what's called literature or writing on the Web has incited a great deal of self-indulgence and youthful experimentation, it has also made it possible, I find, to distribute the best work you can find by the best writers who are willing to give their work to you.

DLB: And why is the Web unique for that?

McNamara: Well, now we get back to where we started. It's relatively inexpensive. And you can make the work look as handsome as it does in a literary journal. It's really a very easy thing to put together, technically that is.

DLB: Well, how does that make you feel? Here's this medium that's so simple and relatively inexpensive and that allows you to keep your intentions about publishing pure, and yet in this case, people from China, Europe, and elsewhere have access to the journal. That's not like those idealistic poets you talked about, printing up stapled pamphlets and selling them for a dollar. Publishing on the Web isn't like anything else.

McNamara: No, it's not like anything else. I was curious and excited to learn who would want to read the authors I had to offer and where they would be doing it. And yet I'm not surprised we've been found out. It's as Odile Hellier said, there will always be people out there—it's just a matter of getting to those people, of letting them know there are other people thinking the same way, and that good books and good writers are still here to be read. In this way, at this time, I think the Internet serves that purpose quite well.

DLB: Archipelago in five years?

McNamara: I hope it will be paying for itself and paying its writers. But since I really don't know what the Web will be like in five years, it's hard to predict what will happen to *Archipelago*. We'll just have to wait and see.

The State of Publishing

Clay Reynolds

It has not been our practice at the DLB Yearbook to publish material that has already been published elsewhere. This piece, by Texas novelist Clay Reynolds, is an exception to that rule. This past year was marked by news of and controversy about recent developments and new directions in the publishing world and by more troubles for writers, especially writers of midlist fiction. (See "Book Reviewing and the Literary Scene.") There were significant articles and feature stories on the changing publishing scene in The New York Times, *the* Wall Street Journal, *the* Nation, *and the* New York Observer, *and an issue of* The New Yorker *(16 October) was devoted to the publishing scene. Especially important in that issue, Ken Auletta's "The Impossible Business" dealt with the complex business of contemporary publishing. What concerned everybody was (and remains) the fate of American literature in the hands of the giant international conglomerates of which the major American publishers are now a small and beleaguered part. The attempts to earn (for the first time in publishing history) double-digit percentages of profit, and within the short term; the increasing power and dominance of the big bookstore chains—Barnes and Noble, Borders, Books-a-Million, and so forth—taken together with the precipitous decline in the number of independent bookstores; the severe competition even the chains are facing, coming from Internet shopping sites such as Amazon.com; the growing number of books returned to publishers from all these sources; the new kinds of austerity which in some cases involved canceling large numbers of book contracts; all these things were much in the spotlight.*

What has been missing in this ongoing debate is the point of view of the American writer, at least outside the establishment center in New York City. This other point of view is a provincial one to be sure. But most American writing today, though it must inevitably come through New York, does not come from it, arriving instead from the far-flung provinces of this huge nation.

The question was—who is speaking for the writer?

One answer came in the Spring/Summer 1997 issue of the Texas Review, *a literary quarterly from Sam Houston State University in Huntsville, Texas—an excellent little magazine with a small circulation. We feel that Reynolds's piece is an important document in the continuing discussion and that his point of view deserves more attention than*

Clay Reynolds

publication in a university-based literary magazine might offer.

Here, then, for the record, is Clay Reynolds's article from The Texas Review, *with a brief response by George Garrett.*

In an industry that trades on rumors of disaster, the reports flying around New York (which I use here as a synecdoche for major publishing houses anywhere) are positively holocaustic. If you believe half what you hear, you'd probably take that new word processor you bought for Christmas and heave it into the nearest lake, then truck on down to the highway department and see if there are any openings on the crew that goes about and picks up roadkills. At least that's steady work, has good benefits, and you don't lie awake nights worrying about what it'll be like tomorrow. In the world of books, tomorrow is a source of constant anxiety for everyone involved.

Although agents and editors advertise on the Internet soliciting new writers, most will settle in over a tall stiff drink in the bar and shake their head sadly over the dark omens emanating from New York.

Here's a sampling of what's making the rounds:

"X House has declared a six-month moratorium on
    new acquisitions."
"Y, Inc. isn't going to accept any new manuscripts until
    1998."
"Z Books has a backlog from last July and is scheduling
    books ready now for sometime in 1999."
"Nobody's buying anything that's not a guaranteed
    Best Seller anymore."
"The western is dead."
"Crime fiction is dead."
"No advance above $3,000 will be paid to any writer."

Though some of these dismal pronouncements may be exaggerated—at least insofar as the specific publishers involved are concerned—they're often close to the truth. Most publishers do have enormous backlogs, and some books that have been in galleys since last summer haven't yet been scheduled, may not be scheduled until next fall, may not be published for two or three years. Rising paper costs, diminishing consumer demand, and increasingly fewer independent bookstores are also putting the squeeze on the entire book business; and the situation isn't likely to improve as more and more people turn to the Internet or World Wide Web for their reading matter.

The sad truth is that these days fewer and fewer publishers are buying quality books simply because they are quality books. As huge new bookstores, mega-chains, continue to grow with the rapidity of fast food shops across the country, "Mom and Pop" operations are being systematically squeezed out. Even well-heeled local or regional chains are pulling in their horns, closing stores, regrouping in the face of barracuda-like competition from mega-corporations which increasingly are controlling the retail end of the book business.

It would seem that such growth would indicate an upsurge in the number of books being sold, but this simply isn't happening. These mega-stores sell a lot of other stuff . . . from maps to placemats, bookmarks to totebags, even coffee and bread mixes; they make their real profit by providing atmos-

phere, a place to hang out, to talk about writing or books, not to buy. One New York agent noted that the local mega-store has become the most "chic pickup place" in the NYU area.

The stores have become more than social gathering centers, however. They stage readings and lectures, all of which benefits writers to some extent, but which are really designed to make their stores the center of the book world in their community. But they don't sell many books.

Actually, the owners make more profit from CD, tape and video sales or rentals than they do from books, and periodicals also constitute a huge part of their daily sales figures. (But maybe not for long; books aren't the only thing being affected by electronic media; one source at *Library Journal* privately told me that he estimates that by the year 2000, fewer than 25% of the magazines published in this country, including his own, will be available except through electronic media; why go out and buy and carry home, read, and throw away that which can be downloaded and read in a matter of minutes, then merely deleted, zapped back into the electricity?)

More to the point of this essay, though, new books, recent releases, those books that depend on immediate retail sales for their writers' survival, sometimes constitute less than 25% of retail book sales. Last year, according to a mega-store manager in Amarillo, more people bought reprints of *Moby Dick* and *Paradise Lost* than bought Best Sellers for retail list price. And why should they when Wal-Mart sells the same book for 40% less?

For a time, mall bookstores had something of a lock on the book business, and they did sufficient damage to independents. Waldenbooks, for example, grew with enormous speed. In 1969, the chain boasted only sixty-nine outlets; in 1992, more than 1200 were open for business. B. Dalton followed suit, and wholly-owned regional subsidiaries sprang up from coast to coast. But overhead in malls kept these operations limited in terms of space and volume; even though they may not know it, mall bookshops' days are numbered, and they will soon be replaced by chicken sandwich and soft pretzel stores in the wake of shiny new competition with friendly, homey atmospheres and easier access.

The new mega-stores—Barnes and Noble, Borders, Hastings—are freestanding operations with espresso shops and pastry bars, lots of ferns, comfy chairs for reading, and free access to major national and even international newspapers. They are meccas for the intellectuals and pseudointellectuals who were once the mainstay of the book business. And they control, to a tremendous extent, what sells, what doesn't, what gets shelf space, what remains unordered in publishers' warehouses.

But retail is retail, and writers and publishers have always been at the mercy of that part of the industry. Distribution is another problem, also, but not one that either the publisher or the writer can do much about. What books are ordered and put onto the retail market for sale are selected according to demographic surveys, market analyses, and individual genre and author histories. The relative quality of an individual title rarely has any impact on such decisions.

The saddest truth is that people who read and read a lot don't buy many books, anyway. If they do, as I say, they're too smart to pay full retail for them; they buy from discount stores, book clubs, half-price and remainder stores, or they subscribe to reading clubs or remainder catalogues; more often, though, they visit public and university libraries. Or they visit the mega-stores. I know of one "avid reader" who has now read everything John Grisham has written without buying a single copy. He merely drops by his nearby mega-store for two hours each evening, selects a title from the shelf, orders a croissant and espresso, then reads a portion of the book before returning it to the display. And this isn't an unusual phenomenon. If one walks through such a store at almost any time of day, patrons are often curled up on the floor, reading. One assistant manager proudly boasted, "We have more people reading here than you'll find in the average library."

The point, however, is that no writer depending completely on retail sales of hardbounds has ever done very well. And the supermarket consumer buys little above the level of what's hot at the moment—romance, western, crime fiction, horror—paperback originals or quick reprints, books that have an average shelf life of about six to eight weeks, anyway. (And even this may be changing. At a recent convention of the Romance Writers of America, it was announced that as many as 125,000 "rack spots"—sites where paperbacks are sold, such as airports, grocery stores, etc.—have been totally shut down. Rack-jobbers—those who wholesale books to such sites—just can't compete with the mega-stores' discounts.)

The new problem, a dilemma that has surfaced in the past half decade or so, is much more serious, and it affects the writer in new and profound ways. Moreover, it's not likely to get any better anytime soon.

Put simply: publishing has changed, and it's changed quickly and dynamically. The business is no longer what it was, even ten years ago. Not to put

too fine a point on it, but to state the problem frankly and honestly, most publishers don't want good books anymore simply because they're good books. That is, they don't want books that have been carefully and artfully crafted, which tell a good story, which present stunning characters, which amuse, scintillate, inspire, enthrall, which are, in other words, "literary." They want books that sell. And for big bucks.

This really shouldn't be surprising. Publishing is just like any other business. It's even like the shoe business. I recently saw an ad in a daily newspaper for a big athletic shoe store. There must have been fifty different brands of shoes advertised as being "on sale." But the funny thing is that except for a brand logo here, a splash of color there, every pair of those shoes is precisely the same as all the others. Each one claims to be "new and improved" over last year's model, but each is exactly like the others in every way except accidents of appearance. None will really provide any wearer with any serious advantage over any other pair of shoes, even an old pair of US KEDS, c. 1959, regardless of the use the individual pair is put to; but there they all are. Each sells for between $70 and $120—the markup is about 50%—and each falls into a marketing category. They'll be displayed in the store according to purpose: for running, walking, hiking, tennis, basketball, racquetball, etc. Some will be amorphously dubbed "cross trainers," which indicates that they might do for two or more similar activities. But the fact is that each consists of a thick and durable manmade sole, a leather or nylon and leather upper, a set of laces, and that's about it. Frankly, most people would be just as well off with a pair of cheap-o sneakers from Wal-Mart; and the funny thing is that from twenty yards away, no one could tell the difference.

Okay, we all know this. If you came along with some new style of shoe that might sell for about the same price but which really was different, that could be used for almost any activity, even just watching TV, bŏt which would cost so much to manufacture that to be competitive it would only provide say a margin of 20% profit, chances are that almost no one would want to accept it and stock it. Why? Because that constitutes risk. And unless the risk is warranted in some way (or unless some outside source is willing to underwrite the risk), it's much better to do precisely what everybody else is doing; take the 50% markup and run.

Besides, how would they market it? There's no place on the wall that simply says, "General Purpose Athletic Shoe." If you doubt that I'm right about this, drop by your favorite mall, walk into an athletic shoe store–you can't go to a general shoe store anymore for athletic shoes–and tell the clerk that you want just a pair of "sneakers," nothing more, nothing special. The clerk will most likely puddle up in bewilderment at your consumptive naiveté.

The world has changed. America has changed. And so has publishing. It was just slower than most to catch on.

Up until ten or twelve years ago, when a writer started out with his first book, he would most likely have an editor who had built his reputation on finding an author, then developing him through a series of books. The writer didn't make a lot of money for the first two, three or four volumes, but he made enough to stay happy, to keep writing, and he built an audience, a readership. The idea was that his fifth or sixth book would be his "breakout," and he would make decent, maybe even big money, maybe win a few prizes, maybe get a movie deal. Then he would be in the publisher's stable, would be loyal to that editor, and over a few decades, he would develop a reputation and a readership that would profit everyone. My publisher (and my agent) outlined that plan for me back in 1986.

It made sense. Many editors did this for writers who later become major names, "household words," "name brands" over the years: Ludlum, LeCarré, etc. Anyway, the writer was now "in the process." It might take three, four, even five books, but his day would come. The editor would carry him through the rough times, groom him for "breakout," and all would be well sooner or later, hopefully sooner.

After twenty-five years with the same publisher, though, one editor of this sort of my acquaintance left to become president of another company, which was a wholly owned but totally autonomous corporation belonging to a "mega-house." This was the editorial equivalent of a "breakout." Now, he could control not a few but a whole company of writers. He was ready to count coup. He brought a half dozen other young writers with him, began developing them in the same way he always had, figured that in ten years he could have the best house in New York. But things changed.

The company in question was, as I say, a wholly owned subsidiary of another publisher, which was itself sold to a non-publishing entity whose primary business, I believe, was to make dog food and which employed a whole raft of MBA's whose jobs were to do nothing but figure profit and loss. Some of them actually read books, surely, but none cared very much about that. What they cared about was reading spreadsheets. After two years,

the books this editor was publishing weren't showing profit–at least not enough profit–and the quarterly reports from the MBA's were not good enough. The editor and company president was fired. Just like that. According to the story, a young corporate assistant vice president from the parent company got off the elevator one Wednesday afternoon and "fired everyone in sight." He also fired the secretaries and the maid. He even tried to fire a messenger boy from a private mail service. Twenty-five editors got the axe that afternoon, and the publishing house, for all intents and purposes, was closed.

One writer under contract for the company said that when he called, all he got was an answering machine. "You could hear the wind howling down the empty halls behind the voice," he said.

Two weeks later, the parent company reopened the subsidiary, but only as an imprint house attached to the parent. (According to another rumor, the VP who did the firing and shut down the house forgot that this was one of the oldest publishing entities in New York; he himself was fired the following Monday.) A corporate vice president was put in charge. She'd never edited a soul, but she had absolute control over how things would be done. And they were done by the spreadsheet and according to the most vicious enemy of writers, "market surveys." MBA's took over the book business, at least in this instance.

The new rules were simple: If a book, any book, didn't turn significant sales numbers, the writer was gone. Even a first book had to "pay out," earn out its advance, or the writer's second book probably wouldn't be published. Also gone were reasonable advances, generous deadlines, and any sense of responsibility on the part of the publisher for the book's success. A new and insidious clause appeared in contract boiler plates, allowing the publisher an effective "quit claim." If a contracted book for any reason failed to meet expectations, however they might be defined, a publisher simply didn't have to accept it. Moreover, the writer was suddenly liable for any advance against royalty paid on the contract's signing. Scary business, that. But writers had no choice. It was sign or walk away to another house that had the same boiler plate. Hard cheese.

Another rule applied to the editorial staff. They weren't to buy any book that didn't either fit into a standard genre category or that didn't have "blockbuster" potential. The latter class applied particularly to books by celebrities and other famous people. "Literary fiction" became the dirtiest word in New York. (To ensure against the possibility that something purely literary might slip through, many publishers then adopted the process of "double backing," which means that any manuscript had to go through a minimum of two readings by separate editors prior to being "pitched" to the editor-in-chief as a potential buy for the company. Individual editorial initiative was—and continues to be—systematically eliminated in favor of committee decisions, where responsibility—and blame—can be diffused.)

At the same time, there was a serious industry-wide downsizing, a bloodletting starting sometime in 1989 and really never stopping. A lot of it had to do with corporate mergers, leveraged buyouts, and simple acquisition of publishing houses by other, larger corporations, some of which had no relationship to publishing whatsoever. In some cases, the houses were bought to close down; in others, they were bought to lose money deliberately; in yet others, publishing houses changed hands more frequently than a baton in a relay race. One agent noted that he had to check *Publisher's Weekly* every week just to find out who owned whom, who was still in business.

The result of this massive shake-up was that editorial numbers in New York were cut by as much as 33%. (Some sources suggested 28%; others said it was more like 45%.) And salaries for lower echelon editorial staff (copy editors, proof readers, publicists and the like), never high in the first place, were cut as well. Thus, today, almost every editor in New York is doing the work three to five other editors were carrying five years ago; many experienced and book-loving individuals have left the industry. And the result of that is a decline in editorial integrity, both from the standpoint of acquisition and from the standpoint of producing quality work on a consistent basis.

And the pressure for demonstrable and quick success mounted along with the workload. Typically, now, an editor has about twenty books on his or her desk at one time, all on serious deadline, and each comes attached to a profit and loss forecast sheet that says exactly what numbers that book has to turn to pay out. If it fails, the writer is gone. If too many of them fail, then the editor is gone. Profit drives the industry, and potential profit determines what will be published, what won't.

But it's worse than that. A freelance copy editor recently related the following to me via an ancient correspondence method using the US Postal Service, which is affectionately known as "snail mail":

I'm doing the copy edit on a new novel by a fairly well established writer with [X House]," he said. "So I'm on the phone to the editor there, and I ask casually, 'How's

his last book doing?' Just making conversation, you know. He says, 'Just a sec.' I hear all these keys clicking, and he comes back on the telephone. 'As of three-thirty today, he's shipped 18,683 copies in hardbound,' he said. 'That's New York time. So he's holding on, but it's too early to tell what the returns might be.'

Reports are that Waldenbooks, among other chains, have already established a computer link to major distributors such as Ingram, and the publishers can, with a few keystrokes, find out precisely how many actual copies of any writer's book have sold at any given hour of the day, how many for full retail, how many for discount, and what the returns are likely to be. By 1997, it is forecast that all the mega-chains will be tied in to the same system, which can be used by editors to negotiate advances and contracts for a writer's next effort.

But, in apparent contradiction to this cold, common-sense approach to doing business, the same houses that are squeezing staff and demanding measurable success from every writer's work will pay millions of dollars for a book by a political figure, movie star, celebrity athlete, convicted criminal or accused felon, even when the supposed author was no closer to the actual manuscript than most of them have been to an actual book since they left school. Ghost writers, slaving away for a fraction of a percent of what the supposed authors are getting, are hard at work for a decimal point of what they might have made a decade ago writing their own books. The supposed authors are raking in the big bucks, and so are the publishing houses. In the meantime, they're quibbling over a few grand paid out to a new writer who is a few months late on a deadline, or whose work might require some editing or management in order to find a place on the publisher's list or whose "up to the moment" sales figures are slightly off the mark. To use a well-coined phrase, New York publishing has become penny wise and pound foolish; and the big loser is the writer. A bigger loser is the reader.

Or possibly the biggest losers are the formerly idealistic young people who became editors, now reduced to a collection of brown-nosing company cogs, fiercely loyal to policy, no longer able to take any pride whatsoever in their product. The catchphrase around the book business is "Nobody edits books anymore. We just catalogue them, manage them, and shove them to copy-edit for processing."

The result of all this is a demand for categories. Every book that comes in has to "fit" some surefire category—see the example of the sneakers earlier. Let's say Editor Al gets a novel submitted he really likes by author Fred. He really likes it, thinks it might have serious literary merit, wants to buy it. He can't, not on his own hook. Even if he's authorized to make an offer (and only a handful of editors are allowed to do that without checking upstairs anymore), to do so constitutes a major risk. If he buys the book on his own authority, and it doesn't turn the right numbers, he could be fired.

So, he needs corporate approval. He takes it upstairs to the corporate VP, who is functioning as editor-in-chief. She doesn't read it, doesn't even glance at the outline. She asks, "what kind of book is it?" Editor Al says, "Well, it's this great story of coming of age. It's about this young boy and this old man. . . ." she interrupts, "No, not what is it about. What kind of book is it?" Al says, "Well, it's this sort of bittersweet story of growing up–" she stops him again. "No! I mean what kind of book is it? Have you seen our catalogue?" Of course he has. "We have crime, mystery, thriller, romance, adventure, horror, western, children's, juvenile, and science fiction. Which of these categories would it go under?"

He shakes his head. "None of them. It's kind of literary. You know, mainstream." She shakes her head. "Best Seller?" He admits that it has potential, but no ironclad guarantee. "Then we don't want it," she says. "Get back to your desk and quit fooling around." End of consideration.

This—well, I based the dialogue on a summary; hey, I'm a writer–actually happened to a writer I know, and it's one of three manuscripts his agent has that are deemed "too literary" to publish with a commercial house. What he means is that they don't fit the categories. There's simply no editor to show it to.

"Commercial" and "Literary" have become opposing terms, contradictions in vernacular that are poles apart. It's not deemed possible, certainly isn't desirable, for any writer to try to do both. If you write "genre" then you're a "genre writer." If you write "literature," then you're a "literary" writer. The only way to bridge the gap is by way of a pseudonym, and that's also becoming harder and harder to do; any writer who finds success in one area is "locked in" with a publisher who specializes in that; if he wants success in another area as well, that means he has to work with two different publishers. Not easy, even when the two houses are owned by the same parent corporation; some agents say it's almost impossible. It's a small industry, and word gets around. No editor wants to hear that "his" writer is making money for another editor at another house. That kind of news can get an editor fired as well.

To put it another way: the "midlist" is dead. And it's probably not saying too much to observe that literary fiction is dead, at least when it's generated by American authors. There's just not enough money in it.

As I say, the irony is that the quality of editorial work is diminishing as well. The average editor in New York, I'm told, starts out at about $25,000 a year. And they're living in Manhattan, where a one-room apartment in a dangerous neighborhood can go for a grand a month, plus utilities. That's less money than a public school teacher can make. (Yet applicants for editorial positions are standing three deep at any employment office in New York. Go figure.)

In exchange for this princely sum, the editor is asked to put in close to eighty hours a week. Advancement is possible, if a Best Seller emerges; but by and large, they work in a sweatshop environment with little hope of anything good coming their way from the companies they work for. Moreover, because of these conditions, the quality of individuals who want to be editors is declining. One has only to look through a few published novels on any bookstore's "recent release" rack to discover that major errors in grammar, fact, style, structure, and even chronology and logic occur with alarming regularity. To put it another way and to quote a major New York agent, "no one knows how to edit, anymore. Maxwell Perkins is dead."

Essentially, and importantly to the writer, no one in New York publishing is going to take a risk on any book that does not appear to be a surefire success. If the author is a brand name (Stephen King), or is some international literary figure (Salman Rushdie, i.e.), who will bring along a sufficient amount of press, hype, or public relations to make it worthwhile, then who cares what the book is about or whether it's any good or not? Quality is something for college professors to debate. We're talking profits here!

Sometimes, being a name brand celebrity isn't enough. The recent Joan Collins case is testimony to that. And that's a million dollar write-off.

Yet it's all connected in a way. Publishers may be willing to pay gazillions for a "quick kill," a book by Newt or Hillary, by a successful general or a moviestar-athlete on trial for murder, even by Anonymous, but taking a chance on a book just because it might be good, because it might earn out and provide a base for another book, build a readership–that's just too risky. Forget it.

It's just plain easier to cut losses than to risk profits. If a book doesn't do well, then cut the author, even if it means having to buy out the contract. For every book published there are as many as 100,000 waiting for consideration, and any one of them might be from the next Tom Clancy or John Grisham or whoever. Hell, one of them might be the next Anonymous.

The point is that publishers aren't buying books anymore, really. They're buying writers, but what's different from before when old-time editors were buying writers to develop is that today publishers want the writers to be able to guarantee confirmation, consistency, and category production. If Elmore Leonard tried to shift from westerns to crime today, he'd probably never make it. One can hear the corporate VP/editor-in-chief now: "Leonard writes westerns, and that's all we want from him. Period." My first editor told me he didn't give a hoot in hell what kind of book my next book was, he wanted it if it was good. And he wanted the next one, too. (He didn't define "good," but I had an idea what he meant.) By the time I was in a position to show it to him, he was out of work, too. His style of editorship, learning in the same school that produced Maxwell Perkins and Jacques Barzun, died. Possibly there are a half dozen other "old timers" left.

Okay, what does this mean for the writers out there who have manuscripts in progress or are even already making the rejection rounds of editors and agents? The answer is that each of them must learn to write for category, to figure out what's hot and to deliver it. They must forget writing well and learn to write popular. They must learn to "color inside the lines," to remain religiously adherent to requirements of formula, length, and plot points. They must abandon any notions they ever had about merely telling a good story with interesting characters. They should be studying what's in the top ten and trying to imitate it, trying to make another pair of sneakers just like all the others, but promising all the while that they will make a reader jump higher, run faster, or play harder than any of a hundred other pairs that are identical in every way.

Moreover, they must be more careful than ever of grammar, style, organization, construction, and all the other elements that editors used to take care of after a book was delivered. If it's wrong in manuscript, it'll be wrong in the galleys; and it'll be wrong in the publication, and reviewers will fall on it with the bloody enthusiasm of feral dogs. Craft is everything today; art doesn't count.

I can sense many of you already arguing that this isn't logical or even so, or that there are exceptions, and you'd be right on all counts. It's great to believe that hard work, perseverance, and a dedicated belief in the quality of one's own work will pay off, that literary attention will succeed, and that quality will triumph over machine-stamped, imitative schlock. Maybe it will. For some. But for most, it will end only in frustration, in honest editors, if there are any left, saying, "I love this, but it just won't work. Not for this house."

But the bottom line, to use the publisher's favorite phrase, is that the way it is is the way it is, and it's not going to change anytime soon; in fact, it will probably get worse. The Nancy Taylor Rosenbergs and Mary Higgins Clarks will inherit the earth, or at least the big contracts. Anyone who tries to sell a book based on literary quality, not on marketability and category appeal, will have trouble, will most likely fail.

If a writer is European, Asian, or Oriental (without the hyphenated American behind it), there's still a chance of success; but if a writer is an American writer, get back. Even African American and Hispanic writers are feeling the pinch. Ernest Gaines' last book, excellent as it was, never even got a paperback out anywhere anyone could find a copy. And distaff writers, while popular at the moment, will probably fade as well. It's no secret that women buy more books than men, but women reading women has never been a reliable trend, according to long-range "market surveys." Female readers, for some reason, tend to prefer male authors. You can learn that by checking any demographic or marketing survey.

(The truth of this is underscored in the experience of a close friend of mine, author of nine "hardboiled crime novels," featuring a serial male protagonist. His books were hot for a few years, but then the scene shifted, and his numbers went down. He was told that the market for "hardboiled crime novels with male protagonists" was dying. So he became pragmatic. He wrote a new book under a female pseudonym, featuring a "hardboiled female protagonist." For all intents and purposes, she's the same character as his male serial hero; in every way except gender and, obviously, the accoutrements and physical dictates of gender; the author is the same guy. But the numbers on the new book went through the roof. Ironically, he can hardly sell anything as himself, but he can sell almost anything he writes as his distaff alter-ego.)

Still, about the only American literary writer who's still producing regularly is a woman: Joyce Carol Oates. But her sales figures are bolstered by Women's Studies programs and feminist and gay groups, all of whom tout and sell her books in conjunction with her personal appearances. She also receives comparatively modest advances, is highly prolific, and supplements her income by teaching in a university and consulting for PBS. The big money losers in the past half decade include John Updike, Saul Bellow, Phillip Roth, E. L. Doctorow, Gore Vidal, John Barth, and the list goes on of "major contemporary American writers" who have failed to put up impressive numbers. Some "great American authors" can't even get contracts, though their names are virtual icons among those who worship the contemporary American literary pantheon. Other writers, the "literary crowd," sponsored to a great extent by the Associated Writing Programs, writers like Rick Bass, Richard Ford, Thomas McGuaine, Craig Leslie, are still publishing with major houses, of course, still winning major literary awards; but the word is that they aren't putting up significant enough numbers to last much longer, and their days are numbered unless they do. They'll probably hang around for a while, even so. But their print runs will begin to shrink as rapidly as their advances, and the editorial interest in their work will most likely wane.

Other "literary writers" are signing contracts for about a tenth of what some romance writers make per book for a straight sale. If their work isn't picked up and taught in college, it probably won't be long before they're back to the keyboard, trying to figure how to bring "Jessica and Lance" together in some exotic location for another steamy, bodice ripping, heavy breathing scene and to get back into the game. Many of these writers are solid with major publishers, tied in to a system that will tolerate them so long as they break even somehow, mostly because, for the moment at least, these publishers are continuing to maintain the facade of integrity, trying to convince the reading world that they really do care about books, not merely about profits. But the reaction among agents and writers who know is simple: "Yeah, right."

Probably in their hearts, they do care. But at last word, American Express wasn't accepting heartfelt messages in lieu of hard cash for monthly payments.

But that's the position most writers must find if they wish to play this game. The problem is that it's getting harder and harder even to get in, to stay in, and to make money once you are in. As I said, almost every contract issued now has an "escape clause" in it, an effective "quit claim" that puts the responsibility for a book's success on the writer's shoulders, even if the publisher fails to promote it one bit. An editor told me, "they're turning us into a low-rent Hollywood. We're supposed to make 'B' movies and sell each one like it's *Gone With the Wind*." Another editor said that it's worse than that. "More thought goes into a pilot for a TV commer-

cial," he said, "than effort goes into editing a new book."

Once again, I anticipate objections. I'm sure many might ask about the recent success of such movies as *Sense and Sensibility, The Scarlet Letter, Huck Finn,* etc. Doesn't the success of these films and others of a literary bent indicate a public hunger for quality? Well, it might. But it probably doesn't. You must bear in mind that along with *Sense and Sensibility*'s success is an even more successful movie about an Australian talking pig. And, to be honest, apart from the hype surrounding the Academy Awards and other exercises in Tinsel Town's mutual admiration society, films like this are comparative losers up against blockbuster action flicks, movies that pander to the categories as Hollywood defines them.

Moreover, the authors of classic stuff like this are dead. There's no one to demand big authorial contracts or residual payments, no one to complain when the Hollywood writers futz around with the script, cut out characters, alter plots, endings, or even entire works. The resemblance between some of these films and the works they are "based on" often never goes beyond the similarity of the titles.

So why bother writing at all? Why not just get into a warm tub and open up a fat vein rather than slave away writing a book no one will want? The results of the former action won't be particularly stimulating, but at least there's a finite sense of purpose about it. The answer is that writing is still, at bottom and in spite of the narrowminded, profit-mongering, myopic and frightened editors' and publishers' demands, an art, an impulse; it's one of the oldest forms of human expression there is. At the moment the Philistines are in charge of the temple, the money changers in charge of what will or will not be seen and read; but most of us who continue to assault it with our best work keep hoping that somehow, somewhere, there will be a breakthrough, a sudden awareness that quality, care, and talent are more valuable than crass imitation or the quick buck.

I certainly continue to hope. And I hope for all the real writers in the world that it will someday come true.

George Garrett responds:

It seems to me that Clay Reynolds is right on the money, right as rain, in his unflinching, hardnosed piece–"The State of Publishing." He is also brave. Nobody likes to hear the truth. Somebody said (who was it? beats me) that telling the truth is like firing a revolver in a crowded room. We really aren't easy with the truth.

Truth is, I often think that things are even worse than Clay's vision. Worse than we can imagine. But he has told it well and accurately. Using his persuasive argument as a base, I want to add a couple of observations. First off, there is the matter of fact that even as the situation is slowly and surely deteriorating, just as Clay describes it, there is nevertheless some literary publishing going on at the big commercial houses. Some anyway. Never mind why. For the publishers it seems to be more a matter of advertising and general visibility than anything else. These literary books are, after all, regularly reviewed in the principal newspapers and magazines. So, essentially, it's all a form of relatively cheap advertising. The blockbusters generally don't need and don't receive much review space or serious reviewing. Literary titles live and die on the strength or weakness of their reviews. They are, most of them, "review driven." All of which works to make book reviews of literary books very important to the publishers and, as well, to the cadre and corps of literary journalists and reviewers. The working publicists need reviews and interviews (on radio, TV, in print) to justify their jobs and to minimize the inevitable losses involved with all things literary. They work to maintain the image, if not the reality, of the publisher's reputation. As in most aspects of contemporary corporate life—social and political life as well—image is always more important by far than reality (if any).

What all this adds up to (among other things) is an odd kind of collaboration, often bordering on collusion, among publishers, the literary press, the academies where there is still some place for literary books, and, alas, the writers themselves. The way it works is by means of an assumed literary establishment, a national consensus, manifest in a hierarchy of literary celebrity. Which may or may not have anything whatsoever to do with sales and/or literary quality. In the American publishing world, unlike that of the first quarter, perhaps even the first half of this century, the greatest energy and dedication are devoted and expended on maintaining the literary status quo as much as may be possible. New talents, new voices, are from time to time recognized, invited, and admitted; but otherwise the whole system is designed to allow for as little change as possible. Thus the kind of rediscovery of the masters of the first generation of the 20th century that we witness in the late 1940s and 1950s is not likely ever to happen again. Thus, also, those writers who have somehow stumbled into places at the banquet table of the literary status quo are not likely to be the least bit generous to their fellow writers. They don't even read each other. The sense of a larger community of letters, beyond the fringes of the little community of the lucky, does not exist any longer.

None of these things tends to bring out the best in our writers. For the few bones available they snarl and fight like feral dogs. It is, above all, not a time conducive to serious questions or to the examination of the assumptions and follies at the heart of our lives. Few of our writers dare to do anything more interesting or risky than to preach blandly and safely with a rosary of cliches, to the long-since converted. Literary writing, at least for the survivors, is not a career of danger and daring. Our best and brightest have become "company men" just as in the old Soviet Union the writers, with towering exceptions like Solzhenitsyn and Brodsky, sold their souls for some potage and comfort. Remember what Solzhenitsyn told a graduating class at Harvard—how we in the West don't need any state censors because the intellectual status quo does a fine and dandy job in keeping the deepest questions unasked and the most serious problems untouched. There is no incentive to challenge the prevailing orthodoxy, either in literary form or content. There is no good reason to take a stand against what is popular.

One of the things that I fear may result from the present state of things, even if, by new technology, by better and smaller publishing practices, by some hoped-for sea-change, publishing should somehow again become an honest and honorable (and sensible) enterprise, engaging the interests of real people of real character and intelligence, even so, the writers, ourselves, either defeated or tainted by the corruption of the system, would not be worthy or able to rise to such an occasion.

On a bad day, I sometimes allow myself the liberty of thinking that maybe it is just as well that literary art is dying. Meantime, however, like all the others, I continue to persist, practicing the ancient and honorable craft, aiming always (even here and now) for art and even for the grace beyond it.

Book Reviewing and the Literary Scene

George Garrett
University of Virginia

Publishers say they're doing badly, yet they pay $5 million for books that their sales force tells them aren't going to work and don't.

> —Leonard Riggio, CEO of Barnes &
> Noble Inc., quoted in the *New
> York Observer* (4 August).

Whatever joy there once was in the otherwise frightening process of publishing a book—nurturing of concerned editors, ceremonies of publication day, a sense of celebration at the end of a long and arduous task—is gone today.

> —Mary Lee Settle, "Works of
> Art or Power Tools."

It helps to be beautiful.

> —Morgan Entrekin, quoted in *The New
> York Times* (11 January).

The thing about books is that they are different from slalom races. One success does not take away from the next.

> —Ann Roiphe, "Literary Pups Snap Savagely At
> Top Dogs," *New York Observer* (27 October).

Summing up the year in "A Feast of Literary Delights" (*Newsweek,* 5 January 1998), reviewers Malcolm Jones Jr. and Ray Sawhill compared the current literary scene to what they viewed as the high point of the 1960s, when "Writers in the mid-60s stood at the red-hot center of things." In contrast, "Writers today dwell in an uneasy shadowland somewhere between the wax museum and the midway." Nevertheless, after allowing for some unpleasant facts—huge celebrity advances that did not earn out, declining sales overall, the losing battle against the chain stores and superstores being fought by the independents, the amazing percentage of returns (50 percent and more), etc.—they ended on an upbeat note, citing the extraordinary success of some smaller presses (Steerforth, Ecco, Chronicle), the impact of Oprah's Book Club, and, above all, as exemplary of the "best season, both critically and commercially in years," the remarkable atten-tion and success gained by three literary novels: *Cold Mountain* (Grove/Atlantic), *Mason & Dixon* (Holt), and *Underworld* (Scribner).

What the two *Newsweek* reviewers do not mention (among other things) is that all three of these books received massive and expensive promotion by their publishers and that of the three only *Cold Mountain* achieved success commensurate with the expensive efforts of promotion and publicity. I cannot recall in my lifetime any literary novel which received the kind of orchestrated attention that *Underworld* earned: prominent and prompt reviews (almost simultaneous nationwide) by prominent writers and reviewers in almost all the publications that review books. *VLS,* the literary supplement of *The Village Voice,* put Don DeLillo's photo on the cover and named him "Mister America." Praise (and featured position) was lavish in the major newspapers, magazines, literary magazines, and on the Internet. And, indeed, for all this sound and fury, this explosion of enthusiasm (Adam Begley of the *New York Observer,* 15 September, announced that *Underworld* would win *all* the prizes and predicted that DeLillo would earn the Nobel Prize), *Underworld* had a brief life on the best-seller lists, nothing close to *Cold Mountain,* which sat atop most lists for more than half a year and at this writing remains high on the lists. *Cold Mountain* also won the National Book Award over the favored *Underworld,* causing even more orchestrated publicity for the latter, which, at the least, may help *Underworld* to win one or more of the other major prizes.

Perhaps more to the point than the *Newsweek* summary of where we are now was a major and widely discussed article by Ken Auletta in *The New Yorker* (6 October)—"The Publishing World: The Impossible Business." (By the way, in 1997 *The New Yorker* again became a major player in the literary scene with both its book reviews and literary journalism, a condition attested to by the surprising number of advertisements for new books in its pages. Many publicists have shifted the advertising of literary books from *The New York Times Book Review* to *The New Yorker.*) Auletta's article was first-rate journalism, offering significant numbers, pertinent interviews, and thoughtful judgment; while not the last word on the subject, it is the best piece so far on the contemporary pains of American publishing: "People in the adult-trade-publishing industry are again talking about a crisis, but this one seems different from the crisis of any other period in modern book publishing. Today people seem to be losing interest in the business itself–or, at least, in the business as we've known it." Auletta deals in detail with the major problems confronting American publishing today: the buying and selling of publishing houses by their conglomerate owners (including the possibility that books retailer Barnes and Noble may be in the market for a publishing company of its own); the fact that even the most successful publishers earn small profits compared to other "contest businesses" and seem unlikely to change that situation or to reduce significantly the basic costs of publishing; the "punishing" expense of high advances that are not earned out; the problem of returns from the retailers; the serious influence of marketing considerations on editorial decisions; the increasing importance of the Internet, not only for retail sales, but as a primary means of publication; and the contagion of "the Hollywood mentality." On 29 September several of the people discussed and quoted in the Auletta article (including Auletta himself) gathered to form a panel for an invitation-only audience at the New York Public Library–Morgan Entrekin of Grove/Atlantic; Michael Naumann of Holt; Leonard Riggio, CEO of Barnes and Noble; and writer Cynthia Ozick. Their topic was "Book Publishing: Dead or Alive?" (See Doreen Carvajal, "Much Hand Wringing With Gloves Off, At A Publishing Debate," *The New York Times*, 1 October.) Essentially this discussion and question-and-answer session covered much of the same ground as the Auletta article–the past long gone, the present a sea of troubles and troublesome numbers, and the future altogether uncertain. With one surprise. Big-time bookseller Riggio made a strong case for mid-list authors from his particular point of view: "In the middle I don't think the average publisher understands the depth to which people are embracing serious literature."

If Auletta's article was the best outline and summary of the present literary scene (from the publishers' point of view, at least), the writers' part in all this–the view from the trenches–was mostly to be found in the special publications aimed at and for writers. Among the best of these are the revamped *Authors Guild Bulletin,* which offers Campbell Geeslin's excellent column "Along Publishers Row"; *The National Book Critics Journal; AWP Chroni-*

cle; *Poets & Writers; American Poet* (the journal of the Academy of American Poets); and the *Journal of the Poetry Society of America.* Of course, *Publishers Weekly* (*PW*), which celebrated its 125th anniversary in 1997, is the bible of the business. With its news of the industry, of the coming and going of people and publishers, of trends and prizes; its forecasts of the new books, early reviews which can make or break; its interviews with authors deemed worthy of attention, *PW* is preeminent. If there is any weakness, from the writer's or the reader's point of view, it is that over the years *PW* has become more and more a part of the establishment that it is to scrutinize. Perhaps it is the hard times for publishers, but, for whatever the reason, *PW* has circled the wagons and busily defends the publishing establishment and, coincidentally, the literary establishment as well. At the end of this century and millennium *PW* seems to have a vested interest in the status quo. Nothing wrong with that except that it is not a good place to look for new and original ideas, discoveries or rediscoveries. Still, all of us need what it gives us. To ask for more would be ungrateful.

Both tactical and strategic battles are handled by certain major newspapers. Among these are the principal reviewing media–*The New York Times, The New York Times Book Review, The Washington Post, Washington Post Book World, Washington Times, Chicago Tribune, Los Angeles Times, Boston Globe, Wall Street Journal,* and others. As a matter of course and basic literary journalism they deal with the publishing scene as part of their limited coverage of the literary world. Perhaps the best, certainly the most extensive, coverage of the literary and publishing scenes is to be found in *The New York Observer.* There are frequently several news and feature stories about the publishing scene as well as reviews of books making a name and a mark on that scene. For example, the 8 December issue offered three full-scale, front-page stories–Lorne Manly's "Can Mort Rescue the Amazing Harry?," concerning the move of Harold Evans from boss at Random House to media chief for Mortimer Zuckerman's publications, including *U.S. News & World Report,* the *New York Daily News, Atlantic Monthly,* and *Fast Company;* Celia McGee's "Publishing" column; "Ann Godoff's Power Play Was Not a Random Move," dealing with Evans's successor at Random House; and Philip Weiss's "J. D. Salinger Girlfriend Breaks the Glass Ceiling," focusing on the announcement by Joyce Maynard of her intention to write about the affair she had with J. D. Salinger some twenty-five years ago. There was also a book review of *The Making of a Chef* (Holt) by Michael Ruhlman and a column, "Off the Record," about the serious financial problems of the youth-oriented magazines *George* and *Swing.* Again and again during the year the *Observer* published "cutting edge" and often outrageous literary journalism. For example, there is the 13 October issue with two lengthy articles linked together under the general title, "Twilight of the Great Literary Beasts": one, by critic Sven Birkerts, trashing several literary dignitaries–"Roth, Mailer, Bellow Running Out of Gas"; the other, by cult figure David Foster Wallace–"John Updike, Champion Literary Phallocrat, Drops One; Is This Finally the End for Magnificent Narcissists?" This, in turn, led to a response by one of the *Observer*'s regular columnists, Anne Roiphe, in the 27 October issue–"Literary Pups Snap Savagely At Top Dogs": "What we really have here is the primitive competitiveness of males who want to urinate on the books placed on the front tables of Barnes & Noble in order to signify territorial ownership." An earlier piece (2 June), by Warren St. John, "The Secret Selling of Thomas Pynchon: Marketing *Mason & Dixon:* Best-Selling Work of Genius, or Great American Doorstop?," may well be the most thorough exploration of the ways and means of the selling of literary fiction to date.

Literary News From 1997: A Collage

If Stephen King, John Grisham, and Michael Crichton got together, they'd become one of the top three publishers overnight.

> –Morgan Entrekin, quoted in *The New Yorker* (6 October).

It is not possible to begin to mention all the news, or even very much of it, that marked the year. And yet one can honestly and fairly note some of the things that seemed to me to be important at the time and, taken together, seem to characterize the year gone by.

Perhaps the most extraordinary happening was the huge and mostly unanticipated success of *Cold Mountain.* They expected this first novel to do reasonably well, but nobody had any hope that a serious, literary novel, or *first* novel, would be the most successful book of the year, outdoing even the blockbusters. Of course the book was vigorously promoted and more so when it began to catch on. But nobody has yet offered an acceptable explanation of why all this took place. Perhaps the only adequate explanation is that of Marty Asher, editor of Vintage Books: "There's this strange fairy dust that sprinkles down from the ether and just kisses a

book and it seems to have landed on this one. It's just a beautiful thing to behold."

In October the Round Reading Room of the British Library was closed after serving writers and readers for 140 years. (See Sarah Lyall, "In Hallowed Room, Last Page is Turned," *The New York Times,* 25 October.)

All year long publishers, writers, and above all literary journalists publicly worried about the marketplace for books. In May *The Wall Street Journal* pointed out that sales of hardcover books fell 4.4 percent in 1996 with no sign of potential improvement in 1997. Revenue growth in publishing, overall, was 1.8 percent, not nearly enough to keep conglomerates happy. And during the first three months of 1997 HarperCollins sustained losses of more than $7 million, resulting in a reorganization of the company and the cancellation of 106 book contracts. Writing in *Washington Post Book World,* 1 June, Marie Arana-Ward had this to say in "Views From Publishers Row": "One thing is clear: A great paradox is at work in the marketplace of books. On the one hand, there are blockbusters whose fates are impervious to reviews, driven by personalities, Hollywood afterlives, and author appearances on television talk shows. On the other, there are books whose futures are played out on the review page—with lesser-known authors, potentially long shelf lives and better shots at the literary prizes."

Speaking of prizes, in addition to *Cold Mountain*'s Charles Frazier, the winner, the following writers were finalists for the National Book Award: Diane Johnson for *Le Divorce,* Ward Just for *Echo House,* Don DeLillo for *Underworld,* and Cynthia Ozick for *The Puttermesser Papers.* Conspicuously missing and the cause of some public grousing were Philip Roth for *American Pastoral* and Thomas Pynchon for *Mason & Dixon.* (Representatives from Holt refused to attend the affair when Thomas Pynchon was not named a finalist.) The 1997 Lannan Literary Awards gave novelist William H. Gass its Lifetime Achievement Award of $100,000. Other fiction writers who received Lannan Awards were John Banville ($75,000), Anne Michaels ($75,000), and Grace Paley ($75,000). Oprah Winfrey, whose newly formed Oprah's Book Club had turned seven books, including two novels by Kaye Gibbons, into best-sellers overnight, received the *Literary Marketplace*'s Person of the Year Award. Anthony Hecht won the $100,000 Tanning Prize given by the Academy of American Poets for lifetime achievement. Judges were Debra Gregor, John Hollander, Heather McHugh, Mark Strand, and Harold Bloom. Poet Adrienne Rich was awarded a 1997 Medal for the Arts but turned it down publicly, writing in a letter to Jane Alexander of the National Endowment of the Arts: "The radical disparities of wealth and power in America are widening at a devastating rate. A president cannot meaningfully honor certain token artists while the people at large are so dishonored." Her position in her letter (published in the *Los Angeles Times Book Review,* 3 August) earned her a tomahawk chop in the September issue of *The New Criterion.* In "A Rich Harvest of Muddle," editor-critic Hilton Kramer wrote: "We have given some thought to the possibility that Rich was actually an expert parodist and that this was her masterly send-up of the arty eco-feminist P.C. productions that are now such a conspicuous feature of NEA–sponsored cultural projects. Alas, no. Rich's grim earnestness makes that attractive possibility of parody implausible." Another prize that came to nothing in 1997 was the winner of the Yale Series of Younger Poets. Poet W. S. Merwin, acting as judge of the seven hundred book-length entries, concluded that none was worthy of publication. Other years in which there was no winner of this prize are 1943, 1949, 1954, and 1965. (See David Streitfeld, "And the Winner Isn't . . . ," *Washington Post,* 3 October.)

Tina Brown, at the helm of *The New Yorker,* must have experienced a change of heart in 1997. Certainly, after an earlier austerity, there was an abundance of literary material in the magazine. Perhaps she reasoned that people who might be drawn to read her publication are most likely readers in a general sense as well. At any rate, there was more literary action and more literary subject matter this year than the year or so before. Some of these were rather surprising. For instance, on 18 August *The New Yorker* published excerpts from the journals of the late William S. Burroughs, his thoughts about life and art ("Maybe on the basic level of truth there just isn't any more to say.") and his final note written to himself and posterity on the day before he died: "Love? What is it? Most natural painkiller. What there is. LOVE." Another surprise arrived in the form of an old-fashioned profile of poet Jorie Graham, replete with poems and a more-than-full-page photograph—"Big Poetry," by Stephen Schiff, *The New Yorker* (14 July): "She has also been elaborately championed by the most powerful poetry critic in America, the Harvard professor Helen Vendler [who also writes regularly for *The New Yorker*], whose ardently argued views sometimes baffle those who don't share them. Vendler and Graham have become friends, and Graham sometimes seeks out Vendler's response to her poems before publishing them." *The New Yorker* also became a contributing player in the massive

and widespread hype for DeLillo and his novel, publishing a profile (and picture) of the author in David Remnick's "Exile on Main Street" (15 September). Another unusual piece, echoing the style of the "old" *New Yorker,* was John Updike's "Me and My Books" (3 February): "A master set of the forty Knopf hardcovers sits in a polychrome row opposite my desk. They are stripped of their jackets and marked up with typos and second thoughts toward some ultimate perfected edition. Somewhere in their several million pondered, proofread, printed words I must have done my best, had my say."

Esquire magazine made some copy, if not headlines, when its editor, Edward Kosner, rejected David Leavitt's bought-and-paid-for, scheduled-for-April story, "The Term Paper Artist."

While he was still the main man at Random House, Harold Evans organized a series of literary breakfasts, one of which, to celebrate the reissue of *Appointment in Samara* (1934), brought together Shelby Foote, Fran Lebowitz, Louis Begley, and Gay Talese to honor its author, the late John O'Hara. Harold Evans, husband of *The New Yorker*'s Tina Brown and president and publisher of the Random House Trade Publishing Group, resigned from that position to go to work for Mort Zuckerman, owner of a string of newspapers and magazines. Evans was replaced by Ann Godoff. Random House also made news when it first delayed, then re-edited Peter Watson's *Sotheby's: The Inside Story* in response to considerable legal pressure and threats of a libel suit by Sotheby's attorneys. Writes Jeffrey Hogrefe ("Random House Bows to Pressure From Sotheby's, Cleanses Expose," *New York Observer,* 1 September): "When it was pointed out that such changes seemed to give Sotheby's a more positive spin in light of the rather serious allegations presented in the book, Mr. Vaughan [Samuel S. Vaughan, editor at large] took the high editorial road. 'The editorial additions were done in part to reflect the response from Sotheby's,' he said. 'But I wasn't so much concerned with getting Sotheby's position. I was concerned with getting our edition right and as complete as it could be.'"

In his regular (and thorough and inclusive) column, "Along Publishers Row," Campbell Geeslin informed us that a manuscript by Arthur Conan Doyle of *The Sign of Four* fetched $519,500 at auction. That figure seems modest enough and well spent when compared with some of the advances against royalties paid out by publishers for blockbusters that soon went to the remainder shelves: $3.5 million to Johnnie Cochran (from Random House) for his autobiography; $2.5 million to Dick

Morris (also from Random House); $4.5 million paid to O. J. Simpson prosecutor Marcia Clark by Viking. Comic Jay Leno contributed to the heavy losses incurred by HarperCollins with his $4 million advance on *Leading with My Chin.* A somewhat different story was the news of Stephen King's decision to leave Penguin Putnam and to search out a new publisher and, the story went, an advance of at least $17 million on his new horror novel, *Bag of Bones.* But in the end (7 November) it was announced that King's book will be published by Simon and Schuster with a "token" advance of only $2 million, compensated for by the new publisher's "enthusiasm" for the writer and his work.

Among the deaths of literary figures in 1997 were two suicides which aroused sorrow and considerable publicity. They were Michael Dorris, novelist and husband to the writer Louise Erdrich, and J. Anthony Lukas, a much-admired reporter and author of nonfiction (elected president of the Authors Guild in 1997), whose 1986 book on desegregation in Boston, *Common Ground,* had won him the Pulitzer Prize, the National Book Award, and the National Book Critics Circle Award. He had also won a Pulitzer Prize in 1968 for *The Two Worlds of Linda Fitzpatrick.* His latest book, *Big Trouble* (Simon and Schuster), 875 pages and eight years in the making, dealing with an early-twentieth-century murder trial, was published posthumously in September. There was a great deal of journalism about his death. One of the best pieces was Doreen Carvajal's "Survived by His Book," *The New York Times* (12 October). Michael Dorris proved, on close examination of his life, to be a complex and often contradictory character, a man as troubled by his self-image as by the domestic problems which helped to drive him to ground. The most thorough and thoughtful appraisal was "Michael Dorris's Troubled Sleep" (*New York,* 16 June), by Eric Konigsberg: "Dorris was known for his public generosity toward other authors. He said he would not negatively review any books by Indian authors, because the field needed support. In truth, says Mark Anthony, a friend of the couple's, 'in dozens of conversations on the subject, I never heard Michael utter a nice word about another Indian writer.'" Dorris's posthumous book was the novel *Cloud Chamber* (Scribners).

J. D. Salinger, often written about as a recluse who hates publicity, found himself in the papers and magazines for two separate reasons this year. First there was the prospect of a new book by Salinger. Here is Campbell Geeslin's account in "Along Publishers Row" (*Authors Guild Bulletin,* Summer): "NEAR MISS? After a flurry of articles about the upcoming publication of a J. D. Salinger novel, *Hapworth 16, 1924, Book Publishing Report* said in February that Publisher Robert Lathbury of Orchises Press announced that the project had been delayed indefinitely." Not canceled, but delayed. This book was in fact the republication of an uncollected short story published in 1965. Perhaps the most unwelcome attention to Salinger came in the form of the announcement that a onetime close friend, Joyce Maynard, was writing an account of her relationship with Salinger: "Joyce Maynard, the novelist and journalist, whose first love was J. D. Salinger, plans to break a 25-year silence about her nine-month relationship with the reclusive author by writing about it in a memoir" (*Washington Post,* 22 November).

As usual in any given literary year there were public and private quarrels aplenty. The National Book Award (NBA) created hard feelings among any number of the literate. David Streitfeld set the tone before the awards were announced in "Frazier vs. DeLillo In Title Fight," *Washington Post* (16 October): "In the most interesting prize competition in ages, two extremely popular, highly praised and widely different novels will face off for the National Book Award this year." The *Publishers Weekly* (24 November) account of the NBA affair, while allowing that the choice of *Cold Mountain* "was greeted with some astonishment," pointed out that Frazier is a great admirer of DeLillo's art. Celia McGee focused on the noticeable absence of people from Henry Holt and Company (publishers of Thomas Pynchon's *Mason & Dixon,* which was not nominated) at the occasion, quoting Holt's president Michael Nauman—"I wasn't there because the jury chose not to put Thomas Pynchon into its list of finalists. . . . How could they say, to hell with one of the greatest writers produced in this century?" ("Nauman Nixes N.B.A. Because of Pynchon Snub," *New York Observer,* 1 December). There were other lively quarrels. Bill Glauber, writing for the *Baltimore Sun* (syndicated in the *Charlottesville Daily Progress,* 14 December) followed the yearlong epistolary mud wrestling between British stars John le Carré and Salman Rushdie back and forth in the pages of *The Guardian.* In the "Correspondence" section of the revamped *Los Angeles Times Book Review* (24 August) there was a fine multisyllabic dustup between poet John Ashberry and Alexander Theroux over a review which Theroux had written earlier. Theroux had the last word: "Obscurantism is morally wrong precisely for the lie it tells in the pretense of coming forward with the truths it simultaneously—and always posturingly—refuses to divulge."

Other fights were in the courts. Patricia Cornwell was sued for invasion of privacy. An unprecedented Nevada defamation award (based chiefly on catalogue copy) in a suit brought by Steve Wynn against Lyle Stuart, publisher of Barricade Books, resulted in a judgment against Stuart of $3 million, together with a restraining order barring any distribution from the warehouse. Another defamation and invasion of privacy suit was brought against Stuart in Kentucky (see Doreen Carvajal, "Defamation Suit Leaves Small Publisher Near Extinction," *The New York Times,* 8 October). In an ongoing lawsuit African American writer Barbara Chase-Riboud sued Steven Spielberg's Dreamworks for $10 million for plagiarizing material from her 1989 novel *Echo of Lions* and using it in the movie *Amistad*. The response by Dreamworks was that the material for the movie was gathered from historical documents as well as a 1953 novel, *Slave Mutiny,* by William A. Owens. Dreamworks further argued that Chase-Riboud herself had plagiarized material from *Slave Mutiny.* Chase-Riboud was quoted as saying, "I'm doing this not only for myself. I'm doing this for all writers." (See Bernard Weinraub, "Filmmakers of 'Amistad' Rebut Claim by Novelist," *The New York Times,* 4 December; also by the same reporter–"Judge Rejects Author's Plea to Block Film By Spielberg," *The New York Times,* 8 December; also: Sharon Waxman, "Judge Allows Release Of Spielberg's 'Amistad'," *Washington Post,* 9 December; and Celia McGee, "Novelist Sues Dreamworks Over Story Behind Amistad," *New York Observer,* 17 November.) In a separate event not involving any lawsuit, romance writer Janet Dailey admitted to plagiarizing some material from writer Nora Roberts for her own novels *Aspen Gold* and *Notorious* (see *Publishers Weekly,* 4 August).

Also in the bad-news department: the Association of Authors Representatives expelled agent Natashia Kean from their ranks for creating a fake auction for *The Piper's Sons* by Bruce Ferguson.

In the current literary scene it proved to be better for some writers with mid-list track records to adopt pseudonymns and to start over. Veteran writer of thrillers David Bayer wrote *The Magician's Tale* (Putnam) and sold it for an advance of $1 million as "David Hunt." A lot of publicity greeted the discovery that K. C. McKinnon, author of the popular novel *Dancing at the Harvest Moon* (Doubleday), for which she received a large advance and a first printing of 200,000 copies, was in fact mid-list writer Cathie Pelletier. (See Judy Quinn, "K. C. McKinnon Uncovered," *Publishers Weekly,* 13 October; also Celia McGee, "Who Is K. C.

McKinnon? Just Ask Cathie Pelletier," *New York Observer,* 6 October.)

Of all the comings and goings within the publishing business two seemed to be particularly meaningful. William Strachan, editor in chief at Holt and widely regarded as one of publishing's best and brightest, resigned to become president and director of the Columbia University Press, a move which might suggest changes on both sides of the equation. Similarly Adam Bellow, Saul Bellow's son, gave up the editorship of the Free Press, perhaps, as Celia McGee put it, "a casualty of false hopes they raised for a Tory-ish publishing explosion" (see "Basic Books To Be Bought; Bellow Bows Out at Free Press," *New York Observer,* 7 July).

In the world of book reviewing there were fewer changes than one might have imagined. Two major pages hired new editors who, in turn, slightly remodeled their publications. Elizabeth Taylor took over at the *Chicago Tribune,* and Steve Wasserman left Times Books to become editor of the *Los Angeles Times Book Review.* And after two years of having no book pages, the *San Diego Union-Tribune* began to publish an eight-page Sunday book section under the guidance of Rick Levinson, senior editor for special sections.

A final note about subtle shifts and changes in the book-reviewing scene. Tabloid-size and regional, in a general rather than a strict way, several publications are thriving. Already four years old, *The Boston Book Review* is first-rate and influential– the Boston area is good book-reading and -buying country, and there are plenty of good writers in the area to call on for reviews. Just so is *Brightleaf,* in its first year, coming from Raleigh, North Carolina. Edited and published by David S. Perkins, formerly book editor for the *Raleigh News & Observer, Brightleaf* has a good mix of reviews, literary journalism, and articles drawing on the abundant available talent in the central North Carolina area. In response to the first issue Shelby Foote wrote: "All in all, I found it the best-balanced view of the South and its literature I've encountered in ages."

Literary Journalism

The significance of literary journalism, as distinguished from book reviewing and serious criticism, continues to grow. Publishers would in general prefer an interview, a profile, or a general topic that will allow the literary journalist to focus on particular books and writers, instead of the conventional book review that, with its characteristic of judgment, is uncontrollable and can easily cause as much or more harm in the brief life of a contemporary literary book than it can offer aid and comfort. Similarly, newspapers and magazines of all kinds seem to be willing to allot more space to literary journalism, which may claim to pass as "news," than they are willing to increase, or even maintain, the space given over to book reviews.

As for the best of the bunch, someone especially active and excellent for the *Yearbook* to single out and salute, the gold star (if there were one) could easily, and again, go to David Streitfeld of *The Washington Post,* who has been praised in the past in these pages for the quantity and quality of his literary journalism. But there are others around and about the scene who have contributed a great deal to our understanding of the contemporary literary scene. One of these people, someone whose literary journalism throughout the year was routinely first-rate, is Celia McGee, whose regular "Publishing" column gave the best coverage and response to the New York publishing scene. An outstanding reporter as well as a thoughtful and witty commentator, she easily earns the 1997 *Yearbook* salute for literary journalism.

Streitfeld is close as a runner-up. He is especially good on the subtle nuances of fame and reputation and in the difficult, shifty definitions of literary "success." If he has a serious failing, it is that, for all his interest in establishing the guidelines of success and failure, he seems to be completely unaware of or, anyway, unable to conceive of the idea that any number (the majority, if truth and fact are to be known) of contemporary American writers work at their art and craft almost completely outside the precincts of the establishment, with its conventional rewards and punishments. It would seem almost impossible to understand the contemporary scene without being aware of the work, however marginal it may seem, of many greatly gifted American writers whose example helps maintain the high standards of their more-successful colleagues. This, in itself, is a major story he has missed. Moreover, there is, inevitably, a certain hostility toward writers who go on working in spite of the yawning indifference of critics and publishers hewing to the bottom line, a feeling that these people are serving only to clutter up the scene. As Streitfeld wrote (*Washington Post Book World,* 28 December), speaking as much for his fellow critics and journalists as himself: "It's an act of supreme ego to spend a year or two creating a lengthy piece of prose—something the world doesn't need and will never miss if it doesn't appear—and then expect people to pay $24 or so for it." But what of those (many, many) who work for the joy and challenge

of it and ask for nothing and expect less? What harm have they done?

Add to it the problem faced by literary journalists of all kinds—that they are ill equipped to do the one great thing reporting can do best, that is to *discover* anything, to make *discoveries,* precisely because of their symbiotic relationship with the establishment and because the subjects of their attention must have already established themselves before they can be given space and consideration. Celia McGee, to an extent, escapes this funhouse of mirrors because she has the New York publishing scene (more a zoo than a funhouse) as her principal subject.

The larger question posed, and probably not to be answered in this world or (one hopes) the next, is whether or not there is any reality at all outside of, separate from, the clamor and clatter of publicity which is the daily fare of literary journalists in this century's final decade. Looking hard at things, one is tempted to believe that image is all, the only "reality" there is. But if so (returning to our large population of mute, inglorious Miltons), then who are all these others?

Here, at any rate, are some of the outstanding pieces of literary journalism from 1997:

Roger Angell, "Marching Life," *The New Yorker* (22 and 29 December). Profile of the late V. S. Pritchett: "Fiction need not always confirm our knowing, irony-abraded wariness; sometimes we need it to motor along life's outer possibilities, to provide the jolts and swerves that keep us awake, against all odds, and for the next part of the trip."

Ken Auletta, "The Impossible Business," *The New Yorker* (6 October). One of the most significant articles about the contemporary publishing business in a long time. This one has impact: "In 1991, nearly a third of all consumer adult titles were sold in independent bookstores, but in the last six years that figure has plunged. Today a mere 18.6 percent are sold in the bookstores that were once the sentimental, if not the financial, heart of the industry—a figure equal to the number sold through book clubs. Today, nearly a quarter of all books are sold through superstore chains like Barnes & Noble and the Borders Group, and these outlets account for about forty percent of adult hardcover trade books."

Marie Dawson, "The Listening Ear," *The World & I* (October 1997). Profile of Eudora Welty: "These days, Welty's life is quiet and peaceful; there are few demands on her time. She enjoys attending the public readings of her work held locally and receiving visits from her brother Walter's family and cherished friends. She also savors the small events that make life joyful, such as her daily drive around Jackson with Daryl Howard, the vibrant companion who takes care of her, and eating ice cream for dessert."

Rozanne G. Epps, "Another World," *Style* (25 March). Article—and one of the few so far concerning this serious candidate for the Nobel Prize in Literature—on the books of Ismail Kadare: "Even if you are not particularly interested in Albania, Kadare is worth the trouble it will take to find his books in bookstores and libraries. He lives in France and his novels, written first in Albanian, have been translated into French and then into English. The French revere him and have made him one of only 12 non-French members of the French Academy of Moral and Political Sciences. Slowly, slowly, we are beginning to appreciate him also."

Malcolm Jones Jr. and Ray Sawhill, "A Feast of Literary Delights," *Newsweek* (5 January 1998). A summation of the year; the trials and tribulations of the publishing industry; nevertheless a year with significant literary pleasures for readers who care: "It is hard to despair of American publishing in a year when three such distinguished and challenging novels (Charles Frazier's *Cold Mountain,* Don DeLillo's *Underworld,* Thomas Pynchon's *Mason & Dixon*) not only appear on bestseller lists, but, in the case of 'Cold Mountain,' sell well over a million copies. Moreover, there was even more reason to smile last month when a modest amount of sideline brawling broke out over the National Book Awards."

Celia McGee, "Big Fun in Frankfurt: King Jumps Viking's Ship," *New York Observer* (3 November): "Here is the interesting wrinkle in Mr. King's makeup: While measuring himself financially against the likes of Mr. Clancy, he remains enthralled by literary cachet. Hence his representative's approach to such publishers as Alfred A. Knopf, Farrar, Straus & Giroux and Scribner."

Celia McGee, " 'I Am Not a Crook!' Barnes & Noble Head Lets Loose," *New York Observer* (4 August): "Leonard Riggio, the chief executive officer of Barnes & Noble Inc., likes to play hard to get, especially when reporters call to inquire about a common publishing complaint: the amount of books the mammoth bookseller returns to publishing houses, big and small. Since numerous publishers have been crushed by returns this year, reportedly as high as 40 percent in some cases, chains such as Barnes & Noble, Borders Books & Music, and Books-a-Million have come under increased fire from publishers."

McGee, "Susan Sontag Stonewalls Norton's Biographers," *New York Observer* (21 July): "The Rollyson-Paddock Team has a contract with W. W. Norton & Company, which plans to publish the biography in two years. The working title, *Susan Sontag and the Way We Live Now: A Life,* is an allusion to both Ms. Sontag's controversial *New Yorker* story of the same title about AIDS and to Anthony Trollope's dissection of the foibles and feints of nineteenth century English society."

Robert Stone, "American Dreamers: Melville and Kerouac," *New York Times Book Review* (7 December): "The overwhelming gratifying element in 'On the Road' for its contemporary readers was the dream, the promise of life more abundant to the young American adventurer, the intrepid traveler. Thirty or so years before, 'The Sun Also Rises' had offered similar dreams, though it made them appear more difficult of access."

Ron Rosenbaum, "The Man in the Glass House," *Esquire* (June). Article about J. D. Salinger and the announced publication of his story—"Hapworth 16, 1924": "The accumulation of comic exotic speculations about Salinger and Pynchon is testimony in a way to the compelling hold their forms of silence still have over us. In a publicity-mad, celebrity-crazed culture, they have become in effect the Madonna and Michael Jackson of Silence, celebrities for their reticence and their renunciation of celebrity, for their Bartleby the Scrivener–like great refusal, the resounding echo of their silent 'I would prefer not to.'"

Donald Seacrest, "Grace Is Preparation," *The World & I* (January 1998). Profile of Charles Frazier, author of *Cold Mountain,* by a friend of twenty years. There were, during the year, many interviews and profiles of Frazier. But this one's very likely the best, certainly the most revealing: "For Chuck grace is a matter of preparation. Certainly the preparation includes doing the market research. Doing the stylistic research. . . . It also requires, however, that the traveler, the writer, and the reader pay attention."

David Streitfeld, "James Salter, Writer's Writer," *Washington Post* (27 August). Profile of James Salter: "Salter is an unusual case among novelists. They tend either to become successful, in which case they keep on writing, or their books go unreviewed and out of print and agents and publishers don't bother returning their phone calls, in which case they find other, more worthwhile pursuits. Salter's sales have never been great—none of his books has ever had more than 12,000 hardcovers printed—but he has kept at it."

David Streitfeld, "A Story That Speaks Volumes: They've Got Lots of Space, Lots of Books, But Where Are the Readers?," *Washington Post* (24 September). Article on the impact of superstores on bookselling and publishing: "Instead of expanding the market, the superstores seem to be mostly cannibalizing what's already there, whether by killing independents or closing B. Dalton (owned by Borders) and Walden (owned by Barnes & Noble), stores that used to be in every mall in the country."

In a class by itself (not surprisingly) was Gore Vidal's review of Seymour Hersh's *The Dark Side of Camelot* (Little, Brown) for *The New Yorker* (1 December). The stance of Vidal as an insider, as "kissing kin" to the Kennedys, was that Hersh didn't know the half of it–that it was a lot worse than Hersh or his critics in the press imagined: "For some reason Hersh's 'revelations' are offensive to many journalists, most of whom are quick to assure us that though there is absolutely nothing new in the book (what a lot they've kept to themselves!), Hersh has 'proved' nothing. Of course, there is really no way for anyone ever to prove much of anything, short of having confessions from the participants, like the four Secret Service men who told Hersh about getting girls in and out of Jack's bed."

Robert Wilson, "A Subversive Sympathy," *Atlantic Monthly* (September). Appreciation of the short stories of Peter Taylor: "Taylor wrote perhaps a hundred stories, many of which appeared in his eight collections; three novels, two book-length plays; and perhaps a dozen shorter plays, and although the themes and settings of these many works of course varied, his larger subjects were related to this sense of himself as a rebellious son. His persistent theme was how the world into which he had been born, lodged between the Old South and the New–that is the world of his parents' generation, born in the nineteenth century and living well into the twentieth–failed to live up to the illusions of either."

James Wolcott, "Me, Myself, and I," *Vanity Fair* (October). Critique of "the new confessional school of writing known as 'creative non-fiction'": "The new confessionals are tonally and psychologically different from what's come before–needier, reedier, the worst of them evincing a flayed, righteous, yet willowy sense of grievance that's like *Mein Kampf* on spiritual retreat, while others piddle away into pointless passive aggressive chat."

Gold-Star Reviews

Our (metaphorical) gold-star laurel wreath for outstanding and distinguished book reviewing for 1997 is to be divided between two excellent critics who have reviewed widely and well. The first is Steven G. Kellman of the University of Texas–San

Antonio, author and editor of seven books, more than two hundred critical articles in quarterlies and literary magazines, several hundred book and movie reviews in newspapers and magazines (*The New York Times Book Review, Washington Post, TLS, Atlanta Journal-Constitution, Atlantic Monthly, The Nation, The Village Voice,* etc.) and currently writing a biography of Henry Roth. Kellman's range–he is professor of comparative literature–and productivity make him an influential force in contemporary book reviewing and criticism. Gold-star reviews of prominent writers in 1997, for the *Atlanta Journal-Constitution* alone, place him in the front ranks of 1997 reviewers. Among other books he reviewed for that paper were Philip Roth's *American Pastoral* (Houghton Mifflin); *The Actual* (Houghton Mifflin), by Saul Bellow; Norman Mailer's *The Gospel According to the Son* (Random House); Paul Theroux's *Kowloon Tong* (Houghton Mifflin); and *Echoes of an Autobiography* (Doubleday) by Naguib Mahfouz. A double-barreled review, "Life with Mailer, Bellow as an ordeal"–a review of *The Last Party* (Barricade) by Adele Mailer and *Handsome Is* (Fromm International) by Harriet Wasserman– nailed hides to the wall: "'The Last Party' is an often tedious account of marriage to America's most prominent young author as a series of joyless bacchanalia, whose participants are so stupefied by alcohol and drugs that they are barely recognizable as the nation's cultural elite." Another review offered this conclusion about Harriet Wasserman's tell-all book about Saul Bellow: "But the mere existence of 'Handsome Is,' its author's decision to switch from 'agent's to writer's hat,' is testimony to dual betrayal. . . . When a prominent Jewish author stabs in the back the woman who cherishes him, expect at least a book."

Less prolific, but certainly no less influential, is the critical work, found mostly in book reviews, of novelist (*The Corpse Dream of N. Petkov* and *Going to Patchogue*) Thomas McGonigle. McGonigle, a regular for the *Washington Post Book World, Los Angeles Times Book Review, Chicago Tribune Books,* and others, is especially knowledgeable and discerning, dealing with modern and contemporary European literature. Among his genuinely outstanding reviews of 1997 one would want to include his reviews of *A Book of Memories* (Farrar, Straus) by Peter Nadas (*Washington Post Book World,* 20 July); *Dreams of My Russian Summers* (Arcade) by Andrei Makine (*Los Angeles Times Book Review,* 24 August); *Slander* (Nebraska) by Linda Le (*Washington Post Book World,* 2 March); and, for the *Los Angeles Times,* his funny and sympathetic accounting of Jean Echenoz's *Big Blondes* (New Press): "This French novel is different.

You don't have to think of that squat dour gnome Sartre or of boring novels only poorly paid academics can understand. Liam O'Flaherty said once that the only place to learn French is in bed and not alone."

Adam Begley, "In DeLillo's Hands, Waste Is a Beautiful Thing," *New York Observer* (15 September). Review of *Underworld* (Scribner): "Spiff up the superlatives, the big book is here. Don DeLillo's *Underworld* will win him all the awards and place him first in line among American candidates for the Nobel Prize in Literature. While the brass band strikes up a triumphal march, I'm happy to pitch in with the best praise I know: This novel will make you feel lucky to be alive and reading."

Doris Betts, "Lost in Translation," *Brightleaf* (September–October). Review of *Women With Men* (Knopf) by Richard Ford: "Ford's ear for our slangy speech and thought, his insight into the problems of Americans of a certain age, with their sense of failed promise, make him one of our finest contemporary realists. But in these stories the sameness of the themes, overlapping and echoing, did grow a bit wearisome."

Sven Birkerts, "Malamud's Way," *Boston Sunday Globe* (7 September). Review of *Bernard Malamud: The Complete Stories* (Farrar, Straus): "Given his range and his conspicuous gifts, how is it that Malamud is not widely admired, more frequently cited? Why does he now seem a background figure to Bellow, say, or Cheever, or O'Connor herself? I fear that the explanation may be a simple one. The author has become identified—and not without reason—with the world of the Jewish immigrant. . . . But the world of our fathers is eclipsed. The impulse of our times—more than ever I think—is to leave that past, to get away from those awkward places of origin. Younger readers especially do not seem to be looking for gloomy riches from the old world. And the status of a writer like Malamud must suffer. Even a grand collection like this will not change the situation dramatically. One can only hope that the work will gather back some of the true readers, that they will confirm the stature of this sorrowful yet luminous teller of tales."

David A. Bovenizer, "Beyond All the Shouting," *Chronicles* (January 1998). Review of *Nashville 1864* (J. S. Sanders) by Madison Jones: "Madison Jones has created one of the finest fictional recollections of boyhood ever written. Moreover, he makes the time, the countryside, the way of life, and—not least—the war present to the imagination and the senses. He captures what it meant (and still may mean) to be a Southerner, as well as, more particularly, a Tennessean."

Jewell Spears Brooker, "Insight into America's Most Tragic War," *Tampa Tribune-Times* (29 June). Review of *Nashville 1864:* "The language of 'Nashville 1864' is lean and elegant, the narrative pace excellent, the exploration of themes sensitive and intelligent. This is Madison Jones at his best, and at his best he has few equals in the history of American fiction."

Richard Dyer, "Higgins Hones His Touch," *Boston Globe* (9 September). Review of *A Change of Gravity* (Houghton Mifflin) by George V. Higgins: "Higgins is as dodgy as some of the customers he writes about; where he's going doesn't really matter as much as how he gets there, and there are plenty of surprises along the way, along with some hilarity and some unmasked pain; the skewer of irony twists above the licking flames of hell, and there is little hope of heaven."

Scott Heim, "The Passion of Darcey Steinke," *Voice Literary Supplement* (Fall). Review of *Jesus Saves* (Atlantic Monthly) by Darcey Steinke: "Few authors understand America's darkest fears and obsessions like Darcey Steinke. Steinke is the sort of novelist who examines the public fascination with little girls like Katie Beers and JonBenet Ramsey, who reads between the lines of true-crime paperbacks to find fresh insight into the now commonplace tragedies of our contemporary grotesque."

Michiko Kakutani, "Of America as a Splendid Junk Heap," *The New York Times* (16 September). Review of *Underworld* (Scribners) by Don DeLillo: "Though the novel is laugh-out-loud funny at times, Mr. DeLillo's impulse is motivated in these pages by a new willingness to probe beneath the surface of his characters' lives; his hero's chronic alienation is even given a history and a source. Indeed, 'Underworld' demonstrates—much as Thomas Pynchon's novel did earlier this year—that this bravara master of cerebral pyrotechnics also knows how to seize and rattle our emotions."

Steven G. Kellman, "Too Much Paradise," *Pakn Treger* (Fall). Review of *The Puttermesser Papers* (Knopf) by Cynthia Ozick: "Puttermesser's comically cumbersome name—German for butterknife—suggests a certain lack of affect. . . . Born in the Bronx, both Puttermesser and Ozick are bookish urban Jews for whom New York is a city 'crazed by mental plenitude.' Unlike Ozick, though, Puttermesser is solitary and childless, a homely golem designed to help the author probe a hostile universe."

John Lukacs, "The Condottiere," *Chronicles* (October). Review of *André Malraux: A Biography* (Forum) by Curtis Cate: "Malraux's relationship with women is interesting enough to be essential. . . . He was very handsome, which was not only an asset when it came to women: it helped him to stand out in a crowd of dowdy intellectuals, together with this ability to speak startlingly, rapidly and well. He was attractive rather than admirable; impressively interesting rather than interestingly impressive. He pretended that art was the proposition of his life, whereas it was his life that was an artistic proposition."

D. T. Max, "Schmuck With Underwood Makes the Literary Pantheon," *New York Observer* (22 September). Review of *Nathanael West: Novels and Other Writings* (Library of America): "The star-starved fans have long since rioted and burned down the stupid system, helped, it turned out, by the greed of the stars themselves. In my apartment building there is a press agent who hasn't had a client in years and a trinket salesman who says he is an actor. We are all locusts now."

Thomas McGonigle, "Heady Hungarian Rhapsodies," *Washington Post Book World* (20 July). Review of *A Book of Memories* (Farrar, Straus) by Peter Nadas: "*A Book of Memories* is one of those truly moral books, a novel written out of and within this century dominated by the malignant two-headed coin of the organized fascist and communist lie, and where the familiar literary response has echoed Pilate's, right down to the washing of the hands. However, there have been those rare novels—*Pushkin House,* by Andrei Bitov, *Paradiso* by Jose Lezama Lima, and *The Master of Margarita* by Mikhail Bulgarov come to mind and are now joined by *A Book of Memories.*"

McGonigle, "Memory Speaks," *Los Angeles Times Book Review* (24 August). Review of *Dreams of My Russian Summers* (Arcade) by Andrei Makine: "Praised by the French for the purity of its prose, language uncontaminated by euphemisms or jargon, the book comes to English readers in a translation that is wonderful and modestly eloquent. The story will resonate for many Americans with immigrant backgrounds who have experienced or imagined a grandmother who does not speak English and spends most of her time in the kitchen."

Rick Moody, "Surveyors of the Enlightenment," *Atlantic Monthly* (July). Review of *Mason & Dixon* (Holt) by Thomas Pynchon: "The first electrifying difference about *M & D* is the astonishing voice of its narration. Pynchon has elected to write his new novel in an eighteenth-century English idiom. To say this is risky is to understate, and get the voice here is not only elegiac and credible, but also powerfully moving and unexpected, especially given the very contemporary language of the Pynchon novels that have preceded it."

Joyce Carol Oates, "Future Tense," *The New Yorker* (8 December). Review of *Toward the End of Time* (Knopf) by John Updike: "Though in some ways the most inventive of his myriad fictions, Updike's new novel is, like *The Poorhouse Fair,* at heart a wholly realist work, saturated in memory, emotion, meditation, and that staple of realistic fiction human relations. It is often inspired, and funny, 'futurist' detail serves the function of ectoplasmic daubs on a photograph."

Carolyn See, "Writing With a Brogue," *Washington Post* (26 September). Review of *An Irish Eye* (Viking) by John Hawkes: " 'An Irish Eye' is probably politically incorrect, racist, discriminatory, and a few other things, but it has—within its fable form—a ring of crazy truth. . . . It's some story! Foundlings and luck and misery and high spirits. Hawkes writes it with affection, and it's a pleasure to read."

Walter Sullivan, "Behind the Iron Mask: Joseph Blotner's *Warren,*" *Virginia Quarterly Review* (Autumn). Review of *Robert Penn Warren: A Biography* (Random House) by Joseph Blotner: "Blotner's job as a biographer was to give us Warren, to render him not only as the great writer that he was, but as a complicated and often secretive human being. This Blotner has done admirably, and the result of his consummate skill, his thorough research, his solid construction of his narrative, his graceful and concretly detailed writing, is a Red Warren developed in a completeness and angularity that will enlighten even some of Warner's oldest and closest friends."

Tomahawk Chops

Until a few years ago Tomahawk Chops (strongly negative reviews) were few and far between. It was often argued that the book reviewers were too cozy and too gentle with the publishing business. Others argued that, with limited space available for book reviewing in newspapers and periodicals, silence should be the correct treatment accorded to bad and indifferent books. All that has changed. More and more negative reviews are appearing and doing so almost everywhere. It is no trick to find them and not difficult to come up with a list like this one of the best of the bunch for this year's *Yearbook.* Perhaps one surprise in 1997 was the number of rough reviews of work by prominent writers handed out by Michiko Kakutani, reviewer for *The New York Times,* who blasted icons such as Ann Beattie, Denis Johnson, Norman Mailer, and Joyce Carol Oates, all of whom had earlier earned her praise. Maybe she was just a little cranky in 1997. . . .

Brooke Allen, "The Gospel of Norman," *The New Criterion* (June). Review of *The Gospel According* to the Son (Random House) by Norman Mailer: "*The Gospel According to the Son* shows that Mailer is still more concerned with his place in a tradition than with the actual quality of his work; for all its high-flown ideas it is a flimsy, careless, shoddy piece of writing, and a cynical effort to create excitement by addressing a subject about which many people feel passionately. That he himself does not feel passionately is evident from the clear lack of effort he has put into his work."

Allen, "Period Ironies," *New Criterion* (September). Review of *Mason & Dixon* (Holt) by Thomas Pynchon: "It has always seemed to me that if someone writes a novel that is long, obscure, and pretentious enough, the fashionable world will rise in a body and proclaim it a masterpiece, and this is exactly what happened with Pynchon's eight-hundred-page, all but unreadable tome."

Michiko Kakutani, "Like Mother, Alas, Like Daughter," *The New York Times* (29 August). Review of *Man Crazy* (Dutton) by Oates: "Although more than a dozen people in this novel die horrible and, in some cases, truly gruesome deaths, Ms. Oates tacks on one of her contrived happy endings. It is an absurd conclusion to an inept and gratuitously lurid story—an embarrassing performance, particularly for a writer of Ms. Oates's experience and talents."

Kakutani, "The Mystical and the Damned on the Lost Coast," *The New York Times* (12 August). Review of *Already Dead* (HarperCollins) by Denis Johnson: "It is hard to understand why a writer as gifted as Mr. Johnson would want to use other people's ideas or words. He'd be better off, by miles, relying upon his own talents—talents that are nowhere to be found in this inept, repugnant novel."

Kakutani, "Swapping Family Tedium for Ruthless Narcissism," *The New York Times* (24 April). Review of *My Life, Starring Dara Falcon* (Knopf) by Ann Beattie: "An ill-conceived experiment, 'My Life, Starring Dara Falcon' must surely mark a low point in this gifted writer's career."

William Logan, "Hardscrabble Country: Verse Chronicle," *The New Criterion* (June). Review of work by several poets:

. . . Of Charles Wright's *Black Zodiac:* "Wright threatens to open a minimart of metaphysics. His poems are full of vague notions and vaguer discontents. It's not that I'm deaf to metaphysics; it's that these conundrums were old a century ago—the poets they were alive for are the dust of our anthologies."

. . . Of Mary Oliver's *West Wind:* "A poetry so limited in its means and devastated in its imagining is also deadened to its responsibilities—it's as if poetry meant nothing but a few gestures toward the sentiment of meaning. A Baroque revival must be right around the corner."

. . . Of Robert Bly's *Morning Poems:* "*Morning Poems* has a dozy complacency (you feel some of it was written before waking). The book is composed of simple declarative sentences, full of 'wisdom' and 'sentiment'; as if these were ingredients found in any supermarket; and like a Disney cartoon they're full of talking mice, talking cars, talking cats, talking trees. The poems peter out at sonnet length, the appetite for poetry exhausted where the appetite for breakfast begins."

Ralph Lombreglia, "The Life of Job in Exurbia," *Atlantic Monthly* (June). Review of *American Pastoral* (Houghton Mifflin) by Philip Roth. "A story has to work as a story before it can work as an allegory. If one accepts the novel's dramatic premise and then makes a list of seemingly essential scenes, one finds very few of them are directly portrayed in the book."

Laurie Morrow, "Isn't It Romantic," *The World & I* (September). Review of *The Blue Flower* (Houghton Mifflin) by Penelope Fitzgerald: "Fitzgerald's allusions to German Romanticism disguise the fundamental shallowness of this work. Writing passionlessly about a philosophical movement that celebrates passion, Fitzgerald tosses in some philosophical in-jokes, like doggy treats for rolling over on command, perhaps to suggest that hers is a cynical vision of romanticism but certainly to reassure her readers of their sophistication. To provide a patina of profundity, she has her protagonist offer in stilted, tedious dialogue, philosophical allusions to account for his actions and feelings."

Timothy Noah, "Tom Wolfe's Sour Note," *U.S. News & World Report* (1 September). Review of Tom Wolfe's audio novella, *Ambush at Fort Bragg:* "The trouble is not that Wolfe flunks political correctness. Satire isn't supposed to be PC, and Wolfe has never been so. . . . Wolfe's brilliant mastery of dialects, perhaps unsurpassed by any other American writer save Mark Twain, is deliciously antithetical to multicultural hypersensitivity. Nor is the trouble that Wolfe is a conservative; Christopher Hitchens, a left-leaning journalist, complained in *Mother Jones* some years back that Wolfe avoids conservative targets, but there's no law against that. The problem is that Wolfe seems to be saying something about homosexuals that isn't just rude, it's vicious."

Joe Queenan, "Some '60s Things Reconsidered," *Wall Street Journal* (8 September). Review of *Heretic's Heart* (Beacon) by Margot Adler: "Ms. Adler's brief involvement with the civil-rights movement was the last time in her life that she would back a winning horse. She went off to Cuba as part of the Venceremos Brigade, only to discover that some of the cadres were more interested in sex than in advancing the cause of the proletariat. She fell in love with Camus and Franz Fanon, always a bad idea. Mostly, she spent the remainder of her youth actively despising the land of her birth."

Carolyn See, "American Culture's Trial by Ire," *Washington Post* (15 August). Review of *Resentment* (Doubleday) by Gary Indiana: "There's something in this narrative to offend everybody. Graphic gay sex and dastardly murders abound; there's so much human excrement that it almost functions as a separate character. Everything we hold most dear (What things? Everything!) is gleefully held up by the author to limitless scorn and contempt."

See, "Devoutly Ever After," *Washington Post* (20 June). Review of *The Sharp Teeth of Love* (Knopf) by Doris Betts: "It's not as though Betts can't write, she can! But it *is* as though the novelist here got kidnapped by a Theologian on speed."

Carol Tavris, "It's Empty at the Top," *New York Times Book Review* (7 September). Review of *When Work Doesn't Work Anymore* (Delacorte) by Elizabeth Perle McKenna: "After successfully climbing the corporate ladder, she discovered that the bottom-line mentality of modern business, coupled with the crass materialism of American consumer culture, can crush your soul, erode your values, devour your family life and deaden your libido. This is a surprise? Anyone remember 'Death of a Salesman'? 'What Makes Sammy Run'? 'The Man in the Gray Flannel Suit'?"

David Foster Wallace, "John Updike, Champion Literary Phallocrat, Drops One; Is This Finally the End for Magnificant Narcissists," *New York Observer* (13 October). Review of *Toward the End of Time* (Knopf) by John Updike: "Besides distracting us with worries about whether Mr. Updike might be injured or ill, the turgidity of the prose also increases our dislike of the novel's narrator. . . . This dislike absolutely torpedoes *Toward the End of Time,* a novel whose tragic climax (in a late chapter called 'The Deaths') is a prostate operation that leaves Turnbull impotent and extremely bummed."

James Wolcott, "The Odd Couple," *Wall Street Journal* (9 May). Review of *The Last of the Savages* (Knopf) by Jay McInerney: "All of the literary biggies Mr. McInerney invokes (Mailer, Fitzgerald, even Mark Twain) can't camouflage the fact that this is a novel that thinks in mushy platitudes, especially when it's dispensing important life lessons.

Kenneth Dale McCormick

(25 February 1906 – 27 June 1997)

Anne Hutchens McCormick

With the death of Kenneth Dale McCormick on 27 June 1997 the lengthy life of a special man with panache, joy in his work, and love of his friends and colleagues came to a close, as did an era of book publishing and editorial wisdom spanning across sixty years.

From his youngest days growing up in small southern Minnesota towns where his father was a Methodist minister and later in Salem, Oregon, where he attended high school and college, his first loves were music—particularly the piano, which he played as a good amateur—and books. All his life he would attribute the love of a good story to hearing his parents read aloud to each other as he sat and listened. Among his favorites were the works of Willa Cather, David Grayson, Ray Stannard Baker, and Gene Stratton Porter.

Imagine the energy and expectations of this young man on his graduation from Willamette University in Salem, Oregon, as he departed a state he loved and hitchhiked across the country to be in a place he would come to love more than even he could have believed. It was New York City, where his long career at Doubleday and Company became the focus of his life.

When he arrived in New York in 1928, he worked first at the Twenty-third Street YMCA Library, then at the old Colony Bookstore, and in due course became a clerk in the Doubleday Book Shop chain, first in New York and then for two years in Philadelphia. He would later say these were the longest two years of his life. But he took that job because his salary was raised from eighteen dollars to thirty-five dollars per week, and it was a luxury even to have a job in 1932. He was noticed by a Doubleday salesman named George Seifert who covered the Philadelphia shop, in part because Ken had written articles for *Publishers' Weekly* on how, in his opinion, a bookstore should be run. He always felt that his experience in the shops was a key factor in his book-publishing education. Seifert recommended him to the main Doubleday office in Garden City, New York, for an opening in the Promotion Department. Ken spent two years as assistant promotion manager, where his salary was sixty dollars a week; it was 1933. The company was run with an iron hand by Nelson Doubleday Sr., son

Kenneth McCormick (photograph by Alex Gotfryd)

of the founder, Frank Nelson Doubleday. In 1935 the entire promotion department was let go with the exception of Ken McCormick. He became the first reader of unsolicited manuscripts in the editorial department. The first year he read twenty-five hundred submissions and paid the price in exhaustion and ulcers. But he was invited to become an assistant editor. As part of his new duties he represented five or six other aspiring young editors at meetings—which he felt was a fine idea because he was speaking for several colleagues' projects and ideas. In 1937 he was appointed associate editor.

The editorial offices moved to Manhattan, the heart of hardcover trade-book publishing. His model/inspiration was Maxwell Perkins, legendary editor for Charles Scribner—a man he would in time come to know well and continue to revere. A. Scott Berg's biography *Max Perkins, Editor of Genius* (1978) begins with a meeting at which Ken is a moderator of a publishing class to which Perkins comes to speak.

The first best-seller he developed and handled was Oscar Levant's *A Smattering of Ignorance* (1939). The author was a popular panel member of *Information Please,* a radio quiz show. Ken's original project for him was a biography of Victor Herbert, which Levant declined, promising instead a book of essays on topics of interest to him. It was written with music critic Irving Kolodin. Ken was always proud of this title and remained sensitive to the importance of titles in general.

In 1942 he was appointed editor in chief of the trade department. Somerset Maugham, who was living in the United States during World War II, suggested to Nelson Doubleday that he offer Ken this position. For several years he was the youngest editor in chief in town. This part of his career was interrupted when he went into the air force, the office of flying safety. At Headquarters Squadron in Winston-Salem, N.C., he helped publish detailed books of flight instruction for prospective pilots. Here he met several men who went on to publishing careers; among them was Walter Bradbury, who became a distinguished editor at Doubleday.

In 1945 Ken returned to New York and Doubleday and began a professional relationship that would become one of the most successful in the publishing world. LeBaron (Lee) Barker stepped down from the editor-in-chief position he had held temporarily while Ken was in the air force, allowing Ken to resume his old job. Realizing the contributions of Barker, Ken felt a joint decision-making process would work best for all, and so began the years of success for the "Ken and Lee team." In 1948 while continuing as editor in chief he was made a vice president of the company. He would later acknowledge that he probably should not have been an officer of the company: "I'm just not enough of a financial person."

He had a wonderful time finding authors, working with those who wanted him to be their editor—whether a new name or well known. The stories of some of these discoveries were interesting and frequently amusing. He felt triumph in finding new talent, sometimes in unusual places. In the 1950s his children played with Grace Paley's youngsters. He would pick up his own at her home, and find her working on a small table, writing short stories. He asked to see a couple of them, and the result was a book which became a classic of its kind and a favorite of many readers—*The Little Disturbances of Man* (1959). He waited a long time for some contracted books to finally arrive—sometimes years, such as Alex Haley's *Roots* (1976)—but there was no denying that often the waits were worthwhile, and patience was its own reward.

As the years went by, he worked with books that reflected his many and varied interests. His first love was fiction and a good story; and he could list Ilka Chase, Edna Ferber, Irving Stone, Allen Drury, Leon Uris, Max Shulman, Fannie Hurst, Robert Lewis Taylor, Paul Gallico, Nelson Algren, and James T. Farrell among the many he nurtured and befriended professionally and personally. His innate sense of humor led him to Jean Kerr's writings and to *Please Don't Eat the Daisies* (1957); Clare Barnes's *White Collar Zoo* (1949); Charlotte Chandler's biography of Groucho Marx,

Hello, I Must Be Going (1978); and to Beatrice Lillie and Noel Coward.

A lifelong Democrat, he managed to edit the works of many political figures with impartiality—Richard Nixon's *Six Crises* (1962); Dwight D. Eisenhower's *Crusade in Europe* (1948); and later *The White House Years* (1963-1965); *Harry Truman's Memoirs* (1955-1956)—and later books with Robert F. Kennedy, Pierre Salinger, Earl Warren, Averell Harriman, Robert Murphy, and Andreas Papandreou. His continuing love of music led to the memoirs of Sir Rudolf Bing, *5000 Nights at the Opera* (1972); Gregor Piatigorsky's *Cellist* (1965); and Gary Graffman's *I Really Should Be Practicing* (1981). Public figures—Jacques Cousteau, Lowell Thomas, Louis Nizer, Otto Preminger, Colleen Moore, James Cagney, Hedda Hopper—offered new challenges, but above all new insights into the world at large. They fed his curiosity and his constant wish to know more about a wide range of issues, places, people, and topics.

In a piece written in 1982 in the *Willamette Scene* (his university's paper), the writer Ralph Wright said:

> McCormick is always looking for the best in each writer and he sees each writer differently. McCormick does not engage in conversation about this writer being good, this one being a hack, or this one being overrated. He respects them all for the talents they have. It is easy to see why he is one of the best liked editors in the business. Part of the answer to his popularity would be that self-effacement. He doesn't talk about himself; he talks about the writer.

For years he covered the British publishing scene; he loved the trips and in particular the London Doubleday office where staff members had actually known one of his favorite authors, Arnold Bennett. He was always generous on his return in sharing the news about what went on in England (and from time to time France) with the New York staff. Colleagues enjoyed the stories about Norah Lofts, Daphne du Maurier, Robert Graves, Winston Graham, Vita Sackville-West, Sir Harold Nicholson (one of his favorite authors), and Frank Swinnerton. Several English publishers became close friends of his, and he loved entertaining them when they visited New York.

Ken McCormick was devoid of snobbery; he never forgot his roots. His father, John Dale McCormick, was a Methodist minister receiving an advanced degree at Drew University in Madison, New Jersey, when Ken was born in 1906. Six months later they moved to Minnesota, where McCormick had a series of pastorates until the 1919 move to Oregon. For a long time his salary was eighteen hundred dollars a year, but Ken, who was an only child, always felt they were wealthy. His parents were both from large families; he had many aunts, uncles, and cousins full of love for each other. His trips to his paternal grandparents in Idaho where they had been water pioneers extended this family geniality and advanced Ken's great affection for the West.

His sense of fairness was an extension of this family life. It manifested itself through his work on industry committees, where he was a leader of many efforts associated with reading, writing, and publishing for industry, the government, and the library community. He was well known as a civil libertarian. He was the founder of and an early chairman of the Freedom to Read Committee of the Association of American Publishers, a First Amendment Committee; a member of the Defend Your Freedom to Read Committee; chairman of the Media Coalition; a director of the American Book Publishers Council; and a member of the International Freedom to Publish Committee. He also served several years as chairman of the ABPC Committee of Reading Development. He was invited to several National Library Week Committees and to a Government Advisory Committee created by President John F. Kennedy. He taught publishing courses at New York University and later a creative-writing course at Columbia University. Several of his students were later published. In 1975 he contributed to the Columbia University Oral History Program on Communication, a series of nine lectures with Louis Sheaffer. He was a frequent lecturer and delivered "Editors Today," the twelfth of the R. R. Bowker Memorial Lectures at the New York Public Library in 1948.

In 1984 the ninth annual Curtis Benjamin Award was presented to Ken McCormick, then a senior consulting editor for Doubleday, at the annual meeting of the Association of American Publishers. The press release at the time of the award quoted one publisher as saying,

> No other editor/publisher in American history has been responsible for so many good, successful and lasting books; no one else has brought so much reading pleasure to so large and varied an audience. . . . McCormick's influence has gone beyond his direct editorial contribution. During his tenure at Doubleday, Mr. McCormick is said to have been responsible for the development of countless individuals who are now respected editors in major publishing houses throughout the United States. Those who call themselves graduates of Ken McCormick University refer to his zest for literature, his respect for talent, his patience and kindness, as integral to the training he offered in the precepts of the craft of the editor.

He was described by his colleagues at the time in this way:

> Although he is a trade or general publisher, his concerns have encompassed the entire industry and the whole wide world of books—text, technical and scientific, children's books. His mind is a model of democracy in action. He is the finest affirmation of what an editor/publisher should be. His intelligence, his generosity and his character have made of editing an honorable and enviable profession.

After retiring as editor in chief in the early 1970s and becoming a senior consulting editor at Doubleday, Ken took on a new project. Daniel Boorstin, then Librarian of Congress, had asked for the Doubleday papers. Three days a week for several years, Ken and Louise Thomas, former publicity director of Doubleday, sorted 155 full boxes of old correspondence from the earliest Doubleday days (1897) through the mid 1980s. Until her death they weeded and annotated the material before sending it to the Library of Congress, where there is now a Ken McCormick Collection containing his correspondence and that of his publishing forebears. The other two days a week Ken worked with the New York office of the Franklin Library, the book division of the Franklin Mint, where he judged books for selection for the Signed First Edition series until 1989.

With Hamilton Darby Perry, Ken was the editor of a 1990 volume titled *Images of War: The Artist's Vision of World War II,* published by Crown Publishers. Herbert Mitgang of *The New York Times* called it "a highly original and historic work, which provides a rare worldwide portrait of the home and war fronts."

In 1990 he began to lose his eyesight, a terrible irony for a man with his book history. Books on Tape provided his "eyes"—the way to read new books and reread old favorites. His family and friends continued to read to him until the end of his life.

In 1995 John Sargent, once a Doubleday editor and later president of the company, said of Ken, "He was the most talented editor I ever worked with. He had a knack of treating a first novelist with the same attention, care, sympathy, editorial skill and enthusiasm as he would treat Irving Stone or Robert Graves or Eisenhower; they became equally his admirers and friends."

Tribute from Garry Wills

Ken McCormick was the editor every author dreams of—and yet I found him early in my writing career. Or, rather, he found me. Though he had long been the famous editor of famous authors (authors like Dwight Eisenhower), he had an eye out for new arrivals on the scene. He bought my contract from another publishing house and offered me a long-term multibook arrangement. When we were working on one of my books, he gave the impression that nothing was more important to him—the kind of attention others told me they received, too. Problems disappeared as soon as he became aware of them. He published more of my books than any other editor, and the only thing that could have ended our partnership (but not our friendship) was his retirement, made necessary by eye trouble. Recognized as publishing's great gentleman, he was a boon not only to me and his other authors but also to the entire world of books.

Stephen Vincent Benét Centenary

Charles Schlessiger

Stephen Vincent Benét died in 1943 at the age of forty-four. More than fifty years later, as we approach the centenary of his birth, his reputation is secure.

Looking through the file of permission requests to use his short stories and poems over the years, one can't help but be impressed by the number of times his work—including "The Devil and Daniel Webster" and extracts from *John Brown's Body* (1928)—has been included in textbooks and in anthologies.

To commemorate the centenary of Benét's birth a stamp will be issued in his honor by the U.S. Postal Service. The Museum of Modern Art will present a program examining both Benét's movie career and Hollywood's adaptations of his work. It will include D. W. Griffith's first talking film, *Abraham Lincoln,* for which Benét wrote the screenplay, and William Dieterle's *The Devil and Daniel Webster* and Stanley Donen's *Seven Brides for Seven Brothers,* both of which are based on Benét short stories. Also to be shown is Jorvis Ivens's *Power and the Land,* a documentary for the Rural Electrification Administration with a commentary by Benét. The Beinecke Library at Yale University will present a Benét exhibit.

A group of enthusiasts and well-wishers headed by Joan Campion, a regional historian, and Patricia MacAndrew, a dance historian, have formed the Stephen Vincent Benét Centennial Committee. Based in Bethlehem, Pennsylvania, the town of Benét's birth, the committee has scheduled a series of events to honor him. Starting in February there will be a fiddle contest, inspired by the poem "The Mountain Whippoorwill," and in the following months, as part of "John Brown's Bus Tour," a trip to Harpers Ferry, West Virginia, and to the battlefield of Gettysburg.

In his review of Charles Fenton's *Stephen Vincent Benét; The Life and Times of an American of Letters,* Orville Prescott wrote in *The New York Times:*

> When Stephen Vincent Benét died in 1943 at the age of 44, the loss to American Letters was beyond calculation. One of the fine poets of the twentieth century, he was the only American poet who was read with enthusiastic admiration by a national audience. One of the finest and most original writers of short stories of his time, he

combined fantasy, folklore and the American past into a succession of superb tales written with such shining craftsmanship that they, too, were the delight of hordes of readers. What Benét might have written had he been granted threescore years and ten is beyond conjecture. What he did accomplish in his busy, harassed and gallant life was an enduring triumph.

Tributes

David Garrett Izzo

I suppose the only way to describe Steve would be to say that if I had a chance to be some other person whom I had known in my lifetime, I would have preferred to have been Stephen Benét, not anyone else.

—William Sloane, Benét's friend

In this year, the centennial of his birth, it should be noted that Stephen Vincent Benét, in his time, was as popular as any writer in America, principally through his short stories in mass-circulation periodicals such as *The Saturday Evening Post.* (See *DLB 102.*) He was both a critically esteemed artist and a superlative entertainer who wrote for the popular audience and gave them what they wanted—poignant, heart-tugging, exhortatory fables with direct narratives, archetypal caricatures, and punchy finales. Countless teenagers have read his most widely anthologized short story, "The Devil and Daniel Webster" (1937), in which the great lawyer-orator defends a farmer who sold his soul to "old Scratch." Many more have been inspired by reading his fantasy/science-fiction classic, "By the Waters of Babylon." In 1928 his Pulitzer Prize–winning Civil War epic in verse, *John Brown's Body,* established Benét's status as a distinctly American writer and solidified a reputation that began years before when he graduated from Yale in 1919 and was known as a wunderkind all over the Northeast. His undergraduate classmate Thornton Wilder recalled that at Yale, Benét was "the whole power" of the *Yale Literary Review.* As a writer with a social consciousness Benét produced short stories and poems that influenced many during his life and, later, the generation after World War II, which was moved by his populist emotionalism.

For example, Margaret Mitchell, author of *Gone With the Wind,* profoundly admired *John Brown's Body* and in a letter to Benét called it "my favorite poem, my favorite book. I know more of it by heart than I do any other poetry. It means more to me, is realer than anything I've ever read." Benét's story "The Sobbin' Women" (read Sabine Women) was the basis for the popular film musical *Seven Brides for Seven Brothers.* Country songster Charlie Daniels said that his award-winning song about a fiddle-playing devil meeting his match was inspired by Daniels's high-school reading of a Benét poem that is also about a fiddling contest and is called "The Mountain Whippoorwill." Dee Brown's landmark book, *Bury My Heart at Wounded Knee,* a chronicle of the tragic history of Native Americans, took its title from the last line of Benét's 1930 poem "American Names." The speaker of the poem, while acknowledging his European antecedents, declares America to be his true home even though it has faults that should be recognized and addressed:

> I shall not rest quiet in Montparnasse.
> I shall not lie easy in Winchelsea.
> You may bury my body in Sussex grass,
> You may bury my tongue at Champmedy.
> I shall not be there. I shall rise and pass.
> Bury my heart at Wounded Knee.

Perhaps Benét's greatest influence has been on that subgenre of science fiction concerned with future worlds reduced to rubble and few survivors after an apocalyptic holocaust. In 1937 Benét's short story "By the Waters of Babylon" originally established the dominant traits of this sci-fi category. Saying that this "clever, sentimental, post-holocaust [story] was responsible for creating many of the cliches of that sub-genre which became so popular after the Second World War," *The Science Fiction Encyclopedia* gives due credit to Benét. Sci-fi historian Paul Carter summarizes it:

> The island of Manhattan is tabooed as a Dead Place: "The north and the west and the south are good hunting ground, but it is forbidden to go east." In the story, John, son of John, tribesman of the Hill People, sets forth on a journey comparable to the vision-quests of the young American Indian braves back in the days before the coming of the white man. The waking dream John has by the medicine fire before he goes, and the omens he sees along the trail, convince him he must break the taboo against visiting the dead places. Just the same, when he comes to the great river Ou-dis-sun

(Hudson), he sings his death-song [thinking he may not come back] before rafting over to New York. There beside a heap of stones and shattered columns, down near where Wall Street used to be, John finds a white, tie-wigged marble image of a god. "His name was ASHING, as I read on the cracked half of a stone," John relates. "I thought it wise to pray to ASHING, though I do not know that god." In 1937, with Spain, China, and Ethiopia in smoking ruins, Stephen Vincent Benét surmised that [the world's] downfall would come by war. His hero refers back to "the time of the Great Burning when fire fell out of the sky."

"By the Waters of Babylon" was meant to be a warning about the coming threat of fascism that became World War II; yet it also forecast the 1950s fear of nuclear destruction. Countless times from the 1950s to the present other writers have adopted and extrapolated this theme of postapocalyptic futures that Benét initiated. This tale displays Benét's penchant for telling stories as social parables, a penchant on which many other writers of his era also acted. Benét, whose social concern was nurtured in his childhood, was at the forefront of this effort and exemplified the role of the man of letters as a humanist and public activist.

Benét (of Spanish, not French, ancestry) was the son of a military man, Col. James Walker Benét, whom his son had in mind when he remarked, "I cannot agree with those who say that the military mind is narrow and insensitive." According to biographer, Charles A. Fenton, Benét's father was, "articulate, civilized, and widely read," and his mother, Frances, was "talented and lovely; the fluency of their children [as writers] was foreshadowed in her immense correspondence and occasional verse." Indeed, Stephen's older siblings, William and Laura, also became writers. Both parents were progressive and encouraged progressiveness in their three children.

Because Benét's father was a career army officer, he and his family moved about often: Bethlehem, Pennsylvania; Watervliet, New York; Rock Island, Illinois; Augusta, Georgia; and more. This diverse view of the United States later informed and colored his writing. In 1918 he had enlisted in the army, but he was honorably discharged due to poor eyesight and fragile health resulting from a childhood attack of scarlet fever. At Yale, where he graduated in 1919, Benét and classmate Thornton Wilder saw and were greatly impressed by populist poet Vachel Lindsay. Lindsay once said: "I love the heroic. I hate the game of puncturing heroics that is so popular nowadays." Benét and Wilder could have said it as well, and when Lindsay died in 1931, Benét wrote a poem, "Do You Remember Springfield?," which praised Lindsay and chastised those who had scorned Lindsay's idealism.

Benét earned an M.A. from Yale in 1920 and received a traveling fellowship that enabled him to go to Paris that same year. (See *DLB 2*.) He married Rosemary Carr at the end of 1921 and began his career as a writer of poems, short stories, novels, and book reviews. In fact, even before he attended Yale, Benét had already achieved literary recognition with a first book of poetry, *Five Men and Pompey,* published in 1915 when he was seventeen years old. More poetry followed, and a first novel, *The Beginning of Wisdom* (1921), added to his emerging reputation.

Critic John Peale Bishop included this novel in a review that considered it to be as significant as F. Scott Fitzgerald's *The Beautiful and the Damned* and John Dos Passos's *Three Soldiers. The Beginning of Wisdom,* Bishop wrote, "is a picaresque novel of a young man who successively encounters God, country and Yale," and Benét—who was only twenty-two—had "the courage and skill to write beautifully. He has so rare a skill with color, so unlimited an invention of metaphor, such humorous delight in the externals of things, so brave a fantasy." By 1926 he had written three more novels, two more volumes of poetry, and short stories.

In 1926–1927 Benét received the Guggenheim Fellowship, which enabled him to devote himself to writing *John Brown's Body,* winner of the Pulitzer Prize for poetry in 1929. Southern poet and critic Allen Tate said of *John Brown's Body,* "If professional historians, particularly those of the Northern tradition, will follow Mr. Benét's [Jefferson] Davis, a distorted perspective will soon be straightened out. Nowhere else has Lee been so ably presented." For the first time a best-selling epic earned Benét substantial income, which was all lost by the end of 1929 in the stock market crash that precipitated the Great Depression.

Benét and the rest of the Western world had to focus attention in the 1930s on the Depression and the rise of fascism/Stalinism in Europe. Here begins the public activism that Benét pursued to the end of his life, as did his Yale classmates Thornton Wilder and Archibald MacLeish. Benét's benevolence was both public and private, and he was generous with or without fanfare.

Benét was a benefactor to emerging writers, particularly when he was the editor of the *Yale Series of Younger Poets,* which required him to read dozens of manuscripts and make one selection per year. Among his discoveries were writers such as Norman Rosten, Muriel Rukeyser, James Agee, Margaret Walker, Joy Davidman, Paul Engle, and Edward

Weismuller. Later, Weismuller said of Benét, "It seemed to me that I owed the real beginning of my career to him. He was a very wise person, utterly kind; only seeing him and having him glad to see me, willing to talk to me, meant a great deal. A great man, talking to me as though we were both quite ordinary people! Obviously it was possible to be a poet and a human being too; I had hoped it was, but how, at that time, is one to know?"

Benét understood the young writer's struggle and always tried to help when he could: "I have been thinking about the Yale series to this effect," he wrote to the Yale Press. "It seems rather disproportionate to pay me $250 for reading the mss. when the lucky boy or girl who wins the competition can only make, at the most, $100 if he completely sells out the 500 copies of his book. I therefore suggest that you pay me $150 and pay the winner of the competition the other $100 . . . after all, I'm old and tough." And so it was.

In fact, because of Benét's own need for income, he worked at a furious pace and wrote short stories that both met his high standards and had the wide appeal needed to satisfy editors of popular magazines. He fully understood the struggle to earn a living, especially during the Depression. According to Fenton, Benét "could not insulate himself against the grim depression winters in New York. He was stricken by the sight of white-collar workers wielding relief shovels in their shabby overcoats. 'They were not used to digging,' Benét wrote. 'You could tell by their shoulders.'"

Benét actively supported President Franklin Delano Roosevelt and the New Deal, and he insisted that "At the moment every element I dislike most in the country [Marxists, fascists, the indifferent rich] are allied against Roosevelt, [who] has made his purpose plain and united all the pigs and Bourbons against him, which is fine." An activist government, for Benét, was something very American to believe in and share: "If you're a liberal," he said, "that means you're always out on a limb. It isn't very comfortable, on the limb, but then God never intended liberals to be comfortable. If he had, he'd have made them conservatives. Or radicals."

As time went on, Benét's frustration began to sound, if not radical, angry: "It is horrible to see the nervous violence of the comfortable ones once they get the idea that one cent of their precious money is being touched. It makes you feel degraded. The [so-called] patriots and lovers of America who put their money in Newfoundland holding companies—the descendants of signers who talk about people on relief as if they were an inferior breed of dog. What a sorry class of rich we have here—their only redeeming feature is their stupidity." The energy of Benét's anger was then put to good use. For the first time, his stories and verse began to use the American past as parables for the present.

His story about the young George Washington, "Man from Fort Necessity," appeared in *The Saturday Evening Post,* and in it the unwarranted vitriol of the people toward Washington is analogous to the attacks on Roosevelt. In "Silver Jemmy," Thomas Jefferson and Aaron Burr are presented as prototypes of Roosevelt and demagogue Huey Long. These parables began a steady output of stories using the spirit of a liberal America to proselytize for the New Deal as the model of democracy in action. In 1936 Benét's volume of poems *Burning City* was an outburst of patriotic indignation. Here, in addition to reminding Americans of their populist heritage in an "Ode to Walt Whitman" and paying tribute to Vachel Lindsay in "Do You Remember Springfield?," Benét addresses the threat to the United States that had emerged in the totalitarianism of Europe. In "Ode to the Austrian Socialists," "Litany for Dictatorships," "Metropolitan Nightmare," and more, he not only tells of the actual European reality, but also warns of the potential for a homegrown fascism that could evolve from public indifference borne of the alienating effects of the mechanized city. An angel in a gas-mask warns:

> You will not be saved by General Motors or the pre-
> fabricated house.
> You will not be saved by dialectic materialism or the
> Lambeth Conference.
> You will not be saved by Vitamin D or the expanding
> universe.
> In fact, you will not be saved.

Increasingly, Benét advocated the responsibility of the writer as citizen:

> If the artist believes, I think he should state his belief. . . .
> He ought to think and think hard. For neither his
> freedom of speech nor his liberty of action will
> automatically preserve themselves. They are part of
> civilization and they will fall if it falls. And he has a
> responsibility to his own art, and that is to make it great.
> I doubt if he can do so by blacking himself out.

In 1937 Benét's role as a writer of parables took on more importance with the publication of "The Devil and Daniel Webster" in *The Saturday Evening Post*. The demand for it soon moved Benét to produce a book version, then an opera libretto and also a screenplay for a movie. Its popularity continued to solidify Benét's role as a national spokesman for democracy. When, in 1939, the conflict in Europe began, he said, "I hope we stay out of it. On the other hand, I'd

sell the allies all the munitions possible–I don't want us to have to build a two-ocean fleet against time." Benét was prophetic, as the United States was put in exactly this position after the bombing of Pearl Harbor. Thus Benét became a writer for democracy at the service of his country, and he reflected on the personal and professional consequences this might bring: "If what I am writing today . . . will hurt my eventual reputation as a writer–very well, then let it. I can't just sit on my integrity as a writer, like a hen on a china egg, for the duration." He did not sit, writing pro-American, antifascist fiction and verse. He also scripted radio plays for national broadcast: "We Stand United," "Listen to the People," "Letter from a Worker," Dear Adolph (a continuing series), "They Burned the Books," and many more. He refused remuneration and requested that any fees he might receive be given to the USO. Benét advocated that a national democratic government should serve its people, and he refuted those who wanted less government in one letter to a friend:

> If national government is merely a "necessary evil" why
> the hell should anybody bother trying to set up any sort of
> international government? I think one of our great
> troubles has been this idea that "government" is
> something high-sounding and far-off and scary that gets
> after you with a club–that it's outside of and removed
> from the normal life of the citizen–that it's something you
> yell for help in a very bad jam and curse out the rest of the
> time. It isn't. Government is the people and the people are
> government. It isn't something some man from Mars
> called a "politician" does to you–it's what we do to and for
> ourselves to get the way of life we want and believe in. If
> we don't like the men who run it, we can get them
> changed–if we don't like the laws they make we can get
> laws changed–but we can't do either by sitting back on
> our rears and remarking, "The best government is the
> government that governs least." That was never true of
> any civilization more complex than that of the free
> hunter–and while I might like to be a free hunter, I know I
> can't be . . . I don't know how you get an ideal
> government–but I'm perfectly sure you don't get it by
> regarding it as a dose of salts or an inevitable doom
> overtaking the innocent taxpayer. To the men who
> founded this union, the republic they envisaged and the
> government they devised meant something–a great and
> daring experiment and a roof for the people and a flag out
> on the wind. I want to get back to that idea and to the
> pride that was in that idea. I am tired of apologizing for the
> American experiment. In addition, that American
> government is precisely and exactly a howling success by
> any standard now existing on the planet. It is full of
> defects, it is still what we make it. But it works.

On 13 March 1943 this man of fragile health who worked tirelessly for his country died of a heart attack at the age of forty-four.

In Benét's centennial year his legacy is one of the popular artist who never lost touch with his heart and with real people in a complex world. His stories, novels, and poems deal with universal themes that transcend time and place and can be read now as meaningfully as when they were originally written. This is the mark of a true writer. *John Brown's Body,* "The Devil and Daniel Webster," "By the Waters of Babylon," "The Blood of the Martyrs," "Freedom's a Hard-Bought Thing" (about a runaway black slave before the Civil War), "Jacob and the Indians," *Western Star* (his verse epic of Europe's road to America), and many more works will still be read in the Benét bicentennial.

Rosemary and Stephen Vincent Benét

Douglas Moore
Reminiscences of Stephen Vincent Benét

I cannot remember actually having met Steve Benét at New Haven. We were five classes apart; while I stayed on to do some graduate work during his freshman and sophomore years and we undoubtedly ran into each other, all that comes to mind now is his reputation. There was plenty of that.

Yale at that time was transforming itself from athletic eminence and traditional philistinism to a center of creative literature. Before us had gone Sinclair Lewis, William Rose Benét, and Thomas Beer. In my class there was Archibald MacLeish and shortly after were to come Philip Barry and Thornton Wilder. Steve came in like a whirlwind. The rumor traveled fast that in the entering freshman class in 1915 there was to be a poet who had already published a book of verse. This was heady news in the Elizabethan Club, where the chosen few met to drink tea, a beverage previously unheard of under the elms, and sit at the feet of such visiting celebrities as William Butler Yeats, Tagore, Alfred Noyes, and Vachel Lindsay. John Farrar, editor of the *Yale Literary Magazine,* and afterwards Steve's friend and publisher, describes his first meeting with the new phenomenon, badly in need of a haircut and pitching pennies on the floor of the freshman dormitory. We heard reports of his reckless behavior—one man testifies to this day of having picked him out of a snowdrift into which he had blundered more or less permanently on his way home from a meeting of kindred spirits. Such diversions did not however interrupt his productivity, for the year before graduation he published a second volume, this one sponsored by the august Yale University Press, and his reputation was secured.

It was in the Montparnasse section of Paris that we became close friends. This was a time in the first of the twenties, before the Hemingway era, when the Café du Dome and the Rotonde were still neighborhood bistros where you could get breakfast chocolate and croissants and have a beer in the evening without feeling that you were part of a literary movement. Steve was around writing his first novel, and I was a student at the Schola Cantorum. This was also my honeymoon, and my wife and I were able to provide sausage and waffles and other nostalgic foods for undomesticated Americans. Steve liked to work at our apartment in the Rue de la Grande Chaumière, and once or twice a week there were gatherings when we played charades, paper games, and wrote letters to the Paris edition of the *Herald Tribune.* This was particularly entertaining because the paper would print anything, and we managed to start several controversies on purely hypothetical issues, defending each side with equal heat. One unfortunate pianist from Texas who had received an unfavorable review from the music critic who happened to be a friend of ours got his friends to write letters of protest. We took up the issue. Steve wrote as a simple doughboy who couldn't understand why the performance was considered so bad. "What could have been more or less impressive," he inquired, "than his rendering of Chopin's grand old funeral march?"

One day we met a young woman who worked on the paper. She was a wonderful combination of shyness and sedateness, fancy and irony, and lovely to look at. That was Rosemary Carr, who married Steve in 1921. It was easy to see at once how things were going to turn out, but we were all concerned to help as much as we could. I remember a long walk back from Montmartre with Steve, trying to convince him that he was worthy of her. There was another friend of Steve's who made a specialty of understanding other men's wives and fiancées. He assured Rosemary that marriage would ruin Steve's career. When Steve heard about this, he was angrier than I have ever seen him. He was perhaps the most charitable man that I have ever met, and his loyalty to his friends was a fierce one; but this time everything went overboard, and when the storm had cleared, the engagement looked fairly assured.

After the Paris days my wife and I went to Cleveland, the Benéts to New York. Steve began the arduous task of earning a living by writing. We managed to see something of each other as our families grew and occasionally collaborated again in the light-hearted Paris manner. One such collaboration was at the Playhouse in Cleveland in 1923 when we put on an evening of Polyphonic Poetry, alleged to be the latest artistic movement in Paris and accompanied by formidable lectures on the poetical and musical issues involved. The theory was that poetry had now reached the stage when a single line no longer had meaning, and verses should be combined in the contrapuntal manner to reveal new beauties. Steve wrote a polypoem which was supposed to combine the ultramasculine with the ultrafeminine point of view. The masculine one began, "Son of the North, the North am I whelped in a forest where werewolves cry–Woof." At the same time the feminine poem, read by Rosemary, was going on "My soul is curved like a cockle shell, a wee small thing with a fragrant smell." The audience was not entirely convinced as to the artistic merit of the movement, except for some of the musicians, who said that this was really an important idea.

One of the most attractive things about Steve was his relish of nonsense. We could sit for hours and improvise stories, passing it on to the next person when a particularly difficult situation had developed. He was the sort of person with whom you could talk endlessly or sit comfortably and say nothing. Everything in his manner was effortless and reassuring. One summer we shared the same studio. I liked to work mornings and Steve afternoons. We generally met at the changeover. There was one day when we were both invited to an all-day tennis match. Steve firmly declined because of pressure of work, but I went along. The next morning when I arrived at the studio every piece of furniture was decorated with typewritten quotations, all of them admonitions as to the value of industry and the perils of sloth. I am sure he enjoyed the afternoon much more than a tennis match.

When Steve received a Guggenheim award in 1926 he had reached a point of exhaustion in short-story writing. Five or six of them would provide a year's income, but it was a form of drudgery, especially at first. He said that he was happy now to forget writing for money and was

going to devote himself to an epic poem that he had long wanted to write. The result of the two years in Paris was *John Brown's Body,* which in addition to establishing him in the front rank of American poets also made him a small fortune.

When he arrived back in America, having won the Pulitzer Prize and achieved distribution by the Book-of-the-Month Club, he was a national hero to be met by reporters at the ship and in demand by all the culture clubs of the country. I went to meet him with some trepidation. Celebrity sometimes does disagreeable things to old friends. They acquire a professional manner, a personal vagueness useful in extricating one from old contacts. I should never have worried about Steve. As the years went on, he became a national institution, but there was never evidence of change in his friendships. He may have tried to protect himself by not enlarging the circle, but the old warmth and generosity and gaiety never varied.

Although Steve wrote poems about music, praising it highly, I never felt he was greatly attracted to it. In the last years he developed an interest in Haydn symphonies, but he was never a concert- or opera-goer. I had set some of his verse to music–"The Ballad of William Sycamore," "Perhaps to Dream," and "Adam was My Grandfather"–and he was always pleased and encouraging. My dream however was to persuade him to do the libretto for an opera. Finally I managed to interest him in doing a piece for high-school performance. This was in 1937 when the Gebrauchsmusik idea was in the air. We talked over story possibilities, somewhat limiting when you are setting out to appeal to high school students, and he decided that the supernatural was the one topic that was sure. We pondered between "The Canterville Ghost" and "The Legend of Sleepy Hollow" and finally chose the latter. The libretto turned out very well even though everything had to take place in a single set and indoors, quite a feat for this particular story of a midnight ghostly rider. The music was ready at the end of the summer, and we had the pleasure of seeing it well mounted by the Bronxville High School in 1938.

It was during a trip to Boston to see about the publication of *The Headless Horseman* (that was what we called it) that Steve suggested the possibility of making a musical version of "The Devil and Daniel Webster." He said that the story had been dramatized by others in several versions, and he wanted to do one of his own but felt that the story needed musical treatment. I was a little worried as to this particular story for fear it might be said to resemble Faust; but I realized that if I was going to have an opera from him, this would have to be it.

We started at once to discuss how to treat the story. Steve had no idea how to go about writing a libretto, and I made matters only worse by giving him the opera version of *Othello* to read as a sample. Finally we agreed to block it out together and then for him to write exactly what he wanted and I would try to work it out. There was no love interest in the story, and this had of course to be inserted into any right-thinking opera. So it was decided to make Jabez, who had sold his soul to the Devil, a much younger man and to have the action take place on the very evening when he was taking a young bride, now reassured by his new prosperity. During the opening chorus with the wedding party, Scratch the Devil makes his appearance as one of the wedding guests, and the predicament of Jabez is revealed, to the horror of everyone including the bride and Webster, who has honored the occasion by his presence. After that the story line could be followed exactly with the added poignance of the loyalty under this fearful situation of Mary, the bride.

We were working separately, and each few days a fresh batch of the manuscript arrived. Everything went beautifully. Obviously some of it was to be sung and some would have to be spoken, but that was perfectly good opera tradition. When we came, however, to Webster's speech which persuades the diabolical jury to release Jabez, we both had trouble. Steve in the story had written about the speech and could say it was overwhelmingly eloquent; now he had actually to write it. He succeeded magnificently. I shall never forget the excitement of first reading it, but then I found myself in an even worse dilemma. Webster after all was an orator, and this was an oration. Oratory is close to singing, so close in fact that it would seem absurd to turn Webster into a baritone soloist. And yet this was the climax of the opera. After prayerful thought I decided to have it spoken against a background of music, interjections by the jury in chorus, and instrumental music which would heighten as the oratory became more fervid. This worked fairly well, although I was reproached by several critics for making the music play too modest a part in the scene.

We were fortunate in having a quick and sumptuous performance by the American Lyric Theatre in 1939 with Fritz Reiner conducting, John Houseman directing, and scenery designed by Robert Edmond Jones. Since then the opera has been played in many cities of the United States.

I had hoped that Steve could be encouraged to do another opera libretto because he was pleased with this result, but the coming of the war involved him so deeply in patriotic work that he never got around to it. He told me that after the war we should do a romantic opera with all stops pulled, and he also had a ballad opera in mind. The only collaboration we did again was a version of his "Prayer for the United Nations" in 1942. He wrote this prayer at the request of President Roosevelt and made some changes for me when I expressed an interest in setting it for chorus.

His death came crushingly and unexpectedly to us all in the spring of 1943. It was some comfort to discover that he had completed the first part of his second planned epic, *Western Star,* which was published the year after his death. He had been so generous of his time to others and to his country that the hours to work on this cherished project must have been hard-won.

During the years that I knew him, Steve changed very little. Perhaps his slender figure stooped with arthritis and his gait became less assured, but the other things were always there: the somewhat owlish face with warm, brown eyes behind thick lenses; the high forehead, prominent ears, drawling and somewhat nasal voice; the quick understanding; the characteristic slouch in the chair; even the delight in penny candy and detective-story fiction. His and Rosemary's pets were important and durable. One, an aristocratic and capricious Sealyham named Jinny, was the mother of several distinguished puppies, one of which came to us. Another, a lovely yellow Persian cat named Goldilocks, also became a cherished member of our family.

Two things rooted in Benét's nature were his love of his wife and his intense love of his country. Whatever he has written in poetry, prose, or drama is colored by these two great passions. His work will live as an expression of all that is most beautiful in the human spirit.

Thornton Wilder Centenary at Yale

(July–September 1997)

Christa Sammons
Beinecke Rare Book and Manuscript Library

The Beinecke Rare Book and Manuscript Library at Yale University observed Thornton Wilder's centenary in 1997 with a conference and major exhibition about his life and works.

Exhibition

Thornton Wilder graduated from Yale in 1920 and in the early 1940s began to give his papers and correspondence to his alma mater. Now the world's largest gathering of such materials, Yale's Wilder archive was the source of the exhibition *Thornton Wilder: A Centennial Celebration,* on view at the Beinecke Rare Book and Manuscript Library between early July and 20 September. The display, which featured books, manuscripts, correspondence, and such memorabilia as photographs, playbills, and posters, was prepared by Patricia C. Willis, curator of the Yale Collection of American Literature, with the assistance of Yale graduate students Dwight Zscheile and Maria Malkiewicz.

Four of Wilder's best-known works were represented in the exhibition by a full range of materials, extending from the author's notes and manuscripts to evidence of the reception the works received here and abroad. Early notes for *The Bridge of San Luis Rey* (1927), for instance, included outlines for chapters that are not part of the published novel and a notebook titled "The Growth of the Bridge of San Luis Rey," in which Wilder discussed his use of the seventeenth-century French letter writer Mme. de Sévigné as a model for the Marquesa de Montemayor. A 1732 English edition of Mme. de Sévigné's letters was on view, as well as an edition of Prosper Mérimée's *Le Carrosse du Saint Sacrement.* In a late letter to Dennis M. Cunningham, Wilder recalled that he had seen a production of the Mérimée play (originally published in 1829) around 1921 and that its main character, a Peruvian actress, had provided the model for Camilla Perichole in *The Bridge.*

Wilder received considerable amounts of fan mail, a selection of which was on display, often with replies written by his sister Isabel. Comments about *Our Town* (1938) included a handwritten letter from Albert Einstein, who compared the play to the *Odyssey* and to *Hamlet* and added "mathematical physicist" after his signature by way of identifying himself.

The section of the exhibition devoted to *Our Town* brought together many letters by Wilder himself in which he commented both on the meaning and on the staging of the play. Covering a thirty-year span, the letters ranged from one written to his mother in 1937, while he was in Zürich working on the play ("echoes of you are all thru the play"), to a meditation of 1967 ("I have always felt certain that a large part of the effectiveness of the original production came from the emergence of Grovers Corners—not from an abstract 'non--place,' but from that homely even ugly 'rehearsal stage'").

Memorabilia relating to various productions and adaptations of *Our Town* were on display, among them photographs of Wilder as the Stage Manager (he played the part for two weeks during the first staging of the play in 1938) together with the copy of the script from which Wilder learned the part.

In 1943 *The Skin of Our Teeth* earned Wilder a third Pulitzer Prize. Among the exhibited sources of the play were Plato's *Critias* (although Wilder admitted to inventing the Critias quotation in Act 3) and Aristotle's *Metaphysics* as excerpted in a 1916 anthology edited by Robert Seymour Bridges. Wilder's process of composition was illustrated by emended scripts, a handwritten "Memo" on "Sabina as a Beauty," and letters in which the author commented on his intentions and on the reception of the play. Writing to Amy Wertheimer in the year of the play's publication, for instance, Wilder explained that he "wrote in

Poster for the Wilder centenary exhibition and symposium

the moral and crossed the t's and dotted the i's" because early readers of the play had found it defeatist.

In an amusing letter to his brother Amos, Wilder noted that the novel *The Eighth Day* (1967) was like "Little Women as tho' it were written by Dostoyevsky." "I borrow from everything I've known," he adds. In other letters he named Teilhard de Chardin, Søren Kierkegaard, and Carl Jung among his sources. The exhibit included Wilder's own Bible, open to Isaiah 40:3 ("The voice of him that crieth in the wilderness, Prepare ye the way of the Lord, make straight in the desert a highway for our God"), a passage Wilder dis-

cussed at length in letters to Amos Wilder and in reference to *The Eighth Day*.

The exhibition also presented material relating to Wilder's lesser-known works—his novels *The Cabala* (1926); *The Woman of Andros* (1930), based on the *Andria* of Terence; *Heaven's My Destination* (1935), about a born-again textbook salesman, in which Wilder drew on his own experiences traveling the country as a lecturer in 1929; *The Ides of March* (1948), a novel about Julius Caesar that was made into a play by Jerome Kilty in the 1960s; *The Alcestiad* (1955); and the semi-autobiographical *Theophilus North* (1973). *The Merchant of Yonkers* (1938), a play written just after the resounding success of *Our Town,* was also featured in this section of the exhibition. *The Merchant* was reworked as *The Matchmaker* in 1954 and became the basis of the musical *Hello, Dolly!*

Various fragments of an autobiographical manuscript by Wilder were on display, including accounts of his early schooling in China, his student days at Yale, and a meeting with Sigmund Freud in the 1930s. At the end of one of the fragments is a passage Wilder crossed out: "this book is not an autobiography. Autobiographies are better left to those of a precise and tenacious memory. Mine is a random thing; it retains or expunges in a manner beyond my control."

Thornton Wilder came from a family of writers, and visitors to the Beinecke could also view a small exhibition of photographs, books, manuscripts, and letters documenting the careers of the "other" Wilders. Thornton Wilder's father, Amos Parker Wilder, an editor and journalist, wrote on political topics and on his experiences as American consul general in Hong Kong during the first decades of the twentieth century. His mother, Isabella Niven Wilder, published poems. Three of Thornton Wilder's siblings were writers as well: his brother Amos Niven wrote poetry and studies in the field of theology; his sister Charlotte was the author of two volumes of poetry; and his sister Isabel published three novels.

Symposium

On 18 September 1997 a Thornton Wilder centenary symposium took place at Yale, sponsored by the Beinecke Library, the Yale School of Drama, the Department of English, the Theater Studies Program, and the Whitney Humanities Center. The conference was organized by Patricia C. Willis, curator of the Yale Collection of American Literature. Scholars, actors, directors, authors, students, and Wilder's friends and relatives met for a day to exchange insights and perspectives on the playwright and his work.

Several subjects recurred during the meetings—Wilder's neglect by academics in contrast to his continuing popularity, especially on the amateur stage; the related question as to why Wilder is missing from many recently published anthologies; Wilder's minimalism; his stagecraft; the "Norman Rockwell" stereotype in contrast to the darker mood of Wilder's later works; and Wilder's universal themes as a key to communality.

Jackson Bryer (University of Maryland) chaired two sessions, which included papers by Tatiana Kaba-

nova (Bishkek, Kyrgyzstan, "Thornton Wilder: The Writer as Reader"), Peter Valenti (Fayetteville State University, "Thornton Wilder, Sol Lesser, and the Demands of Hollywood Narrativity in *Our Town*"), Martin Blank (The College of Staten Island, CUNY, "Shadow of a Doubt: A Study of Authorship, Twinship, and the Nature of Evil"), and Christopher J. Wheatley (The Catholic University of America, "Acts of Faith: Thornton Wilder and His Critics").

The second session included statements by Howard M. Stein (Columbia University) on Wilder's departure from realism and by Joseph W. Reed (Wesleyan University), who returned to the theme of Wilder's collaboration with Alfred Hitchcock. Penelope Niven, who is currently working on a new biography of Wilder, offered thoughts on the art of writing biography. Paul Lifton (North Dakota State University) discussed Wilder as a spokesperson for communality. Edward Burns (William Paterson College) spoke about Wilder's relationship to James Joyce, in particular his interpretation of *Finnegans Wake* (1939), while Irena Babushkina (Moscow State Institute of International Relations) explored the relationship of Wilder's novel *The Eighth Day* to Russian literature.

Six students of acting from the Yale School of Drama gave dramatic readings of two one-act plays from Wilder's series The Seven Deadly Sins. In *Bernice* ("Pride" in the series) an embezzler just released from prison is advised by his maid Bernice how to kill off his criminal identity and assume a new one for the sake of his children. In *The Wreck on the Five-Twenty-Five* ("Sloth" in the series) humor and imagination lead Mr. Hawkins to perceive the ordinary anew, without taking the long journey he had dreamed of. Habituated perception—not the 5:25—is derailed. The readings were directed by Liz Diamond, assistant professor of directing at the Yale School of Drama and director of the 1997 Yale production of *The Skin of Our Teeth* (1942). Both one-act plays were recently published in the *Yale Review.*

The conference session "Remembering Thornton Wilder" was moderated by Wilder's nephew A. Tappan Wilder. Sally Begley, who called herself Wilder's courtesy niece, remembered Wilder's encouragement to her as a young woman. John Barnett, the last of Wilder's lawyers from the Wiggin and Dana firm, identified Wilder humorously as the "ideal client"—one who was rarely in town. Mr. Barnett's firm began to manage Wilder's finances and literary rights in the late 1920s. Caroline Rollins was Wilder's neighbor in Hamden, Connecticut. She recalled Christmas Eve 1960, when Wilder came to visit and read his play *The Long Christmas Dinner* (1931). F. J. O'Neil judged his twenty-five-year acquaintance with Wilder "the sunniest friendship of my life." O'Neil remembered sending Wilder the paper, pen, and magnifier that allowed him to write *Theophilus North* (1973) despite failing eyesight. Mary Hunter Wolf's archetypal Wilder experience was encountering the author, a few weeks before his sudden death, at a Chinese restaurant in New Haven. Wilder threw his arms around her and said, "Remember me!" Theodore Mann recounted his experiences producing three of Wilder's cycle plays at the Circle in the Square Theater. Heinrich von Staden, who knew Wilder during the author's last few years, created a vivid picture of the playwright's voracious hunger for learning, especially in Professor von Staden's field, classics. The actor Jerome Kilty recalled Wilder's participation in theater activities at Harvard shortly after World War II. Kilty collaborated with Wilder on the dramatization of *The Ides of March.*

The Wilder symposium concluded with a lively panel discussion titled "Thornton Wilder and American Playwrights." With Liz Diamond as moderator, John Guare, A. R. Gurney, and Donald Margulies explored Wilder's stagecraft, the peculiarities of his reception, his influence, and the meaning he has for contemporary audiences. All three playwrights spoke of their indebtedness to Wilder. Comparisons between Wilder and his contemporaries, such as Eugene O'Neill and Tennessee Williams, were explored, and Wilder's influence was noted on current authors, for instance Christopher Durang. Guare, who has just written the introduction to an edition of Wilder's short plays, remarked that the darkness of these works contrasts with the redemptive mood of plays such as *Our Town* and that Wilder needs to be reinterpreted in light of this and other paradoxes embedded in his life and work.

Archive

The Thornton Wilder Collection at Yale's Beinecke Rare Book and Manuscript Library, the world's largest collection of his manuscripts and correspondence, was founded by deposits and gifts from the author and his sister Isabel. The archive contains extensive Wilder correspondence, including family letters and correspondence with friends, writers, organizations, theaters, periodicals, publishers, and agents. Among Wilder's correspondents were such individuals as Sigmund Freud, Paul Hindemith, Gertrude Stein, and Alice B. Toklas. The Thornton Wilder Papers include holograph manuscripts and typescripts of virtually all of his works as well as large gatherings of photographs and printed ephemera. These archival materials are complemented by the Beinecke Library's exhaustive collection of Wilder's printed works in English and in translation.

Information about the Beinecke Library, its exhibitions, collections, and programs, may be found at the library's website (http://www.library.yale.edu/beinecke/brblhome.htm).

Michael M. Rea and the Rea Award for the Short Story

George Garrett
University of Virginia

Michael M. Rea established the Rea Award for the Short Story in 1986, the only literary award in the United States focusing exclusively on that genre. Aware that the short story was a long-neglected art form in the world of literature and publishing, he felt that it needed revitalizing. As he said in an interview with Connecticut's *Litchfield County Times,* "the basic thrust of the award is to foster a literary cause–to ennoble the form, to give it prestige." The recipient of the Rea Award is nominated and selected by a jury of three, each a notable literary figure.

To administer the annual award, Michael Rea established the Dungannon Foundation. The prize originally was $25,000 and is now $30,000. The Rea Award for the Short Story is not given for a specific title, but rather for literary power, originality, and influence on the genre, to honor a writer who has made a significant contribution to the short-story form. To qualify, a candidate must be a U.S. or Canadian citizen. Michael Rea traced his love of the short story back to his Irish forebears. "The Irish were great storytellers," he said. The Dungannon Foundation is named for his paternal hometown in Northern Ireland.

Born on 19 January 1927, he was the son of Henry Oliver Rea and Margaret Moorhead of Pittsburgh, Pennsylvania. From 1948 to 1952 he attended the University of Virginia, graduating with a B.A. in English. From 1952 to 1969 he was vice president of the Oliver Tyrone Corporation, a family real estate firm in Pittsburgh. From 1970 to 1979 he was active in real estate in the Washington, D.C., area. There he later founded Harrea Broadcasting, which owned and operated radio stations in Pennsylvania and Maryland. In 1980 he moved to New York City and subsequently bought a home in Washington, Connecticut, which became his primary residence. From that time on, he immersed himself in art and rare-book collecting and publishing. His library includes several hundred volumes of first-edition short-story collections.

In 1986, the first recipient of the Rea Award for the Short Story was Cynthia Ozick. Since then, the following writers, each nominated by a different panel of jurors, have won the Rea Award: Robert Coover (1987), Donald Barthelme (1988), Tobias Wolff (1989), Joyce Carol Oates (1990), Paul Bowles (1991), Eudora Welty (1992), Grace Paley (1993), Tillie Olsen (1994), Richard Ford (1995), Andre Dubus (1996), and Gina Berriault (1997).

The jurors meet annually in New York City to select the winner. Except for the goal of excellence and the most general guidelines, Rea gave his jurors independence and, in fact, did not participate in the meetings and was not present at the judging process. When they had chosen a winner and notified Michael Rea, he joined them for a private luncheon celebration. During that luncheon, he would telephone the winner, so he could personally break the news.

In July of 1996 Michael Rea died of a heart attack at his country home in Washington, Connecticut. In the obituary published in *The New York Times* on 3 August ("Michael M. Rea, 69, A Collector of Art and First Editions," by Lawrence Van Gelder) we learned a little more about his life: that he had joined the U.S. Marine Corps at seventeen and served in north China at the end of World War II; that he was a collector of American paintings and sculpture and served as a trustee of the Solomon R. Guggenheim Museum, the Corcoran Gallery of Art, and the Norton Museum of Art in Palm Beach; and that through his publishing company, Sweetwater Editions, he published many books, including an edition of Isaac Bashevis Singer's *Satan in Goray* with engravings by Ira Moskowitz and *Early Stone Sculpture,* a book about New England tombstone art. Rea also edited an anthology, *The American Story: Short Stories From the Rea Award* (Ecco Press, 1994). This book consists of twenty-one stories by Rea Award winners and nomi-

Michael M. Rea (photograph by Elizabeth Richebourg Rea)

nees selected by seven Rea Award jurors–Stanley Elkin, Joyce Carol Oates, Shannon Ravenel, Joy Williams, Tobias Wolff, Ann Beattie, and Cynthia Ozick.

After his death it was announced that, under the guidance of his widow, the photographer Elizabeth Richebourg Rea, the Rea Award will continue, as will the other activities of the Dungannon Foundation, which include support for writers-in-residence at various colleges and universities. Dedicating the 1997 Rea Award, the first following his death, as a tribute to Michael Rea, Mrs. Rea selected a special jury composed of three previous winners of the award–Cynthia Ozick, Tobias Wolff, and Andre Dubus.

The jury offered the following citation:

IN MEMORIAM: MICHAEL M. REA
1927–1996

The 1997 Rea Award for the Short Story stands as a superlative tribute and memorial to its founder, Michael M. Rea, and continues as his splendid legacy. In honoring the American short story, and in establishing a significant award for its most distinguished contemporary representatives, Michael Rea sought to celebrate a consummate art with consummately generous devotion. Constituting the highest form of national recognition accorded exclusively to the short story, the Rea Award

embodies its creator's passionate homage to literary achievement.

The jury selected Gina Berriault (1926–), a native Californian of Russian Jewish immigrant parents. She is the author of four novels and three collections of short stories, including most recently *Women in Their Beds: New and Selected Stories* (Counterpoint), a book that in 1996 also won the National Book Critics Circle Award, the PEN/Faulkner Award, and the Bay Area Reviewers Award. Her stories have won several O. Henry prizes and have appeared in such magazines as *Harper's Bazaar, Esquire, Mademoiselle, Paris Review, The Threepenny Review,* and *Ploughshares.*

The recent recognition given to Gina Berriault was of special significance in bringing her to the awareness of the American reading public. In the citation honoring Berriault, the judges wrote: "Her stories astonish–not only in their range of character and incident, but in their worldliness, their swift and surprising turns, their penetration into palpable love and grief and hope. Her sentences are excitingly, startlingly juxtaposed; and though her language is plain, the complexity of her knowing leads one into mysteries deeper than tears. To discover Berriault is to voyage into uncharted amazements."

Tributes

Cynthia Ozick

The cost of founding the Nobel Prize for Literature was dynamite and war. The Michael M. Rea Award for the Short Story was established by a man of letters whose life, both before and after the invention of his prize, was fixed on the explosive power of a small-scale art. The Rea Award seems to me to be the purest of all prizes—an act of homage and love and gratitude for the protean short story, for its narrow deeps and alpine glimpses. The short story *is* the art of the glimpse: the whole of life seized in the brilliant blink of a sovereign eye. And a short story is a more difficult form than a novel, just as a novel is more difficult than an epic, and a haiku more demanding than a sonnet. The smaller the form, the greater the pressure for perfection. That is why Michael himself, and the spirit of his prize, are on the side of the consummate.

It was my privilege and honor—and I confess I was stupefied—to be the first recipient of the Rea Award for the Short Story. I remember the annunciatory telephone call: I expected Michael Rea to be an intimidating, even a fearsome, philanthropist. Instead I heard the shy and modest voice of a man who was himself a striving writer of stories, though I did not learn that until much later. When, soon after the astonishment of that call, I finally met Michael and Elizabeth Rea, I read in the eyes of both of them all the imperatives of what was once unashamedly called Beauty, meaning, as Keats meant it, Truth. Nowadays we try to veil that word, and sometimes say Insight instead. But both words are appropriate to Michael and Elizabeth Rea: Beauty and Insight.

By now the Rea Award is an indispensable American institution and a coveted American prize. It is our little Nobel—little only in the sense that it addresses the short form. But it is as large as Michael Rea's heart, and no recipient of the Rea Award has ever encountered anything larger, or more capaciously literary, than that.

Andre Dubus

On Good Friday of 1996 I woke with a mild stomach illness, and went back to sleep. Sometime that morning I heard a man's voice on my answering machine in the dining room, down the hall from where I slept. I did not know his voice and did not pick up the phone. I slept, and woke at noon, worrying about money. I had a little over two thousand

dollars left in the account I live on. To get through the next twelve months I needed another twenty-two thousand, though I receive fifteen hundred a month, in retirement and social security checks. This is absurd; it even feels immoral, though usually my only luxuries are music, books, movies, and sometimes a pipe. I remember when a thousand a month paid for everything, and I remember many years when I did not earn a thousand a month. I think of Haiti; I think of other places.

After making the bed and dressing I played the answering machine. The man whose voice was on it was Michael Rea. I knew of the Rea Award, had hoped for a few years to receive it, but I did not know that it came from a man named Rea. He called me Andre and said he would call me again. I did not want him to, this stranger. I wanted to rest and heal and find some money without plundering from the mutual fund in Texas, emergency money I pretend is not there. At one o'clock I got saltines and Coca-Cola and the cordless phone and went to the couch and turned on the television for a Red Sox game. In the early innings the phone rang and I answered.

"Andre? This is Michael Rea. Do you know me?"

He sounded happy. I was not in the mood for a happy stranger, calling an unlisted number during a ball game when I was tired and nauseated.

"No. Am I supposed to?"

"I'm sitting here with George Garrett and Jayne Anne Phillips and Barry Hannah. Do you know them?"

"I know George and Jayne Anne. I've never met Barry. Where are you? In a bar?"

"We're in my living room. I'm calling to give you the Rea Award."

"Oh my God."

"It used to be twenty-five thousand, but I've raised it to thirty this year."

Tears were on my cheeks. I said, "You can't believe how much I need thirty thousand dollars."

"I know you do."

Then he told me he had been a marine at the end of World War II, stationed in China. I asked him what outfit he had been in.

"Eleventh Marines."

"So was *I*," I said. "At Camp Pendleton."

The next week I got the check and took my family to a Japanese restaurant to celebrate. I lived on the money for over a year, after Michael was dead, and I was grateful for it, month after month, thinking of him as my brother marine who loved stories. *Semper fidelis,* Michael, and thank you.

The next week I got the check and took my family to a Japanese restaurant to celebrate. I lived on the money for over a year, after Michael was dead, and I was grateful for it, month after month, thinking of him as my brother marine who loved stories. *Semper fidelis,* Michael, and thank you.

Bill Henderson

I will remember Michael always as a guy who saw something in me nobody else did. What was that? I was bone poor but I didn't know how to ask for money and I was too proud to apply for a grant (and depend on some fool committee to approve or disapprove of my plans) and I was far too lazy to do any of the paperwork involved with any of the above in any case. Michael sensed that, I think. Or maybe it was just my laziness he sensed. In any case, he had a way of coming up to me at a party and saying, "Bill, how can I help you?" At that I'd manage to blurt out, "Well I can always use some money." And sure enough he would send a little something (the first time) and a lot of something (the last time, only months before his death). Michael never knew it, but that last time bailed me out. I had spent the evening at his apartment, an evening for the Rea Award, and I talked with Dan Halpern, mostly about how miserable the lit. pub. biz. was (returns were devastating that year, averaging almost 80 percent for some titles industry wide). I didn't know it then, but Dan was in as bad shape as I was. Michael didn't hear us crying the blues to each other, but as I walked to the door—that last time—he put his hand on my shoulder and said, "Bill, how can I help you?"

We will all remember him for his vision, for his love of the short story, and for the terrific parties that he and Elizabeth gave for the Rea Award winners, but for me those words linger. "How can I help?"

And he did. And that's why Pushcart lived to celebrate its twenty-fifth year. Without Michael, nada.

I, and hundreds of authors, praise you, Michael.

Frank Conroy

When Michael Rea, who was at that time a stranger to me, called to ask if I would serve on the panel for the Rea Award for excellence in the short story, I asked what the award was all about. (This was many years ago, when the program had just started.) He described himself as a friend of the arts

who had established a small foundation to support the arts with the help of advice from practicing artists, all of which sounded fine to me. "But why the short story?" I asked, genuinely curious. There was a pause. "During the war they more or less kept me sane" (I paraphrase). "In a combat zone you didn't have time to read anything long." That was World War II he was talking about. I'm sure others have remembered his words, but I must mention them. There was something in his voice, something completely straightforward in his manner, and I instantly believed him. Why wouldn't you, you may ask. Well, life and a good deal of experience with philanthropy had taught me to take the professed goals and motivations of various organizations and individuals with a large grain of salt. Vanity, politics, narcissism, and a relish in the exercise of power had been the rule rather than the exception, sadly enough, as the late Gerald Freund—and who would know better?—pointed out in many contexts.

My first meeting with Mike Rea confirmed what I'd sensed in his voice. He looked at me with his intense blue eyes as we shook hands and I had the spooky feeling that he was looking past my appearance and into what I will call for want of a better word my character. He had a calmness, did Mike, a gravitas—and intuitively I trusted him. This turned out to be the right reaction.

In New York, and later when he came for a short visit to Iowa City, we had wonderful talks. What can I say? There was simply no bullshit to the man, no hidden agendas, no role playing. He was exactly what he appeared to be—a generous and very smart man who knew that doing good required thought and effort, and was in fact much harder to accomplish than might appear at first glance. (In this regard he resembled James Michener.) He seemed not particularly interested in talking about himself, and yet did, in a collapsed fashion, when he sensed he should, simply to get it out of the way. He had done very well in business; the arts had tangibly enriched his life; and now that he was in the last stretch he wanted to be of service. I believe he was unaware of what I take to be the rare purity of his position—to him it was simply common sense.

To know Mike was to take a tonic against cynicism. I've known very few people about whom that can be said. A true American gentleman.

Daniel Halpern

Michael invited me to a party he gave in 1989 for Tobias Wolff, winner of that year's Rea Award for the Short Story. As it turned out, I had just edited a collection of short stories which Michael had picked up. When he introduced himself, he said, "I just read your anthology—you like the form?" Michael was always quick to the point. "Does a rock sink?" I believe I replied, coming immediately under the influence of his keep-it-brief, spirit-of-the-thing approach. "Good," he said. "You want to be a judge for the Rea Award?" "Sure," I said, keeping things fast and simple between us.

His love for the story never flagged, nor did his belief in focused and intense brevity, which may be one of the reasons he favored this genre. The short story was his cause and—along with art—his great love in life. It was Jorge Luis Borges, a favorite of Michael's, who wrote, "Unlike the novel, a short story may be, for all purposes, essential."

I have known few people in the literary world who felt as strongly as Michael did about the short story—perhaps only Borges and Ray Carver (I didn't know Anton Chekhov)—but certainly very few others.

In 1993 we published *The American Story,* an important collection of stories, edited by Michael, to acknowledge the contribution of the Rea Award. His anthology included the winners of the prize as well as the finalists. It represented, in effect, the American canon of postwar writers, with work by every major American practitioner of the short story.

The Rea Award for the Short Story has been given annually to celebrate those writers who have made "a significant contribution to the short story." Michael's award has been a significant encouragement to writers. You may think writers such as Donald Barthelme, Eudora Welty, and Paul Bowles don't need acknowledgment of this sort—but if you believe this, you'd be wrong. To be honored by your peers—in the tasteful way that was always Michael's way—*matters . . . has* made a difference to every writer singled out by the Rea Award. It was how Michael acknowledged—and honored!—those writers he loved most.

Stuart Dybek

With Michael Rea's passing, American arts and culture lost a tremendous friend.

I feel fortunate that I had the opportunity to meet him. I served as one of the judges for the Rea Award in short fiction. The award reflected both Michael Rea's special affection for and deep knowledge of the short-story form. He wasn't a man who did things in half-measures; his great enthusiasm and vitality wouldn't allow for that. He was engaged

in the award process, and that process reflected his balance of seriousness of purpose and high-spirited good humor. Here was a benefactor who acted not out of noblesse oblige, but out of joy.

The judging process also reflected Michael Rea's fair-minded, straightforward personality. I came away from the experience with an enormous amount of respect for him. He possessed the intelligence and energy to fully participate in the extensive reading that was required and in the give-and-take discussions, and he had the wisdom to allow the judges he had selected to finally arrive at their own decisions.

I had breakfast with him one morning and it wasn't long before I realized that I was in the company of one pretty good storyteller. I remember the writers we talked about and the stories we traded about fishing and life in Florida. His observations, whether about fishing or writing, were shrewd and grounded in experience.

The Rea Award remains the premier award for short fiction in the United States. Michael Rea saw to it that the award was conducted at a level that properly honored a great American art form. It is fitting that the Rea Award now also serves to honor the memory of Michael Rea.

Joyce Carol Oates

There are works which wait, and which one does not understand for a long time; the reason is that they bring answers to questions which have not yet been raised; for the question often arrives a terribly long time after the answer.

These striking words of Oscar Wilde are as applicable to certain individuals as to works of art. Michael Rea, with his generous and judicious commitment to the short story, and his presence in the literary community, is one of these individuals.

Michael Rea has been a model of generosity, largeness of spirit, and literary taste; his intense interest in and support of the short story has been enormously appreciated by practitioners of this difficult art. One of the most prestigious literary awards in America is the Rea Award for the Short Story, initiated by Michael Rea in 1986. Since its inauguration, the Rea Award has acquired a distinguished reputation. I was greatly honored to be a recipient of the award several years ago; I felt it to be immensely encouraging.

At Princeton University I've been using Michael Rea's excellent *The American Story,* a gathering of strikingly diverse and engaging short stories assembled by winners of the Rea Award, and edited by Michael Rea. I believe that Michael would be pleased, and stimulated, if he could overhear student discussions arising from this provocative anthology.

George Garrett

I want to add a brief personal note to this gathering of tributes to the late Michael Rea. I served as one of the judges for the award, and, because of his great enthusiasm and his integrity, it was an altogether pleasant experience. Later he pointed out to me a favorite quotation of his, from Guy de Maupassant's introduction to Flaubert—*Etude sur Flaubert,* which, I think, is appropriate to end here:

> The profound and delicious joy which leaps to the heart before certain pages, before certain phrases, does not come only from those who have written them; they come from an absolute compatibility of expression and idea, from a sensation of harmony, of secret beauty, eluding for the most part the judgment of the many.

Tobias Wolff

When I heard of Michael Rea's death, I felt a sorrow out of all proportion to the time I had actually known him: a few meetings, over a period of seven or eight years. Yet I counted him a friend. We all now and then recognize a comrade from the first encounter, and in Michael's case that recogni-

tion was especially vivid because of his directness and honesty. He did not hide himself in detachment, banter, or irony; he was present—there to be known, if you cared to know him.

Michael was not an uncomplicated man (no one with his history and intelligence could be), but he had kept something of the boy about him in his curiosity and enthusiasm. He knew a lot, yet he was less interested in what he knew than in knowing more, discovering some new passion. I remember his account of his time in China as a marine; what really stayed with him, he said, was the memory of coming upon Maupassant's short stories for the first time.

He loved stories. I've known people who loved them as much as Michael did, but no one who loved them more. He seemed to have read everyone with any claim to distinction in the form, and could call up the smallest details from his reading. His largesse with writers was both legendary and a matter of fact, but he was equally generous in the quality of his attention to their work. When he talked about stories, you could see that they were as real a world to him as this world, and as essential.

Even as our stories became his stories, some of his became mine. When I think of him now, I think of a young man, far from home, alone in his barracks, his spirit suddenly roused by a French prostitute's defiance of all the oppressions of circumstance and power. That young man was my friend, and I miss him.

Dawn Powell, Where Have You Been All Our Lives?

Dillon Teachout
Princeton University

Wish I could change publishers—not to make money but to be quietly, decently published as honest work, worthy of intelligent attention.

—Dawn Powell, from a 1931 diary entry

During her lifetime Dawn Powell never received the attention she felt she deserved. She frequently complained that reviewers didn't understand her work, though she was often favorably reviewed by some of the leading critics of her day. As she moved from publisher to publisher—Maxwell Perkins at Scribners was among her several editors—sales of her books were almost always disappointing: none of her fifteen novels had an initial printing of more than five thousand copies, and few saw second printings. Powell often blamed her publishers for this neglect. Writing in her diary in 1940 she bemoaned the "lack of any ad or announcement, the silence from the publishing end, the all too familiar signals of another blank shot." Now, more than thirty years after her death, with the republication of nine of her novels and the first publication of her diaries by Steerforth Press, it would appear that Dawn Powell not only has found a permanent publishing home but has lately been receiving all of the attention she craved, from reviewers and readers alike.

Born in Mount Gilead, Ohio, in 1897, Powell moved to New York City in 1918, where she lived until her death in 1965. She was close to John Dos Passos and Edmund Wilson, knew Ernest Hemingway (who called her "a better wit than Dotty Parker, who cries too much"), and was a vibrant member of the New York literary set. During her long writing life she produced what John Updike has called "deft, funny, knowing, compassionate, and poetic" works—novels, stories, and plays. Most of her novels are set in New York and satirize everyone from business tycoons to artists and writers and poseurs from every walk of life. She took particular pleasure in attacking the literary establishment and had vicious fun pillorying publishers and editors. She also wrote several novels

Dust jacket for a volume published as part of the effort to revive Powell's literary standing

set in her native Ohio, and these have a different feel, evoking the realism of Sherwood Anderson and Willa Cather. Whatever the setting, "her stories are simple, her plot twists are many and her characters are bursting with dreams and doing their best to exceed or deny their limits," wrote the critic Margo Jefferson.

With her death it seemed likely that her literary legacy would be buried with her. Then in 1987 Gore Vidal wrote a glowing piece on Powell for the *New York Times Review of Books* in which he proclaimed that "in her lifetime she should have been as widely read as, say, Hemingway or the early Fitzgerald or the mid O'Hara or even the late, far too late, Katherine Anne Porter." There directly followed a small flurry of publishing activity for the lost writer. In 1989 the Quality Paperback Club issued a fat trilogy of Powell's satirical novels, *Angels on Toast, The Wicked Pavilion,* and *The*

Golden Spur, and all three novels were then broken out in separate trade editions by Vintage. Two years later a new, regrettably short-lived publisher in New York, Yarrow Press, reissued two more Powell novels, *A Time To Be Born* and *The Locusts Have No King.* While the Yarrow books attracted some review attention and eventually sold out their first and only printings, the Vintage books quickly went out of print and Dawn Powell appeared to be slowly sinking back into literary obscurity.

Early in 1994 Michael Moore, one of the four partners in the then one-year-old Steerforth Press, was visiting New York City in order to introduce the start-up publishing company to literary agents and was hoping to return to South Royalton, Vermont, with a book or two to publish. He was in the offices of the agent Melanie Jackson, who, Moore recalls, was most charming as she regretted she had nothing on her table that might be suitable for the Steerforth list. "Except I have this," she said, reaching for a manuscript buried in a pile. "Have you ever heard of Dawn Powell? One of my clients has this mad notion of reissuing Powell in cloth. But no one is going to undertake this," she said in a doubtful tone. "Not after that Vintage flop." Moore had heard of Powell, had read the Vidal piece years before, and had subsequently read two of her novels. He also knew of Jackson's client, Tim Page, who was then the music critic for the *New York Newsday,* before that newspaper's retreat back to the Long Island suburbs. (He has since become chief music critic for the *Washington Post* and this year was the winner of the Pulitzer Prize for criticism.) Page, an avid reader of fiction, had also discovered Powell through the Vidal article, collected all of her books, and written a piece on her for *Newsday.* It was while working on this piece that he found himself drawn into the life of his subject, meeting Powell's institutionalized son and eventually playing an instrumental role in helping to clean up Powell's disordered literary estate. The book Page had assembled was a collection of her work that included two novels—the two Dawn Powell had considered her best work—a New York satire, *Turn, Magic Wheel* (1936), and one of her Ohio novels, *Dance Night* (1930), along with a selection of her short fiction and an autobiographical sketch written toward the end of her life, "What Are You Doing In My Dreams?"

Moore left with the collection, but he recalls being more than a little doubtful about the project, and particularly about Page's insistence that the book be published in hardcover. Back in Vermont

when opening the box, he also came upon a rejection letter written by the well-known editor of one of America's most distinguished publishing houses suggesting all the reasons a second attempt at a revival could never work. But Moore read the books, liked what he found, and passed them along to his partners, Chip Fleischer and the writers Thomas Powers and Alan Lelchuk, who each found something to admire in Powell. They decided to move forward with the project, and on Page's condition that Powell be published in cloth this time. They gave the omnibus the title *Dawn Powell At Her Best.*

On the day the book was officially published, a laudatory review appeared in the daily *New York Times* by the critic Margo Jefferson. She began: "So, we say to ourselves, another nearly forgotten writer exhumed, cleaned up, reissued and put on display with endorsements from Edmund Wilson, Diana Trilling, and Gore Vidal. Then a friend says no, read her, and we do, and here it is, that infinitely distinguished thing, a dead writer so full of charm and derring-do that literature's canon makers should sit back, smile, and say, Dawn Powell, where have you been all our lives?"

"That day the review came out the phone never stopped ringing–friends from New York calling to congratulate us," says Moore. "It was more than a review, it was a great embrace of this book, of this writer." Other equally enthusiastic reviews followed, including a long piece in *The New Yorker* by Updike, who agreed that Powell was "too good a fiction writer . . . to be forgotten." This was the kind of serious attention the young Steerforth Press had been hoping to attract for their books–and Dawn Powell, it seemed, had finally become "worthy of intelligent attention."

This was by no means the end of the Dawn Powell/Steerforth story. Tim Page, who was by then at work on a biography of Powell, suggested that her diaries also deserved to be published. Powell had kept extensive diaries from 1931 until her death, and their tone and content were just as compelling and witty as the writing in her novels. "When I first read Page's edited typescript," Moore remembers, "I quite believed this was her best work—and one of the best and truest stories of the writer's life I had ever read."

In the fall of 1995 Steerforth published *The Diaries of Dawn Powell: 1931–1965,* at the same time reissuing the first paperback edition of Powell's most autobiographical novel, *My Home Is Far Away* (1944), both of them with introductions by Page. Excerpts from *The Diaries* had already run in *The New Yorker* prior to the book's publication, and soon thereafter the two books appeared together on the front cover of *The New York Times Book Review*. Inside, the reviewer called Powell's *Diaries* no less than "one of the outstanding literary finds of the last quarter-century" and declared the novel "one of the permanent masterpieces of childhood, comparable with *David Copperfield, What Maisie Knew* and the early reminiscences of Colette." In the following weeks *The Diaries* received generous notice in most of the nation's metropolitan dailies, in magazines and literary journals, and finally, as a fitting bookend, in another long essay on Powell by the writer who had begun it all, Gore Vidal, again writing for the *New York Review of Books*.

Steerforth has since published its own editions of Powell's *Angels on Toast, The Wicked Pavilion, The Locusts Have No King,* and *A Time To Be Born,* and this season brought out *The Golden Spur* and another of her Ohio novels, *Come Back to Sorrento* (first published in 1932 as *The Tenth Moon,* a title given to the book by its publisher and one Powell never liked). There may be a third chapter in the Powell/Steerforth story when Tim Page's biography of the writer is published by Holt, now planned for the fall of 1998. Steerforth will issue *The Diaries* in paperback at the same time and has plans to break out the two novels from *At Her Best*—*Dance Night* and *Turn, Magic Wheel*—into separate paper editions.

The press's success with Dawn Powell led indirectly to another publishing project for Steerforth. In 1995 a lawyer, Leonard Goldstein, called from New York to make a plea for another dead and long-forgotten writer, Isabel Bolton. He told Moore of having come across the Powell books, and he believed Bolton was equally worthy of rediscovery. He also said that he was in a losing battle with lung cancer but was determined to see this writer back in print as his last living act.

"It was a most strange call," says Moore. "I'd never heard of Isabel Bolton. None of us had. But I could hear his passion for her, and what could I say? I asked him to send me the books." The three Bolton novels–*Do I Wake or Sleep* (1946), *The Christmas Tree* (1949), and *Many Mansions* (1952)–passed between the Steerforth editors over the next several months, and in the fall news came of Goldstein's death. It wasn't until the middle of the follow-ing year that Steerforth decided to go forward with the Bolton project.

Little is known about Bolton. Her real name was Mary Britton Miller, the name under which she wrote children's books, poetry, and an unmemorable novel. Then in 1946, at the age of sixty-three, she took on the pen name Isabel Bolton and published *Do I Wake or Sleep*. The novel was highly praised by both Edmund Wilson writing for *The New Yorker* and by Diana Trilling for the *Nation*. Trilling went so far as to call Bolton "the best woman writer of fiction in this country today" and was even more enthusiastic about Bolton's next novel, *The Christmas Tree*.

Steerforth decided to publish all three Bolton novels in a single volume, reintroducing Bolton as they had Powell with *At Her Best*. The book came out in late October under the title *New York Mosaic*, and at this writing the reviews are still coming in. Writing for the *Los Angeles Times*, Vivian Gornick put Bolton in the company of Virginia Woolf, Jean Rhys, and Djuna Barnes, and Vidal weighed in once again in the *New York Times Review of Books*. Steerforth has already sold foreign rights to Britain's Virago Press.

Asked if Steerforth plans to make a niche out of publishing "dead women writers," Moore is emphatic in his reply. "Not at all," he says. "Our commitment is to publish serious books by good writers, and both of these women happened to more than qualify." Steerforth is not interested in being the "Dawn Powell Press," he points out, and despite the space that her work fills in the catalogue, Steerforth has published many other books of note in its four-year history, including three first novels.

Now that Dawn Powell has become a steady backlist author for the small press, "there are the obvious ironies," notes Moore: "Dawn Powell finally getting all of this attention thirty or forty years too late for her sake, finally becoming a backlist author after her life of agonizing obscurity. And us, through her, suddenly getting all of this attention." Perhaps equally important, Powell has gained from her posthumous association with Steerforth the respect and loyalty from her publisher that she found so elusive in her lifetime. Says Moore, "In the end, I like her. I like her story. I like her sensibility." The endurance of this most recent revival has proved that for Powell, Steerforth's efforts have not been just another blank shot.

The Thomas Wolfe Society

Ted Mitchell
Thomas Wolfe Memorial, Asheville, N.C.

PUBLICATIONS OF THE THOMAS WOLFE SOCIETY: Thomas Wolfe, *London Tower,* edited by Aldo P. Magi (1980);

Wolfe, *The Proem to "O Lost,"* edited by John L. Idol Jr. (1980);

Madeleine Boyd, *Thomas Wolfe: The Discovery of a Genius,* edited by Magi (1981);

Wolfe, *The Streets of Durham,* edited by Richard Walser (1982);

Wolfe, *K-19: Salvaged Pieces,* edited by Idol (1983);

Wolfe, *The Train and the City,* edited by Richard S. Kennedy (1984);

Holding on for Heaven: The Cables and Postcards of Thomas Wolfe and Aline Bernstein, edited by Suzanne Stutman (1985);

Wolfe, *The Hound of Darkness,* edited by Idol (1986);

Aldo P. Magi and Richard Walser, *Wolfe and Belinda Jelliffe* (1987);

William B. Wisdom, *The Table Talk of Thomas Wolfe,* edited by John S. Phillipson (1988);

Wolfe, *The Starwick Episodes,* edited by Kennedy (1989);

Wolfe, *Thomas Wolfe's Composition Books: The North State Fitting School 1912–1915,* edited by Alice R. Cotten (1990);

Wolfe, *The Autobiographical Outline for Look Homeward, Angel,* edited by Lucy Conniff and Kennedy (1991);

Wolfe, *Thomas Wolfe's Notes on Macbeth: The University of North Carolina, English 37, Winter Quarter 1919,* edited by William Grimes Cherry III (1992);

Wisdom, *My Impressions of the Wolfe Family and of Maxwell Perkins,* edited by Magi and David J. Wyatt (1993);

Wolfe, *[George Webber, Writer]: An Introduction by a Friend,* edited by Idol (1994);

Magi, *Portraits of a Novelist: Douglas Gorsline and Thomas Wolfe* (1995);

Wolfe, *Antaeus, or A Memory of Earth,* edited by Ted Mitchell (1996);

Maxwell Perkins, *"Always Yours, Max," Maxwell Perkins Responds to Questions about Thomas Wolfe,*

together with his *Scribner's and Tom Wolfe,* edited by Alice R. Cotten (1997).

Following a suggestion by the late Richard Walser (North Carolina State University) and Duane Schneider (Ohio University), admirers of Thomas Wolfe as well as collectors, librarians, and scholars began working in 1978 to form the Thomas Wolfe Society. Spearheading the campaign, John S. Phillipson and Aldo P. Magi continued working through the spring and summer of 1979, and the society was formally founded in October 1979 during the Thomas Wolfe Fest at St. Mary's College in Raleigh. Professor Schneider, a driving force behind the newly formed society, became its first president in April 1980, when the society held its initial meeting in Asheville, North Carolina.

The purpose of the society is to encourage general interest and scholarly study of Wolfe's career and work, and it has long had a large following outside of academe. The society gives scholars, critics, and readers the opportunity to share knowledge of Wolfe's writings and life through its publications and annual meeting. It also undertakes special projects to promote its goals and purposes. The society's current president is Frank C. Wilson (University of North Carolina, Chapel Hill); vice president is Mary Aswell Doll (Our Lady of Holy Cross College, New Orleans).

From the outset the society has held its meetings in places associated with Wolfe's life and works, such as Asheville and Chapel Hill, North Carolina; Cambridge, Massachusetts; and New York City. Other sites include the Hudson River valley–the setting of scenes in *Of Time and the River* (1935)–and Richmond, New Orleans, Gettysburg, and Baltimore (the city where Wolfe died in 1938). The society scheduled its 1997 meeting in Munich, Germany, a city Wolfe loved and where he was injured in an Oktoberfest brawl in 1928, an event preserved in *The Web and the Rock* (1939). Future meetings will be held in Chapel Hill (1998), New York City (1999), Asheville (2000), and New Orleans (2001). The society also actively participates in the annual Thomas Wolfe Festival in October in Asheville, an event sponsored by the Tho-

Front cover of the introductory biography published in 1997

mas Wolfe Memorial and the North Carolina Department of Cultural Resources. In addition, the society is affiliated with the American Literature Association.

The Thomas Wolfe Review, the journal of the society, is the product of a University of Akron professor, the late John S. Phillipson, and Wolfe enthusiast Aldo P. Magi of Sandusky, Ohio. The journal is published twice a year and carries articles and notes about Wolfe and his circle. It also features news and announcements of interest to society members. Terry Roberts (University of North Carolina, Chapel Hill) is editor; Magi serves as editor emeritus. The editorial staff includes Deborah A. Borland, Joseph M. Flora, and John L. Idol Jr.

The Thomas Wolfe Society also commits itself to an annual publication, many of which have become collector's items. These special publications, for the most part, are drawn from materials in the Thomas Wolfe collections at Harvard University and the University of North Carolina at Chapel Hill. Its first effort was modest, a reprinting of Wolfe's "London Tower," a piece that had first appeared in an Asheville newspa-

per in 1925. Among the publications that followed have been Madeleine Boyd's "The Discovery of a Genius," an account of how *Look Homeward, Angel* (1929) was placed by Wolfe's first agent; and a facsimile of the dummy prepared by Scribners announcing the publication of Wolfe's second (but aborted) novel, "K-19." Wolfe's unpublished writings alternate each year with biographical publications.

Unpublished works by Wolfe have become important society publications. They include: *The Hound of Darkness* (1986); *The Starwick Episodes* (1989); *Thomas Wolfe's Composition Books: The North State Fitting School, 1912–1915* (1990); *The Autobiographical Outline for Look Homeward, Angel* (1991) *[George Webber, Writer]: An Introduction by a Friend* (1994); and *Antaeus, or A Memory of Earth* (1996).

Another project of the Thomas Wolfe Society is the placing of memorial plaques at sites directly linked to Wolfe's life and works. Plaques have been placed at Riverside Cemetery in Asheville, where Wolfe is buried; at the Johns Hopkins University hospital, where he died in 1938; and at 5 Montague Terrace, one of his residences in Brooklyn Heights. The society has recently undertaken an effort to see that Wolfe is honored by a postage stamp on his one-hundredth birthday (in the year 2000).

The society also awards citations of merit for exceptional scholarly or creative work on Wolfe. Thanks to the generosity of Paul Gitlin (executor of Wolfe's estate), the society annually awards the Zelda Gitlin Literary Prize to the author of the outstanding scholarly article on Wolfe published during the preceding calendar year. The Thomas Wolfe Student Prize is awarded annually to a graduate or undergraduate student submitting the best essay on Wolfe.

Through the generosity of Adelaide Wisdom Benjamin (whose father donated his superb collection of Wolfe manuscripts to Harvard University), the society has established the William B. Wisdom Grant in Aid of Research. These grants provide travel and living expenses for scholars and students working in the William B. Wisdom Collection of Thomas Wolfe in the Houghton Library, Harvard University, where the majority of Wolfe's original manuscripts are preserved. Consideration is also given to applicants using the Thomas Wolfe Collection at the University of North Carolina at Chapel Hill. Candidates working on dissertations are especially encouraged.

Membership in the Thomas Wolfe Society is open to any person, business, corporation, or educational institution. The society issues an annual proceedings and membership list, including an account of the annual society meetings, and abstracts of the papers given at the annual meeting. David Strange of

Bloomington, Indiana, edits *The Proceedings and Membership List of the Thomas Wolfe Society.*

Membership now hovers around six hundred members, including those in Europe and Asia, especially Japan. Applications for membership and yearly dues of $30 should be sent to David Strange, Thomas

Wolfe Society Membership, P.O. Box 1146, Bloomington, IN 47402-1146. Students can obtain a membership for $10. Lifetime memberships are available at $500. For their dues, members receive the spring and fall issues of *The Thomas Wolfe Review* and the annual special publication.

The Thomas Wolfe Collection at the University of North Carolina at Chapel Hill

Alice R. Cotten
Library of the University of North Carolina at Chapel Hill

The Thomas Wolfe Collection, part of the North Carolina Collection at the library of the University of North Carolina at Chapel Hill, includes printed materials, correspondence, manuscripts, photographs, memorabilia, scrapbooks, clippings, and audiovisual items by and about Thomas Clayton Wolfe (3 October 1900–15 September 1938).

Wolfe, who was born in Asheville, North Carolina, was a student at the University of North Carolina in Chapel Hill from 1916 until his graduation in 1920. Though he originally did not want to attend the state university, preferring Princeton or the University of Virginia, Wolfe grew to love the campus and wrote fondly of his days there. His involvement in drama, student publications, fraternity life, and the overall intellectual life of the campus increased each year, culminating in his editorship of the *Tar Heel,* the student newspaper, in his senior year. After leaving Chapel Hill, Wolfe went to Harvard to study playwriting, receiving a master of arts in 1922. From 1924 to 1930 he occasionally taught at Washington Square College of New York University, traveled widely in Europe, and wrote. *Look Homeward, Angel,* his first novel, was published in 1929 to critical acclaim. While on a tour of the western United States in the summer of 1938 Wolfe became ill in Seattle. He was later taken by train to Johns Hopkins, where he died of tuberculosis of the brain on 15 September, just prior to his thirty-eighth birthday.

The unexpected death of this native son of North Carolina shocked the campus community. As early as October 1938 the *Carolina Magazine* published a commemorative issue with tributes by students, faculty, and others, including Maxwell Perkins and Edward Aswell, Wolfe's two editors. As the campus sought to find an appropriate memorial

Always yours,

Max

Edited by Alice R. Cotten

Front cover of the volume of letters about Thomas Wolfe written by Maxwell Perkins to Wolfe's putative biographer

to Wolfe, it seemed obvious that one fitting legacy would be a collection of manuscripts and books written by Wolfe. The library had already begun collecting Wolfe's published works, including his undergraduate articles, poems, and essays published in campus magazines.

Early in 1939 dramatist Paul Green and university librarian Carl White began separate attempts to secure the manuscript of *Look Homeward, Angel* for the university. Wolfe had given this manuscript to Aline Bernstein, who had made it possible for him to write his novel, and she donated it to an auction to benefit exiled German writers, stipulating that the purchaser must donate the manuscript to an appropriate institution. Both Green's and White's belated attempts failed. Book dealer Gabriel Wells purchased the manuscript in February 1939 and donated it to Harvard University soon thereafter.

After this disappointment a group led by Paul Green in Chapel Hill began a fund-raising drive to raise five thousand dollars to purchase from the Wolfe estate the other literary remains of Thomas Wolfe for the library at the University of North Carolina. This effort fell far short, raising only slightly more than four hundred dollars, over half of which came from Wolfe's former college classmate Benjamin Cone. Private collector William B. Wisdom of New Orleans purchased this massive collection and donated it to Harvard in 1947, where it joined the *Look Homeward, Angel* manuscript. Once again Chapel Hill had failed to secure a significant offering of Thomas Wolfe's manuscripts. In October 1939 poet Arthur Davison Ficke donated to the library a four-page letter on Harvard Club stationery that Wolfe had written him in response to Ficke's letter praising *Look Homeward, Angel*. This was the first manuscript letter from Thomas Wolfe that the library acquired.

In 1950, after extensive correspondence with librarian Charles Rush and Wolfe's literary executor Edward Aswell, the brothers and sisters of Thomas Wolfe, led by Mabel Wolfe Wheaton and Fred Wolfe, gave to the library a large collection of family correspondence, photographs, memorabilia, and printed materials in memory of their parents, W. O. and Julia E. Wolfe. This initial family gift, later designated as the CW Series, forms the core of the Thomas Wolfe Collection at Chapel Hill. The family made additions to the papers periodically, culminating with a gift in 1981 from the estate of Fred Wolfe, who died in 1980, the last of Thomas Wolfe's siblings.

The collection in Chapel Hill is second in size only to the collection at Harvard's Houghton Library. Whereas the Harvard collection has almost all of the literary material, the University of North Carolina has extensive family correspondence. The CW Series, containing about twenty-nine hundred items, includes more than two hundred letters from Wolfe to his mother. These letters have been published in two editions. One, edited by John Skally Terry, was published by Scribners in 1943; another, edited by C. Hugh Holman and Sue Fields Ross, was published by the University of North Carolina Press in 1968. The collection also includes correspondence between Wolfe and other family members, particularly his brother Fred and sister Mabel, as well as with friends and acquaintances. In addition to the correspondence, this series includes some school and college notebooks, typed and autograph manuscripts, passports, diplomas, and other memorabilia of Thomas Wolfe. The composition books from Wolfe's days at a private school in Asheville were published in 1990 by the society as *Thomas Wolfe's Composition Books: The North State Fitting School, 1912–1915,* edited by Alice R. Cotten.

One of the most significant items in the collection is the typescript of the speech that Wolfe gave at Purdue University on 19 May 1938. (This was published in 1964 as "Thomas Wolfe's Purdue Speech: Writing and Living" and again in 1983, along with *The Story of a Novel,* as *The Autobiography of an American Novelist.*) Pages 18–24 are missing from this 63–page typescript and are among the Wolfe papers at Harvard.

In addition to the correspondence and manuscripts in the collection the initial family gift included photographs. The photograph collection has grown from other sources and today contains almost five thousand images, including about two hundred of Wolfe. Photographs and drawings are housed in and administered by the North Carolina Collection's Photographic Archives. The Thomas Wolfe Collection also includes paintings and other artwork related to Wolfe. A significant recent acquisition is the set of drawings done by Douglas Gorsline for the 1947 Scribners illustrated edition of *Look Homeward, Angel.*

Memorabilia include costumes from the original 1919 University of North Carolina student production of Wolfe's play, "The Return of Buck Gavin," a bud vase that Wolfe gave his sister Mabel as a wedding present, an alarm clock used by Wolfe, and similar objects. These items, designated as "keepsakes," are housed in and administered by the North Carolina Collection Gallery.

Another major addition to the Wolfe collection arrived in 1954 when the family of John Skally Terry, a classmate of Wolfe's at the University of North Carolina who also lived in New York during the time Wolfe lived there, donated items that Terry had gathered during the years he was collecting materials for his proposed biography of Wolfe, a biography that was never written. This series, given the designation CW1, contains correspondence to and from Terry about Thomas Wolfe, Terry's notes on Wolfe, copies of some of Wolfe's correspondence, interviews with former students of Wolfe, minutes of the Thomas Wolfe Biography Club at New York University, a transcript of Terry's interview with Wolfe's mother, and fifteen responses of Maxwell Perkins to questions Terry asked him about his relationship with Wolfe. Because of the significance of Maxwell Perkins, Wolfe's editor at Scribners, the society in 1997 published these fifteen letters commenting on Wolfe's life and work. *Always Yours, Max,* edited by Cotten, prints the complete text of Perkins's responses, includes several facsimiles, and provides notes to explain some of the references.

Series CW2 was created to accommodate smaller but significant additions to the Wolfe collection from various sources. It includes nearly five hundred items, including original letters from Wolfe to friends and professional associates. Additional items of note in this series are materials gathered by Richard Walser for his publications related to Wolfe, letters from American authors giving their appraisals of *Look Homeward, Angel,* letters from Vardis Fisher to Elizabeth Nowell and copies of her responses, and a portion of the galley proof of *Of Time and the River* with corrections in Wolfe's hand.

Series CW3, the Edward Aswell Series, documents Aswell's activities as administrator of the estate of Thomas Wolfe from 1947 until 1958. It includes about twenty-three hundred items. Series CW4 includes the correspondence and administrative documents of the librarian and the curator of the North Carolina Collection at the University of North Carolina Library, documents relating to the Thomas Wolfe Collection. Series CW5, the Fred William Wolfe Series, contains about six thousand items, including family and personal correspondence, legal documents, family memorabilia, and materials related to the Thomas Wolfe Memorial Association and the restoration of the Old Kentucky Home, the Asheville boardinghouse owned by Wolfe's mother.

Two major collections were added in 1990. One, the collection that was formerly at St. Mary's College, Raleigh, North Carolina, is designated Series CW6. Among its holdings are the papers of Asheville journalist George McCoy; the papers of Edgar E. (Jim) Wolfe, focusing on the Pennsylvania roots of Thomas Wolfe; and additional materials of Wolfe scholar Richard Walser. This collection also includes some original Wolfe letters, first editions of Wolfe's novels, and general works of and related to

Wolfe. Dr. and Mrs. John O. Fulenwider collected much of this material and donated it to St. Mary's. In addition the collection contains recordings of sessions of the Thomas Wolfe Fests held at St. Mary's.

William Hatchett and his wife, the poet Eve Braden, from Memphis, Tennessee, were friends of Fred Wolfe and over many years amassed a large collection of materials about Thomas Wolfe, including family letters, photographs, clippings, photocopies of articles by and about Wolfe, and memorabilia. This collection was acquired by the North Carolina Collection after Mr. Hatchett's death and is designated Series CW7.

The most recent series, CW8, is the Aldo P. Magi Series. The series began with a gift in Magi's honor, a postcard sent in June 1935 from Wolfe to William Weber, publicity director at Scribners. Since then the series has attracted additional gifts. These include some calling cards and Christmas cards relating to Wolfe and more than two hundred letters of condolence sent to the Perkins family after the death of Maxwell Perkins in 1947.

The North Carolina Collection attempts to collect Wolfe comprehensively, seeking all editions and printings of Wolfe's works, published books and other printed materials about Wolfe, audiovisuals related to Wolfe, and, where appropriate, photographs, correspondence, and manuscript material of or related to Wolfe. For example, a recent purchase was an advance review copy of *Look Homeward, Angel* in tan Kraft paper wrappers. Some items are received as gifts. A gift of several presentation copies of Wolfe's works to members of his family included the copy of *Look Homeward, Angel* that Wolfe inscribed to his mother. Another recent purchase is a manuscript, "What a Writer Reads," which is written by Wolfe entirely in pencil. Edited and cut substantially, this was published in the December 1935 issue of *The Book Buyer.*

A guide to the Thomas Wolfe Collection was prepared by Frances A. Weaver in 1980 and is updated as needed; a copy is available in the reading room. The North Carolina Collection also maintains a computerized index to correspondence in its Thomas Wolfe Collection. A description of the Wolfe collection and images of some of its manuscripts and photographs are featured on the North Carolina Collection's Internet website. Access to materials in the CW Series, and to portions of other series, requires written permission from the executor of the estate of Thomas Wolfe. Those planning to use the collection should write or call in advance of a visit. A small room in the front of the North Carolina Collection's reading room is devoted to exhibiting materials from the Thomas Wolfe Collection.

William Seward Burroughs

(15 February 1914 – 2 August 1997)

Matt Theado
Gardner-Webb University

See also the Burroughs entries in *DLB 2: American Novelists Since World War II; DLB 8: Twentieth-Century American Science-Fiction Writers; DLB 16: The Beats: Literary Bohemians in Postwar America; DLB Yearbook: 1981;* and *DLB 152: American Novelists Since World War II, Fourth Series.*

BOOKS: *Junkie,* as William Lee, bound with *Narcotic Agent,* by Maurice Helbrant (New York: Ace, 1953; London: Digit, 1957); as William Burroughs (New York: Ace, 1964; London: Olympia/New English Library, 1966); unexpurgated edition as William S. Burroughs, *Junky* (New York: Penguin, 1977);

The Naked Lunch (Paris: Olympia, 1959); published as *Naked Lunch* (New York: Grove, 1962; London: Calder/Olympia, 1964);

The Exterminator, by Burroughs and Brion Gysin (San Francisco: Auerhahn Press, 1960);

Minutes to Go, by Burroughs, Sinclair Beiles, Gregory Corso, and Gysin (Paris: Two Cities, 1960; San Francisco: Beach, 1968);

The Soft Machine (Paris: Olympia, 1961; revised and enlarged edition, New York: Grove, 1966; second revision and enlargement, London: Calder & Boyars, 1968);

The Ticket That Exploded (Paris: Olympia, 1962; revised and enlarged edition, New York: Grove, 1967; London: Calder & Boyars, 1968);

Dead Fingers Talk (London: Calder/Olympia, 1963);

The Yage Letters, by Burroughs and Allen Ginsberg (San Francisco: City Lights Books, 1963; enlarged, 1975);

Nova Express (New York: Grove, 1964; London: Cape, 1966);

Roosevelt after Inauguration, as "Willy Lee" alias WSB (New York: Fuck You Press, 1964); enlarged as *Roosevelt after Inauguration and Other Atrocities* (San Francisco: City Lights Books, 1979);

Health Bulletin: APO-33, a Metabolic Regulator (New York: Fuck You Press, 1965); republished as *APO-33 Bulletin: A Metabolic Regulator* (San Francisco: Beach, 1966);

William Burroughs in 1983 (photograph by Kate Simon)

Time (New York: "C," 1965);

Valentine's Day Reading (New York: American Theatre for Poets, 1965);

So Who Owns Death TV?, by Burroughs, Claude Pélieu, and Carl Weissner (San Francisco: Beach, 1967);

Entretiens avec William Burroughs, by Burroughs and Daniel Odier (Paris: Belfond, 1969); translated, revised, and enlarged as *The Job: Interviews with William S. Burroughs* (New York: Grove, 1970; London: Cape, 1970; second revision and enlargement, New York: Grove, 1974);

The Last Words of Dutch Schultz (London: Cape Goliard, 1970; revised and enlarged edition, New York: Viking/Seaver, 1975);

Ali's Smile (Brighton, U.K.: Unicorn, 1971); published in an enlarged edition as *Ali's Smile/Naked Scientology* (Göttingen: Expanded Media Editions, 1973);

Electronic Revolution 1970–71 (Cambridge: Blackmoor Head, 1971; enlarged edition, Göttingen: Expanded Media Editions, 1972);

The Wild Boys: A Book of the Dead (New York: Grove, 1971; London: Calder & Boyars, 1972);

Exterminator! (New York: Seaver/Viking, 1973; London: Calder & Boyars, 1975);

Mayfair Academy Series More or Less (Brighton, U.K.: Urgency Rip-Off, 1973);

White Subway (London: Aloes, 1973);

Brion Gysin Let the Mice In, by Burroughs, Gysin, and Ian Sommerville, edited by Jan Herman (West Glover, Vt.: Something Else, 1973);

Port of Saints (London: Covent Garden, 1973; revised edition, Berkeley: Blue Wind Press, 1980);

The Book of Breathing (Ingatestone, Essex, U.K.: OU, 1974; Berkeley, Cal.: Blue Wind Press, 1975);

Sidetripping, by Burroughs and Charles Gatewood (New York: Strawberry Hill, 1975);

Snack . . . , by Burroughs and Eric Mottram (London: Aloes, 1975);

Cobble Stone Gardens (Cherry Valley, N.Y.: Cherry Valley Editions, 1976);

The Retreat Diaries, with *The Dream of Tibet,* by Ginsberg (New York: City Moon, 1976);

The Third Mind, by Burroughs and Gysin (New York: Seaver/Viking, 1978; London: Calder, 1979);

Doctor Benway: A Passage from The Naked Lunch (Santa Barbara, Cal.: Morrow, 1979);

Ah Pook Is Here and Other Texts (London: Calder, 1979; New York: Riverrun, 1982);

Blade Runner (A Movie) (Berkeley, Cal.: Blue Wind Press, 1979);

The Soft Machine, Nova Express, The Wild Boys: Three Novels (New York: Grove/Outrider, 1980);

Cities of the Red Night (New York: Holt, Rinehart & Winston, 1981; London: Calder, 1981);

Early Routines (Santa Barbara, Cal.: Cadmus, 1981);

The Streets of Chance (New York: Red Ozier, 1981);

A William Burroughs Reader, edited by John Calder (London: Pan/Picador, 1982);

The Place of Dead Roads (New York: Holt, Rinehart & Winston, 1983; London: Calder, 1984);

The Burroughs File (San Francisco: City Lights Books, 1984);

Queer (New York: Viking, 1985; London: Pan, 1985);

The Adding Machine: Collected Essays (London: Calder, 1985); republished as *The Adding Machine: Selected Essays* (New York: Seaver, 1986);

The Cat Inside (New York: Grenfell, 1986);

The Western Lands (New York: Viking/Penguin, 1987; London: Pan, 1987);

Interzone (New York: Viking, 1989);

My Education: A Book of Dreams (New York: Viking, 1995; London: Pan, 1995).

PLAY PRODUCTION: *The Black Rider: The Casting of the Magic Bullets,* with songs by Tom Waits, Hamburg, Thalia Theater, 31 March 1990; New York, Brooklyn Academy of Music, December 1993.

William Seward Burroughs died on 2 August 1997, about twenty-four hours after suffering a heart attack. He was eighty-three. The author of the once-banned *Naked Lunch* (1959), who lived much of his life in New York City, Mexico City, North Africa, Paris, and London, spent his last sixteen years in Lawrence, Kansas, 270 miles west of Saint Louis, where he was born.

For a person with a notorious reputation–he was arrested twice for his complicity in killings and several more times for possession of drugs and firearms and was sometimes referred to as the "Godfather of Punk"–Burroughs spent the final years of his life in relative tranquillity. In *William Burroughs: El Hombre Invisible* (1993) biographer Barry Miles describes Burroughs's comfortable life in a small, white frame house as orderly and routine in a period when Burroughs generally avoided drugs and sex and doted on his cats. During this time Burroughs confined most of his writing to brief journal entries. Less than two months before his death he wondered in his journal if "there just isn't any more to say" by any writers. He told a *New York Times* interviewer in November 1996 that he "had run out of things to say." His journal suggests that his search for "the final answer," a search that had led him to the jungles of Central America and to the opium dens of Morocco, was ultimately a "receding image." In his last journal entry, on the day before he died, he was not thinking of books or writing or final answers at all. Burroughs, whose writerly image conveyed frequently a cold-blooded, almost insectlike presence, questioned the nature of love and concluded that love "is the most natural pain killer."

Despite his loss of intrigue with writing, Burroughs had maintained his interest in painting and in creating "shotgun art": in pursuing spontaneity and freedom from constraints, Burroughs would discharge a shotgun at his "canvass," usually a rectangular board. He occasionally enjoyed this activity with artist Ralph Steadman or writer Hunter Thompson, and frequently sold the results. He never lost his interest in the subjects that attracted some readers while repelling others. Miles reports that among the books scattered around Burroughs's living room were such titles as *Basic Stick Fighting* and *How To Kill, Vol. V.* and magazines such as *Gun World, Soldier of Fortune,* and *UFO Universe.* Another late visitor noted the piles of "*Amityville Horror*–style trashy books about exorcism and ghosts." To the end of his life Burroughs cleaved to the image of a tormented but supremely curious person who explored the dark side of the human consciousness. Perhaps he ventured into these zones of experience since he felt that, as things stand, people are not advancing toward any noble goals. His deep pessimism challenged even that of the aged Mark Twain: "We have been abandoned here on this planet ruled by lying bastards of modest brain power. No sense. Not a modicum of good intentions. Lying worthless bastards." Miles concludes his biography with Burroughs's assessment of the human condition as "a vast mudslide of soulless sludge." Burroughs may be remembered as an artist who despaired of the human situation as a malady, an affliction on the earth, yet he moved through his life as one who felt deep emotional ties for his friends and loved ones and who wrote for the sake of others, that they might see the control that governments, religions, greedy human beings, and their own cravings for drugs, sex, or power often hold over them.

The obituaries were respectful. *The New York Times* called Burroughs a "renegade writer of the Beat Generation who stunned readers and inspired adoring cultists" and whose books "always interested the critics." The *Lawrence Journal-World* observed that although some readers dismissed *Naked Lunch* as "undecipherable garbage," others praised the book as "literary genius." *Rolling Stone* acknowledged Burroughs as a "cultural force" who "challenged the codes and norms of society." The Associated Press release cited Burroughs's publicist Ira Silverberg: "The passing of William Burroughs leaves us with few great American writers. His presence in the American literary landscape was unparalleled." Burroughs is an indelible cultural icon largely because his influence carries beyond the literary world. *Wired News,* an Internet news source, proclaimed that "net denizens received the news of the death of William Burroughs . . . as a loss of one of their own," even though Burroughs rarely used the Internet and did not even have an E-mail address. Nonetheless, Burroughs had spent much of his career subverting censorship, a prominent issue on the Internet, and he had created "Interzone," a fantasy place that served him as Yoknapatawpha County served William Faulkner, and that parallels the lawless freedom of the Internet. Burroughs often quoted Hassan i Sabbah, who reportedly said, "Nothing is true, everything is permitted," a phrase that partly defines Burroughs's concept of Interzone and illuminates the Internet as well.

Other obituaries mentioned the effect Burroughs had on musicians over a span of three decades. Few writers have had the impact on a wholly different artistic genre that Burroughs had on music. Musicians and songwriters David Bowie, Lou Reed, Patti Smith, and Michael Stipe all acknowledged Burroughs's influence. Morris Dickstein, a writer and English professor at the City University of New York, said that Burroughs gave these musicians "techniques to get inside the dark side of the mind. He explored the fantastic, the irrational, so he freed them from a pretty rational form of literary narration." Burroughs opened doors to these musicians also by dredging up taboo subjects, such as his own heroin addiction and homosexuality. He did more than influence them; he collaborated with rock groups such as Ministry and R.E.M. and with Kurt Cobain of Nirvana; he appeared in videos by U2; and he lent his haunting Midwest drawl as a voice-over narration on performance artist Laurie Anderson's cult album, "Mister Heartbreak." His introduction to the music scene began early. Burroughs's face appears among the eclectic crowd of people gathered on the cover of the Beatles' album *Sergeant Pepper's Lonely Hearts Club Band,* and Burroughs is generally credited with coining the phrase *heavy metal,* a name of a variety of rock music. Probably the best known of Burroughs's infiltrations of pop music is via Steely Dan, a band that took its name from a sexual aid in *Naked Lunch.* When one adds his appearances in advertisements for GAP brand clothes and for Nike athletic shoes, one can see that clearly the public embraced Burroughs in a way that goes beyond the recognition usually associated with writers. A Nike spokesperson said of Burroughs, who is probably the least athletic pitchman Nike could have used, "When he came onto the scene, what he was doing in literature was the equivalent of what Nike had done in the athletic world in terms of pushing the limits and taking risks and doing things differently." People who never read a book by Burroughs came to recognize him as a celebrity.

Still, Silverberg's hyperbolic assessment of Burroughs's literary importance is understandable. After the publication of *Naked Lunch,* Burroughs's most famous and notorious book, J. G. Ballard called Burroughs "the most important writer to emerge since the Second World War," and jacket blurbs on the Grove Press first paperback reprint convey Norman Mailer's estimation that Burroughs is "the only American novelist today who may conceivably be possessed by genius." Karl Shapiro called *Naked Lunch* "one of the most important pieces of literature of our time." Burroughs's hallucinatory style and jarring juxtapositions perfectly suited him in his own great quest, the battle against control. Burroughs believed that language is a virus and that words and images are instruments of control that allow evil forces to impose their will over people. Taking the enemy head-on, Burroughs sought to battle the control of language by manipulating the medium itself.

Another force that confronted Burroughs was that of censorship. His first book, *Junkie* (1953, as William Lee), a hard-boiled narrative of drug addiction, includes none of the experimental writing or pornographic subjects that make up *Naked Lunch,* although some of the themes carry over into the later book. But in 1965 *Naked Lunch* was banned in Boston, deemed obscene by Superior Court Judge Eugene Hudson of Massachusetts. In 1966 the Massachusetts Supreme Court ruled that the book was "grossly offensive" and cited the author's own judgment that it was "brutal, obscene and disgusting." Even though the book may appeal to "the prurient interest of deviants," the Massachusetts Supreme Court also found that the book had redeeming social importance in a decision based in part on the testimonies of Allen Ginsberg, Norman Mailer, and John Ciardi. Jennie Skerl, author of the first book-length English-language study of Burroughs's work, points out the significance of this court decision for all writers: "*Naked Lunch* was the last literary work to be subjected to a major censorship trial in the United States and marked the end of an era that began in the 1870s when the crusader Anthony Comstock persuaded federal and state governments to create and enforce stricter obscenity laws. . . . *Naked Lunch* was the final step in eliminating censorship of the printed word in the United States today." By turning his dark fantasies into published prose, Burroughs felt he had exorcized the demons that possessed him during his drug addiction and that he had emerged "clean as a lamb." Although the book

was denounced by some critics as "psychopathological filth," Burroughs felt that he had sought to "make people aware of the true criminality of our times" and to force readers to a "frozen moment," as the title insists, "when everyone sees what is on the end of every fork." His breakthrough as a writer came in his ability to describe this moment while subverting the language of description through juxtaposition and nonlinear narrative. Despite his lengthy—and almost untrackable—bibliography and his appearances in music and in films, Burroughs will be remembered most for *Naked Lunch.*

William Burroughs was born in 1914, a grandson of the inventor of the first reliable adding machine. His mother traced her family's lineage to Robert E. Lee. Though well known and fairly well off, the family was not a part of Saint Louis society. They sold most of their stock in the invention before the Burroughs Adding Machine Company could have made them rich, yet it was also the sale of stock that saw the family through the Depression. Burroughs grew up in an upper-middle-class, protected environment. In the midst of this lackluster setting, though, young Burroughs began to display the dark tendencies that would later make him famous. For example, he wrote a brief story called "The Autobiography of a Wolf." He would later recall that adults tried to correct his title; surely he must have meant "Biography of a Wolf," but he would not listen to them. He noted, too, in his journal years later that a childhood friend's father likened his appearance to that of a "sheep-killing dog." In his early teen years he discovered Jack Black's *You Can't Win,* the autobiography of a petty thief who moves through an underworld of whorehouses, opium dens, and hobo haunts. Despite his involvement in crime, Black stays true to his own code of honor. This book inspired Burroughs to his own later adventures—including drugs—and influenced him, too, by the way its direct narrative style revealed scenes without sensationalizing or apologizing for them.

Burroughs attended private schools and went to Harvard University when he was eighteen and, as an English major, studied the typical fare: Milton, Wordsworth, Chaucer, Shakespeare (with George Lyman Kittredge), and Coleridge. He did not enjoy his time there, and later he preferred not to refer to his Harvard experiences. As a graduation present his parents gave him a $200-per-month allowance. With this money he traveled to Europe and enrolled briefly in the University of Vienna medical school. While there, he made one of the first quirky decisions that would perplex his family; he married Ilse Klapper, a German Jew who was stranded in Dubrovnik, so that she could flee to the United States. Upon their arrival they dissolved the marriage, and Burroughs reunited with a childhood friend, Kells Elvins. They lived together (without a sexual relationship, though Burroughs knew that he himself was a homosexual by this time) in an apartment in Cambridge where they began to collaborate on stories. Typically these stories originated with the two men acting out scenes and carrying their premises to the furthest imaginable extremes, primarily for their own amusement. Soon they were writing their "routines" down, and in this way Dr. Benway, one of Burroughs's most memorable characters, was born.

Burroughs avoided the draft in 1942 and moved to Chicago, where he worked briefly as an exterminator. Burroughs relied on these experiences later in his writing, particularly in his book *Exterminator!* (1973). Just as importantly, he was beginning to define himself by his morbid occupations. He found a great amount of humor in the image of himself as a serious professional going from apartment to apartment to kill bugs. He was beginning to carve out his character in the combination of humor and horror.

While Burroughs was in Chicago, two Saint Louis friends came to visit him. The arrival of Lucien Carr and David Kammerer—and their subsequent luring of Burroughs to New York—changed Burroughs's future and probably the course of American literature, at least as far as Burroughs's influence on it goes. In 1943 Burroughs was living in Greenwich Village when Carr introduced him to a Columbia University friend, Allen Ginsberg. Shortly thereafter Carr also set up the meeting between Burroughs and Jack Kerouac, another friend that Carr knew from his association with Columbia. Through a chain of other acquaintances Burroughs met Herbert Huncke, a Times Square junkie, who introduced Burroughs to heroin. Huncke is also generally credited with bringing the word *beat* into popular use. According to Steve Watson, author of *The Birth of the Beat Generation,* "In the drug world, 'beat' meant 'robbed' or 'cheated' (as in 'a beat deal'). Huncke picked up the word from his show business friends on the Near North Side of Chicago, and in the fall of 1945 he introduced the word to William Burroughs, Allen Ginsberg, and Jack Kerouac." Kerouac, with his keen sense of catchy phrases, commandeered the expression as the name of the generation that included his new visionary but disenfranchised friends. At about the same time Kerouac also recognized the potential depth of the phrase *naked lunch,* when he heard Ginsberg misread a Burroughs piece that included *naked lust.* In the coming decade and beyond, these men would influence each other and propel one another's writing ca-

reers until they became established as the core of the Beat Generation. In fact, Burroughs credits Kerouac's persistence in persuading him to become a writer: "You can't walk out on the Shakespeare squad, Bill."

Kerouac and Ginsberg looked up to Burroughs as a teacher. Harvard-trained, well traveled, and well read, knowledgeable not only of Shakespeare but also of writers unknown to the two younger men, they saw in Burroughs an example of a man who pursued his own education in actual experience. Kerouac dramatized Burroughs as Bull Lee in his best-selling novel *On the Road* (1957):

> It would take all night to tell about Old Bull Lee; let's just say now, he was a teacher, and it may be said that he had every right to teach because he spent all his time learning. . . . He was an exterminator in Chicago, a bartender in New York, a summons-server in Newark. In Paris he sat at café tables, watching the sullen French faces go by. In Athens he looked up from his *ouzo* at what he called the ugliest people in the world. In Istanbul he threaded his way through crowds of opium addicts and rug-sellers, looking for the facts. In English hotels he read Spengler and the Marquis de Sade. In Chicago he planned to hold up a Turkish bath, hesitated for two minutes too long for a drink, and wound up with two dollars and had to make a run for it. He did all these things merely for the experience. Now the final study was the drug habit.

Shortly after Kerouac wrote the above description, he and his friends were shocked to learn that while living in Mexico City, Burroughs had shot and killed his wife, the former Joan Vollmer, with a .38 caliber pistol while drunkenly acting out a William Tell routine. The *New York Daily News* headline on 8 September 1951 read, "Heir's Pistol Kills His Wife; He Denies Playing Wm. Tell." Burroughs spent only a few weeks in jail, but now, at age thirty-seven, he underwent an important transformation. For years afterward he would avow that if his wife had not died—a victim, he came to believe, of the Ugly Spirit that had possessed him and with whom he battled for control—then he never would have become a writer. Kerouac had long encouraged Burroughs to write, but except for the routines he wrote with Kells Elvins and a collaborative effort with Kerouac, he had written little that reassured him that he should continue. Now he decided to finish a project that had already been well under way. By 1953 he had completed *Junkie* (which would be republished with its current title, *Junky*). The prose was unadorned, modeled on that of Dashiell Hammett and Jack Black: "My first experience with junk was during the War, about 1944 or 1945. I had made the acquaintance of a man named Norton who was working in the shipyard at the time. . . . Norton was a hard-working thief, and he did not feel right unless he stole something every day from the ship-yard where he worked. A tool, some canned goods, a pair of overalls, anything at all. One day he called me up and said he had stolen a Tommy gun. Could I find someone to buy it? I said, 'Maybe. Bring it over.'"

In the subsequent years Burroughs wrote an-other novel, *Queer* (1985), which is also autobio-graphical and given similar treatment, and he col-lected letters to Ginsberg he had written about his adventures in the South American jungles, where he searched for yage, a medicinal plant that he hoped would grant spiritual insight. Neither book was pub-lished until years later. Meanwhile, Burroughs transformed himself as a writer and made the leap into highly individualistic, experimental writing that probed the recesses of his nightmare world of addiction and the battle for control. Living now in Tangier, Morocco, he typed incessantly, strewing pages across the floor of his rented room. At first the results were mystifying, even to him. As he wrote in a letter to Ginsberg in December 1954, "I am dis-couraged about my writing. It seems impossible for me to write anything salable, or, in fact, anything that achieves artistic unity or wholeness. What I have written sounds like the notes for a novel, not the novel itself. . . . All I can write is pieces of a novel, and the pieces don't fit together." Burroughs tried to redeem his writing efforts by collating all his notes and routines and centering the results around an intensified version of Tangier, which he began to call "Interzone." Burroughs reveled in the freedom he found in Tangier. He indulged liberally in his fa-vorite deviant behaviors: drugs and sex with young boys. He wrote a letter to Allen Ginsberg in which he referred primarily to his deportment but also obliquely to his approach to writing: "I am progress-ing towards complete lack of caution and restraint. Nothing must be allowed to dilute my routines." Kerouac visited Burroughs in Tangier in early 1957 and lent his typing skills to Burroughs's project. Later Kerouac complained that he had to stop typ-ing *Naked Lunch* because of recurrent nightmares of "great long balonies" coming out of his mouth. Af-ter Kerouac left, Ginsberg and Alan Ansen stayed with Burroughs and finished the typing and the somewhat arbitrary ordering of sections. Ginsberg dedicated *Howl* (1956) in part to Burroughs, "author of [yet unpublished] *Naked Lunch,* an endless novel which will drive everybody mad."

Naked Lunch was first published in Paris by Olympia Press in 1959. Olympia Press owner Maurice Girodias kept in business by publishing pornographic stories in the Traveller's Companion series, but he also published works by avant-garde writers or works that were too racy for mainstream American publishers. For example, Girodias pub-lished Vladimir Nabokov's *Lolita,* which was then published by Grove Press in America. *Naked Lunch* followed the same path. After successfully defend-ing Henry Miller's *Tropic of Cancer* in an obscenity lawsuit Grove Press agreed to publish *Naked Lunch* in the United States. In addition to the recognition that the obscenity trial in Boston brought to the book and its author, Jennie Skerl points out that the book "attracted the attention of serious readers . . . when Mary McCarthy and Norman Mailer praised the book highly at the Edinburgh International Writer's Conference in 1962" and that the praise led to highly visible reviews, some of which were strongly negative.

Burroughs continued to experiment with liter-ary form. Most notably, he began to explore the pos-sibilities of the "cut-up" technique. He sought to bring the collage of visual arts to the writer's desk by writing a passage of prose and then juxtaposing the lines with another piece of prose, written by himself or another writer. Readers tend to have mixed views about the results. Kerouac believed that Burroughs's success as a writer ended after *Na-ked Lunch* when he began the cut-up technique. Bur-roughs hoped to free himself from the control that language imposes by relinquishing his own rein over his meanings and by arbitrarily combining words. The results conjure up the distinctive and pe-culiar world of William Burroughs:

> through the open window trailing swamp smells and old newspapers—orgasm addicts stacked in the attic like muttering burlap—the mattress molded on all sides masturbating afternoons reflected; "Difficult to get out" —word and image skin like a rubber toy dusted with grey spine powder—Blue notes of Pan trickled down silver train whistles—calling the imprisoned Jinn from copulation space suits that clung to his muscle lust and burning sex skin—The green fish boys dropped their torture of spectral presence and like fish left the garden through clear water—Tentative beings followed the music membrane of light and color—Pipes of Pan trickled down sleeping comrade of his childhood—

(from *The Ticket That Exploded,* 1962). The outcome can be beautiful, troubling, bizarre, and baffling at the same time.

Burroughs's bibliography speaks for itself. He produced a large number of works over a long and productive career, continually breaking out in new directions, originating a body of work that defies categorization. Like other literary geniuses, his effect can be measured by the number of writers who came after him and derived their styles in part from his influence. For Burroughs, one can track more than writers; musicians and artists as well as movie makers cite his persuasion, and his influence is felt, too, in popular culture. Barry Miles notes that although many readers and critics recognize Burroughs as a great American writer, "it is his newspaper image as the homosexual junkie pornographer who shot his wife in a bizarre William Tell act that still attracts and fascinates the public." Whether or not one agrees with Ira Silverberg's high praise–that Burroughs's "presence in the literary landscape was unparalleled"–one must certainly find that Burroughs was a force, and one whose position in literature will continue to be redefined over the coming years.

Letters:

Letters to Allen Ginsberg, 1953–1957, edited by Ron Padgett and Anne Waldman, introduction by Ginsberg, preface by Burroughs (New York: Full Court Press, 1981);

The Letters of William S. Burroughs, 1945–1959, edited by Oliver Harris (New York: Viking, 1993).

Interviews:

Gregory Corso and Allen Ginsberg, "Interview with William Burroughs," *Journal for the Protection of All Beings,* no. 1 (1961): 79–83;

Conrad Knickerbocker, "William Burroughs," in *Writers at Work: The Paris Review Interviews, Third Series,* edited by George Plimpton (New York: Viking, 1967), pp. 143–174;

Robert Palmer, "Rolling Stone Interview: William S. Burroughs," *Rolling Stone,* 108 (11 May 1972): 48–53;

Gerard Malanga, "An Interview with William S. Burroughs," *Beat Book,* 4 (1974): 90–112;

John Tytell, "An Interview with William Burroughs," in *The Beat Diary,* no. 5, edited by Arthur and Kit Knight (California, Pa.: A. & K. Knight, 1977), pp. 35–49;

Victor Bockris, *With William Burroughs: A Report from the Bunker* (New York: Seaver, 1981);

Jennie Skerl, "An Interview with William S. Burroughs (4 April 1980, New York City)," *Modern Language Studies,* 12 (Summer 1982): 3–17.

Bibliographies:

Miles Associates, *A Descriptive Catalogue of the William S. Burroughs Archive* (London: Covent Garden, 1973);

Jennie Skerl, "A William S. Burroughs Bibliography," *The Serif,* 11 (Summer 1974): 12–20;

Michael B. Goodman, *William S. Burroughs: An Annotated Bibliography of His Works and Criticism* (New York: Garland, 1975);

Joe Maynard and Barry Miles, *William S. Burroughs: A Bibliography, 1953–1973* (Charlottesville: University Press of Virginia, 1978);

Goodman and Lemuel B. Coley, *William S. Burroughs: A Reference Guide* (New York & London: Garland, 1990).

Biographies:

Bruce Cook, "The Holy Monster," in his *The Beat Generation* (New York: Scribners, 1971), pp. 165–184;

William Burroughs Jr., *Kentucky Ham* (New York: Dutton, 1973);

John Tytell, *Naked Angels: The Lives and Literature of the Beat Generation* (New York: McGraw-Hill, 1976), pp. 36–51, 111–140;

Ted Morgan, *Literary Outlaw: The Life and Times of William S. Burroughs* (New York: Holt, 1988);

Barry Miles, *William Burroughs: El Hombre Invisible* (New York: Hyperion Press, 1993).

References:

Alan Ansen, *William Burroughs: An Essay* (Sudbury, Mass.: Water Row, 1986);

Michael Bliss, "The Orchestration of Chaos: Verbal Technique in William Burroughs' *Naked Lunch,*" *enclitic,* 1 (Spring 1977): 59–69;

Clive Bush, "An Anarchy of New Speech: Notes on the American Tradition of William Burroughs," *Journal of Beckett Studies,* 6 (Autumn 1980): 120–128;

Gérard Cordesse, "The Science-fiction of William Burroughs," *Caliban,* 12 (1975): 33–43;

Edward Halsey Foster, *Understanding the Beats* (Columbia: University of South Carolina Press, 1992);

Laszlo Géfin, "Collage Theory, Reception, and the Cutups of William Burroughs," *Perspectives on Contemporary Literature,* 13 (1987): 91–100;

Michael B. Goodman, *Contemporary Literary Censorship: The Case History of Burroughs' "Naked Lunch"* (Metuchen, N.J. & London: Scarecrow Press, 1981);

James Grauerholz, *On Burroughs' Art* (Sante Fe, N.M.: Gallery Casa Sin Nombre, 1988);

Ihab Hassan, "The Literature of Silence: From Henry Miller to Beckett and Burroughs," *Encounter,* 28 (January 1967): 74–82;

Hassan, "The Subtracting Machine: The Work of William Burroughs," *Critique,* 6 (Spring 1963): 4–23;

Anthony Channell Hilfer, "Mariner and Wedding Guest in William Burroughs' *Naked Lunch,*" *Criticism,* 22 (Summer 1980): 252–265;

Richard Kostelanetz, "From Nightmare to Serendipity: A Retrospective Look at William S. Burroughs," *Twentieth Century Literature,* 11 (October 1965): 123–130;

David Lodge, "Objections to William Burroughs," in his *The Novelist at the Crossroads and Other Essays in Fiction and Criticism* (Ithaca, N.Y.: Cornell University Press, 1971), pp. 161–171;

Robin Lydenberg, *Word Cultures: Radical Theory and Practice in William S. Burroughs' Fiction* (Urbana: University of Illinois Press, 1987);

Lydenberg and Jennie Skerl, *William S. Burroughs at the Front: Critical Reception, 1959–1989* (Carbondale: Southern Illinois University Press, 1991);

Mary McCarthy, *The Writing on the Wall and Other Essays* (New York: Harcourt, Brace & World, 1970), pp. 42–53;

Frank D. McConnell, "William Burroughs and the Literature of Addiction," *Massachusetts Review,* 8 (Autumn 1967): 665–680;

Eric Mottram, *William Burroughs: The Algebra of Need,* revised edition (London: Boyars, 1977);

Cary Nelson, "The End of the Body: Radical Space in Burroughs," in his *The Incarnate Word: Literature and Verbal Space* (Urbana: University of Illinois Press, 1973), pp. 208–229;

Neal Oxenhandler, "Listening to Burroughs' Voice," in *Surfiction: Fiction Now . . . and Tomorrow,* edited by Raymond Federman (Chicago: Swallow Press, 1975), pp. 181–201;

Donald Palumbo, "William Burroughs' Quartet of Science Fiction Novels as Dystopian Social Satire," *Extrapolation,* 20 (Winter 1979): 321–329;

Alvin J. Seltzer, "Confusion Hath Fuck His Masterpiece," in his *Chaos in the Novel, the Novel in Chaos* (New York: Schocken, 1974), pp. 330–374;

Steven Shaviro, "Burroughs' Theater of Illusion: *Cities of the Red Night,*" *Review of Contemporary Fiction,* 4 (Spring 1984): 64–74;

Skerl, *William S. Burroughs* (Boston: Twayne, 1985);

Tony Tanner, "Rub Out the Word," in his *City of Words: American Fiction 1950–1970* (New York: Harper & Row, 1971), pp. 109–140;

John Tytell, *Naked Angels: The Lives and Literature of the Beat Generation* (New York: McGraw-Hill, 1976);

Nicholas Zurbrugg, "Burroughs, Barthes and the Limits of Intertextuality," *Review of Contemporary Fiction,* 4 (Spring 1984): 86–107.

Papers:

Primary collections of Burroughs's papers are located at the Ohio State University, Arizona State University, the University of Kansas, Columbia University, and the University of Texas at Austin. Other locations include Northwestern University, Princeton University, and Syracuse University.

1997 Booker Prize

Merritt Moseley
University of North Carolina at Asheville

The Booker Prize, awarded each year to "the best full-length novel of the year," is Britain's best established and most prestigious literary award. Sponsored by Booker–McConnell PLC, a food distribution company, it is worth £20,000 to the winner. Five or six finalists (the "shortlist") are announced in August or September, and then, after a tension-building two months, the winner is revealed in a gala ceremony at London's Guildhall, which is also broadcast live over television to a large audience.

The 1997 Booker Prize, announced on the evening of 14 October, went to Arundhati Roy's first novel, *The God of Small Things* (London: Flamingo; New York: Random House). This was both surprising and unsurprising. Bookmakers (who handle a lot of betting on the Booker Prize, unlike any American counterpart) had made Bernard MacLaverty's *Grace Notes* (London and New York: Norton) the favorite, at 2–1, with the second favorite Jim Crace's *Quarantine* (London and New York: Viking), at 3–1, followed by Roy at 7–2. On the other hand, cynical observers pointed out that Roy, as a photogenic Indian woman whose book had received strong publicity (for instance, she had a central position in a *New Yorker* photograph illustrating "India's leading novelists" despite the handicap of not having published a novel when the photograph was made), had a good chance to win irrespective of the quality of her novel. Many considerations go into the Booker decision, which is made by a committee and is very closely scrutinized throughout the process of selection.

Richard Todd, in his *Consuming Fictions: The Booker Prize and Fiction in Britain Today* (London: Bloomsbury, 1996), writes that "it is surely evident that it is precisely by 'getting it wrong' that the Booker survives. . . . Every decision, in other words, must be more or less contentious." Not only the winner but also the shortlist—that is, the list of 5 or 6 finalists, chosen from a "long list" of somewhere between 100 and 120 books read by the five-judge panel and announced about two months before the

Dust jacket for the 1997 Booker Prize novel

Booker itself is awarded—stimulates plenty of disagreement.

This year, as usual, much of it was about notable omissions; the consensus was that the two most deserving novels not put on the shortlist were Ian McEwan's *Enduring Love* and John Banville's *The Untouchable*. *Enduring Love* is a powerful and touching story of a man involved by strange accident in a situation where he is being stalked by someone with a homoerotic religious mania but cannot make anyone believe him. It may be McEwan's best book. Irish author Banville, in *The Untouchable,* has written

338

an elegant, lightly fictionalized account of the Establishment figure Antony Blunt, who, while Keeper of the Queen's Pictures, was revealed to have been a Russian spy. McEwan, like his near contemporaries Martin Amis and Julian Barnes, has been routinely overlooked by Booker panels.

Of course, in any year there are more than six books published that deserve consideration for an award, so pointing out omissions is easy. What is more vehement is the general critical dismissal of most or all of the shortlisted books. Jason Cowley of the London *Times* wrote that 1997 "has not been an exceptional year for the British, or indeed the Commonwealth novel," and admits, grudgingly, that "the 1997 shortlist is not without value." And Cowley was on this judging panel. This is an astonishingly modest act of praise for one of the five people responsible for creating the list. The London *Sunday Times* critic, uninvolved, commented on the list's "showing a surprising aversion to complexity, sophistication, intensity, ambitiousness, intelligence, and stylistic brilliance" and thought it omitted all but one of the outstanding books eligible for the award. Paul Levy, who covers the Booker for *The Wall Street Journal,* wrote that "this year's shortlist, as flawed as those of previous years, has the additional demerit of being dull." Catherine Lockerbie, literary editor of *The Scotsman,* damned the list as "lamentably banal."

One reason for the unsatisfactory list may be the horse-trading among the judges, who are a fairly miscellaneous lot anyway. As usual, in 1997 they included academics, literary journalists, and novelists who had no book eligible, and it is quite clear that much compromising goes on. Another reason—or so many observers would claim—is the literary gerrymandering or quota system that some critics believe is in operation—though all judges deny it. Each list, they say, will include at least one Celtic (Irish or Scottish) novel, one exotic (Indian or African) book, a decent number of women, some sort of historical pastiche, and often an antipodean author. This year's obscure Australian Madeleine St. John replaced a previous Booker winner, the famous Australian Peter Carey, whose novel *Jack Maggs* (which was also a historical pastiche, being a rewriting of the story of Magwitch in Charles Dickens's *Great Expectations,* 1861) was a surprising omission. Other categories include the "Hampstead novel," about domestic difficulties among middle-class Londoners. St. John's *The Essence of the Thing* (London: Fourth Estate) is a Hampstead novel, even though it is set in Notting Hill Gate. Levy thinks that in 1997 the judges again demonstrated "the consistent liking of Booker juries for body fluids—snot, blood,

vomit—and for scabs." Childhood sexual abuse often features in shortlisted novels, too.

The 1997 Booker judges may have been misguided in choosing a dull group of six novels or in overlooking more deserving books; but they must be given credit for daring in choosing new authors. Two of the six shortlisted books were their authors' first works; and St. John, almost completely unheard-of, has been publishing fiction only since 1993. Moreover, nobody on the list had ever been nominated for the Booker Prize before. In 1996, by contrast, three of the five shortlisted authors, including the eventual winner, had been nominated before.

The God of Small Things is a first novel, written by a woman who in many ways is not even a writer—aside from this novice effort, her field is architecture. The other first novel is Mick Jackson's *The Underground Man* (London: Picador; New York: Morrow), a "fictionalization" of the oddities of John Cavendish Bentinck-Scott, the fifth Duke of Portland, a genuine Victorian eccentric. He had an impressive system of tunnels dug beneath his estate in Nottinghamshire, to which he used to descend by various lifts and in which he used to career around in a carriage, either to visit the further reaches of his property or just for fun.

The novel consists of imagined passages from his Grace's journal interleaved with accounts by his servants, architects, and others who can comment on his behavior, including rumormongers who know nothing about him. The novel records his increasing weirdness: he takes to midnight frolics, naked, in a part of his estate called the Wilderness; he is increasingly troubled by a dream of his drowned twin brother; and he develops delusions. Near the end he writes:

> After a minute a rough piece of paper appeared under my door with, *Is Your Grace ill?* scribbled on it in pencil. "Not at all," I whispered at the door.
> Another note. *Then why does Your Grace hide away?*
> There was no satisfactory way of answering this last question, so I let the tight, round silence speak for itself, and after a minute or two he left me alone.
> Well, I have my voices to be getting along with. I find that if I come within twenty yards of another mortal their thoughts tend to interfere with my own. Yesterday I heard a farmer in Derbyshire complaining about his dinner. "This meat is too tough," he said.

This is a really promising topic, but Jackson has not done enough with it. Though the ending is sad, the story of an extreme eccentric who has enough money to indulge his eccentricities ought to be good for more humor than the little bits of amusement Jackson gets out of this. This is a completely worthy but minor work.

Madeleine St. John's *The Essence of the Thing* (London: Fourth Estate) is easily the most trifling of these books. The title comes from this reflection on marmalade: "The balance between bitter and sweet was the essence of the thing." In this story of love problems among young Londoners, Nicola comes back to their shared flat to be told, coldly, by her lover Jonathan that he no longer loves her and she should move out. The working out of this situation makes up the book. She is inconsolable; her friends commiserate with her and tell her Jonathan is a bastard; and both sets of parents are dumbfounded. She gets her life together, develops independence, slugs Jonathan, finds another flat, even lands a good job at the other end of the country; at the end Jonathan is, somehow, transformed (like Torvald Helmer in Henrik Ibsen's *A Doll's House,* 1879) and clearly wants her back. But nothing doing.

Reviewers commented on the banality and pointlessness of this little book and its obviousness. We might also note its predictability; the desperately brittle dialogue of the choral couples who discuss Nicola and Jonathan's breakup; the pointless rearrangement of chronology; and the sheer bad writing. Almost the most frequently used word is *alright,* which is not a word, and the analysis rises, or descends, to this sort of thing: "He was no longer the lover, comrade, companion she had known, but a frighteningly unreckonable creature as of faery." St. John may be the most interesting *novelist*–in her fifties, she published her first book in 1993; she is Australian and reclusive; she reportedly had a mysterious affair with an American academic–but hers is the least interesting novel.

Turning to the experienced authors, we find Tim Parks's *Europa* (London: Secker and Warburg). Jerry Marlow, an Englishman teaching English in Italy, abandons his family the night before his daughter's eighteenth birthday to join a busload of other foreign lecturers who are on their way to Strasbourg to lobby the European parliament about keeping their jobs. Jerry does not feel strongly about this, rather acknowledges they are underworked and overpaid, but has a feeling of solidarity. He feels sorry for Vikram Griffiths, the rather ridiculous Welsh-Indian leader of the group. Moreover, his former mistress is on the bus too, and he goes along to be with her, to spy on her, to make himself jealous about her (at one point fantasizing that she is having an affair with his daughter, more often tormenting himself with the knowledge that she sleeps with Georg, another of the foreign lecturers, also on the bus), even hoping to reunite with her. Furthermore, the bus is full of young Italians, most of them girls, and is referred to by other lecturers as "the shag-wagon." This is a sort of Euro-novel, moving across borderless states into the heart of the "European community." It is amply skeptical about that organization. This passage gives the flavor of Parks's sometimes tumultuous prose:

> When Vikram Griffiths begins to speak, the girl in the seat in front of me, whose great brown eyes are of course like those of a million other Italian girls, not to mention Spanish and Greek and doubtless other races too, by which I mean to say, unique, splendid, eminently replaceable, swivels on her seat to pay attention, and what I'm telling myself now, slightly right of centre in the back seat of this packed coach, assailed by Vikram Griffiths' efficiently amplified, demotic voice, what I'm telling myself is that I truly am in this now, in this coach I mean, like it or not, for twelve hours and then the two nights in Strasbourg and then twelve hours in the coach again on the way back, not to mention the danger that it could well be more than twelve hours, depending on traffic and circumstances beyond your control. . . .

Vikram Griffiths ends up hanging himself. Jerry thinks of finding work with the European parliament. He calls his daughter. This novel is all, or almost all, atmosphere and character and situation (hopeless love, self-loathing, acting against one's own interests) and not much about plot.

Parks lives in Italy and works as a teacher and translator in addition to writing fiction and nonfiction books about Italy. He has won the Somerset Maugham Award, the Betty Trask Award, and the John Llewellyn Rhys Memorial Prize. He is an established name, though never nominated for the Booker before. In Jerry Marlow he has created an unlikable protagonist who cannot be bothered to learn the names of the Italian girls but refers to them as various different kinds of "tottie"–Opera-tottie, Sneaky-tottie, Plottie-tottie, Tittie-tottie.

As well as being the betting favorite, Bernard MacLaverty's *Grace Notes* was the best book on the shortlist. It is a sensitive study of artistic creation, family tensions, and Irish history in the person of Catherine McKenna. She is the daughter of a publican in a town near Belfast. A Catholic, she has grown up among sectarian troubles; hearing the Protestants pound their giant, Lambeg drums, apparently a peculiarly Protestant instrument, on the anniversary of the Battle of Boyne–described contemptuously by her father as a form of mindless fanaticism–makes a great impression on her. As the novel opens, she has come home for her father's funeral. Clearly she is estranged from her mother; it gradually comes out that she has a daughter whom her mother knows nothing about. She has lost her faith, lost her family connection, and somewhat given up her music. She was a prizewinning composition student, given a prize for study in Glasgow, and sent to Kiev for study with an older composer. Part one ends.

Part two takes place more than a year earlier; in it Catherine is living with loutish Dave on a Scottish island and is pregnant. She goes to Glasgow and has the baby, returns, and eventually leaves Dave, who is irresponsible and a drunkard. She composes a mass, incorporating the Lambeg drums of her childhood, which is played over the BBC radio: and this is her triumph.

There is beautiful writing in *Grace Notes,* especially sensitive about art. Catherine is thinking about her mass:

Cre
Do
In
Un
Um
De
Um

Seven in all. That was her. A mythic number. Seven little claps in all. Catherine Anne McKenna. Mysterious. The first voice like a precentor. Followed by others, each of whom is a precentor to the rest. Grace notes—notes which were neither one thing nor the other. A note between the notes. Notes that occurred outside time.

The attitude toward the Troubles is complicated; the automatic Catholic sympathies of Catherine McKenna's family are undermined by the violence of the IRA bombing campaign.

One sly reviewer noted that MacLaverty has not published a novel since 1983 and found it unsurprising that the novel was about the difficulties of artistic creation. Still, if not a *great* novel, it is nevertheless a very good one, and Booker-worthy.

Jim Crace's *Quarantine* is this year's historical—or biblical—pastiche, though it is not done in a meretricious or exploitative way. Showing considerable research, it is set in Judea in the first century and includes Jesus Christ as a character. This is an ambitious undertaking, and Crace succeeds in it well. He is an original writer whose previous works have demonstrated his versatility; *Continent,* published in 1987, was a series of interlinking stories based on—or creating—an imaginary geography. Opinions sharply divided on *Quarantine.* Eileen

Battersby, in the *Irish Times,* declared that "*Quarantine* should win this, and so justify Booker if only by introducing this fine writer to a wider, new audience"; while Paul Levy commented more coolly that it "tells us a good deal about surviving in the desert, Semitic languages, primitive weaving and trading practices."

The 1997 Booker Prize–winner, Arundhati Roy's *The God of Small Things,* was referred to by one caustic reviewer as "this year's identikit Indian novel." This is unfair, perhaps, though it is easy to see why reviewers might say so. From the announcement of the list there was excited discussion of Roy's chances, and she became surrounded by an enormous cocoon of extraliterary fact and fancy. It is a fact that she is a beautiful woman, in a way exotic by British standards if not to Indians; a Christian from the state of Kerala in India, she is a practicing architect and screenwriter who had never written fiction before. In interviews she demurred at comparisons with other writers and insisted that she is so poorly read that she writes outside of traditions. The story of the English publisher who read the manuscript and flew out to India immediately, *without getting his vaccinations,* to sign her to a contract emphasized the importance of this book.

Then there was the persecution of her book by intolerant clerics—so reminiscent of the troubles Salman Rushdie's 1988 shortlisted *The Satanic Verses* endured from militant Shiites. Roy's novel turns on an illicit sexual affair between a middle-class Christian woman and an Untouchable, and thus, for zealous defenders of the caste system (which ostensibly has not existed since Gandhi's time but for many people obviously still does), it violates all sorts of sexual, political, and religious laws. Roy is being prosecuted in an Indian court for her offense.

I think Roy succeeded at least in part because in 1995 Rushdie's *The Moor's Last Sigh* made the shortlist but missed the prize, and in 1996 the same happened to Rohinton Mistry's *A Fine Balance.* That these two books were the best candidates in their year may have created an Indian momentum, or a compensatory decision, even though they are both also much better than *The God of Small Things.*

But what is the book like? It is the somewhat fragmented account of the lives of Indian-Christian twins, Rahel and Estha, whose lives, and that of their mother, are clearly blighted by something bad that happened in their childhood. The circling around this traumatic event (though we know from almost the beginning of the book that it is the death of their cousin Sophie Mol, we do not know how it happened) and the related adult event of their mother's disgraceful love for a forbidden man make up the swirling narrative of the novel.

Though it is engaging enough, *The God of Small Things* is troublingly amateurish in various ways. One of these is its typographical archness: "A few mornings ago she had opened her window (for a Breath of Fresh Air) and caught them red-handed in the act of Returning From Somewhere"; "Their prer NUN sea ayshun was perfect." Related to these is a sort of imperfectly committed or partially realized magic realism:

> Ammu was asleep and looked beautiful in the barred-blue streetlight that came in through the barred-blue window. She smiled a sleepsmile that dreamed of dolphins and a deep barred blue. It was a smile that gave no indication that the person who belonged to it was a bomb waiting to go off.
>
> Estha Alone walked heavily to the bathroom. He vomited a clear, bitter, lemony, sparkling, fizzy liquid. The acrid aftertaste of a Little Man's first encounter with Fear. Dum dum.

> He felt a little better. He put on his shoes and walked out of his room, laces trailing, down the corridor, and stood quietly outside Rahel's door.
>
> Rahel stood on a chair and unlatched the door for him.
>
> Chacko didn't bother to wonder how she could possibly have known that Estha was at the door. He was used to their sometimes strangeness.

Nevertheless, alongside its story of a tragic misalliance there is considerable good writing about India, and a part of its geography and culture less familiar to westerners than the Bombay of Rushdie and Mistry. It is worth noting that Roy's novel began 1998 as the fifth highest-selling hardback novel in Britain (no other shortlisted book appears on the bestseller list), so the buyers are endorsing the Booker judgment. And, like most human enterprises, the Booker Prize arises out of a mixture of motives; it is not just about art but about discussion of fiction (hence, controversy), publicizing authors, and selling books.

Louisiana State University Press

Kristin Bryan
Louisiana State University Press

Founded in 1935, Louisiana State University Press, one of the oldest and most prestigious publishing houses in the South, is a nonprofit organization committed to the publication of scholarly and general-interest books. The professional and support staff of the press, some thirty-five members, is dedicated to acquiring, editing, producing, and marketing books of enduring significance. Governing the press imprint is an editorial board appointed from the faculty. As the publishing branch of Louisiana State University, the press is a partner in LSU's educational and cultural pursuits.

Widely regarded as the preeminent source of books about the South–its history, its literature, its politics, its culture–LSU Press publishes some eighty books each year and has more than one thousand titles in print. The press's editorial program focuses on the humanities and social sciences, with special consideration placed on Southern history and literature. Its backlist includes such distinguished names as C. Vann Woodward, John Hope Franklin, and Dan Carter in history, and Cleanth Brooks, Louis D. Rubin Jr., and Lewis P. Simpson in literary studies; but the press is also proud of its role in publishing younger scholars who promise to be leading figures of the next generation.

In addition to its emphasis on Southern subjects, the press is strongly committed to excellence in other areas. Particularly notable is the poetry program, which produces twelve new volumes a year and is one of the largest and most critically acclaimed in the country. LSU Press is also celebrated for its work in the fields of political science, African American history, Latin American studies, and music.

The press also publishes important books about Louisiana and the Gulf region. Various aspects of the state's history and culture, as well as its considerable natural gifts–wildflowers, birds, mammals–have been effectively and handsomely treated under the LSU Press imprint. This strong emphasis on regional publishing was established by Marcus M. Wilkerson, the first director of the press. It was under Wilkerson's leadership that the press set off in the direction it still in many ways follows today.

Three major ventures that have proved of great importance to the press and the scholarly community were initiated during the years of Wilkerson's directorship (1935 to 1953). Established in 1938, the Southern Biography series includes such notable titles as *Mary Boykin Chesnut* (1981), by Elisabeth Muhlenfeld; *James Henry Hammond and the Old South: A Design for Mastery* (1982), by Drew Gilpin Faust; and *Breckinridge: Statesman, Soldier Symbol* (1992), by William C. Davis. Edited by Wendell Holmes Stephenson and Fred C. Cole in its early years, T. Harry Williams in the 1950s, 1960s, and 1970s, and then William J. Cooper Jr., this celebrated series has been published since 1995 under the leadership of Southern historian Bertram Wyatt-Brown.

Another of Wilkerson's successes was the arrangement with the Littlefield Fund for Southern History that made LSU Press publisher of the multivolume *A History of the South* (1947–). Written by prominent scholars such as Woodward, Charles W. Sydnor, E. Merton Coulter, George Brown Tindall, and Numan V. Bartley, the ten volumes published in the series to date (with volume two still to come) are an indispensable guide to the history of the region.

Also during Wilkerson's tenure, works resulting from the Walter Lynwood Fleming Lectures in Southern History began appearing on LSU Press publication lists. Inaugurated by the LSU history department in 1937, the Fleming Lectures bring a distinguished historian to the university every year to present three lectures on some aspect of Southern history. LSU Press has published, usually in revised and expanded form, thirty-three sets of Fleming Lectures, including John Hope Franklin's *A Southern Odyssey: Travelers in the Antebellum North* (1976), Frank L. Owsley's *Plain Folk of the Old South* (1982), and James M. McPherson's *What They Fought For, 1861–1865* (1994). Other historians published in the series include Avery O. Craven, David M. Potter, Eugene D. Genovese, Don E. Fehrenbacher, Drew

*L. E. Phillabaum, director of Louisiana State
University Press*

Gilpin Faust, James Axtell, Eric Foner, and Woodward.

Donald R. Ellegood, who served as director from 1954 to 1963, added many distinguished titles to the press's list. Shortly after his arrival at LSU Press, Ellegood met the political philosopher Eric Voegelin, who was then a member of the LSU faculty, and established the press's role as the primary publisher of Voegelin's work, including the five-volume *Order and History* (1956–1987), and of his *Collected Works* (now in process).

During this time the historian T. Harry Williams published two books on Confederate general P. G. T. Beauregard with the press and also became an active supporter and adviser. Woodward's famed *The Burden of Southern History* (1960) originated as a result of Ellegood's proposal to Woodward that the press publish a collection of his essays. A list in jazz history was initiated; some textbooks were developed; and the press ventured briefly into the publication of phonograph recordings with a collection of folklore prepared by Harry Oster. Ellegood also cultivated projects in the fields of geography, political science, and recent history so the press could engage issues of contemporary concern in the national and international arenas.

In 1963, when Ellegood left for the University of Washington Press, Richard L. Wentworth was promoted to the directorship. Wentworth made several notable contributions to the press. He established the Southern Literary Studies series in 1965. Edited for twenty-eight years by Rubin, and now by Fred Hobson, this renowned series explores the richness of Southern letters from colonial times to the present. It includes works by eminent critics, such as C. Hugh Holman, Andrew Lytle, and Thomas Daniel Young, about the most influential figures in Southern literature, among them Walker Percy, Robert Penn Warren, Kate Chopin, Allen Tate, Eudora Welty, and William Faulkner.

Created in 1968, the Library of Southern Civilization, in the words of its editor, Lewis P. Simpson, "was conceived as a scholarly response to the idea of the South as a civilization, especially as this idea is expressed in historical and literary records either not heretofore published or no longer easily available." The first title to appear in the series, *Twelve Years a Slave* (1968), by Solomon Northup, one of the press's best-sellers, exemplifies its commitment to publishing valuable firsthand sources of enduring historical importance. Other classic works in this vital series include *Brokenburn: The Journal of Kate Stone, 1861–1868* (1972) and new editions of the Agrarian manifesto *I'll Take My Stand* (1977); *Lanterns on the Levee: Recollections of a Planter's Son* (1974), by William Alexander Percy; and *Swallow Barn; or, A Sojourn in the Old Dominion* (1986), by John Pendleton Kennedy. In 1965 LSU Press was chosen by the Jefferson Davis Association to publish a definitive multivolume edition of the Confederate president's personal and official papers. Wentworth persuaded Potter to compile his most significant essays about the South, published in 1968 as *The South and Sectional Conflict*. He also acquired, while it was still a dissertation, Dan T. Carter's *Scottsboro: A Tragedy of the American South* (1979), winner of the Bancroft Prize in History.

Another significant contribution made during this period was the institution, in 1966, of the Louisiana Paperbacks series, making LSU Press the first paperback publisher in the South. Another important decision that would have a lasting impact was the creation of the poetry program in 1964.

When Wentworth moved on to the University of Illinois Press in 1970, Charles East was named director. East added to the press's already distinguished reputation with the publication of Thomas Lawrence Connelly's superb two-volume history of the Army of Tennessee, *Army of the Heartland* (1967) and *Autumn of Glory* (1971); *The Diary of Edmund Ruffin* (1972–1989), in three volumes; and A. J. Liebling's colorful *The Earl of Louisiana* (1970). He also continued the publication of original poetry and short fiction and initiated the Louisiana Bicentennial Reprint Series.

East resigned in 1975 to devote his attention to editing and writing. The current director, Leslie E. Phillabaum, succeeded East with several clearly defined goals. He resolved to expand the list to at least fifty titles per year and to increase the sales volume to a million dollars, and in just over five years he met these objectives. In 1982 he moved the press offices from Hill Memorial Library, which it had occupied for more than twenty years, to the newly renovated French House.

Another early goal that Phillabaum pursued was the enhancement of the press's national image. He proudly acknowledges that he began with a winner; the press had long been recognized as a leading Southern publisher. But he now wanted the press to be recognized as the best publisher in the South and as one of the major publishers in the nation. Toward that end, he has sought to broaden the overall focus of the press's program while maintaining and strengthening its core.

The press has indeed achieved national, even international, stature. LSU Press books have been awarded prestigious prizes (over one hundred in the last fifteen years), including three Bancroft Prizes, two Avery O. Craven Awards of the Organization of American Historians, five Charles S. Sydnor Awards of the Southern Historical Association, two Fletcher Pratt Literary Awards of the New York Civil War Round Table, ten Roanoke-Chowan Awards for Poetry, and four Lamont Poetry Selections of the Academy of American Poets. Since 1981 LSU Press publications have been the recipients of a National Book Award for Poetry (and have been finalists on three other occasions) and three Pulitzer Prizes—one for fiction, for *A Confederacy of Dunces* (1980), by John Kennedy Toole; and two for poetry, for *The Flying Change* (1985), by Henry Taylor, and *Alive Together* (1996), by Lisel Mueller. The press itself has earned several accolades for its publishing program, including a Carey-Thomas Honor Citation from *Publishers Weekly* for creative publishing and an American Association of State and Local History Award of Merit.

In the Phillabaum years LSU Press, while expanding the scope of its established series, has also instituted several new ones to reflect the diversity of its growing list. The Pegasus Prize for Literature was established by Mobil Corporation to introduce readers to distinguished works of fiction from nations whose literatures are rarely translated into English. Since 1980 LSU Press has published translations of the prizewinning volumes. Denmark, the Ivory Coast, Indonesia, Turkey, and Portugal are some of the countries whose novelists have been acknowledged by the Pegasus committee. The work of the Netherlands' Cees Nooteboom is now widely published in English as a result of the prize; *The Year of the Frog* (1993), by Martin Simecka of the Slovak Republic, received a *Los Angeles Times* Book Prize in

Dust jacket for the surprise best-selling novel and Pulitzer Prize winner published by the press in 1980

1994; and New Zealander Keri Hulme's *The Bone People* (1985) won the British Booker Prize in 1985.

The Miller Center Series on the American Presidency, launched in 1981 under the editorship of Kenneth W. Thompson and James Sterling Young and supported by the White Burkett Miller Center for Public Affairs at the University of Virginia, consists of analytic works on the presidency. Titles in the series include Thompson's *The President and the Public Philosophy* (1981), Don K. Price's *America's Unwritten Constitution: Science, Religion, and Political Responsibility* (1983), and Erwin C. Hargrove's *Jimmy Carter as President: Leadership and the Politics of the Public Good* (1988).

The aim of the Political Traditions in Foreign Policy series, also edited by Thompson, is the restoration of philosophical and historical thought to the study of politics and international relations. Introduced in 1985 with the publication of *Toynbee's Philosophy of World History and Politics*, by Thompson, and *Foreign Policy in the Early Republic: The Law of Nations and the Balance of Power*, by Daniel G. Lang, the volumes in this series attempt to formulate a unifying body of theory on foreign policy.

In the late 1980s and early 1990s the Eisenhower Center at the University of New Orleans regularly held conferences on world issues and sponsored oral history projects on this century's wars. Books resulting from these ventures are published in the Eisenhower Center Studies on War and Peace, edited by Stephen E. Ambrose and Günter Bischof. *Voices of D-Day: The Story of the Allied Invasion, Told by Those Who Were There* (1994), edited by Ronald J. Drez, and *The Pacific War Revisited* (1997), edited by Bischof and Robert L. Dupont, are two of the titles published since the series' 1992 inception. Under the directorship of Douglas Brinkley, the center's activities and publications have broadened in scope. The new Eisenhower Center for American Studies has given rise to such titles as *YA/YA!: Young New Orleans Artists and Their Storytelling Chairs (And How to Ya/Ya in Your Neighborhood)* (1996), by Claudia Barker.

One of the more-popular recent additions to the press's program has been Voices of the South, a series whose purpose is to reissue previously out-of-print works, primarily fiction, by the South's finest writers. Authors published in the series to date include many of the leading writers of the twentieth-century South, such as Lee Smith, Fred Chappell, Elizabeth Spencer, Ellen Douglas, Peter Taylor, Warren, Evelyn Scott, Shirley Ann Grau, George Garrett, and Willie Morris. Introduced in 1994, the Modernist Studies series, edited by Rima Drell Reck, offers innovative works from a wide range of interrelated fields, such as literature, art history, architecture, photography, urbanism, and cultural anthropology. The first title in the series was John G. Hutton's amply illustrated *Neo-Impressionism and the Search for Solid Ground: Art, Science, and Anarchism in Fin-de-Siècle France*, followed by Marja Warehime's *Brassaï: Images of Culture and the Surrealist Observer* (1996) and Donald Pizer's *American Expatriate Writing and the Paris Moment: Modernism and Place* (1996).

In 1996, with its poetry program at a critical and commercial peak, the press announced its Southern Messenger Poets series. Edited by Dave Smith, this new series of works by natives of, or transplants to, the South already boasts the work of T. R. Hummer, James Seay, Claudia Emerson Andrews, and Reginald Gibbons. An active supporter of American poetry for more than thirty years, LSU Press publishes distinguished contemporary poets, among them James Applewhite, Chappell, Kelly Cherry, Brendan Galvin, Margaret Gibson, Susan Ludvigson, Lisel Mueller, Marilyn Nelson, David R. Slavitt, Dabney Stuart, Henry Taylor, and Garrett. The press also publishes the winner of the Walt Whitman Award of The Academy of American Poets, which is given annually to an American poet for a first collection. Previous winners include Alison Hawthorne Deming, Nicole Cooley, Joshua Clover, and Barbara Ras.

Horizons in Theory and American Culture, edited by Bainard Cowan and Joseph G. Kronick, explores the dimensions of theory in American literature and culture and emphasizes the interdisciplinary nature of literary studies. Other series established during this productive time were the Pennington Center Nutrition series and the T. Harry Williams Center for Oral History series.

A new multidisciplinary series from the press, Conflicting Worlds: New Dimensions of the American Civil War, edited by T. Michael Parrish, will include works that explore the Civil War era in the most creative and expansive ways possible. Among the first titles that will be published in this series are *Lincoln and Davis* by Kenneth H. Williams; *Service, Hardships, Battle, and Defeat: A Reassessment of War and the Confederate Soldier* by Carl H. Moneyhon; and *A Black Patriot and a White Priest: Race, Religion, and Radicalism in the Civil War* by Stephen J. Ochs.

LSU Press is one of the largest and most successful publishers of books on the Civil War, with more than one hundred titles on the subject in print. Classic titles such as Ezra J. Warner's *Generals in Gray: Lives of the Confederate Commanders* (1959) and *Generals in Blue: Lives of the Union Commanders* (1964), Bell Irvin Wiley's *The Life of Johnny Reb: The Common Soldier of the Confederacy* (1994) and *The Life of Billy Yank: The Common Soldier of the Union* (1994), and Stephen Z. Starr's three-volume *The Union Cavalry in the Civil War* (1979–1985) are popular in the North and the South, in the United States and abroad.

Another prominent element of the press's list is African American history. In the last two decades distinguished historians such as John Hope Franklin, Eric Foner, Eugene D. Genovese, Gwendolyn Midlo Hall, David Blight, and Winthrop D. Jordan have produced major works in this field with LSU Press. In 1997 the press published *My Life and an Era: The Autobiography of an African American Lawyer in Early Oklahoma*, by Buck Colbert Franklin, John Hope Franklin's pioneering father, and a paperback edition of Carl T. Rowan's *South of Freedom*, the classic account of his journey through the South during the summer of 1951. Biographies of many important African Americans—including Marcus Garvey (1985), Archibald Grimké (1993), Carter G. Woodson (1993), and A. Philip Randolph (1996)—have been published by the press, along with penetrating examinations of significant events in the history of race relations, such as *Death in a Promised Land: The Tulsa Race Riot of 1921* (1992), by Scott Ellsworth, and *Anatomy of a Lynching: The Killing of Claude Neal* (1992), by James R. McGovern. The press also publishes significant work by and about black literary figures such as Nella Larsen, Claude McKay, Jean Toomer, Toni Morrison, and Ernest Gaines. *A History of Afro-American Literature: The Long Beginning, 1746–1895,* by Blyden Jackson, came out in 1989, prompting one critic to declare it a "masterwork of literary scholarship."

The press's commitment to literary studies has been strong since its first decade, when titles by Brooks, Warren, Kenneth Burke, and Robert Heilman appeared under its imprint. A major achievement in the press's literary program was the publication in 1990 of *The History of Southern Literature,* coedited by Rubin, Simpson, Thomas Daniel Young, Blyden Jackson, and Rayburn Moore, the consummate single-volume reference book on literature from the American South. The press has not neglected, however, the study of national and international literatures. Its list is notable for important critical studies of writers as diverse as Henry James, Walt Whitman, Ford Madox Ford, Virginia Woolf, Wallace Stevens, and William Carlos Williams.

Abundant in nature, culture, and history, Louisiana is a rich resource for valuable publishing projects, and LSU Press has successfully tapped into that resource over the years, particularly with its illustrated books. Photographer David King Gleason's *Plantation Homes of Louisiana and the Natchez Area* (1982) reveals, through 120 full-color photographs, the beauty and grandeur of these

monuments from a lost era. *The Gulf Coast: Where Land Meets Sea* (1984), by the wildlife photographer C. C. Lockwood, offers a splendid pictorial representation of the natural wonders available to Louisianans via the coastline; *Discovering Louisiana* (1986), also by Lockwood, is a paean to the state's diverse habitats, from the hills and piney woods in the north to the thousands of miles of shoreline in the south. Neil Johnson's *Louisiana Journey* (1997) is a visual exploration of the state. With 150 black-and-white photographs, *Elysium—A Gathering of Souls* (1997), by Sandra Russell Clark, evokes the mood of New Orleans cemeteries. Randolph Delehanty's *Art in the American South* (1996), an illustrated chronicle of the South's visual legacy, is a showcase of 250 works from the vast collection of New Orleans entrepreneur Roger Ogden. A full-color celebration of Louisiana music is on display in photographer Philip Gould's *Cajun Music and Zydeco* (1992).

Nearing its sixty-fifth year of excellence in publishing, LSU Press continues to expand in interesting directions. The year 1997 was one of the most exciting in the press's lively history: *Intimate Enemies,* by Christina Vella, landed on the front page of *The New York Times Book Review*; Marilyn Nelson's *The Fields of Praise* was selected as one of the five finalists for the National Book Award in Poetry; and Mueller won the Pulitzer Prize in Poetry for *Alive Together.*

Perhaps author and historian C. Vann Woodward had much of this impressive history in mind when he said, "LSU Press has maintained a level of quality and good work that has made it one of the outstanding presses in the nation and the best in the South."

John Updike on the Internet

Charles Brower

John Updike became, as he put it, an "elderly white-haired writer gingerly stepping out into cyberspace, whatever that is." Accepting an invitation from Amazon.com, the Internet's largest bookseller, Updike contributed the first paragraph of a story titled "Murder Makes the Magazine" to appear on Amazon's website. Each day for six weeks a paragraph was added from submissions by Internet users, with each selected contributor receiving a prize of $1,000. Updike would provide the concluding paragraph. To sweeten the pot each entry, whether selected for inclusion in the story or not, qualified its author for a grand prize of $100,000, to be awarded at the end of the contest. The winner, Dean Routh, was not one of the story's chosen contributors.

The relay-race approach to fiction writing is not new. In the 1930s a group of writers composed mysteries under the collective byline of "the Detection Club." In 1969 the novel *Naked Came the Stranger* proved to be a best-seller once it was revealed that its author, "Penelope Ashe," was actually a pseudonym, a prank perpetrated by twenty writers. More recently, Carl Hiaasen, Elmore Leonard, James W. Hall, and other Florida writers teamed to write the best-selling *Naked Came the Manatee* (1996), a parody of the Detection Club mysteries. But the Internet added a new dimension to this literary form, greatly multiplying the speed with which entries could be submitted from around the globe, as well as the number of potential participants with more or less instant access to the contest. By the end of the contest Amazon had received more than 360,000 entries.

Some critics questioned why Updike was willing to participate in this venture on Amazon's behalf when the author himself was barely familiar with the new realm of cyberspace. He does own a computer that he uses for reviews and shorter writing, but he prefers composing on typewriters: "The difficulty of making corrections focuses your attention in a healthy way." He has no fax line or access to the Internet. He sent the first installment of the story to Amazon by U.S. Mail. In *The New York Times* on 2

August Mel Gussow speculated that "undoubtedly he is being paid a sizable advance" for his participation in the endeavor; Updike told *USA Today* that he received $5,000, about as much as he would make for a story appearing in *The New Yorker*. Yet Updike, whose postnuclear fantasy *Toward the End of Time* (composed with pad and pencil) also appeared in 1997, likely benefited from the worldwide media attention "Murder Makes the Magazine" received: "This has gotten more ink than my last six books."

Updike told *The New Yorker* in August 1997, he began "Murder Makes the Magazine" in 1960, intending the story as a "whimsical report from the interior" of *The New Yorker* itself. But in part because of his uneasiness over even a frivolous betrayal of that magazine's legendary circumspection, he abandoned the effort after thirteen pages, and the fragment lay in his files for nearly forty years. When Amazon approached him, Updike gave the fate of his protagonist, Miss Tasso Polk, middle-aged editor at "The Magazine," over to forty-four fellow contributors. The winning entries were judged by a panel of six editors selected by Amazon, according to Updike "the real narrative artists" of the story, whose daily task was to sift through the myriad potential plot directions. In the first week alone they were flooded with more than eighty thousand entries. The resulting story is a freewheeling, almost coherent combination of murder, secret chambers, hypnotism, and catnapping.

Updike's opening might not rank with his best material, but it proved to be a fruitful inspiration to his on-line collaborators:

Miss Tasso Polk at ten-ten alighted onto the olive tiles of the nineteenth floor only lightly nagged by the sense of something wrong. The Magazine's crest, that great black M, the thing masculine that had most impressed her life, echoed from its inlaid security the thoughtful humming in her mind: 'm.' There had been someone strange in the elevator. She had felt it all the way up. Strange, not merely unknown to her personally. Most of the world was unknown to her personally, but it was not strange. The men in little felt hats and oxblood shoes who performed services of salesmanship and accountancy and research and coordination for the firms

(Simplex, Happitex, Technonitrex, Instant-Pix) that occupied the seventeen floors beneath the sacred olive groves of The Magazine were anonymous and interchangeable to her but not strange. She could read right through the button-down collars of their unstarched shirts into the ugly neck-stretching of their morning shaves, right through the pink and watery whites of their eyes into last night's cocktail party in Westchester, Tarrytown, Rye, or Orange, right through their freckled, soft, too-broad-and-brown hands into adulterous caresses that did not much disgust her, they were so distant and trivial and even, in their suburban distance from her, idyllic, like something satyrs do on vases. Miss Polk was forty-three, and had given herself to The Magazine in the flower of her beauty. Since the day, a nervous bride, when she had been led to a desk in whose center was set a bouquet of sharpened pencils in a water glass, she had ridden the elevator two dozen thousand times.

In the hands of Updike's subsequent co-authors Miss Polk's insulated life quickly takes a change for the mysterious, although the stranger in the elevator is shelved for the time being. Miss Polk finds in her office a message from her eccentric Uncle James, world traveler and self-proclaimed descendant of James K. Polk. Unlike the girls in the typing pool, Miss Polk doesn't return personal calls on company time. But again her spinsterish reflections are interrupted, this time by the entrance of The Magazine's editor, Mr. Evermore, who is not only Miss Polk's mentor but also was for a brief time her lover. (Miss Polk's feelings toward Evermore tend to become a little unfocused as the story progresses, floating somewhere between still-smoldering passion, sentimentality, and utter loathing.) Before Evermore can share a piece of dire news, he's interrupted by the ringing of the phone, and a strange voice warns Miss Polk that Evermore can't be trusted. Evermore tells Miss Polk that Marion Hyde Merriweather, the owner of The Magazine, has committed suicide and left ownership of The Magazine in dispute. But the phone call and a note from Merriweather she discovers in her desk leave Miss Polk wondering if she can trust Evermore.

Complications proliferate as Miss Polk decides to investigate the mystery herself. She attempts to contact her Uncle James, whose penchant for quoting Euripides is introduced at this point and run with by various contributors to the story. At Merriweather's mansion the strange man from the elevator finally reappears. As Miss Polk follows, he enters the house from the back, goes to the dead man's library, and takes a volume of Poe from the shelf. Inside the house Miss Polk meets Evermore again. As it turns out, Evermore knows the stranger: he is Franklin Boyce, cofounder with Merriweather of

The Magazine and the man to whom ownership is to revert should Merriweather die intestate.

Leaving the two men to a suspiciously chummy reunion, Miss Polk goes off to find Merriweather's cat, who leads her to a hidden VCR and a taped message from Merriweather. Soon Miss Polk finds herself hypnotized, and she is confronted with the entire ring of conspirators—Evermore, Boyce, her Uncle James, and, most surprisingly, Marion Merriweather himself, who had faked his suicide. They have made Miss Polk their pawn in a complicated scheme (so complicated the exact motive is never clear) to boost The Magazine's circulation. Further, she learns upon awakening from her trance that someone (Merriweather?) also intends to frame the despised Evermore for Merriweather's murder. By now Miss Polk is understandably confused. As she leaves the mansion, "night fell and the city quieted." Allowing even for daylight saving time, Miss Polk was in the mansion musing over Poe an awfully long time, and the reader can only wonder about the whereabouts of the "various reporters, police officers, and curious neighbors" who had been there when she arrived. But as Updike generously observed in *The New Yorker*, "of course there were inconsistencies, which occur even with a single writer."

Miss Polk returns home to find that her cats, Helen and Menelaus, are missing although Merriweather's cat Mauser is there; he bears a note instructing her to return to the Karleton Hotel, site of her youthful indiscretion with Evermore. There she sees Merriweather, who the world still believes is dead. (Perhaps no one recognizes him because now he has a "bulky form," while before he was described as bony and Howard Hughes–like.) No matter, because by the time Miss Polk can make it to the seventh floor Merriweather really is dead. The killer would seem to be Evermore, but Uncle James and Boyce soon prove to be on hand, as well. They all want a key that Merriweather had included in the note he sent to Miss Polk, which, it turns out, opens a safety-deposit box containing the entire worth of The Magazine's pension fund in bars of platinum. In a slyly self-deprecating passage, Boyce reveals that The Magazine had fallen on hard times because "all those people that used to pore over its scrupulously edited, fact-packed pages now cruise the Internet, communicating interactively with a world of electronic buddies. Print has become a mug's game." As Miss Polk's payoff in the scheme, Boyce offers her editorship of The Magazine, to which she responds, "The Godhead fires, the Soul attains, huh?" She promises to think about it, but really only wants her cats back. The platinum is not in the lockbox, Miss Polk realizes, but in "the thick old books in Merriweather's study, under the television set. They seemed uncannily heavy when I handled them." As for the exact circumstances of Merriweather's murder, Miss Polk leaves it to the police to figure out, "along with the other sort of nitpicking detail these blue-uniformed numbskulls were paid to do."

Updike was then left with the daunting task of concluding the tale. As he observed, his on-line collaborators had "served up lots of red herrings. And a lot of male characters, so that my spinster heroine finds herself with this suddenly jammed dance card. . . . When the last entry was in place, I just tried to tie up some of the loose ends and to reward Tasso Polk for her patience." In his concluding submission, posted on 12 September, Updike affirms the value of stability in Miss Polk's life, reminding the reader that all the story's events happened in a single eventful day: "The Magazine, at any rate, would enjoy an infusion of embezzled platinum. The issues would issue forth, mug's game or not. Pencils would be sharpened, spelling would be checked. And tomorrow, at ten-ten—or perhaps, in deference to today's shocks to her accustomed routine, ten-twenty—she would be there." Updike's last contribution to the story came as something of an adventure, "a hair-breadth escape from cyberspace": "As it happened, I was in New York the day my finale came due, and I had to write it on a strange laptop, with a program I didn't know. The screen kept disappearing, or jumping sideways. When I came to print it out, the printer ignored the punctuation. Still, I got it done."

Despite his participation in the endeavor, Updike remained ambivalent about the Internet's literary merits. As he told USA Today, "it doesn't seem terribly real to me. I don't want to be crusty, but to me if it's not in a book, I can't take it fully seriously." Although Internet users are obviously engaged with the written word, the style of writing is "linear and hasty": "the communication that goes on is like telephone calls, only down in print." Yet he professed to be reassured by the number of literary allusions in "Murder Makes the Magazine": to Shakespeare and the classics, to Poe, to the conventions of British drawing-room mysteries. As Updike observed to The New Yorker, "A lot of the mystery takes place, classically, in a library full of old books"—although tellingly hidden behind the books are a television and VCR. In the end, if we can infer from the conclusion he supplied, perhaps Updike considered his foray into cyberspace "a larky thing to do" before returning like Miss Polk to his daily writing routine. When asked if he was considering further on-line collaborations, he replied that he was content to let another author "stick his head into the mouth of the electronic lion."

References:

Mel Gussow, "John Updike, Impresario of Fictional Relay Race," New York Times, 2 August 1997, pp. 14, 16;

Gussow, "Whodunit and Who Wunit: The Plot Quickens," New York Times, 13 September 1997, pp. 16, 19;

Bob Minzesheimer, "Updike in the teeth of technology," USA Today, 11 September 1997, pp. 1D, 2D;

Noah Robischon, "Updike.com: A Novel Effort," Entertainment Weekly, 400 (10 October 1997): 100;

John Updike, "A Writer at Large," New Yorker, 73 (29 September 1997): 31–32.

Author Websites

Robert Weibezahl

Internet proponents, touting its potential as an information resource, claim that sometime in the not-too-distant future everyone from schoolchildren to Ph.D. candidates will be able to tap into the collections of the great libraries of the world without ever leaving the comfortable environs of their ergonomically correct keyboards. While these visionaries may be overlooking possible roadblocks over issues of who owns information and whether it should be disseminated for free when there is the possibility of making a buck off it, there is no denying that the Information Superhighway is here to stay and that it can be used as a powerful research tool.

But the web can be an unwieldy and extremely capricious instrument of knowledge. Anyone who has spent even a little time exploring cyberspace has felt the blade of its double-edged sword—the lure of seemingly endless information on one hand and voracious time consumption on the other. Researching on the web can become a labyrinthine journey as one site leads to another and then another, all of highly uneven quality and, sadly, occasionally of suspect reliability. A web search can lead to many frustrating dead ends or, maybe worse, can become an exercise in procrastination as the web surfer finds him- or herself wandering to unrelated sites that look interesting but have nothing to do with the project at hand. (True, this can happen in a library, too, but the ease of skipping hither and yon on the Internet makes distraction much, much easier.) Also, websites are subject to the whims of their creators, and while those sponsored by legitimate institutions are on the whole useful, it is not the case across the board, and even sites with sterling academic credentials behind them can prove disappointing. For the nonexpert looking for facts, an inaccurate website can be worse than no website at all.

There are thousands of author-related webpages out there, and any search engine can point to information on everything from *Beowulf* to the latest John Grisham work. There are places where you can read the complete texts of classic works, pin down an appropriate quotation, find extensive scholarly bibliographies, obtain an overview—some-times an extensive overview—of an author's life and work, and even chat with others who visit the site and count themselves fans. The sites are maintained by university literature departments, libraries, graduate students, professional societies, and, perhaps most notably, by members of the general public who cannot get enough of an adored writer.

Where does one begin when invited to take a look at the boundless offerings about authors on the web? I limited my search to authors writing in English, and, looking at my final lineup, that has resulted in mostly English and American writers, with a few Irish thrown in for good measure. By attempting to cover a reasonably broad spectrum in period, style, and substance, my selection may seem idiosyncratic, if not wholly subjective. Some of the choices were dictated by what is available and, equally, by what is not. For instance, there are so many on-line sources on Shakespeare that narrowing the field to one or two proved impossible, and a fair look would have been an article in itself. Personal favorites such as Muriel Spark and E. M. Forster yielded nothing of great interest. In recognition of his centenary, I tried to find a webpage on Thorton Wilder and came up with naught. So I settled on websites for twenty-one writers, some who wrote in the eighteenth century, some at work today.

My literary cyber tour begins with William Wordsworth, for no other reason than that he is the focus of an impressive website, *TCG's Wordsworth Page* (http://www.usd.edu/~tgannon/words.html), put together by Thomas C. Gannon. Someone looking for a solid introduction to the English Romantic poet needs to look no further than this site. Gannon provides a short biography of the poet, a listing of the original publication dates of Wordsworth's chief volumes of poetry, an adequate bibliography of secondary sources, and links to related sites. Gannon, a graduate student in English Romantic literature, started the website while earning his master's degree at the University of South Dakota. He claims to be "a true amateur lover of the Sage of Grasmere," and he displays his somewhat irreverent enthusiasm by answering a series of frequently asked questions ranging from "William Who?" and "What's Wordsworth's greatest poem?" to "Isn't a Hollywood movie of Wordsworth's life in the works?" (Gannon's answer: No. But William Hurt is holding his breath.)

One of Gannon's links leads to the *Project Bartleby Archive* (http://www.columbia.edu/acis/bartleby/), a site started by Steven van Leeuwen in 1993 at Columbia University. Bartleby features the complete texts of some thirty-five disparate literary works, all of which have entered into the public domain, including Wordsworth's *Complete Poetical Works,* F. Scott Fitzgerald's *This Side of Paradise,* Agatha Christie's *The Mysterious Affair at Styles,* Eugene O'Neill's *Beyond the Horizon,* Bernard Shaw's *Pygmalion,* and poetry by Edna St. Vincent Millay, D. H. Lawrence, A. E. Housman, W. B. Yeats, and Emily Dickinson. Users can search a word or phrase to find where or how often it appears in a work. *The New Bartleby Library* (http://www.bartleby.com/) is a new site that continues the project although it currently contains only selected works by Theodore Roosevelt.

Given the Jane Austen craze that has descended upon the land, I was not surprised to find a minor deluge of websites devoted to Hampshire's most famous daughter. The best I could find is the *Jane Austen Information Page* (http://www.pemberley.com/janeinfo/janeinfo.html), which was put together by Henry Churchyard, a graduate student at the University of Texas, Austin. It offers a wide selection of information on the author, her writings, and related materials. There is an annotated *Pride and Prejudice* as well as a wide assortment of electronic texts (E-texts) of some of Austen's lesser-known light verse, stories, juvenilia, and incomplete manuscripts. Genealogical charts for the characters in the novels, pictures of the author, the *Encyclopedia Britannica* entry on Austen, and even "Some failed pick-up lines from Jane Austen" (lines used in humorous scenes from the novels when young men are trying unsuccessfully to impress young women) are at your electronic fingertips here. For scholarly inquiry, the site includes a biography; bibliographies of Austen's work, of Jane Austen sequels, and of articles and dissertations; and links to sixteen other Austen webpages. A useful feature of the *Jane Austen Information Page* is a search page that allows users to enter keywords that will search the texts of all six of the major novels, along with *Lady Susan* and *The Watsons.*

My search for Austen pages led to the site created by Mitsuharu Matsuoka at Nagoya University in Japan, who also maintains interesting pages on Charles Dickens, George Gissing, Elizabeth Gaskell, and others. *The Gaskell Web* (http://ernie.lang.nagoya-u.ac.jp/~matsuoka/Gaskell.html) is a site well put together for a writer often overlooked. It features links to E-texts of Gaskell's writings and articles and publications about Gaskell from around the world as well as a good supply of other academic resources. While still under construction, the site promises soon to provide criticisms for the novels, including *Mary Barton, Cranford,* and *North and South* as well as Gaskell's *Life of Charlotte Brontë.*

Nathaniel Hawthorne (http://www.tiac.net/users/eldred/nh/hawthorne.html), maintained from New Hampshire by Eric Eldred, a self-described "independent amateur," is a good example of a user-friendly site (and with its beautiful color reproduction of an oil-on-canvas portrait of the author by Charles Osgood, it is among the more eye catching). The home page links to complete texts, reproduced graphically using HTML (Hypertext Markup Language) for most of Hawthorne's works, as well as to *Personal Recollections of Nathaniel Hawthorne* by Horatio Bridge (1893). The texts are annotated—*The House of the Seven Gables* links, for example, include a 1950 introduction by Basil Davenport, illustrations, notes and commentary, a glossary, a time line of dates, a list of places mentioned in the text, and a link to an on-line discussion of the book. There are even lesson plans for teachers. A comprehensive section on the life of the writer includes biographical writings by his contemporaries; a bibliography of Hawthorne biographies; articles on his friendships with Herman Melville, Henry David Thoreau, and William Dean Howells; and the memorial poem by Henry Wadsworth Longfellow.

Not surprisingly, Edgar Allan Poe is another Internet favorite, considerably outdistancing even Austen in the sheer number of sites dedicated to his life and work. In conjunction with an article titled "The Electronic Poe" in *Poe Studies* (Volume 30, Numbers 1 and 2 for 1997), Heyward Ehrlich, associate professor of English at Rutgers University, has created *A Poe Webliography* (http://andromeda.rutgers.edu/~ehrlich/poesites.html), which is a good starting point. It provides web sources for plain electronic texts (including Charles Baudelaire's translation, *"Le Masque de la mort rouge"*); hypertexts at the University of Virginia, the University of Michigan, and the Oxford English Dictionary Online Library; library special collections and databases; secondary material and parodies; historical sites, exhibits, and associations; and general literary indexes and resources. *Edgar Allan Poe's House of Usher* (http://www.comnet.ca/~forrest/), offers a less academically oriented introduction, discussing an array of Poe-related esoterica and supplying links to scores of other sites. *The Poe Decoder* (http://www.poedecoder.com/), is "a project started by a small group of Poe enthusiasts to make criticism and information on Poe and his work available on the Internet." It features essays on some of Poe's stories and a serviceable short biography.

If Walt Whitman were at work today, he would most assuredly embrace the Internet as a great democratic disseminator, so perhaps the biggest disappointment of my research was in discovering the dearth of comprehensive material on the web about our populist master. The only site of any substance that I found is *The Walt Whitman Hypertext Archive* (http://jefferson.village.virginia.edu/whitman/), which is still under construction. This project is codirected by Kenneth M. Price, professor of English and American Studies at the College of William and Mary, and Ed Folsom, professor of English at the University of Iowa and editor of the *Walt Whitman Quarterly*. When completed, the archive promises to offer hypertext reproductions of all the published versions of *Leaves of Grass* although right now they are limited to the complete 1891–1892 edition and the "Song of Myself" entries from 1855 and 1881–1882. Although there is a category listing for biographical material, none is provided, and clicking on "Notebooks and Letters" leads only to the Thomas Biggs Harned Collection at the Library of Congress. For current bibliography information the site provides a list only of articles and books published since 1985. This archive has the potential to be a valuable Whitman resource, but it has a long way to go toward that objective.

Mark Twain fares better than Whitman, in no small part thanks to the efforts of Jim Zwick and his website: *Mark Twain from the Mining Company* (http://marktwain.miningco.com/mbody.htm), part of a network of five hundred sites on a wide range of topics. Each site is led by an expert, and the network is operated by General Internet in New York City. Zwick, author of *Mark Twain's Weapons of Satire: Anti-Imperialist Writings on the Philippine-American War* (Syracuse University Press, 1992) and numerous articles about Twain, is clearly an enthusiastic and knowledgeable champion of the author. Although commercially sponsored—which means that users must accept advertisements in the margins—this extensive site combines a friendly format that will not daunt the general reader with fairly comprehensive links to serve more-academic visitors. The home page spotlights weekly feature articles and connects to a gallery of photos of Clemens's life, an events calendar, a Mark Twain chat room, associations, and an on-line newsletter. Clicking on "net links" brings up a lengthy index of everything from asso-

ciations and biographies to sources for used and rare books.

Mark Twain E-texts abound, and Zwick provides an alphabetical list of links to all Mark Twain books available on the Internet as well as excerpts and translations, maxims and quotations, a long litany of shorter writings, and speeches. Other links describe manuscript collections, provide teaching resources, and offer discussions on everything from whether *Huckleberry Finn* is a racist book to Mark Twain's enduring influence on popular culture. The site reproduces a healthy selection of Mark Twain criticism, obituaries and memorials from the year of the author's death, and reviews of recent Mark Twain scholarship. This site is, hands down, the example that all web masters should study before embarking on a literary website.

Frustration abounds for Oscar Wilde fans searching the web for a comprehensive look at his work. *Oscariana* (http://www.jonno.com/oscariana/1.html), which bills itself as "the life and times of Oscar Wilde," is really just a primer that glides cursorily through the more-tragic highlights of his life. Created and maintained by John d'Addario, an independent scholar, it is a time-consuming site which requires users to "page through" the site to encounter one excerpt or citation at a time (for example, the content of one entire page is the ambiguous quotation, "I am not English. I am Irish—which is quite another thing"). The point of the site seems to be to celebrate Wilde's homosexuality and to assail the Victorian society that destroyed him because of it. Even so, I'm not sure what purpose—political, historical, or literary—it serves to adorn an excerpt from an 1892 letter by Wilde to Robert Ross with a very modern, pointedly seductive photograph of a naked young man reading. Serious students of Oscar Wilde's poetry and fiction will be better served by sticking to the primary sources, and a satisfactory amount of it is reproduced in the Bartleby Archive and also at http://www.bibliomania.com/Fiction/wilde/stories/index.html.

Virginia Woolf Web (http://www.aianet.ne.jp/~orlando/VWW/index.shtml) is another paean to a great English writer and is maintained by Japanese devotees, in this case Hiroko Fukushima and Tae Yamamoto of Osaka. While its format is a little confusing and its electric-blue background is hard on the eyes, there is solid material to be found in it. Under the heading "Life and Works of Virginia Woolf" there is a chronology and bibliography as well as photographs of the author by Man Ray and of her mother, Julia Jackson, by Julia Margaret Cameron. There are links to E-texts through the Oxford Text Archive, Oxford Online Library, and Project Gutenberg, and to Woolf-related mailing lists, societies, and collections. A noteworthy feature is that this site offers a well-assembled list of hyperlinks to information on the Modernist movement in art and literature in general and to the remarkable number of artists who share Woolf's 1882 birth year—James Joyce, Wyndham Lewis, Igor Stravinsky, Umberto Boccioni, George Braque, and Edward Hopper. The site can also be viewed in Japanese.

Also from Japan, created by Professor Eiichi Hishikawa at Kobe University, are straightforward, attractive webpages dedicated to eleven modern English-language masters—W. H. Auden, Hart Crane, T. S. Eliot, Robert Frost, James Joyce, Robert Lowell, Marianne Moore, Ezra Pound, Wallace Stevens, William Carlos Williams, and W. B. Yeats—that serve as good jumping-off points for further inquiry. He also offers links to Internet resources on more than 150 poets writing in English.

Hishikawa's *William Butler Yeats* page (http://www.lit.kobe-u.ac.jp/~hishika/yeats.htm.) reproduces an encyclopedia entry on the poet, as well as a bibliography of the more-important general studies of Yeats's life and work. There are links to other Yeats sites, mostly featuring E-texts of many of his poems; to the *Yeats Society Sligo Home Page* to other links featuring newsletters, publications, and articles; and to organizations and libraries.

Hishikawa does the same for *James Joyce* (http://www.lit.kobe-u.ac.jp/~hishika/joyce.htm), reproducing a concise biography and bibliography from the *Academic American Encyclopedia*. There is less E-text of Joyce's actual writing on the web, no doubt due to copyright issues, but there is an unusual link to an audio sample of Joyce reading from a Caedmon recording. Along with links to The James Joyce Centre Dublin and *James Joyce Quarterly,* the site links to *Work in Progress: A website Devoted to the Writings of James Joyce* (http://www.2street.com/joyce/).

A much more academic site maintained by R. L. Callahan of Temple University, *Work in Progress* bills itself as "the original Joycean website . . . a constellation of resources available to enthusiasts and scholars of the work of James Joyce." In this audaciously conceived site Callahan's considerable ambition is to show how the web is the natural successor to Joyce's all-encompassing literary vision, as put forth in his introduction:

> Our present technology encourages us to rethink the notion of "text" in radical ways. Many of those familiar with the fictions of James Joyce, however, recognize that late-twentieth century reformulations of textuality are not entirely without precedent. Intricately self-reflexive and densely allusive—or, to use terminology appropriate to this medium, containing multiple links to both inter-

nal and external documents—Joyce's work anticipates so-called hypertext. Likewise, the encyclopedic urges of *Ulysses* and *Finnegans Wake* resemble the Internet's impetus towards boundless inclusion. The metaphor of a spider's web has often and appropriately been used to describe Joyce's writings, . . . and fittingly the same metaphor has been used to describe the interconnected tangle of text on the 'Net, called the World Wide Web. The Web—which we might perhaps regard as our present-day, perpetually protean epic text—thus appears to hold a number of affinities to Joyce's work.

Given its attempt to re-create a Joycean texture, this site can seem a bit daunting when first encountered, at least by someone possessing non-Joycean bearings. But once the user gets past clever, pun-laden headings such as "Mind your hats goan in," "Fly by those nets," or "Who's getting it up?," there is a wealth of good information to be found. The on-site resources include a biographical time line, information about discussion groups, maps of Dublin, a gallery of Joyce images, and even a digitized audio recording of Joyce reading from *Finnegans Wake*. The site boasts a hypertext journal of Joyce criticism, *Hypermedia Joyce Studies,* but in the late fall of 1997 an issue dated August 1995 was the most recent posting. The index to off-site links is fairly extensive, with connections to relevant articles located elsewhere on the Net, and to an *Irish Times* site that celebrates Bloomsday 1997, to University College Dublin, and to the University of Trieste's Joyce site, among others.

The great American triumvirate of the first half of this century, Faulkner, Fitzgerald, and Hemingway, is represented on the web with varying degrees of success. The year 1997 marks the centenary of Faulkner's birth, and, fittingly, the University of Mississippi's *William Faulkner on the Web* (http://cypress.mcsr.olemiss.edu/~egjbp/faulkner/faulkner.html), keeps users apprised of celebratory events. This superb, quite extensive, easy-to-navigate site offers a good introduction to Faulkner and directs users toward many additional resources. There is a feature called "Faulkner QuickLink" that will jump to information about the specific work a user selects. To help readers untangle Faulkner's interconnected novels, there is a Yoknapatawpha Timeline (which currently goes from 1540 to 1865, but it promises eventually to bring readers up to 1962), a glossary, and character biographies. There are plot summaries for all the novels, short stories, essays, and speeches, and for twelve of the novels there are supplementary listings of genealogical charts, character lists, and recommended critical works. (The *As I Lay Dying* bibliography lists twenty-two articles.) There are also pages of Faulkner trivia, such as the fact that his Nobel Prize acceptance speech was heralded by the press as a triumph despite the fact that the thickly accented writer stood too far from the microphone and few could hear it. When this site and its time lines, genealogies, and cross-references are completed, it will serve as an irreplaceable resource for Faulkner scholars and devotees.

Almost as extensive as the Faulkner site is the *F. Scott Fitzgerald Centenary* site (http://www.sc.edu/fitzgerald/index.html). Put together in 1996 by graduate students at the University of South Carolina, but frequently updated, this is a useful site that draws extensively on books, photographs, and related materials from the Matthew J. and Arlyn Bruccoli Collection of F. Scott Fitzgerald at the Thomas Cooper Library, University of South Carolina. After reading a concise preface, users can choose from an array of pages that offer a biography, a detailed Fitzgerald chronology that begins with the births of Scott's and Zelda's parents and ends with Zelda's death in 1948, and bibliographies of works by and about both of the Fitzgeralds. Clicking on "Essays and Articles," one finds only three critical articles, but there are short vignettes about everything from Fitzgerald's football stories to the press book for the 1949 Paramount movie version of *The Great Gatsby*. Also reproduced at this site are twenty-six specimen pages from the out-of-print *The Romantic Egoists* (1974), a pictorial autobiography drawn from the Fitzgeralds' scrapbooks and photo albums. Links to other websites are to mostly broad-based, general literature sites. A nice feature is the E-text of short stories as well as a link to the Bartleby *This Side of Paradise*.

It is surprising to find that Hemingway is not particularly well served by the web. *The Papa Page* (http://www.ee.mcgill.ca/~nverever/hem/pindex.html) offers a general introduction, but it falls short in examining his work or offering any direction for further inquiry. There is a lengthy (for a website) biography, a frequently-asked-questions feature, and even a picture album, but there are no E-text links and none of the bibliographies, summaries, or critical essays that distinguish the Faulkner and Fitzgerald sites. Many of the off-site links are superficial or would seem to hold the interest of a select few. A site called *Sharks in Literature,* for example, is not going to be of much use even if the user is concentrating on *The Old Man and the Sea*. The one intriguing link is to the *Kansas City Star* website, which features some of Hemingway's work for that newspaper at the beginning of his career.

Investigating another trio of American writers—Raymond Chandler, Dashiell Hammett, and James M. Cain—I again found a wide disparity in their presences on the web. Chandler is the only one of the three yet to earn a full-fledged site. *The Raymond Chandler Webpage* (http://www.geocities.com/Athens/Parthenon/3224/index.htm) is the work of Robert F. Moss, a Ph.D. candidate at the University of South Carolina. Still under construction, it offers a chronology, a checklist of the author's works, and a bibliography of secondary sources and critical studies. An "Essays and Criticism" page at present offers just one essay. There is an interesting commentary, however, on the early poetry and prose Chandler wrote while still living in England, and links to other Raymond Chandler resources include a filmography and Joyce Carol Oates's review of the Library of America volume.

One of the off-site links leads to *A Guide to Classic Mystery and Detection* (http://members.aol.com/MG4273/classics.htm), a very impressive undertaking written and maintained by Michael E. Grost, a private individual in Detroit. The site offers a comprehensive, if highly opinionated, survey of three hundred crime-fiction writers. The Chandler section, *Raymond Chandler and His Followers* (http://members.aol.com/MG4273/chandler.htm) features short essays on important influences and on the major works. Grost is, admittedly, not a Chandler adherent—he finds the books gloomy, downbeat, and weak of plot—but his site serves as a good introduction to some of the lesser-known writers who followed in Chandler's wake.

I was astonished to find so little available about Hammett on the web. Grost's pages on *Dashiell Hammett* (http://members.aol.com/MG4273/hammett.htm) are really the best source of information among very limited on-line resources. At this site you can find a list of his works and read short essays about the major works, but, like the Chandler information, it is highly subjective and not really useful for anyone beyond the casual fan. Since this is not really a Hammett website, per se, there are no links to off-site resources. Biographical material is scant and bibliographical information nonexistent.

James M. Cain (http://www2.rmcil.edu/dhaynes/cainbio.htm) merits a single page and is put together by Don Haynes, an instructor at Robert Morris College in Chicago. It features a short biography and even shorter summaries of Cain's first five novels, including *The Postman Always Rings Twice* and *Double Indemnity*. There are also links to a bibliography of books by and about Cain and to critical essays. With all the critical work that has been published on these writers and the hard-boiled genre they pioneered, it would seem that Hammett and Cain deserve more-comprehensive websites. Such an undertaking would probably have to capture the interest of a university, though, before anything approaching the Faulkner or Fitzgerald sites would be constructed. With both of their centenaries come and gone, such a project, sadly, may not be in the cards.

If ever an author presaged the edgy randomness of the World Wide Web, it was William S. Burroughs. A fan, Malcolm Humes, has put together *The William S. Burroughs Files InterWebZone* (http://www.hyperreal.org/wsb/), which apologizes right at the top of its home page for not being comprehensive or up to date. But it does offer bibliographies of books by and about Burroughs; background on the author (including his familial ties to the Burroughs Corporation); lists of recordings, movies, and videos that Burroughs made; trivia; and links to some on-line texts. There are links to eight other sites with Burroughs connections and a memorial written after the author's death on 2 August 1997.

Taking a quick look at websites dedicated to writers who are still at work, I found mostly exercises in fan appreciation. The hagiographic *Doris Lessing: A Retrospective* (http://tile.net/lessing/) put together by Jan Hanford of Oakland, California, offers a complete list of Lessing's books, a list that can be viewed alphabetically, chronologically, or by publisher. Her short stories and short nonfiction pieces can be cross-referenced. The site provides an interview with Lessing by Joyce Carol Oates, and some references to periodicals, essays, articles, and collections. The information is solid, and the site is a suitable launch point for someone wishing to learn a bit more. Ever progressive in her outlook, Lessing herself provides an epigraph that suggests her own willingness to embrace the web as a new medium of publication: "I am so happy to be communicating with people on this newest of new wavelengths which to some older people must seem like a kind of magic."

A site on *Seamus Heaney* (http://sunsite.unc.edu/dykki/poetry/heaney/heaney-cov.html), which is part of the *Internet Poetry Archive* created by Paul Jones and sponsored by the University of North Carolina Press and the North Carolina Arts Council, barely scratches the surface of the Irish poet's work. A handful of poems are reproduced, and there is a biography and select bibliography. Beyond that, there is his Nobel Prize citation and a link to the Swedish Academy site where his Nobel lecture, "Crediting Poetry," is featured. The only feature of this site not readily available elsewhere is Heaney's 1996 commencement address at the University of North Carolina.

Much better views of a contemporary writer can be found at two sites about Salman Rushdie. The first (http://www.crl.com/~subir/rushdie.html), maintained by Subir Grewal, a graduate student at Duke University. It offers a chronology of Rushdie's work; interviews with him; articles and reviews; and links to other Rushdie sites, including George P. Landow's hypertext project from Brown University (http://   www.stg.brown.edu/projects/hypertext/landow/post/rushdie/rushdieov.html). A professor of English and art history, Landow envisions his site as an on-line critical journal with scholarly articles that examine Rushdie's work in its political, religious, social, and literary contexts. Still under construction, this site promises to be quite comprehensive, but the articles currently available are uneven in quality and content. Some are by Landow and other scholars; others are by undergraduates. Nonetheless, there is good information here, far more than is available on the websites of most living writers, and that is unquestionably a step in the right direction for cyberscholars.

Making a general assessment of literature's presence on the web is a Sisyphean task, with so many sites, both good and bad, vying for the reader's attention. Literary websites are, after all, still in their infancy, still evolving. For lovers of the written word, there is a great deal out there to explore. But there are still countless, often inexplicable, gaps in who is represented, or represented well, on the web. And there is ample room for improvement in many of the literary sites that are already available. While it is easy to wish that all the sites were as comprehensive and helpful as those devoted to Twain and Faulkner, the sheer number of sites attempting to bring a favorite writer to the attention of a new generation of readers is encouraging.

Certainly, no one is going to go on-line to read *The Prelude* or *This Side of Paradise* in their entirety, but the presence of these books on the web most assuredly will tantalize lapsed readers (and potential readers) back to the printed word. As proof that literature lovers are out there surfing, I took a look at the number of hits some of the sites had logged. As of late fall 1997, the Wordsworth site had attracted 14,054 visitors; Woolf, 35,262; Faulkner, 80,202; and *The Poe Decoder,* 22,928. The Fitzgerald site reports more than 60,000 visitors. Even Gaskell's humble page had attracted a respectable 6,216 hits.

Surely these numbers reveal something salient about the future of literature, not only in this new medium but also in its oldest guises. A substantial number of the Internet users who are hanging out at these sites must also be reading. It is heartening that in an age when the demise of the written word has become common cant, the very instrument of its impending doom is teeming with tributes to writers great, near great, and good.

Producing *Dear Bunny, Dear Volodya: The Friendship and the Feud*

Harold Augenbraum
Mercantile Library, New York City

On the evening of 19 May 1997, two of the great literary figures of the twentieth century came back to life at the new Century Center Theatre on East Fifteenth Street in Manhattan, when Vladimir Nabokov and Edmund Wilson squared off in Terry Quinn's dramatic adaptation of their thirty-year correspondence, *Dear Bunny, Dear Volodya: The Friendship and the Feud*. The evening of theater was produced as a benefit for and presented by The Mercantile Library of New York and was directed by the author. The play was performed on the theater's proscenium stage, with the main characters moving between desks and lecterns, at which they read excerpts from the letters and diaries, delivered to each other, as if in epistolary dialogue.

An audience of three hundred cheered as William F. Buckley Jr. (Wilson) and playwright Quinn (Nabokov)–a last-minute replacement for an indisposed Dmitri Nabokov–brought to life the often hilarious, often disputatious dialogue of Wilson and Nabokov. Despite a severe case of laryngitis, Dmitri Nabokov greeted the audience from the stage, bringing good wishes from his family, while National Public Radio affiliate WNYC recorded the performance for broadcast in the winter of 1997–1998. Recovered from his illness, Nabokov was able to perform alongside Buckley at a reprise of the production, which took place at the Century Association on West Forty-third Street in Manhattan on 2 December before an equally enthusiastic audience.

The two title characters ("Bunny" was Wilson's childhood nickname and "Volodya" the diminutive of Nabokov's given name) were born within four years of each other, though five thousand miles apart–Wilson in Red Bank, New Jersey, in 1895 and Nabokov in Saint Petersburg in 1899. By the age of twenty-five Wilson had become an editor of *The New Republic* and had launched a writing career that would result in twenty-seven volumes touching on the twentieth century's most critical themes. As the country's de facto "critic laureate,"

Wilson was to play a dominant role in American literary circles from the 1920s until his death in 1972. He enjoyed the respect of the general reading public as well as of his fellow intellectuals, due to his genius for combining an incisive intelligence with an ability to communicate complex ideas. He was among the first to explain to American readers the difficult concepts of modernism (*Axel's Castle,* 1931), the influence of socialism in the Western World (*To the Finland Station,* 1940), and the brutality of geographical displacement (*Apologies to the Iroquois,* 1960). He brought renewed attention to many women authors, including Edith Wharton, and was among the first to write about French Canadian and Caribbean fiction writers.

Vladimir Nabokov was completing his high-school studies when the Russian Revolution broke out, an event that would leave his once-affluent family stateless, homeless, and nearly impoverished. Throughout the 1920s and 1930s he lived primarily in Berlin and Paris, where, under the pseudonym of Vladimir Sirin, he produced ten novels, more than fifty short stories, and a great deal of poetry, drama, and criticism – mostly in Russian for expatriate publications. Nabokov eventually developed a reputation in Europe as one of the most talented émigré writers of his generation, though his work was next to unknown in the Soviet Union and the United States. In 1940 he left France for the United States, with his wife Vera and their six-year-old son Dmitri, only weeks before Paris fell to the Nazis.

While teaching at Wellesley, Harvard, and Cornell, Nabokov established a reputation among American literati for the extraordinary English prose of his novels. Many of these works have since been praised as masterpieces, including *The Gift* (1963), *Bend Sinister* (1947), *Pnin* (1957), *Pale Fire* (1962), and *Ada* (1969). It was his most famous and controversial work, *Lolita* (1955), however, which has been turned into two movies, that brought him public recognition. With the success of *Lolita* Nabokov was able to regain a measure of the

Poster for the performance at the Century Theater

family's affluence, and in the early 1960s he stopped teaching, and he and Vera moved to Montreux, Switzerland, where he died in 1977.

On the suggestion of a relative, in 1940 Nabokov sent to Edmund Wilson several samples of his earliest attempts at writing in English, a language he had learned as a child. Wilson's gracious response to Nabokov's letter initiated a correspondence that ran more than two thousand pages and lasted for thirty years. Yet, in 1965, when Nabokov published his long-awaited English translation of *Eugene Onegin,* following his own editorial principles, Wilson wrote a scathing review for the *New York Review of Books.* Nabokov retaliated; a war of letters ensued; and except for the one or two letters the men exchanged just before Wilson's

death, one of literature's great correspondences came to an end. The letters were edited by UCLA professor Simon Karlinsky and published in 1979.

In the spring of 1995 The Mercantile Library commissioned Quinn to research the journal entries and letters Nabokov and Wilson wrote to or about each other between 1940 (the year Nabokov arrived in the United States) and 1972 (the year Wilson died) and to distill and lend shape to that voluminous account of what many scholars regard as one of modern literature's most celebrated friendships, as well as one of its most bitter feuds. These letters and diaries are important documents in literary and intellectual history.

Using only the writers' words, *Dear Bunny, Dear Volodya* chronicles the bonding and eventual estrangement of Wilson and Nabokov. In language at times warm and insightful, at times shockingly blunt or laced with searing gossip, these two giants of twentieth-century culture trace the literary, social, and political currents running through several decades of American and European thought.

The Mercantile Library production's two stars are William F. Buckley Jr. and Dmitri Nabokov. Buckley is the founder, editor, and currently editor at large of *The National Review;* is host of the long-running public-television talk show *Firing Line;* and has written thirty-seven volumes of fiction, essays, political commentary, and accounts of transatlantic sailing exploits.

Dmitri Nabokov graduated from Harvard, served in the U.S. Army, and then began the vocal studies that would lead to a career in grand opera. In 1960 he took first prize in the basso category of the Reggio Emilia International Opera Competition near Parma, Italy, where the winning tenor was Luciano Pavarotti. (They were awarded a debut together, the following year, in La Boheme.) He has since performed a large repertoire of opera and oratorio roles in major theaters throughout Italy, Spain, France, Germany, Israel, the United States, and South America and has sung recitals at Milan's La Scala and El Liceo in Barcelona. Nabokov is the principal translator of his father's Russian works into English—an effort that recently culminated in his editing of the 1995 Knopf publication *The Stories of Vladimir Nabokov.*

Author Terry Quinn has written a novel (*The Great Bridge Conspiracy* [St. Martin's Press, 1979]), co-authored a biography (*Second Daughter: Growing Up in China, 1930–1949* [Little, Brown, 1984]), and published stories, poems, and essays in national magazines and literary journals. His plays and musical theater works—for which he writes the books, lyrics, and scores (*A Second Chance, Rasputin, A Match Made in Brooklyn, Love Hurts,* and *Georgette's Last Re-*

hearsal)—have had regional and Off-Broadway productions or been broadcast on WNYC and WBAI in New York City and on National Public Radio. He wrote the screenplay for and starred in *It's About Time,* a National Geographic film broadcast on public-television stations across the country.

Dear Bunny, Dear Volodya was commissioned and produced by The Mercantile Library of New York. The library is located on East Forty-seventh Street in Manhattan in an historically restored building designed by Henry Otis Chapman in 1932. In addition to *Dear Bunny, Dear Volodya* the library presented forty-five literary programs in 1997 and published *Edmund Wilson: Centennial Reflections* in association with Princeton University Press. Two years ago the library initiated seminars in U.S. ethnic literatures for New York City high-school teachers and established an annual lecture on French literature. The Mercantile Library has benefited from four National Endowment for the Humanities grants in the past five years as well as several grants from the New York Council for the Humanities and private foundations. Recent speakers have included Richard Howard, Sue Grafton, Mary Gordon, Alain Robbe-Grillet, and Matthew J. Bruccoli. The library is also now the home of the Mystery Writers of America, The Trollope Society of America, the Augustus Saint-Gaudens Memorial, Playwrights Preview Productions, and Arethusa. The Mercantile Library's Writer's Studio, one of three rooms in New York dedicated to workspace for writers, has provided a creative haven for scores of authors since it opened in 1972. The library also houses The Archives of Detective Fiction, an Internet archive.

The library continues to break new ground in bringing fiction and literary criticism to the public. Two books of essays and centennial celebrations for Ernest Hemingway and Alexander Pushkin are planned for coming years.

Department of Library, Archives and Institutional Research, American Bible Society

Mary F. Cordato
American Bible Society

The Department of Library, Archives and Institutional Research of the American Bible Society (ABS) constitutes one of the most important resources of books and records documenting the history of the Bible and Bible-related work. Located at 1865 Broadway in New York City, the holdings are treasure troves for biblical scholars, linguists, historians and art historians, students of printing and binding, bibliographers, and other researchers. The library includes the largest collection of printed Scripture material in the Western Hemisphere. More than fifty-two thousand titles representing more than two thousand languages and dialects dating from the thirteenth century to the present have been catalogued, including classical Bible editions, rare translations, illustrated manuscripts, and exquisitely bound volumes. The library produces an annual "Scripture Language Report," prepared jointly with the British and Foreign Bible Society's Library at Cambridge University, which lists new Scripture publications for the year, and the biennial *Scriptures of the World,* which presents the chronological and geographical spread of Bible translations from the fifteenth century to the present. The archives consist of minutes of the governing board and its committees dating from the ABS's founding in 1816, annual reports, correspondence documenting the ABS's worldwide missionary activities, language files on translations, photographs, a complete run of the *Bible Society Record,* and oral-history transcripts. The archives is also responsible for the ABS's historical essays project.

Founded in New York City in May 1816 as an interdenominational national-based Christian reform group, the ABS mission was and continues to be the circulation of the Scriptures to every man, woman, and child in a language and form each can readily understand and at a price each can afford, without doctrinal note or comment. From the time of its first headquarters located on Nassau Street in Lower Manhattan, the ABS em-ployed the most sophisticated stereotype printing methods for the time, producing inexpensive Bibles in large quantities. The breadth of its work both at home and abroad was widespread, and by 1850 the ABS had become a respected publisher, translator, and distributor of Bibles; was an innovator in the printing trades; and was one of the nation's most successful philanthropies.

Establishing a Scripture library and archives figured strongly in the ABS mission. Following the example of its London counterpart, the British and Foreign Bible Society, founded in 1804, the Board of Managers agreed in January 1817 "that a copy of each edition of the Bible printed for the American Bible Society in their various bindings be deposited in the Society's Biblical Library." In 1836 the ABS appointed its first librarian, the Reverend George Bush, a distinguished Hebrew scholar at New York University. In 1845 the ABS incorporated the library and archives into its bylaws: "There shall continue to be kept a Library of the Society in which shall be placed and preserved all books not for sale, belonging to the Society, all manuscripts and other interesting papers which Society, Board of Managers, Committees, or Corresponding Secretary may deem worthy of preservation. There shall also be placed in the Library a copy of the first edition of every book published by the Society, and a copy of every other edition thereof in which material alteration shall have been made in the stereotype plates."

Throughout the nineteenth century the library's collection grew by gift and an ambitious acquisitions policy. In 1817 New York philanthropist and bibliophile John Pintard and ABS president Elias Boudinot donated classical volumes from their personal libraries, and in the same year Pintard secured gifts of French and Dutch Bibles from the New York Historical Society. In 1823 ABS agent John Nitchie received board approval to "purchase from the British and Foreign Bible Society, from the Russian and other Bible Socie-

THE NEW PRINTING ESTABLISHMENT AND DEPOSITORY OF THE AMERICAN BIBLE SOCIETY, NEW YORK

American Bible Society, Astor Place Building, New York City, circa 1853 (American Bible Society Archives)

ties printing the Scripture in foreign languages, a regular series of the Bibles and Testaments, printed by them, other than in the English language." Other early accessions included an "Ojibway Hymn and Spelling Book" presented by a Wesleyan missionary; a Chinese grammar and New Testament (Canton, 1814) translated by Robert Morrison; the *London Polyglot* (1657), edited by Brian Walton; several reference works and translations from the ABS's overseas representative in Constantinople; and the library and archives of the American Bible Revision Committee. Advances in technology, communication, and book production, together with Bible translation that characterized missionary activity at this time, contributed to the growth of the ABS library. By 1896 the collection had more than fifty-three hundred volumes, including rare—many one of a kind—editions, new translations, commentaries, reference books, and data relating to missions throughout the world, and the library had become a major resource for both ABS translators and external researchers, particularly Bible scholars who used the collection for reference and consultation.

By the middle of the nineteenth century, the concerns of space and security prompted the ABS to consider the library's physical environment. In 1853 the ABS had relocated its headquarters to a nonfireproof building on Astor Place, and managers recognized the ease with which valuable books could be stolen, lost, or destroyed. Their concerns led to the transfer of four thousand books in 1897 to the Lenox Library, a part of the New York Public Library. James Lenox, a prominent rare-book collector and Christian philanthropist, had served as president of the ABS from 1864 to 1871.

With the removal of the bulk of its collection, the ABS continued to expand its library holdings. This growth coincided with administrative changes. In 1928 Eric North, a man with deep commitment to scholarship, was named general secretary, a position he held until 1956. The library, which was part of the translations department, was his responsibility, and in 1935 he appointed Margaret T. Hills assistant librarian. In 1939 Hills was promoted to librarian, a post she held until 1963, when she became secretary for historical research. Both North and Hills recognized the biblical collection's importance as an institutional and scholarly resource as well as a public-relations tool. During their tenure they initiated exhibits and educational outreach programs and actively sought new acquisitions for the Scripture collection. With the relocation of the ABS to its new headquarters at Park Avenue and Fifty-seventh Street in 1936, North requested that the volumes deposited at Lenox be returned to the ABS. By 1940, with the collection reunited, the library numbered more than nine thousand volumes in more than eight hundred languages and dialects. The library also expanded its traditional role as a research collection by publishing reference works, including *The Book of a Thousand Tongues* (New York, 1938; revised 1972), a volume designed to identify languages into which a portion of the Scriptures had been translated. In 1961 Hills published *The English Bible in America* (New York, 1961), a standard reference work that continues to be consulted by biblical scholars today. In 1963 Elizabeth Eisenhart replaced Hills as librarian.

In 1966 the ABS relocated to its present headquarters on West Sixty-first Street, a move that coincided with greater exposure and expansion for the Scripture collection. Plans for the new library included a glass-enclosed, climate-controlled storage area to ensure proper preservation of the rare books. The library was situated and remains adjacent to the ABS gallery, thus giving the collection greater public visibility and access. Library holdings were enriched substantially after the move. In 1967 the ABS purchased eighty books at a major auction held at Sotheby's in London.

During the tenures of North and Hill the ABS evaluated its archival function. Although managers had specified in the 1845 bylaws that the library was responsible for the organization's records, an archives was not formally organized until 1949. At that time North initiated a program to microfilm permanently valuable documents, to discard records of little or no value, and to retain in hard-copy format those manuscripts and papers with historical significance. In 1967 Martha Dobias became the ABS's first archivist.

In anticipation of the ABS's 150th anniversary in 1966, North inaugurated an historical essays project that aimed to explain the programmatic and administrative history of the society from its founding to the present. Since the project's inception in the early 1960s more than seventy-five essays have been researched, written, and catalogued. Older institutional studies provide data and insight into ABS programs and document the development and evolution of its translation, publication, and distribution functions. Newer, more topical working papers are written within professional guidelines set by the American historical profession and examine issues such as women's involvement in the ABS mission, the relationship between African Americans and the ABS, trends in national distribution, and ways in which the ABS celebrated important historical milestones. The essays project continues today within the archives program.

In 1969 the ABS underwent administrative change. The library, which had been part of the translations department, was placed under the direct control of the general secretary. The shift had important implications for the library by giving it greater status and independence within the organization. The position of librarian was upgraded to officer level; a records-management program was implemented; and by 1976 several professional positions, including Scripture cataloguer, periodicals librarian and reference librarian, were added. The archives continued to function as a separate unit within the library. During the 1970s the library and archives also received public exposure when several rare volumes and manuscripts, including the correspondence of Elias Boudinot, were featured in television segments.

Eisenhart's ABS career ended with her retirement in 1980, and the position of library head was not permanently filled until 1983 with the appointment of Boyd Daniels. During his tenure Daniels moved the department in new directions by initiating automation of library holdings and re-evaluating the archives function. In 1989 Peter Wosh, who had served as ABS archivist from 1984, replaced Daniels as director of library and archives. Wosh continued the work in computerized access begun by Daniels and was instrumental in expanding the reference and research functions of both the library and archives. In 1994 institutional research became a third area within the department.

Today the Department of Library, Archives and Institutional Research includes a staff of eleven and is part of the ABS Scripture publications area. It is headed by a director, Mary Jane Ballou, who was appointed in 1995. There are two assistant directors, Liana Lupas, curator of the Scripture collection, and archivist Mary Frances Cordato. The department provides a wide range of services for ABS staff, scholars, and the general public. Library and archives staff respond to hundreds of reference inquiries each year; compile background papers, reports, and trends studies in order to support organization programs and projects; catalogue archival holdings and library acquisitions; maintain and conserve the Scripture and archival collections; conduct tours; and coordinate a records-management program. From its modest beginnings in 1817 the library now has fifty-two thousand volumes, including twelve hundred rare books. A sampling of its holdings includes almost all of the first editions of the English Bible; all of the great polyglot Bibles; milestones in the history of Bible publication, such as the *Erasmus Greek New Testament* (1516), the *Aldine Greek Bible* (1518), and the *German Bible* translated by Martin Luther (1522–1532); first editions of the Bible published in America, including the *Massachusetts* or *Indian Bible* translated by John Eliot (1663), the *German*

Bible published by Christopher Saur (1743), and the *English Bible* published by Robert Aitken (1782); and manuscripts, including a thirteenth-century Latin Bible in microscopic script, a fifteenth-century English New Testament in Wyclif translation, a late fifteenth-century illuminated Armenian manuscript of the Gospels, and a fifteenth-century Torah scroll from the Jewish community of Kai-Feng-Fu in China. The archives consist of more than eighteen hundred linear feet of paper-based records, eighty-seven thousand historical photographs, and eighty-seven hundred roles of microfilm documenting the translation, publication, and distribution functions of the ABS. The library and archives are open all year to ABS staff and outside researchers.

Research in the American Antiquarian Book Trade

Donald C. Dickinson
University of Arizona, Tucson

The antiquarian book trade has a long and honorable history. Librarians and private collectors have been able to develop distinguished holdings of books and manuscripts through the efforts of antiquarian dealers. Members of the trade have used their specialized knowledge to locate, describe, and supply basic and advanced works in all subject disciplines. As a result, scholarship has been served and learning advanced.

In spite of the importance of this role, little serious attention has been given to the history of the antiquarian trade or to the men and women who have contributed to its development. For the researcher who wishes to examine an aspect of the antiquarian book trade, whether in America or Europe, the difficulties are formidable. While related fields such as history of the book, printing, and book collecting have a respectable literature, the antiquarian book trade lacks even the most basic reference tools. There are no bibliographies, indexes, dictionaries, or manuals, and with the exception of Madeleine B. Stern's *Antiquarian Bookselling in the United States: A History from the Origins to the 1940s* (Westport, Conn.: Greenwood Press, 1985) there are no adequate histories. Primary research materials are scarce and difficult to locate.

The periodical literature devoted to publishing and book collecting does provide some help in tracing developments in the antiquarian book trade. From its beginning in 1872 *Publishers Weekly* devoted space to columns such as "Old Book Notes," "Notes for Dealers in Old Books," and "Old Book Chat." Frederick M. Hopkins, Jacob N. Blanck, and Sol M. Malkin carried forward the reporting on buying and selling old and rare books in *Publishers Weekly* until 1947, when that responsibility fell to the new journal *The Antiquarian Bookman*, later *AB Bookman's Weekly*. Between 1900 and 1905 George D. Smith published *The Literary Collector*, an amalgam of reports and articles on book sales, collecting, and dealers as well as binding, manuscripts, and typography. Charles F. Heartman's journals, *The American Collector* (1925–1928) and *The American Book Collector* (1932–1935), supplied brief biographies of notable figures in the antiquarian trade along with a mixture of gossip and opinion. A newer version of *The American Book Collector* reported news from the rare-book world on an occasional basis into the 1980s. In November 1989 the Antiquarian Booksellers' Association of America brought out the first issue of the *ABAA Newsletter*, an important reporting publication on current trade activities as well as a source for reviews and personal memoirs. The *ABAA Newsletter* was preceded by the short-lived *Professional Rare Bookseller* (1980–1984). In spite of the number of journals that have attempted to treat the various aspects of the antiquarian book trade, sustained and systematic coverage has never existed in the past and does not exist today.

A few dealers have published book-length memoirs, and a few more—such as Charles P. Everitt, Harold C. Holmes, Charles E. Goodspeed, H. P. Kraus, David B. Magee, and David A. Randall—have written autobiographical essays. There is little biography—the Edwin Wolf and John F. Fleming study of A. S. W. Rosenbach stands almost alone in that genre. Useful, if selective, information is available in the transcripts produced by various institutions as part of their oral history programs. Columbia University, the University of California at Berkeley, the University of California at Los Angeles, Stanford University, and the Claremont Graduate Colleges, among others, have made efforts to tape the reminiscences of local antiquarian dealers. During the late 1970s, for example, the staff of the Columbia University Rare Book Project conducted interviews with Louis Cohen, Peter Decker, Franklin Gilliam (reminiscences of E. Byrne Hackett), Douglas G. Parsonage, Walter Schatzki, and John Scopazzi. A researcher interested in developing an accurate history of the Lathrop C. Harper firm during the 1930s and 1940s would be hard-pressed to find a more detailed account than that presented in the thirty-page Parsonage interview.

Many dealers left no such record. Influential figures such as Walter M. Hill of Chicago, Charles Sessler of Philadelphia, and George D. Smith of New York are remembered only in brief anecdotal accounts. In their day, the years leading up to and just following World War I, these men dominated auction sales in New York and London and sold millions of dollars' worth of rare books and manuscripts to wealthy private collectors. Tycoons such as Henry E. Huntington, J. P. Morgan, and Henry C. Folger asked for their advice and followed their recommendations. Ideally, the researcher intending to document the lives of Hill, Sessler, or Smith would have a wide assortment of research materials at hand–letters to customers, friends, and colleagues; business records and ledgers; a diary or two with some private revelations; a complete run of the dealers' sales catalogues and lists, with prices realized; scrapbooks and photographs; and an assortment of newspaper articles. Since such materials are rarely available, the search for primary records related to the antiquarian book trade is likely to be frustrating. The multivolume Library of Congress *National Union Catalogue of Manuscript Collections* (1962–to date) provides only a few scattered citations to the personal or business archives of antiquarian book dealers.

In the case of Charles Sessler (1854–1935), for example, researchers will have a difficult time establishing anything beyond the bare outline of his career. The events of the first twenty-five years of his life in Austria are completely unknown. He never published anything about himself or the book trade, and during the thirty-five years that he was active as an antiquarian dealer he issued only one sales catalogue. Contemporaries neglected Sessler almost as much as he neglected himself. Neither Charles F. Heartman, in *The American Book Collector,* nor George S. Sargent, in his regular column on collecting in the *Boston Transcript,* devoted any space to Sessler. Ruth Brown Park, writing for *Publishers Weekly* in November 1929, produced a rather insipid four-page tribute to the dealer on his seventy-fifth birthday, but beyond that one is left with only a few references in A. Edward Newton's *The Amenities of Book Collecting* and some scattered newspaper citations. Sessler did his business directly with collectors, and the papers reflecting those transactions were in most cases not retained. A few institutions, such as the Folger Shakespeare Library in Washington, D.C., and the Henry E. Huntington Library in San Marino, California, do have correspondence files that shed light on Sessler's career. The Free Library of Philadelphia has three scrapbooks of newspaper clippings about Sessler's shop, and the Historical Society of Pennsylvania holds business records for the firm, chiefly from the Mabel Zahn years, 1935 to 1950, after Sessler died.

As literary and historical researchers know, there is no substitute for primary records. In the spring of 1995, in order to determine the location of archival materials on the antiquarian book trade, the author sent a brief questionnaire to some one hundred research libraries and historical societies in the United States and Canada. This inquiry, backed up by a request posted on EX LIBRIS, the electronic forum for those who work with rare books, and a computer search of the archive and manuscript control file of the Research Libraries Information Network (RLIN), produced eighty-three replies. According to a spring 1997 article by Donald C. Dickinson in the *ABAA Newsletter,* typical answers included such statements as "Unfortunately our university has no archival holdings related to bookselling and booksellers. Sounds like a most interesting project." One curator simply wrote, "Sorry, no related material." Book dealers and their heirs have routinely destroyed important business records and correspondence while librarians and curators have been less than energetic about seeking out and protecting such records. For want of staff time and financial resources, the archives that do exist often lack rudimentary cataloguing or indexing.

With primary records in short supply and periodical coverage sporadic, researchers investigating the antiquarian book trade often turn to dealers' sales catalogues. As Roger E. Stoddard recently pointed out in December 1995 in *Papers of the Bibliographical Society of America,* "The base-line for the study of a bookdealer is a record of the catalogues." ("Book Catalogues and Life: A Preliminary Witness," *Papers of the Bibliographical Society of America,* December 1995). A set of catalogues will not only contribute to an understanding of the dealer's specialties but also will reflect current trends in the complex world of buying and selling rare books. If enhanced with accurate notes and careful annotations, catalogues can also stand as bibliographic contributions.

Some catalogues do more than list books for sale. Occasionally they provide an essay on book collecting, a history of a subject field, or an autobiographical sketch of the dealer. One of the few sources of information on the New York dealer James W. Bouton (1847?–1902) is found in the preface to his catalogue 84 (1889), "A Few Words to My Bookbuying Friends." Much is revealed about the inner workings of Dauber and Pine's Bookshop by examining their catalog 100 (1931), "A List of Some Outstanding Books to Which Are Added the Opinions of Seasoned Bibliophiles on the Amenities of Book-collecting at Dauber and Pine's Bookshop." Walter M. Hill (1868–1952) supplied his customers with a thoughtful autobiographical sketch in his catalog 100 (1923).

While catalogues can supply much useful raw material for the researcher, their use is of course limited. Never intended to serve for more than the immediate purpose of selling the books listed, catalogues were and are ephemeral. With a few notable exceptions, they are printed on cheap paper, bound in paper covers, and distributed in limited quantities. The indexing for dealer's catalogues, still in its infancy, presents a daunting challenge. Under constant pressure to set priorities for shelving space, librarians have been, for the most part, unwilling to retain retrospective catalogue collections. Bouton's career provides an example: probably no more than three or four American libraries hold a complete run of his catalogues. It would be helpful if publishers of reprints would continue to issue sets of catalogues for major dealers as they did for Peter Decker, Edward E. Eberstadt, and A. S. W. Rosenbach.

Another limit on the usefulness of catalogues is that they document only some transactions. Sessler's way of doing business was typical: important sales were often made person to person, in the shop, or over the telephone. Many important books never appear in dealers' catalogues. No printed record exists. We know very little, for example, about the negotiations leading up to the extensive purchases made by George D. Smith for Henry E. Huntington at the Henry Poor sales of 1908 and 1909, since both men lived in New York and could settle on bids without resorting to correspondence.

Many areas of the antiquarian book trade invite scholarly investigation. Recent publications—including the Sol M. Malkin lectures and subsequent printed versions by Bernard M. Rosenthal, "The Gentle Invasion, Continental Emigré Booksellers of the Thirties and Forties and Their Impact on the Antiquarian Booktrade" (New York: Columbia University Press, 1987); and Lucien Goldschmidt, "The Scenery Has Changed: The Purpose & Potential of the Rare Book Trade" (New York: Columbia University Press, 1989)—suggest that lively topics abound. In the area of primary materials, the student should be aware of the archive of correspondence and committee reports established by the Antiquarian Booksellers' Association of America.

Many library workers and antiquarian book dealers, in their different ways, have devoted professional attention to improving access to records of the past; it is time that they turned more careful scrutiny on their own transactions. Obviously this would involve a commitment of time and money. Dealers and library staff should plan together for the preservation and organization of business records and correspondence. Once deposited in a library or historical society, these materials must be catalogued and indexed to ensure that they can be used easily. Further, an indexing system for sales catalogues that would accommodate both retrospective and current publications would be extremely important. Dealers need to write about their experiences in the trade and record their recollections for oral history programs. Family members and colleagues of deceased dealers should be encouraged to contribute their memories on tape. The New York area alone could easily provide dozens of people able to add to the body of knowledge on the antiquarian trade. Such a storehouse of information would be invaluable for the historians and biographers of the future.

William R. Emerson
(1923-1997)

William Emerson was a member of the Planning Board for the *Dictionary of Literary Biography* that convened in 1977. He was joined by John Baker, Orville Prescott, Vernon Sternberg, and Alden Whitman: an extraordinary assemblage. Emerson provided the definition of literature that established the *DLB* rationale: "the intellectual commerce of a nation." The publishers relied on his advice for twenty years in connection with the *DLB* and other Bruccoli Clark Layman publications. The association between William Emerson and the *DLB* resulted from the circumstance that Matthew J. Bruccoli reported to him at the National Endowment for the Humanities when Bruccoli was director of the Center for Editions of American Authors. Bruccoli was impressed by Emerson's keen mind and breadth of learning. When Frederick Ruffner invited Bruccoli and C. E. Frazer Clark to organize the *DLB,* they automatically sought Bill Emerson's guidance.

A Little Rock native, Emerson attended Hendrix College and the University of Missouri before World War II; he served as a fighter pilot in Italy and was awarded the Distinguished Flying Cross. He earned a B.A. in history summa cum laude from Yale in 1948 and a Ph.D. from Oxford University as a Rhodes Scholar. After teaching history at Yale from 1951 to 1963—where he published *Monmouth's Rebellion* (1951) and *Operation Pointblank: A Tale of Bombers and Fighters* (1962)—and a stint at the U.S. Naval War College, he served as assistant to the president of Hollins College until 1969. That year he joined the National Endowment for the Humanities as director of research grants. Emerson was appointed director of the Franklin D. Roosevelt Library in Hyde Park, New York, in 1974, retiring in 1991.

—M.J.B.

William Emerson

Literary Awards and Honors Announced in 1997

ACADEMY OF AMERICAN POETS LITERARY AWARDS

HAROLD MORTON LANDON TRANSLATION AWARD

David Hinton, *Landscape Over Zero* by Bei Dao (New Directions), *The Late Poems of Meng Chiao* (Princeton University Press), and *The Selected Poems of Li Po* (New Directions).

JAMES LAUGHLIN AWARD

Tony Hoagland, *Donkey Gospel* (Graywolf).

LENORE MARSHALL – *NATION* MAGAZINE PRIZE FOR POETRY

Robert Pinsky, *The Figured Wheel* (Farrar, Straus & Giroux).

RAIZISS/DE PALCHI TRANSLATION AWARD

Michael Palma, *The Man I Pretend to Be: The Colloquies and Selected Poems of Guido Gozzano* (Princeton University Press).

RAIZISS/DE PALCHI TRANSLATION FELLOWSHIP

No Award.

TANNING PRIZE

Anthony Hecht.

WALT WHITMAN AWARD

Barbara Ras, *Bite Every Sorrow* (Louisiana State University Press).

AMERICAN ACADEMY OF ARTS AND LETTERS AWARDS

ACADEMY AWARDS IN LITERATURE

Charles Baxter, Layne Dunlop, Allen Grossman, Maureen Howard, Jayne Anne Phillips, Luc Sante, Wallace Shawn, Jane Smiley.

MICHAEL BRAUDE AWARD FOR LIGHT VERSE

Robert Conquest.

WITTER BYNNER PRIZE FOR POETRY

Mark Doty.

GOLD MEDAL IN POETRY

John Ashbery.

E. M. FORSTER AWARD IN LITERATURE

Glyn Maxwell.

AWARD OF MERIT FOR THE NOVEL

Richard Ford.

SUE KAUFMAN PRIZE FOR FIRST FICTION

Brad Watson, *Last Days of the Dog-Men* (Norton).

ROME FELLOWSHIP IN LITERATURE

Fae Myenne Ng.

RICHARD AND HINDA ROSENTHAL FOUNDATION AWARD IN LITERATURE

Mary Kay Zuravleff.

HAROLD D. VURSELL MEMORIAL AWARD IN LITERATURE

Elizabeth McCracken.

MORTON DAUWEN ZABEL AWARD FOR CRITICISM

Wendy Lesser.

AMERICAN BOOKSELLERS BOOK OF THE YEAR

ADULT TRADE BOOK

Frank McCourt, *Angela's Ashes* (Knopf).

CHILDREN'S BOOK AWARD

Kevin Henkes, *Lilly's Purple Plastic Purse* (Green Willow).

AMERICAN LIBRARY ASSOCIATION AWARDS

JOHN NEWBERY MEDAL

E. L. Konigsburg, *The View from Saturday* (Jean Karl/Atheneum).

RANDOLPH CALDECOTT MEDAL

David Wisniewski, *Golem* (Clarion).

MARGARET R. EDWARDS AWARD FOR OUTSTANDING LITERATURE FOR YOUNG ADULTS

Gary Paulsen.

CORETTA SCOTT KING AUTHOR AWARD

Walter Dean Myers, *Slam!* (Scholastic).

CORETTA SCOTT KING ILLUSTRATOR AWARD

Jerry Pinckney, illustrator, *Minty: A Story of Young Harriet Tubman* (Dial).

MILDRED L. BATCHELDER AWARD

Farrar, Straus & Giroux, for *The Friends*, by Kazumi Yumoto, translated by Cathy Hirano.

DARTMOUTH MEDAL
The Dictionary of Art (Grove).

ANISFIELD-WOLF BOOK AWARDS

Jamaica Kincaid, *The Autobiography of My Mother* (Farrar, Straus & Giroux).
James McBride, *The Color of Water* (Putnam).

LIFETIME ACHIEVEMENT AWARD
Albert R. Murray.

ANTHONY AWARDS

BEST NOVEL
Michael Connelly, *The Poet* (Little Brown).

BEST FIRST NOVEL (cowinners)
Dale Furutani, *Death in Little Tokyo* (St. Martin's Press).
Terris Grimes, *Somebody Else's Child* (Onyx).

BEST PAPERBACK ORIGINAL
Terris Grimes, *Somebody Else's Child* (Onyx).

BEST SHORT STORY
Eve Sandstrom, "Bugged."

BEST CRITICAL/BIOGRAPHICAL
Willetta Heising, *Detecting Women II* (Purple Moon).

IRMA S. AND JAMES H. BLACK AWARD FOR EXCELLENCE IN CHILDREN'S LITERATURE

Michael P. Waite, *Jojofu* (Lothrop).

JAMES TAIT BLACK MEMORIAL PRIZES

BIOGRAPHY
Diarmid MacColloch, *Thomas Cranmer: A Life* (Yale University Press).

FICTION
Alice Thompson, *Justine* (Canongate Books).
Graham Swift, *Last Orders* (Picador).

BLACK CAUCUS OF THE AMERICAN LIBRARY ASSOCIATION LITERARY AWARDS

FICTION
Florence Ladd, *Sarah's Psalm* (Scribner).

FIRST NOVEL
Sapphire, *Push* (Knopf).

NONFICTION
Nell Irvin Painter, *Sojourner Truth: A Life, A Symbol* (Norton).

OUTSTANDING CONTRIBUTION TO AFRICAN AMERICAN LITERATURE
Albert Murray.

BOOKER PRIZE

Arundhati Roy, *The God of Small Things* (London: Flamingo; New York: Random House).

BOSTON BOOK REVIEW LITERARY PRIZES

BINGHAM POETRY PRIZE
Mark Doty, *Atlantis* (HarperCollins).

REA NONFICTION PRIZE
Denni Covington, *Salvation on Sand Mountain* (Addison-Wesley).

FISK FICTION PRIZE
Joyce Carol Oates, *Zombie* (NAL/Dutton).

BOSTON GLOBE–HORN BOOK AWARDS

FICTION
Kazumi Yumoto, *The Friends* (Farrar, Straus).

NONFICTION
Walter Wick, *A Drop of Water* (Scholastic).

PICTURE BOOK
Brian Pinkney, *The Adventures of Sparrowboy* (Simon & Schuster).

BREAD LOAF BAKELESS PRIZE

FICTION
Katherine L. Hester, *Eggs for Young America* (Middlebury College).

POETRY
Mary Jo Bang, *Apology for Want* (Middlebury College).

JOHN BURROUGHS MEDAL

David Quammen, *The Song of the Dodo* (Scribner).

THE CHRISTOPHER AWARDS

BOOKS
Robert P. Casey, *Fighting for Life* (Word).
Jimmy Carter, *Living Faith* (Times Books).
Patricia Raybon, *My First White Friend: Confessions on Race, Love, and Forgiveness* (Viking).
Jim Doyle and Brian Doyle, *Two Voices: A Father and Son Discuss Family and Faith* (Liguori).
Stephen E. Ambrose, *Undaunted Courage: Meriwether Lewis, Thomas Jefferson, and the Opening of the American West* (Simon & Schuster).

BOOKS FOR YOUNG PEOPLE
Ellen Howard, *The Log Cabin Quilt*, illustrated by Ronald Himler (Holiday House).
Alan Schroeder, *Minty: A Story of Young Harriet Tubman*, pictures by Jerry Pinkney (Dial).
Andrew Clements, *Frindle*, pictures by Brian Selznick (Simon & Schuster).
Patricia Calvert, *Glennis, Before and After* (Atheneum).

Susan Kuklin, *Irrepressible Spirit: Conversations with Human Rights Activists* (Philomel).

COMMONWEALTH CLUB CALIFORNIA BOOK AWARDS

GOLD MEDAL

Gina Berriault, *Women in Their Beds* (Counterpoint).

Donald J. Waldie, *Holy Land: A Suburban Memoir* (Norton).

SILVER MEDAL

John Hart, *Storm Over Mono: The Mono Lake Battle and the California Water Future* (University of California Press).

Ruth Lewin Sime, *Lise Meitner: A Life in Physics* (University of California Press).

David Hill, *Sacred Dust* (Delacorte).

Carolyn Kizer, *Harping On: Poems 1985–1995* (Copper Canyon).

Nancy Farmer, *A Girl Named Disaster* (Orchard).

Robert Hass, *Sun Under Wood* (Ecco).

Ernest J. Finney, *Flights in the Heavenlies* (University of Illinois Press).

Alan Schroeder, *Minty: A Story of Young Harriet Tubman* (Dial).

COMMONWEALTH WRITER'S PRIZES

BEST BOOK

Earl Lovelace, *Salt* (Persea).

BEST FIRST PUBLISHED BOOK

Anne-Marie MacDonald, *Fall on Your Knees* (Simon & Schuster).

FELLOWSHIP OF SOUTHERN WRITERS LITERARY AWARDS

HILLSDALE PRIZE FOR FICTION

Lewis Nordan.

HANES PRIZE FOR POETRY

Yusef Komunyakaa.

CHUBB AWARD FOR FICTION IN HONOR OF ROBERT PENN WARREN

Allen Wier.

BRYAN FAMILY FOUNDATION AWARD FOR DRAMA

Naomi Wallace.

NONFICTION AWARD

Bailey White.

NEW WRITING AWARD

William Henry "Hank" Lewis.

SPECIAL ACHIEVEMENT AWARD

James Still.

CLEANTH BROOKS MEDAL FOR DISTINGUISHED ACHIEVEMENT IN SOUTHERN LETTERS

Dr. Louis D. Rubin Jr.

FIRECRACKER ALTERNATIVE BOOK AWARDS

FICTION

Rob Hardin, *Distorture* (Fc2/Black Ice Books).

NONFICTION

Leslie Feinberg, *Transgender Warriors* (Beacon Press).

POETRY

Linda Smukler, *Home in Three Days. Don't Wash.* (Hard Press).

CHARLES FRANKEL PRIZE IN THE HUMANITIES

Rita Dove, Doris Kearns Goodwin, Daniel Kemmis, Arturo Madrid, Bill Moyers.

GAY, LESBIAN, AND BISEXUAL TASK FORCE OF THE AMERICAN LIBRARY ASSOCIATION LITERARY AWARDS

FICTION

Emma Donoghue, *Hood* (HarperCollins).

NONFICTION

Fenton Johnson, *Geography of the Heart* (Scribner).

GILLER PRIZE

Mordecai Richler, *Barney's Version* (Knopf).

GOVERNOR GENERAL'S LITERARY AWARDS

CHILDREN'S LITERATURE – ILLUSTRATION

Barbara Reid, *The Party,* text by Reid (North Winds Press).

Stéphane Poulin, *Poil de serpent, dent d'araigné,* text by Danielle Marcotte (Editions Les 400 coups).

CHILDREN'S LITERATURE – TEXT

Kit Pearson, *Awake and Dreaming* (Viking/Penguin).

Michael Noël, *Pien* (Editions Michel Quintin).

DRAMA

Ian Ross, *Farewel* (Scirocco Drama).

Yvan Bienvenue, *Dits et Iné* (Dramaturges Editeurs).

FICTION

Jane Urquhart, *The Underpainter* (McClelland & Stewart).

Aude, *Cet imperceptible mouvement* (XYZ Editeur).

NONFICTION

Rachel Manley, *Drumblair—Memories of a Jamaican Childhood* (Ian Randle).

Roland Viau, *Enfants du néant et manageurs d'âmes—Guerre, culture et société en Iroquoisie ancienne* (Editions du Boréal).

POETRY

Dionne Brand, *Land to Light On* (McClelland & Stewart).

Pierre Nepveu, *Romans-fleuves* (Editions du Noroît).

TRANSLATION

Howard Scott, *The Euguelion* (Alter Ego Editions); English version of *L'Eugué*, by Louky Bersianik (Editions La Presse).

Marie José Thériault, *Arracher les montagnes* (Editions du Bor); French version of *Digging Up the Mountains*, by Neil Bissoondath (Macmillan Canada).

DRUE HEINZ LITERATURE PRIZE

Katherine Vaz, *Fado & Other Stories* (Pittsburgh).

HUGO AWARDS

BEST NOVEL

Kim Stanley Robinson, *Blue Mars* (Bantam Spectra).

BEST NOVELLA

George R. R. Martin, "Blood of the Dragon."

BEST NOVELETTE

Bruce Sterling, "Bicycle Repairman."

BEST SHORT STORY

Connie Willis, "The Soul Selects Her Own Society. . . ."

BEST NONFICTION BOOK

L. Sprague de Camp, *Time & Chance* (Donald H. Grant).

IMPAC DUBLIN LITERARY AWARD

Javier Marias, *A Heart So White* (Harvill Press).

INTERNATIONAL ASSOCIATION OF CRIME WRITERS HAMMETT AWARD

Martin Cruz Smith, *Rose* (Random House).

ROBERT F. KENNEDY BOOK AWARD

David M. Oshinsky, *Worse Than Slavery: Parchman Farm and the Ordeal of Jim Crow Justice* (Free Press).

KIRIYAMA PACIFIC RIM BOOK PRIZE

Patrick Smith, *Japan: A Reinterpretation* (Pantheon).

LAMBDA LITERARY AWARDS

EDITORS' CHOICE

Donald Windham.

LANNAN LITERARY AWARDS

LIFETIME ACHIEVEMENT AWARD

William Gass.

POETRY

Ken Smith.

FICTION

John Banville, Anne Michaels, Grace Paley.

NONFICTION

David Quammen.

LENORE MARSHALL POETRY PRIZE

Anthony Hecht, *Flight Among the Tombs* (Knopf).

THE LIBRARY ASSOCIATION LITERARY AWARDS

CARNEGIE MEDAL

Melvin Burgess, *Junk* (Penguin).

KATE GREENAWAY MEDAL

Helen Cooper, *The Boy Who Wouldn't Go to Bed* (Bantam).

LOS ANGELES TIMES BOOK PRIZES

FICTION

Rohinton Mistry, *A Fine Balance* (Knopf).

POETRY

Alan Shapiro, *Mixed Company* (University of Chicago Press).

HISTORY

Neal Ascherson, *Black Sea* (Hill & Wang).

BIOGRAPHY

Frank McCourt, *Angela's Ashes* (Scribner).

SCIENCE AND TECHNOLOGY

Carl Sagan, *The Demon-Haunted World: Science as a Candle in the Dark* (Random House).

CURRENT INTEREST

Peter Maass, *Love Thy Neighbor: A Story of War* (Knopf).

ART SEIDENBAUM AWARD FOR FIRST FICTION

Mark Behr, *The Smell of Apples* (St. Martin's Press).

THE JOHN D. AND CATHERINE T. MACARTHUR FOUNDATION FELLOWS

Luis Alfaro, Lee Breuer, Vija Celmins, Eric L. Charnov, Elouise Cobell, Peter Galison, Mark Harrington, Eva Harris, Michael Kremer, Russell S. Lande, Kerry James Marshall, Nancy A. Moran, Han Ong, Kathleen A. Ross, Pamela Samuelson, Susan A. Stewart, Elizabeth Streb, Trimpin, Loic J. D. Wacquant, Kara Elizabeth Walker, David Foster Wallace, Andrew J. Wiles, Brackette F. Williams.

MACAVITY AWARDS

BEST MYSTERY NOVEL

Peter Lovesey, *Bloodhounds* (Myslenous Press).

BEST FIRST MYSTERY NOVEL

Dale Furutani, *Death in Little Tokyo* (St. Martin's Press).

BEST MYSTERY SHORT STORY

Carolyn Wheat, "Cruel & Unusual," in *Guilty as Charged: A Mystery Writers of America Anthology* (Pocket Books).

BEST CRITICAL/BIOGRAPHICAL WORK

Willetta L. Heising, *Detecting Women 2: Reader's Guide and Checklist for Mystery Series Written by Women* (Purple Moon Press).

MOBIL PEGASUS PRIZE FOR LITERATURE

Mário de Carvalho, *A God Strolling in the Cool of the Evening* (Louisiana State University Press).

MODERN LANGUAGE ASSOCIATION PRIZES

PRIZE FOR A FIRST BOOK

Marc Redfield, *Phantom Formations* (Cornell University Press).

John Rogers, *The Matter of Revolution* (Cornell University Press).

PRIZE FOR INDEPENDENT SCHOLARS

Graham Robb, *Unlocking Mallarmé* (Yale University Press).

JAMES RUSSELL LOWELL PRIZE

Joseph Roach, *Cities of the Dead* (Columbia University Press).

ALDO AND JEAN SCAGLIONE PRIZE FOR A TRANSLATION OF A LITERARY WORK

No Award.

MINA P. SHAUGHNESSY PRIZE

James Crosswhite, *The Rhetoric of Reason* (University of Wisconsin Press).

MYSTERY WRITERS OF AMERICA EDGAR ALLAN POE AWARDS

GRAND MASTER AWARD

Ruth Rendell.

BEST MYSTERY NOVEL

Thomas H. Cook, *The Chatham School Affair* (Bantam).

BEST FIRST MYSTERY NOVEL BY AN AMERICAN AUTHOR

John Morgan Wilson, *Simple Justice* (Doubleday).

BEST ORIGINAL PAPERBACK MYSTERY NOVEL

Harlan Coben, *Fade Away* (Dell).

BEST FACT CRIME BOOK

Darcy O'Brien, *Power to Hurt* (HarperCollins).

BEST CRITICAL/BIOGRAPHICAL WORK

Michael Atkinson, *The Secret Marriage of Sherlock Holmes* (University of Michigan Press).

BEST YOUNG ADULT MYSTERY

Willo Davis Roberts, *Twisted Summer* (Atheneum).

BEST JUVENILE MYSTERY

Dorothy Reynolds Miller, *The Clearing* (Atheneum).

BEST MYSTERY SHORT STORY

Michael Malone, "Red Clay" (*Murder for Love* / Delacorte).

BEST MYSTERY MOTION PICTURE

Sling Blade, by Billy Bob Thornton (Miramax).

ROBERT L. FISH MEMORIAL AWARD

David Vaughn, "The Prosecutor of DuPrey" (*Ellery Queen's Mystery Magazine*, January).

ELLERY QUEEN AWARD

François Guerif.

RAVEN AWARD

Marvin Lachman.

NATIONAL BOOK AWARDS

FICTION

Charles Frazier, *Cold Mountain* (Atlantic Monthly).

NONFICTION

Joseph J. Ellis, *American Sphinx: The Character of Thomas Jefferson* (Knopf).

POETRY

William Meredith, *Effort at Speech: New and Selected Poems* (Triquarterly Books).

YOUNG PEOPLE'S LITERATURE

Han Nolan, *Dancing on the Edge* (Harcourt Brace).

MEDAL FOR DISTINGUISHED CONTRIBUTION TO AMERICAN LETTERS
Studs Terkel.

NATIONAL BOOK CRITICS CIRCLE AWARDS

FICTION
Gina Berriault, *Women in Their Beds* (Counterpoint).

NONFICTION
Jonathan Raban, *Bad Land* (Pantheon).

BIOGRAPHY/AUTOBIOGRAPHY
Frank McCourt, *Angela's Ashes* (Scribner).

POETRY
Robert Hass, *Sun Under Wood* (Ecco).

CRITICISM
William Gass, *Finding a Form* (Knopf).

NONA BALAKIAN CITATION FOR EXCELLENCE IN REVIEWING
Dennis Drabelle.

IVAN SANDROF AWARD FOR LIFETIME ACHIEVEMENT IN PUBLISHING
Albert Murray.

NATIONAL MEDAL OF ARTS

Edward Albee, Sarah Caldwell, Harry Callahan, Zelda Fichandler, Eduardo "Lalo" Guerrero, Lionel Hampton, Bella Lewitzky, Vera List, Robert Redford, Maurice Sendak, Stephen Sondheim, The Boys Choir of Harlem.

NEW YORK PUBLIC LIBRARY HELEN BERNSTEIN AWARD FOR EXCELLENCE IN JOURNALISM

David Quammen.

NOBEL PRIZE FOR LITERATURE

Dario Fo.

SCOTT O'DELL AWARD FOR HISTORICAL FICTION

Katherine Paterson, *Jip: His Story* (Lodestar).

ORANGE PRIZE

Anne Michaels, *Fugitive Pieces* (Knopf).

LAWRENCE O'SHAUGHNESSY AWARD

Eavan Boland.

PEN AMERICAN CENTER LITERARY AWARDS

PEN/MARTHA ALBRAND AWARD FOR FIRST NONFICTION

Mark Doty, *Heaven's Coast* (HarperCollins).

PEN/BOOK-OF-THE-MONTH CLUB TRANSLATION PRIZE
Ronald de Leeuw, ed. and trans., *The Letters of Vincent Van Gogh* (Viking).

ERNEST HEMINGWAY FOUNDATION/PEN AWARD FOR FIRST FICTION
Ha Jin, *Ocean of Words* (Zoland).

PEN/FAULKNER AWARD
Gina Berriault, *Women in Their Beds* (Counterpoint).

PEN/JERARD FUND AWARD FOR A NONFICTION WORK IN PROGRESS
Judy Blunt, *Winter Kill.*

PEN/NORMA KLEIN AWARD
Rita Williams-Garcia.

PEN/ROGER KLEIN AWARD
Kate Medina.

PEN/RALPH MANHEIM MEDAL FOR TRANSLATION
Robert Fagles.

PEN AWARD FOR POETRY IN TRANSLATION
Edward Snow, trans., *Uncollected Poems of Rainer Maria Rilke* (Farrar, Straus & Giroux).

PEN/SPIELVOGEL-DIAMONSTEIN AWARD FOR THE ART OF THE ESSAY
Cynthia Ozick, *Fame and Folly* (Knopf).

RENATO POGGIOLI TRANSLATION AWARD FOR A WORK IN PROGRESS
Ann McGarrell, tr., *The Face of Isis,* by Vittoria Ronchey.

ROGER KLEIN FOUNDATION CAREER ACHIEVEMENT AWARDS
Carol Houck Smith and Alan D. Williams.

PEN CENTER USA WEST LITERARY AWARDS

CHILDREN'S LITERATURE
Peg Kehret, *Small Steps: The Year I Got Polio* (Albert Whitman).

FICTION
William T. Vollmann, *The Atlas* (Penguin).

NONFICTION
Jonathan Raban, *Bad Land* (Pantheon).

POETRY
Bob Kaufman, *Cranial Guitar* (Coffeehouse Press).

RESEARCH NONFICTION
Edward Humes, *No Matter How Loud I Shout* (Touchstone).

TRANSLATION
Maryellen Toman Mori, *Kangaroo Notebook* (Vintage).

ANTOINETTE PERRY AWARDS

PLAY
Alfred Uhry, *The Last Night of Ballyhoo*.
MUSICAL
Titanic.

PULITZER PRIZES

BIOGRAPHY
Frank McCourt, *Angela's Ashes* (Scribner).
CRITICISM
Tim Page, *The Washington Post*.
FICTION
Steven Millhauser, *Martin Dressler: The Tale of an American Dreamer* (Crown).
GENERAL NONFICTION
Richard Kluger, *Ashes to Ashes: America's Hundred-Year Cigarette War, the Public Health, and the Unabashed Triumph of Philip Morris* (Knopf).
HISTORY
Jack N. Rakove, *Original Meanings: Politics and Ideas in the Making of the Constitution* (Knopf).
POETRY
Lisel Mueller, *Alive Together: New and Selected Poems* (Louisiana State University Press).

SHAMUS AWARDS

BEST NOVEL
Robert Crais, *Sunset Express* (Hyperion Press).
BEST PAPERBACK ORIGINAL
Harlan Coben, *Fade Away* (Dell).
BEST FIRST NOVEL
Carol Lea Benjamin, *This Dog For Hire* (Walker).
BEST P.I. SHORT STORY
Lia Matera, "Dead Drunk," published in *Guilty as Charged: A Mystery Writers of America Anthology* (Pocket Books).

LILLIAN SMITH BOOK AWARDS

FICTION
Charles Frazier, *Cold Mountain* (Atlantic Monthly Press).
NONFICTION
John M. Barry, *The Great Mississippi Flood of 1927 and How It Changed America* (Simon & Schuster).

TEXAS INSTITUTE OF LETTERS LITERARY AWARDS

BOOK PUBLISHERS OF TEXAS AWARD FOR BEST BOOK FOR YOUNG PEOPLE
J. A. Benner, *Uncle Comanche* (Texas Christian University Press).
BRAZOS BOOKSTORE SHORT STORY AWARD IN MEMORY OF BILL SHEARER
Daniel Stern, "The Passion According to St. John by J. S. Bach" (*New Letters*).
CARR P. COLLINS AWARD FOR NONFICTION
Nolan Porterfield, *Last Cavalier: The Life and Times of John A. Lomax* (University of Illinois Press).
FRIENDS OF THE DALLAS PUBLIC LIBRARY AWARD FOR THE BOOK MAKING THE MOST SIGNIFICANT CONTRIBUTION TO KNOWLEDGE
Rick Bass, *The Book of Yaak* (Houghton Mifflin).
O. HENRY AWARD FOR JOURNALISM
Debbie Nathan, "The Death of Jane Roe" (*Village Voice*).
JESSE JONES AWARD FOR FICTION
Sandra Scofield, *A Chance to See Egypt* (HarperCollins).
NATALIE ORNISH POETRY AWARD IN MEMORY OF WAYNE GARD
Isabel Nathaniel, *The Dominion of Light* (Copper Beech).
LON TINKLE AWARD FOR LIFETIME ACHIEVEMENT
Cormac McCarthy.
STEVEN TURNER AWARD FOR FIRST BOOK OF FICTION
Kathleen Cambor, *The Book of Mercy* (Farrar, Straus & Giroux).

THURBER PRIZE

Ian Frazier, *Coyote vs. Acme* (Farrar, Straus & Giroux).

WHITBREAD PRIZES

BIOGRAPHY
Diarmaid MacCulloch, *Thomas Cranmer: A Life* (Yale University Press).
FIRST NOVEL
John Lanchester, *The Debt to Pleasure* (Picador).
NOVEL
Beryl Bainbridge, *Every Man for Himself* (Duckworth).

POETRY
>   Seamus Heaney, *The Spirit Level* (Faber & Faber).

BOOK OF THE YEAR
>   Seamus Heaney, *The Spirit Level* (Faber & Faber).

CHILDREN'S BOOK OF THE YEAR
>   Anne Fine, *The Tulip Touch* (Hamish Hamilton).

WHITING WRITERS' AWARDS

Jo Ann Beard, Connie Deanovich, Erik Ehn, Forrest Gander, Jody Gladding, Suketu Mehta, Ellen Meloy, Josip Novakovich, Robert Pinsky, Melanie Rae Thon, Mark Turpin.

Necrology

Acker, Kathy – 30 November 1997
Alden, Jerome – 4 May 1997
Amin, Mustafa – 13 April 1997
Anderson, William [Francis Desnaux] – 6 February 1997
Awdry, Reverend Wilbert Vere – 21 March 1997
Balakian, Anna – 12 August 1997
Barfield, Owen – 14 December 1997
Baum, Allyn – 17 May 1997
Becker, Jurek – 14 March 1997
Bogard, Travis – 5 April 1997
Botwin, Carol – 15 April 1997
Branscum, Robbie Tilley – 24 May 1997
Brown, William Slater – 22 June 1997
Burnett, Murray – 23 September 1997
Burroughs, William S. – 2 August 1997
Caidin, Martin – 24 March 1997
Callado, Antonio – 28 January 1997
Carver, Catharine – 11 November 1997
Christopher, Matt – 20 September 1997
Cordell, Alexander – 9 July 1997
Danly, Robert Lyons – 27 April 1997
Daves, Joan – 25 June 1997
David, Lester – 10 November 1997
Dickey, James – 19 January 1997
Dietz, Lew – 26 April 1997
Dorris, Michael – 11 April 1997
DuBois, William – 16 March 1997
Duncan, Harry – 18 April 1997
Eastlake, William Derry – 1 June 1997
Edel, Leon – 5 September 1997
Elman, Richard – 31 December 1997
Emerson, William R. – 2 June 1997
Fehrenbacher, Don E. – 13 December 1997
Fine, Donald I. – 14 August 1997
Flower, Desmond [John Newman] – 7 January 1997
Forrest, Leon – 6 November 1997
Geng, Veronica – 24 December 1997
Gerrard, Roy – 5 August 1997
Gill, Brendan – 27 December 1997
Ginsberg, Allen – 5 April 1997
Granger, Percy – 10 March 1997
Grierson, Margaret – 12 December 1997
Hahn, Emily – 18 February 1997
Halsey, Margaret – 4 February 1997
Hanff, Helene – 9 April 1997
Harrington, Alan – 23 May 1997
Heider, Werner – 27 May 1997

Henry, Marguerite – 26 November 1997
Hrabal, Bohumil – 3 February 1997
Humphrey, William – 20 August 1997
Huxley, Elspeth – 10 January 1997
Ignatow, David – 17 November 1997
Jacobi, Carl – 25 August 1997
Kane, Robert S. – 10 November 1997
Katz, Leslie George – 18 April 1997
Kingsley, Dorothy – 26 September 1997
Kirchner, Merian L. – 25 September 1997
Klein, Arthur – 7 April 1997
Kopelev, Lev Z. – 18 June 1997
Koshland, William A. – 7 May 1997
Kramer, Aaron – 7 April 1997
Lampell, Millard – 3 October 1997
Laughlin, James – 12 November 1997
Lee, Laurie – 14 May 1997
Levertov, Denise – 20 December 1997
Lorant, Stefan – 14 November 1997
Loynaz, Dulce María – 27 April 1997
Lu, Cary – 24 September 1997
Lukas, J. Anthony – 5 June 1997
Maillart, Ella – 27 March 1997
Mannix, David – 29 January 1997
Mason, Richard – 13 October 1997
Matthews, William – 12 November 1997
McCord, David – 13 April 1997
McCormick, Kenneth D. – 27 June 1997
Mellow, James R. – 22 November 1997
Merrick, Elliott – 22 April 1997
Merril, Judith – 12 September 1997
Michener, James A. – 16 October 1997
Modarressi, Taghi – 23 April 1997
Montgomery, George – 7 April 1997
Moskowitz, Sam – 15 April 1997
Moss, Carlton – 10 August 1997
Nardy, Manuel – 5 May 1997
Norman, Dorothy – 12 April 1997
Noyes, Newbold Jr. – 18 December 1997
Olding, Dorothy – 14 May 1997
O'Neill, Charles Kendall – 19 June 1997
Petry, Ann – 28 April 1997
Pike, R. E. – 7 August 1997
Pinget, Robert – 25 August 1997
Pope, Dudley – 25 April 1997
Pritchett, V. S. – 20 March 1997
Raeburn, Ben – 9 April 1997
Resnicow, Herbert – 4 April 1997

Riggs, Dionis C. – 20 April 1997
Robbins, Harold – 14 October 1997
Rosten, Leo – 19 February 1997
Rowse, A. L. – 3 October 1997
Royko, Mike – 30 April 1997
Sandburg, Margaret – 12 April 1997
Schwartz, Bernard – 23 December 1997
Shumway, Floyd Mallory – 12 November 1997
Sinyavsky, Andrei – 26 February 1997
Slocum, John J. – 12 August 1997
Smith, Charles E. – 7 December 1997

Troup, Stuart – 4 June 1997
Tutuola, Amos – 8 June 1997
Vale, Eugene – 2 May 1997
Wannous, Saadallah – 15 May 1997
Weaver, Warren – 20 February 1997
Wedgwood, Dame Cicely Veronica – 9 March 1997
Wertenbaker, Lael Tucker – 24 March 1997
Whiteside, Thomas – 10 October 1997
Wolfert, Ira – 24 November 1997
Yoder, John Howard – 30 December 1997
Young, Thomas D. – 29 January 1997

Checklist: Contributions to Literary History and Biography

This list is a selection of new books on various aspects of literary and cultural history, including biographies, memoirs, and correspondence of literary people and their associates.

Alldritt, Keith. *W. B. Yeats: The Man and the Milieu*. New York: Clarkson Potter, 1997.

Assouline, Pierre. *Simenon: A Biography,* translated by Jon Rothschild. New York: Knopf, 1997.

Auster, Paul. *Hand to Mouth: A Chronicle of Early Failure*. New York: Holt, 1997.

Bach, Gerhard and Blaine Hall, eds. *Conversations with Grace Paley*. Jackson: University Press of Mississippi, 1997.

Benedetti, Jean, ed. *Dear Writer, Dear Actress: The Love Letters of Anton Chekhov and Olga Knipper*. Hopewell, N.J.: Ecco Press, 1997.

Berkeley, Elizabeth M., ed. *William and Henry James: Selected Letters*. Charlottesville: University Press of Virginia, 1997.

Blotner, Joseph. *Robert Penn Warren: A Biography*. New York: Random House, 1997.

Bonazzi, Robert. *Man in the Mirror: John Howard Griffin and the Story of* Black like Me. Maryknoll, N.Y.: Orbis Books, 1997.

Boulton, James T., ed. *The Selected Letters of D. H. Lawrence*. Cambridge & New York: Cambridge University Press, 1997.

Bowker, Gordon. *Through the Dark Labyrinth: A Biography of Lawrence Durrell*. New York: St. Martin's Press, 1997.

Brown, Rita Mae. *Rita Will : Memoir of a Literary Rabble-Rouser*. New York: Bantam, 1997.

Brown, W. Dale. *Of Fiction and Faith: Twelve American Writers Talk about Their Vision and Work*. London: Aurum, 1997.

Chapple, J. A. V. *Elizabeth Gaskell: The Early Years*. Manchester, U.K.: Manchester University Press, 1997.

Clapp, Susannah. *With Chatwin: Portrait of a Writer*. London: Cape, 1997; New York: Knopf, 1997.

Cooper, David D., ed. *Thomas Merton and James Laughlin: Selected Letters*. New York: Norton, 1997.

Costello, Bonnie, Celeste Goodridge, Cristanne Miller, eds. *The Selected Letters of Marianne Moore*. New York: Knopf, 1997.

Dickens, Charles. *My Early Times,* compiled by Peter Rowland. London: Aurum, 1997.

Dyer, Daniel. *Jack London: A Biography*. New York: Scholastic, 1997.

Ezenwa-Ohaeto, *Chinua Achebe: A Biography*. Bloomington: Indiana University Press, 1997.

George, Susanne K. *Kate M. Cleary: A Literary Biography with Selected Works*. Lincoln: University of Nebraska Press, 1997.

Glasgow, Joanne, ed. *Your John: The Love Letters of Radclyffe Hall*. New York: New York University Press, 1997.

Greene-Gantzberg, Vivian. *Biography of Danish Literary Impressionist Herman Bang*. Lewiston, N.Y.: Edwin Mellen Press, 1997.

Grosskurth, Phyllis. *Byron: The Flawed Angel*. Boston: Houghton Mifflin, 1997.

Hadda, Janet. *Isaac Bashevis Singer: A Life*. New York: Oxford University Press, 1997.

Harrison, Antony H., ed. *The Letters of Christina Rossetti: 1843–1873*. Charlottesville: University Press of Virginia, 1997.

Hill, Christine M. *Langston Hughes: Poet of the Harlem Renaissance*. Springfield, N.J.: Enslow, 1997.

Hindus, Milton, ed. *Selected Letters of Charles Reznikoff 1917–1976*. Santa Rosa, Cal.: Black Sparrow Press, 1997.

Hockaday, Mary. *Kafka, Love and Courage: The Life of Milena Jesenska*. Woodstock, N.Y.: Overlook Press, 1997.

Hoffman, Andrew. *Inventing Mark Twain: The Lives of Samuel Langhorne Clemens*. New York: Morrow, 1997.

Jarvis, Adrian. *Samuel Smiles and the Construction of Victorian Values*. Thrupp, Stroud, Gloucestershire: Alan Sutton, 1997.

King, Reyahn, Sukhdev Sandhu, James Walvin, and Jane Girdham. *Ignatius Sancho: An African Man of Letters*. London: National Portrait Gallery, 1997.

Kramer, Jane. *Allen Ginsberg in America,* revised edition. New York: Fromm International, 1997.

Lear, Linda J. *Rachel Carson: Witness for Nature*. New York: Holt, 1997.

Lessing, Doris. *Walking in the Shade: My Autobiography, 1949–1962*. New York: HarperCollins, 1997.

Lieblich, Amia, Devorah Baron, and Naomi Seidman. *Conversations with Dvora: An Experimental Biography of the First Modern Hebrew Woman Writer,* translated by Chana Kronfeld. Berkeley: University of California Press, 1997.

Lindfors, Bernth, ed. *Conversations with Chinua Achebe*. Jackson: University Press of Mississippi, 1997.

Mahfouz, Najib. *Echoes of an Autobiography,* translated by Denys Johnson-Davies. New York: Doubleday, 1997.

Maguire, Roberta S., ed. *Conversations with Albert Murray*. Jackson: University Press of Mississippi, 1997.

McCall, Bruce. *Thin Ice: Coming of Age in Canada*. New York: Random House, 1997.

Molvaer, Reidulf K. *Black Lions: The Creative Lives of Modern Ethiopia's Literary Giants and Pioneers*. Lawrenceville, N.J.: Red Sea Press, 1997.

Moran, Marsha, Patrick Moran, and Norah K. Barr, eds. *M. F. K. Fisher, a Life in Letters: Correspondence, 1929–1991*. Washington, D.C.: Counterpoint, 1997.

Mosley, Charlotte, ed. *The Letters of Nancy Mitford and Evelyn Waugh.* Boston: Houghton Mifflin, 1997.

Murray, Nicholas. *A Life of Matthew Arnold.* New York: St. Martin's Press, 1997.

Myer, Valerie Grosvenor. *Jane Austen: Obstinate Heart.* New York: Arcade, 1997.

Myerson, Joel, ed. *The Selected Letters of Ralph Waldo Emerson.* New York: Columbia University Press, 1997.

Nokes, David. *Jane Austen: A Life.* New York: Farrar, Straus & Giroux, 1997.

Peters, Margot. *May Sarton: A Biography.* New York: Knopf, 1997.

Ramsdale, Katherine. *Dean Koontz: A Writer's Biography.* New York: Harper Prism, 1997.

Reynolds, Michael. *Hemingway: The 1930s.* New York: Norton, 1997.

Rilke, Rainer Maria. *Diaries of a Young Poet,* translated by Edward Snow and Michael Winkler. New York: Norton, 1997.

Salamo, Lin, and Harriet Elinor Smith, eds. *Mark Twain's Letters: 1872–1873.* Berkeley: University of California Press, 1997.

Schmidgall, Gary. *Walt Whitman: A Gay Life.* New York: Dutton, 1997.

Seshachari, Neila C., ed. *Conversations with William Kennedy.* Jackson: University Press of Mississippi, 1997.

Todd, Janet M. *The Secret Life of Aphra Behn.* New Brunswick, N.J.: Rutgers University Press, 1997.

Todd, Olivier. *Albert Camus: A Life,* translated by Benjamin Ivry. New York: Knopf, 1997.

Tomalin, Claire. *Jane Austen: A Life.* New York: Knopf, 1997.

Williams, Susan Millar. *A Devil and a Good Woman, Too: The Lives of Julia Peterkin.* Athens: University of Georgia Press, 1997.

Yardley, Jonathan. *Misfit: The Strange Life of Frederick Exley.* New York: Random House, 1997.

Contributors

Betty Adcock ....Raleigh, North Carolina
Michael Allin ....East Hampton, New York
James Applewhite ....Duke University
Harold Augenbraum ....Mercantile Library
Judith Baughman ....University of South Carolina
Richard Bausch ....George Mason University
Tracy Simmons Bitonti ....University of South Carolina
André Bleikasten ....University of Strasbourg
David Bottoms ....Georgia State University
Charles Brower ....Columbia, South Carolina
Matthew J. Bruccoli ....University of South Carolina
Kristin Bryan ....Louisiana State University Press
Frederick Busch ....Sherburne, New York
Hayden Carruth ....Munsville, New York
R. V. Cassill ....Providence, Rhode Island
Frank Conroy ....Iowa City, Iowa
Mary F. Cordato ....American Bible Society
Alice Cotten ....University of North Carolina, Chapel Hill
James Gould Cozzens
Donald C. Dickinson ....University of Arizona, Tucson
R. H. W. Dillard ....Hollins College
Andre Dubus ....Haverhill, Massachusetts
Stuart Dybek ....Kalamazoo, Michigan
A. Nicholas Fargnoli ....Molloy College
Irvin Faust ....New York, New York
Leslie Fiedler ....State University of New York, Buffalo
William Foltz ....University of Hawaii
Doreen Fowler ....University of Mississippi
Peggy L. Fox ....New Directions
George Garrett ....University of Virginia
Michael Patrick Gillespie ....Marquette University
Kenneth Graham ....Columbia, South Carolina
Michael Groden ....University of Western Ontario
Daniel Halpern ....Ecco Press
Robert W. Hamblin ....Southeast Missouri State University
Bill Henderson ....Pushcart Press
George V. Higgins ....Boston University
Caroline C. Hunt ....College of Charleston
John Iggulden ....Bellingen, New South Wales, Australia
John T. Irwin ....University of Georgia
David Garrett Izzo ....Chapel Hill, North Carolina
William Jovanovich ....San Diego, California

Stephen James Joyce ....*Paris, France*
Terence Killeen...The Irish Times
Howard Kissel..New York Daily News
Donald S. Klopfer
John E. Lane ....*Wofford College*
Michael L. Lazare ....*New Milford, Connecticut*
Peter H. Liddle ....*University of Leeds*
Gordon Lish ....*New York, New York*
Anne Hutchens McCormick ....*Alfred A. Knopf, Inc.*
Walt McDonald..*Texas Tech University*
Thomas McHaney ....*Georgia State University*
Lauren McIntyre ....The New Yorker
Michael Millgate ....*University of Toronto*
David Minter...*Emory University*
Ted Mitchell..*Thomas Wolfe Memorial*
Douglas Moore
Willie Morris...*Jackson, Mississippi*
Merritt Moseley...*University of North Carolina at Asheville*
Albert Murray..*New York City*
Joyce Carol Oates...*Princeton University*
Cynthia Ozick ....*New Rochelle, New York*
Kelli Rae Patton...*Unterberg Poetry Center*
Clay Reynolds
Christa Sammons..*The Beinecke Library, Yale University*
Donato Santeramo ....*Queen's University*
Charles Schlessiger ....*New York, New York*
Patrick Scott ....*University of South Carolina*
Fritz Senn..*Zurich James Joyce Foundation*
Judith L. Sensibar...*Arizona State University*
John Simon..New York Magazine
Hans Skei ....*University of Oslo*
Dave Smith ....*Louisiana State University*
William Styron..*Roxbury, Connecticut*
Ernest Suarez ....*Catholic University of America*
Mary Jo Tate ....*Ripley, Mississippi*
Dillon Teachout ....*Princeton University*
Matt Theado..*Gardner-Webb University*
John F. Thornton...*New York, New York*
Mona Van Duyn...*Saint Louis, Missouri*
Robert Weibezahl ....*Venice, California*
Philip Weinstein ....*Swarthmore College*
Judith Wittenberg..*Simmons College*
Tobias Wolff ....*Stanford University*
Herman Wouk ....*Palm Springs, California*

Cumulative Index

Dictionary of Literary Biography, Volumes 1-191
Dictionary of Literary Biography Yearbook, 1980-1997
Dictionary of Literary Biography Documentary Series, Volumes 1-16

Cumulative Index

DLB before number: *Dictionary of Literary Biography,* Volumes 1-191
Y before number: *Dictionary of Literary Biography Yearbook,* 1980-1997
DS before number: *Dictionary of Literary Biography Documentary Series,* Volumes 1-16

A

Anyidoho, Kofi 1947- DLB-157

Anzaldúa, Gloria 1942- DLB-122

Anzengruber, Ludwig
1839-1889 . . . . DLB-129

Apess, William 1798-1839 . . . . DLB-175

Apodaca, Rudy S. 1939- DLB-82

Apollonius Rhodius third century B.C.
. . . . DLB-176

Apple, Max 1941- DLB-130

Appleton, D., and Company DLB-49

Appleton-Century-Crofts DLB-46

Applewhite, James 1935- DLB-105

Apple-wood Books DLB-46

Aquin, Hubert 1929-1977 . . . . DLB-53

Aquinas, Thomas 1224 or
1225-1274 . . . . DLB-115

Aragon, Louis 1897-1982 . . . . DLB-72

Aralica, Ivan 1930- DLB-181

Aratus of Soli circa 315 B.C.-circa 239 B.C.
. . . . DLB-176

Arbor House Publishing
Company DLB-46

Arbuthnot, John 1667-1735 . . . . . . DLB-101

Arcadia House DLB-46

Arce, Julio G. (see Ulica, Jorge)

Archer, William 1856-1924 . . . . DLB-10

Archilochhus mid seventh century B.C.E.
. . . . DLB-176

The Archpoet circa 1130?-? DLB-148

Archpriest Avvakum (Petrovich)
1620?-1682 . . . . DLB-150

Arden, John 1930- DLB-13

Arden of Faversham DLB-62

Ardis Publishers Y-89

Ardizzone, Edward 1900-1979 . . . . . DLB-160

Arellano, Juan Estevan 1947- DLB-122

The Arena Publishing Company DLB-49

Arena Stage DLB-7

Arenas, Reinaldo 1943-1990 . . . . . . DLB-145

Arensberg, Ann 1937- Y-82

Arguedas, José María 1911-1969 . . . . DLB-113

Argueta, Manlio 1936- DLB-145

Arias, Ron 1941- DLB-82

Arishima, Takeo 1878-1923 . . . . . . DLB-180

Aristophanes circa 446 B.C.-circa 446 B.C.-
circa 386 B.C. DLB-176

Aristotle 384 B.C.-322 B.C. DLB-176

Ariyoshi, Sawako 1931-1984 . . . . . . DLB-182

Arland, Marcel 1899-1986 . . . . DLB-72

Arlen, Michael
1895-1956 . . . . DLB-36, 77, 162

Armah, Ayi Kwei 1939- DLB-117

Der arme Hartmann
?-after 1150 . . . . DLB-148

Armed Services Editions DLB-46

Armstrong, Richard 1903- DLB-160

Arndt, Ernst Moritz 1769-1860 . . . . . DLB-90

Arnim, Achim von 1781-1831 . . . . . DLB-90

Arnim, Bettina von 1785-1859 . . . . . DLB-90

Arno Press DLB-46

Arnold, Edwin 1832-1904 . . . . DLB-35

Arnold, Edwin L. 1857-1935 . . . . . . DLB-178

Arnold, Matthew 1822-1888 . . . . DLB-32, 57

Arnold, Thomas 1795-1842 . . . . DLB-55

Arnold, Edward
[publishing house] DLB-112

Arnow, Harriette Simpson
1908-1986 . . . . DLB-6

Arp, Bill (see Smith, Charles Henry)

Arpino, Giovanni 1927-1987 . . . . . DLB-177

Arreola, Juan José 1918- DLB-113

Arrian circa 89-circa 155 . . . . DLB-176

Arrowsmith, J. W.
[publishing house] DLB-106

The Art and Mystery of Publishing:
Interviews Y-97

Arthur, Timothy Shay
1809-1885 . . . . . . DLB-3, 42, 79; DS-13

The Arthurian Tradition and Its European
Context DLB-138

Artmann, H. C. 1921- DLB-85

Arvin, Newton 1900-1963 . . . . DLB-103

As I See It, by
Carolyn Cassady DLB-16

Asch, Nathan 1902-1964 . . . . . . DLB-4, 28

Ash, John 1948- DLB-40

Ashbery, John 1927- DLB-5, 165; Y-81

Ashburnham, Bertram Lord
1797-1878 . . . . DLB-184

Ashendene Press DLB-112

Asher, Sandy 1942- Y-83

Ashton, Winifred (see Dane, Clemence)

Asimov, Isaac 1920-1992 . . . . . DLB-8; Y-92

Askew, Anne circa 1521-1546 . . . . . DLB-136

Asselin, Olivar 1874-1937 . . . . DLB-92

Asturias, Miguel Angel
1899-1974 . . . . DLB-113

Atheneum Publishers DLB-46

Atherton, Gertrude 1857-1948 . . DLB-9, 78, 186

Athlone Press DLB-112

Atkins, Josiah circa 1755-1781 . . . . . DLB-31

Atkins, Russell 1926- DLB-41

The Atlantic Monthly Press DLB-46

Attaway, William 1911-1986 . . . . . . DLB-76

Atwood, Margaret 1939- DLB-53

Aubert, Alvin 1930- DLB-41

Aubert de Gaspé, Phillipe-Ignace-François
1814-1841 . . . . DLB-99

Aubert de Gaspé, Phillipe-Joseph
1786-1871 . . . . DLB-99

Aubin, Napoléon 1812-1890 . . . . . . DLB-99

Aubin, Penelope 1685-circa 1731 . . . . DLB-39

Aubrey-Fletcher, Henry Lancelot
(see Wade, Henry)

Auchincloss, Louis 1917- DLB-2; Y-80

Auden, W. H. 1907-1973 . . . . . DLB-10, 20

Audio Art in America: A Personal
Memoir Y-85

Audubon, John Woodhouse
1812-1862 . . . . DLB-183

Auerbach, Berthold 1812-1882 . . . . . DLB-133

Auernheimer, Raoul 1876-1948 . . . . . DLB-81

Augustine 354-430 . . . . DLB-115

Austen, Jane 1775-1817 . . . . DLB-116

Austin, Alfred 1835-1913 . . . . DLB-35

Austin, Mary 1868-1934 . . . . . . DLB-9, 78

Austin, William 1778-1841 . . . . DLB-74

Author-Printers, 1476–1599 . . . . . . DLB-167

Author Websites Y-97

The Author's Apology for His Book
(1684), by John Bunyan DLB-39

An Author's Response, by
Ronald Sukenick Y-82

Authors and Newspapers
Association DLB-46

Authors' Publishing Company DLB-49

Avalon Books DLB-46

Avancini, Nicolaus 1611-1686 . . . . . DLB-164

Avendaño, Fausto 1941- DLB-82

Averroëö 1126-1198 . . . . DLB-115

Avery, Gillian 1926- DLB-161

Avicenna 980-1037 . . . . DLB-115

Avison, Margaret 1918- DLB-53

Avon Books DLB-46

Awdry, Wilbert Vere 1911- DLB-160

Awoonor, Kofi 1935- DLB-117

Ayckbourn, Alan 1939- DLB-13

Aymé, Marcel 1902-1967 . . . . DLB-72

Aytoun, Sir Robert 1570-1638 . . . . . DLB-121

Aytoun, William Edmondstoune
1813-1865 . . . . DLB-32, 159

B

B. V. (see Thomson, James)

Babbitt, Irving 1865-1933 . . . . DLB-63

Babbitt, Natalie 1932- DLB-52

Babcock, John [publishing house] DLB-49

C

H

I

K

L

N

P

438

S

447

X

Y

Z

ISBN 0-7876-2519-1

90000